"It's no secret that most textbooks on International Relations are written by Western scholars and offer a mainly Western perspective. This comprehensive and well-written volume is a major step towards building a Global IR, and deserves to be used in class-rooms around the world."

— Amitav Acharya, American University, USA

"The stories and theories we encounter in the field of International Relations are often presented as having 'global' or 'universal' reach. Yet quite to the contrary they often reflect very particular experiences, viewpoints and understandings of the world. This highly anticipated textbook shows how approaching international relations from the per-spective of researchers and students from the 'global South' matters for thinking through international politics more comprehensively, carefully and realistically. This text will pro-vide an invaluable resource for thinking, practicing and studying IR as the field's Euro-centric framings of the world are challenged, shifted and decolonized."

— Milja Kurki, Aberystwyth University, UK

"This is the first textbook to approach international relations as experienced and theor-ized in the global South. It brings non-Western stories to the center of knowledge pro-duction, breaking with rigid classifications to reflect on the diversity of experiences of the international. This is a bold and emancipatory textbook that will have a lasting effect on the way we teach IR everywhere."

— Manuela Lavinas Picq, Universidad San Francisco de Quito, Ecuador,
and Amherst College, USA

"This new textbook is a generous gift to teachers and students of IR. While the first impression might be that it is 'only' a solution to the much bewailed problem that stu-dents in the global South have been fed irrelevant introductions to the discipline, it is actually a very productive and stimulating way to also teach mainstream and 'Northern' concepts in a topical way. This is the textbook for teaching IR in and for all of the world."

— Ole Wæver, University of Copenhagen, Denmark

International Relations from the Global South

This exciting new textbook challenges the implicit notions inherent in most existing International Relations (IR) scholarship and instead presents the subject as seen from different vantage points in the global South.

Divided into four sections, (1) the IR discipline, (2) key concepts and categories, (3) global issues and (4) IR futures, it examines the ways in which world politics have been addressed by traditional core approaches and explores the limitations of these treatments for understanding both Southern and Northern experiences of the "international." The book encourages readers to consider how key ideas have been developed in the discipline, and through systematic interventions by contributors from around the globe, aims at both transforming and enriching the dominant terms of scholarly debate.

This empowering, critical and reflexive tool for thinking about the diversity of experiences of international relations and for placing them front and center in the classroom will help professors and students in both the global North and the global South envision the world differently. In addition to general, introductory IR courses at both the undergraduate and graduate levels it will appeal to courses on sociology and historiography of knowledge, globalization, neoliberalism, security, the state, imperialism and international political economy.

Arlene B. Tickner is a Professor of International Relations in the School of International, Political and Urban Studies at the Universidad del Rosario, Bogotá, Colombia. Her main areas of research include sociology of knowledge in the field of International Relations and the evolution of IR in non-Western settings, Latin American and hemispheric security, and Colombian foreign policy. She is the co-editor (with David Blaney and Inanna Hamati-Ataya) of the Routledge book series, Worlding Beyond the West. In addition to her academic work, she writes a weekly newspaper column in the Colombian daily, *El Espectador*.

Karen Smith teaches International Relations at Leiden University in the Netherlands. She also remains affiliated as an honorary research associate with the University of Cape Town, South Africa, where she was based as an associate professor until 2017. Her research focuses on contributions to IR theory from the global South, South Africa's foreign policy and changes in global order.

Worlding Beyond the West

Series Editors

Arlene B. Tickner, *Universidad del Rosario, Colombia*, **David Blaney**, *Macalester College, USA* and **Inanna Hamati-Ataya**, *Cambridge University, UK*

Historically, the International Relations (IR) discipline has established its boundaries, issues and theories based upon Western experience and traditions of thought. This series explores the role of geocultural factors, institutions and academic practices in creating the concepts, epistemologies and methodologies through which IR knowledge is produced. This entails identifying alternatives for thinking about the "international" that are more in tune with local concerns and traditions outside the West. But it also implies provincializing Western IR and empirically studying the practice of producing IR knowledge at multiple sites within the so-called "West."

International Relations from the Global South

Worlds of Difference

Edited by Arlene B. Tickner and Karen Smith

LONDON AND NEW YORK

First published 2020
by Routledge
2 Park Square, Milton Park, Abingdon, Oxon OX14 4RN

and by Routledge
52 Vanderbilt Avenue, New York, NY 10017

Routledge is an imprint of the Taylor & Francis Group, an informa business

British Library Cataloguing-in-Publication Data
A catalogue record for this book is available from the British Library

Library of Congress Cataloging-in-Publication Data
Names: Tickner, Arlene B., 1964- editor. | Smith, Karen, 1974- editor.
Title: International relations from the global South : worlds of difference / edited by Arlene B. Tickner and Karen Smith.
Description: Abingdon, Oxon ; New York, NY : Routledge, 2020. |
Series: Wording beyond the West | Includes bibliographical references and index.
Identifiers: LCCN 2019055069 | ISBN 9781138799097 (hardback) |
ISBN 9781138799103 (paperback) | ISBN 9781315756233 (ebook)
Subjects: LCSH: International relations–Textbooks. | International relations–Philosophy. | Developing countries–Foreign relations. | Developing countries–Politics and government.
Classification: LCC JZ1242 .I5764 2020 | DDC 327.09172/4–dc23
LC record available at https://lccn.loc.gov/2019055069

ISBN: 978-1-138-79909-7 (hbk)
ISBN: 978-1-138-79910-3 (pbk)
ISBN: 978-1-315-75623-3 (ebk)

Typeset in Times New Roman
by Swales & Willis, Exeter, Devon, UK

Contents

Figures

Tables

Boxes

Contributors

Navnita Chadha Behera is a Professor of International Relations in the Department of Political Science at the University of Delhi, India. Her areas of research include knowledge production in IR outside the West, IR theory, security and conflict and political violence.

Pinar Bilgin is a Professor of International Relations at Bilkent University, Turkey. She is the author of *The International in Security, Security in the International* (Routledge, 2017) and co-editor of the *Routledge Handbook of International Political Sociology* (Routledge, 2017) and *Asia in International Relations* (Routledge, 2017). With Monica Herz, she is also the co-editor of the Palgrave book series, Critical Security Studies in the Global South.

David L. Blaney is G. Theodore Mitau Professor of Political Science at Macalester College, United States. With Naeem Inayatullah, he authored *International Relations and the Problem of Difference* (Routledge, 2004) and *Savage Economics: Wealth, Poverty and the Temporal Walls of Capitalism* (Routledge, 2010). He is currently working with Naeem on two companion volumes on liberal International Political Economy and Marxist thought.

Asli Calkivik is an Assistant Professor in the Department of Humanities and Social Sciences at Istanbul Technical University, Turkey. She received her PhD degree in Political Science at the University of Minnesota. Her work focuses largely on international relations and political theory, and critical security studies.

Carolina Cepeda-Másmela is an Assistant Professor in the Department of International Relations at the Universidad Javeriana, Bogotá, Colombia. She obtained her PhD in political science from the Universidad de los Andes. Her main areas of research and teaching are theories of international relations, social movements and transnational collective action.

Aparna Devare is an Assistant Professor in the Department of Political Science at the University of Hyderabad, India. She teaches courses in IR. Her areas of interest are colonialism and international relations, religion, nationalism and politics. Her book *History and the Making of a Modern Hindu Self* (Routledge, 2011) deals with themes of religion, secularism and nationalism through key Indian nationalist figures.

Matías Franchini is a Professor of International Relations in the School of Political Science, Government and International Relations at the Universidad del Rosario, Bogotá, Colombia. His main areas of research are global environmental governance, the governance of the Anthropocene in Latin America, and the international political economy of climate change. He is the co-author of *Brazil and Climate Change: Beyond the Amazon* (Routledge, 2018).

John M. Hobson is a Professor of Politics and International Relations at the University of Sheffield, UK. He is a fellow of the British Academy and author of nine books, the latest of which is *Multicultural Origins of the Global Economy: Navigating beyond the Western-centric Frontier* (Cambridge University Press, 2020).

Cristina Yumie Aoki Inoue is a Professor in the Institute of International Relations at the University of Brasília, Brazil. She is member of the Earth System Governance, Scientific Steering Committee and of the Active Learning in International Affairs Section of the International Studies Association. Her main areas of research are global environmental politics, transnational relations and international development cooperation.

Laura Kemmer is a PhD candidate in urban anthropology at Hafen City University, in Hamburg, Germany. She studies the emergence of urban collectivities through affective "bonds" and the "political matters" of public transport in Brazil. Her recent publications include "Free Riding Rio: Protest, Public Transport and the Politics of a Footboard," *City & Society* (forthcoming) and "Promissory Things: How Affective Bonds Stretch Along a Tramline," *Distinktion: Journal of Social Theory* (2019).

Alina Kleinn is a consultant for the UNESCO International Institute for Educational Planning, based in Buenos Aires. She is the author of a chapter of the volume *Globalizing International Relations: Scholarship amidst Divides and Diversity* (Palgrave Macmillan, 2016).

L.H.M. Ling served as Associate Dean of Faculty Affairs at the New School for Public Engagement (NSPE) and at the time of her passing in 2018, was an Associate Professor at the Milano School of International Affairs, Management, and Urban Policy at The New School, United States. Her research focused on developing a post-Western, post-Westphalian approach to world politics through the notion of "multiple worlds" or worldism. As the author of numerous academic books and articles, plays and a novel, Lily's work will continue to be a driving force in critical IR for many years to come.

Luisa Linke-Behrens holds a PhD in International Relations from Freie Universität Berlin, Germany, where she has held positions as Research Assistant and Project Coordinator. She now works at the Senate Chancellery of Berlin.

Nizar Messari is an Associate Professor in International Studies at Al Akhawayn University in Ifrane (Morocco) and Vice President for Academic Affairs at the same institution. His areas of interest are IR theory and critical security studies. He has worked and published on topics related to migration and refugee studies since 2010.

Sabine Mokry is a PhD candidate in the Political Science Department at Leiden University, Netherlands. Her dissertation analyzes the conditions under which Chinese social actors, specifically think tankers, scholars and lobbyists, influence China's foreign policy priorities. She obtained two Master's degrees from Freie Universität Berlin, one in International Relations and one in China Studies.

Amy Niang is a Senior Lecturer of International Relations at the University of the Witwatersrand. Her areas of research include the history of state formation, the notion of "the international" in theory and practice, and Africa in/and international relations. She is the author of *The Postcolonial African State in Transition* (Rowman & Littlefield, 2018).

Joao Pontes Nogueira is an Associate Professor of International Relations at the International Relations Institute, Pontifical Catholic University of Rio de Janeiro, Brazil. His fields of interest include IR theory, international political sociology, humanitarianism, international inequality and the role of cities in world politics.

Ingo Peters is an Associate Professor and Executive Director of the Center of Transnational Studies, Foreign and Security Policy at the Otto-Suhr-Institute for Political Science, Department of Political and Social Sciences, Freie Universität Berlin, Germany. His teaching and research interests include German foreign policy, European security and European Union foreign policy, transatlantic relations, European security institutions and IR theory.

Carolina M. Pinheiro holds a Master's degree in International Affairs from the Julien J. Studley Graduate Program, Milano School of International Affairs, Management, and Urban Policy at The New School, United States. With a background in law and diverse activities ranging from grassroots advocacy representing indigenous populations to serving as a finance attorney, her research interests encompass creative intersections between different world views and the art of listening to navigate them.

Karen Smith teaches International Relations at Leiden University in the Netherlands. She also remains affiliated as an honorary research associate with the University of Cape Town, South Africa, where she was based as an Associate Professor until 2017. Her research focuses on contributions to IR theory from the global South, South Africa's foreign policy and changes in global order.

Vineet Thakur is a University Lecturer in History and International Relations at Leiden University, the Netherlands. He is the author (with Peter Vale) of *South Africa, Race and the Making of International Relations* (Rowman & Littlefield, 2020), *Postscripts on Independence: Foreign Policy Discourses in India and South Africa* (Oxford University Press, 2018) and *Jan Smuts and the Indian Question* (University of KwaZulu-Natal Press, 2017).

Arlene B. Tickner is a Professor of International Relations in the School of International, Political and Urban Studies at the Universidad del Rosario, Bogotá, Colombia. Her main areas of research include sociology of knowledge in the field of International Relations and the evolution of IR in non-Western settings, Latin American and hemispheric security, and Colombian foreign policy. She is the co-editor (with David Blaney and Inanna Hamati-Ataya) of the Routledge book series, Worlding Beyond the West. In addition to her academic work, she writes a weekly newspaper column in the Colombian daily, *El Espectador*.

Peter Vale is a Senior Fellow at the Centre for the Advancement of Scholarship at the University of Pretoria, South Africa. He was the founding director of the Johannesburg Institute for Advanced Study, and is Nelson Mandela Professor of Politics Emeritus, Rhodes University. His latest book is *South Africa, Race and the Making of International Relations* (with Vineet Thakur) (Rowman & Littlefield, 2020). Currently, he researches cartoons and international relations, how the international came to South Africa and the social responsibility of higher education.

Wiebke Wemheuer-Vogelaar is a Post-doctoral Researcher at the Freie Universität Berlin, Germany. She initiated the project "Global Pathways: Knowledge Diffusion in IR Research" at FU Berlin and worked previously on similar projects at that institution and at the College of William and Mary, United States. She is the co-editor of the volume *Globalizing International Relations: Scholarship amidst Divides and Diversity* (Palgrave-Macmillan, 2016) and the co-author of several journal articles on the sociology of International Relations.

Preface

This book has been a long time coming. For over 15 years, a group of colleagues working throughout the world on distinct facets of what is loosely described as non- or post-Western International Relations, has frequently expressed our discomfort with the field of IR and its textbooks for addressing varied experiences of world politics in a meaningful way with our students. A typical challenge faced by professors of IR, particularly in global South classrooms, but increasingly in the North too, is how to teach theories, concepts and issues in ways that make sense to students, given the strong disconnect that exists between what we have grown accustomed to labeling the "ABC" or the "canon" of the discipline, on the one hand, and lived realities on the ground, on the other.

In April 2012 we finally decided to do something about this. At the International Studies Association (ISA) annual convention in San Diego, Pinar Bilgin, Nizar Messari, Karen Smith and Arlene B. Tickner sat down in a random coffee shop and talked through what a textbook written from the global South, and of use both there and in the North for understanding IR and international relations[1] in all of its diversity, would look like and who we might recruit to actually write it. We were fortunate enough to receive the generous support of Nizar's institution, Al Akhawayn University, to hold a first authors' workshop in Ifrane, Morocco, in October 2012, at which an initial contributor pool delivered preliminary presentations, discussed in greater detail the contents of our "dream" textbook, and tried out our ideas on some of the university's IR students. In Ifrane we were joined, among others, by Lily (L.H.M.) Ling, who became a tireless source of support for the project and collaborated temporarily as one of the textbook's co-editors (as did Nizar). Thanks to Lily's efforts, the Julien J. Studley Graduate Program in International Affairs at The New School hosted a second workshop in New York in October 2013, at which more refined chapter drafts were presented and commented upon by both textbook contributors and New School professors. Subsequently, we presented our collective work in panels at the annual ISA conventions in Toronto (February 2014) and New Orleans (March 2015) and at the EISA in Sicily (2015), where we were genuinely surprised at the amount of enthusiasm that the textbook idea generated among our academic peers, many of whom have continued to ask about it regularly.

On more occasions than we would like to remember, we were ready to throw in the towel on this project. In addition to the comings and goings of potential chapter authors, as the project advanced our ideas changed in terms of what we were doing, whether it was a textbook of alternative theorizing, a more general critical reading of international relations from the perspective of the global South or both, for which audiences (undergraduate, graduate, global South, global North or all of the above), and how best to achieve this. We are grateful to those who encouraged us not to give up, and deeply appreciative of all our contributors' patience, understanding and commitment, as well as that of our editors at Routledge. During those times when it seemed as if the textbook would never come to fruition, Lily liked to remind us that doing something different as compared to the dozens of other publications available for teaching IR was a tall order, given the disciplining functions of IR. In particular, providing students with a minimal roadmap to dominant approaches in the field – as is customarily expected in a "textbook" – while avoiding making those same approaches the center of attention or the main focus of critique, is surprisingly difficult. The fact that after so many years nothing analogous to this textbook has yet appeared seems to prove the point. We think that Lily – who departed this world way too soon in 2018 – would find this quite amusing.

Now that we have (finally) completed the textbook, which admittedly is a bit different from what we might have envisioned eight years ago, we are hopeful that it will help professors and students alike to identify alternatives within IR and international relations and to envision the world(s) differently.

Note

1 In the volume we distinguish between International Relations (IR) as the field of study and international relations as a practice.

1   Introduction

International Relations from the global South

Karen Smith and Arlene B. Tickner

A familiar saying about the field of International Relations (IR) is that it is not very "international," given the pervasiveness of Western (mainly Anglo-American) modes of thought, nor much about "relations," except for those that exist between states, especially world powers. By way of justification, neorealist theorist, Kenneth N. Waltz (1979: 72) once claimed that

> [i]t would be as ridiculous to construct a theory of international politics based on Malaysia and Costa Rica as it would be to construct an economic theory of oligopolistic competition based on the minor firms in a sector of an economy.

In his critical historiography of IR, John Hobson (2012) traces the origins of such myopia to scientific racism in the 18th and 19th centuries, showing how the main canons of (Westphalian) world politics are rooted in the perspectives and experiences of white, European men (a similar argument is developed in Chapter 4). This Eurocentric background, according to Hobson, accounts for both the intellectual and the material domination of the West in IR.

And yet, the claim that world politics may look different depending on the geocultural site from which one views it has become commonplace in IR. During the past two decades, growing scholarly interest in the global South and the non-West has led to a number of literatures that have sought to: (a) critique the supposed "universality" of categories such as sovereignty, the state, secularism and security; (b) analyze distinct IR concepts as they have actually been experienced, problematized and theorized in distinct parts of the world; and (c) identify different non-Western concepts that may shed light on world politics beyond existing disciplinary lenses (by way of illustration, see Neuman 1998; Dunn and Shaw 2001; Gruffydd Jones 2006; Acharya and Buzan 2010; Nayak and Selbin 2010; Cornelissen et al. 2012; Tickner and Blaney 2012).

Although significant contributions have been made by critical theories of distinct stripes, including feminism, poststructuralism, queer theory, postcolonialism and decoloniality, to our understanding of the social and situated nature of knowledge, and of the diverse perspectives on the world derived from them, the question of what an IR rooted in the experiences of the global South and the non-West might actually look like has been less explored, especially in the realm of teaching (for more on this issue, see Chapter 2).

It could be said that a growing "decolonializing" mood is permeating the IR discipline, generating impatience and discontent with much of the conventional work being done in North American and European universities (Gruffydd Jones 2006; Taylor 2012). Many in IR, particularly a growing number of younger scholars and students (including those still in undergraduate and graduate programs), are hungry for materials to enrich their knowledge in a way that helps them to see how the world looks from diverse places. A characteristic challenge that many of the contributors to this volume share when teaching IR both in or centered around the global South is precisely the disconnect that we sense between the theories customarily used to analyze world politics, the field's key concepts, categories and themes as determined by those theories, and lived realities outside the West and North. However, deeply entrenched disciplinary logics operate in such a way that even scholars who acknowledge the problematic and exclusionary nature of the field, and support efforts to decenter or globalize it, continue to use conventional texts in their syllabi, and to present students with a limited, Western-centric account of IR. As explained briefly in the Preface, it is with this quandary in mind that the idea for our textbook emerged.

Despite the fact that doing IR "differently" has become increasingly embraced as an idea, be it through distinct critical lenses, alternative concepts, or diverse methods such as narrative (Inayatullah and Dauphnee 2016), actual engagement in such an effort – the "how to" question – continues to pose considerable challenges. More so than other fields of knowledge, and as suggested by Waltz's quote, IR has largely limited itself to the study of issues of relevance to the global North. When we try to think and write differently about international relations, we find ourselves constrained by the boundaries created by decades of gatekeeping and attempts at constructing and maintaining an independent field of study, not to mention the rules that customarily underwrite "scientific" narratives in general (Inayatullah 2013). These boundaries relate to what knowledges are regarded as important (in terms of subject matter), where knowledge comes from (both geographically speaking and in terms of how it is made, a question of epistemology), and how and where "serious" knowledge is published and presented.

The stories that textbooks tell

As Kim Nossal (2001) reminded us nearly 20 years ago, textbooks play an essential role in constructing the way in which the story of international relations is told and in introducing students to specific ways of thinking about the world. Even when they do not engage explicitly with theory, textbooks suggest what subject matters do and do not legitimately form part of the discipline of IR. In foregrounding certain issues, others are inevitably left out, implying that they are unimportant to the concerns of IR and to the workings of the international system. They also suggest which authors' analyses should be considered authoritative.

It is important to challenge the view that there is a self-contained, existing field of IR "out there" and that the purpose of a textbook is simply to introduce students to it. This contention implies that textbooks play no role in constructing the field, when in fact they do. In particular, by emphasizing certain topics, framing them in a particular way and privileging some approaches to understanding the world, thus excluding many others, textbooks bestow upon students ready-made lenses through which to see international relations, which inevitably constrains the ability to think creatively about potential alternatives. As has been pointed out repeatedly, due to the nature and power dynamics that are operative within the global production of knowledge (Tickner 2013), IR textbooks are predominantly American or Western-centric, including not only their authors and publishing houses, but inevitably their content. The implications of this include the perception that only the views of Western scholars are important to the discipline of IR and, by extension, that only they can legitimately engage in theorizing (with non-Western scholars and students limited to being consumers of Western knowledge). It also "confirms" that international relations revolve around the West, and Western interests. As noted by Nossal (2001: 6), the main storyline as told by many textbooks is thus that world politics cannot be understood unless the United States is at the center.

While a number of introductory International Relations textbooks claim to be sensitive to global South concerns and/or to "alternative" readings of world politics, a common element that is largely missing from all of them are the views and scholarly voices from the global South. Our volume aspires to fill this gap by problematizing the issue of *perspective* as a theoretical, methodological and pedagogical problem that should be placed at the core of classroom debates, instead of being a secondary or subsidiary matter. Namely, it offers students a textbook that challenges the implicit notions inherent in most existing IR textbooks and, instead, presents international relations as seen from different vantage points in the global South. Its chapters are authored mainly by scholars who are either from and/or based in the global South, and whose primary goal is to provide an alternative or complementary reading of IR derived from the experiences of the non-core. We have tried to include perspectives that are not normally found in standard IR textbooks – including alternative origins of the discipline and views on the state and security that do not have their roots in the West or North. In doing so, we challenge conventional notions about which and whose narratives matter. In this sense, the knowledge-making exercise practiced in this textbook seeks to shift the point of departure from singular and exclusionary narratives towards multiplicity and discovery, thus showing that other ways of doing IR are possible.

The importance of multiple stories

Nigerian writer Chimamanda Ngozi Adichie gave a TED talk in 2009 called "the danger of a single story" that has since been viewed by over 18 million people (watch it here: www.ted.com/talks/chimamanda_adichie_the_danger_of_a_single_story?language). Her message resonates strongly with the singular readings of the world (re)produced in many IR textbooks. Although Adichie focuses largely on the problematic effects of simplistic narratives about Africa that condense the entire continent into oftentimes derogatory adjectives such as "backwards," "uncivil" or "corrupt," she alerts us to the impossibility, if not the dangers, of reducing people, places and problems to single, fixed explanations and categories by exploring her own biases concerning Mexico.[1]

Within the field of IR, and notwithstanding increased self-reflection and self-consciousness concerning our academic practices, many scholars continue to ignore how their own perspectives – derived from myriad socio-cultural factors, including gender, race, class, academic training, institutional location and where they live – may lead them to prioritize one particular view. This is also characteristic of Eurocentrism (to be discussed further in the next section), which assumes not only that the West lies at the core of the world, but that its ideas and experiences are universalizable. The result is that we base our understandings on an incomplete history, in which agency is denied to many marginalized actors, and in which the worldviews, actions and experiences of a small percentage of the world's population are prioritized. Stories from other parts of the globe are subsequently left out because they are believed to be of no consequence. That is, they do not provide credible accounts of the world, at least not as the West understands it. By listening only to some stories and being led to believe that they are the only important ones, we as scholars of IR are missing out on potentially important insights.

With this void in mind, our textbook is filled with a wealth of stories. Indeed, most of the chapters begin with a story, an example or an anecdote that puts into relief situations and encounters in global politics that the tools offered to us by conventional IR are poorly equipped to understand, and that beg to be accounted for distinctly in order to make better sense of the world(s) around us. Contrary to scholarly prose, stories allow us to lower our guard, avoid trying to fit things into accepted categories and stop asking questions such as "what is this an instance of?" or "what theory does this reflect?" When they contain ideas or behaviors that contradict predominant modes of understanding the world, stories also play a more emancipatory function through the jolts they produce to accepted ways of knowing and categorizing the world. In this fashion, they turn conventional academic analysis on its head by generating openness towards new and oftentimes unexpected situations (if not feelings) that are often "explained away" by dominant conceptual lenses. "This relaxed transportation ... allows us a sense ... that multiple valuable positions exist on any issue" (Inayatullah 2013: 194–5), thus opening space for the creative and transgressive power of diversity and difference.

This textbook is premised largely on the argument that the global South's encounter with the "international" has been mediated by its particular (and dependent) mode of insertion into the world system, thus making its experiences distinct. However, a second underlying theme is that the invisibility of the global South within dominant narratives about world politics has been a key enabling factor of the singular, universalizing stories of the West, such as the formation of its civilizational ideal or the idea of the modern nation-state. This is not a call for particularism, but rather an invitation to transcend the Western-centrism within which IR has historically been embedded, and to make visible and give legitimacy to alternative worlds. Accordingly, the contributors to the textbook ask questions such as: how has the global South dealt with the epistemic violence that is mainstream IR? What is the meaning of sovereignty to those who have experienced colonialism and imperialism? How can we re-imagine the "international" when the global North sets its norms, institutions and practices? What does it mean to give voice to the world's silenced voices? Does it mean to necessarily hold critical views on IR? In addition to focusing on how geocultural differences influence the experience, problematization and conceptualization of world politics, the textbook asks: how should we teach this global South IR?

Defining our terms

Although this textbook does not assume prior knowledge of the main theoretical debates in the field of International Relations, many of our contributors refer to both "conventional" IR theories and to a number of terms more prevalent within "critical" IR circles (including feminism, poststructuralism, postcolonialism and decoloniality). It is to a broad definition of some of the latter that we now turn.

Conventional, mainstream, disciplinary IR

Many of the textbook chapters establish contrasts between global-South-driven approaches, on the one hand, and "conventional," "mainstream" or "disciplinary" IR on the other. Although diverse contributors may use such terms in slightly different ways in order to highlight distinct facets of the dominant strains of International Relations, they largely operate as synonyms in that they all underscore the idea that IR is a field of study in which certain understandings of the world predominate and various gatekeeping practices (among them specialized publications, scholarly associations and academic training) are in place that "discipline" potential members and reproduce such domination.

By way of general distinction, by mainstream or conventional IR we refer to scholarship that centers on specific research topics (largely rooted in the experiences of the West and the North, as discussed previously), that defends a positivist idea of science (consisting of empirical observation and the testing of hypotheses and causal claims about a world "out there"), and whose adherents share ontological assumptions about what the "international" *is* and epistemological ones about how to build knowledge about it (Steans 2003: 432). In turn, we share Ling's (2017: 4–7) description of disciplinary IR as a domain of hypermasculine, Eurocentric whiteness that is rooted in realist and liberal modes of relating to the world, and that assumes that the West and North America are the main origins (and drivers) of international relations. For her, the Peace of Westphalia (1648) and the resulting Westphalian state system are thus one of disciplinary IR's main founding myths.

North, South, West, non-West

In this textbook, many references are made to the "West," "non-West," "global North," "global South," "third world," "core" and "periphery." We are cognizant of the varied interpretations that might exist of these terms, the boundary problem entailed in their use as dichotomies, and the potential risks of deploying them to refer to very diverse parts of the world (including the danger of treating diverse places as homogeneous). Placing the terms initially in quotes is meant to acknowledge the contingent nature of their construction and their eventual overlaps. For example, the "West" certainly does not refer to a geographical location alone since "Western" hegemony in IR and world politics spans the globe. Similarly, some of the "third world" or "global South" could be considered part of the "West," as occurs in the case of Latin America. Given this understanding, and in order to provide a less cumbersome text for the reader, we refrain from putting the terms in quotes in the remaining sections of this chapter and subsequent ones.

Broad categories are never unproblematic, but if we use them carefully, whilst historicizing and contextualizing, they can be useful analytical tools. In the specific case of this textbook, they allow us to focus on what distinct parts of the world defined variously as the periphery, third world, non-West or global South, have in common. For instance, while those who study modernity have established clear links between Western colonizers and the non-Western colonized, global capitalism continues to operate in such a way that distinguishes between core and periphery, or North and South. Additionally, core–periphery- or North–South-like dynamics are also palpable in academic practice, where exclusion from the production of IR knowledge, and in some cases, a deliberate silencing, are apparent.

Within fields such as IR, we have seen an evolution from the use of first/third world to West/non-West to global North/global South, the latter being the preferred paired terms today. What all these concepts share is that they are invoked in antithesis to the West, a concept that also has multiple meanings, ranging from being a predominantly geographical indicator to referring to religion (Christianity), political ideology (liberalism) and development. As O'Hagan (2002) points out, while we often see reference to "the West" in IR, both in theory and practice, scholars are not necessarily referring to the same conception, and may refer to material, normative or other dimensions. She divides the impact of the West on modern IR into three key elements (the West as an actor, the West as an institutional model and the West as an intellectual foundation) (O'Hagan 2002: 9). These different elements are present to a greater or lesser degree in each of the references to "the West" that you will encounter in this book. The latter (the West as an intellectual foundation) is perhaps most directly relevant to our project, in the sense that this book is an attempt to challenge the Western-centrism or Eurocentrism (discussed below) so prevalent in the discipline of IR.

It is also important to note that these terms are always contextual and never static. During the Cold War, for example, the West was contrasted to the East, whereas today it is contrasted to the "non-West" (see for example, Acharya and Buzan 2010) or the "global South" which includes Asia, Africa and Latin America. In some cases, "Western" is also regarded as a euphemism for "white."

The term "global South," which is the preferred one in this volume, has less of a negative connotation as the parts of the world that make up this broad category are identified not only in terms of their non-Westernness. While the global South is sometimes used to refer to countries based on economic indicators (for example, World Bank classification), we use it in a broader sense, in line with Dados and Connell (2012: 13), who affirm that it "[f]unctions as more than a metaphor for underdevelopment. It references an entire history of colonialism, neo-imperialism, and differential economic and social change through which large inequalities in living standards, life expectancy, and access to resources are maintained." Therefore, for us, global South also denotes those parts of the world that have largely been absent in terms of contributing to our understanding of international relations. While it has (sometimes) been studied, it has not been viewed in mainstream IR as having the agency to make substantive theoretical contributions, but at most to provide the raw empirical data that can then be analyzed by scholars in the North, much the same as raw materials are exported from the global South to be turned into manufactured goods elsewhere, only to be sold back. The idea of the South as a region of distinctive intellectual production is articulated, among others, in Boaventura de Sousa Santos' "epistemologies of the South" (discussed more extensively in Chapter 17) and Raewyn Connell's "Southern theory" (Dados and Connell 2012: 13; in the specific case of IR, see among others, Aydinli and Biltekin 2018 on "homegrown theories"). Many chapters in this textbook similarly explore the global South's agency, for example in terms of resistance by actors generally perceived to be marginalized victims, to global power or proactive measures designed to create other worlds.

In sum, and echoing Asli Calkivik's discussion of foreign policy in Chapter 11, global South is used in this textbook not only as a geopolitical label, but also as a distinctive political positionality and an ethical subjectivity.

Eurocentrism

At the heart of the debate about the need to globalize International Relations and to make it more inclusive, lies a critique of Western-centrism or Eurocentrism, two terms that are often conflated. In the specific case of IR, authors such as Steve Smith (2002) also refer to the American-centrism that characterizes the field in order to describe U.S. dominance, as discussed in a previous section.

It is important to keep in mind that there are different understandings of Eurocentrism. You might want to take a quick look now at the distinct ways in which Pinar Bilgin and John M. Hobson perceive it in Chapters 10 and 12. Eurocentrism is understood here as the limitations engendered by theorizing from a particular narrative on "European" experiences to study the rest of the world. For example, concepts that form the core of IR (such as sovereignty and statehood) have been derived from a narrow European experience, and yet have acquired status as universal categories. The effect is that, as students of international relations, we are limited in terms of understanding the world based on Eurocentric accounts.

Eurocentrism is evident in IR in that the themes, theories and preoccupations of the field largely reflect the history of the West (Gruffydd Jones 2006: 3). The result is that certain forms of knowledge (which originate in the West) dominate the field. In addition, Western knowledge and theories are perceived to be universal, while knowledge originating in the global South is regarded as particular and therefore inferior. The idea that some forms of knowledge are universal while others are localized or particular has been challenged by numerous postcolonial and decolonial scholars, who point out that all knowledge is hybrid, multilayered and intertwined (see Chapter 3 for more on this issue). An important part of the anti-Eurocentric critique in IR is the rejection of the Westphalian narrative that underlies both the field of IR and the practice of international relations (Kayaoglu 2010; Ling 2014).

Epistemic violence

The term "epistemic violence" originates from Spivak's (1988) reference to hegemony's dismissal, silencing and/or erasing of alternative perspectives, particularly those developed by the "subaltern." It is described in further detail in Chapter 2. As postcolonial scholars have pointed out, colonialism was not only about political domination but also about cultural (and psychological) domination, which involved the denigration of knowledge systems that were different and deemed to be inferior to that of modern Western science that, in the words of Santos et al. (2007: xviiii), was granted "epistemological privilege." This also had implications for understandings of what constitutes legitimate knowledge. Entrenchment of dichotomies such as modern/traditional, scientific/unscientific, rational/irrational has served to facilitate the domination of Western knowledge while the knowledges of the colonized were deemed irrational, unreliable, unscientific and therefore illegitimate (Lily Ling and Carolina Pinheiro develop this discussion more in Chapter 17).

However, epistemic violence is never completely triumphant. Indeed, postcolonial and decolonial theorists, as well as many of our textbook contributors, amply demonstrate the resilience of local cultures, languages, religions and ways of life to survive despite hegemonic, colonizing attempts to the contrary, thereby ensuring the interwoven, interstitial legacies that make world politics what it is today (see Chapters 3, 6, 9, 12, 15 and 17 in particular). This does not mean that "epistemicide" (Santos et al. 2007) – the systematic suppression and destruction of subaltern knowledges – does not occur, but rather, that subaltern logics and practices are still alive, despite unequal conditions, and consequently, that they continue to make worlds (or in the words of some, a pluriverse) on a daily basis.

Epistemic violence also operates in such a way that we customarily measure ourselves against dominant notions of what IR is and is not. In the specific case of this textbook, we are wary of the potential of the field's allegedly "key" concepts and categories – around which the distinct chapters are largely structured – to do harm themselves. By starting with a story, instead of a summary of how conventional IR approaches each topic, our aim is precisely to unsettle and to "decenter" such dominant narratives.

Decentering and counterpoint

"Decentering" and "counterpoint" can be considered methods for countering epistemic violence. Although not explicitly mentioned throughout much of the textbook, most of the chapters implicitly practice them. While both seek to unsettle the hierarchical power operations that place dominant (Western or Northern) experience at the center of historical narratives, as well as politics, economics and what not, they also address the problem of how to communicate with an "Other" who is significantly different from one's Self, and how to recognize that the Other or the "stranger" is also always within us (Nandy 1983).

The act of decentering challenges the alleged existence of a center from which legitimate knowledge is deemed to originate and is oftentimes used with reference to Eurocentrism or Western-centrism, although it largely originated in feminist thinking. According to Nayak and Selbin (2010: 4), "to decenter IR from its Northern/Western anchors requires us to challenge the politics, concepts, and practices that enable certain narratives of IR to be central." An important element of globalizing and pluralizing International Relations is recognizing the role that the global South has played in shaping world politics and recognizing the work that scholars from the global South have done, with an eye to identifying distinct starting points for talking about the world. This textbook does both.

As David L. Blaney discusses in Chapter 3, drawing upon the work of Edward Said, a method of "counterpoint" highlights in turn the intertwined and overlapping trajectories that exist between past and present, and colonizers and colonized. By creating awareness of the complex connections that exist between things, a "contrapuntal" reading makes visible knowledges and histories that have been occulted or repressed, thus offering an alternative means and an *ethos* for (re)envisioning global politics (see too, Bilgin 2016).

Structure and rationale

Many distinct approaches to structuring this textbook were proposed and debated among our contributors. In the end, we decided that authors would write their chapters based on concepts and issues, with some exceptions. Many of these are well-known categories such as order, war, security, sovereignty and foreign policy, that are not only familiar to mainstream IR scholars but that are also at the core of their work. We are conscious of the potential problems inherent in using them, as described previously, and as highlighted by Nayak and Selbin (2010: 9) in their decentering project. One of the aims of the chapters, however, is to problematize these concepts, and through engaging with how they have traditionally been used, ask whether they are relevant to thinking about IR in the global South, and to envisioning IR differently. Related to this are questions concerning how concepts travel and whether they have multiple origins and can therefore be considered Western at all (see Chapter 12 for elaboration of this idea in the case of globalization). We are also interested in how concepts have and can be rearticulated in diverse contexts.

The book also does not start from a position of simply rejecting the existing IR canon but instead chooses to engage with it, something that will undoubtedly elicit skepticism from some critical scholars who feel that this serves to continue privileging the West. By placing conventional and alternative treatments of key IR concepts, categories and problems side by side, in counterpoint, we might say, the book offers a broad understanding of the "international" in different parts of the world, especially the global South. Furthermore, it is unique in its insertion of IR knowledge within a context of epistemic violence and geocultural epistemologies, of understanding the global politics of international thinking informed by both post-positivist epistemologies and global power analysis.

The textbook is divided into four parts that address: (1) the IR discipline, (2) key concepts and categories, (3) global issues and (4) IR futures. In Chapter 2, Wiebke Wemheuer-Vogelaar, Ingo Peters and co-authors Laura Kemmer, Alina Kleinn, Luisa Linke-Behrens and Sabine Mokry, argue that widespread agreement about the shortcomings of mainstream IR for understanding world politics has yet to permeate International Relations teaching in any meaningful way. The authors offer a comprehensive mapping of what they call "global" or "globalizing" IR, consisting of diverse strands of critique that seek to interrogate IR as U.S. social science, expose Western-centrism, identify alternative disciplinary practices and conceptual frameworks emerging from the global South, and develop a non- or post-Western IR. Like us, they are wary of the potential dangers of simply "adding on" the global South as an appendage to existing pedagogical exercises, and thus offer ways of bringing "global" IR into the classroom with an eye to generating awareness and sensitivity to geocultural bias, epistemic violence and diversity.

Chapters 3 and 4, authored by David L. Blaney, and Peter Vale and Vineet Thakur, respectively, illustrate what decolonizing and decentering International Relations might mean in practice by recovering alternative narratives and histories of the discipline. Blaney makes use of the method of counterpoint, discussed above, to highlight the multiple and entangled perspectives that are necessarily at play in all worldly encounters. With this goal in mind, he explores the "when," the "where" and the "what" of International Relations through three distinct narratives: the stereotypical story of Eurocentric IR, the invasion of North America and the Chinese One Belt, One Road initiative. One of the key takeaways of this exercise is a more nuanced understanding of international relations as shifting spaces of (human) interconnection and intermingling, in which multilayered, overlapping histories and trajectories coexist.

In turn, Vale and Thakur claim that imperialism and racism are inscribed in the very DNA of International Relations, and call for further inquiries to show how, in addition to questions of war, order, anarchy and state sovereignty, colonial administration and race account for the origins of IR in both Europe and the United States. Rather than Aberystwyth University in Wales, or the U.S., where the discipline is said to have emerged in the aftermath of the First and Second World Wars, respectively, the authors trace its appearance to South Africa, where organizational ideas related to the reformulation of British empire were first tried out.

Part 1 constitutes an initial provocation to "unlearn" IR as it has been conventionally narrated and taught. Instead, and following Blaney's closing invitation, these chapters illustrate how the "what" of IR can be expanded when the "when" and the "where" are interrogated critically. Parts 2 and 3 of the textbook continue to disturb (or decenter) the discipline's "master narratives" by beginning each chapter with a story or an anecdote that puts into relief the misfit between canonical understandings of IR's concepts, categories and themes, and the ways in which these are experienced in concrete settings across the global South and the North.

As suggested previously, the purpose of these stories is to both lower the readers' guard and to decenter, which amount to quite a different exercise than simply "adding on" global South voices to already existing IR knowledges. Only then do the chapters examine conventional approaches to each concept or issue. In doing so the authors offer a brief intellectual history of IR in its dominant version. In the third and perhaps most substantive part of each chapter, alternative approaches to the categories or issues included in the textbook are offered with the goal of highlighting both the limitations of traditional tools and the peculiarities of dealing with such topics in the global South. Each chapter therefore offers a systematic "intervention" into key IR concepts, categories and issues that aims at both expanding the horizons of our understanding and enriching the original and dominant terms of the debate.

Part 2 includes chapters on order and ordering (Chapter 5, Karen Smith), the "international" (Chapter 6, Amy Niang), war and conflict (Chapter 7, Arlene B. Tickner), the state and sovereignty (Chapter 8, Navnita Chadha Behera), secularism, nationalism and religion (Chapter 9, Aparna Devare), security (Chapter 10, Pinar Bilgin) and foreign policy (Chapter 11, Asli Calkivik).

In turn, Part 3 explores a number of international relations issues, including globalization (Chapter 12, John M. Hobson), inequality (Chapter 13, Joao Pontes Nogueira), migration (Nizar Messari), resistances (Carolina Cepeda-Másmela) and socio-environmentalism (Cristina Yumie Aoki Inoue and Matías Franchini).

As it would be impossible to do justice to the richness of content present in each author's analysis in such a brief Introduction, at the risk of gross simplification we limit ourselves here to a number of common themes that we see running through these chapters. First, in many ways, the "international" in its distinct guises is largely an extension of racialized, colonial (and gendered) practices conceived as a result of Western imperialism. As underscored by Latin American decolonial writers such as Anibal Quijano (2010), colonial domination did not end with decolonization but was essentially transformed into a regime he describes as the "coloniality of power," which continues to uphold global hierarchies of identity, development and knowledge. For example, Western-based conceptions of order, sovereignty, peace and security, and the absence thereof, constitute dichotomies through which the countries of the North and the South are customarily represented, act to fuel anxieties about the disruptive effects of the global South for the international order and oftentimes justify distinct forms of intervention in the global South.

Second, historicizing concepts and issues that singular narratives have monopolized and naturalized is a crucial step in overcoming epistemic violence and in recovering alternative histories and knowledges. By decentering our gaze away from Eurocentric or Northern narratives, the agency of distinct Southern actors, their knowledges of the world and their distinctive protagonism in diverse global processes, comes into view.

Third, the rigid classification schemes that we customarily use to portray complex and constantly changing social practices result largely from Eurocentrism, colonialism and more recently, liberal forms of "pluralism" that all subsume difference as particular forms of allegedly universal projects. Echoing the need for greater contrapuntal sensitivity, many of the chapters in Parts 2 and 3 underscore the co-mingling of diverse traditions related to religion, political community, peace and conflict, and others, thus making visible the multiplicity that is always at play in worldly encounters.

Fourth, another of the main insights offered by these chapters is that allegedly "universal" ideas and categories rooted in provincial European history, and normalized and globalized through practices such as colonialism, are a fiction everywhere as they fail to capture the lived realities of most people, both in the global South and the North. Indeed, as Devare reminds us in Chapter 9, this may well be the largest "fault line" in today's world.

In Part 4 (Chapter 17), L.H.M. Ling and Carolina M. Pinheiro offer a vision for an alternative IR future by suggesting that distinct actors of the global South learn to converse among themselves, rather than gesturing regularly towards the West and the North. They liken this strategy, which is derived from Ling's idea of worldism and Santos' epistemologies of the South, to creative chatting among friends. They provide an example through a conversation between Daoism and Andean cosmovision, both of which uphold a similar notion of relationality. One of the key messages that we derive from the authors' exercise is the need to make visible both multiple understandings, and distinct forms of being in and with the world.

How to use this textbook

The idea of non-Western or global IR has been gaining traction within the field for over a decade now and has slowly begun to appear as a topic of study in undergraduate and graduate courses alike. And yet, as we have noted in this Introduction, the gap between scholarly research focused on decentering and pluralizing the study of international relations, and IR teaching, continues to be considerable (see Chapter 2). Given that this textbook is aimed at students and educators located in both the global North and the global South, we expect that its use will vary in these two broad geopolitical contexts. At the risk of gross simplification, we hope that Northern students will become more sensitive to why and how the South experiences the international differently but also, where important commonalities or points of potential intersection may lie. Ideally, Southern students will encounter a textbook that speaks more directly to them, with concepts and examples that are less distant, and that potentially resonates with their own experiences of and perspectives on world politics.

More generally, we envision the textbook being used in several different ways. First, it is meant to serve as the main text in undergraduate-level International Relations courses, at institutions in both the global South and North. Given that the distinct chapters offer general "state of the art" treatments of the subject matter addressed, in those courses that aspire to provide students with "the basics" in terms of the main debates within disciplinary IR, the textbook can easily be combined with supplemental readings or be used alongside more traditional texts. Second, the textbook will complement undergraduate International Relations theory courses by offering alternative readings of key IR concepts and categories. Third, in the global North in particular, the textbook is meant to be essential reading for a growing number of courses offered on diverse matters related to world politics and/in the global South.

In advanced IR courses, we envisage the textbook serving two distinct purposes: to teach IR differently by bringing in global South experiences and readings of the "international" to the forefront; and to interrogate the theoretical, conceptual and pedagogical frames used by conventional IR textbooks. In other words, we hope that the textbook provides educators with an empowering, critical and reflexive tool for reflecting on the diversity of experiences of international relations and for placing it front and center in the classroom.

For this same reason, we think that the textbook will also be useful in graduate courses that include a mix of Western/Northern students and overseas ones, where some engagement with distinct cultural traditions, geopolitical concerns and ways of knowing is necessary and rarely achieved through conventional texts (which are either narrowly grounded in Western perspectives or in Western readings of non-Western ones).

In addition to general, introductory IR courses at both the undergraduate and graduate levels, the textbook, or some of its chapters, might appeal to courses on sociology and historiography of knowledge, globalization, neoliberalism, security, the state, imperialism and international political economy.

Remaining challenges

We are at a stage today where the Western story appears wanting. It can no longer provide us with satisfactory ways of understanding what is going on in the world, if indeed it ever was capable of such a feat. Fortunately, as the different chapters in this textbook will attest, there are countless unexplored ways of thinking about the world from the global South. If we want to advance a more nuanced and meaningful understanding of international relations, this is where we should be looking. Although squarely situated within the perspectives of the global South with an eye to showing how key concepts, categories and global issues can be conceived of differently, as many of our contributors argue, this textbook is not only equipped to speak of the South, but also of the wider world, including the North, and our knowledge of it.

One challenge of existing IR scholarship that we have not addressed is that of language. The discipline remains an Anglo-centric one, with the majority of books and articles published in English. While English is not the mother tongue of most of our authors, all chapters are written in this language in order to reach as wide an audience as possible. It would have been a radical departure indeed to publish a multilingual textbook, but this is simply not practically possible (yet). However, in an attempt to expose readers to scholarship not published in English, some authors have drawn on and referenced sources published in other languages. In light of the enduring hegemony of global knowledge production, this indeed remains a pending debt. Our hope is that the textbook will subsequently be translated into other languages.

Finally, we are well aware that this textbook, like all others, is simply another attempt at constructing IR. We do not claim to be accurately representing the full extent of the discipline nor of global South experiences and readings of the world, mainly because we do not believe that this is possible or desirable. Our hope is that you, our readers, both teachers and students, will engage with the textbook critically, questioning the views taken by the different authors, counterposing them to your own views, and in doing so, building your own stories of international relations that make sense to where you find yourselves in the world, confident in the knowledge that there is never just one story (nor for that matter, one world), but always multiple ones.

Note

1 For those who are interested, you might also take a look too at "African Men Hollywood Stereotypes," produced by the NGO Mama Hope, www.mamahope.org/media/

References

Acharya, Amitav and Barry Buzan (eds) (2010) *Non-Western International Relations Theory*, London: Routledge.

Aydinli, Ersel and Gonca Biltekin (eds) (2018) *Widening the World of International Relations: Homegrown Theorizing*, London: Routledge.

Bilgin, Pinar (2016) "'Contrapuntal Reading' as a Method, an Ethos, and a Metaphor for Global IR," *International Studies Review* 18(1): 134–146. doi:10.1093/isr/viv018

Cornelissen, Scarlett Fantu Cheru and Timothy Shaw (eds) (2012) *Africa and International Relations in the 21st Century*, Houndmills: Palgrave Macmillan.

Dados, Nour and Raewyn Connell (2012) "The Global South," *Contexts* 11(1): 12–13. doi: 10.1177/1536504212436479

Dunn, Kevin and Timothy Shaw (eds) (2001) *Africa's Challenge to International Relations*, Houndmills: Palgrave Macmillan.

Gruffydd Jones, Branwen (ed) (2006) *Decolonizing International Relations*, New York: Rowman & Littlefield.

Hobson, John (2012) *The Eurocentric Conception of World Politics: Western International Theory, 1760–2010*, Cambridge: Cambridge University Press.

Inayatullah, Naeem (2013) "Distance and Intimacy: Forms of Writing and Worlding," in Arlene B. Tickner and David L. Blaney (eds) *Claiming the International*, London: Routledge, pp. 194–293.

Inayatullah, Naeem and Elizabeth Dauphnee (eds) (2016) *Narrative Global Politics*, London: Routledge.

Kayaoglu, Turan (2010) "Westphalian Eurocentrism in International Relations Theory," *International Studies Review*, 12(2): 193–217. doi:10.1111/j.1468-2486.2010.00928.x

Ling, L.H.M. (2014) *The Dao of World Politics: Towards a Post-Westphalian, Worldist International Relations*, New York: Routledge.

Ling, L.H.M. (2017) "Introduction," in Pinar Bilgin and L.H.M. Ling (eds) *Asia in International Relations*, London: Routledge, pp. 1–9.

Nandy, Ashis (1983) *The Intimate Enemy*, Delhi: Oxford University Press.

Nayak, Meghan and Eric Selbin (2010) *Decentering International Relations*, London: Zed Books.

Neuman, Stephanie (ed) (1998) *International Relations Theory and the Third World*, London: Palgrave Macmillan.

Nossal, Kim Richard (2001) "Tales that Textbooks Tell: Ethnocentricity and Diversity in American Introductions to International Relations," in Robert M.A. Crawford and Darryl S.L. Jarvis (eds) *International Relations: Still an American Social Science? Toward Diversity in International Thought*, Albany, NY: State University of New York Press, pp. 167–186.

O'Hagan, Jacinta (2002) *Conceptualizing the West in International Relations: From Spengler to Said*, Houndmills, Basingstoke: Palgrave.

Quijano, Anibal (2010) "Coloniality and Modernity/Rationality," in Arturo Escober and Walter Mignolo (eds) *Globalization and the Decolonial Option*, London: Routledge, pp. 22–33.

Santos, Boaventura de Sousa, Joao Arriscado Nunes and Maria Paula Meneses (2007) "Opening up the Canon of Knowledge and Recognition of Difference," in Boaventura de Sousa Santos (ed) *Another Knowledge Is Possible: Beyond Northern Epistemologies*, London: Verso, pp. xviii–lxi.

Smith, Steve (2002) "The United States and the Discipline of International Relations: 'Hegemonic Country, Hegemonic Discipline'," *International Studies Review* 4(2): 67–86.

Spivak, Gayatri Chakravorty (1988) "Can the Subaltern Speak?" in Cary Nelson and Lawrence Grossberg (eds) *Marxism and the Interpretation of Culture*, Champaign, IL: University of Illinios Press, pp. 271–313.

Steans, Jill (2003) "Engaging from the Margins: Feminist Encounters with the 'Mainstream' of International Relations," *British Journal of Politics and International Relations* 5(3): 428–454.

Taylor, Lucy (2012) "Decolonizing International Relations: Perspectives from Latin America," *International Studies Review* 14(3): 386–400. doi:10.1111/j.1468-2486.2012.01125.x

Tickner, Arlene B. (2013) "Core, Periphery and (Neo)imperialist International Relations," *European Journal of International Relations* 19(3): 627–646. doi:10.1177/1354066113494323

Tickner, Arlene B. and David L. Blaney (eds) (2012) *Thinking the International Differently*, London: Routledge.

Waltz, Kenneth (1979) *Theory of International Politics*, Reading, MA: Addison-Wesley.

Part 1

Discipline

2 The global IR debate in the classroom

Wiebke Wemheuer-Vogelaar, Ingo Peters, Laura Kemmer, Alina Kleinn, Luisa Linke-Behrens and Sabine Mokry[1]

Introduction: it's the classroom, stupid!

"Not only do common International Relations theories lack truly international characteristics, the discipline of IR understood as a social group does as well." This is what our syllabus' first sentence declared. Our teaching experiment started with a graduate student's term paper on "non-Western IR" in a traditional International Relations (IR) course at Freie Universität Berlin, Germany. Realizing what a vivid debate on global IR[2] was out there, the student, Wiebke Wemheuer-Vogelaar, and the lecturer, Ingo Peters, decided to bring it into the classroom by teaching the graduate seminar "Locating the 'I' in IR: Non-Western Contributions to International Relations Scholarship." The seminar introduced the sociology of IR literature and identified problems and theories from beyond the "West." Not only the seminar's content was new: during the course, a student–lecturer synergy, characterized by mutual learning, constructive openness and intellectual curiosity, developed that motivated us to take our discussion beyond the classroom. Given that the students' papers contained original research relevant to the global IR debate, Wiebke and Ingo decided to edit a volume based on carefully selected student papers (Wemheuer-Vogelaar and Peters 2016). What followed was a series of author workshops with external reviewers; a workshop at the College of William & Mary, Williamsburg, Virginia; and, finally, a presidential roundtable at the International Studies Association Annual Convention 2015 in New Orleans. And yet, despite the project's topical nature, the publication of our book has long been impeded by the structural gatekeeping mechanisms we criticize: who wants to publish a book most of whose contributors have not (yet) earned a graduate degree?

Our story illustrates how the global IR debate can be included in teaching and how students can contribute to the discipline. We conceptualize this debate along literature that addresses the discipline's geo-epistemological dimensions and the epistemic violence inherent in ignoring them, thereby aspiring to rethink IR as a global discipline. In this chapter, we, the students and lecturers of this graduate seminar and authors of the aforementioned volume posit that the IR research community's efforts to create a more inclusive discipline can only be permanent if this debate is taken to the classroom. University classes constitute an important social space to initiate changes in theory production. Based on our unique learning experience, we want to map the academic debate, discuss how it does (or does not) play out in IR teaching, and demonstrate the benefits of including students into the move towards a globalized IR.

At the center of the discipline today, the global IR debate has established that mainstream IR falls short of providing adequate analytical tools to capture global international relations and that it systematically excludes traditions from beyond the West. However, this recognition has not yet reached the IR classroom (Carvalho et al. 2011; Lupovici 2013). In fact, most IR syllabi around the world convey a nearly identical account of what IR is and how it evolved. Textbooks perpetuate the "myths of 1648 and 1919" and persistently define the grand paradigms of realism, liberalism, Marxism and constructivism as the discipline's core curriculum (Wæver 1996; Nossal 2001; Schmidt 2002; Carvalho et al. 2011). Students are currently socialized into a Western hegemony that the discipline struggles to lay off; they grow into the discipline without reflecting on geo-epistemology and epistemic violence (see Box 2.2). The marginalization of global IR in teaching will lead students to regard it as irrelevant and will, hence, perpetuate our current, undesirable situation.

BOX 2.1 NON-WESTERN? POST-WESTERN? GLOBAL?

Scholars use numerous terms for referring to challenges to traditional IR; all of them carry heavy connotations and reflect both intellectual and political aspirations. The term "non-West" that was used early on in the debate (e.g. Acharya and Buzan 2007) usually refers to a geographical or geopolitical distinction from the West, but was soon criticized for reinforcing the dichotomy between the "West" and "the rest" that it sought to overcome (e.g. Bilgin 2008; Hutchings 2011; Shilliam 2011). Both, "post-Western IR" and "global IR" carry a desire to transcend the IR discipline in its current form. While post-Western IR clearly distances itself from "Western" IR and embodies a rather radical move to create critical and less Eurocentric IR theory (e.g. Shani 2008), global IR aims at recreating IR as a global discipline. Acharya (2014, 2016) stresses that global IR constitutes "an aspiration for greater inclusiveness and diversity in our discipline" built upon pluralistic universalism and world history (Acharya 2016: 649).

We suggest a new way of teaching IR and especially IR theory. Similar to the calls for including critical theory into IR teaching via critical pedagogy (Neufeld and Healy 2001; Hagmann and Biersteker 2014) and postcolonial perspectives via engaged pedagogy (Madge et al. 2009), we propose "to bring the global IR debate in" and to go beyond the classroom with student research projects. IR courses should sensitize students to geo-epistemological biases and epistemic violence while allowing for a collective reflection on the discipline. This approach can bear fruit because students are by definition "learning" and thus could more easily "unlearn" the discipline's traditional cleavages. Because of their limited socialization into the discipline, they have a good instinct for epistemic violence and new ideas of how to make IR more diverse, plural and inclusive. Teaching should embrace this potential and establish an environment of mutual learning, in which students and lecturers discuss as equals and student research is considered a valuable addition.

In practice, we imagine the following. First, IR courses should discuss what traditional IR theories *cannot* do in addition to what they can do. In what cases do they "not fit?" Second, courses should incorporate meta-questions and elements of the sociology of IR. Who contributes to the discipline? For whom do they write and why? What are the discipline's mechanisms of reproduction? Third, syllabi should include examples of IR from outside the canon. How do they compare to traditional IR theories? What can we learn about IR in and beyond the West? Fourth, since textbooks have "the capacity to shape theoretical understandings of world politics" (Nossal 2001: 168), those that deviate from the standard narrative should inform IR courses, at least in a supplementary way. Finally, if opportunities arise to make student research accessible to a wider audience, they should be embraced because it can constitute a substantial contribution to the field: being less familiar with disciplinary habits, students are more likely to challenge norms and to move beyond the beaten track.

To build our case, this chapter progresses as follows. First we explore the global IR debate literature in three strands according to their main questions, central aims and methods. The chapter then establishes and problematizes the global IR debate's absence from IR classrooms by reviewing syllabi and major textbooks. Finally, we explore the benefit of including students into the move towards global IR and describe our way of achieving it.

Mapping the global IR debate[3]

We conceptualize the global IR debate as the body of literature that addresses the discipline's geo-epistemological dimensions and the epistemic violence inherent in ignoring these. An example comes from prioritizing knowledge produced in one geo-epistemological context over all others. Global IR, therefore, is more to us than the way Amitav Acharya has defined the concept (2014, 2016; see Box 2.1). As we will show, this debate has been going on for over 30 years but has gained momentum only in the past five to ten. Although all global IR contributors share a basic dedication to the core themes of geo-epistemology and epistemic violence, (see Box 2.2.) they do so with different foci and by different means. Consequently, different strands of argumentation have developed, which we conceptualize as: first, a *pre-debate* on IR as an "American social science"; second, a *conceptual-normative strand* raising awareness for IR's Western-centric character; and third, an *empirical strand* with case studies on IR knowledge practices in different countries and regions beyond the West. These strands are neither independent of each other nor follow a strict chronological order. However, they are distinct in the questions they raise and the methods they apply to address them (see Table 2.1).

BOX 2.2 GEO-EPISTEMOLOGY AND EPISTEMIC VIOLENCE

Emerging from the geography of knowledge literature (e.g. Harding 1998; Preston 2003; Agnew 2007), *geo-epistemology* denotes the boundedness of knowledge and its production to the contextual time and space in which it occurs. Thus, there is no universal way of producing knowledge and no particular (regional) epistemology can claim superiority. To create a more inclusive and diverse IR, we need to become aware of these geo-epistemologies and direct attention towards how IR is practiced around the globe (see most prominently Tickner and Wæver 2009).

Epistemic violence, put forward by postcolonial scholars, describes the act of imposing a particular (in this case Western-centric) knowledge on other parts of the world (Spivak 1994). This process entails determining what we can know and how we can know it, creating hierarchies between different kinds of knowledge and its production contexts, and ultimately denying the agency of non-Western regions in producing IR knowledge. Thereby, they are constituted as the "Other" in the discipline.

Table 2.1 The global IR debate

Strand	Main question	Central aims	Method	Representative contributions
"American social science"	Is IR an "American social science"?	Identify factors that shape IR; case studies on Western alternatives to U.S. IR	Critical analysis; empirical case studies based on sociology of science	Hoffmann (1977) Wæver (1998) Friedrichs (2004) Kristensen (2015b) Turton (2015)
Conceptual-normative	What is Western-centric about IR? How to overcome its biases?	Raise awareness for the dominance of Westphalian narratives in IR theory and practices; suggest alternative conceptualizations of the international	Critical de- and re-construction of IR concepts, theories and practices	Inayatullah (2004) Bilgin (2008) Tickner (2003) Tickner (2013) Hobson (2009, 2012) Chen (2012) Worlding Beyond the West, volumes 2 and 3 Acharya (2014, 2016)
Empirical	How is IR practiced beyond the West?	Describe how IR is "done" in countries and regions beyond the West	Case studies; partially paired with quantitative data analyses, including citation analysis	Aydinli and Mathews (2000) Huang (2007) Worlding Beyond the West, volume 1 Acharya and Buzan (2007) Sharma (2010) Maliniak et al. (2018) Wemheuer-Vogelaar et al. (2016) Kristensen (2015a)

Pre-debate: IR as an "American social science" and Western responses

Long before the first claims about Western-centrism in IR were uttered in the early 2000s, a debate about the preponderance of U.S. authors, theories and epistemologies had evolved. In 1977, Stanley Hoffmann published his now famous article, "An American Social Science: International Relations." He argued that the discipline could not have evolved as it did anywhere but in the United States. The ensuing strand of the global IR debate is therefore characterized by reactions to Hoffmann (1977), which vary in their degree of disagreement and the methods used to disprove his arguments. Focusing on European and other Western counter-examples, its key message was: there is good IR from Europe and Canada too!

For Hoffmann, "intellectual predispositions" explain why the discipline materialized in the U.S. after World War II. This includes a general strengthening of the social sciences, their modeling after the natural sciences and the influx of scholars from Europe whose philosophical training and personal experiences provided them with a sense of history that made them ask big questions. This resolute account has provoked many reactions, most prominently, Ole Wæver's (1998) "The Sociology of a Not So International Discipline ...." Wæver points towards a substantive diversity among European IR communities

(Friedrichs 2004; Jørgensen and Knudsen 2006) and argues that every country can develop its distinct approach towards IR (Crawford and Jarvis 2001). Nevertheless, the American "way of doing IR," driven by positivist epistemologies and realist theories, has been regarded as the discipline's leading narrative.

Younger European scholars have recently started to counter the claim of U.S. dominance through case studies on, among others, the dominance of single institutions of higher education in the U.S. and Europe (Kristensen 2015b) and the strong influence of émigré scholars on ostensibly "American" IR (Rösch 2014). In contrast to these approaches that placed knowledge producers center-stage, Turton (2015) recently called for distinguishing between U.S. dominance in terms of people (i.e. authors, editors) and content (i.e. theories, epistemology, methods). This means that, while IR journals and editorial boards are indeed filled with U.S.-based scholars, the IR field is not necessarily U.S.-centered (for a counter claim see Smith 2002). This pre-debate thus suffers from a strong commitment to analyzing IR on the nation-state level (Porter 2001) and the omission of connecting its critique to the vivid discourse on hegemonic knowledge production outside of IR (for example, Harding 1998). The second strand has addressed both these gaps.

The conceptual-normative strand: Western-centrism in IR

During the past decade, the Eurocentric responses to Hoffmann's article have been comple- mented by a vivid conceptual-normative literature on "IR beyond the West."[4] In aiming to uncover "Western" (not only U.S.) hegemony in IR scholarship, this literature suggests alter- native conceptualizations that are more sensitive to social and political realities in the global South/East. While contributors to this strand agree that there should be an alternative IR, they disagree on more concrete details. The search for non-Western alternative IR theories began optimistically but stalled when the hidden theories waiting to be "discovered" and integrated into mainstream IR failed to materialize or, if found, failed to impact mainstream discourses (Acharya and Buzan 2007). These difficulties are rooted in expectations of what such non-Western IR theory should look like: conceptually exotic, but epistemologically and ontologically fit for mainstream consumption (Shilliam 2011).

Consequently, many authors shifted away from searching for such theories to iden- tifying gate-keeping practices that prevent such alternative theoretical approaches and narratives from emerging at all or from entering IR's disciplinary core. The overall dominance of the "Westphalia narrative" in IR theorizing (Chakrabarty 2000; Inaya- tullah 2004; Hobson 2009; Kayaoglu 2010) places actors other than states (for example indigenous peoples) or forms of international (non-)cooperation other than intergovernmental institutions (e.g. transnational interaction among civil society actors) in inferior positions by declaring these as epiphenomena of international rela- tions. The same restrictions apply to alternative ways of doing research and the types of knowledge that are regarded as valid contributions (Nayak and Selbin 2011; Chen 2012; Tickner and Blaney 2013). This intellectual gate-keeping is reinforced by struc- tural barriers, such as biased peer-review systems (Salager-Meyer 2008), the predom- inance of English as the *lingua franca* of IR publishing (D'Aoust 2012) as well as the brain-drain and socialization effects caused when scholars from beyond the West seek degrees in the West (Tickner 2013). These and similar practices serve to repro- duce the core–periphery system and stifle a more globalizing development of the entire field.

Yet, there are alternatives. While some authors have argued for establishing non-Western (often national) schools of IR as a means of provincializing mainstream IR theorizing (Song 2001; Makarychev and Morozov 2013), others developed new theories based on local sources of knowledge or post-Western theorizing (see Box 2.3). Theories that draw on local sources of knowledge, such as ideas of local leaders, religious thoughts or conceptions from local or global history, often aim at explaining locally specific phenomena and might do so in traditional terms of (IR) theorizing. Post-Western theories, by contrast, typically aim at radically transcending all local ideas, aiming for an alternative outlook on the world as a whole (Ling 2014). Yet another approach is to critically de- and re-construct single key IR narratives, for example concepts like the "state" and "sovereignty" (see Part 2 of this volume; Neuman 1998; Murithi 2007; Tickner and Blaney 2012).

BOX 2.3 NON-/POST-WESTERN IR THEORIES

Over the past decade, numerous attempts have been made to translate local sources of knowledge into IR theorizing. Such studies draw on non-Western political, religious and economic philosophies as well as local history or reinterpret global events from a non-Western perspective. Examples include:

- Giorgio Shani (2008) suggests two concepts from Islam and Sikhism – *Umma* and *Khalsa Panth* – as a base for "post-Western" theorizing. Both terms refer to deterritorialized, translational communities of believers, which Shani uses to transcend Western IR's universalist notion of international relations among sovereign nation-states.
- Khong (2013) applies the tributary system, with China at the center of nations that pay tribute in return for protection, to contemporary policies in the United States of America, thereby representing a rather unique instance of using "non-Western" sources of knowledge to explain a case of Western foreign policy.
- Recently, IR scholars have (re-)discovered the transformative potential of the Latin American decolonial perspective for key IR concepts (Grosfoguel 2007; Shilliam 2011; Taylor 2012). Decolonial perspectives also have a growing relevance for African IR, inquiring into the position of African states and society in the colonial world system and their collective subjectivity (Ndlovu-Gatsheni 2013).
- Several IR scholars and human rights advocates have promoted an African conceptualization of human rights based on *ubuntu* (e.g. Tutu 1999; Masina 2000), a notion common to many African societies referring to humanness through sharing, compassion and mutual belonging: "I am because we are." If globalized, this concept could serve as an ethical guidance for international human rights law and practice (Smith 2009; Murithi 2007).

The empirical strand: practicing IR beyond the West

Parallel to the conceptual-normative strand, literature developed that described and analyzed IR as practiced beyond the West. Contributors presented specific IR practices to illuminate what geo-epistemological diversity looks like in action. One important cornerstone of this strand is the first volume of the "Worlding Beyond the West" series, edited by Arlene B. Tickner and Ole Wæver (2009: 1). In their introduction, the editors state:

> ironically, when this [critiquing of IR] is done without a concrete study of non-dominant and non-privileged parts of the world, it becomes yet another way of speaking from the center about the whole ... In order to transcend this state of affairs, it is necessary to actually know about the ways in which IR is practiced around the world.

However, in spite of having compiled 16 different case studies around the world, the editors had to conclude that the discipline is practiced more homogenously than expected. This finding reinforced the normative warnings about the West's intellectual hegemony within the debate's second strand, but also encouraged paying attention to small differences and forms of localization, i.e. the adaption of potentially hegemonic concepts and practices to local contexts (Acharya and Buzan 2007). As Pinar Bilgin (2008: 6) illustrates: we need to develop an awareness of what is "almost the same but not quite."

When studying entire IR communities (Fonseca 1987; Lebedeva 2004; Huang 2007; Hadiwinata 2009; Sharma 2010), this level of sensitivity may be hard to achieve due to the number of aspects which have to be taken into account or the complexity of their interconnectedness. A number of scholars have therefore turned their attention toward smaller units: national or regional IR journals (Aydinli and Mathews 2000; Kristensen 2015a), university syllabi (Hagmann and Biersteker 2014; Colgan 2016; Grenier and Hagmann 2016) and the socio-academic hierarchies involved in local theorizing (see further on the empirical study of IR, Wemheuer-Vogelaar 2014; Wemheuer-Vogelaar and Peters 2016).

Currently, the largest empirical endeavor on IR's geo-epistemological dimensions is the Teaching, Research and International Policy (TRIP) project at the College of William & Mary in the United States. TRIP has been analyzing theoretical, methodological and epistemological diversity in IR journals (Long et al. 2005) since 2004, beginning with only U.S.- and Europe-based journals but since 2013 including journals from China, Japan and Latin America. In addition to investigating the published discipline, TRIP has been conducting regular national surveys of IR scholars in (currently) 32 countries, inquiring into scholars' teaching and research practices as well as their perceptions of developments in the discipline and international politics (Maliniak et al. 2012; Aydin and Yazgan 2013; Wemheuer-Vogelaar et al. 2016). Despite being a rich and useful data source on IR as a discipline, TRIP has been criticized for only partially succeeding in adapting its empirical research arguments to the study of power relationships and epistemic violence discussed in strand two of the debate (however, see Maliniak et al. 2018 for a shift into this direction). Moreover, the survey might be regarded as an unintentional tool for normalizing U.S./Anglophone interpretations and practices of IR. Its data should therefore be carefully (re)interpreted with these arguments in mind.

This brief description of the global IR debate illustrates the diversity of approaches and blooming variety of opportunities for established, as well as younger, scholars to contemplate the inner structures of their own discipline. After all, IR scholars remain students at all career stages. We believe that a globally informed IR discipline is the form of the discipline that can make the biggest difference in real-world politics. It is therefore worth the effort to engage in more inclusive and reflective research, be it when conceptualizing seminar papers or conference contributions.

The absence of the global IR debate from the classroom

Although the debate outlined above has received growing attention, it has not yet entered IR classrooms. Instead, curricula and syllabi remain U.S.-centered, and leading textbooks seldom problematize the discipline's geo-epistemological biases. Drawing on postcolonial studies and the sociology of IR, we will show why these tendencies pose problems both for students' learning and for the discipline's development before discussing strategies to overcome them.

Empirical evidence for the debate's absence from the classroom

An examination of a number of textbooks used, according to TRIP survey respondents, in the "best" IR programs reveals that they do not address the discipline's geo-epistemological biases. Instead, these biases are reinforced. All the textbook authors have a Western background and work at Western universities, primarily in the United States and the United Kingdom. The textbooks trace the discipline's history back to Ancient Greece or the Westphalian Peace (Mingst 2013; Baylis et al. 2014) and introduce realism, liberalism, constructivism, Marxism, feminism and poststructuralism (Burchill and Linklater 2001; Art 2008; Brown and Ainley 2009; Kegley and Shannon 2011; Mingst 2013; Baylis et al. 2014). Only one of them discusses postcolonialism (Dunne et al. 2006). Regardless of their scope, none of the textbooks introduce the global IR debate. While some chapters do cite authors born outside the West, such as Pankaj Ghemaway (Art 2008) or Mahbub ul Haq (Baylis et al. 2014), these authors have all been socialized into Western academia through their Western university education. More importantly, the textbooks neither allow for the systematic incorporation of thinking that goes beyond Western-centric approaches nor encourage students to challenge their assumptions.[5] Against this backdrop, it does not come as a surprise that publications on IR teaching, such as Matthews and Callaway's (2014) recent examination of the role of theory in 18 IR textbooks published since 2011, do not mention approaches from beyond the West at all.

More systematic investigations of IR syllabi reveal a similar picture. Hagmann and Biersteker (2014) examined the readings assigned in IR theory classes at 23 graduate programs in the U.S. and Europe. After coding syllabi from 2007/2008 for paradigmatic orientation, national base, language, gender and date of publication, they found that in the United States, instructors "overwhelmingly assign only works developed within the intellectual and socio-political context of the U.S." (303). In other countries, instructors choose either only U.S. works or a mix of U.S. works and works from their respective countries of origin. Publication language reinforces this impression. In the United States and United Kingdom, lecturers almost exclusively assign works in English (Hagmann and Biersteker 2014).[6]

Scholars' answers in the TRIP survey corroborate these findings: more than half of the assigned material in introductory IR courses is from the U.S. and for U.S. respondents, the proportion climbs to almost three quarters (Maliniak et al. 2012). Likewise, Hagmann and Biersteker (2014: 303) find that "most remarkably, overall, none of the 23 schools surveyed here draws on non-Western scholarship to explain international politics." They conclude that "world politics as it is explained to students is exclusively a kind of world politics that has been conceptualized and analyzed by Western scholars" (Hagmann and Biersteker 2014: 303). While this finding is alarming, the study itself seems to suffer from similar limitations since it only investigates IR programs from the U.S. and Europe.

Problematizing and overcoming the debate's absence from the classroom

Scholars working within postcolonial studies and the sociology of IR show *why* the absence of the global IR debate from the classroom is a problem and offer strategies for overcoming it. Postcolonial scholars were the first to reveal the Western dominance in knowledge production (Mudimbe 1988; Hall 1992; Said 1993; Spivak 1994; Chakrabarty 2000; Mignolo 2002). Their perspectives helped to explain why IR usually includes case studies *about* countries beyond the West, hence treating them solely as objects of study and not as sites of knowledge production. In assuming that the phenomena studied elsewhere could be analyzed with the same "Western" categories, they were presented either as exotic/different or as (defective) copies of supposedly "Western" phenomena. Consequently, no need was seen for studies *from* these countries to contribute to theory production. Studies such as Acharya and Buzan's (2007), who concluded that there are no fully fledged IR theories from outside the West, have reinforced this "division of labor" between theorizing and theorized regions by omitting the role that epistemic violence plays in universalizing Western criteria for theory production (Kristensen 2015c).

The notion of *epistemic violence* has played a major role in explaining the systematic exclusion of non-Western thought in academic knowledge production. Asking "Can the subaltern speak?" Gayatri Chakravorty Spivak (1988) was among the first academics to argue that Western dominance results from the fact that "subalternized" and therefore socially excluded populations, especially women, were rarely allowed to speak for themselves in scientific communities. Rather, their ability to produce and articulate knowledge was delegitimized by the proclaimed need for a "translation" by Western mediators.[7] More specifically, the practice she criticizes consists of imposing the "predictive Eurocentric scenario onto large parts of the globe" (Spivak 1988: 142), thereby depriving the colonized of their position of epistemological actors and forcing them into the position of the Other.

This alerts us to the violence inherent in many IR concepts such as "modernity" and "progress," which build on the construction of non-Western counterparts as "premodern" and "backward" departures from the Eurocentric viewpoint of linear and universal history. Equally, the postcolonial concern with discourse does not imply the ignoring knowledge production's material effects.[8] Drawing from studies on imperial history and literature (Mignolo 1995), philosophy and cartography (Maldonado-Torres 2004), as well as relations of class, race and gender (Quijano 2000; Lugones 2007) and migration histories (Grosfoguel 1994), these scholars have shown how the social sciences have always been interwoven with and constitutive of material exploitation, cultural domination and epistemological violence. Colonial and imperial domination would have been impossible without the European scientific representation of the colonized people as (racially and culturally) inferior or as perennially "lacking ... civilization, ... development, ... democracy" (Ndlovu-Gatsheni 2013: xi). Taking this argument to the level of (social) scientific knowledge production, acknowledging that Europe was "military, economically and culturally entangled for centuries" (Boatcă 2011: 26) with its (former) colonies implies that there have always been influences from beyond the West on supposedly "Western" concepts.

Consequently, IR teaching needs to be aware of the potential of its categories, concepts and practices to be harmful. Postcolonial scholarship urges students to reflect critically on their discipline and their own positions within the context of knowledge production and reception by making them aware of their potential role as agents of epistemic violence. As a concrete strategy, many postcolonial scholars call for the epistemic delinking from, or "unlearning of," Western concepts and theories and the revalidation of different local and heterogeneous epistemologies (derived from mythology, oral traditions, embodied experience, etc.), thereby bringing the experience of the subaltern to the center of knowledge production (Mignolo 2007). While some emphasize the singularity and heterogeneity of subaltern experiences (Bhabha 1994) or imply the appropriation of essentializing concepts (Spivak 1996), others go as far as to envision a "universal project" of connecting the diverse experiences of colonial subjects (Mignolo 2011).

Thus, in the classroom, approaches from beyond the West cannot be simply "included" in the canon, but the very base of knowledge production needs to be changed. Pursuing similar objectives, scholars working on the sociology of IR have more recently developed conceptual and methodological tools to analyze the social forces behind asymmetries in knowledge production (Adler 2011; Camic et al. 2011; Büger 2012; D'Aoust 2012). Christian Bueger (2012: 103) argues that in analyzing epistemology, scholars' everyday social practices need to be examined. He draws attention to material and social contexts, financial and human resources, and the impact of socialization and disciplinization, and he calls for examining negotiations about relevance, significance, instruments and methods along with required institutions and techniques. In the classroom, students should therefore be introduced to the "realities of scientific practices," particularly to the different stages of the research process and its associated problems, instead of being served the "finished product" of scholarly knowledge. Ideally, they will then be enabled to question the discipline's common narratives and to criticize common norms, such as the practices of peer review or application processes.

By unmasking its involvement in global relations of power and violence, these perspectives show how the IR discipline is not neutral but reflects geo-epistemological biases. By incorporating the perspectives introduced above into teaching, students can grasp the ways in which the discipline reproduces gate-keeping mechanisms, upholds the intellectual and material superiority of the core and is constitutive of hierarchies. It furthermore allows students to understand how categories and binaries reduce social complexity by depicting simplified, homogenized and contained entities as non-negotiable truths.

The global IR debate in the classroom

So far, we have abstractly problematized the absence of the global IR debate in the classroom. In this section of the chapter, we discuss the value that participatory teaching and student ownership can contribute to the global IR project.

Participatory teaching in IR: a lecturer–student perspective

Teaching classes on global IR in a way that does justice to the topic is not an easy task. In the case at hand, we argue that it was the open and participatory character of teaching which enabled both lecturers and students to move beyond their initial assumptions and advance an independent understanding of the challenges prevalent in the global IR debate.

Our classroom experience[9] started with a *tour de table* inquiring about the participants' disciplinary backgrounds. Strikingly, most students reported that their earlier engagements with IR centered on variations of realism/neo-realism. Consequently, the classes started out with critical reflections on epistemology and ontology as well as on the debate surrounding IR as an "American social science." Paralleling the global IR debate's second strand, the classes then discussed Western-centrism in IR. To sensitize students to structural and intellectual barriers, we focused on gate-keeping practices. In this context, the more we used the terms "West" and "non-West," the more skeptical we, instructors and students alike, became of their appropriateness. This feeling was deeply linked to the class's international composition: many students came from what could be labeled the "non-West" but could not identify with it due to the arbitrariness of such geographic categories (see Box 2.4). Our first attempt to tackle this challenge was to use the terms in quotation marks. This method did not solve the unease many of us felt as we tried to fit scholarly diversity into homogeneous containers. In a second step, we therefore substituted them with speaking about "locality" instead, thereby marking experiences, including "Western" history, as local and non-universal particulars, without assuming a false homogeneity.

BOX 2.4 MOVING FROM FIXED CATEGORIES TO NETWORK ONTOLOGIES

If we are interested in retracing scientific knowledge production, the discipline's actors, relevant geographical locations, gate-keeping practices and the maintenance of fixed analytical categories, such as West/non-West, can be obstructive. Rather than departing from the assumption of pre-identifiable representational groups, such as "the non-West," "the Asian/African/Latin American perspective," or "the indigenous people from locality XY," deconstructive and post/decolonial approaches can be based on network ontologies (Deleuze and Guattari 1987; Castells 1996). In order to avoid reducing the complexity of actors and mechanisms of knowledge production to homogeneous entities, network ontology starts with mapping their complex interrelations and shifting patterns of inclusion and exclusion. For example, labeling a Peruvian scholar, who has studied and worked both in Peru and the U.S. and has worked with scholars from around the world, as "non-Western" can be quite misleading. Instead, a nuanced analysis of her academic biography would reveal her situatedness more clearly.

These theoretical and conceptual reflections were followed by sessions on IR practice beyond the West and on local IR. Student groups chose particular countries or regions and researched how IR is "done" there, bringing in personal or academic interests and language skills. With regard to IR theorizing from beyond the West, this "freedom of choice" proved difficult. In the first seminar, students were simply asked to search for "non-Western IR theories." When we came up with theorizing produced by professors tenured or at least educated at elite universities in the United Kingdom (i.e. Ali Mazrui) and the U.S. (i.e. Walter Mignolo), our first reaction was to conclude that we simply had not searched deeply or widely enough. We were frustrated that nothing new appeared, but from today's perspective, we must admit that this attitude was both naïve and presumptuous (although far from unique as we learned later: Tickner and Blaney 2012). Firstly, we did not know enough about the state of "non-Western" thought in IR since little literature was available. Secondly, we continued to struggle with the categories we had been using and which had proven problematic: if "Western" and "non-Western" did not adequately describe our object of study, what exactly were we looking for? And, to further complicate things, what qualified as *theory*? The empirical-analytical understanding of theory explaining social phenomena did not match our growing interest in critical or deconstructive theorizing, nor did a narrow focus on "big" IR theories such as realism, liberalism or institutionalism allow us to appreciate the wide scope of interdisciplinary theorizing on international relations. While the existing literature suggested some criteria (Acharya and Buzan 2007), it was too ambiguous and Western-centered to offer us good guidance. For example, distinctions such as "pre-theory" and "full-fledged theories" seemed to reproduce a positivist and exclusive understanding of what counts as global IR theorizing.

To circumvent this issue, the lecturers adjusted some expectations for the subsequent seminar sessions and encouraged the students to explore texts with some theoretical component on different policy areas or academic concepts that made use of local sources of knowledge. This worked out much better. However, what helped most was the increase of such approaches in accessible Anglophone journals and edited volumes after 2011 (see Box 2.3; Naghibzadeh 2012; Tickner and Blaney 2012; Zhang 2012).

Student reactions to the seminars illustrated what stakes we all had in decentering Western hegemony. Asked to comment on the class, they expressed how much they appreciated this form of participatory and reflective teaching. The feedback confirmed that the approach was groundbreaking, both in terms of content and pedagogy. One student, for example, said that it was the first time he had "tangled with IRT [IR theory] beyond just positivism and the three big 'isms'," and another described how she was not usually encouraged to question the theories she studied. Students found the seminars unusually challenging but also inspiring and rewarding. A third student noted: "the creative part in this class requires a huge amount of intellectual independence, but it is worth the effort!"

Both the lecturers' and students' reflections on the classes demonstrated that the way IR is typically taught and studied had restrained their thinking about the subject. One student expressed how "through the class I was able to see how much my educational background had influenced my thinking of what a 'non-Western' IR theory might look like, and I realized that I had not been as open-minded as I had thought." As the dead ends, which our prefixed biases and dichotomies had maneuvered us into, were addressed collectively, both lecturers and students learned their lessons for improving their quality of teaching and research.

The class led to a sustainable change in our mindsets and attitudes towards the field of IR. This was most strongly reflected in the research of those students who chose to write a term paper. In fact, the majority of papers were so good that we decided to move beyond the classroom. Through author workshops and group peer reviews, we transformed the papers into an edited volume (Wemheuer-Vogelaar and Peters 2016).

BOX 2.5 BEYOND THE CLASSROOM: PRACTICING GLOBAL IR DIFFERENTLY

The participatory and reflective nature of our seminars allowed us to contribute our insights to the scholarly debate: while transforming our term papers into an edited volume, we sought to apply the classes' conclusions to our own research, using self-referential authorship in order to avoid the pitfalls of IR's parochial center, among other strategies. In terms of content, a first set of chapters focuses on the dividing lines and gate-keeping mechanisms of the discipline. Having to use the discipline's problematic dichotomies in order to discuss them, they base their inquiry on their own situatedness as scholars and problematizing the self–other constructions in the discipline. A second set of chapters presents empirical examples of IR scholarly practice beyond the West, analyzing the publishing practices of national IR communities. The third set of chapters was originally intended to engage with alternative, non-Western IR theorizing. However, realizing the problematic nature of exploring complex theoretical traditions under the homogenized label of "non-Western," the authors decided to engage in a process of *unlearning* instead. The chapters therefore deconstruct key categories of the discipline with the help of critical perspectives hitherto marginalized or excluded from IR theorizing. The collective research project beyond the classroom has yielded unexpected results: our approach for practicing global IR differently has not only allowed us to transcend the prevalent fixed ontologies (see Box 2.4), but we have also opened up spaces for power-sensitive and self-situated approaches to studying a globalizing discipline.

Conclusion

A key conclusion that has emerged from the overall project presented here is that bringing the global IR debate to the classroom involves acknowledging the role that today's students play in shaping tomorrow's scientific discourse as well as their eagerness and potential to move beyond the beaten track. The students' feedback, summarized above, underlines the importance of addressing the politics of knowledge production at an early stage of tertiary education. Their enthusiasm and engagement challenge the norm of offering introductory IR classes which simplify the discipline's diversity and point towards a more proactive concept of studying.

As young scholars who are new to disciplinary wisdoms and conventions, students are open-minded and willing to challenge the alleged truths they are confronted with. If they aim at an academic career, they have a particular interest in critically interrogating the discipline's boundaries before being fully socialized into its underlying assumptions and in questioning its partially parochial set-up that will increasingly lose its ability to explain a globalized world. Those of us striving to engage in international relations practically by working for governments, international institutions, non-governmental organizations (NGOs) or transnational enterprises will also be critical of an IR that does not prepare them for the complexity and sensitivity of different contexts. As Joseph Stiglitz' (1998) critique of the World Bank has shown, international institutions basing their policies on one-sided, empiricist and modernist assumptions do tremendous harm in global politics. The same counts for the development of IR as a discipline. As long as certain approaches, traditions of thoughts and ways of producing knowledge are systematically ignored, IR will remain parochial in its explanatory scope, insufficient in its knowledge base and generally exclusionary.

Evaluating our project with a sociology of knowledge approach, we argue that the intensive exchange, the closely knit student group, the extended time period, the lack of hierarchies, the feeling of ownership and personal investment has allowed us to pursue our project with a curiosity, passion and seriousness that both students and teachers rarely experienced in our academic careers. The group dynamics have encouraged us to offer each other radical but constructive critiques and have empowered us to move beyond the parochialism of the discipline and explore its alternatives. Moreover, by actively practicing global IR, we have encountered some of its gate-keeping mechanisms ourselves, contributing to a deeper understanding of IR's exclusionary practices. IR could therefore benefit vastly if scholars and teachers viewed themselves as life-long students, as the lecturers in our classroom experience did. Their openness towards the students' contributions and their willingness to reconsider both curriculum and concepts according to our discussions enabled them to tackle some of the discipline's shortcomings.

Through participatory teaching and student ownership we have embarked on a reflexive process of unlearning previously absent from our personal experiences, departments' course offerings and IR curricula. We have come to understand that it is impossible to dissociate the *what* from the *how*. Our academic and cultural socialization influences what we are prepared to question and what we take for granted. Rendering these assumptions and perceptions visible is a first step towards a more reflexive knowledge production in IR. If these aspirations are taken seriously, we can hope for a more nuanced, negotiated, fluid and contested view of the global.

Questions for discussion

1. Why is IR criticized for being an "American" or "Western" discipline?
2. What were the global IR debate's major turning points?
3. In the light of the global IR debate, what bothered you about your introduction to IR? Why?
4. Why is it problematic that the global IR debate as an important research trend has so far been largely excluded from the classroom?
5. Keeping in mind the experiences of translating a seminar into research projects, what would you imagine your own project to look like?
6. If you could design your own IR course, what would definitely be listed on the syllabus?

Notes

1 We are very grateful for Julita Dudziak's research assistance and Anchalee Rüland and Sandra Bätghe's tremendously helpful comments on the draft. We also thank Jack Galloway and Rabea Heinemann for their editing services. Laura Appeltshauser was originally one of the authors of this chapter. Unfortunately, we lost track of her after graduation and were unable to obtain her author information. We honor her contribution to this chapter and could not have done it without her!

2 While we acknowledge Amitav Acharya's use of the term "Global IR" (2014, 2016), we understand what we call the "global IR debate" to include much more than his work. That is, we do not endorse Acharya's particular agenda but rather use the term to refer to IR around the globe.

3 The discussion that follows adheres largely to the arguments presented in Wemheuer-Vogelaar and Peters (2016: 1–27).

4 Many authors in the second strand of the debate have a global South/East background, marking a shift not only in the debate's content but also in the agency of the debaters.

5 Jenny Edkins and Maja Zehfuss's textbook *Global Politics: A New Introduction* (2013) approaches IR from a new perspective and introduces students to key issues in global politics drawing on a wide range of disciplines including sociology, postcolonial studies and geography. However, the TRIP survey data show that it has not (yet) been used in the discipline's most prestigious programs.

6 At the Institut d'études politiques de Paris (Science Po), a significant proportion of the mandatory readings are in French, in Moscow's MGIMO around half of the material is in Russian, and in different German universities around a third of the required readings are published in German. At CEU Budapest and EUI Florence no readings written in Hungarian and Italian were assigned (Hagmann and Biersteker 2014: 13).

7 Three excellent examples for the "refusal to listen" to subaltern women are given by Julia Roth in *Occidental Readings, Decolonial Practices: A Selection on Gender, Genre, and Coloniality in the Americas* (2014). She explains how colonial and gender hierarchies play out in the relations between "Western interpretive communities," such as biographers, publishers or art critics and three Latin American women – namely Frida Kahlo, Victoria Ocampo and Rigoberta Menchú.

8 An important example is the Latin American decolonial perspective which has evolved around Ramón Grosfoguel, Maria Lugones, Nelson Maldano-Torres, Walter Mignolo and Aníbal Quijano. For a more detailed explanation of decolonial thinking, see Box 2.3.

9 The two six-month classes "Locating the 'I' in IR: Non-Western Contributions to International Relations Scholarship" at Freie Universität Berlin were co-taught by Ingo Peters and Wiebke Wemheuer-Vogelaar, while the shorter seminars at the College of William & Mary were taught by Wiebke alone. All co-authors of this chapter were participants from Freie Universität, while the student quotes in the following sections come from William & Mary students.

Further reading

Bueger, Christian (2012). "From Epistemology to Practice: A Sociology of Science for International Relations," *Journal of International Relations and Development*, 15(1): 97–109. Conceiving science as a social practice, Bueger establishes that sociology of IR helps to understand knowledge that informs political decision-making, to illuminate power plays within the discipline and to strengthen self-evaluation and education.

Carvalho, Benjamin de, Leira Halvard and John Hobson (2011). "The Big Bangs of IR: The Myths that Your Teachers Still Tell You about 1648 and 1919," *Millennium – Journal of International Studies*, 39(3): 735–758. Although historical and historiographical scholarship has deconstructed the narratives that international relations emerged through the peace of Westphalia and that the discipline emerged after World War I, they still play a key role in IR classrooms and are deeply linked to the discipline's Eurocentric meta-narrative.

Hagmann, Jonas and Thomas J. Biersteker (2014). "Beyond the Published Discipline: Toward a Critical Pedagogy of International Studies," *European Journal of International Relations*, 20(2): 291–315. Building on a concise summary of the sociology of IR, Hagmann and Biersteker set a new focus on IR teaching by investigating syllabi from American and European universities and find substantial differences between the instructed and the published discipline.

Mhurchú, Aoileann Ní and Reiko Shindo (eds) (2016). *Critical Imaginations in International Relations*, London: Routledge. This edited volume discusses one key concept traditionally used in IR per chapter and thereby addresses the limitations of its state-centered approach. It provides a provocative view on the discipline and is well suited to function as a corrective companion to many more traditional IR textbooks and volumes.

Seth, Sanjay (ed.) (2013). *Postcolonial Theory and International Relations: A Critical Introduction*, London: Routledge. The edited volume shows how the postcolonial lens radically alters the understanding of global politics' core concepts such as the international political economy through an examination of slavery, finance or war.

Shilliam, Robbie (ed.) (2011). *International Relations and Non-Western Thought: Imperialism, Colonialism and Investigations of Global Modernity*, New York: Routledge. The chapters sketch the historical depth and contemporary significance of non-Western thought for modernity by drawing on a rich diversity of movements and traditions, including political Islam and Japanese humanism.

Vale, Peter (2014). "If International Relations Lives on the Street, What Is It Doing in the Classroom?" *International Relations*, 28(2): 141–158. Arguing from a South African perspective, Vale points out that IR remains directed by and towards knowledge courts of the global North, a reality underpinned by the primacy of English, which closes off perspectives of the international written in other languages.

Vasilaki, Rosa (2012). "Provincialising IR? Deadlocks and Prospects in Post-Western IR Theory," *Millennium – Journal of International Studies*, 41(1): 3–22. Originally submitted to the journal as a student paper, Vasilaki's contribution discusses "post-Western IR," focusing on postcolonialism through a discussion of Chakrabarty's "Provincializing Europe" and criticizes the postsecular stance endorsed by postcolonial epistemology.

References

Acharya, Amitav (2014) "Global International Relations (IR) and Regional Worlds," *International Studies Quarterly*, 58(4): 647–659. doi:10.1111/isqu.12171

Acharya, Amitav (2016) "Advancing Global IR: Challenges, Contentions, and Contributions," *International Studies Review*, 18(1): 4–15. doi:10.1093/isr/viv016

Acharya, Amitav and Barry Buzan (2007) "Why Is There No Non-Western International Relations Theory? An Introduction," *International Relations of the Asia-Pacific*, 7(3): 287–312. doi:10.1093/irap/lcm012

Adler, Emanuel (2011) "International Practices," *International Theory*, 3(1): 1–36. doi:10.1017/CBO9780511862373

Agnew, John (2007) "Know-Where: Geographies of Knowledge in World Politics," *International Political Sociology*, 1: 138–148. doi:10.1111/j.1749-5687.2007.00009.x

Art, Robert J. (ed.) (2008) *International Politics: Enduring Concepts and Contemporary Issues*, New York: Pearson Longman.

Aydin, Mustafa and Korhan Yazgan (2013) "Türkiye'de Uluslararası İlişkiler Akademisyenleri Eğitim: Araştırma Ve Uluslararası Politika Anketi – 2011 (Survey International Relations Faculty in Turkey: Teaching, Research and International Politics – 2011)," *Uluslararası İlişkiler*, 36(9): 3–44.

Aydinli, Ersel and Julie Mathews (2000) "Are the Core and the Periphery Irreconcilable? The Curious World of Publishing in Contemporary International Relations," *International Studies Perspectives*, 16(1): 33–51. doi:10.1111/1528-3577.00028

Baylis, John, Steve Smith and Patricia Owens (eds) (2014) *The Globalization of World Politics. An Introduction to International Relations*, Oxford: Oxford University Press.

Bhabha, Homi K. (1994) *The Location of Culture*, London: Routledge.

Bilgin, Pinar (2008) "Thinking Past Western IR?" *Third World Quarterly*, 29(1): 5–23. doi:10.1080/01436590701726392

Boatcă, Manuela (2011) "Global Inequalities: Transnational Processes and Transregional Entanglements," *DesiguALdades Working Paper Series No. 11*. Berlin.

Brown, Chris and Kristen Ainley (2009) *Understanding International Relations*, London: Palgrave Macmillan.

Büger, Christian (2012) "From Epistemology to Practice: A Sociology of Science for International Relations," *Journal of International Relations and Development*, 15(1): 97–109. doi:10.1057/jird.2011.28

Burchill, Scott and Andrew Linklater (2001) *Theories of International Relations*, London: Palgrave Macmillan.

Camic, Charles, Neil Gross and Michèle Lamont (eds) (2011) *Social Knowledge in the Making*, Chicago, IL and London: University of Chicago Press.

Carvalho, Benjamin de, Halvard Leira and John M. Hobson (2011) "The Big Bangs of IR: The Myths that Your Teachers Still Tell You about 1648 and 1919," *Millennium – Journal of International Studies*, 39(3): 735–758. doi:10.1177/0305829811401459

Castells, Manuel (1996) *The Information Age: Economy, Society and Culture. Volume 1: The Rise of the Network Society*, Oxford: Blackwell.

Chakrabarty, Dipesh (2000) *Provincializing Europe: Postcolonial Thought and Historical Difference*, Princeton, NJ: Princeton University Press.

Chen, Ching-Chang (2012) "The Im/Possibility of Building Indigenous Theories in a Hegemonic Discipline: The Case of Japanese International Relations," *Asian Perspectives*, 36(3): 463–492.

Colgan, Jeff D. (2016) "Where Is International Relations Going? Evidence from Graduate Training," *International Studies Quarterly*, 60(3): 486–498. doi:10.1093/isq/sqv017

Crawford, Robert M.A. and Darryl S.L. Jarvis (eds) (2001) *International Relations – Still an American Social Science? Toward Diversity in International Thought*, Albany, NY: State University of New York Press.

D'Aoust, Anne-Marie (2012) "Accounting for the Politics of Language in the Sociology of IR," *Journal of International Relations and Development*, 15(1): 120–131. doi:10.1057/jird.2011.30

Deleuze, Gilles and Felix Guattari (1987) *A Thousand Plateaus: Capitalism and Schizophrenia*, Minneapolis, MN: University of Minnesota Press.

Dunne, Timothy, Milja Kurki and Steve Smith (2006) *International Relations Theories*, Oxford: Oxford University Press.

Edkins, Jenny and Maja Zehfuss (eds) (2013) *Global Politics: A New Introduction*, London and New York: Routledge.

Fonseca, Gelson (1987) "Studies on International Relations in Brazil: Recent Times (1950–80)," *Millennium – Journal of International Studies*, 16(2): 273–280. doi:10.1177/03058298870160020401

Friedrichs, Jörg (2004) *European Approaches to International Relations Theory: A House with Many Mansions*, New York: Routledge.

Grenier, Félix and Jonas Hagmann (2016) "Sites of Knowledge (Re-)production: Toward an Institutional Sociology of International Relations Scholarship," *International Studies Review*, 18(2): 333–365. doi:10.1093/isr/viw006

Grosfoguel, Ramón (1994) "World Cities in the Caribbean: The Rise of Miami and San Juan," *Review (Fernand Braudel Center)*, 17(3): 351–381.

Grosfoguel, Ramón (2007) "The Epistemic Decolonial Turn," *Cultural Studies*, 21(2): 211–223. doi:10.1080/09502380601162514

Hadiwinata, Bob S. (2009) "International Relations in Indonesia: Historical legacy, Political Intrusion, and Commercialization," *International Relations of the Asia-Pacific*, 9(1): 55–81. doi:10.1093/irap/lcn026

Hagmann, Jonas and Thomas J. Biersteker (2014) "Beyond the Published Discipline: Toward a Critical Pedagogy of International Studies," *European Journal of International Relations*, 20(2): 291–315. doi:10.1177/1354066112449879

Hall, Stuart (1992) "The West and the Rest: Discourse and Power," in Bram Gieben and Stuart Hall (eds) *Formations of Modernity*, Cambridge: Polity Press, pp. 275–320.

Harding, Sandra (ed.) (1998) *Is Science Multicultural? Postcolonialisms, Feminisms, and Epistemologies*, Bloomington and Indianapolis, IN: Indiana University Press.

Hobson, John M. (2009) "Provincializing Westphalia: The Eastern Origins of Sovereignty," *International Politics*, 46(6): 671–690.

Hobson, John M. (2012) *The Eurocentric Conception of World Politics: Western International Relations Theory, 1760–2010*, Cambridge: Cambridge University Press.

Hoffmann, Stanley (1977) "An American Social Science: International Relations," *Daedelus*, 106(3): 41–60. doi:10.1007/978-1-349-23773-9_9

Huang, Xiaoming (2007) "The Invisible Hand: Modern Studies of International Relations in Japan, China, and Korea," *Journal of International Relations and Development*, 10(2): 168–203. doi:10.1057/palgrave.jird.1800124

Hutchings, Kimberly (2011) "Dialogue between Whom? The Role of the West/Non-West Distinction in Promoting Global Dialogue in IR," *Millennium – Journal of International Studies*, 39(3): 639–647. DOI:10.1177/0305829811401941

Inayatullah, Naeem and David Blaney (2004) *International Relations and the Problem of Difference*, New York: Routledge.

Jørgensen, Knud Erik and Tonny Brems Knudsen (eds) (2006) *International Relations in Europe: Traditions, Perspectives and Destinations*, London and New York: Routledge.

Kayaoglu, Turan (2010) "Westphalian Eurocentrism in International Relations Theory," *International Studies Review*, 12(2): 193–217. doi:10.1111/j.1468-2486.2010.00928.x

Kegley, Charles W. and L. Blanton Shannon (2011) *World Politics: Trend and Transformation*, Boston, MA: Wadsworth.

Khong, Y.F. (2013) "The American Tributary System," *The Chinese Journal of International Politics*, 6(1): 1–47.

Kristensen, Peter Marcus (2015a) "International Relations in China and Europe: The Case for Inter-regional Dialogue in A Hegemonic Discipline," *The Pacific Review*, 28(2): 161–187. doi:10.1080/09512748.2014.948568

Kristensen, Peter Marcus (2015b) "Revisiting the American Social Science: Mapping the Geography of International Relations," *International Studies Perspectives*, 16(3): 246–269. doi:10.1111/insp.12061

Kristensen, Peter Marcus (2015c) "How Can Emerging Powers Speak? On Theorists, Native Informants and Quasi-officials in International Relations Discourse," *Third World Quarterly*, 36(4): 637–653. doi:10.1080/01436597.2015.1023288

Lebedeva, Marina M. (2004) "International Relations Studies in the USSR/Russia: Is There a Russian National School of IR Studies?" *Global Society*, 18(3): 263–278. doi:10.1080/1360082042000221478

Ling, L.H.M. (2014) *Imagining World Politics: Sihar & Shenya, a Fable for Our Times*, London and New York: Routledge.

Long, James D., Daniel Maliniak, Susan Peterson and Michael J. Tierney (2005) "Teaching and Research in International Politics: Surveying Trends in Faculty Opinion and Publishing." Paper presented at the Annual Meeting of the International Studies Association, Honolulu, Hawaii, March 1st–5th, 2015.

Lugones, Maria (2007) "Heterosexuality and the Colonial/Modern Gender System," *Hypatia*, 22(1): 186–209. doi:10.1111/j.1527-2001.2007.tb01156.x

Lupovici, Amir (2013) "Me and the Other in International Relations: An Alternative Pluralist International Relations 101," *International Studies Perspectives*, 14(3): 235–254. doi:10.1111/j.1528-3585.2012.00473.x

Madge, Clare, Parvati Raghuram and Patricia Noxolo (2009) "Engaged Pedagogy and Responsibility: A Postcolonial Analysis of International Students," *Geoforum*, 40(1): 34–45. doi:10.1016/j.geoforum.2008.01.008

Makarychev, Andrey and Viatcheslav Morozov (2013) "Is Non-Western Theory Possible? The Idea of Multipolarity and the Trap of Epistemological Relativism in Russian IR," *International Studies Review*, 15(3): 328–350. doi:10.1111/misr.12067

Maldonado-Torres, Nelson (2004) "The Topology of Being and the Geopolitics of Knowledge," *City: Analysis of Urban Trends, Culture, Theory, Policy, Action*, 8(1): 29–56. doi:10.1080/1360481042000199787

Maliniak, Daniel, Susan Peterson, Ryan Powers and Michael J. Tierney (2018) "Is International Relations a Global Discipline? Hegemony, Insularity, and Diversity in the Field," *Security Studies*, 27(3): 448–484. doi:10.1080/09636412.2017.1416824

Maliniak, Daniel, Susan Peterson and Michael J. Tierney (2012) "TRIP Around the World: Teaching, Research, and Policy Views of International Relations Faculty in 20 Countries." Williamsburg, VA: The Institute for the Theory and Practice of International Relations, College of William & Mary, Williamsburg, Virginia.

Masina, Nomonde (2000) "Xhosa Practices of Ubuntu for South Africa," *Traditional Cures for Modern Conflicts: African Conflict Medicine*: 169–181.

Matthews, Elizabeth and Rhonda Callaway (2014) "Where Have All the Theories Gone? Teaching Theory in Introductory Courses in International Relations," *International Studies Perspectives*, 16(2): 1–20. doi:10.1111/insp.12086

Mignolo, Walter D. (1995) *The Darker Side of the Renaissance: Literacy, Territoriality, and Colonization*, Ann Arbor, MI: University of Michigan Press.

Mignolo, Walter D. (2002) "The Geopolitics of Knowledge and the Colonial Difference," *Social Epistemology: A Journal of Knowledge, Culture and Policy*, 19(1): 111–127. doi:10.1215/00382876-101-1-57

Mignolo, Walter D. (2007) "Delinking: The Rhetoric of Modernity, the Logic of Coloniality and the Grammar of Decoloniality," *Cultural Studies*, 21(2–3): 449–514. doi:10.1080/09502380601162647

Mignolo, Walter D. (2011) *The Darker Side of Western Modernity: Global Futures, Decolonial Options*, Durham, NC and London: Duke University Press.

Mingst, Karen A. (2013) *Essentials of International Relations*, New York: W.W. Norton.

Mudimbe, Valentin Y. (1988) *The Invention of Africa, Gnosis, Philosophy, and the Order of Knowledge*, Bloomington, IN: Indiana University Press.

Murithi, Tim (2007) "A Local Response to the Global Human Rights Standard: The Ubuntu Perspective of Human Dignity," *Globalisation, Society, and Education*, 5(3): 277–286.

Naghibzadeh, Ahmad (2012) "A Persian-Muslim Approach to Diplomacy," *Iranian Review of Foreign Affairs*, 2(4): 81–98.

Nayak, Meghana and Eric Selbin (2011) *Decentering International Relations*, New York and London: Zed Books.

Ndlovu-Gatsheni, Sabelo J. (2013) *Empire, Global Coloniality and African Subjectivity*, New York and Oxford: Berghahn Books.

Neufeld, Mark and Teresa Healy (2001) "Above the 'American Discipline': A Canadian Perspective on Epistemological and Pedagogical Diversity," in Robert M.A. Crawford and Darryl S.L. Jarvis (eds) *International Relations: Still an American Social Science?* Albany, NY: State University of New York Press, pp. 243–253.

Neuman, Stefanie (1998) *International Relations and the Third World*, London: Palgrave Macmillan.

Nossal, Kim Richard (2001) "Tales that Textbooks Tell: Ethnocentricity and Diversity in American Introductions to International Relations," in Robert M.A. Crawford, Darryl S.L. Jarvis (eds) *International Relations: Still an American Social Science?* Albany, NY: State University of New York Press, pp. 167–187.

Porter, Tony (2001) "Can There Be National Perspectives in Inter(national) Relations?" in Robert M.A. Crawford and Darryl S.L. Jarvis (eds) *International Relations: Still an American Social Science?* Albany, NY: State University of New York Press, pp. 131–147.

Preston, Christopher J. (2003) *Grounding Knowledge: Environmental Philosophy, Epistemology, and Place*, Athens, GA: University of Georgia Press.

Quijano, Anibal (2000) "Coloniality of Power, Eurocentrism and Latin America," *Neplanta: Views from the South*, 1: 533–580. doi:10.1177/0268580900015002005

Rösch, Felix (2014) *Émigré Scholars and the Genesis of International Relations: A European Discipline in America?* Houndmills, Basingstoke, Hampshire: Palgrave Macmillan.

Roth, Julia (ed.) (2014) *Occidental Readings, Decolonial Practices: A Selection on Gender, Genre, and Coloniality in the Americas*, Tempe and Trier: Bilingual Review Press and WVT Verlag.

Said, Edward (1993) *Culture and Imperialism*, London: Chatto & Windus.

Salager-Meyer, Françoise (2008) "Scientific Publishing in Developing Countries: Challenges for the Future," *Journal of English for Academic Purposes*, 7(2): 121–132. doi:10.1016/j.jeap.2008.03.009

Schmidt, Brian (2002) "On the History and Historiography of International Relations," in Walter Carlsnaes, Thomas Risse-Kappen and Beth A. Simmons (eds) *Handbook of International Relations*, London and Thousand Oaks, CA: SAGE Publications, pp. 3–22.

Shani, Giorgio (2008) "Toward a Post-Western IR: The Umma, Khalsa Panth, and Critical International Relations Theory," *International Studies Review*, 10(4): 722–734. doi:10.1111/j.1468-2486.2008.00828.x

Sharma, Devika (2010) "Mapping International Relations Teaching and Research in Indian Universities," *International Studies*, 46(1–2): 69–88. doi:10.1177/002088171004600206

Shilliam, Robbie (2011) "The Perilous but Unavoidable Terrain of the Non-West," in Robbie Shilliam (ed.) *International Relations and Non-Western Thought*, New York: Routledge, pp. 12–26.

Smith, Steve (2002) "The United States and the Discipline of International Relations: Hegemonic Country, Hegemonic Discipline," *International Studies Review*, 4(2): 67–85. doi:10.1111/1521-9488.00255

Song, Xinning (2001) "Building International Relations Theory with Chinese Characteristics," *Journal of Contemporary China*, 10(26): 61–74. doi:10.1080/10670560125339

Spivak, Gayatri Chakravorty (1988) "Can the Subaltern Speak?" in Cary Nelson and Larry Grossberg (eds) *Marxism and the Interpretation of Culture*, Champaign-Urbana, IL: University of Illinois Press, pp. 273–313.

Spivak, Gayatri Chakravorty (1994) "Can the Subaltern Speak?" in Patrick Williams and Laura Chrisman (eds) *Colonial Discourse and Post-Colonial Theory: A Reader*, New York: Columbia University Press, pp. 66–111.

Spivak, Gayatri Chakravorty (1996) *The Spivak Reader: Select Works of Gayatri Chakravorty Spivak*, New York and London: Routledge.

Stiglitz, Joseph E. (1998) *More Instruments and Broader Goals: Moving toward the Post-Washington Consensus*, Helsinki: UNU/WIDER.

Taylor, Lucy (2012) "Decolonizing International Relations: Perspectives from Latin America," *International Studies Review*, 14: 386–400. doi:10.1111/j.1468-2486.2012.01125.x

Tickner, Arlene B. (2003) "Seeing IR Differently: Notes from the Third World," *Millennium*, 32(2): 295–324. doi:10.1177/03058298030320020301

Tickner, Arlene B. (2013) "Core, Periphery and (Neo)imperialist International Relations," *European Journal of International Relations*, 19(3): 627–646. doi:10.1177/1354066113494323

Tickner, Arlene B. and David Blaney (eds) (2012) *Thinking International Relations Differently*, New York: Routledge.

Tickner, Arlene B. and David L. Blaney (eds) (2013) *Claiming the International*, London: Routledge.

Tickner, Arlene B. and Ole Wæver (eds) (2009) *International Relations Scholarship Around the World*, New York: Routledge.

Turton, Helen (2015) *International Relations and American Dominance: A Diverse Discipline*, London: Routledge.

Tutu, D. (1999) *No Future Without Forgiveness*. New York: Doubleday.

Wæver, Ole (1996) "The Rise and Fall of the Inter-Paradigm Debate," in S. Smith, K. Booth and M. Zalewski (eds) *International Theory: Positivism and Beyond*, Cambridge: Cambridge University Press, pp. 149–185.

Wæver, Ole (1998) "The Sociology of a Not so International Discipline: American and European Developments in International Relations," *International Organization*, 52(4): 687–727. doi:10.1162/002081898550725

Wemheuer-Vogelaar, Wiebke (2014) "Bibliometric Studies of International Relations as a Global(izing) Discipline: An Analytical Review," paper presented at the Annual Conference of the International Studies Association, March 26–29, 2014, Toronto.

Wemheuer-Vogelaar, Wiebke, Nicholas J. Bell, Mariana Navarrete Morales and Michael J. Tierney (2016) "The IR of the Beholder: Examining Global IR Using the 2014 TRIP Survey," *International Studies Review*, 18(1): 16–32. doi:10.1093/isr/viv032

Wemheuer-Vogelaar, Wiebke and Ingo Peters (eds) (2016) *Globalizing International Relations: Scholarship Amidst Divides and Diversity*, London: Palgrave Macmillan.

Zhang, Feng (2012) "The Tsinghua Approach and the Inception of Chinese Theories of International Relations," *Chinese Journal of International Politics*, 5(1): 73–102. doi:10.1093/cjip/por015

3 Where, when and what is IR?[1]

David L. Blaney

Introduction

The growing intensity of calls for decolonizing International Relations (IR) reflects a restless desire for alternative modes of scholarly and pedagogical practice (see Chapter 2). Fixing on what alternatives a decolonizing IR offers remains a bit difficult to specify, though growing ink is being spilt towards this end.[2] Surely, decolonizing the field means redressing or overturning the dominance of colonial epistemological violence in the field by recovering alternative histories and knowledges. Recovering these histories and knowledges requires that we re-specify our object of inquiry and the very field that we teach. This is necessarily a demanding, complex and multifarious task. Here I can only offer some preliminary thoughts about re-imagining the object of IR as more encompassing of the human condition in all its variety and interconnection.

I organize this inquiry around three questions: When is IR? Where is IR? What is IR? The answers to such questions are interlinked, as we shall see. I try to illustrate this in relation to a stereotypically Eurocentric account of the field, identifying the spatial, temporal and social ontological demarcations, however problematic, of IR. But we also find possibilities here that point beyond. To further specify the boundaries of our stereotypically Eurocentric IR, I briefly consider two additional "cases" that might demarcate IR differently: reflections centered on the conquest and colonization of the Americas, where North America might be the central site and model for IR and the spatial, temporal and social ontological specificities of an IR centered on the Silk Road. Together, these "cases" allow us to think differently about the domain of IR: no longer centered on Europe and more attentive to the varieties of forms of social and political life and their interactions and interconnections.

I take some inspiration for this effort from Edward Said. Said (2004: 26; also 52–4) explains that our rejection of Eurocentrism need not entail a rejection of forms of humanism, embracing "the human mind *tout court*," where we start with the premise that there are "multiple learned traditions in the world," multiple "cultures" and "geniuses," all central to "human history as a continuous process of self-understanding and self-realization." That said, Said (2004: 47–8, 54–6) warns against simply pluralizing the humanistic project of recovering and counterpoising non-European traditions to European traditions since such multicultural projects too easily fall into a "nativism" or "exclusivism" that ignore the "complex intermingling" constitutive of traditions historically and omnipresent today in a world of movement and mixing. Rather, as Ilieva (2018: 4–5) notes, Said gestured towards "the necessity of multiple perspectives" and claimed that "only a multi-layered narrative could confront the subtleties and complexities of the cross-cultural encounter."

One account of that "multilayered narrative" emerges in Said's *Culture and Imperialism* (1993: 51), where he suggests a method of "counterpoint" for reading history and human literary and scholarly production. While he means to keep our attention on the variety of human experience, Said (1993: 32) insists that we "think through and interpret together experiences that are discrepant, each with its particular agenda and system of external relationships, all of them coexisting and interacting with others." A multilayered narrative brings to light alternative histories and knowledges that may have been lost or repressed. But it does so, Said (1993: 61) emphasizes, by highlighting the "integration and connections between the past and the present, between imperializer and imperialized, between culture and imperialism," or "overlapping territories" and "intertwined histories" that can be understood only "from the perspective of the whole of secular human history." Let's try and capture something like this spirit of reading by counterpoint in the following three "cases."

Eurocentric IR, its implausibility and the other within

We usually begin our stories of international relations with answers to questions of where, when and what. We start by locating international relations in a particular place and time: the emergence of the states-system in Europe. And we think about the content of international relations as interactions of sovereign states, especially among Great Powers, largely in Europe (see Walker 1993; Inayatullah and Blaney 2004). But, if we look closely, we can see a more multilayered narrative that emphasizes more varied units and interconnections, including imperial relations, not only separable states.

For example, the Peace of Westphalia of the 17th century is quite difficult to see as inaugurating a system of sovereign states, given the diversity of kinds of units involved and the general ambivalence of the principles supposedly articulated by the series of peace treaties bringing the 30 Years' War to an end.[3] And the world is hardly a unit at this time, politically or economically, though by some accounts a world-system organized along capitalist lines has already emerged.[4] The Vienna system of the 19th century manages somewhat greater plausibility as a founding moment of a balance of power states-system, or perhaps in Bull's terms an "international society" with its own norms and practices (Bull 1977). But not, Bull admits, a worldwide society of states (Bull and Watson 1984), since international society is limited to European climes. This is an era of conquest and defense, pacification and resistance, and civilizational standards for acceptance of states or societies into international society. Most of the non-European world remains excluded or included only as colonized peoples and territories or as part of colonial economies.

Most conventional textbooks begin the story of international relations as a discipline in the European interwar period.[5] Europe had suffered economic crises, a devastating war and the beginnings of the fraying of empire, with the rise of self-determination as a principle. Maybe we can begin here and speak convincingly of and organize a discipline around a states-system, the problem of war and peace, the building of international institutions to secure cooperation in security and economic affairs. We might speak of a Paris System[6] as a founding moment with greater plausibility than we could with reference to a Peace of Westphalia or Vienna.

But then even our interwar Paris system of the 20th century is far from a worldwide society of states. Much of Asia and Africa remain colonies and the principle of self-determination is repudiated by the major empires and gradually embraced as a form of resistance by many in the colonies.[7] And the "liberal" international political and economic institutions that mark this, still European, international society are poised on the cusp of crisis and collapse. International relations might best be seen as inter-imperial relations, including the fact that "international" finance and trade are interlaced with colonial economic practices (see Chapter 4).

It might be more convincing to argue that IR's object of inquiry – a state system – is put fully in place with the process of decolonization, so that the later part of the 20th century is really the distinctive setting for IR. But those in the discipline (like Mearsheimer 2014), who seek to make timeless generalizations, seem compelled to extend by analogy the logic of anarchy and competition/cooperation among great powers to the warring states period in China, the Greek city states, and treat Thucydides, Machiavelli, Hobbes, with nods to various Chinese and Indian thinkers, as articulating a trans-historical realist tradition. Plus, by foregrounding the existence of independent states, IR pushes into the background the ways that the world might better be described in a language of capitalist or imperial connection in which the self-determination associated with the idea of sovereignty is unavailable for most states or peoples (Inayatullah and Blaney 1995; see too, Chapter 8).

It is clear that even work situated squarely and perhaps self-consciously within European traditions, opens up very different stories than those in IR committed to a picture of the states-system or a timeless science of anarchy. Instead, stories of global relations and interconnections, of empire and various forms of resistance to empire, seem the more relevant and universal categories. So, let's try beginning somewhere else.

The invasion of North America

Even when we start with empire or the capitalist world system, Eric Wolf (1982) warns that we face the danger of placing Europe at the center of the world and eclipsing the histories and agency of actors in what became parts of European empires or subordinated regions within global capitalism (see Chapter 6). Without denying the crucial impact of European colonization, authors like Wolf, including Abu-Lughod (1989), Stavrianos (1981), Frank (1998), Hobson (2004) and Anievas and Nişancioğlu (2015), write against such Eurocentric histories and work to restore a sense of history and agency to non-Europeans.

Francis Jennings (1975) aims to do something similar for the Amerindians of eastern North America, though more careful and detailed studies set across the continent are now available, as I indicate with examples in notes. Jennings stresses the Amerindians' symbiotic relationship with European invaders, though without ignoring the "staggering price in lives, labor, goods, and lands" that the Indians ultimately paid (41). In quite close parallel to Wolf, Jennings begins not with empty lands, as in the colonial imaginary, but a North America full of "ordinary human beings" whose "actions and reactions do not seem so difficult to infer from both circumstances and the available documentary evidence" (62–7). As Calloway (2003: 2) puts it, what we call North America was "a series of Indian homelands," each existing "at the center of a kaleidoscopic world" of homelands, settled and moving and adapting populations.[8]

Early Native Americans appear quite skilled, living partly by hunting, fishing and foraging, as dictated by general and local climate and topography (Calloway 2003: Chapter 1). But as a warming climate and local conditions allowed, most groups produced agricultural surpluses that promoted consistent population increases until struck by unfamiliar diseases transported by European adventurers and invaders. Though lands were not owned in a European sense, native groups "were as tied to particular localities as Europeans" and well understood that the Europeans wanted land (Calloway 2003: 67, 82). Despite ties to "particular localities," Amerindians were not isolated but connected by a continent-wide trade system long before Europeans arrived[9] and managed complex systems of diplomacy that operate according to principles that are recognizable as a form of international politics, but seem to defy the spatial mappings of the IR imaginary (see Box 3.1).

BOX 3.1 ANISHINAABE INTERNATIONAL RELATIONS

Hayden King (2018) identifies a specifically indigenous, in this case, Anishinaabe, theory and practice of international politics that is routinely and systematically discounted as proper international relations. Diplomacy was central to relations among the closely related peoples of the Great Lakes. These practices continued into relations with Europeans and ongoing struggles around the self-determination of Anishinaabe groups in relation to the governments and societies of the United States and Canada. Emphasizing continuity across these periods obscures the very different understandings of identity and self-determination on which Anishinaabe diplomacy depended and may, still in part, depend. Instead of claims of exclusive sovereignty by distinct nations, Anishinaabe "practiced a politics that emphasized shared jurisdiction and inclusive or mobile sovereignty," reflected in the exchange of gifts, wampum belts, that represented the reciprocities, relations and boundaries (not strict borders) embodied in treaties (146–7). Rather than treaties among "nations," which Hayden takes to be a "grotesque caricature" useful to settler states, identities were conceived as overlapping networks that extended outward from a center – a heart – that linked groups and only loosely demarcated territories (142–3). This diplomacy can be thought of as among nation-states only to the extent that we extend a picture of anarchy to the time and place where it doesn't belong.

Amerindians responded to the European invasion with an ordinary combination of direct resistance, retreat, tactical alliances with other groups against the Europeans and with the Europeans against other Indian groups, and attempts to gain by supplying European demands for goods in order to acquire European goods previously unavailable (Jennings 1975: 14, 62–7). For example, Amerindians were incorporated as energetic actors in the global circuits of the fur trade, including producing many of the maps that traders followed (Calloway 2003: 8–15). Indians provided much of the labor involved in trapping, initial processing of hides and transportation crucial to the world market in furs, investing in fur production in return for iron and steel implements beyond local technology to produce (Jennings 1975: 85–6, 89–90, 102). Though equally seeking their advantage as traders and consumers in this world market, the trade was, as Jennings (1975: 87) points out, "a means of unstable symbioses for two societies": "For Indians the advantages of the trade were local and temporary."

But over the long term the commercial transformation of their society implied, in Jennings' terms, its "decay." He lists disease and growing conflict as important, but key is that "the Indians became dependent upon the Europeans who controlled the market's functioning in America" (87–8). As Europeans advanced a process of capital accumulation through the trade, Indians lost assets when hunting areas were depleted and the complexity of the local economy declined: "Indian industry became less specialized and divided as it entered into relations of exchange with European industry." Intertribal trade decreased, credit arrangements put Indian producers in permanent debt and growing European economic prosperity allowed the extension of a property regime that secured legal titles to land for Europeans and the police power to enforce that dispossession on Indian groups (85–7, 102, 129–33).[10] "In legal terms," as Jennings puts it, "they lost both sovereignty and property" (129). With dispossession, Indians "lost all hope of finding any niche in the society called civilized, except that of servant or slave" (145). This stark conclusion could be seen to ignore contemporary and continuing struggles for land and sovereignty that might involve re-conceiving sovereignty and property (see more on this below and Box 3.2).

Indian resistance to Europeans appears in Jennings' story as the actions (however desperate) of "ordinary human beings." In pre-invasion conditions, Indian villages were relatively peaceful by comparison with European cities and towns; justice among parties was negotiated instead of meted out through civil "revenge," as in so-called "civilized justice" (147–9). Jennings quips that "Indians never achieved the advanced stage of civilization represented by the rack and the iron maiden" (163). Intertribal warfare occurred along the frontiers shared by groups, though this fell far short of the total war practiced by Europeans (in Mexico, the 30 Years' War, or in North America in displacing the native groups; see Inayatullah and Blaney 2004, Chapters 1 and 2), and territorial boundaries generally survived despite defeat (150–7). Indians proved themselves no more sadistic than Europeans, though cruelty increased in response to European depredations. Intertribal wars did increase in incidence and ferocity as groups were displaced onto the territories of others and competed for control of shrinking hunting and trapping grounds (159–60, 162–8). These wars only intensified as Indians became allies and "expendable surrogates" in inter-imperial competition in North America (168).[11]

Though a focus on empire and imperialism might lead us to begin the timeline of international relations with Columbus and the European conquest, that move would limit our vision to the period in North America when European agency enters the frame. Nor is the conquest the moment when the Amerindians overcome their localism and join a wider world; North American groups are already connected to far-flung networks that move goods, peoples and ideas along pathways connecting central nodes around the continent. But we also cannot simply transpose notions of state and nation to this context, incorporating North America fully within the familiar spatial contours of international relations. Though we find recognizable, albeit diverse, practices of conflict, war, alliances and diplomacy, the units exercising agency or broader authority vary a great deal. We might capture the diversity of forms of political authority in terms like "city-states," "confederal republics" and "empires." We also find smaller-scale units only loosely connected to the larger systems of authority, encompassed at some points but independent at others. Borders might appear as frontiers that are not finely demarcated by contemporary standards but are broadly known and respected. Central political authority waxes and wanes and some groups and their rulers displace others, shifting populations and the nodes around which flows occur. This is a world of settled life and mobility, the extension and evasion of central control, and containment and flows of people, goods and practices. This is not a picture of isolated peoples, whatever the scale and degree of territorial boundedness; North America can only be described in the multilayered narrative Said suggests, which places differences and interconnection and overlapping spaces and traditions in counterpoint.

Too often, however, our accounts begin with Columbus and the conquest, but we can read this world in Said's humanistic practice as well, as one of cultural encounters and overlaps produced by imperial connections. Todorov's Bahktinian-inspired work (1986) that sees the conquest in large part as communicative encounters is the most familiar text for IR scholars. For Todorov, practices of mass slaughter, colonial ideology and administration, and anti-colonial thinking are not simply brought to the continent but developed and refined in the Americas.[12] More broadly, Nederman (2000) sees Las Casas' Christian critique of colonial cruelty as crucial to articulating ideas of civilization and equality; Crawford (1994) sees Iroquois cooperation as a model security regime; and Anaya (1996) and Keal (2003) see international law as both a reflection of the European need to legalize the encounter and lasting evidence of the moral failure of international law as a practice. Even more broadly, Weatherford (1988) pictures the encounter in the Americas as producing much of what we take to be modern. Not only do flows of silver prompt "money capitalism," but we can trace our foods and the technologies we use to produce them, our medicines, our political forms and our ideas of freedom and liberty, the shape of our cities, as all having their source in the Americas. And we may find a source and continued inspiration in Amerindian traditions for American pragmatism, a workable environmental ethics and a critique of the market (Pratt 2002; Cheyfitz 2009; Blaney and Inayatullah 2010: Chapter 7, respectively). Speaking about a European world or self apart from the Americas seems impossible; instead, we find ourselves on Said's terrain of the "complex intermingling" of human creativity and experience in which "past and present" and "imperializer and imperialized" participate. I would also invoke a principle perhaps reflecting Said's emphasis on interconnection: self and other are not so polarized, even across oppressor and oppressed; the other is not only outside but also within (Inayatullah and Blaney 2004).

But the present need not be read only as how the conquest produced modern law or society in which the Native American groups figure as historical influences but not as living contemporaries. These groups have not vanished; they remain part of the political landscape of the present in North America. Struggles around land, identity and sovereignty continue, always raising questions about on whose terms, or in whose image, will self-determination be understood or nationhood conceived (Deloria 1984; Biolsi 2005; Wilkinson 2005; Ranco and Suagee 2007; Johnson 2008; Barker 2011; Coulthard 2014; Lightfoot 2016). The implications of these ongoing struggles might be to reimagine not just the relations between existing states and Indian nations, but our ideas of statehood or political authority itself, suggesting that these nations may be spatially located both within and beyond the existing states and in both the same and different times than the current states. This vision of territoriality and rule seems to involve spatial and temporal dislocations that force us to see, as Said suggests, a joining of past and present coexisting in our multilayered narrative of human prospects. More specifically, the present borders and legal mechanisms of settler state sovereignty would coexist in time with the pre-existing homelands and governance practices of an era prior to European invasions. Accommodating spaces that are part of the state and not (and part of the state's time and not) would extend our ideas of the multiplicity of nations occupying the territory of existing states beyond current multicultural conceptions. This would open us to the multiplicity and complexity of relationships that suggest simultaneously multiple and overlapping sovereignties. Applying the logic of the states-system to North America effaces not only a multilayered narrative but narrowly circumscribes our political options within the imaginary of a Eurocentric IR (see too Chapter 8).

Or we might shift to another region beyond Europe, but one in which the dominance of the Chinese state might suggest the enduring relevance of the state system. But this conclusion is premature: a simple state imaginary unravels when we place the past and present of the Chinese state and the surrounding regions in counterpoint.

On belts and roads

China's recent "One Belt One Road" initiative locates its foreign policy in a regional setting, extending beyond East Asia to Central and Southeast Asia. This gesture means to remind readers of a long history of the Silk Road, both on land and sea, in which China played a putatively central role.[13] Here, the Silk Road functions, as Chin (2013: 195) explains, as a "geopolitical chronotope" that becomes "a condition or strategy for geopolitical thought and action." For some Western analysts, One Belt One Road can be nothing other than the assertion of state power: a quest for regional hegemony and, beyond that, a direct challenge to U.S. power that prompts worries about great power conflict if not the inevitability of war predicted by theories of a Thucydides trap.[14] Chinese analysts often draw from a similar repertoire, though often, if not invariably, offering more defensive readings of Chinese strategies.[15] All these analysts frame the possibilities of peace and war in relation to the time and space of the European state system or international society, but now extended as a global system. The relevance of IR as conventionally taught seems preserved despite the geographical shift to Asia.

On closer examination, however, the Silk Road may not be so readily appropriable for nationalist purposes. As opposed to the imagined Eurasian networks of highways, trains and trans-shipment infrastructure, moving vast amounts of Chinese cargo, the historical *imaginary* of the Silk Road is a contested story. Reading in counterpoint, we might begin with 19th-century thinkers who imagine Asia not as a world of sovereign states, but as a space on which European imperial designs might be written. Chin (2013: 196) traces the invention of the Silk Road to "Immanuel Kant's cosmopolitan 'right of common possession of the surface of the earth,'" including a note in his geographical writings, describing the silk trade between "the People of Ser" and Europe. More potent in inventing the Silk Road, including coining the term itself, was the German traveler and geographer, Ferdinand von Richthofen, who saw the "Silk Road" as part of a scientific recovery of Ptolemy's geographic writings and the plotting of a "measurable route" from China to Afghanistan. But more than simple scientific curiosity, Richthofen's geography was a "German blueprint" for rail links between China and Europe, "designed" to overcome the opposition of the Qing government to any foreign transportation projects (Chin 2013: 202). Once in circulation in both European and, later, Chinese sources, Chin (2013: 196; see also 217–9) explains that the idea of the Silk Road "offers a template for modern international commerce" and, according to Yo-Yo Ma's orchestral Silk Road Project, "a modern metaphor for sharing and learning across cultures, art forms and disciplines."

But the meaning of the Silk Road is open and contested. As Chin (2013: 195) summarizes the discussion:

In Chinese-language media and China studies the Silk Road generally begins with China's official diplomacy in Central Asia in the second century BCE and inserts China into an enduring world history of "open" empires instead of isolated civilizations. In Central Asian studies, by contrast, the Silk Road begins with Indo-European migrations four millennia ago and ends with Russian and Qing imperial expansion into Central Asia in the seventeenth century. This latter-most Silk Road makes Central Eurasian pastoral nomads the political center, rather than the middle-man, of an interconnected world history.

We might best understand the Silk Road as a political and cultural imaginary that, when placed in a larger and multilayered narrative, reveals a vast and interconnected social, cultural and economic space, for which China may or may not serve as the center, as we shall see (see Chapter 12).

For example, though Valerie Hansen (2012) centers her recovery of the history of the Silk Road on the interconnections of China with a wider world, she deflates our image of the land-route Silk Road as a major source of commerce. She explains that "the 'road' was not an actual 'road' but a stretch of shifting, unmarked paths across massive expanses of deserts and mountains," and "the quantity of cargo transported along these treacherous routes was small." Nor was trade the primary purpose for most travelers, who included "artists, craftsmen, missionaries, robbers, and envoys"; the largest group were refugees. What flowed along with people and a few trade goods were "ideas," "artistic motifs" and "technologies." In this respect, the Silk Road was principally a space of *cultural* engagement – between China and South and West Asia – occupied by a cosmopolitan community of Buddhists, Manicheans, Zoroastrians, Jews and Christians (Hansen 2012: 5, 167, 238). Adding the maritime routes across Southeast Asia and the Indian Ocean into the Arabian Sea and the Mediterranean, as does Liu (2010), may increase our estimation of the role of commerce in connecting the ends of the system: China on one side and Rome on the other. But the major impact, as Said might insist, was cultural interconnection – the spread and "complex intermingling" of commercial, artistic and religious ideas.

If we map these longer temporalities of the flows and interconnections of an imagined Silk Road, several possible spatial imaginaries emerge, none of which crystalize neatly or simply into a world of states. We might join Chaudhuri (1990: Chapter 2) in constructing the relevant unit as the Indian Ocean – as a flowing material and mental unit; as a durable, if differentiated, "totality" made up of Chinese, Indian, Islamic and Southeast Asian civilizational zones surrounding and interconnected via the Indian Ocean. Chaudhuri follows Braudel's work (1972, 1973) on the Mediterranean as a relatively enduring civilizational zone in carefully documenting the material *and* mental structures that persist below the surface of everyday life, organizing the patterns and rhythms that governed social activities into a relative unity over time and space (Chaudhuri 1990: 5–10).

The point for Chaudhuri, however, is not simply that contemporary historians can identify a unit for which external and internal limits are set by a particular geographical, climatic and social materiality. Rather, it is that individuals of the time recognized that they occupied a complex but interconnected whole in time and space. For example, in chapters on industry, agriculture and forms of political authority, Chaudhuri suggests that a sense of shared space is constructed partly in terms of stories of origins of a way of life or system of rule around which identities might circulate. That way of life was given a topographical grounding in relatively common systems of cropping of cereal grains and water management that might be counterpoised to more nomadic forms of life that set an external limit to the Indian Ocean civilizations. The advantages of Indian Ocean industrial producers in cost, quality and variety over other regions favored their goods for local consumption as well as export into the circuits of trade that flowed across the world from and around production and staging centers. All these gave a centricity to the zone and a sense of shared superiority in these arts. The geographical extension of a sense of identity and difference was also set by possibilities for travel along the routes and infrastructure established for trade within and beyond the Indian Ocean (Chaudhuri 1990: 31, 117, 147). By juxtaposing past and present we might see in East and Southeast Asia, just as we did in North America, spaces and flows or fluidity and containment as our objects of analysis, instead of a simplistic notion of states as territorial containers (Chua 2018; Inayatullah and Blaney 2018).

Or, when thinking of this extended space of the Indian Ocean, we might as counterpoint take note of those who, in order to escape taxation, conscription and the burdens of settled agriculture, relocated to the upland areas of Southeast Asia that James Scott (2009) calls "Zomia." The presence of these "peripheries" or "shatter zones" across Southeast Asia (and universally, Scott asserts) disrupts narratives of the centrality of states and central governance. As Scott (2009: Chapter 1) contends, these populations evaded full or even partial control from the center and established distinctive cultural economies around swidden-agriculture, hunting and foraging. The persistence of such peripheries helps makes sense of the current "enclosure" going on across Southeast Asia and the world, in which mountain and forest spaces are mapped, forced to conform to standardized property regimes, and more fully incorporated into national plans and development strategies. Anna Tsing's *Friction* (2004) explores these mountain and forest spaces and peoples, though in Indonesia,[16] that similarly disrupt easy narratives (see Box 3.2). Tsing's multilayered stories are about walking through forests as part of hiking clubs, forest dwellers' cultivation practices, a local classification of biodiversity and small-scale miners and migrants seeking farm land to squat. She describes geologists and environmental scientists studying the forests as sites for mining or preservation, respectively, government officials registering property, representatives of Indonesian and Japanese firms seeking control of minerals or supplies of rattan, and the ultimate denuding of some forests and the conservation of others, but nearly invariably displacing the forest peoples. Though intimate portraits, Tsing knows these stories are also about supply chain capitalism, dispossession and deforestation, global democracy and environmental movements, national development plans and international development agencies. She uses these familiar terms and notions, but also refuses to accept them at face value. No global process moves across space without *friction*, without intersecting with and being shaped by the contours of local politics, ecologies and ways of life. We cannot read them but in counterpoint, as Said recommends. For Tsing, national development practices are not simply the actions of pre-existing states according to international frames, but about producing the state and the nation in relations that often forcibly incorporate those that have previously evaded the rule of empires and kingdoms. To speak of global capitalism, norms or institutions requires stories of complex intermingling with the local that never quite reproduce global logics, even as those stories cannot be told without reference to the varied practices we link together and call international or global.

BOX 3.2 WEEDINESS AND THE IN-BETWEEN

Tsing (2004: Chapter 5) explores the space of an inhabited forest, which is not properly pristine forest, nor properly farms. This space in-between, a space of "weediness" provides an interpretive challenge for an ethnographer and a political challenge for environmental activists and a state committed to national development. For the state, it is a wasted space, not used to its maximal purpose as commercial agriculture or industrial forest. For environmental activists, the inhabited forest is already damaged by the long human presence and alteration, its very weediness a product of a vast number of small, targeted interventions to foster fruit trees, honey production by bees, to restore the fertility of the ground. No longer available for preservation, the forest becomes an object of sustainable forestry practices. Here, there is a partial convergence of the state and the environmental activist; neither can tolerate the weediness of Zomia that falls outside of centralized management. Difference exceeds the categories of the state and the activist.

In a similar narrative, but from the west of China, Christopher Beckwith (2009) examines the Silk Road in relation to the cultural and political space of Central Eurasian empires.[17] Quite strikingly, China is not at the center of the interconnected story. For Beckwith, "the Silk Road was not in essence a commercial transportation network at all. It was the entire Central Eurasian economy, or socio-economic-political-cultural system," made up of "the nomadic pastoral economy, the agricultural 'oasis' economy, and the Central Asian urban economy" (264, 28; see also 328). The Silk Road and the entire Central Eurasian socio-economic system co-existed with, and became possible, only via a series of peace treaties with the states and empires peripheral to the system, like the Chinese and Umayyad dynastic states (27). In contrast to the more formal states or empires actually *peripheral* to the "Silk Road" system, political rule was organized initially around "the sociopolitical-religious ideal of the heroic lord and his *comitatus*, a war band of his friends sworn to defend him to the death" (12). Political and economic forms, including an almost fully monetized trading system, and far more fully monetized than the Chinese economy (158),[18] encompassed a vast "multi-ethnic" and "multicultural" population (158, 326). Though usually pitted against the image of modern state practices, as backward or barbarous, these steppe peoples and empires and their transnational and transcultural political and economic systems arguably herald modern forms of governance and contemporary economic and cultural globalization (see Weatherford 2004; Neumann 2013). The implication is that the origins of the state system, or modernity generally, might lie in a "where" outside of Europe, and in a "when" well before its usual/linkage to the Peace of Westphalia.

Further, one of the key "items" that flowed along the Silk Road was religion, particularly Buddhist ideas, practices and imagery. We might read the space of Silk Road, then, less as socio-economic or political economic, but as a socio-cultural, in this case Buddhist, space, as does the project by Prapin Manomaivibool and Shih Chih-yu (2016). Shih (2016a) sets the tone by arguing that analyses of China's position in Asia have emphasized Confucian sources of thought and practice, obscuring the importance of Buddhist sources (Shih 2016a: i). Such work, importantly, also decenters China, since Buddhism is not China's to possess or interpret. He also decenters the state, since it is the relations built around or shaped by Buddhist identities, principles and connection that suggest less threatening possibilities for China and its neighbors than claims about Confucianism as Chinese state identity or as a blueprint for Chinese regional hegemony (Shih 2016a: i, iii–vi). Consistent with Shih's earlier argument (2013), the essays collected here (Ikeda 2016; Marwah 2016; Nguyen and Shih 2016; Singh and Wallis 2016, for example) claim that Chinese identity is understood and negotiated only in complex relations or, in Said's terms, intermingling with its various neighbors, so that there is no singular China and no singular China threat. Thinking through China's international relations from a position centered on a Buddhist space and understanding Chinese thought, whether Daoist or neo-Confucian, as inflected by this Buddhist space produces a distinctly relational understanding of international relations and balancing behavior (Shih 2016b; Shih et al. 2019; see too Chapter 17), not a simple translation or imposition of a purported trans-historical realist logic into contemporary East and Southeast Asia. This is the time or "when" of Buddhism, where something thought as past, the spread of Buddhism across the Central Asian frontiers, is intimately connected to the present of a Buddhist relational space. States may not disappear in the present of this Buddhist space, but the place of states can be understood only as part of a multilayered narrative of counterpoint and interconnection.

Conclusion: so what is IR?

In a bold move, Justin Rosenberg (2016: 135) recently called for a radical re-imagining that begins with a broad conception of the "international" that extends the where and when of IR (see too, Chapter 6). IR might be given a sounder footing, he argues, if rooted in an "elemental fact" that sounds much like Said's humanism: "human existence is not unitary but multiple" and that multiplicity is "distributed across numerous interacting societies." Rosenberg stresses how starting with "societies" means that we should conceive the object of IR not simply as a world of multiple polities, but see it as a world of multiple social, economic and cultural spaces that interconnect and, perhaps, intermingle. He does recognize that the notion of society might be misleading, since it can be taken to imply a clearly circumscribed and homogeneous entity. But with the language of multiplicity and difference, he means, as I did above in the two cases, to suggest a more open understanding of the kinds of units into which humans may organize themselves. And, as above, Rosenberg (2016: 136–9) insists that multiplicity and difference have always been accompanied by "coexistence," "interaction" and therefore also "combination," by which he means no unit's history is ever "linear or self enclosed." Instead of separate units with their own development paths, as implied by accounts built on the spatial demarcations of the states-system, "[a]ll societies must therefore be ongoing combinations of local patterns of development with external influences and pressures of all kinds." He uses this formulation to suggest that though we might still see the "social world as a whole," that whole involves processes of inter-societal relations, not individualized states or societies (139–41).

Rosenberg's vision of IR as a study of the world and its peoples in all their variety, interactions and intersection has much to recommend it. As hinted above, Rosenberg's reformulation of IR seems broadly consistent with Said's humanism and its embrace of human multiplicity, interconnection and overlap. But we might worry about Rosenberg's embrace of the idea of development, which seems still to bear the weight of Marxist modernity (see Blaney and Tickner 2017b) – the idea that there is some notion of material/ social development that we can use to encompass the variety of societies, their interactions, intersections and combinations. It is not clear at all that Said would link his notion of humanism to an idea of development, though he certainly sees the human mind as engaged in multiple processes of self-understanding and realization.

The "cases" I have introduced here reinforce the feeling that Rosenberg's vision of difference does not reach far enough. For example, we might read the encounters in North America as a story of difference and interaction with distinctive forms of combination resulting in modern North American diets and modes of political organization. But we might also see that modern North America appears not simply as a combination, but also as an attempt at erasure. Though the societies and values and visions of the Amerindians have not vanished but live and serve as inspiration for continuing political struggles and may serve as resources for critical reflection on modern developmental lifeways (Blaney and Inayatullah 2010), they also need to be understood in counterpoint to modernity. It also is not clear that Scott's "Zomia" or Tsing's forest and mountain peoples would see themselves in Rosenberg's understanding of development. Indeed, we might read Scott and Tsing to suggest that it is precisely processes of development these "societies" have willfully evaded or escaped, though escape has grown more difficult in the present (see too, Chapter 15). Similarly, Shih's identification of a space of Buddhist relationality certainly does connect and combine societies, but he seems to imagine the world as a space of cultural flows and interconnections that might resist claims about development as capturing the human condition. Chaudhuri's examination of the Indian Ocean as a site of material and cultural life and Beckwith on the Silk Road as the Central Asian polity fit better within Rosenberg's vision of different but combined development.

Even following conventional practice that locates the "where" of IR in Europe, or in its extensions in the U.S., we cannot sustain the idea that a state system forms the object of analysis of the discipline. Beginning with Europe suggests we put empire and imperial practices at the center of our work, unless we limit our temporal focus to the "when" of the late 20th century. And, even then, we could sustain a focus on separable states only by ignoring the relations and flows that interconnect the world into a capitalist global division of labor. Shifting the "where" of our investigation by centering on North America or the Silk Road only reinforces the sense that centering IR around the idea of a state system fails us, particularly as it also shifts our sense of the "when" and "what" of IR. Prior to the European invasions, North America does offer a vision of multiple "homelands," bounded by frontiers, but not strictly bordered in the way of today's sovereign states. These homelands interacted and overlapped extensively, with exchanges of goods and cultural influences spanning the entire continent. It would be difficult to describe this space of relations and flows as a state system, though practices of rule, trade and diplomacy are recognizable. North America becomes divided finally into the recognizable states of Mexico, Canada and the United States in the 19th century, but speaking of North America only as states would mask the presence of populations subjugated by the settler populations that made those states. This remains a story of colonial relations and continued anti-colonial struggles. And the time of the present contains the pasts of pre-imperial North America and eventual conquest and empire and the present of state borders and rule. The "Silk Road" points similarly to a space of flows and interconnection that unsettles less multilayered historical narratives of statehood and contemporary state ideologies. The space of flows might be contained within a political, geographical and cultural space, like the Indian Ocean, that highlights the importance of central authority, or it might focus attention on the polities of the steppes, that might be the more legitimate ancestors of modernity than the old empires of Asia or the European monarchies. We might find more radical difference in counterpoint and connection to the idea of modern secular statehood in the shatterzone of those evading central authority in Zomia or a Buddhist relational zone in which states are enveloped. In either of the latter two cases, we are far from the state system as *the* object of inquiry. We are now on the terrain of marginal zones in relation to centers and religiously demarcated spaces in relation to the assumed secular rationalism of state logic. Taking our cases together, we find that, as we move across time and space, the question of the "what" of IR seems newly open.

Study questions

1. Why do we choose certain points as the beginnings of international relations? What intellectual or political reasons might motivate such choices?
2. Or, more specifically, why do scholars in IR hold so strongly to a Eurocentric narrative of the state system?
3. What are the political or policy implications of such choices? How would we act differently in a world of multiplicity and connection than in a state system?
4. What are the various forms of political rule and social organization introduced by the chapter? Can we identify cases of the persistence of these varied forms in the present?
5. Some narratives of global multiplicity and interconnection resist organizing human history around the idea of development. What do we gain by abandoning this idea? What do we lose?

Notes

1   Xian Lu, Lan Yaqing and Luo Zhantao provided research assistance during the summer of 2018.
2   See Tucker (2018) for a helpful recent discussion. Blaney and Tickner (2017a) point to Robbie Shilliam's work (2015) as an important decolonial effort within IR.
3   See, for example, Osiander (2001). We might follow on this thought and diversify our idea of units and still see our object of inquiry as IR. See Ferguson and Mansbach (1996), who classify a variety of political and social forms under the label "polities," and, more recently, see Rosenberg (2016) who favors the term "society."
4   Of course, this account is disputed. Maybe capitalism arrives much later and global capitalism not until the more complete European colonization of the globe. See the varying accounts of Wallerstein (1976, 1980); Ellen Meiksins Wood (2017 [1999]); and Timothy Mitchell (2002) to suggest how contentious the idea of a capitalist world system.
5   Obviously, I don't favor this view. See Inayatullah and Blaney (2004) for an articulation of IR's creation myth in relation to the 30 Years' War and the conquest of the Americas.
6   See Weitz (2008) on the civilizational notions and the forced movements of people associated with the recognition (or construction of) sovereign states in the interwar period.
7   See Schmidt (1998) and Vitalis (2015) on the central place of race relations and colonial administration in early 20th-century IR. See also, Chapter 4.
8   Many such accounts are available. For example, Calloway (2003) begins with an extended discussion of "The West Before 1500" that serves as both the "ancient" and more recent history of peoples and their responses to Spanish invasion from the south and the U.S. army and settlers from the east. See also Richter (2001), Du Val (2006).
9   On trade and market centers, see, for example, Fenn (2014) on the Mandan and Young and Fowler (2000) on the Mississippian center of Cahokia.
10 See also White (1983). Jennings' language is reminiscent of Third World theories of dependency and unequal development that reached prominence in the 1960s and 1970s. The most prominent Latin American dependency theorists, at least because their work was available in English, included Cardoso and Faletto (1979), Sunkel (1969, 1973), Furtado (1969, 1970) and Dos Santos (1970). Theorists of unequal development, such as Rodney (1974) and Amin (1976, 1979), make closely associated claims.

11 The geopolitics of North America during the process of European colonization included varying conflicts and alliances (Nye 1968; Richter 2001; Taylor 2002; Calloway 2007), shifting of populations (Warren 2014), the rise and fall of empires (White 1991; Gwynne 2010), Amerindian refinement of their own theories and practices of treaty-making (Williams 1997), and mixed results of efforts to create a united front against the outside invaders (Dowd 1992).

12 Others have mapped the terrain of encounter. See Greenblatt (1993), Pagden (1993) and Mason (1990) as examples.

13 See recent Xi speech at (http://en.ndrc.gov.cn/newsrelease/201503/t20150330_669367.html). The implications for China's relations with various regions are discussed by Blanchard (2017), Tukmadiyeva (2013) and Fallon (2015).

14 Mearsheimer (2014) and Allison (2017).

15 Some Chinese analysts share the offensive realist vision of China's foreign policy, but many put more weight on the defensive motives for national policy, either in securing a regional role or to secure China's national identity in regional context (Lynch 2013).

16 Though somewhat beyond Scott's "Zomia," Tsing's work is recognizably connected with his account (see Greenhouse 2011).

17 Neumann (2013: 78–97).

18 Chin (2014) finds that coinage and quantitative theories of money emerge in the Han Dynasty around the need for currency exchange and foreign, not domestic, commerce, which are both submerged in "Confucian" ideas of propriety.

Further reading

Anievas, Alexander and Kerem Nişancioğlu (2015) *How the West Came to Rule: The Geopolitical Origins of Capitalism*, London: Pluto. This book gives a non-Eurocentric story about Western dominance. The initial theory chapter is a bit heavy, but the various chapters that document the importance of particular times and regions, for example, the Atlantic slave trade and the gradual control by Europe of trade in the Pacific, are crucial to understanding the rise of capitalism.

Lightfoot, Sheryl (2016) *Global Indigenous Politics: A Subtle Revolution*, London: Routledge. Documents the rise of a global indigenous movement and the distinctive ways this movement does international or transnational relations.

Scott, James C. (2009) *The Art of Not Being Governed: An Anarchist History of Upland Southeast Asia*, New Haven, CT: Yale University; and Tsing, Anna Lowenhaupt (2004) *Friction: An Ethnography of Global Connections*, Durham, NC: University of North Carolina. Both authors disrupt any easy assumption of the naturalness of the state or capitalist development. Scott's work provokes us by identifying *escaping rule* as a political process usually neglected by social scientists. Tsing is a wonderful storyteller and it is easy to be carried away. But pay attention to the way these stories are always challenging our unquestioning recourse to universal notions, like development, the state, capitalism, transnational social movement, even as she shows how these notions achieve a kind of universality by travel, realizable only in the friction that occurs as they touch down in particular places.

Wolf, Eric R. (1982) *Europe and the People Without History*, Berkeley, CA: University of California Press. An inviting read and a good, if not quite comprehensive, picture of the world at both 1500 and as it evolved with European expansion and the rise of capitalism. Its weakness is that Africa is given short shrift in the text.

References

Abu-Lughod, Janet L. (1989) *Before European Hegemony: The World System A.D. 1250–1350*, New York: Oxford University Press.

Allison, Graham (2017) *Destined for War: Can America and China Escape Thucydides's Trap?* Boston, MA: Houghton Mifflin Harcourt.

Amin, Samir (1976) *Unequal Development: An Essay on the Social Formations of Peripheral Capitalism*, New York: Monthly Review Press.

Amin, Samir (1979) *Imperialism and Unequal Development*, New York: Monthly Review Press.

Anievas, Alexander and Kerem Nişancioğlu (2015) *How the West Came to Rule: The Geopolitical Origins of Capitalism*, London: Pluto.

Barker, Joanne (2011) *Native Acts: Law, Recognition, and Cultural Authenticity*. Durham, NC: Duke University Press.

Beckwith, Christopher I. (2009) *Empires of the Silk Road: A History of Central Eurasia from the Bronze Age to the Present*, Princeton, NJ: Princeton University.

Biolsi, Thomas (2005) "Imagined Geographies: Sovereignty, Indigenous Space, and American Indian Struggle," *American Ethnologist* 32(2): 239–59. doi:10.1525/ae.2005.32.2.239

Blanchard, Jean-Marc (ed) (2017) *China's Maritime Silk Road Initiative and South Asia: A Political Economic Analysis of Its Purposes, Perils, and Promise*, Basingstoke: Palgrave.

Blaney, David L. and Naeem Inayatullah (2010) *Savage Economics: Wealth, Poverty, and the Temporal Walls of Capitalism*, London: Routledge.

Blaney, David L. and Arlene B. Tickner (2017a) "Worlding, Ontological Politics and the Possibility of a Decolonial IR," *Millennium* 45(3): 293–311. doi:10.1177/0305829817702446

Blaney, David L. and Arlene Tickner (2017b) "IR in the Prison House of Modernity," *International Politics* 31(1): 71–5. doi:10.1177/0047117817691349

Braudel, Fernand (1972) *The Mediterranean and the Mediterranean World in the Age of Phillip II*, Volume I, New York: Harper and Row.

Braudel, Fernand (1973) *The Mediterranean and the Mediterranean World in the Age of Phillip II*, Volume II, New York: Harper and Row.

Bull, Hedley (1977) *The Anarchical Society: A Study of Order in World Politics*, New York: Columbia University.

Bull, Hedley and Adam Watson (eds) (1984) *The Expansion of International Society*, Oxford: Clarendon.

Calloway, Colin G. (2003) *One Vast Winter Count: The Native American West Before Lewis and Clark*, Lincoln, NE: University of Nebraska.

Calloway, Colin G. (2007) *The Shawnees and the War for America*, New York: Penguin.

Cardoso, F.H. and E. Faletto (1979) *Dependency and Development in Latin America*, Trans. M. M. Urquidi, Berkeley, CA: University of California Press.

Chaudhuri, K.N. (1990) *Asia before Europe: Economy and Civilisation of the Indian Ocean from the Rise of Islam to 1750*, Cambridge: Cambridge University Press.

Cheyfitz, Eric (2009) "Balancing the Earth: Native American Philosophies and the Environmental Crisis," *Arizona Quarterly* 65(3): 139–62. doi:10.1353/arq.0.0045

Chin, Tamara (2013) "The Invention of the Silk Road, 1877," *Critical Inquiry* 40(1): 194–219. doi:10.1086/673232?mobileUi=0

Chin, Tamara (2014) *Savage Exchange: Han Imperialism, Chinese Literary Style, and the Economic Imagination*, Cambridge, MA: Harvard University Press.

Chua, Charmaine Siuwei (2018) *Containing the Ship of State: Managing Mobility in an Age of Logistics*, Unpublished: University of Minnesota.

Coulthard, Glen (2014) *Red Skin, White Mask: Rejecting the Colonial Politics of Recognition*. Minneapolis, MN: University of Minnesota Press.

Crawford, Neta C. (1994) "A Security Regime among Democracies: Cooperation among Iroquois Nations," *International Organization* 48(3): 345–85. doi:10.1017/S002081830002823X

Deloria, Vine, Jr. (1984) *The Nations Within: The Past and Future of American Indian Sovereignty*, New York: Pantheon.

Dos Santos, Theotonio (1970) "The Structure of Dependence," *American Economic Review* 60(2): 231–36.

Dowd, Gregory Evans (1992) *A Spirited Resistance: The North American Indian Struggle for Unity, 1745–1815*, Baltimore, MD: Johns Hopkins University.

Du Val, Kathleen (2006) *The Native Ground: Indians and Colonists in the Heart of the Continent*, Philadelphia, PA: University of Pennsylvania.

Fallon, Theresa (2015) "The New Silk Road: Xi Jinping's Grand Strategy for Eurasia," *American Foreign Policy Interests* 37: 140–47. doi:10.1080/10803920.2015.1056682

Fenn, Elizabeth A. (2014) *Encounters at the Heart of the World: A History of the Mandan People*, New York: Hill and Wang.

Ferguson, Yale H. and Richard W. Mansbach (1996) *Polities: Authority, Identities, and Change*, Columbia, SC: University of South Carolina Press.

Frank, Andre Gunder (1998) *ReOrient: Global Economy in the Asia Age*, Berkeley and Los Angeles, CA: University of California Press.

Furtado, Celso (1969) "U.S. Hegemony and the Future of Latin America," in J. de Castro Horowitz and J. Gerassi (eds), *Latin American Radicalism: A Documentary Report on Left and Nationalist Movements*, New York: Random House, pp. 33–43.

Furtado, Celso (1970) *Obstacles to Development in Latin America*, Garden City, NY: Anchor.

Greenblatt, Stephen (ed) (1993) *New World Encounters*, Berkeley and Los Angeles, CA: University of California Press.

Greenhouse, Carol J. (2011) "Review Symposium. State, Power and Anarchism: A Discussion of *The Art of Not Being Governed*," *Perspectives on Politics* 9(1): 88–92. doi:10.1017/S1537592710003336

Gwynne, S. C. (2010) *Empire of the Summer Moon*, New York: Scribner.

Hansen, Valerie (2012) *The Silk Road*, Oxford: Oxford University Press.

Hobson, John M. (2004) *The Eastern Origins of Western Civilization*, Cambridge: Cambridge University Press.

Ikeda, Josuke (2016) "(Re)creating China: Sinology, The Kyoto School and the Japanese View of the Modern World," in Prapin Manomailvibool and Chih-yu Shih (eds), *Understanding 21st Century China in Buddhist Asia: History, Modernity and International Relations*, Bangkok: Chulalongkorn University, pp. 3–20.

Ilieva, Evgenia (2018) "The Historicity of Exile: Said, Auerbach, and the Return to Philosophical Hermeneutics," Unpublished: Ithaca College.

Inayatullah, Naeem and David L. Blaney (1995) "Realizing Sovereignty," *Review of International Studies* 21(1): 3–20. doi:10.1017/S0260210500117498

Inayatullah, Naeem and David L. Blaney (2004) *International Relations and the Problem of Difference*, New York: Routledge.

Inayatullah, Naeem and David L. Blaney (2018) "Units, Markets, Relations and Flow: From Bargaining Units to Unfolding Wholes," in James Caporaso (ed), *Oxford Research Encyclopedia of Politics*, pp. 1–22. doi:10.1093/acrefore/9780190228637.013.272

James, Anaya S. (1996) *Indigenous Peoples in International Law*, Oxford: Oxford University Press.

Jennings, Francis (1975) *The Invasion of America: Indians, Colonialism and the Cant of Conquest*, Chapel Hill, NC: University of North Carolina Press.

Johnson, Jay T. (2008) "Indigeneity's Challenges to the White Settler-State: Creating a Thirdspace for Dynamic Citizenship," *Alternatives* 33(1): 29–52. doi:10.1177/030437540803300103

Keal, Paul (2003) *European Conquest and the Rights of Indigenous People: The Moral Backwardness of International Society*, Cambridge: Cambridge University Press.

King, Hayden (2018) "Discourses of Conquest and Resistance: International Relations and Anishinaable Diplomacy," in Randolph B. Persaud and Alina Sajed (eds), *Race, Gender, and Culture in International Relations: Postcolonial Perspectives*, London: Routledge, pp. 132–54. doi:10.4324/9781315227542

Lightfoot, Sheryl (2016) *Global Indigenous Politics: A Subtle Revolution*, London: Routledge.

Liu, Xin-ru (2010) *The Silk Road in World History*, Oxford: Oxford University Press.

Lynch, Daniel C. (2013) "Securitizing Culture in Chinese Foreign Policy Debates: Implications for Interpreting China's Rise," *Asian Survey*, 53(4): 629–52. doi:10.1525/as.2013.53.4.629

Marwah, Reena (2016) "Buddhism in Nepal and Sri Lanka Perspectives: Contextualizing China's Soft Power Diplomacy," in Prapin Manomailvibool and Chih-yu Shih (eds), *Understanding 21st*

Century China in Buddhist Asia: History, Modernity and International Relations, Bangkok: Chulalongkorn University, pp. 71–100.

Mason, Peter (1990) *Deconstructing America: Representations of the Other*, New York: Routledge.

Mearsheimer, John J. (2014) *The Tragedy of Great Power Politics*, New York: W.W. Norton.

Mitchell, Timothy (2002) *Rule of Experts: Egypt, Technopolitics, Modernity*. Berkeley, CA: University of California.

Nederman, Cary (2000) *Worlds of Difference: European Discourses of Toleration, c. 1100-c. 1550*, University Park, PA: Penn State University.

Neumann, Iver (2013) "Claiming the Early State for the Relational Turn: The Case of Rus' (Ca. 800–1100)," in Arlene B. Tickner and David L. Blaney (eds), *Claiming the International*, London: Routledge, pp. 78–97.

Nguyen, Tran Tien and Chih-yu Shih (2016) "Buddhist Influence in Vietnamese Diplomacy toward China: Lessons from the History of Religion," in Prapin Manomailvibool and Chih-yu Shih (eds), *Understanding 21st Century China in Buddhist Asia: History, Modernity and International Relations*, Bangkok: Chulalongkorn University, pp. 45–69.

Nye, Wilbur Sturtevant (1968) *Plains Indian Raiders: The Final Phases of Warfare from the Arkansas to the Red River*, Norman, OK: University of Oklahoma.

Osiander, Andreas (2001) "Sovereignty, International Relations, and the Westphalian Myth," *International Organization* 55(2): 251–87. doi:10.1162/00208180151140577

Pagden, Anthony (1993) *European Encounters with the New World: From Renaissance to Romanticism*, New Haven, CT and London: Yale University Press.

Pratt, Scott L. (2002) *Native Pragmatism: Rethinking the Roots of American Philosophy*, Bloomington and Indianapolis, IN: University of Indiana.

Ranco, Darren and Dean Suagee (2007) "Tribal Sovereignty and the Problem of Difference in Environmental Regulation: Observations on 'Measured Separatism' in Indian Country," *Antipode* 39(4): 691–707. doi:10.1111/j.1467-8330.2007.00547.x

Richter, Daniel K. (2001) *Facing East from Indian Country: A Native History of Early America*, Cambridge, MA: Harvard University Press.

Rodney, Walter (1974) *How Europe Underdeveloped Africa*, Washington, DC: Howard University Press.

Rosenberg, Justin (2016) "International Relations in the Prison House of Political Science," *International Relations* 30(2): 127–153. doi:10.1177/0047117816644662

Said, Edward W. (1993) *Culture and Imperialism*, New York: Alfred A. Knopf.

Said, Edward W. (2004) *Humanism and Democratic Criticism*, New York: Columbia University Press.

Schmidt, Brian (1998) *The Political Discourse of Anarchy: A Disciplinary History of International Relations*, Albany, NA: SUNY Press.

Scott, James C. (2009) *The Art of Not Being Governed: An Anarchist History of Upland Southeast Asia*, New Haven, CT: Yale University Press.

Shih, Chih-yu (2013) "Sinic World Order Revisited: Choosing Sites of Self-Discovery in Contemporary East Asia," in Arlene B. Tickner and David L. Blaney (eds), *Claiming the International*, London: Routledge, pp. 98–117.

Shih, Chih-yu (2016a) "Introduction: Transcending China via Buddhism," in Prapin Manomailvibool and Chih-yu Shih (eds), *Understanding 21st Century China in Buddhist Asia: History, Modernity and International Relations*, Bangkok: Chulalongkorn University, pp. i–xviii.

Shih, Chih-yu (2016b) "The Two States of Nature in Chinese Practice of Non/Intervention: Buddhism, Neo-Confucionism, and Modernity," in Prapin Manomailvibool and Chih-yu Shih (eds), *Understanding 21st Century China in Buddhist Asia: History, Modernity and International Relations*, Bangkok: Chulalongkorn University, pp. 123–52.

Shih, Chih-yu, et al. (2019) *China and International Theory: The Balance of Relationships*, London: Routledge.

Shilliam, Robbie (2015) *The Black Pacific: Anti-Colonial Struggles and Oceanic Connections*, London: Bloomsbury. doi:10.1080/00064246.2016.1223487

Singh, Swaran and Kaziah Wallis (2016) "Buddhism as a Solution to 'China Threat Theories'? Chinese Diplomacy and the Case of Chinese Tooth Relic in Myanmar," in Prapin Manomailvibool and Chih-yu Shih (eds), *Understanding 21st Century China in Buddhist Asia: History, Modernity and International Relations*, Bangkok: Chulalongkorn University, pp. 101–22.

Stavrianos, L. S. (1981) *Global Rift: The Third World Comes of Age*, New York: William Morrow.

Sunkel, O. (1973) "Transnational Capitalism and National Disintegration in Latin America," *Social and Economic Studies*, 22(1): 132–76.

Sunkel, Osvaldo (1969) "National Development Policy and External Dependence in Latin America," *Journal of Development Studies*, 6(1): 623–48. doi:10.1080/00220386908421311

Taylor, Alan (2002) "The Divided Ground: Upper Canada, New York, and the Iroquois Six nations, 1783–1815," *Journal of the Early Republic* 22(1): 55–75.

Todorov, Tzvetan (1986) *The Conquest of America: The Question of the Other*. New York: Harper and Row.

Tsing, Anna Lowenhaupt (2004) *Friction: An Ethnography of Global Connections*, Durham, NC: University of North Carolina Press.

Tucker, Karen (2018) "Unraveling Coloniality in International Relations: Knowledge, Relationality, and Strategies for Engagement," *International Political Sociology* 12(3): 215–32. doi:10.1093/ips/oly005

Tukmadiyeva, Malika (2013) "Xinjiang in China's Foreign Policy toward Central Asia," *Connections*, 12(3): 87–108. doi:10.11610/Connections.12.3.05

Vitalis, Robert (2015) *White World Order, Black Power Politics: The Birth of American International Relations*, Ithaca, NY: Cornell University Press.

Walker, R.B.J. (1993) *Inside/Outside: International Relations as Political Theory*, Cambridge: Cambridge University Press.

Wallerstein, Immanuel (1976) *The Modern World-System: Capitalist Agriculture and the Origins of the European World-Economy in the Sixteenth Century*, New York: Academic Press.

Wallerstein, Immanuel (1980) *The Modern World System II: Mercantilism and the Consolidation of the European World-Economy, 1600–1750*, New York: Academic Press.

Warren, Stephen (2014) *The Worlds the Shawnee Made: Migration and Violence in Early America*, Chapel Hill, NC: University of North Carolina Press.

Weatherford, Jack M. (1988) *Indian Givers: How the Indians of the Americas Transformed the World*, New York: Crown.

Weatherford, Jack M. (2004) *Genghis Khan and the Making of the Modern World*, New York: Crown.

Weitz, Eric D. (2008) "From the Vienna to the Paris System: International Politics and the Entangled History of Human Rights, Forced Deportations and Civilizing Missions," *The American Historical Review* 113(5): 1313–43. doi:10.1086/ahr.113.5.1313

White, Richard (1983) *The Roots of Dependency: Subsistence, Environment, and Social Change Amont the Choctaws, Pawnees, and Navajos*, Lincoln, NE: University of Nebraska Press.

White, Richard (1991) *The Middle Ground: Indians, Empires, and Republics in the Great Lakes Region. 1650–1815*, Cambridge: Cambridge University Press.

Wilkinson, Charles (2005) *Blood Struggles: The Rise of Modern Indian Nations*, New York: Norton.

Williams, Robert A. (1997) *Linking Arms Together: American Indian Treaty Visions of Law and Peace, 1600–1800*, Oxford: Oxford University Press.

Wolf, Eric R. (1982) *Europe and the People without History*, Berkeley, CA: University of California Press.

Wood, Ellen Meiksins (2017 [1999]) *The Origins of Capitalism: A Longer View*, London: Verso.

Young, Biloine Whiting and Melvin L. Fowler (2000) *Cahokia: The Great Native American Metropolis*, Urbana and Chicago, IL: University of Illinois Press.

4 IR and the making of the white man's world

Peter Vale and Vineet Thakur

> The problem of the twentieth century is the problem of the color line.
>
> W.E.B. Du Bois (1996 [1900])

> I went to a school modeled on British public schools. I read lots of English books there; *Treasure Island* and *Gulliver's Travels* and *Prisoner of Zenda,* and *Oliver Twist* and *Tom Brown's School Days* and such books in their dozens. But I also encountered Rider Haggard and John Buchan and the rest, and their "African" books. Africa was an enigma to me. I did not see myself as an African in those books. I took sides with the white men against the savages. In other words, I went through my first level of schooling thinking I was of the party of the white man in his hair-raising adventures and narrow escapes. The white man was good and reasonable and smart and courageous. The savages arrayed against him were sinister and stupid, never anything higher than cunning. I hated their guts.
>
> Chinua Achebe (2009)

Introduction

The very first act of International Relations (IR) was to exclude. To understand this, we must begin with the discipline's natal story: the founding of the Department of International Politics at the (then) University of Wales in Aberystwyth – now, Aberystwyth University. It tells of the

> generous endowment of £20,000 given by David Davies, as a memorial to the students killed and wounded in the First World War. Davies was moved by a global vision, forged in the fires of war, aimed at repairing the shattered family of nations and, more ambitiously, to redeem the claims of men and women in a great global commonwealth – the League of Nations.
>
> Aberystwyth University (2017)

In fact, Davies was not the only one who funded the Chair; he was only one of the three people who contributed an equal amount. The other two were women, Davies' sisters, Gwendoline and Margaret (Haslam 2000: 57). So, while crediting David alone with "redeem[ing] the claims of men *and women* in a great global commonwealth," Aberystwyth continues to erase women from its founding moment. This itself is quite revealing of a narrative of exclusion on which IR builds its disciplinary identity.

BOX 4.1 LANGUAGE AND COLONIZATION

H. Rider Haggard (1856–1925) and John Buchan (1875–1940) wrote some of the most popular adventure novels of their time. Haggard is popularly remembered for *King Solomon's Mines* and *She*, while Buchan's *Prester John* and *The Thirty-Nine Steps* were among the most influential novels. These books, steeped in colonial stereotypes, were widely read and recommended in public schools. Interestingly, both of these authors also spent considerable time in South Africa; Buchan was, in fact, a member of the Milner's Kindergarten (which we will discuss below) and later became Canada's governor general.

To read IR's story further is to go beyond the "great unwashed" of Victorian novelists, i.e. the common men and women IR wanted to rescue from the ravages of war. In this story of redemption, we now stumble onto the "savages" of the Edwardian novelists, Ryder Haggard and John Buchan. After all, these were also bound into IR's hope for a better world, the League of Nations. However, they were not to be treated as equal citizens of the great commonwealth for which early IR longed, but were tethered to the League's project in second- and third-class carriages. As the Darwinist language of the time, expressed in Article 22 of the League Covenant, makes clear, the "strenuous conditions of the modern world," had compelled "advanced nations" to take up the responsibility for governing those whose historical misfortune was to have been colonized by the losing parties of the "Great War."

Anthony Anghie's work has demonstrated that the League institutionalized the idea that "sovereignty could be graded, as implied by the classification of mandates into A, B and C, based on their state of political and economic advancement" (Anghie 2005: 148; also see Pedersen 2015). But there was more to this than meets the legal eye because the position a political community occupied on the Mandate ladder depended on where it stood on the plane of race. So, under the Mandate system, Asians were accorded their own "nations" – they were derivative and conjured, certainly, but they were still nations; Africans and other indigenous groups were parceled out as tribal societies – to be ruled over by the civilized. So, the ranking was not only colonial, it was explicitly racial.

Quite correctly, the institutionalized racism of the League and its Mandate system is identified with a man whose own academic writing had endorsed neo-Lamarkian "scientific racism" and who actively carried out racial segregation during his term in high office (de Carvalho et al. 2011: 750). This was America's 28th president, Woodrow Wilson, whose duplicity at the League of Nations was reflected in his approach to African Americans in the United States itself. As the African American scholar, Rayford Logan (1928: 426), caustically commented:

> it is … one of the enigmas of history that Mr. Wilson should have been so vitally interested in the welfare of Bantus, Oulofs, Manidingoes, Doualas, and other tribes of which he had never heard while he remained deaf to the pleas of black peons in the country under his direct administration.

But Logan was perhaps too generous to Wilson. The U.S. president's call for granting self-determination was restricted to the relatively civilized Eastern Europeans and excluded non-white races (de Carvalho et al. 2011: 750).

In recent years, many scholars have explored this blighted past and made a broader point about the discipline of IR: race and imperialism were inscribed into the very DNA of the discipline. The works of John Hobson (2012) and Robert Vitalis (2015) are particularly revealing in this regard. In the "historical turn" carried in the works of David Long and Brian Schmidt (2005), Nicolas Guilhot (2014), Errol Henderson (2013), Duncan Bell (2007), among others, the façade of benign internationalism of IR's founding narrative has been authoritatively exposed.

But further probing of the discipline's imperial and racial origins of IR is important for several reasons (Bell 2009; see too, Chapter 6). For one thing, as always, the past writes the present. In all academic disciplines, epistemological categories are determined on the basis of original understandings. So, IR is said to be thematically concerned with questions of world order, anarchy, security, sovereignty, state system and so on. This is because these are assumed to be central to the primary question in IR: why do wars happen? But while this may have been the discipline's core founding challenge, as more scholars turn to the archives, it is increasingly clear that "race" was another of its natal concerns. Indeed, as the African American scholar W.E.B. Du Bois had argued, "race" or "color" was one of the fault lines around which understandings of global conflict were structured.

In the U.S. case, the discipline explicitly originated from the field of "colonial administration" (Vitalis 2015). Likewise, in Britain and its white settler colonies, both academic and political understandings of the "international" were steeped in deeply racial thinking (Long and Schmidt 2005). At least in one case that we have studied, South Africa, the efforts towards institutionalizing IR nationally were driven by the desire to perfect a system of "native administration." In fact, it was the success of social anthropology as a field that supposedly studied natives and their administration objectively that inhibited the early growth of IR in institutional and political life (Thakur and Vale 2019: 43).

While the founding narrative of IR is always cast as a deeply moral tale, as many thinkers including Achebe remind us, we need to constantly ask: who is telling the story? We are likely to find a different story about IR in the German South-West Africa (now Namibia), which was mandated to (the then Union of) South Africa, than in London, which (certainty formally) saw the move as enhancing the prospects for peace. As the old adage – often called Miles' Law points out – "Where you stand depends on where you sit."

Thus, critical thinking begins with thinking about the world in different ways. So, perhaps we should look at IR's natal moment not by the purported high-mindedness of building international peace but through a prism which was located not in the high corridors of global power but at the grubby, dusty rock face of a gold mine in Johannesburg. And this is the task we set for ourselves in this chapter.

Unlike most discussions which begin with World War I as the setting for the emergence of IR as a disciplinary field, we begin with the Anglo-Boer war. This war, we would argue, set the stage for an ideational and institutional reformulation of the British empire. For imperial enthusiasts, we will focus in particular on Lionel Curtis and on how South Africa became a laboratory of the empire where new ideas and institutions could be fleshed out. The South African model of a segregated state was then "kicked up," first to the level to the British empire (or the British commonwealth, as it was now called), and eventually to the world state. These ideas were then circulated, molded and formalized through networks of people and institutions across the British empire. Indeed, IR as a "scientific study" emerged primarily through the same networks. In noting the racial character of the discipline, we also discuss how E.H. Carr's framing of the "first great debate" invariably erases race from disciplinary memory, giving us a racially sanitized version of IR.

"The romance of the veld"

The first war of the twentieth century, the Boer war (1899–1902), was fought over access to the gold mines of Johannesburg in the country which would come to be known as "South Africa." The South African War (as the war was also known) inaugurated the decline, if not the end, of *Pax-Britannica*, the glorious Victorian phase in which Britain's empire had commanded the globe (see Box 4.2). Although Britain emerged victorious from the war, it was weakened and felt increasingly insecure about its power and moral authority. Joseph Chamberlain, the secretary of state for the colonies, had stated just prior to its outbreak that the Boer war posed a question about Britain's continued existence as a great power in the world. But, as it turned out, the most industrialized nation in the world took three long years to defeat a largely peasant population, despite pouring in 450,000 troops into the war from the length and breadth of its empire. The war, the largest that Britain fought between the Napoleonic Wars and World War I, exhausted Britain militarily, financially and morally (a liberal journalist G.P. Gooch (1907 [1901]) asked, "what … does it profit a state if it gain[s] the whole world and lose[s] its own soul?").

BOX 4.2 THE SOUTH AFRICAN WAR

The Second Anglo-Boer War (1899–1902), also called the South African War, was fought between the British empire and the two Afrikaner republics – Transvaal and Orange Free State. Known as the first war of the twentieth century, this was also the last war among the white settler colonial communities within the British empire. It had a tremendous global significance, as it informed narratives of nation-building not just in Britain and South Africa, but also New Zealand, Australia, Canada and India.

"Imperialism," the term that until the Boer war had been considered a noble force for both peace and progress, had morphed into something increasingly intolerable. The left-liberal journalist John Hobson's book, *Imperialism: A Study* (1902), was the first sustained critique of naked imperialism and helped to turn the idea of imperialism "[in]to a status of partial abuse" (Koebner and Schmidt 1964: 221–249).

Anxieties over military weakness and a resulting ideological vacuum generated fears about the decline of the British "race." So, for instance, the reverses in the war were attributed to the industrialized, emasculated British soldier. A notion grew that the slums and squalor of industrial Britain had produced "a stunted, narrow-chested, easily wearied [dweller] … with little ballast, stamina or endurance" (Masterman 1907 [1901]: 8). This had emerged, so the argument went, during the same period as the best Britons had sailed to the "other Englands," as the Oxford historian and empire enthusiast J.A. Froude (1886) called the settler colonies.

These fears played into an increasing lack of confidence in Britain's view of itself as a global power. Britain had already been told-off from the Atlantic by the United States in the Venezuelan affair and felt increasingly threatened by the rise of Germany and Japan in the Indian Ocean and the Pacific. Out of this sense of military and ideological crisis emerged a new fantasy, the idea of "new imperialism," in which imperial enthusiasts saw an opportunity to tailor the Britain-centered empire into a broader white commonwealth. The drift towards this idea had begun during the Boer war when the so-called "daughters of the empire" – other settler colonies – had fought alongside the British against the Boers (see Box 4.3).

BOX 4.3 IMPERIAL ANXIETIES

Over two successive crises in 1895 and 1902–03, United States forced Britain (and other continental powers) to accept the Monroe Doctrine in the Americas, by disallowing the latter's coercion in Venezuela. Furthermore, while the Royal British Navy continued to be the largest, rapid naval modernization by Germany and Japan challenged Britain's dominance in the Atlantic and Pacific Oceans. Between 1907 and 1909, Roosevelt's "Great White Fleet," aimed at displaying America's blue water capability, travelled across the world and received warm welcome in the white British dominions, in particular. This also worried British policy makers.

In essence, "new imperialism" called for a broader federal structure of the empire where the white settler colonies would join with Britain to strengthen the task of governance across the empire. So, instead of the emphasis falling as before on Britain as a ruling state, much was now made of the "British race." The most assiduous champion of this ideological turn was the imperial pro-consul, Alfred Milner, whose thoughts are captured in the following:

> My patriotism knows no geographical but only racial limits. I am a British Race Patriot … It is not the soil of Britain, dear as it is to me, which is essential to arouse my patriotism, but the speech, the tradition, the spiritual heritage, the principles, the aspirations of the British race. They do not cease to be mine because they are transplanted. … I feel myself as a citizen of the Empire. I feel that Canada is my country. Australia my country, New Zealand my country, South Africa my country, just as much as Surrey or Yorkshire.
>
> (quoted in Schwarz 2011: 99)

As a result, the settler colonies provided not only a hope for a stronger empire, militarily speaking, but they also buttressed various threads of thinking on the three levels of imperial being: empire, state and society. While race as a marker of identity was expressed in the idiom of the "British race" or "Anglo-Saxon race" (to use Cecil John Rhodes' phrase) to provide an imperial identity, "race" was also elevated into an issue of the emerging "British world" (to use a phrase from Leo Amery) in another way. Unlike the British state itself, the white settlers continuously grappled with the "native problem," as it was commonly called. This trope drew upon a common history of genocidal wars, and the perennial fear of being "swamped" by the natives. In an influential book, the Oxford historian Charles Pearson captured these fears in the following words:

> the day will come, and not perhaps far distant, when the European observer will see the globe girdled with a continuous zone of black and yellow races, no longer too weak for aggression or under tutelage, but independent, or practically so, in government, monopolizing the trade of their own regions, and circumscribing the industry of the European.
>
> (quoted in Plaut 2016: 50)

With white settler colonies at the imperial table, "native administration" and "native problem" became truly imperial issues, to the extent that imperial unity was often achieved by diluting British liberal opinion and its concerns about the treatment of non-white populations (Plaut 2016).

Once the empire was reimagined as an organic union of white settler colonies, its conflicts were naturally arranged along racial lines between whites and non-whites. From being essentially an issue of domestic politics concerning the frontiers of empire, race whirled to form its central organizing principle. Accordingly, we will argue below, Southern Africa became a laboratory of the empire: where a new conception of sovereign association could be tried, tested and, finally, elevated to the international level. And hence the ideas that "birthed" IR emerged from these very frontiers. To this "romance of the veld" (as Bill Schwarz calls this imperial fascination with the frontiers and borrowing of ideas) we will now turn.

The clothes of new imperialism: Brit-Boer-Bantu

Lord Alfred Milner, the quintessential "British race patriot," was also the architect of the Boer war. At its end, he added to his portfolio as high commissioner the administratorship of the two conquered Boer republics, Transvaal and Orange River Colony. His task was to unite disparate entities of what was then often loosely called "southern Africa" into a single polity.

To serve this end, Milner recruited graduates from his alma mater, Oxford, in the hope of creating (what he saw) as a modern industrial state out of a medieval hierarchy (Nimocks 1968: 18). This group included several individuals who would become important players in the history of empire. But our interest will fall on only one individual: Lionel Curtis.

Although Milner was to leave southern Africa five years before the unification of South Africa, these young apparatchiks – often derisively called, "Milner's Kindergarten" – worked behind the scenes to bring the four southern Africa colonies, Transvaal, Orange River, Cape Colony and Natal, together in the form of a "closer union." For the Kindergarten, the closer union of South Africa was to be achieved through an elite-driven process of knowledge creation and its dissemination. These would later provide the seeds for the discipline of IR.

But before we see how these took root, we must traverse both political history and the career of Lionel Curtis.

In August 1906, Curtis who was then assistant colonial secretary responsible for municipal affairs in Johannesburg, set about writing a document that was to lay out the barebones of a new state in South Africa. Called the *Selborne Memorandum*, the document appeared in mid-1907 with the aim of igniting discussions on the possibility of creating a single "sovereign" unit across southern Africa (William 1925). The *Selbourne Memorandum* was certainly not the first time such a possibility had been proposed. Indeed, British policy in the region had flirted with the same idea since the late 1850s but the context and content of its enunciation was different. In the aftermath of the Boer war, Britain controlled all of southern Africa, including the former Afrikaner republics and the African kingdoms.

Although the *Selborne Memorandum* laid out a formal case for a federal union, there was no clarity about what shape (or form) the political union in southern Africa would take. This clarity was to be provided by the deliberations of a members-only association, which was known by the moniker *The Fortnightly Club*. Organized by Curtis and others in Johannesburg, 40-odd British devotees of empire met more than two-dozen times between October 1906 and May 1908 under the auspices of The Fortnightly Club to discuss issues of empire, race and federal union and, in particular, to address the issue of statehood in southern Africa.

Some of the central questions that engaged this process were explained by Curtis himself in a paper he presented to the Club in May 1907. In it, he framed the question of South Africa in the wider context of the political form of the empire (Curtis 1907). In this paper, he called for laying a more sustained theoretical argument of political rule in the British empire. As he argued, empire building "was the result of many different causes and motives to which the sea-faring habits of the British race gave free play" (Curtis 1907). The empire was driven by contingency rather than by any grand scheme of colonization. So it was that American colonization was a result of religious persecution; Canadian colonization grew out of the fear of American republics; Australia was a dumping ground for convicts; South Africa was "acquired simply as the commercial half-way house to India," and India itself was colonized to "provide it with a government compatible with the maintenance of the great commercial interests." Consequently, rather than a unified approach to the imperial project, Britain has had to implement more practical solutions to secure the colonies from internal and external worries. The mandarins of empire, Curtis argued, were not afforded a theoretician's distance and abstractness to consider the question of political rule from a scientific and objective vantage point. In other words, the empire needed a theory of political rule (Curtis 1907).

For him, South Africa was "the microcosm in which human problems can be studied as a physicist studies the forces of nature in the test-tube of a laboratory" (Curtis 1923: 80), and thus provided as an ideal setting for experimenting on broader scheme for imperial unity. However, imperial unity was not important for its own sake. As he was to argue in his writings over a five-decade long career, the British empire demonstrated the possibility that war can be made obsolete. Indeed, from 1910 onwards, he referred to the British empire as the British commonwealth, a loose federation of dominions and dependencies which through creation of a multinational community has eliminated war as a function of politics.

War itself, according to his understanding, was primarily caused by the competition among higher races for access to resources and raw material in the non-Western world. In this, he in fact pre-empted both Du Bois and Lenin, who later made the same argument. For Curtis, the "ultimate problem of the world" was the racial one. Peace was conditioned upon finding a scheme of reconciliation among and between the three chief races of the world – Europeans, Asians and Africans – all at different stages of human evolution. South Africa, being the country that truly represented this imperial as well as global reality, was ideally placed to provide such solutions to the world.

Hence, a theory of political rule within the empire, and eventually the world, had to be thrashed out first in the South African veld. A theory that would not only unite the white communities – Brits and Boers in South Africa – but also find a more sustainable arrangement between Europeans and non-Europeans.

In his 1907 paper, Curtis first elaborated on his view of the empire. The empire, according to him, was chiefly composed of two levels of civilization, modern and ancient. Modern civilizations were those which had developed faculties of change in human organization. Europeans came under the modern civilization category because they had adapted to change and showed significant progress in developing institutions of self-government. However, various European cultures had developed at different speeds which created an internal hierarchy. Unsurprisingly, Curtis believed that Britain was the most developed because it had perfected the art of self-government and free institutions. Other races – the Germans and the French, for instance – were on a lower scale but they were capable of self-development in order to build better institutions. Ancient civilizations, for their part, were culturally and politically static, and were without any internal capacity for political change. As a result, autocracy remained the most functionally viable and popularly accepted form of rule in these cultures. The divide was exacerbated by an understanding that there was no hope of these societies becoming modern. Unlike other social Darwinists who would argue that the non-Europeans could be pulled over to the modern era through a "civilization mission," Curtis argued here that the principles of progress – externally or internally driven – only work within modern societies (Curtis 1907).

Drawn together, these arguments were not new and expectedly collapsed any distinctions between terms such as civilizations, cultures, races and societies, but their end point departed from the Victorian liberal reasoning on one important point. Unlike others of his generation, Curtis did not suggest that the British rule was good because it would act as a civilizing influence on the non-Europeans. On the contrary, he believed that the attempts at civilizing non-Europeans were often counter-productive because instead of the civilized pulling up the non-civilized, the superior races were more likely to be pulled down if they were to co-habit with non-Europeans. Indeed, as several other papers in this Club argued, South Africa provided a different challenge from other white dominions and the United States, where non-whites were in minority and numerically insignificant because of genocidal wars. In South Africa the specter of a civilized black majority evoked sharp worries about "reverse extinction" of whites. In other words, while the colonial discourse had until now justified colonial genocides as a natural culmination of the contact of "civilized" whites with "uncivilized" non-whites in the manner of the "survival of the fittest," a black majority that had not only resisted for centuries and fought back against whites in South Africa, but also proliferated abundantly raised serious questions about the validity of this thesis. Indeed, the fears were reversed. The white minority now worried that they were the ones under the threat of extinction. Furthermore, in its racial composition South Africa approximated the empire in general, and thus pre-figured what could be expected at the imperial scale.

In response, Curtis proposed a three-tier framework for political rule in the empire. The first tier comprised colonies which were composed of purely European populations – Canada, Australia and New Zealand. The second – India, say – was a colony with an almost wholly non-European population. The colonies in South Africa, which contained a significant European settler community together with an overwhelming non-European population, were considered as the third tier (Curtis 1907).

He argued that Canada, Australia and New Zealand which were "almost empty before they were occupied by Europeans" should enjoy full self-government (Curtis 1907). These colonies were to be encouraged to "exercise the most direct control over their own administration." There was only a negligible aboriginal population which "constitute(s) no social or political danger" and the white community "can be trusted to look after ... [indigenous people] ... as they look after kangaroos and elk, as a sort of national curiosity" (Curtis 1907).

Because India was almost wholly populated by non-Europeans the only form of rule that the people understood was autocracy. The problem with this, however, was that all power was concentrated in one person. In Curtis's view "the human conscience is atrophied by the exercise of unbridled ... power over others," which is why this kind of autocracy degenerates into despotism which permitted no political freedoms. The solution was not democracy, but a mediated form of autocracy – the mediation was provided by an efficient colonial bureaucracy which was accountable to public conscience in Britain. This public oversight over bureaucratic rule would be "sufficiently remote to prevent constant interference but near enough to prevent free government from degenerating into despotism" (Curtis 1907). This kind of thinking married the best of Weberian bureaucracy with assumptions about Oriental autocracy.

South Africa was plainly different: not only was its "European" population significant, but its predominantly African population was also "less capable of self-government than those in India." Furthermore, within these communities there were major social cleavages which other colonies did not face. The European community was divided between the British and the Boer: a division which straddled the two extremes of "civilization" within the broad category of Europeans. Amongst the non-Europeans, to complicate matters, a significant population of Asians were relatively more advanced than the other group, the Africans. The Asians demanded rights commensurate with their position in their countries of origin, while the latter had only a rudimentary conception of political rule (Curtis 1907).

Viewed in this way, the issue of South African statehood was intricately tied to the very nature of the empire. This was because South Africa encapsulated the central concerns – peace and racial order – that the empire faced. Like the empire, peace and racial order in South Africa was contingent on bringing together different white "races" towards a single identity while at the same time confronting a majority of non-Europeans who were asserting their claims for rights. The challenge of creating a sovereign state in southern Africa, comprising of the four colonies, would require the fusion of the Boer and the Brit into a single "nation" in order to end the fissures that had caused the Boer war. It was equally important to devise a southern Africa-wide policy of native administration. Curtis's preferred solution for the latter was the idea of "segregation," i.e. a form of indirect bureaucratic rule.

The acclaimed historian, Martin Legassick (1995: 45), suggested that Lionel Curtis was the first to use the term "segregation" in South Africa. There is some debate over the initial use (Dubow 1995: 147–148), but South African historians agree that the theoretical case for segregation as a state-building ideology was only made authoritatively in the first decade of the twentieth century, and the deliberations in Curtis's Fortnightly Club article was one of the clearest theoretical expositions.

Two other crucial figures from the Club who developed segregationist ideas in South Africa were Howard Pim (later one of the founders of the South African Institute for Race Relations) and Philip Kerr (later the first editor of *The State* and *The Round Table*, more on them below). This is a crucial point because not only does this particular idea of segregation become the precursor to the later policy of apartheid, but it is also presented as a model of indirect rule across the British empire. Indeed, the League of Nations mandate system was also inspired from this idea, as we will explore below.

"Imperial chain of being": South Africa, the British commonwealth and world state

Statehood came to South Africa in 1910. Although the grunt work was done by Afrikaner politicians like Jan Smuts and Louis Botha, Curtis and the Milner's Kindergarten played an important role, or at least took sufficient credit for it. Just prior to the formation of the Union of South Africa, the Kindergarten created (what was called) the Association of Closer Union Societies in September 1908. Known as the "Closer Union Societies," its primary function was to propagate the idea of common statehood. At their peak, 64 such societies were active across the region. In addition, a bilingual journal – called *The State/De Staat* – was launched in January 1909. They also produced two different sets of books which fostered the possibility of a regional political formation. These were called *The Government of South Africa* (which consisted of two volumes) and *The Framework of the Union*. Through these initiatives, Curtis and the Kindergarten attempted to spread the "gospel" of a political union, which took into consideration their racial schemes of white unity against their African subjects and creating schemes of native administration based on segregation.

Several members of the Kindergarten, including Curtis and Kerr, left for England soon after it was clear that a political union was to be established. As Curtis wrote, the Kindergarten had "acted as an advance party of sappers[1] sent out to build a vital section of the road over which the main force will have to travel later on" (quoted in Nimocks 1968: 114). Imperial union, or a federal empire, was to be this main road.

The Kindergarten now reproduced their South African methods on an imperial scale. Over the next few years, they created an empire-wide community of imperial enthusiasts, called the Round Table movement, which replicated the South African Closer Union Societies. They started a journal of this movement, *The Round Table*, which was completely modelled on *The State*. In 1915 and 1916, Curtis produced two books titled *Problem of the Commonwealth* and *The Commonwealth of Nations*, which proposed a scheme for turning the hierarchical British empire into a federated union. Not surprisingly, he replicated his three-tier scheme of political rule, with one major difference. In these years, he had changed his ideas about the potential of Asians (Indians, in particular) to adapt to Western political institutions. He now believed that Asians could be taught self-government, and thus, they could one day become self-governing just like Europeans. However, these schemes for self-government for them still had to be designed by Europeans. Indeed, he himself designed one for India; he called it dyarchy – which was incorporated into the 1919 Montagu Chelmsford reforms designed to gradually introduce self-government in India. However, his ideas about

Africans and indigenous peoples remained the same. A 1914 internal Round Table memo, drafted initially by Curtis but then revised by Edward Grigg – then the co-editor of Round Table and later the governor of Colonial Kenya – stated:

> the salvation of the more backward races [Africans] is not to be achieved by Euro-peans repudiating the task of control, but only by exercising control from first to last in the interest of the lower races as well as the higher.
>
> (The Round Table Papers 1914: 20)

Curtis's British commonwealth – and it is important to remember that he was the first thinker to conceptualize this idea – not only established peace between the white domin-ions but also between whites and non-whites in the colonies by devising appropriate sys-tems of governance. Consequently, the British commonwealth was not only preserving the future of the white race, but also presenting a model on which a world government ought to be based.

In 1918, he wrote an article titled "Windows of Freedom" for the Round Table where he first fleshed out the idea of mandates (Curtis 1918), which Jan Smuts supposedly picked on for his longer pamphlet, *The League of Nations*. Another crucial person in devising the mandate scheme was Philip Kerr, Curtis's Kindergarten colleague who was also the first editor of *The Round Table*, who actually drafted Article 22 which set out the mandate system. This was, in fact, an international application of Curtis's revised three-fold conception of the empire. The white nations come together as equal partners in a global scheme of governance. The equality of Asian nations (except "honorary whites" such as Japan) is deferred to a future date – consigned to the "waiting room of history," as Dipesh Chakrabarty (2000) has argued – although notionally they are acknowledged as capable of making a transformation into modern nationhood. Africans and indigenous people are, however, considered designed for perpetual subjection. Since they were deemed capable of polluting the white race through continual contact, a more indirect and segregated rather than direct form of government required relations of trusteeship. The whole scheme is in its character very South African, which draws on the very specific experience of Curtis, Smuts and Kerr.

After the end of World War I, as his schemes of imperial unity floundered mostly because dominion nationalism pushed for further decentralization of empire, Curtis turned his attention to more global concerns. Indeed, both Curtis and Kerr became ardent champions of the world federation in the 1920s and 1930s. Curtis's own ideas were fleshed out in a three-volume study published between 1934 and 1937, titled *Civitas Dei* (1938).

Curtis here summons a heady admixture of Christian *agape* and British *noblesse oblige* and sets out a vision of a world commonwealth which, he argued, would be the final embodiment of the principles of Christianity. For him, the commonwealth was based on the principle of mutual obligation of all citizens towards others. This was in contrast to an autocratic state where the duty was only owed only to the sovereign. Hence, the latter was naturally inferior to the former.

Although an exemplary polity, the first commonwealth in Greece perished because it had refused to extend this principle of mutual duty beyond racial and territorial frontiers, such as to the gentiles and barbarians. Like an organism, as the common-wealth stopped to grow, it degenerated. In contrast, the British empire had found a way to continuously expand its boundaries to include even people of other races.

This was done through a two-way interpretation of this "sense of duty" towards others: fraternal and paternal. In the British commonwealth, members of the British race had a fraternal sense of duty towards each other, but they also had a paternal duty to uplift the lower races up on the scale of civilization. The British commonwealth, thus, provided a better model for a world state than any other form of commonwealth or empire. The U.S. commonwealth, for instance, was based on a conception of self-interest and thus, like the Greeks, refused to extend the principle of mutual duty to others. Germany and its empire were premised on autocratic assumptions of the duty of individuals only towards the sovereign.

Hence, a world commonwealth could only grow out of the British experience. The British commonwealth thus not only provided the model for the world state, but also would serve as its organic core (Lavin 1995). The world commonwealth would encourage peace among the European powers in exactly the same way that its British precursor had fostered peace among Britain and the white settler colonies. As it did this, it would also uplift the lower races by bringing them under the tutelage of the government of the world commonwealth. And in that fashion, the world commonwealth or state would fulfill both its instrumental (peace) as well as moral (racial uplifting) functions.

But South Africa, of course, remained a life-long model; it was after all the only real success that Curtis ever experienced. When asked about the putative idealism of his world state scheme towards the end of his life, Curtis reminded his critics of the successes this kind of thinking achieved in the uniting of South Africa. That was a political union formed in the aftermath of a devastating war, in which four colonies – two British, two Boer – had willingly joined forces to form a singular state. From an academic standpoint, this may seem an idealist project, but it was achieved largely, as Curtis and his friends in the Round Table often reminded each other, through the initiative and tireless work of an epistemic group, Milner's Kindergarten.

Lionel Curtis and the invention of IR?

Although a little-explored figure in disciplinary history, Curtis's imprint in how IR is studied and imagined far surpasses many others. Indeed, Curtis is perhaps known less for his ideas and more as an institutional builder. Technically, he was only one of the many recognized founders of the Royal Institute of International Affairs, but as the place which came to be known as Chatham House once admitted, he was the founder in "a special and unique way" (RIIA 1952).

It was Curtis who initially organized meetings of U.S. and British representatives on the sidelines of the Paris Peace Conference in 1919 where a "joint institute" with branches in England and the United States was conceived. However, when the Americans did not show much enthusiasm for this form of association, the British members founded an independent British Institute in 1920. As Chatham House was to admit, both the "labour and inspiration for the Institute" came from Lionel Curtis (RIIA 1952). In the years that followed, Curtis sustained the work of this Institute almost single-handedly by garnering the necessary funding. He conceived of this, and a series of other institutes that were later opened across the world, as "laboratories for the scientific study of international questions" (Curtis 1945: x). These include IR think-tanks in the United States, Australia, Canada, New Zealand, South Africa and India. In the words of the Canadian merchant banker, Edward Robert Peacock (1871–1962), the greatest contribution … [of Lionel Curtis] is this conception of his that the scientific method must be applied to the study of international affairs. In founding the Institute, he did for international affairs what was done for science when the Royal Society was founded.

(RIIA 1932: 66)

Elsewhere, with our collaborator, Alex Davies, we have told how Curtis sharpened the "scientific method" in the field that he had first brought to his work in South Africa (Thakur et al. 2017).

Robert Vitalis (2005) has claimed that the journal, *Foreign Affairs* (which started publication in 1909 as *The Journal of Race Development*), was the first IR journal, but *The Round Table* could very well claim that status, too. This is because it commenced publication in the same year. Importantly for the claims made in this chapter, both the Round Table movement and its journal, were modelled on the "Closer Union Societies" and *The State*, which had begun life in South Africa.

But the imprint of Curtis – and the Round Table – on IR is not just institutional and methodological. He was also influential in the realm of ideas. We have noted above the role Curtis played in advancing ideas related to the British commonwealth, the League of Nations and the world state. He also played a pivotal role in drafting constitutional roadmaps for India and Ireland, for which a British member of parliament scathingly called him "the man who created dyarchy in India and anarchy in Ireland" (Brand 1944).

Curtis was linked not only to IR's hinterland of discourses about "race" but also to British idealism, the two of which being mutually reinforcing. Curtis indeed was the epitome of British "idealism" which E.H. Carr had criticized in his *Twenty Years Crisis* (1946 [1939]). Importantly, British idealism was firmly embedded in a racialized understanding of the world which has been written out of disciplinary narratives.

To substantiate this argument, let us consider IR's first great debate briefly. This "great debate" allegedly took placed between "realists" and "idealists." Several IR scholars have pointed to how the first great debate is itself a great myth (Schmidt 1998; Wilson 1998; Quirk and Vigneswaran 2005), but the myth itself, and its originator E.H. Carr, distort the debate in a spectacular way, whether unintended or contrived. In the *Twenty Years Crisis*, Carr had claimed that "nearly all thinking, both academic and popular, on international politics in English-speaking countries" was "idealist." Indeed, he was unrelenting in his criticism of visionary schemes such as world federation and collective security, which he called "quack remedies" (Haslam 2000: 81). According to Carr, all scientific disciplines evolve in stages of development. Idealism, which he equated with moral pronouncements about world politics, exhibited the primitive or utopian stage of development in IR, while "realism," which was based on facts and existing reality, was an advanced stage. Thus, the British idealists as they advanced their schemes of world government were guilty of preferring morals over realities, *ought* over *is*, and thus fundamentally misunderstood how global politics operated. While Carr mentioned a number of such thinkers in his book, including Alfred Zimmern, Woodrow Wilson, Norman Angell, among others, one name conspicuously absent is that of his Chatham House colleague, Lionel Curtis. It was certainly impossible for Carr to miss Curtis's book *Civitas Dei*, considering the former started writing his text just after Curtis's final volume hit the market, was eventually reviewed in 110 papers around the world, was translated into many languages and also adorned the shelves of politicians across the globe such as the British Queen, Hitler and the South African Afrikaner politician D.F. Malan. Indeed, no other thinker of the interwar era fits Carr's description of an idealist better than Curtis (with the possible exception of Philip Kerr).

Whatever the reasons for this omission, Carr's book is in fact a direct rejoinder to Curtis and his conceptions of the world commonwealth. Importantly however, by referring to Curtis and other British thinkers as moralists or idealists, the terms of debate are set to exclude the otherwise immoral, racial dimension of this thinking. The agenda of the debate is set between idealists/realists, in which the former are christened moralists. Curtis's racialized thinking is only indicative of the broad thread that runs across the writings of the British idealists or moralists of this era, including Alfred Zimmern, Gilbert Murray, Arnold Toynbee, Philip Kerr, Leo Amery and Leonard Woolf, among others. Their implacable faith in the values of the British empire, namely liberal democracy and self-governing institutions, was always complemented by their justifications of colonialism and racism under the guise of imperial responsibility. These ideas, which were so central to the founding of both IR's most prestigious institutions and as an intellectual practice, were suffused with the goal of the creation of a global racial empire. But since the disciplinary narrative is set along moralist/realist lines, race goes missing from disciplinary narratives. From this perspective, perhaps the most relevant critique of these idealist schemes among British public intellectuals came from George Orwell.

On the eve of World War II and just around the time Carr published his book, Orwell asked of the idealists:

> what would really be happening if [the scheme of a Union of World's democracies] were put into operation. The British and French empires, with their six hundred million disenfranchised human beings, would simply be receiving fresh police forces; the huge strength of the USA would be behind the robbery of India and Africa. ... *all* phrases like "Peace Bloc.", "Peace Front", etc. contain some such implication; all imply a tightening up of the existing structure. The unspoken clause is always "not counting niggers". For how can we make a "firm stand" against Hitler if we are simultaneously weakening ourselves at home? In other words, how can we "fight fascism" except by bolstering up a far vaster injustice?
>
> (Orwell 1939)

BOX 4.4 LANGUAGE AND DECOLONIZATION

Chinua Achebe (1930–2013) and Ngugi Wa Thiong'o (1938–), two of the greatest modern writers, have reflected on the role of English language and decolonization. Ngugi famously argued that language was a carrier of culture and a tool of self-definition. English as the language of the colonizer was thus a tool of control, leading to the perpetual colonization of the mind. Achebe disagreed. He argued that if "language was a weapon," it could also be used to generate new solidarities and throw away the colonizer.

Conclusion

The African philosopher V.Y. Mudimbe once famously called anthropology "the scientific advisor to colonialism," because it spoke colonial bureaucratese (on language, see Box 4.4). Likewise, IR was the scientific advisor to the "new imperialism" of the early twentieth century. It provided a language and finesse well suited to imperial desires. War, peace, commonwealth and world government became the conceptual markers through which colonialism of the past was made palatable. Disciplinary amnesia about these issues, evident in everyday renderings of the "origins" of IR in classrooms across the world, allows the discipline to present its past in a narrative of high idealism. The origins story, as Carvalho, Leira and Hobson (2011: 736) tell us, appears to be "complete and settled as if it was carved in stone." The narrative comes to us as an inherently moral one, one where finding global peace was the central driving force for the discipline's "birth."

This internal peace of the discipline can, and must, be disturbed. The question of voice becomes crucial here. Who is telling the story and whose voice is being recorded? At first glance the non-West seems absent in the "IR for world peace" narrative. But on further probing, one registers its presence as the perpetual recipient of IR's violence (see too Chapter 6). Therefore, every story has to be read with caution – nay, deep suspicion – more so in a discipline such as IR, which, as Sankaran Krishna (2001) argues, relies necessarily on an abstract way of thinking and purposely discourages ventures into archives. For students and scholars in the global South, the process of reclaiming IR would begin by not just disturbing the master narrative, but also by presenting alternative stories (on this, see Chapter 3).

Questions for discussion

1. Why is it important to study disciplinary history?
2. Can one understand concepts such as war, peace or world state in abstract?
3. Are your IR course syllabi filled with white men? Can you think of why?
4. What do adventure novels tell us about the world?
5. Do alternative narratives of disciplinary history help us understand IR better?
6. What are the ways in which we can decolonize IR?

Note

1 A sapper is a soldier who is sent ahead on a variety of engineering duties to create the requisite infrastructure to facilitate the advance of the army.

Further reading

Ashworth, Lucian (2014) *A History of International Thought. From the Origins of the Modern State to Academic International Relations*, London: Routledge. DOI: 10.4324/9781315772394. An excellent and readable account of the evolution of Western international thought and how it has shaped the predominantly Anglophone discipline of IR.

Dyvik, Synne, Jan Salby and Rorden Wilkinson (2017) *What's the Point of International Relations?* New York and London: Routledge. DOI: 10.4324/9781315201467. A recent edited volume which, as the title suggests, takes stock of the discipline, its history and its silences.

Guilhot, Nicolas (ed.) (2011) *The Invention of International Relations Theory: Realism, the Rocke-feller Foundation, and the 1954 Conference on Theory*, New York: Columbia University Press. A fine collection of essays that attempts to gauge the influence of a remarkable gathering of key IR scholars in May 1954.

Morefield, Jeanne (2005) *Covenants without Swords: Idealist Liberalism and the Spirit of Empire*, Princeton: Princeton University Press. With a focus on two "idealists," Gilbert Murray and Alfred Zimmern, Morefield interrogates the enduring tension between universalism and empire in liberal thinking.

Rösch, Felix (ed.) (2014) *Émigré Scholars and the Genesis of International Relations. A European Discipline in America?* Basingstoke: Palgrave Macmillan. DOI: 10.1057/9781137334695. Is American IR really a German social science? This volume focuses on the contribution of German émigré scholars in the making of the field.

References

Aberystwyth University (2017) "About Us: History," Aberystwyth University website, www.aber.ac.uk/en/interpol/about/history/, accessed 22 August 2017.

Achebe, Chinua (2009) "African Literature as Restoration of Celebration," in *The Education of a British-Protected Child*, New York: Penguin, pp. 107–123.

Anghie, Antony (2005) *Imperialism, Sovereignty and the Making of International Law*, Cambridge: Cambridge University Press. DOI: 10.1017/CBO9780511614262

Bell, Duncan (2007) *The Idea of Greater Britain: Empire and the Future of World Order, 1860–1900*, Princeton, NJ: Princeton University Press.

Bell, Duncan (2009) "Writing the World: Disciplinary History and Beyond," *International Affairs*, 85(1): 3–22. DOI: 10.1111/j.1468-2346.2009.00777.x

Brand, R.H. (1944) "Letter to Ivor Macadam, 14 January 1944," MS Eng Hist. c. 853, f. 25, Bodlean Library, Oxford.

Carr, E.H. (1946 [1939]) *The Twenty Years' Crisis 1919–1939: An Introduction to the Study of International Relations*, London: Macmillan.

Chakrabarty, Dipesh (2000) *Provincializing Europe: Postcolonial Thought and Historical Difference*, Princeton: Princeton University Press.

Curtis, Lionel (1907) "The Place of Subject People in the Empire," 9 May, Fortnightly Club Collection, A 146, Wits Historical Papers, Johannesburg.

Curtis, Lionel (1918) "Windows of Freedom," *The Round Table*, 8(3): 1–47.

Curtis, Lionel (1923) "'The Union of South Africa'," in Philip Kerr and Lionel Curtis (eds) *The Prevention of War*, New Haven: The Institute of Politics and Yale University Press, pp. 77–106.

Curtis, Lionel (1938) *Civitas Dei: The Commonwealth of God*, London: Macmillan.

Curtis, Lionel (1945) *World War: Its Cause and Cure*, London: Oxford University Press.

de Carvalho, Benjamin, Halvard Leira and John M. Hobson (2011) "The Big Bangs of IR: The Myths that Your Teachers Still Tell You about 1648 and 1919," *Millennium: Journal of International Studies*, 39(3): 735–758. DOI: 10.1177%2F0305829811401459

Du Bois, W.E.B. (1996 [1900]) "The Present Outlook for the Darker Races of Mankind," in Eric Sundquist (ed) *The Oxford W.E.B. Du Bois Reader*, Oxford: Oxford University Press, pp. 47–54.

Dubow, Saul (1995) "The Elaboration of Segregationist Ideology," in William Beinart and Saul Dubow (eds) *Segregation and Apartheid in Twentieth-Century South Africa*, London: Routledge, pp. 145–175.

Froude, J.A. (1886) *Oceana: Or, England and Her Colonies*, London: Longmans, Green and Co.

Gooch, G.P. (1907 [1901]) "Imperialism," in C.F.G. Masterman (ed) *The Heart of Empire: Discussions of Problems of Modern City Life in England. With an Essay on Imperialism*, Second edition, London: T. Fisher Unwin, pp. 308–400.

Guilhot, Nicolas (2014) "Imperial Realism: Post-War IR Theory and Decolonization," *The International History Review*, 36(4): 698–720. DOI: 10.1080/07075332.2013.836122

Haslam, Jonathan (2000) *The Vices of Integrity: E.H. Carr, 1892–1982*, London: Verso.

Henderson, Errol (2013) "Hidden in Plain Sight: Racism in International Relations Theory," *Cambridge Review of International Affairs*, 26(1): 1–92. DOI: 10.1080/09557571.2012.710585

Hobson, J.A. (1902) *Imperialism: A Study*, London: J. Nisbet.

Hobson, John (2012) *The Eurocentric Conception of World Politics: Western International Theory, 1760–1910*, Cambridge: CUP. DOI: 10.1017/CBO9781139096829

Koebner, Richard and Helmut Dan Schmidt (1964) *Imperialism: The Story and Significance of a Political Word, 1840–1960*, Cambridge: Cambridge University Press.

Krishna, Sankaran (2001) "Race, Amnesia and Education of International Relations," *Alternatives*, 26(4): 401–424. DOI: 10.1177/030437540102600403

Lavin, Deborah (1995) *From Empire to International Commonwealth: A Biography of Lionel Curtis*, Oxford: Claredon Press.

Legassick, Martin (1995) "British Hegemony and the Origins of Segregation in South Africa 1901–1914," in William Beinhart and Saul Dubow (eds) *Segregation and Apartheid in Twentieth Century South Africa*, Routledge: London, pp. 43–59. DOI: 10.4324/9780203425442

Logan, Rayford W. (1928) "The Operation of the Mandate System in Africa," *The Journal of Negro History*, 13(4): 423–477. DOI: 10.2307/2713843

Long, David and Brian C. Schmidt (eds.) (2005) *Imperialism and Internationalism in the Discipline of International Relations*, Albany, NY: State University of New York Press.

Masterman, C.F.G. (1907 [1901]) "Realities at Home," in C.F.G. Masterman (ed) *The Heart of Empire: Discussions of Problems of Modern City Life in England. With an Essay on Imperialism*, Second edition, London: T. Fisher Unwin, pp. 1–52.

Nimocks, Walter (1968) *Milner's Young Men: The "Kindergarten" in Edwardian Imperial Affairs*, Durham: Duke University Press.

Orwell, George (1939) "Not Counting Niggers," *The Adelphi*, July.

Pedersen, Susan (2015) *The Guardians: The League of Nations and the Crisis of Empire*, Oxford: Oxford University Press. DOI:10.1093/acprof:oso/9780199570485.001.0001

Plaut, Martin (2016) *Promise and Despair: The First Struggle for a Non-Racial South Africa*, Johannesburg: Jacana.

Quirk, Joel and Darshan Vigneswaran (2005) "The Construction of an Edifice: The Story of a First Great Debate," *Review of International Studies* 31(1): 89–107. DOI: 10.1017/S0260210505006315

RIIA (Royal Institute of International Affairs) (1932) "A Tribute to Lionel Curtis: Record of the Proceedings at the Presentation to Chatham House of the Portrait Painted by Oswald Birley, 1 November 1932." MS Eng Hist c. 853, f. 65–68, Bodleian Library, Oxford.

RIIA (Royal Institute of International Affairs) (1952) "Message from the Council of the Royal Institute of International Affairs to Mr Lionel Curtis on His 80th Birthday," MS Eng Hist c. 853, f. 119, Bodleian Library, Oxford.

Round Table Papers (1914) "Whitsdunite Memorandum," MS Eng Hist c. 778, Bodleian Libraries, Oxford.

Schmidt, Brian (1998) *The Political Discourse of Anarchy: A Disciplinary History of International Relations*, Albany: State University of New York Press.

Schwarz, Bill (2011) *Memories of Empire, Vol. 1: The White Man's World*, Oxford: Oxford University Press. DOI: 10.1093/acprof:oso/9780199296910.001.0001

Thakur, V., A. Davis and P. Vale (2017) "Imperial Mission, Scientific Method: An Alternative Account of the Origins of IR," *Millennium: Journal of International Studies*, 46(1): 3–23. DOI: 10.1177/0305829817711911

Thakur, V. and P. Vale (2019) "The Empty Neighbourhood: Race and Disciplinary Silence," in Jenny Edkings (ed) *Handbook of Critical International Relations*, London: Routledge, pp. 34–48. DOI: 10.4324/9781315692449

Vitalis, Robert (2005) "Birth of the Discipline," in David Long and Brian Schmidt (eds) *Imperialism and Internationalism in the Discipline of International Relations*, Albany: State University of New York Press, pp. 159–181.

Vitalis, Robert (2015) *White World Order, Black Power Politics: The Birth of American International Relations*, Ithaca and London: Cornell.

Williams, Basil (ed) (1925) *The Selborne Memorandum: A Review of the Mutual Relations of the British South African Colonies in 1907*, Oxford: Oxford University Press.

Wilson, Peter (1998) "The Myth of the First Great Debate," *Review of International Studies*, 24(5): 1–16. DOI: 10.1017/S0260210598000011

Part 2

Concepts

5 Order, ordering and disorder

Karen Smith

Introduction

In the 1940s, anthropologists were puzzled by a remote tribe in Southern Sudan, known as the Nuer. Their behavior challenged accepted notions of political theory; by living in what Evans-Pritchard (1940: 77) called "ordered anarchy" they defied conventional wisdom about the nature of political rule. In stark opposition to the widely accepted ideas of theorists like Thomas Hobbes,

> order here did not congeal in offices or institutions, in courts or constabularies, in finite territories or fixed geographical borders. It inhered, rather, in virtual grammars of action encoded in the idiom of kinship: in an immanent sociologic of fission and fusion, of relative social distance, that brought people together or forced them apart in situations of conflict.
>
> (Comaroff and Comaroff 2012: 91–92)

This example of a political system without government or a defined territory challenged the Western assumption that humans naturally tend towards a particular form of political order, and that "the absence of structures of state or sovereignty amounts to anarchy" (Grovogui 2006: 5). In addition, Evans-Pritchard describes the kind of order that can be identified as being central to the Nuer as a moral rather than social one:

> We would, therefore, suggest that Nuer political groups be defined in terms of values, by the relations between their segments and their interrelations as segments of a larger system in an organisation of society in certain social situations, and not as parts of a kind of fixed framework within which people live.
>
> (Evans-Pritchard 1940: 149)

While this example speaks of potentially different understandings of what constitutes order at the local or domestic level, it suggests that there is also more than one way to think about order at the level of the international system. In particular, it challenges the widespread assumption in International Relations (IR) that order and disorder are necessarily in opposition to one another, and therefore mutually exclusive. It speaks to certain assumptions in the West about what constitutes order, with any deviation from these preconceived notions being viewed with a sense of anxiety as potentially disruptive and resulting in disorder and chaos. In addition, it suggests that there might be different bases for order, including values and morality, rather than power and violence. This chapter engages with some of these ideas.

In the discipline of IR, the story of how the world came to be ordered the way it is today is usually told from the vantage point of the West (see Chapters 3 and 4). Despite the existence of alternative views of order – whether at the domestic or international level – Western-centric scholarship and political practice (including colonialism) is based on the assumed superiority of the Western understanding of order. Such a hierarchical, linear and ahistoricist approach to order also pervades the study of international relations. In an attempt to engage with and contest this state of affairs, the chapter starts by exploring ways in which the concept of order has been understood within the field of IR. This is followed by a brief overview of the usual story of how the global order came about, and how international institutions function as both constituents and instruments thereof. I also consider the role that the global South has played in constructing but also contesting the current global order. The chapter ends with an exploration of how alternative views can challenge existing perspectives, and how these insights can help us to develop better understandings not only of how orders come about, but also what the elements of a very different order might look like.

Order: a conceptualization

While order is one of the core concepts of the field of International Relations, it is essentially a contested concept, but also one that is often used without being interrogated. In the words of Marc Trachtenberg (2006: 207) it might simply refer to the idea that "international political life is not totally chaotic and that there is instead a certain logic to how things work in this area." Although the media constantly confronts us with examples of global disorder, such as conflict, this is not a representative picture of international relations. Most relations across borders – involving both state and non-state actors – are ordered by rules and norms. Take a few seconds to think about the different types of transnational interactions that occur on a daily basis: agreements between states are signed, companies engage in business dealings, non-governmental organizations cooperate on various issues. Even though we live in a world of territorial, sovereign states that form part of a system that is widely regarded as anarchic (meaning there is an absence of authority above the level of the state) it could be argued that a characteristic of the system is that it is largely marked by order. More specifically, cooperation in the international system is largely institutionalized, meaning it is governed by rules that provide order. One of the things that we are interested in when we study international relations is how this order is created and maintained. In addition, some critical scholars problematize the field's preoccupation with order, and question the way in which order obtains meaning only in contrast with disorder. Relatedly, a number of implications follow from this type of dichotomous thinking, for example that the world can be divided into orderly and disorderly spaces, with the wealthy, industrialized West associated with order and the rest associated with disorder. This thinking is also reflected in anxiety about the end of the Western, liberal order, and assumptions about the inevitable disorder that will accompany the continued rise of non-Western powers.

Notions of order and ordering can also be thought of in a very broad sense. If we think, for example, about how the world is ordered spatially on maps, it is obvious that European cartographers placed Europe at the center of the world, and there it remains. Imagine a map that is turned upside down, or where Africa, or Asia, or Latin America is at the center of the world. How would this change our perspective? Perhaps the simple act of visualizing the world in an alternative way (imagine, for example, a world map where Africa is at the top – see Figure 5.1)[1] might allow us to question existing notions

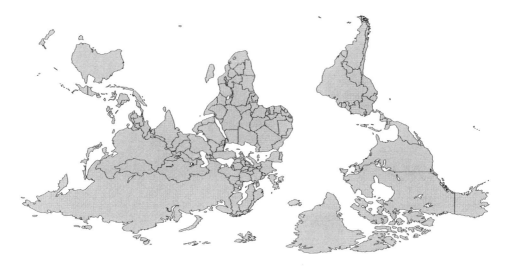

Figure 5.1 Upside-down map of the world
Source: https://philosophipotamus.com/maps/

of core and periphery, of power and marginalization, and to consider the possibilities of a different world order. This is particularly pertinent if we consider that, for much of history, China, India and the Middle East were at the core of the global economy, and that the rise of the West is a relatively recent phenomenon (see Chapter 12; and Abu-Lughod 1989).

Drawing on Robert W. Cox (1981), Hedley Bull (1977) and Robert Cooper (2004), Sanjay Chaturvedi and Joe Painter (2007) distinguish between order as indicating an absence of randomness or haphazardness, and order as the opposite of disorder, indicating a normative preference for order. This sets up a mutually constitutive dichotomy in which order has no meaning but in opposition to disorder, with the former being superior and preferable. One can also distinguish between interpretations of order as referring to something that comes about naturally, versus understandings that view order as something that must be constructed or brought about through rules – in other words – order as procedure, or order as something that is imposed by an authority. Different existing IR theories have diverse views about this.

Neorealists like Kenneth Waltz (1979) are concerned primarily with how there can be order without someone doing the ordering. In what is perceived to be an anarchical international system lacking a legitimate authority above states, order comes about through a balance of power between the great powers. Significantly, this implies that order (and shifts in order) is the result of the capabilities and distribution of power between the most important states. Smaller and less powerful states, not to mention non-state actors, have no relevance for thinking about order. In addition, neorealists also regard war as an important mechanism in the building, destruction and reconfiguration of order. In this understanding, a world of order can therefore still be a world of conflict and violence (see Chapter 7).

In contrast, liberal scholars are primarily interested in how an order that also limits the occurrence of war can be achieved.[2] For example, at the end of World War II, liberal efforts to construct a post-war order that would preserve peace were at the heart of the creation of the United Nations (UN) system. This implies a much more normative understanding of order that is closely related to the notion of international society, as understood by the English school.[3] According to Trachtenberg (2006: 208) international order and international society are often conflated, and refer to "the whole set of norms, relationships and institutions, political, economic and cultural, both international and cross-national, which … introduces a certain element of stability into what would otherwise be a violent, war-prone world." Different liberal theorists are interested in exploring how international law, international institutions and economic interdependence, respectively, can contribute to greater order by constraining states. Liberal institutionalists, like Robert Keohane (1989), for example, focus on the role of institutions and cooperation in constructing order.

Constructivists emphasize the role of ideas, norms and shared meanings in constructing order. Rules – both constitutive and regulative – are regarded as an important element of global order. Well-known constructivist Alexander Wendt (1999) focuses on the process of identity and interest formation, arguing that these are the most important factors in understanding the effects of anarchy and international order. The emphasis is thus on the impact of process, rather than structure on creating and maintaining order. In addition, because constructivists contend that social facts exist because of intersubjectively shared meanings, this implies that world order is not a fixed, but a changing concept.

Marxist theorists,[4] by contrast, focus on economic forces in explaining international relations, particularly the role of the capitalist system in shaping the world and maintaining an unequal order, both within and between states. International institutions are seen as the product of a dominant group of states, dominant ideas and the interests of the capitalist classes, serving to entrench existing relations of dependence. Cox (1983) applies Italian Marxist Antonio Gramsci's notion of hegemony[5] to the international system and looks, for example, at the way in which the United States has managed to maintain a world order that benefits itself by generating consent for that order (even amongst those who are disadvantaged by it). For feminist scholars,[6] the gendered nature of the existing world order manifests itself through the continued marginalization of women across all aspects of life.

The different theoretical approaches briefly outlined above suggest that one can also differentiate between descriptive and normative usages of order, although the distinction is not always clearly discernible. One of the most often cited scholars on order, English school theorist Hedley Bull, distinguishes between patterned regularity and purposive order, defining world order as "those patterns or dispositions of human activity that [achieve and] sustain the elementary or primary goals of social life among mankind as a whole" (1977: 20). This definition assumes that there is consensus among humankind about common goals, an idea that we will return to later. Alternatively, one could argue that all understandings of order necessarily entail normative assumptions. For example, Peter Jones (2010) contends that the contractarian way of thinking that we know from the work of Hobbes, Rousseau and Kant assumes that we must enter into a social contract, which entails rules or deliberate ordering, to avoid a situation of chaos. This is founded on a dichotomous way of thinking that assumes that if there is no order, there must be disorder.

As outlined above, many mainstream IR scholars think about world order in a unidimensional way. Realists, for example, prioritize stability, take a state-centric view, and therefore engage in endless debates about whether we are currently in a uni-, bi- or multi-polar world, and which of these would be preferable. This represents a very narrow view of order and does not ask questions about who benefits from this order, what kind of order would entail a qualitatively better life for the majority of the world's people, or what kind of order would be more just. Other scholars (see Box 5.1) have engaged in debates about the interplay between order and justice. We will return to this issue later, but for now, let us turn to the predominantly Western story of how the current dominant order came into being, and the role of institutions in maintaining this order.

BOX 5.1 ARE JUSTICE AND ORDER RECONCILABLE?

Throughout history, there have been calls for a more just global order. Such calls, however, raise questions about whether order and justice are in fact reconcilable, and what a just order would entail. According to Bull (1984) justice and order are separate objectives, and the pursuit of the former might jeopardize the latter. As an example, the pursuit of justice in the form of human rights could entail interference in the affairs of another state, which could lead to instability in the international order. Based on fear that justice could undermine order, Bull therefore prioritized the latter. Alternatively, scholars like John Rawls argue that justice is not only reconcilable with but essential for order (Jones 2010: 121). His thinking is based on the notion that only when all members of the international society regard it as just will there be stability and order. Even if we agree that a different, and particularly a more just global order is desirable, we might not easily agree on what exactly would constitute a just order. Amartya Sen's (2009) work on what the elements of a less unjust society might be can be useful for us in thinking about what might constitute a more just global order. Would it be an order in which there is greater economic equality between people, or would it be an order in which everyone's human rights are protected equally? Can a more just global order be achieved within the sovereign state system, or does it require a different governance system such as a world government? This raises complex questions such as whether states are capable of moral conduct (see Jones 2010: 116). What do you think?

A brief history of the current global order

The ideas on which the current global order and its accompanying institutions are built are hundreds of years old. Political communities throughout history have tried to establish rules for interacting with their neighbors. Many political philosophers have written about alternatives to living in an anarchic state of nature, including means of resolving disputes peacefully and inter-state cooperation. Although the standard international relations and political theory literature tells us mostly about the ideas of European philosophers, including the so-called peace plans from the thirteenth century onwards (for example, Kant's 1795 *Perpetual*

Peace), similar ideas can also be found in non-Western traditions, for example in the writing of the Chinese scholar Confucius or the Indian philosopher Kautilya (1992).

According to mainstream IR, the foundations of the current world order – territorial sovereignty and the juridical equality of states – were laid at the Peace of Westphalia.[7] Over the centuries, institutions and norms relating to diplomacy, commerce and the conduct of war were developed and served to institutionalize the European order, which was eventually spread across the globe (Kupchan 2012: 66). Mentioned less frequently in IR textbooks is that empires played an important role in ordering the world, with examples of deliberate ordering perhaps most obviously visible in the indiscriminate carving up of the African continent through the drawing of borders by the colonial powers during the late nineteenth century (Burbank and Cooper 2010).

The imposition of a racial order was another important part of the colonial project, establishing a hierarchy based on race (see Chapter 3). This was closely tied to European ideas about the superiority of their civilization, which allowed Europe to assert "its right to lead the world on the basis of a set of supposedly universal rules" (Mazower 2012: 71). The rules of what became known as the international society did not apply to what were regarded as the uncivilized/unrecognized peoples and parts of the world. Admission to international society – or parts of it – was dependent on perceptions of civilization and abiding by Western rules. Ironically, Japan was only recognized by the West after it defeated Russia in the 1905 war. Mazower (2012: 72) quotes a Japanese diplomat who, at the time, said, "We show ourselves at least your equals in scientific butchery and are at once admitted to your council tables as civilized men."

The fact that the current global order is not only marked by inequality, but that this inequality is compounded by racial discrimination is rarely acknowledged. Part of the reason for the lack of attention paid to race in mainstream IR scholarship has to do with the fact that, formally, institutions of global governance are built on principles of racial equality and human rights. Similarly, although colonialism as an explicit political, economic and cultural order has ended, colonial strategies have been rearticulated in the post-1945 period, and racialized structures of social power remain entrenched (Sahle 2010: 22; see Chapter 6 for an example of postcolonial Franco–African relations).

During the twentieth century we saw the unraveling of empires, with significant implications for global order. Changes were also deliberately made to the Western order after World Wars I and II, overseen by the U.S. and its allies. The balance of power system was replaced with a collective security system (first under the League of Nations and subsequently under the UN), underpinned by democratic governance and human rights. The post-WWII order included the creation of the Bretton Woods institutions aimed at regulating currency stability and free trade, as well as regional security alliances like the North Atlantic Treaty Organization (NATO). All these elements combined to form what is today referred to as the liberal order, consisting of a liberal economic structure, a multilateral system of global governance centered on the UN system and including the Bretton Woods institutions, and the notion that liberal democracy is the only legitimate form of government. In summary, the United States and its allies built a post-war international order, which was consolidated by the end of the Cold War. As Ikenberry and Wright (2008: 3) note, "America and the West have laid down the rules and institutions of the post-war world. They have been its creators, owners, managers, and chief beneficiaries."

What is problematic is that in discussions of current and future global order, this liberal order is often conflated with global order more generally. Although a liberal international order has arguably become the dominant order, this does not mean that it is the only one, or that it was never contested. Acharya (2014) reminds us that many parts of the world, including China and India, only recently subscribed to some elements of the liberal order. Similarly, throughout the Cold War, the Soviet Union promoted a very different vision of global order, which was supported by many third-world states. Marxist internationalism, for example, was but one alternative of what some have referred to as the profusion of mid-nineteenth-century visions of world order. Even within the United States, there were competing visions of post-war global order, ranging from ambitious ideas of global governance involving supranational organizations to others that were primarily concerned about an economics order that would ensure an open trading system (Ikenberry 2001: 176). These examples underline Alker et al.'s (2001: 1) contention that the world is simultaneously being shaped by a multiplicity of coexisting world orders, present not only in different regions of the world, but even within countries, and at any given time.

Global institutions have been crucial instruments in establishing and upholding particular world orders. While one could argue theoretically about the importance of institutions in shaping the behavior of states and the nature of the international order, it would be almost impossible to disregard the fact that institutionalization has been a central aspect of the post-1945 world order. While Keohane and Murphy (1992: 871) define institutions as "persistent and connected sets of rules (formal and informal) that prescribe behavioral roles, constrain activity and shape expectations" (including formal organizations,[8] international law and norms), Cox adds another dimension to the definition, holding that institutions are also "[A] means of stabilizing and perpetuating a particular order" (1981: 136). As already mentioned, part of global ordering is the establishment of rules that actors are expected to abide by if they want to participate in it. Rules are regarded as necessary to produce and maintain order and have become a type of admission ticket to global political recognition, participation in the global trading system, access to international development assistance and so forth. During the twentieth century, international law (a codified form of rules that are authoritative and binding) became an essential tool of ordering the world.

Despite the deliberate silences regarding the role of colonialism and racism in the history of global order, the Western story of order has other limitations. The first is that it neglects to include stories about non-Western contributions to the development of global order. This means that we are not able to think about alternative future global orders if we are constrained by a parochial Western-centric perspective about how the current order was constructed in the first place. As Stuenkel (2016: 10) emphasizes, a "Western-centric worldview leads us to underappreciate not only the role non-Western actors have played in the past … and play in contemporary international politics, but also the constructive role they are likely to play in future." Secondly, it limits itself to ways of thinking about order that originate in the West and does not incorporate alternative ideas and stories from the rest of the world. In order to construct a more inclusive story about order we therefore need to address these two constraints. We will start by revisiting history and exploring some ways in which the global South played an active role in shaping many of the elements that form part of the current global order.

The role of the global South

It can be argued that, from the vantage point of most countries of the developing world, the current order is one that has been imposed on them, one that is associated with inequality and injustice, but one that they have also been complicit in upholding, partly because they have not had much choice in the matter. First, it was forcibly implemented through, for example, colonialism, and later more indirectly through the conditionalities associated with decolonization, international loans and aid, and the process of neoliberal globalization. It must also be noted, however, that some elites from the global South benefited and continue to benefit from supporting the existing order and maintaining the status quo, even if this undermines the wellbeing of their citizens.

While, undoubtedly, many aspects of the order were violently imposed on the rest of the world through centuries of colonialism and imperialism, other parts of it are not uniquely Western in origin, while some were in fact primarily driven by the non-West. This challenges the view held by many participants in the current debates about the future of global order who assume that the current order, in all of its manifestations, is the sole creation of the West. It follows from this view that alternative conceptions of order emerging from outside of the West will therefore necessarily be different to those that have come from the West. Underlying this are further assumptions about the Western origin of the order's foundational principles. Work done by scholars like Bilgin (2008) and Hobson (2012) show that, in fact, many norms and practices associated with the West have multiple origins (see too, Chapter 12). The foundational principle of the self-determination of nation-states, for example, was the outcome of decades of struggle by colonized people against colonial oppression and for freedom and the right to govern themselves. It was not the Western colonial powers that one day decided to give up on the idea of empire and to allow their colonies to become independent states.

Individuals from the global South played an important role in post-World War II discussions about the post-war order. Grovogui's (2006) work on the proposals for world order by a group of African intellectuals is a case in point. Human rights are an aspect of global order that is generally assumed to be Western in origin. However, when French delegate Rene Cassin spoke about the European roots of human rights, the Kuomintang Chinese delegate on the Human Rights Commission (HRC), Peng-Chun Chand, responded that the European enlightenment philosophers had borrowed these ideas from Confucianism (Sluga 2013: 101). Relatedly, it was delegates from the newly independent Haitian republic that suggested the adjective "universal" be added to what became the Universal Declaration of Human Rights (Sluga 2013: 101). This also applies to other areas of post-war ordering. Contradicting the commonly held view that the Bretton Woods system was the outcome of predominantly Anglo-American negotiations, Helleiner (2014) argues that delegates from countries of the global South played a much more prominent role in influencing the outcome of the Bretton Woods conference. Delegates from places like China, India, Brazil and Mexico took part in an extensive North–South dialogue about the global financial order and played an important role in negotiating the development content of Bretton Woods. Unfortunately, this history has largely been sidelined, following the fact that the U.S. subsequently turned its back on much of the development content of the Bretton Woods agreements (Helleiner 2014: 3). These examples underline Stuenkel's (2016: 2) point that "key events in the history of global order, such as the transition from empire to multilateral order made up of nation-states, were not Western-led processes but products of intense bargaining between Western and non-Western actors." The agency of non-Western peoples in the construction of certain aspects of the current global order must therefore not be neglected. At the same time, we should not dismiss the coercive nature of order building, specifically the role of military and economic power in the creation and maintenance of today's global order (Stuenkel 2016: 3).

We should also recognize that the global South has and continues to play an important role in the institutions of global ordering. One of the reasons is that, in an unequal international system, it did not have much of a choice but to conform to the institutions created predominantly by the West. This is only a part of the story, however. Less powerful states tend to be much more inclined to multilateralism and working through institutions than their more powerful counterparts. Part of the reason is, of course, that being a part of international institutions allows states to pool their resources and form coalitions against stronger states. It also allows them to draw global attention to their common interest. From a purely practical position, an organization like the UN provides a setting where developing states can conduct bilateral and multilateral diplomacy with several international actors. Based on their growth in numbers following decolonization, the states of the global South were able to use institutions like the UN to raise issues of common concern, and to legitimize new norms around anti-racism, anti-colonialism, self-determination and development. For example, in order to strengthen their collective economic influence in the UN, developing nations created the Group of 77 in 1964, at the end of the first session of the UN Conference on Trade and Development (UNCTAD). The impetus behind the creation of UNCTAD was the belief that the existing international financial institutions did not have the interests of developing states at heart. Developing states thus viewed these instruments of global order – particularly the UN system – as an important vehicle to advance their interests.

Despite the examples mentioned above, most of the instruments of global order – the rules that regulate almost all aspects of international relations – were created by an exclusive club of states and continue to serve their interests. This is largely because the decision-making bodies within the organizations that make, maintain, monitor and enforce these rules continue to be unrepresentative of the world at large. States from the global South have largely been excluded from exercising power in bodies like the UN Security Council, or economic institutions like the International Monetary Fund, the World Bank or the G7. This inevitably leads to questions of legitimacy and justice. Why should an exclusive club of states make decisions on behalf of the majority of the world's population? This question is at the core of challenges posed to the dominant order by developing states, which we will turn to next.

Challenges to the "Western" order

During the 1960s and 1970s, unified action by developing states brought about gradual changes to existing global rules and organizations. For example, it was largely due to pressure from the global South that membership of the UN Security Council was enlarged in 1965 from 11 to 15, and the UN Economic and Social Council (ECOSOC) from 18 to 27 and later 54 (in 1973). While concerted efforts were undertaken within the UN system to create a greater voice for Southern states in shaping the global order, at the same time, calls for an alternative order were underway outside of the UN. In the inter- and post-war decades, most of the newly independent African and Asian states seemed keen to form bonds with their counterparts in the global South in order to pro- mote common interests. During the early part of the twentieth century, there were a series of organizations and meetings that collectively challenged the colonial order. Examples include the Intercolonial Union, consisting of colonials from different parts of the French empire (Goebel 2015: 187) and the League against Imperialism, which organ- ized the Brussels conference of 1927 that brought together anti-imperialists from around the world (Goebel 2015: 199). The Bandung conference of 1955 laid the foundation for the establishment of the Non-Aligned Movement (NAM), based on the assumption that newly independent states after decolonization would be able to develop a new and more principled approach to international relations, without having to ally themselves with either of the two superpowers. Founded in Belgrade in 1961, the organization also expressed its opposition to all forms of colonialism and imperialism, and its support for the decolonization and self-determination of remaining colonies. The NAM was essen- tially premised on an alternative to the dominant realist views on international order prevalent at the time, which were based on balance of power politics in a bipolar system. The principle of non-alignment can rightfully be recognized as an alternative set of principles to govern relations between states, thereby constituting an alternative view of order. By 1970, the NAM's focus on decolonization made way for concerns of a more economic nature. This opened the doors for the Latin American states that could now identify with the NAM's criticism of the inequities inherent in the global economic system. Concerted calls for a New International Economic Order (NIEO) reflected the global South's dissatisfaction with the existing global order, particularly what they regarded as its unjust nature, and represented an attempt to promote an alternative view of world order.

Building on Bandung and UNCTAD, the 1966 Tricontinental Conference (officially known as the Solidarity Conference of the Peoples of Africa, Asia and Latin America) extended the Afro-Asian anti-imperialist and non-aligned movement to the Americas. It was a much larger gathering than Bandung (with more than 500 representatives from the national liberation movements, guerrillas and independent governments in attendance in Havana). The conference was also much more ambitious in terms of articulating a more radical agenda that linked anti-imperialism with a wider challenge to capitalism, hence promoting a more just global order.

Based on these examples, one might draw the conclusion that, while Western notions of order are predominantly based on securing stability and security, non-Western notions are focused more on the socio-economic and qualitative aspects of order. While this may be true to some extent, we should be careful of falling into the trap of generalizing and dichotomiz- ing. In this regard, it is important to note that there have also been attempts to conceptualize alternative world orders based on, amongst other things, economic justice, in the West. The World Order Models Project (WOMP), for example, took a normative, principled approach to world order thinking, and was aimed at bringing about a just world order. WOMP theorist Richard Falk, for example, constructed a multi-dimensional definition of world order as

the study of international relations and world affairs that focuses on the manner in which mankind can significantly reduce the likelihood of international violence and create minimally acceptable conditions of worldwide economic well-being, social justice, ecological stability, and participation in decision-making processes.

(Falk 1983: 44)

It should also be mentioned that attempts to influence global order and promote the interests of the global South were not only made at the international level. Several regional and sub-regional organizations were also created to address the specific concerns of their members. Examples include the Organization of African Unity (now the African Union), the League of Arab States and the Association of South East Asian Nations (ASEAN). In fact, one could contend that regionalism is an essential element of order in the global South, something we will come back to.

Despite predictions by some scholars like Ikenberry (2010) that the current global order is here to stay and that states from the global South will simply be co-opted into it, one could argue that the global South is challenging the liberal international order in ways that go beyond simply demanding more representation in the UN Security Council. While Ikenberry questions those who propose that a different path to modernity (besides the Western, liberal one) is possible (2010: 510), there are signs that the contemporary international order is characterized by increasingly multi-varied views about future global order. This development relates to the emergence of so-called rising powers from the global South. Scholars differ on which states qualify, but generally China and India are included, and sometimes states like Turkey, Mexico, Indonesia and so forth. The economies of these states have been growing at an impressive rate,[9] with potentially significant implications for governance beyond the realm of the economic. This has led observers to ask questions about the potential impact these states could have on the existing global order (see Box 5.2).

BOX 5.2 THE EMERGING POWERS AND A CHANGING GLOBAL ORDER

In light of the increased economic power of emerging powers like China, the interesting question becomes whether this will be accompanied by an increase in the influence they can exert on the mechanisms of global order. Will they be happy to maintain the existing order, or are they likely to try to change it? Or will they create their own alternative institutions? In trying to answer these questions, it might be useful to disaggregate the liberal order into different components. While a state like China seems to be committed to aspects of the current order, like the importance of multilateral institutions and economic interdependence, as well as environmental protection and clean energy, it is less supportive of the promotion of liberal democracy and human rights. For example, China is also presenting developing countries with an alternative model of state-led economic development – and therefore an alternative path to modernity. Together with other rising powers like India, it is also challenging existing Western models of development assistance, insisting on development partnerships and non-conditionality. It is also creating what Stuenkel (2016) calls a "parallel" structure of global governance. The BRICS (Brazil, Russia, India, China and South Africa) grouping can be regarded as one such alternative global governance grouping which, despite the obvious differences between its members, is united in a common goal of an alternative world order. Two institutions that have been created as alternatives to the Western-dominated Bretton Woods institutions include the New Development Bank (NDB) and the Asian Infrastructure Investment Bank (AIIB).

So, despite the apparent hegemony of the existing world order, this does not mean that it is not being contested, that alternative visions of order do not exist, or that social forces in the global South have no agency in their encounter with the material forces, ideas and institutions that sustain this order (for a discussion of resistances to the neo-liberal global order, see Chapter 15). One of the reasons why we are not familiar with many of these contestations and alternatives is that they have been silenced by the dominant narrative of the omnipresent and universal liberal global order.

In thinking about ways in which existing understandings of order can be challenged, we should not limit our conceptions of what potential contributions or challenges could look like to radically new ideas or theories. New insights can be gained from challenging existing theory, by drawing on concepts unfamiliar to the Western canon, but also by building on, adapting and reinterpreting existing understandings. If we look closely at what is currently happening in the world, for example with regard to the behavior of emerging powers as discussed in Box 5.2, this will provide us with the empirical basis from which to develop new frameworks for thinking about international relations. It would appear that contrary to Ikenberry's premise that emerging states will simply be co-opted into the liberal order, we are currently seeing a rearticulation or reinterpretation of the liberal order by non-Western states, rather than simply a wholesale acceptance or rejection of it. Recognizing such revisions as constituting legitimate alternative theoretical contributions opens up a number of different avenues for theorizing. For example, the work of scholars such as Ayoob (2002) or Escude (1998), who have adapted existing neorealist theory to make it more relevant to the experiences of the global South (calling their versions "subaltern realism" and "peripheral realism," respectively) are a case in point.

Alternative ways of theorizing order

One of the problems with the way in which existing theories conceive of order is that they are not very helpful in explaining current changes or making sense of order outside of a Westphalian state system. Qin (2018: 69) refers to a study by Hui (2005), who argues that balance of power only applies to a sovereignty-based, individually oriented international system. This means it cannot help us to understand other forms of thinking about order that are not based on states or individualism. The limitations of state-centrism and an individualist ontology are elaborated below.

Challenging territoriality and state-centrism

One result of the dominance of the Westphalian, territorial nation-state-based conception of order so prevalent in IR is that our conception of order is limited to one created and maintained by territoriality delineated actors, what Agnew (1994) calls the "territorial trap." Mainstream IR largely accepts that the Treaty of Westphalia initiated an international system of sovereign territorial nation-states. Despite the by now recognized historical inaccuracy of this claim, together with a neglect of current geographical and socio-political realities around the world, the Westphalian model remains the dominant framework for analysis in IR. Existing IR theories are underpinned by a fixed conception of bounded territory which reinforces an absolute view of space, and overlooks the contributions of peoples' spiritual, cultural and political connections to space (see Chapter 8). This is reflected in conventional maps, which only present one system of organization and one representation of global space (see Figure 5.1). In contrast, in many parts of the world, clearly stipulated boundaries are not common, and territory is understood to be flexible and identified by historical use and occupation, harvesting patterns and agreements with neighbors. In contrast to fixed territorial understandings of space, indigenous understandings are broader in what they refer to and in how they encompass indigenous groups across states. For example, the term *Inuit Nunangat* represents all Inuit territories across the Arctic and comprises of all space including the land, sea and ice (Rodon 2014: 19 in Mitchell 2019: 35). Traditional Inuit maps also reflect ideas about space in a manner that does not delineate states or owned areas. They are usually drawn in the air or snow, often memorized by features like *sastrugi* (snow ridges) with route distances measured by days of travel (Olson 1994: 216 in Mitchell 2019: 35). Relatedly, the emphasis on *terra* or earth as being at the core of order is prioritized in traditional IR, to the detriment of other elements like air, water and fire. In contrast, Lily Ling (2014: 103) claims that in Daoist philosophy, water, representing fluidity instead of rigidity, can be regarded as a counterhegemonic force to the Westphalian territorial world order. Such ideas are common to indigenous worldviews across the world, where humans are not unique but emanate from the same spiritual source as other natural phenomena such as animals, rivers, the sun and the moon (see also Chapter 17).

A related result of a worldview based on the territorial nation-state system is the neglect of non-state actors. Most Western debates about world order focus on the role of states as the constituent units. The state is regarded as the sole transmitter of order, which is also reflected in the workings of global intergovernmental institutions, in which states make and enforce the rules, to the exclusion of non-state actors. It is assumed that disorder is inevitable in all places that are not restrained by the authority of a state. This limits our understanding of the breadth of actors involved in world ordering. It is thus important that, when we think of alternative forms of world order, and particularly the forces that may bring about a new order, we should not be constrained by a state-centric perspective. An essential aspect of the changing order is the complex dynamics of political ordering that create highly uneven articulation processes between the state and spaces that are not controlled by formal governments. The role of non-state actors in maintaining and potentially transforming world order therefore needs to be investigated more, for in today's non-polar world, there are many power centers (including international organizations, corporations, militia, criminal networks) beyond states.[10] If we consider, for example, the destabilizing impact of non-state actors like ISIS or Boko Haram on both regional and global order, it becomes clear that states are not the only actors engaged in creating, maintaining or disrupting order.

With regard to the role of non-state actors, Africa arguably presents a particular challenge to state-centric theory. There are spaces on the continent where the state has never exerted an exclusive monopoly on the use of force, and where its power has and is still being met with hostility. Sub-state actors such as warlords are not merely exceptions to the state system but should be seen as constituting an alternative practice to it. Crises in the Middle East and elsewhere remind us that this phenomenon is not limited to Africa, and that in fact, such polycentric orders can be found in many world regions. They are based less on abstract principles and rather on local cultural patterns. This relates to Acharya's idea (2011: 632) that in trying to think differently about IR, we should focus on the local construction of global order. The work of Hannah Pfeiffer (2019) on different local Islamist interpretations of world order is a case in point. She challenges the view that there is one Islamist position on order that violently opposes the "Western" world order, arguing instead that Islamist discourses, too, are "marked by inner contestation, [and] rivalling claims for what order should look like" (Pfeiffer 2019: 101). By investigating how Islamist groups such as Hezbollah construct world order, she finds both continuity and rupture with Western discourses. Such views should be explored further, with more research needed that focuses on how order is perceived and interpreted in different local contexts.

Sub-state actors are not the only alternative to state-centrism. Mazrui, for example, argues that the idea of continental unity has special significance in African political consciousness, originally based on racial pride, and later developed into continental pride (1974: 121), which has also resulted in a sense of continental jurisdiction. In other words, African problems should be resolved by Africans. To this end, he argues that "[t]he world order most favored by African diplomatic thought would put a special value on the principles of political independence for each continent or region and the principle of economic independence between countries and regions" (Mazrui 1974: 132). This focus on regionalism as an essential aspect of global order, and the role of regional organizations in the management of global governance is emphasized in the writing of many African thinkers. This ties in with Acharya's (2014) conception of a future global order as consisting of multiple regional orders, instead of one homogenous global order.

Besides their emphasis on state-centrism, another limitation of existing Western approaches is that they are based on an individualist ontology. Such an ontology inevitably leads to states and other actors being viewed as autonomous, independent actors that only act in self-interest.

Different ontological starting points

If, instead, we consider Qin's (2018) argument, namely that Western and Chinese conceptions of the world are radically different due to their dissimilar ontological starting points, then this opens up exciting new possibilities for approaching international relations differently. In summary, he contends that while Western thinking, based on the Western philosophical tradition, starts with an ontological individualism, Chinese thinking is based on a relational conception of the world (see Chapter 17). The idea of a relational world as "defined by the fundamental relatedness of human beings" (Qin 2018: 114) is similar to the worldview Tieku (2012) subscribes to when he writes about African conceptions of statehood and international politics. He argues that African states are based on collective rather than individualist societies, and that this influences the way African states behave in the international system. This has profound implications for thinking about many taken-for-granted ideas in traditional IR, and for thinking about order.

If we start from the basis of collectivist and relational thinking, this helps us to move beyond the constraints of the individualist, self-interested rationality that mainstream theory assumes to be the driving force behind state action. This, in turn, allows us to imagine a world order that is not primarily based on the interests of individual states, but rather on the collective interests of the world's people. For those of us trained in the Western tradition of realpolitik, this may seem idealistic and naïve. However, if we believe that theory not only reflects but also shapes reality, and that how we think about the world has the power to influence it, then it is certainly worth a shot. Here the African worldview of *ubuntu* (see Box 5.3), which also informs Tieku's work, offers a potential entry point into thinking about a more normatively informed world order. The *ubuntu* belief in the intrinsic value of the collective and the interconnectedness of individuals and states in the global system suggests the possibility of a global order where the emphasis is on ordering in the interests of improving the lives of all the people rather than only some, or order as an end in itself. These ideas also resonate strongly with similar worldviews from other parts of the world, including the Andean cosmovision as described by Lily Ling and Caroline Pinheiro in Chapter 17. This suggests that there are many commonalities between non-Western worldviews that can form the basis for alternative ways of thinking not only about global order, but international relations more generally.

BOX 5.3 *UBUNTU*

The term *ubuntu* is a word from the Nguni language family, which comprises Zulu, Xhosa, Swati and Ndebele. However, variants of it exist in many sub-Saharan African languages. Expressed in Zulu as "*umuntu umuntu ngabantu*" or "a person is a person through other people," it refers to the idea that the individual is inextricably part of the whole, in fact, is identical with the community. It presents "respect, hospitality, reciprocity, connectedness, and interdependence as the ethical tools for creating a sustainable social order" (Ngcoya 2009: 1). It speaks to our interconnectedness, our common humanity and the responsibility to each other that flows from our connection. This suggests that a collectivist worldview is much more aligned with more normative interpretations of order that take into account elements such as justice, equality, etc. The notion of *ubuntu* assumes that when the order in a community has been disturbed, for example through conflict, it requires a collective effort to restore a sense of order. This means that everyone is responsible for everyone else, not because of a sense of duty, but because they are inseparably connected. In the same way, an injustice to one is an injustice to all. This stands in stark contrast with the individualist, self-interested understanding of personhood that dominates Western thinking. When applied to international relations, such thinking results in analyses based on assumptions of self-interested behavior by actors, including a normalizing of the different forms of violence that permeates all aspects of global politics. An acceptance of this status quo by practitioners and scholars serves to perpetuate the continuation of a world order characterized by inequality, injustice and violence, and undermines attempts at cooperating in the interests of humanity as a whole rather than interests driven by territorially based nationalism and global capital.

On order versus disorder

In conclusion, when IR scholars speak of the international or global order, they are usually referring to the Western-led international order of states that has become synonymous with international relations and the international system as a whole. This is, in turn, based on a Western understanding of order, as the opposite of disorder or chaos. As we have discussed, thinking about the world in terms of dichotomies is characteristic of the West, but less prominent in non-Western worldviews. For example, in Daoist philosophy, the well-known black and white yin and yang elements (see Figure 17.1) are seen not as opposites but rather as complementary. Importantly, they both contain elements of one another, emphasizing the notion that thinking in binary, oppositional terms is not helpful to understanding the world. If we allow ourselves to be less categorical about the distinction between order and disorder, perhaps we can imagine something that is neither entirely orderly nor disorderly, at least not in the sense that the two are necessarily regarded as mutually exclusive. If we relate this to the current debates about the future of world order, which largely center on whether the current order will be replaced by a world of disorder, this enables thinking about a range of alternative futures that may or may not include order in the existing, Western sense, but may include forms of order that are based on different principles than the ones we have become accustomed to. Only when we allow ourselves to think outside of the existing box of IR can we truly begin to imagine a different, and better, world order.

Questions for discussion

1. Do you think that people in different parts of the world have different ideas about what global order looks like, and what its purpose is?
2. Does the alternative to order have to be disorder?
3. Is global order something that occurs naturally, or does it have to be constructed?
4. What would a more just global order look like?
5. Can a more just global order be achieved within the sovereign state system, or does it require a different system of governance, such as a world government?
6. Do you believe that rising powers like China pose a threat to the current global order?

Notes

1 For more alternative world maps see https://worldmapper.org/.
2 See, for example, Michael Doyle (1997).
3 See, for example, Hedley Bull (1977).
4 For example, Immanuel Wallerstein's world systems theory (2004).
5 Marxist scholar Antonio Gramsci's understanding of hegemony provides us with an interesting answer to the question of why states cooperate and comply with global rules. He argues that an important part of hegemony is not coercion but spreading of values of the dominant group throughout society (especially the subordinate classes) to become accepted as their own.
6 See, for example, Peterson and Runyan (2010); Tickner (2001).
7 These claims about the origin of sovereignty and the state system have been disputed by scholars like Teschke (2003). See Chapters 3 and 4.
8 International organizations are generally defined as formal, continuous structures with international membership, active in three or more states, and with a permanent headquarters or secretariat. There are, of course, a wide variety of international organizations, and many attempts have been made to distinguish between them. Generally, the simplest way to classify international organizations is to divide them into intergovernmental organizations (IGOs) and

international non-governmental organizations (INGOs). Intergovernmental organizations are often the fora where states create the rules that regulate various aspects of global interaction.

9 In recent years, however, growth in many of the countries previously designated as "rising" or "emerging" (including Brazil and South Africa) has stagnated. Together with severe political and other domestic challenges, this has led to questions about their ability to influence regional and global orders.

10 This argument it not unfamiliar to IR scholars, including liberal theorists, who have emphasized the importance of looking seriously at actors beyond the state. See, for example Milner and Moravcsik (2009).

Further reading

Acharya, Amitav (2018) *Constructing Global Order*, Cambridge: Cambridge University Press. This book focuses on the agency of states and other actors from the global South in the building of global order, focusing on the role of ideas.

Ling, L.H.M. (2014) *The Dao of World Politics: Towards a Post-Westphalian, Wordlist International Relations*, Abingdon and New York: Routledge. Ling deconstructs the existing Westphalian world, and helps us to imagine a world order not based on violence, coercion and inequality but rather on peace, respect and care.

Qin, Yaqing (2018) *A Relational Theory of World Politics*, Cambridge: Cambridge University Press. Drawing on insights from Chinese philosophy, Qin presents an alternative understanding of world politics, based on a collectivist rather than an individualist epistemology.

Stuenkel, Oliver (2016) *Post-Western World*, Cambridge: Polity Press. Stuenkel explores what the rise of non-Western powers means for the future of global order.

References

Abu-Lughod, Janet (1989) *Before European Hegemony: The World System A.D. 1250–1350*, Oxford: Oxford University Press. DOI: https://doi.org/10.2307/3115605

Acharya, Amitav (2011) "Dialogue and Discovery: In Search of International Relations Theories Beyond the West", *Millennium: Journal of International Studies*, 39 (3): 619–637. DOI: https://doi.org/10.1177/0305829811406574

Acharya, Amitav (2014) *The End of American World Order*, Cambridge: Polity Press. DOI: https://doi.org/10.1002/polq.12315

Acharya, Amitav (2016) "'Idea-Shift': How Ideas from the Rest of the World Are Shaping Global Order", *Third World Quarterly*, 37 (7): 1156–1170. DOI: https://doi.org/10.1080/01436597.2016.1154433

Agnew, John (1994) "The Territorial Trap: The Geographical Assumptions of International Relations Theory", *Review of International Political Economy*, 1 (1): 53–80.

Alker, Howard, Tahir Amin, Thomas J. Biersteker and Takashi Inoguchi (2001) "Twelve World Order Debates which Have Made Our Days," paper presented at the Russian International Studies Association, Moscow: MGIMO University, 20–21 April. Available online: http://isanet.ccit.arizona.edu/archive/worldorder.html (accessed 16 September 2013).

Ayoob, Mohammed (2002) "Inequality and Theorizing in International Relations: The Case for Subaltern Realism", *International Studies Review*, 4 (3): 27–48.

Bangura, Abdul Karrim (2012) "From Diop to Asante: Conceptualizing and Contextualizing the Afrocentric Paradigm", *The Journal of Pan African Studies*, 5 (1): 103–125.

Bilgin, Pinar (2008) "Thinking Past 'Western' IR?", *Third World Quarterly*, 29 (1): 5–23. DOI: http://dx.doi.org/10.1080/01436590701726392

Braveboy-Wagner, Jacqueline Anne (2009) *Institutions of the Global South*, London: Routledge. DOI: https://doi.org/10.4324/9780203018422

Bull, Hedley (1977) *The Anarchical Society: A Study of Order in World Politics*, 2nd ed., New York: Columbia University Press.

Bull, Hedley (1984) *Justice in International Relations, the 1983–84 Hagey Lectures*, Waterloo, Ontario: University of Waterloo.

Burbank, Jane and Frederick Cooper (2010) *Empires in World History: Power and Politics of Difference*, Princeton: Princeton University Press.

Chaturvedi, Sanjay and Joe Painter (2007) "Whose World, Whose Order? Spatiality, Geopolitics and the Limits of the World Order Concept", *Cooperation and Conflict: Journal of the Nordic International Studies Association*, 42 (4): 375–395. DOI: https://doi.org/10.1177/0010836707082646

Comaroff, Jean and John L. Comaroff (2012) *Theory from the South: Or, How Euro-America Is Evolving Toward Africa*, Boulder and London: Paradigm. DOI: https://doi.org/10.1080/00664677.2012.694169

Cooper, Robert (2004) *The Breaking of Nations: Order and Chaos in the Twenty-first Century*, London: Atlantic Books.

Cox, Robert W. (1981) "Social Forces, States, and World Orders: Beyond International Relations Theory", *Millennium: Journal of International Studies*, 10: 126–155. http://journals.sagepub.com/doi/abs/10.1177/03058298810100020501

Cox, Robert W. (1983) "Gramsci, Hegemony and International Relations: An Essay in Method", *Millennium: Journal of International Studies*, 12 (2): 162–175. DOI: https://doi.org/10.1177/03058298830120020701

Deng, Francis M. (2010) "From 'Sovereignty as Responsibility' to the 'Responsibility to Protect'", *Global Responsibility to Protect*, 2: 353–370. DOI: https://doi.org/10.1163/187598410X519534

Doyle, Michael (1997) *Ways of War and Peace*, New York: W.W. Norton.

Dunn, Kevin (2001) "MadLib #32: The (*Blank*) African State: Rethinking the Sovereign State in International Relations Theory" in Kevin Dunn and Timothy Shaw (eds) *Africa's Challenge to International Relations Theory*, Basingstoke: Palgrave, pp. 46–63. DOI: 10.1057/9780333977538

Escude, Carlos (1998) "An Introduction to Peripheral Realism and Its Implications for the Interstate System: Argentina and the Condor II Missile Project" in Stephanie G. Neuman (ed) *International Relations Theory and the Third World*, Houndmills: Macmillan, pp. 55–75.

Evans-Pritchard, Edward Evan (1940) "The Nuer of the Southern Sudan" in Meyer Fortes and Edward Evan Evans-Pritchard (eds) *African Political Systems*, London: Oxford University Press, pp. 272–296.

Falk, Richard (1983) *The End of World Order: Essays on Normative International Relations*, New York: Holmes & Meier.

Goebel, Michael (2015) *Anti-Imperial Metropolis, Interwar Paris and the Seeds of Third World Nationalism*, Cambridge: Cambridge University Press. DOI: https://doi.org/10.1017/CBO9781139681001

Grovogui, Siba (2006) *Beyond Eurocentrism and Anarchy: Memories of International Order and Institutions*, Houndmills, Basingstoke: Palgrave Macmillan.

Helleiner, Eric (2014) *Forgotten Foundations of Bretton Woods: International Development and the Making of the Postwar Order*, Ithaca: Cornell University Press.

Hobson, John (2012) *The Eurocentric Conception of World Politics – Western International Theory, 1760–2010*, Cambridge: Cambridge University Press. DOI: https://doi.org/10.1017/CBO9781139096829

Hui, Victoria Tin-bor (2005) *War and State Formation in Ancient China and Early Modern Europe*, Cambridge: Cambridge University Press.

Ikenberry, John (2001) *After Victory: Institutions, Strategic Restraint, and the Rebuilding of Order after Major Wars*, Princeton: Princeton University Press.

Ikenberry, G. John (2010) "The Liberal International Order and Its Discontents", *Millennium: Journal of International Studies*, 38 (3): 509–521. DOI: https://doi.org/10.1177/0305829810366477

Ikenberry, G. John and Thomas Wright (2008) *Rising Powers and Global Institutions. A Century Foundation Report*, New York: The Century Foundation. DOI: https://doi.org/10.1080/13600826.2012.682277

Jones, Peter (2010) "The Ethics of International Society" in Duncan Bell (ed) *Ethics and World Politics*, Oxford: Oxford University Press, pp. 111–129.

Kauṭilya (1992) *The Arthashastra*, New Delhi and New York: Penguin Books.

Keohane, Robert (1989) *International Institutions and State Power: Essays in International Relations Theory*, Boulder: Westview.

Keohane, Robert and Craig Murphy (1992) "International Institutions" in M.E. Hawkesworth and Maurice Kogan (eds) *Encyclopedia of Government and Politics, vol. 1*, London: Routledge, pp. 871–886.

Kouassi, Edmond Kwam (2008) "Negotiation, Mediation and Other Non-Juridical Ways of Managing Conflicts in Pre-Colonial West African Societies", *International Negotiation*, 13 (2): 233–246. DOI: https://doi.org/10.1163/157180608X320225

Kupchan, Charles A. (2012) *No One's World: The West, The Rising Rest, and the Coming Global Turn*, Oxford: Oxford University Press. DOI: 10.1093/acprof:osobl/9780199739394.001.0001

Lake, David A. (2010) "Rightful Rules: Authority, Order, and the Foundations of Global Governance", *International Studies Quarterly*, 54 (3): 587–613. DOI: https://doi.org/10.1111/j.1468-2478.2010.00601.x

Leander, Anna (2006) "Paradigms as Hindrance to Understanding World Politics", *Cooperation and Conflict: Journal of the Nordic International Studies Association*, 41 (4): 370–376. DOI: https://doi.org/10.1007/978-3-658-23975-6_1

Ling, L.H.M. (2014) *The Dao of World Politics: Towards a Westphalia, Worldist International Relations*, New York: Routledge.

Mazower, Mark (2012) *Governing the World: The History of an Idea*, New York: Penguin Press. DOI: https://doi.org/10.1017/S0922156514000314

Mazrui, Ali A. (1974) "Africa and Diplomatic Thought and Supra-Nationality" in Ali A. Mazrui and Hasu H. Patel (eds) *Africa: The Next Thirty Years*, Sussex: Julian Froedman Publishers, pp. 121–133.

Mazrui, Ali A. (1981) "The Moving Cultural Frontier of World Order: From Monotheism to North-South Relations", *Alternatives*, 7 (1): 1–20. DOI: https://doi.org/10.1177%2F030437548100700101

Mazrui, Ali A. (1990) *Cultural Forces in World Politics*, London: James Currey. DOI: https://doi.org/10.2307/524891

Milner, Helen V. and Andrew Moravcsik (eds) (2009) *Power, Interdependence, and Nonstate Actors in World Politics*, Princeton: Princeton University Press.

Mitchell, Robyn (2019) "Views from the Arctic: Broadening International Relations beyond Its Prevailing Assumptions", unpublished MA thesis, Leiden University.

Neuman, Stephanie G. (1998) "International Relations Theory and the Third World: An Oxymoron?" in Stephanie G. Neuman (ed) *International Relations Theory and the Third World*, Houndmills: Macmillan, pp. 1–15.

Ngcoya, Mvuselelo (2009) "Ubuntu: Globalization, Accommodation, and Contestation in South Africa," Dissertation submitted in partial fulfilment of the requirements for the degree of Doctor of Philosophy in International Relations, Washington DC: American University.

Olson, D. (1994). *The World on Paper: The Conceptual and Cognitive Implications of Writing and Reading*, Cambridge: Cambridge University Press.

Peterson, V. Spike and Anne Sisson Runyan (2010) *Global Gender Issues in the New Millennium*, 3rd ed, Boulder: Westview Press.

Pfeiffer, Hanna (2019) "Beyond Terrorism and Disorder: Assessing Islamist Constructions of World Order" in Adiong, Nassef Manabilang, Raffaele Mauriello and Deina Abdelkader (eds) *Islam in International Relations*, Abingdon and New York: Routledge, pp. 100–123. DOI: https://doi.org/10.4324/9781315513577

Qin, Yaqing (2018) *A Relational Theory of World Politics*, Cambridge: Cambridge University Press. DOI: https://doi.org/10.1017/9781316869505

Rodon, Thierry (2014) "Inuit Diplomacy: Reframing the Arctic Spaces and Narratives" *Special Report on The Internationalization of Indigenous Rights: UNDRIP in the Canadian Context*, Waterloo: Centre for International Governance Innovation, pp. 17–23. Available online at www.cigionline.org/sites/default/files/indigenous_rights_special_report_web.pdf

Sahle, Eunice N. (2010) *World Orders, Development and Transformation*, Houndmills: Basingstoke: Palgrave Macmillan. DOI: 10.1057/9780230274860

Sen, Amartya (2009) *The Idea of Justice*, Harvard: Harvard University Press.

Sluga, Glenda (2013) *Internationalism in the Age of Nationalism*, Philadelphia: University of Pennsylvania Press. DOI: 10.1177/0265691410376497

Stuenkel, Oliver (2016) *Post-Western World*, Cambridge: Polity Press. DOI: https://doi.org/10.1111/padr.12107

Teschke, Benno (2003) *The Myth of 1648: Class, Geopolitics and the Making of Modern International Relations*, London: Verso. DOI: 10.1057/palgrave.ip.8800175

Tickner, A. (2001) *Gendering World Politics: Issues and Approaches in the Post-Cold War Era*, New York: Columbia University Press.

Tieku, Thomas Kwesi (2012) "Collectivist Worldview: Its Challenge to International Relations" in Scarlett Cornelissen, Fantu Cheru and Timothy Shaw (eds) *Africa and International Relations in the 21st Century*, Houndmills: Palgrave Macmillan, pp. 36–50. DOI: 10.1057/9780230355743

Trachtenberg, Marc (2006) "The Problem of International Order and How to Think About It", *The Monist*, 89 (2): 207–231. DOI: https://doi.org/10.5840/monist200689221

Wallerstein, Immanuel (2004) *World-Systems Analysis: An Introduction*, Durham: Duke University Press.

Waltz, Kenneth (1979) *Theory of International Politics*, Reading: Addison-Wesley.

Wendt, Alexander (1999) *Social Theory of International Politics*, Cambridge: Cambridge University Press.

6 The international

Amy Niang

The story of the French African colonial franc

Fourteen independent states in West and Central Africa use the CFA franc – originally the French African colonial franc – a currency regime established in 1945 and pegged to the former French franc, and to the euro since 2000.[1] The CFA franc agreement is an anachronistic, colonial arrangement that places postcolonial African countries in a state of permanent economic subordination to France. According to the CFA currency cooperation, the French Treasury keeps 50% of the foreign exchange reserves of the CFA zone countries in a special operations account and in return it guarantees a fixed parity of the CFA franc to the euro.[2] France also holds a veto on the boards of the CFA central banks in West and Central Africa. However, 11 out of the 14 member states of the franc zone are on the list of the least developed countries (LDCs). If the economic woes of member states are not attributable to the currency arrangement but rather to poor economic governance, low investment and other structural and institutional problems, it remains that the CFA regime maintains an artificially low inflation rate, discourages exports given an over-inflated CFA franc and restricts concerned African states' capacity to elaborate and pursue autonomous economic and monetary policies. The currency arrangement also provides France with a political leverage that has often been activated against "non-compliant" leaders. The chapter uses this example to show how the "international" is necessarily an extension of the colonial in a postcolonial world.

Introduction

Eric Wolf starts his book, *Europe and the People without History* (1982), with a series of examples that make apparent a fundamental fact, namely the basic interconnectedness of the world's regions and peoples through travel and trade, diplomacy and political allegiance, military and political domination as early as the 15th century. However, implicit in conventional accounts is the idea that interconnectedness was the result of a particular kind of encounter, of humans and "zombies," Christians and heretics, subjects and serfs, superior and inferior "races." It was, moreover, an encounter framed by the two-fold objective of power and profit that propelled European states to the global stage starting in the 15th century and intensifying in the 18th and 19th centuries. The global history movement, of which Wolf's study is an emblematic foretaste, shows how Eurocentric accounts repressed a number of innovative dynamics, and presented static and homogenous histories of worlds encountered. Wolf's argument goes against a teleological account of the superior morality of an entity called "the West" that developed autonomously, if not in opposition to other societies (Wolf 1982: 5). The global history perspective is relevant to International Relations, a discipline whose ontology is something called "the international." Despite being a malleable and diffuse category (Hurrell 2016), the latter has come to constitute the referent-object of the discipline, if not its organizing principle.

Historically, understandings of the "international" were hinged upon analyses of war and anarchy as two elements that have a bearing on state conduct outside national borders. The discipline itself emerged out of an intellectual taxonomy that made concerns over the "domestic" and the "international" two distinct endeavors (Carr 1939). The international thus came to represent the area of interactions between states and other political entities, but also the limits as well as the product of such interactions. But the international is also informed by the West's attempts to make sense of its own trajectory in global history and to construct corresponding narratives. It therefore carries the marker of Western anxieties, the relics of an expansionist past and aspirations for a Western subjectivity. This is apparent in the way in which race and sovereignty play out in overlapping and antagonistic ways. Nowhere is this fact more glaring than in attempts to institute a postcolonial sovereignty in formerly colonized territories. Thus, while the sovereignty principle is an inescapable frame of organization, it rests upon, and is hampered by, racial conceit.

In fact, one cannot discuss the topographies of the international in any satisfactory manner without engaging the notion of race as one of its unthought foundations. As Henderson (2013: 27) eloquently puts it, "racism informs IR theory mainly through its influence on the empirical, ethical and epistemological assumptions that undergird its paradigms." Such an influence is explicit in the "privileging [of] the experiences of 'superior' peoples and their societies and institutions" (Henderson 2013: 27). The first argument that the chapter therefore seeks to make is that the epistemology and the ideology of the international rest upon the internalizing of a set of ontological discourses pertaining to difference, more crucially to racial difference. In other words, the international can be seen as the substantiation of historically unstable but deeply engrained views of an object of knowledge, an ontological field that is framed in structures of racism. Recent calls for a postcolonial or decolonial outlook and politics in the study of International Relations (IR) and practice of international relations are calls for the regenerative reconnection with the untold history of the discipline, but also an exploration of its potential envisaged from a non-Western perspective.

The second argument the chapter seeks to make is that colonial practice consecrated sovereignty as the teleological starting point and the origin of a discipline (see Chapter 8 for a discussion of this concept). Interestingly, the Franco–African (post)colonial pact provides the most staggering example of how the canonical force of the sovereign outlook has been normalized through two main sources: incorporation and differentiation. Sovereignty was not the proverbial "invention on which it was impossible to secure a patent" (Anderson 2006: 69) but rather a historical form of differentiation in a community of putative equals. The incorporation of the formerly colonized in a divergent community of "equal" entities reveals two broad aspects of the discipline that are important to the discussion at hand: on the one hand an attachment to a notion of sovereignty as an organizing principle that frames the horizon of the international, and the notion of race as a basic scaffolding that sustains the framework of ideas and practice in IR on the other hand.

Two aspects of postcolonial Franco–African relations are important for my argument. The first is France's attempt to reinvent empire in the 1940s through the institution of the Franco-African Community. This is the focus of the first section. The second is the institution of a series of mechanisms articulated around "development aid" and the CFA franc arrangement (described above) as a substitute for colonial governance. One way to think critically about the oddity of the franc zone arrangement in a world of presumed sovereignties is to reflect on the nexus between colonization, race and the making of the international, the focus of the second section. The third section reflects on the international at the intersection of race and coloniality in order to bring into focus the role of hierarchy and differentiation as two dimensions of the international order (see too, Chapters 5 and 13). I conclude the chapter with a discussion of alternative avenues of inquiry that require confronting "the geography of reason" (Gordon 2011) as a way of elucidating a framework of interdependence that is deeply skewed by racial conceit.

A discipline and its (self-)accounts

Conventional IR accounts are predicated upon the existence of distinct "sovereign" entities, a distinction, therefore, between a "domestic" and an "international." As R.B.J. Walker puts it:

> The conditions under which we are now able or unable to conceive of what it might mean to speak of world policy, and thus of the spatiotemporal rearticulation of practical community, are largely defined in terms of assumptions enshrined in the principles of state sovereignty.
>
> (Walker 1993: 21)

The sovereignty principle as a determinant of, and value framework for, international relations plays a key function. It serves to establish an idea of the domestic as an "authentic" experience and the international as vague and unpredictable. The international is therefore necessarily conceptualized in relation to ideas of sovereignty (see Chapter 8).

In the 1960s, the emancipation of formerly colonized societies constituted a radical break in international relations. Colonial subjects became autonomous from an alienating regime. Their sovereignty became safeguarded under international law and a host of conventions and treaties. The gradual liberalization of trade, first under the General Agreement on Tariffs and Trade (GATT) and then under the World Trade Organization (WTO) framework, ensured that these states were able to trade and exchange fairly and competitively in a world where capital, knowledge, goods and people could move freely. In the end, according to the conventional account, colonialism and empire would merely be seen as a short interlude with little consequences for the future of these states. In other words, race and geography no longer mattered to state identity. There were no longer hierarchies, neither symbolic nor racial. It was also implied that liberation from colonial rule gave birth to a new cognitive framework in which the sovereign rights of small and big states dictated respect for their independence and non-interference in their different national pursuits (see Chapter 13).

Conventional accounts depoliticize postcolonial relations to the extent that development aid and other forms of interventions are often presented as political arrangements meant to support the integration of former colonies into global economic and political processes through "technical assistance" in the context of "global solidarity." They rarely connect aid with colonial practices of *mise en valeur* as delineating colonial powers' understanding of what African "development" should be for, namely to enhance the capacity of colonies to better produce raw material and improve the purchasing power of their inhabitants as potential consumers of Western products. As Escobar (1995) and others have shown, colonial *mise en valeur* was implemented at the colonies' own cost.

Another dimension lies in the depoliticization of intervention in postcolonial politics. As a matter of example, despite available evidence of American Central Intelligence Agency (CIA) and French and Belgian secret services' complicity – if not initiation – in the *coup d'état* that toppled Patrice Lumumba and his subsequent gruesome torture and assassination by a firing squad, few analyses in fact integrate this type of intervention from the perspective of postcolonial politics as a terrain of continuity of colonial politics.[3] As the first prime minister of an independent Congo, Lumumba was keen to make Congo's independence translate into a capacity to make sovereign decisions. He was punished for daring to think and act outside of the script of the colonial compact. The latter has continued to frame and contain African sovereignty in postcolonial times (see Box 6.1).

BOX 6.1 PATRICE LUMUMBA

A charismatic autodidact who became an international symbol of the fight for Africa's independence from colonialism, Patrice Lumumba was born as Elias Okitasombo on July 2, 1925, in Onalua, a village in East Kasai. He went on to establish a political party that led the fight for independence, which the Belgians reluctantly conceded in 1958. Until independence, the Congo had been a vast, profitable colony subject to a brutal history of Belgian rule, notably under King Leopold II in the late 19th century. Two years later, following a decisive win for Lumumba's Congolese National Movement in the country's first democratic elections, he was elected as the first prime minister of an independent Congo. Soon after, however, the provinces of Katanga and South Kasai, backed by Belgian funding and troops, rebelled against the central government and declared themselves independent in July 1960. In this way, Belgian mining interests were protected and a large part of the economic wealth was cut off from the central government.

In the end, Lumumba only ruled for four months. Following a military coup, the 36-year-old was ousted by troops loyal to the head of the army, Joseph Mobutu, who later spent 30 years as president. Lumumba was confined, and then taken to the secessionist province of Katanga, where he was tortured and executed by firing squad. In 2001, the Belgian Parliament agreed to establish a commission of enquiry to "determine the exact circumstances of the assassination of Patrice Lumumba and the possible involvement of Belgian politicians" (Belgian Chamber of Representatives 2001). The resulting report[4] found that there were plans to kill Lumumba, and that "some members of the then-government and some Belgian figures of the time irrefutably played a part in the events that led to the death of Patrice Lumumba." Following the report, the Belgian government admitted in 2002 to having had "undeniable responsibility in the events that led to Lumumba's death." However, the government did not take full responsibility and issued a public pardon of the Belgians involved in his assassination. The report furthermore confirmed that, after Congo had become sovereign and independent on June 30, 1960, "this did not stop Belgium and a number of other countries from intervening directly in its internal affairs," and that "the Belgian government showed little respect for the sovereign status of the Congolese government."

African sovereignty after decolonization

Beyond historical interest, an analysis of the project of the Franco-African Community serves to subject the colonial encounter to theoretical scrutiny. In the 1940s, as the desire for emancipation was being articulated in different modes across the French colonial world, a number of French and African elites sought to reform the colonial relationship in a federal union (*union francaise*). This union was variously called the Franco-African Community, *la Communauté*, or the French African Union (see Box 6.2).

BOX 6.2 THE FRANCO-AFRICAN COMMUNITY

The Franco-African Community (also the French Community, *Communauté franco-africaine*) was a project of federation elaborated in the 1940s by French and African politicians as a successor to the French colonial empire. The Community was a diluted version of the *Union française* (up to 1958), which sought to institutionalize non-racialism in a political, economic, ideological and epistemic, multinational project. As a political association between a former colonizer and its former colonies, it carried the contradictions on the one hand of a desire for self-determination variously expressed by African nations, and an aspiration to transcend colonial relations on the other hand. Given the lack of consensus on the form, the jurisdiction and the political attributes of the imagined community, an institutional compromise was eventually adopted between Felix Houphouet Boigny's proposal for a federation and Leopold Sedar Senghor's idea of confederation but without any specific juridical status. The Union was constituted on the basis of a false equality. The constitution of the Union consolidated French sovereignty and deactivated the possibility of a pooling of sovereignties. It maintained in the public domain (*domaine commun*) the most crucial sectors of governance, namely defense, foreign affairs, economic, especially currency policies and control over the exploitation of natural resources. It thus tremendously curtailed African sovereignties and preserved colonial configuration. In the constitution of the Fifth Republic, there was no longer a French empire or French colonies. Instead there was a Greater France that comprised Metropolitan France, overseas departments and territories with differentiated claims to a sovereign existence. In the end, the project failed largely because the coloniality of power/knowledge and being continued to determine postcolonial relations in this reconfigured empire.

The project of the *Communauté* reflected France's desire to preserve its prerogatives and to control former colonies' entry into the global "community of nations." The experiment of the *Communauté* contained both the overriding logic of the day and recessive aspects of colonial modernity. As such, its assigned status as an entry point for prospective African states posed fundamental questions to the morality of the universal and also the continued governance of racial difference. In the early days of African independence, the *Communauté* was to be the institutional bulwark that could prevent former colonies from falling into Cold War wrangling. Beyond political expediency, the *Communauté* was constituted as an internationalist ideal "marshaled as a moral challenge" to national isolation(ism)

(Malkki 1994: 56). But the experiment of the Community and the policy of economic "cooperation" through the CFA franc regime (discussed below) was only possible because of the relative success of the colonial school that socialized African elites through political parties and intellectual circles. When necessary, France fiercely combated anti-colonial politicians through dirty practices, ostracization and assassinations.

Frederick Cooper (2014) and others have made the argument that neither straightforward independence nor the nation-state was a preferred outcome of decolonization, at least in former French West Africa. What does this mean? Principally two things. Firstly, that anti-colonial thinkers sought to extend and to problematize the parameters of Western thought by inscribing themselves into Western philosophical traditions as reluctant heirs. Secondly, in looking at divergence and hierarchy as overarching patterns of practice in international relations, the project of Franco-African Community, despite its glaring paternalism, offered something of a revolutionary possibility in the context of consolidating postcolonial states. For one key actor of this period, "the choice in favor of the nation(state) would be a form of regression,"[5] thus pointing to the greater ethical virtue of a multinational polity.

Many African activists invested in the idea of *Communauté* imagined a federal polity that was at once diverse and inclusive and could transcend the immoralities of empire.[6] For France, the reinvention of the relationship with the colonies was the condition for a preservation of its sovereignty. This reframing could moreover only make sense within the broader context of shifting political balances at the global level: beyond the East/West divide, the emerging Third World movement was articulating a new basis for a global morality that further threatened the weakening power of Western countries. The new configuration provided as many opportunities and constraints for strategic political entrepreneurs (Turpin 2008: 46).

However, the French promise of *liberté, égalité, fraternité* was a possibility in a hypothetical future, therefore a goal whose attainment remained both utopian and ominous. In fact, De Gaule's understanding of "federation" was neither literal nor legal (Turpin 2008: 55–6). From his perspective, France was to remain a sovereign state empire that granted fragments of sovereignty to colonized territories. That attachment to France as a global state was rather daunting. For some observers, Britain managed to "creatively extricate" itself from the frills of empire while France remained "hopelessly bogged down" in it (Niebuhr 1959: 117). In postcolonial Francophone Africa, France is a sovereign state that continues to conduct itself with an imperial mindset.

The main impediment to the establishment of a post-imperial union was France's relentless desire to keep African colonies in a subservient position. The failure of the project of *Communauté* was the combined effect of two facts. First, the attempt by France to extend "freedom" to its former colonies within an unequal, hierarchically ordered regime. Second, France fell into a common imperial hubris, which is a determination for empire to outlive everything "including its own purpose" (Gordon 2011: 98). The denial of moral equivalence can be seen at work in the implementation of a two-tier system of citizens and subjects whereby the *sine qua none* to upliftment was necessarily through assimilation into French ways (Cooper 2014). In the end, the independence of former colonies came, in some ways, too suddenly for the survival of the project of a community. Colonizers had imagined colonialism would last much longer. By and large, however, the Community remained in the Gaulian stronghold and therefore a geopolitical instrument for the global affirmation of France. This would be made possible by "an organically centered construction" that was a far cry from the federation favored by African intellectuals (Turpin 2008: 55).

France's design to "bring into civilization" former colonies was framed through this particular trusteeship. This strategy was consistent with a belief that the same *mission civilisatrice* that made France responsible for the upliftment of its former colonies also made it, along with other Western powers, responsible for transforming and civilizing the international society (Henderson 2013: 87–8). The path to upliftment, however, entailed continued exploitation and expropriation of resources. An important question arises here, namely: what are the conditions of sovereignty for postcolonial states in a context of flawed/compromised decolonization? Given the above, to see in the conflicting interpretations of self-determination a mere problem of phrasal ambiguousness is to miss a greater point to do with ideological closure; for formerly colonized peoples could claim rights from an imperial global to a post-imperial global only as and when they could join the society of states as *sovereign*. Once categories of domination and imperial governance, whether colonization, annexation, overlordship, trusteeship, mandate or protectorate, were partially exhausted and no longer justifiable under evolving international law, the transformation process that was to turn subjects into citizens under a different governance regime was greatly hampered.

The invention of development aid: neocolonialism as decolonization

From its early days, development assistance was presented as a depoliticized, benign form of intervention. Former colonial governors reinvented themselves as "technical assistants" who could claim field knowledge and expertise in all things African – a sure asset in development work. However, from the perspective of African agents, "being known" is a determinism that constrains their capacity to exist in a post-imperial world other than as former colonial subjects turned junior partners.

The technicization of the discourse of development aid provided the parameters for the legitimization of the continued involvement of a corps of former colonial administrators in postcolonial transactions (Meimon 2007: 15). The Union of Administrators of Overseas France oversaw the conversion of its agents and their reinsertion into development assistant jobs. Development aid emerged as an immediate outcome of the end of empire and it remained an imperial strategy designed to repackage and institutionalize its moral, economic and political purposes. The old civilizing mission in fact found a new life in development aid. A first consequence of neocolonial transactions is, therefore, that the international can only exist as an extension of the colonial, at least for those formerly colonized.

The continued interference of former imperial powers in postcolonial African states and social processes constitute key counterpoints to European accounts of decolonization as a successful transfer of sovereignty to African states.[7] France's strategy in particular has been to maintain continuity despite African independence through the reinvention of the *mission civilisatrice* on the basis of a new grammar bestowed with a multilateral dimension. France interfered in democratic processes using political mechanisms and military force. Regime change was always an open possibility and therefore part of the French arsenal of intervention, as has been amply demonstrated by the assassinations of Lumumba to Qaddafi.[8] Four mechanisms were activated, which aimed to maintain continuity beyond colonization.

First, France systematically signed non-reciprocal cooperation agreements at the time of transfer of sovereignty. The objective was to rein in African sovereignty at the very time of inception.[9] The second mechanism was the quasi-systematic establishment of secret military defense agreements with virtually all Francophone African states, either as part of cooperation agreements or separately from these.[10] More often than not, defense agreements were a guarantee that friendly governments would be maintained in power and that coups against unfriendly governments could be legally justified, hence their secret nature.

The third mechanism was the instrumentalized use of both technical and financial assistance as a *monnaie d'échange* (bargaining chip) in hegemonic consolidation. The fourth mechanism was the "institutionalization of a privileged zone of influence," in other words the political and economic fencing off of the *pays du champ* as a "privileged zone of solidarity" (Meimon 2007: 17–19).[11] These various mechanisms are the precursor of Francafrique, which is today the object of much criticism in African civil society circles. Ultimately, at the end of the colonial period, the invention of development aid as the extension of international solidarity turned out to be a godsend for France's plan to reign in Francophone African sovereignty. The institutionalization of technical assistance enabled a form of decentered governance as a strategic articulation of what Mazower calls "the end game of empire" (2009: 14). Even the liberatory claims of self-determination movements became invested in the narrative power of the sovereignty discourse.

As Meimon (2007: 4) explains:

> *[Cette] dynamique hegemonique s'entend ici comme un system de "domination" (Herrschaft) a pretension "ethique", "civilisatrice", "evangelisatrice" ou "assimilationiste", suscitant l'obeissance et l'adhesion, autant qu'un regime de "force" (Macht) fonde sur la crainte, et renvoie en ce sens a la question de la legitimation de la relation post-coloniale.*[12]

According to this author, development aid became an important aspect of postcolonial reconfiguration, in other words *"une variable d'ajustement imperial ou postcolonial"* (2007: 4).[13] The CFA franc arrangement, however, became by far the most coercive dimension of such legitimation for it provided direct French control over economic structures, political processes and unfettered access to natural resources. The franc zone constitutes a staggering example of a profound restructuring that altered the postcolonial economies of former French colonies. It started as a customs union in 1933 as a strategy to mitigate the effects, on empire, of the financial crisis of 1929. Despite being a stable currency, the CFA is chronically overvalued; the lack of fluctuation provides little flexibility. In consequence, the arrangement provides limited incentive for entrepreneurship and innovation, let alone investments and intra-African capital flow.[14] In 2008, during the financial crisis when the French government had to bail out its banks, it dipped into the fund to do so. Francophone Africa's economic lag relative to Anglophone Africa is partly a function of this colonial arrangement.

Les pays du champ thus emerged as a zone of privileged economic and financial transactions that firmly maintained France's relevance in Africa. As a result of the above, admission of former African colonies into the "international community" was necessarily mediated by former colonial powers. In restructuring the parameters of political governance and the economic structures of independent Africa in the image of imperial ambitions, the (post)colonial pact erases presumed distinctions that are meant to be performed by sovereignty and foreign policy. France has *de facto* two foreign policy regimes. The first one is the culmination of various strategies to maintain former colonies under close control. This is the backbone of France's geopolitical status in the world. Put differently,

France is considered a superpower because of its influence in Africa. As a matter of fact, the reason France was granted a permanent seat on the United Nations Security Council had strictly to do with France's imperial history. All of this explains why the discipline of International Relations is relatively underdeveloped in France and French scholars were never associated with turf wars across different IR schools of thought. This gap is however partly compensated by a rich anthropological and ethnological tradition that underpins the constitution of African studies in France.

The larger point that emerges out of postcolonial transactions sketched above is that the postcolonial condition of Francophone Africa is one of independence without decolonization and sovereignty without self-determination. In order to understand how Franco–African relations as described above account for a making of the international as a steady process of hierarchization and differentiation (alterity), one needs to turn to decolonial theories.

The (post)colonial pact sought to institute a very linear and enduring dependence of African states vis-à-vis France whereby the former provides natural resources, exclusively and for the benefit of metropolitan France, and import, almost exclusively, manufactured products from the latter. This economic configuration is sustained by military and political transactions entrenched in mechanisms that are not subject to any democratic control but rather normalized in opaque networks that shape a logic of elite formation. The (post)colonial pact is the outcome of the institution of a "special relationship," the carrier of a colonial affect that mobilizes and harnesses a grammar of difference. By way of illustration, one can conceive of French foreign policy as a dual, hierarchical system: the Quai d'Orsay (Foreign Ministry) and the Ministry of Cooperation (formerly the Ministry of Colonies). "Cooperation" sanctions postcolonial transactions with former African colonies while "diplomacy" is reserved for the Western world. French foreign policy in Francophone African was always folded into the life and afterlives of empire, in the same manner that since the 19th-century beginnings of the discipline of IR, foreign policy was also about race and empire for the United States. This configuration raises obvious questions to do with the inside/outside division in IR, the relationship between IR and the colonial and that of the international order and racial hierarchy.

The international at the intersection of race and coloniality

Race-thinking as mentalscape of IR: a dual bind

Racial thinking is not only evident in the practices that constitute the international, as outlined above through the example of France's relations with its former colonies. The discipline of International Relations was itself erected on foundations constituted by a fundamental anxiety about race as the organizing principle of encounter and interactions (Mills 1997; Vitalis 2015). In other words, the epistemology and the ideology of "the international" rest upon the internalizing of a set of ontological discourses pertaining to difference, more crucially to racial differences. In fact, it can be safely said that all IR theories have something to say about the self/other boundary and the policing of boundaries. Whether race is acknowledged as an explicit category of social thought or not, it structures the delineation of such boundaries. Critical theorists have greatly contributed to taking IR out of enlightenment chronologies and developmental time (Inayatuyllah and Blaney 2018). However, Vitalis and Morefield among others have shown how the imperial categories of "race" and "civilization" inform fundamental assumptions about the nature and the constituting categories of the international (see Chapter 4). Racial and civilizational arguments however became "largely subsumed within the politics of internationalism and its more capacious cousin, globalization" (Gorman 2017). By and large, normative lines of differentiation and social domination, of world power, are closely linked to the framing of an intellectual field: International Relations = race studies.

Coloniality is most intensely at work in the deployment of the notion of anarchy. The latter would be the state that inheres in the (dis)oganization of "inferior races." The attachment to a vision of anarchy as the "natural" state of world affairs therefore reflects a concern that is deeply entrenched in a racist mindset. Historically, this vision has been articulated as a matter of mission, a "burden," that white nations have to enlighten and to bring into the fold of civilization non-white peoples so as to contain the anarchy that afflicts their polities. This burden was executed through the pillage of resources, the enslavement of Africans and Indians, the subjugation of non-Western populations for centuries and the elaboration of institutions that perpetuated the domination by the West of the non-Western world (Henderson 2013: 85). A concern about anarchy is particularly acute among realist and liberalist IR scholars but is not limited to them. That the notion of anarchy informs and suffuses paradigmatic formulations of the discipline constitutes an enduring factor in the justification of the ethical superiority of the West. For Sampson in particular, Africa was always the unthought inspiration for the paradigm of anarchy (Sampson 2002 in Henderson 2013: 86–7).

Like the New World, Africa needed to be "pacified" in order to remedy its ungovernability. The founders of the discipline of IR in the U.S. saw race as the defining feature of civilizational difference. Some of them believed that racial development was analogous to human development and therefore went through different phases of infancy and maturity. Their research topics reflected an interest in race as a category that intimately informed and determined politics. There is an indubitable echo to W.E.B. Dubois' (1903) contention that race was the most important dividing line of the 20th century, albeit for a different set of reasons. Thus, early IR in the United States was very much understood as the administration, the governance of "races" and the maintenance of separate models of difference for different "races" (on this point, see too Chapter 4). International Relations was not about the study of relations among global units called states but rather about the relations between races as working units. In this configuration, empire was to mediate race relations in order to avoid full-blown race wars. Security was therefore uniquely conceived as a capacity to contain race coherence and homogeneity from potential spillover and for advanced races not to be derailed by backwards ones. IR was precisely the discipline that would rationalize and explain how this was to be achieved. It thus became a discipline that indirectly promoted Eurocentrism (see Box 6.3).

BOX 6.3 *WHITE ORDER, BLACK POLITICS*

In *White World Order, Black Power Politics*, Robert Vitalis (2015) examines the origins of International Relations in the United States using archival material and a critical reading of the early scholars and debates that gave a direction to the discipline. He shows that International Relations was supposed to provide a conceptual framework for the preservation of white supremacy in a context that was becoming increasingly global, multiracial and interdependent. Essentially, in the early 20th century, Vitalis argues, "international relations meant race relations."

The founders of what was to become the discipline of International Relations recon-ditioned imperial ideas of cultural development, racial superiority/inferiority and civilizational divergence into precepts for racial administration and imperial expan-sion. More specifically, these scholars invested their expertise as intellectual structure to America's imperial design in the Pacific and in the Americas. There are two aspects to the story that Vitalis excavates. One aspect is about imperialism and racial subjec-tion. The other aspect is about the history of the Howard School of International Rela-tions associated with scholars as prominent as Merze Tate, W.E.B. DuBois, Ralphe Bunche, Rayford Logan, Alaine Locke, Eric William and E. Franklin Frazier. If the Howard School is virtually unknown in IR history, it is because it neither adheres to its common accounts nor supports the premises or agenda of the discipline.

Race and the international: an enduring coloniality

Eurocentrism was and remains the ideological conceit and a specific form of ethnocentrism that enabled Europe to classify, hierarchize and reorder human beings and societies (Amin 2009: 177–9; Ndlovu-Gatsheni 2013a: 332–3; see too, Chapter 12). The invention and pro-duction of categories of humans and sub-humans, and the desire to stabilize one category of humans over others undergirded European conquest of the Americas, Asia and Africa (Gordon 2011: 96). The justification for conquest often took the form of a normative ration-alization of the need for a different morality and therefore a different set of rules for different categories of humans. Contractarian scholars such as Hobbes and Locke, Rousseau and Kant elaborated theories of moral order in the post-Reformation moment at a time marked by European ascendency to imperial hegemony (Henderson 2013: 80–4).[15] Errol Henderson has usefully demonstrated the role of racism and race thinking and the impact, more generally, of a "racial contract" in historical and contemporary conceptualization of anarchy as the the-oretical touchstone of the discipline. Conceptions of anarchy have justified white supremacist views on the inherent superiority of whites over non-whites, and the necessary responsibility of whites to pacify non-white societies by uplifting them, and in shaping an international order in which their leading status remains unchallenged (see Chapter 5).

For Anibal Quijano (2007: 170),

> the large majority of the exploited, the dominated, the discriminated against, are pre-cisely the members of the "races," "ethnicities," or "nations" into which colonized populations were categorized in the formative process of that world power, from the conquest of America and onward.
>
> (Quijano 2007: 169)

Coloniality thus determines ontological rifts and lines of power in practice. More insidious than the material, external imposition, colonial domination was most effective in its aftermath. For colonial domination blunted the colonized's capacity to produce a culture and meaning that is not mediated by the colonizer's symbolic frameworks and modes of knowing and being.

According to Quijano, the European paradigm of coloniality emerged out of the socio-cultural conflicts in Europe. At the very least, these conflicts reveal the fact that "the emergence of the idea of the 'West' or of 'Europe' is an admission of identity – that is, of relations with other cultural experiences, of differences with other cultures"

(Quijano 2007: 173). Further, beyond the process of othering that has been central to the formation of European cognitive principles and rational thinking, Ashis Nandy (1983) shows that the reluctance to acknowledge the enduring other in the (whole) self precludes both a process of healing for the colonizer deeply motivated by misplaced arrogance, and an intellectual leap toward emancipated constructions of knowledge.

According to Maldonado-Torres (2007: 243), "in a way, as modern subjects we breathe coloniality all the time and every day." The expansion of Euro-modernity from the shores of the Mediterranean to the Americas in the 15th century articulated a new system/series of relations whose geopolitical significance partly lay in the organized collapse of various centers "not simply from the force of ideas but sword and musket" (Gordon 2011: 95–6). This collapse was a part of the elaboration of a new global cartography. For Quijano and others, the constitutive condition of coloniality is this: coloniality occurs when Europeans "deprive Africans of legitimacy and recognition in the global cultural order dominated by European patterns" (2007: 170). In the Americas, the subjugation of the high cultures of the Inca, the Aztec and other nations by European colonizers turned these "into illiterate, peasant subcultures condemned to orality; that is, deprived of their own patterns of formalized, objectivized, intellectual, and plastic or visual expression" (Quijano 2007: 169–70).

Coloniality is informed by a "'racial' [ethnographic] social classification of the world population under Eurocentered world power" (Quijano 2007: 171). Coloniality remains "the most general form of domination in the world today, once colonization as an explicit political order was destroyed"; it informs, overall, the cornerstone of global power through the reproduction and the entrenching of patterns of thought and action that stem out of colonial reason and morality (Quijano 2007: 170). In fact, the afterlives of empire and colonialism are being played out continuously and across different planes. They are being played out in the terrain of thought as much as in the terrain of action, in global rivalries as much as in the scramble for markets and the extraction of resources (see Chapters 13 and 15).

The constitutive condition created for the non-West in general is a consistent pursuit of what Ngugi Wa Thiong'o (2006) calls a "quest for relevance." From the very beginning therefore, the structure of epistemic hierarchy/differentiation that presided over the encounter of the West and the non-West gave the former an established identity while setting the latter on a path of uncertain identity. This pursuit is one of recovery, of self in relation to self, not the (other) self thus far bundled unevenly in the image of Europe or as an extension of it. A part of this endeavor is a direct anxiety that results from what the coloniality of being and the coloniality of knowledge have combined to achieve, which is to make whiteness, according to Ndlovu-Gatsheni (2013b: 12), gain greater "ontological density far above blackness."

The absence of perspective?

Under modernity, the temporal taxonomy that allowed Europe to think, the world became the very necessary constraint within which non-European histories could be written. The "theft of history" (Goody 2006) translates across social science disciplines in the use of "a dual modality of historical time, which enabled [scholars] to represent events as at once contemporaneous and non-contemporaneous and thus some conditions as more progressive than others" (Asad 1993: 23, quoting Koselleck 1988: 24). Every single dynamic, every aspect and process of the international remits to a structure of interdependence and intersubjectivity. Yet, European paradigms of knowledge have been sanitized of references to substantive traces of others in the European self on the one hand, the very coloniality of its power structure on the other (Quijano 2007: 174). In other words, the domination of Europe over the rest of the world in the form of subject–object relations is responsible for an alleged "time" gap, namely the problem of coevality often bemoaned by anthropologists (Fabian 2002).

In the post-imperial moment, sovereignty was still associated with ideas of progress and could therefore not quite be turned into a universal principle for unstable institutions and historical contingency. To be sure, Africa's entry into the global realm is indissociable from a history of empire. For scholars like Cemil Aydin (2017), there was no smooth transition from empires to Wilsonianism. There were instead alternative projects grounded in different internationalism(s) such as pan-Islamism, pan-Asianism, pan-Africanism, pan-Arabism and so on and which were not entirely obliterated by the imperial synthesis constituted by the colonial empires (see Chapter 5). The various and competing geopolitical imaginations had important roots in early insights, by former colonial subjects, into alternative global orders. The debate on self-determination touched upon above was important for two main reasons. First, there was the question of how successor polities to Europe's newly "dissolved developing-world empires" were to organize themselves on the basis of a seemingly unaltered principle of sovereign statehood (Husain 2014: 218), in a context whereby the "dynamics of difference" continued to define pretty much the different treatment of states in global institutions of governance (Anghie 2007: 3–4). Second, a discussion of sovereign statehood becomes inevitable in understanding the making of "the international" as framed by the colonial logic and bluntly exemplified in the formation of the League of Nations and the United Nations.

Both the League and the United Nations were not only a product of empire, they were also designed as a framework for the maintenance of control by former colonizers over former colonies, therefore the status quo. For Mazower (2009: 14, 17) the UN in particular "was the product of evolution not revolution." The foundations of the UN are even more disturbing if one considers the very central role played by former South African prime minister, Jan Smuts, in drafting the Charter, especially its rousing preamble. Mark Mazower shows how Jan Smuts' idea of internationalism was imperial and paternalistic in character. Smuts was a fervent defender of an imperial universalism and an ideologue of the racial superiority of whites on top of being a proponent of segregationist policies in South Africa (Mazower 2009: 19; see too, Chapter 4). Both the U.S. and Britain continued to maintain support for Smuts and would entertain no criticism against South Africa's racist policies, in keeping with an economy of affect across white settler colonies, as discussed above.

The possibility of perspective: the geography of reason

In rethinking the logic of relations that mediates the location, status and the quality of the rest in relation to the West, attention also needs to be paid to the unidirectionality of "the international" whereby knowledge is imparted, power exerted and intervention directed from a single perspective. Unidirectionalism is the danger and the product of the single abstract source. This single perspective frames a "geography of power" established by both material power and moral conceit. According to Lewis Gordon (2011), epistemological geography is about the organization, in other words the management of normative life, hence the term "the geography of reason" applies to the framing of constructs. The geography of reason thus delineates the teleological coordinates of progress, civilization, enlightenment with its score of hierarchical subordination and ordering. It explains the (distorted) framework of interdependence that comes across in Eric Wolf's discussion.

The geography of reason defines who is (not) human. It also defines its critiques, for instance postcolonial schools, postmodern perspectives, gender and racial studies and so on. It freezes time even when everything changed drastically at that moment of encounter. As a matter of example, political theory is commonly attached to the territorial state as the normative, the historical and the aspirational limits of universal conceptions of liberty, justice and the good life. The upshot is a theorizing of "the international" as only the stuff of inter-state relations, a viewpoint that further entrenches a reified conception of statehood (Agnew 1994: 59). If anything, postcolonial Franco–African relations demonstrate that such a conception is neither historically true nor possible in the framework of hierarchy and difference.

Unidirectionality impoverishes an account of morality and politics in so far as the human subject remains the product of knowledge. But it is unidirectionalism that drives the production of non-Western subjects in need of liberation and freedom, emancipation and protection, rights and morality; therefore rescue for order, organization and governance (Mutua 2002: 204).

Ultimately however, the object of International Relations is not some vague field but rather the human subject. In that sense, it is no different from other humanities and social science disciplines. If anything, the impulse to differentiate IR from other disciplines in the social sciences has produced precarious constructions. In the context of a globalizing world, the disciplinary endeavor is bewildered and constantly frustrated, for globalization is not just a mechanism but an explanatory framework for rethinking the existential battle between humans and technology. This partly legitimizes much ongoing speculative analysis of a post-humanist IR. If the possibility of a post(imperial) humanism is hinged upon the capacity, for the West, to maintain its vision and its model of the world, this design is undermined by the dispersal of values and ideas, and the knowledge that enables the appropriation of these flows.

In this very configuration, however, some are potentially "international," while others will always remain "local." The transition to the international often operates as the local goes through cultural translation and civilizational leaps in the very global cultural encounters sketched out by Wolf. But the epistemology and the politics of location, will always have to be rethought as this chapter has implicitly suggested. In the same vein, however, it would be aberrant to think of the local as something that is removed from the imaginings of modernity. For "the international" to become a territory of thought in the full sense, the status of the local has to be appreciated in the sense of thinking about location as epistemology and standpoint. But the local has to be seen as something that is neither bound by locality nor tethered to any specific level (local or global) but rather as a standpoint that is grounded in locality (Shaw, Waldorf and Hazan 2010).

Conclusion

The drive for internationalism in the post-1945 era – most emblematically manifest in the development of multilateral institutions of governance – obscures key aspects of the ontology of the international. The latter has been more profoundly shaped by race and colonialism than Wilsonian and post-war internationalist accounts suggest.

This chapter has sought to understand the epistemic status of "the international" in IR. It has argued, among other things, that the notion of sovereignty acts as an unrealized possibility that keeps Africa and the postcolonial world in general apart and out there. The norming of a post-1945 world was articulated on the basis of sovereignty as the politico-juridical horizon of global politics.

Scholars such as Robert Vitalis and Errol Henderson have emphasized the extent to which the racial contract also undergirds thinking, theorizing and key perspectives in the discipline. This chapter thus contributes to a recent effort to show that the boundaries of the discipline are not territorial but rather racial, ethical and ideological. In particular, it uses the examples of race thinking and sovereignty thinking as world-constituting paradigms that frame foundational disciplinary accounts and international practice.

In order to confront this legacy, a reframing of disciplinary knowledge should allow for inbuilt distortions that displace centers of apprehending in order to allow for a deepening of the original purposes of the discipline. To quote the Kenyan scholar Ngugi Wa Thiong'o (1993: 47), "it is time we 'move the centre' of scholarship towards centres long neglected and marginalised and away from histories and epistemologies that privilege and foreground Western thought." In relation to questions touched upon in this chapter, this means that the concepts of race and sovereignty have to be written into a problematized, decentered and reconstructed "international."

Questions for discussion

1. How have practices that constitute the international influenced the development of the disciplines of IR?
2. What does it mean to think about race and colonialism as essential to our understanding of "the international?"
3. To what extent do colonial economic and political configurations continue to shape the conditions of former colonies in a postcolonial world?
4. Are French–African relations typical of postcolonial transactions between former colonizers and former colonies?
5. How does the history of the Franco-African Community and its legacy challenge common accounts of the making of the international community and/or order?

Notes

1 Equatorial Guinea and Guinea Bissau are the only non-Francophone member countries. The franc zone consists of two independent regions: the West African Economic and Monetary Union and the Central Africa Economic and Monetary Community.
2 Foreign reserves stood at 100% at independence and 65% between 1973 and 2005.
3 In Vietnam, attempts to reinstate colonial rule where it had been defeated; in Japan, promotion of crony regimes, clientelism and empire by economic rule.
4 For more information, see the 2001 Report of the Parliamentary Committee of Enquiry in charge of determining the exact circumstances of the assassination of Patrice Lumumba and the possible involvement of Belgian politicians.
5 Assembly of the French Union, debate on a proposition requesting equal treatment of French and Canaques in New Caledonia, Session of April 21, 1948, ANOM/ BiB/50243/1948.
6 Attempts at instituting a British-style self-government were stalled by engrained ideas that even if one could accept the possibility of autonomy, it would have to be contingent upon different "degrees of evolution." A "structural feature of colonial modernity" resided, according

to Wilder, in "the tensions between coexisting policies to abstract and modernise or to differentiate and primitivises subject populations" (2005: 10).

7 Imperial sovereignty had to be preserved at all costs, including the lives of colonial subjects as the massacres of Thiaroye (1944), Sétif (1945) and Madagascar (1947–48) demonstrated all too well.

8 The United States and France at times acted on behalf of the international community using the UN Security Council (UNSC) authorization procedure (France and NATO in Libya; the U.S. in Haiti, etc.) while the UNSC expands the realm of applicability of its resolutions to the domestic prerogatives of certain states.

9 Thus 138 agreements or conventions were signed between 1959 and 1953 and these essentially extended or maintained the jurisdiction of the institutions of the Community (Meimon 2007: 20).

10 According to Meimon, France has over 138 cooperation treaties between 1959 and 1963 that extended the areas of competence of the old *Communauté*; these treaties allowed France to maintain over 60,000 military troops in 90 bases (and garrisons) (Meimon 2007: 20).

11 The expression "*pays du champ*" is evocative of a "field" open for cultivation, of a field yet to be cultivated and developed (hence the need for *mise en valeur*). The expression also evokes a backyard, that is the extension of a core, hence also the expression of *pré-carré*, which delineates a zone of exclusive influence.

12 This hegemonic dynamic should be understood as a system of "domination" (Herrschaft), an "ethical," "civilizing," "evangelizing" or "assimilationist" posture, one that mobilizes obedience and adhesion, as much as a regime based on "force" (Macht) and fear; in that sense it raises the question of the legitimation of the postcolonial relationship.

13 A variable of adjustment, imperial or postcolonial.

14 Eleven of its 14 members of the CFA franc are on the list of least developed countries (LDCs).

15 For Henderson, personhood, for Emmanuel Kant, "is circumscribed by his white supremacism" given that blacks are nowhere near meeting the "minimum requirement for moral agency and thus of personhood."

Further reading

Anghie, Antony (2007) *Imperialism, Sovereignty and the Making of International Law*, Cambridge: Cambridge University Press. This book argues that the colonial confrontation was central to the formation of international law and, in particular, its founding concept, sovereignty.

Cooper, Frederic (2014) *Citizenship between Empire and Nation Remaking France and French Africa, 1945–1960*, New Jersey: Princeton University Press. Cooper explores the archives and debates that led to African independence and attempts to institute a multinational polity to succeed the French empire.

Vitalis, Robert (2015) *White World Order, Black Power Politics. The Birth of American International Relations*, Ithaca: Cornell University Press. This book explores how the origins of the discipline of IR are informed by racial politics and an attempt to maintain white supremacy through imperialism and subjugation.

Turpin, Fréderic (2008) "1958, La Communauté Franco-africaine: un projet de puissance notre héritage de la Ive République et conceptions gaulliennes," *Outre-mers*, 95(358–359): 45–58. This article examines the tensions and contradictions of the promise of emancipation in a context still deeply determined by empire.

References

Agnew, John (1994) "The Territorial Trap: The Geographical Assumptions of International relations Theory", *Review of International Political Economy*, 1(1): 53–80. DOI: 10.1080/09692299408434268

Amin, Samir (2009) *Eurocentrism: Modernity, Religion, and Democracy: A Critique of Eurocentrism and Culturalism*, New York: Monthly Review Press.

Anderson, Benedict (2006) *Imagined Communities: Reflections on the Origin and Spread of Nationalism*, London: Verso.

Anghie, Anthony (2007) *Imperialism, Sovereignty and the Making of International Law*, Cambridge: Cambridge University Press. DOI: 10.1017/CBO9780511614262

Asad, Talal (1993) *Genealogies of Religion. Discipline and Reasons of Power in Christianity and Islam*, Baltimore: John Hopkins University Press.

Aydin, Cemil (2017) *The Idea of the Muslim World: A Global Intellectual History*, Boston: Harvard University Press.

Belgian Chamber of Representatives (2001) "Report of the Parliamentary Committee of Enquiry in Charge of Determining the Exact Circumstances of the Assassination of Patrice Lumumba and the Possible Involvement of Belgian Politicians". Available at www.dekamer.be/FLWB/PDF/50/0312/50K0312006.pdf (Conclusion in English at www.lachambre.be/kvvcr/pdf_sections/comm/lmb/con clusions.pdf).

Carr, E.H. (1939) *The Twenty Years Crisis, 1919–1939: An Introduction to the Study of International Relations*, London: Macmillan.

Cooper, Frederick (2014) *Citizenship between Empire and Nation Remaking France and French Africa, 1945–1960*, New Jersey: Princeton University Press.

DuBois, W.E.B. (1903) *The Souls of Black People*, Chicago: AC McClurg & Co.

Escobar, Arturo (1995) *Encountering Development: The Making and Unmaking of the Third World*, Princeton: Princeton University Press.

Fabian, Johannes (2002) *Time and the Other: How Anthropology Makes Its Object*, New York: Columbia University Press.

Goody, Jack (2006) *The Theft of History*, Cambridge: Cambridge University Press. DOI: 10.1017/CBO9780511819841

Gordon, Lewis (2011) "Shifting the Geography of Reason in an Age of Disciplinary Decadence", *Transmodernity*, 1(2): 95–103.

Gorman, Dan (2017) "All Things to all People? Thoughts on Liberalism and Imperialism", *The Disorder of Things*. https://thedisorderofthings.com/2017/07/18/all-things-to-all-people-thoughts-on-liberalism-and-imperialism/

Henderson, Errol (2013) "Hidden in Plain Sight: Racism in International Relations Theory", *Cambridge Review of International Affairs*, 26(1): 71–92. DOI: 10.1080/09557571.2012.710585

Hurrell, Andrew (2016) "Towards the Global Study of International Relations", *Revista Brasileira de Politica International*, 59(02): e008. DOI: 10.1590/0034-7329201600208

Husain, Aiyaz (2014) *Mapping the End of Empire: American and British Strategic Visions in the Postwar World*, Cambridge: Harvard University Press.

Inayatuyllah, Naeem and David Blaney (2018) "Nandy's Non-Player Dialectics", in Ramin Jahanbegloo and Ananya Vajpeyi (eds), *Ashis Nandy: A Life of Dissent*, Delhi: Oxford University Press India, pp. 197–208.

Koselleck, Reinhart (1988). *Critique and Crisis: Enlightenment and the Pathogenesis of Modern Society*, Cambridge: MIT Press.

Maldonado-Torres, Nelson (2007) "On the Coloniality of Being: Contributions to the Development of a Concept", *Cultural Studies*, 21(2–3): 240–270. DOI: 10.1080/09502380601162548

Malkki, Liisa (1994) "Citizens of Humanity: Internationalism and the Imagined Community of Nations", *Diaspora: A Journal of Transnational Studies*, 3(1): 41–68. DOI: 10.1353/dsp.1994.0013

Mazower, M. (2009) *No Enchanted Palace. The End of Empire and the Ideological Origins of the Unites Nations*, Princeton and Oxford: Princeton University Press.

Meimon, Julien (2007) "L'invention de l'aide francaise au developpement. Discours, instruments et pratiques d'une dynamique hegemonique", *Questions de Recherche*, 21: 1–44.

Mills, Charles (1997) *The Racial Contract*, Ithaca: Cornell University Press.

Mutua, Makau (2002) *Human Rights: A Political and Cultural Critique*, Philadelphia: University of Pennsylvania Press.

Nandy, Ashis (1983) *The Intimate Enemy: Loss and Recovery of Self Under Colonialism*, Delhi: Oxford University Press.

Ndlovu-Gatsheni, Sabelo (2013a) "The Entrapment of Africa within the Global Colonial Matrices of Power: Eurocentrism, Coloniality, and Deimperialization in the Twenty-first Century", *Journal of Developing Societies*, 29(4): 331–353. DOI: 10.1177%2F0169796X13503195

Ndlovu-Gatsheni, Sabelo (2013b) *Coloniality of Power in Postcolonial Africa. Myths of Decolonization*, Dakar: Codesria Book Series.

Niebuhr, Reinhold (1959) "Power and Ideology in National and International Affairs", in W.T.R. Fox (ed), *Theoretical Aspects of International Relations*, South Bend: University of Notre Dame Press, pp. 107–116.

Quijano, Aníbal (2007) "Coloniality and Modernity/Rationality", *Cultural Studies*, 21(2–3): 168–178. DOI: 10.1080/09502380601164353

Sampson, Aaron (2002) "Tropical Anarchy: Waltz, Wendt, and the Way We Imagine International Politics", *Alternatives*, 27(4): 429–457. DOI: 10.1177%2F030437540202700402

Shaw, Rosalind, Lars Waldorf and Pierre Hazan (2010) *Localizing Transitional Justice. Interventions and Priorities after Mass Violence*, Stanford: Stanford University Press.

Turpin, Frédéric (2008) "1958, La Communauté Franco-africaine: un projet de puissance notre héritage de la Ive République et conceptions gaulliennes", *Outre-Mers. Revue d'histoire*, 95(358–359): 45–58.

Vitalis, Robert (2015) *White World Order, Black Power Politics. The Birth of American International Relations*, Ithaca: Cornell University Press.

Wa Thiong'o, Ngugi (1986 [2006]) *Decolonising the Mind. The Politics of Language in African Literature*, Oxford: James Currey Publishers.

Wa Thiong'o, Ngugi (1993) *Moving the Centre: The Struggle for Cultural Freedoms*, Oxford: James Currey Publishers.

Walker, R.B.J. (1993) *Inside/Outside: International Relations as Political Theory*, Cambridge: Cambridge University Press. DOI: 10.1017/CBO9780511559150

Wilder, Gary (2005) *The French Imperial Nation-State: Negritude and Colonial Humanism Between the Two World Wars*, Chicago: Chicago University Press.

Wolf, Eric (1982) *Europe and the People without History*, Berkley: University of California Press.

7 War and conflict

Arlene B. Tickner

Introduction[1]

War is one of the most destructive forms of social behavior, and a stubborn feature of collective group interaction across time and place. The centrality of war to human existence has led to its study in practically all areas of the human, social and natural sciences. International Relations is no exception. Although for years the field focused primarily on large-scale interstate confrontation, since the end of the Cold War the concentration of war in the global South has led to changes in how and where this phenomenon is analyzed. For example, dramatically different violent conflicts such as warfare in former Yugoslavia and the Rwandan genocide reflected what Mary Kaldor (1999) described as "new" wars, in which factors such as globalization, identity and institutional state weakness play a central role. As authors such as Mahmood Mamdani (2002) have argued, however, the role of complex historical triggers, such as colonialism are often glossed over in such (Western) readings. The popular film *Hotel Rwanda* (directed by Terry George 2004) provides a prime example. Let's take a look.

On April 6, 1994, the plane in which Rwandan president, Juvenál Habyarimana, and his Burundian counterpart were traveling was shot down as it approached the Kigawi airport. Several months earlier, Habyarimana, a Hutu, had brokered a peace agreement with the Tutsi rebels that envisioned a power sharing arrangement whose main goal was to overcome decades, if not centuries, of violence between the two groups. Conflicting accounts suggest that the president was targeted either by the Tutsi Rwandan Patriot Front (RPF) rebels, frustrated with the accord's lack of progress, or by Hutu Power extremists who opposed it from the start. The assassination of Habyarimana and subsequent RPF coup triggered a genocide that left as many as one million dead and two million displaced over the span of 100 days. During this time, members of the military and civilian leaders who identified with Hutu Power incited Hutus of all stripes to kill Tutsi "cockroaches" and their sympathizers. The Hutu opposition and those who refused to take part in the killings were also murdered. As Mamdani (2002: 18) suggests, this horrific and unimaginable genocide was neither a localized nor an exclusively elite-driven event, but a collective affair in which Tutsi spouses and children were even massacred by Hutu members of their own families.

Hotel Rwanda represents the genocide as an "exceptional" event rooted in the long-standing clash between Hutus and Tutsis that predated colonialism, but was naturalized by Belgian colonizers (Harrow 2005). In the opening scene, the presenter of the Hutu Power radio station, RTLM, explains his hatred of the Tutsis and invites his listeners to squash the Tutsi infestation, portending the violence to come.

However, when the film's hero, hotel manager Paul Ruserabinga is asked by a U.S. reporter to explain the difference between the two women who accompany him, one a Hutu and the other a Tutsi, he responds that they could be twins, thus hinting that ethnic distinctions are irrelevant. The fact that Paul, himself a Hutu, is married to Tatiana, a Tutsi, reinforces the impossibility that inter-ethnic hatred is the cause of the genocide. As a result, the movie's plot evolves as a story of "bad," "savage" Africans that attack "good," "civilized" ones, reinforcing dominant portrayals of the continent as backwards and irrational, and invisibilizing other ways of understanding the genocide that fail to fit within this narrative (Harrow 2005; Rwafa 2010; Autesserre 2012). The film also gestures towards critique of the inaction and indifference of the United Nations and the international community. But here too, the main takeaway is that the West has a civilizing mission to play in Africa and that it could have prevented the genocide if only it had exercised the appropriate tutelage.

However well-intentioned, *Hotel Rwanda* fixates on a simplistic narrative that reproduces Africa and Africans as inferior "others" and that conceals just as much as it makes visible (Harrow 2005). In his assessment of dominant readings of the Rwandan genocide, Mamdani (2002) argues that the resilience of racialized political identities that were naturalized and institutionalized as a result of colonialism, and the resulting us/them binary, not ethnicity, is at the root of "indigenous" Hutu violence against the allegedly "alien" Tutsis. The Hamitic hypothesis, which assigned racial superiority to certain groups hailing from northern Africa that conquered the continent's allegedly more primitive inhabitants, led to preferential practices and administrative techniques that construed a racialized Tutsi identity. The 1959 Revolution reversed this hierarchy and gave precedence to the Hutus, but the racialized binary sowed through colonization remained intact.

This chapter provides a wide-ranging overview of distinct literatures and theories that have set out to understand the causes of war. Although the study of war and violent conflict encompasses many different angles, including its causes, effects, duration, logics, transformation of the social fabric and termination, the Rwandan genocide suggests that explaining why wars begin and continue to be so prevalent, mainly in the global South, continues to be a key challenge. Following a brief discussion of how to define war, the chapter examines conventional IR approaches to interstate war. It then turns to varied explanations of intrastate conflict in the global South, including state weakness, greed, resources and land, and identity. In the final section, alternative explanations and critiques of standard approaches to war, rooted mainly in postcolonialism and feminism, are developed.

What is war?

Defining war is no small task. Jack Levy and William Thompson (2010: 5) describe it as "sustained coordinated violence between political organizations," largely echoing Carl von Clausewitz's (1989) claim that war is conducted by states (and arguably, other groups), is driven by political objectives and aims to force a contender to act in a specific way through the use of military and other forms of power. Martin Shaw (2009: 101–103) also draws upon Clausewitz in order to develop a sociological definition. Although the author acknowledges that many violent conflicts today stray from the ideal-type described above, he argues that the core logics of "normal" war, including the distinction between combatants and non-combatants, and the use of diverse forms of (violent) power are still useful for theorizing about different types of political violence such as revolution, terrorism and genocide. Shaw considers genocide a specific kind of warfare in which unarmed civilian groups are systematically killed, usually as a byproduct of "normal" war, and that often leads to new phases of warfare.

Conversely, attempts to quantify war and to distinguish it from other forms of violent conflict have been a key facet of positivist research agendas in fields such as IR. For interstate war, the Correlates of War Project developed by David Singer and Melvin Small continues to be the most widely cited, and considers it a violent sustained conflict among two or more states with organized armed forces that produces at least 1,000 battlefield combatant deaths per year. Similarly, the Uppsala Conflict Data Program sets 1,000 combat deaths per year, where each of the warring parties is responsible for at least 10%, as the threshold for intrastate war. In contrast, armed conflict, a term that we will use interchangeably with war in this chapter, in keeping with more qualitative approaches, entails 25 deaths per year.[2]

Notwithstanding these efforts, war is a fuzzy concept. Many definitions fail to capture the complex nature of most violent conflicts in today's world, limited consensus exists as to the usefulness of separating interstate from intrastate wars as discrete categories (as this ignores their potential interaction and interdependence), and the absence of war strictly defined often leads to the mistaken impression that there is peace. Equally important, such definitions fail to account for what war *does* as a political discourse (see Box 7.1).

BOX 7.1 WHAT'S IN A NAME? COLOMBIA AND ITS ARMED CONFLICT

Colombia's armed conflict, which began in the 1950s, is one of the longest lasting in the world and has led to the deaths of over 220,000 people, the disappearance of tens of thousands and the forced displacement of over seven million. Following failed attempts by the government of Andrés Pastrana (1998–2002) to negotiate a peace settlement with the Revolutionary Armed Forces of Colombia (FARC) guerrillas, his successor, Álvaro Uribe (2002–2010) denied the existence of the decades-old armed conflict in Colombia, claiming instead that the country's insurgent groups were terrorists. Although few in Colombia, including the armed forces, ever doubted that there was an ongoing war, the systematic removal of the term "armed conflict" from official discourse and its replacement with words such as "terrorism," "terrorists" and "terrorist threat" had crucial political and legal implications. First, it denied the political origins of the leftist guerrillas, with which future attempts at negotiation were publicly rejected. Second, in addition to depoliticizing the guerrillas, denial of the armed conflict lent itself to the erasure of a key distinction between combatants and non-combatants established in international humanitarian law, by which practices such as extrajudicial killings (which numbered in the several thousands) became licit; as well as the argument that citizens could not remain neutral towards criminal activity and had to take sides. Third, the shift allowed the Uribe government to align Colombia's war with the U.S.-led "global war on terrorism," mainly with an eye to securing greater military cooperation and assistance from Washington, which was forthcoming through a multi-year aid program called Plan Colombia.

Since the 1980s, distinct countries, led by the United States, have waged a "war on drugs" (Marez 2004). In addition to the militarization of policing strategies designed to curtail the threat posed by illicit narcotics and organized crime, peasant communities, who cultivate crops such as coca and poppy, and ordinary consumers are criminalized. In the U.S., the drug war has largely affected the Afro-American community, which comprises the majority of the prison population accused of non-violent drug-related crimes, underscoring its racialized undertones. Philippine president Rodrigo Duterte's (2016–2020) "war on drugs" has justified systematic extrajudicial killings that number over 12,000, according to non-governmental organizations (NGOs) such as Human Rights Watch.

The terrorist attacks of September 11, 2001, in New York and Washington, D.C. also led the United States to declare a "global war on terrorism" (GWOT) (Hershberg and Moore 2002). As argued by Partha Chaterjee (2004: 108) and others, "an unprecedented act of violence was made comprehensible by framing it as an act of war." However, as in the case of the drug war, terrorists are not a conventional enemy. "In the absence of a clear enemy or target, the rhetoric" has frequently slipped "into unconcealed, religious, ethnic and cultural hatred" (Chaterjee 2004: 109) and fueled, among others, anti-Islamic sentiment and Islamophobia around the world. This was in no small part due to the framing of 9/11 as confirmation of Samuel Huntington's (1998) "clash of civilizations" theory, which described the main thrust of conflict after the end of the Cold War as one of "civilizations," leading to clashes between the West and the Islamic East (for further critiques of Huntington, see Chapters 9 and 17). Military interventions in Afghanistan and Iraq, as well as the geographical expansion of the GWOT into the Middle East and North Africa, and South Asia, set in motion a wave of counterviolence that reached its apex with the rise of the Islamic State of Iraq and Syria, ISIS. Although ISIS has been largely vanquished in terms of its territorial control, violence continues unabated in many parts of the Middle East and Afghanistan.[3] As we will now see, the reality-making effects of war discourses are largely overlooked by conventional approaches.

Conventional approaches to war

Since Kenneth Waltz's 1959 book, *Man, the State and War*, the study of interstate war within the field of International Relations has customarily been divided into "levels of analysis," namely, individual, state and international system. As an analytical device the "levels" lens has important shortcomings, including its lack of attention to the interdependence that exists between distinct variables and the fact that many instances of warfare correspond to factors located between and across the three levels. Nevertheless, since most scholars who use conventional approaches to war distinguish themselves from others based upon what "level" they prioritize, the discussion that follows is structured around the three levels.

Individual

Most students of IR will identify the individual level with the first and second of Hans Morgenthau's (2005: 4–7) "six principles of political realism," which claim that the laws of politics are rooted in an unaltered human nature, and that the main driver of human (and by extension, state) activity is the concept of interest defined in terms of power. Realism's pessimism concerning human nature is normally attributed to Hobbes, who explains man's unlimited desire for power in *Leviathan* (1651) in the following way: men are equal by nature and free to pursue their (primarily selfish) desires; power is a basic tool to pursue such desires; equality between men creates mistrust and fear of death; and mistrust and fear of death create a perpetual state of war (state of nature) in which competition, mutual fear and the search for glory are the basic causes of violence.[4]

Contemporary debates on the sources of human aggression tend to be divided along the "nature–nurture" axis, that alleges that such conduct is inherent to human nature or learned via social and cultural factors present in the environment. Ethology, evolutionary biology and primatology are three fields that have advanced arguments concerning animal behavior from the 1960s onward (Cashman 2014). The first, pioneered by authors such as Konrad Lorenz (1966), points to the similarities in the aggressive instincts of all species, linked to the defense of territory, food and reproduction. According to Lorenz, although aggression and violence are spontaneous traits (not environmentally or socially induced), species develop mechanisms to inhibit their use, also as a means of preservation. In the case of humans, the author believed that weapons of mass destruction largely eliminated such inhibitors of violence common to other species, even though rituals of aggression (such as sports) could counteract war by channeling violent impulses elsewhere.

The second, evolutionary biology, also posits, drawing from Darwin's theory of natural selection, that species' behavior, including violence, is an inbred trait related to adaptation and preservation. Richard Dawkins' 1976 theory of the "selfish gene" continues to be a definitive statement in this respect. According to this author (Dawkins 1990), from an evolutionary perspective species act as a result of genes competing to replicate, not necessarily species competing to reproduce or defend territory. Therefore, selfish genes drive species' activity, sometimes acting to the detriment of individual organisms. In the author's view, there is then no human or animal agency, no free will, but just the genetic drive for replication, whereas traits such as altruism and generosity have to be taught. Dawkins refers to these ideas as "memes," the cultural equivalent of genes that are passed from brain to brain.

Primatology is a third strand of thinking that has sought to explain aggression and violence. Jane Goodall is perhaps the most famous primatologist, given her fieldwork with chimpanzees that led her to show that intentional and offensive violence is not particular to just humans. In their work on apes, Richard Wrangham and Dale Peterson (1996) follow up on this finding to show that primates do more than just defend territory in order to survive. Rather, they invade the borders of their neighbors, conduct raids and even commit sexual violence. The authors conclude that such violence can be attributed to "demonic" male behavior, similar to that of human males, in which violence is used to control women, annihilate rival males and maintain patriarchal social structures. In contrast, Wrangham and Peterson (1996) identify the bonobo species, whose DNA is equally shared with humans, as more peaceful and harmonious. Contrary to other chimps, bonobo society is ruled by females, whose shared control over reproduction makes them equal to males. The authors' analysis lends itself to the idea that aggressive state attitudes, as seen in patriotism and war, are the result of the masculine defense of community and/or power, an argument largely supported by feminist theory, as we shall soon see.

Cognitive psychologist Steven Pinker (2002) falls in the middle of the nature/nurture divide. This author describes violence as a social, political, biological and psychological phenomenon. Greater understanding of the human mind is crucial for understanding how human beings make sense of their surroundings and decide to be violent. Instead of viewing aggression as an aberration, Pinker considers it an organized, goal-oriented activity. The human brain has been wired through evolutionary processes to include traits such as fear, revenge and anger, that can incite humans to violence. Nevertheless, the author shows that the human mind and human nature are comprised of diverse impulses that lead to both violent and peaceful conduct, and many things in between. Given that human nature is not just one thing, but a complex system of interacting and dynamic parts and logics, Pinker is confident that nature is not destiny.

In addition to factors residing within people (genetic, biological or otherwise) and personality traits,[5] social psychology also examines environmental and social factors that trigger or increase war's likelihood. Among these, obedience to legitimate authority, the possibility of deflecting responsibility for one's acts, conformity to group pressure and the classification of individuals as non-persons, figure prominently (see Box 7.2).

BOX 7.2 WHY "GOOD" PEOPLE DO "BAD" THINGS

In 1961, social psychologist Stanley Milgram, driven by the need to understand the Nazi war crimes committed during the Holocaust, conducted an experiment to evaluate people's obedience to authority. The experiment consisted of participant volunteers delivering electric shocks to actor "subjects." Volunteers were instructed by a "scientist" to deliver increasingly higher levels of electric shock each time a wrong answer was given. Once shocks reached allegedly painful or lethal levels, the "subjects" would plead each volunteer to stop, scream out in pain and eventually become silent, feigning unconsciousness or even death. Beyond the ethical controversy surrounding the experiment itself, Milgram's findings about people's tendency to obey authority and to not feel remorse about doing harm to others if such harm is in the name of some lofty objective, like "science," has been shown to apply in many other circumstances (although how much people agree with the orders or with the identity of the person giving them may influence their decision too). Ten years later, Philip Zimbardo conducted his now famous Stanford Prison Experiment, in which a mock prison was created with student volunteers assigned the roles of prisoners and prison guards. As the experiment evolved, and with no instruction whatsoever, those students playing the role of prison guards became more and more violent and authoritarian, adopting aggressive, humiliating and sadistic behavior towards the student inmates. In his book, *The Lucifer Effect*, Zimbardo (2006) explores the Abu Ghraib prison tortures committed at this clandestine site by male and female U.S. soldiers and documented extensively with "trophy photos," from a similar perspective. He argues that human behavior is influenced more by situations than by the human mind or genetic makeup. In particular, in external environments characterized by the dehumanization of the "other," anonymity, obedience to authority, the ability to deflect personal responsibility, conformity to group norms and conduct, the exercise of power without oversight, the active commission of violence or evil (intentional actions that harm, demean, dehumanize or destroy), or its passive tolerance or acceptance, become possible. In addition to the heinous crimes in Abu Ghraib, Zimbardo also explains the Rwandan genocide, mass suicide, sexual violence and military and police torture, from a similar lens.

State

Approaches to war located at the state level can be divided into dyadic theories that focus on interactions between pairs of states and monadic (or individual) state features. The democratic (or liberal) peace thesis is by far the dominant explanation of war and peace in International Relations. Democratic peace theorists argue that war is inexistent between democracies due to the political culture and the institutional and structural features that characterize this type of political regime. Namely, democracies are (allegedly) characterized by common values and norms of peaceful conflict resolution, the accountability of elected public officials, free, regular and universal elections, individual rights and freedoms, checks and balances, and a free press, all of which operate to constrain aggressive behavior, at least in relations with like-minded democratic states (Doyle 1996; Russett 1993; Ish-Shalom 2013). Democratic peace theorists also assume that interactions between democracies are viewed in positive sum terms, mutual benefit and cooperation, in large measure due to the economic interdependence that customarily exists between them (Huth and Alee 2004). In contrast, in non-democratic regimes, where political power is not constrained by law nor society, elections (if held) are not free, nor is the press, leaders can repress the population at will, and little to no accountability exists, the use of violence and aggressive behavior is expected internationally (Russett 1993, 2013).

Whereas between democratic states it is assumed that decision makers will apply the same rules of "peaceful engagement" in their dealings among each other, and that shared political culture and institutional logics will allow them to identify win–win scenarios that enable them to overcome dilemmas of collective action that are typical in an anarchical international system (Moravcsik 1997) and that make the use of violence too costly, if not unthinkable, outside such zones of peace, liberal democratic states conduct themselves quite differently. Namely, they are just as, if not more, aggressive than non-democracies in their dealings with the latter (Doyle 1996). Although "the 'liberal' causes for which democracies are willing to fight are always thought of as serving the common good" (Huth and Alee 2004: 196), in practice war and military intervention are usually the result of other strategic, economic and political interests, not the defense of democracy and human rights (see Box 7.3).

BOX 7.3 "DEMOCRATIC" INTERVENTIONISM AND THE RESPONSIBILITY TO PROTECT (R2P)

Following the Cold War's end, the question of whether the "international community" should intervene in (non-democratic) countries in which civilian populations are at risk of grave human rights violations led to a revisioning of Article 2(7) of the United Nations Charter (1945) that considers state sovereignty an absolute right. Following the highly controversial "humanitarian" intervention by the United States in Somalia (1993), and international failure to act to prevent the Rwandan genocide (1994) and the Srebrenica massacre in Bosnia-Herzegovina (1995), the International Commission on Intervention and State Sovereignty (ICISS) was tasked by the UN to devise a more politically acceptable and effective doctrine to uphold basic human rights standards across the globe.

The responsibility to protect (R2P), originally formulated in 2001, switches from the previous language of the "right" of the international community to intervene to one of a "duty" to protect the civilian population, while also redefining sovereignty in terms of state responsibility towards citizens, instead of merely state rights. Its three pillars include the responsibility of the state to protect its citizens, that of the international community to help the state fulfill this obligation and, in instances in which states do not protect their citizens, international responsibility to adopt decisive action, including diplomacy, humanitarian aid and the use of force. For the latter to be legitimately invoked, there must be an existing threat against the civilian population of genocide, ethnic cleansing, violations of international humanitarian law or crimes against humanity, and force must be minimal, extraordinary and temporary.

Although a number of UN Resolutions have made reference to R2P in cases such as Burundi, Congo, Ivory Coast, South Sudan, Central African Republic, Mali, Somalia and Syria, the doctrine faced its main test in Libya in 2011, when the UN Security Council authorized the use of force in that country. Although the alleged objective of the intervention was to respond to atrocious crimes being committed against the Libyan population and to prevent them from worsening, the ulterior motive of most Western powers was to achieve regime change (through the assassination of Muammar al-Qaddafi). Years earlier, when the United States and its "coalition of the willing" invaded Iraq (2003), a similar humanitarian argument was used to justify military action, especially when it was revealed that Saddam Hussein was not producing nor had stockpiles of weapons of mass destruction. More recently, R2P has been called upon to achieve regime change in Syria and Venezuela, even though past experience shows that military intervention, far from being a "solution," tends to prolong civil war, as well as worsen the suffering of those very civilians that the doctrine is allegedly designed to protect.

Additionally, democratic peace theory has little to say about so-called "illiberal" regimes, characteristic of many countries in today's world, both in the global South and the North, in which the causal link between democracy and peace is much less convincing. At the monadic level, non-democracies and democracies tend to act alike when confronted with external or internal crises such as foreign military attacks, declining popularity of leaders and economic stagnation. Namely, they both make frequent use of the "rally round the flag effect," in which citizens are prompted to unite with and defend their leaders in confirmation of nationalist, patriotic sentiments (Lai and Reiter 2005).

International system

Explanations of war located at the level of the international system point to anarchy, on the one hand, and global capitalism, on the other, as two structural features that create conditions conducive to conflict and war. The logic of anarchy is primarily associated with realism. For realists of all stripes (classical, neoclassical, neo, offensive, defensive), a series of features explains the link between anarchy and war (Waltz 1979; Mearsheimer 1994/95: 9–12): (1) the international system is characterized by anarchy, understood as the decentralization of political authority and the absence of global government; (2) in an anarchical system there is no way to control or sanction the actions of states, other than via state activity itself; (3) conflict thus constitutes a natural condition in which war is always a possibility. Within an international system so constituted, realists assume that states fear for their security and survival, as they can never be certain of the intentions of other states (even friendly ones), and act accordingly in terms of "self-help" and the search for (military) power as a means to this end.

Two of the main byproducts of the so-called security dilemma (see Chapter 10) that emerges from each state adopting similar measures to guarantee its security and survival, are the balance of power and arms races, both of which can and have ended in war. For students of the global South, it may seem particularly vexing that global South states too seem to act in the fashion predicted by realism, as the longstanding India–Pakistan nuclear weapons race or conventional arms races in regions such as Latin America appear to suggest. However, subsequent sections of the chapter will show that narrowing discussions of balance of power and arms races to strategic, military concerns ignores the deep links that such logics have with state and society building processes (Abraham 2009) and with the "postcolonial anxiety" (Krishna 1999) that often leads elites to mimic logics practiced by the West/North.

In contrast to the logic of anarchy, which implies decentralization and the relative independence of state "units," global capitalism entails a dramatically different type of ordering, characterized by the hierarchical placing of countries within the international division of labor, interdependence between countries (given this very division) and fluid interaction between the global and the local levels (given that capitalism knows no boundaries). For Marxists, the expansive nature of capitalism and its tendency to domination and exploitation, constitute the main sources of conflict between and within countries, and among distinct social classes, most notably the elite, capitalist class and the working class.

In the case of the international system, Vladimir Lenin's (1917/1975) theory of imperialism as a monopolistic stage of capitalism explains the outbreak of World War I in terms of the increasing scarcity of raw materials and foodstuffs in Europe, excess capital resulting from decreasing rates of return on investments on the continent, and the creation of industrial-financial monopolies resulting from the concentration of capitalist production, all of which led countries such as Great Britain, France and Germany to seek out colonies with an eye to continue expanding. The European partition of the African continent between 1876 and 1900, and the conversion of independent countries such as those of Latin America into what Lenin (1917/1975: 108) describes as "semi-colonies" serving similar purposes of resource extraction and investment, were some of the main results of this process. However, once territorial acquisition was exhausted, imperialist war became almost inevitable, according to the author. As we will see in the next section, capitalist exploitation of natural resources and intrastate war in the global South is a recurring theme.

Immanuel Wallerstein's (2004) world system theory constitutes another attempt to explain the impact of the global capitalist economy on state–society relations at the global and local levels. According to this author, global capitalism creates a division of labor (that includes economic but also intellectual production) that concentrates wealth and development in "core" countries and zones to the detriment of "peripheral" ones. In this sense, core and periphery are strongly interlinked in highly asymmetrical and detrimental relations (Wallerstein 2004: 88). In addition to underdevelopment, inequality and poverty, Latin American dependency theorists also underscore that the negative interdependence resulting from global capitalist logics has profound effects on peripheral states and sovereign statehood (Cardoso 1972; Tickner 2014; on dependence, see Chapters 11 and 13). If indeed, as we will soon discuss in our exploration of intrastate war, what the dominant literature describes as "state weakness" is one of the drivers of internal warfare, neo-Marxist approaches such as world systems theory and dependency may shed light on the colonial and capitalist origins of this problem, even though their main focus is not war.

Constructivism is largely at odds with realist (and Marxist) explanations of war. Constuctivist theorists would not completely disagree that sometimes international anarchy creates conditions of possibility for violent confrontation between states. However, by underscoring the social construction of reality and the varied meanings that states assign to the material world, including other states, the "why" of warfare (and of peace) is quite different. Namely, states relate to each other based upon interests and identities that are not fixed or preordained, but that result from distinct forms of social interaction in which factors such as language and norms play a key role. "Who" a state is thus results from intersubjective meanings that determine its interests and actions, as well as its readings of "who" other states are and how to relate to them.

In his now famous critique of neorealism, Alexander Wendt (1992) suggests that self-help and the security dilemma are not a logical nor inevitable result of anarchy. Rather, different cultures of anarchy emerge from distinct types of intersubjective state identity, some more conducive to violent conflict than others. In this sense, for constructivism not only is the state a socially constructed actor, but war too can be considered a social practice that results from a certain kind of (antagonistic) identity (Wilmer 2002: 51).[6]

Intrastate wars in the global South

Before the Cold War's end, the majority of conventional approaches to war and conflict in the field of International Relations focused on the two world wars and bipolar tensions between the United States and Soviet Union. However, the virtual absence of war and large-scale violent conflict between states, especially the great powers, following World War II and the Korean War, shifted scholarly attention towards intrastate conflicts in the global South.[7] According to the Uppsala Conflict Data Program/Peace Research Institute Oslo (UCDP/PRIO) datasets, these grew steadily between the early 1970s and early 1990s, and peaked to over 50 total in 1992, in large measure due to the dissolution of the Soviet Union and its former satellites, including Yugoslavia.[8] Although the total number dropped thereafter, once again, between 2012 and 2016, the numbers rose to all time highs. This type of war continues to account for almost the totality of violent conflicts in the world. Between the 1990s and 2017, Africa and Asia concentrated lion's share of intrastate conflicts, followed by the Middle East and the Americas. Following the terrorist attacks of September 11, 2001, the U.S. invasion of Afghanistan and Iraq, and the subsequent GWOT, internationalized intrastate conflicts, in which external actors participate actively and provide troop support, have also grown considerably (see Chapter 8).

During the past 20 years, a burgeoning literature has appeared to address the prevalence of internal war. Mary Kaldor's (1999, 2013) "new war" thesis has been the source of many scholarly efforts to theorize civil wars, mostly by way of critique (Kalyvas 2001) and nuancing of the author's arguments. Kaldor maintains that violent conflict in today's world is fundamentally different due to globalization, which has nurtured distinct types of organized violence originating from the crisis of state legitimacy and public revenues, and the privatization of violence. These "new" wars are different from "old" ones in terms of: (1) the actors involved, namely, a complex mix of regular armed forces, guerrillas, paramilitaries, mercenaries and private security contractors; (2) the objectives that are pursued, deriving from the presence of conflicting identities of an ethnic, linguistic or religious nature, instead of geopolitical or ideological goals; (3) the methods employed, which are unrelated to territorial control but rooted instead in control over populations, leading to widespread violence against civilians and forced displacement; and (4) their sources of funding, which are derived primarily from the depredation of resources and wealth (not control over state resources) via pillage, kidnapping, extortion, illicit trafficking and contributions from diasporas (Kaldor 1999). This latter point is key to the author's claim that in "new" wars the distinction between politically driven armed activity and local and transnational criminal behavior is extremely blurry.

Although the space of this chapter is insufficient to provide an exhaustive survey of the distinct approaches that exist to intrastate war, four recurring themes are visible in the literature: state weakness and statebuilding, the role of natural resources, identity-based divisions and sociopolitical grievances.

State weakness and statebuilding

Numerous authors have long argued that a nexus exists between the absence of stateness and intrastate conflict (for example, Zartman 1995; Holsti 1996; Reno 1998; Kaldor 1999; Rotberg 2004; Marten 2012; see too, Chapter 8). Their central argument is that states that lack the ability to exercise basic functions such as the monopoly over violence, territorial control, the exercise of legitimate and centralized authority, and the provision of basic goods (including security) are prone to the emergence of distinct forms of power contestation and violence. Following the terrorist attacks of 9/11, it became almost "commonsense" that the absence of "law and order" and the presence of "ungoverned spaces" in weak state contexts provided fertile ground for criminal and terrorist activity.

In addition to state weakness, the literature also points to incomplete statebuilding processes as a related cause of civil war, in keeping with Charles Tilly's (1992) claim that in the European context, war made the state and vice versa. Essentially, Tilly argues that war contributes to state formation by creating the need to extract resources and revenues from the local population and economy, which in turn requires the use of repression to eliminate rivals and to organize extractive activities more efficiently. This leads to the creation of agents of repression (militaries), to administrative structures required to manage resources and ultimately, to the forging of collective (national) identities.

In discussing the conditions of state formation in the global South (or third world) Mohammed Ayoob (1995) takes issue with Tilly's predatory theory by arguing that "postcolonial" states were borne out of dramatically different (and ultimately unfavorable) processes. Namely, in contrast to Europe, the statebuilding process has been comparatively fast (spanning years instead of centuries), did not make use of wide-scale violence, was conducted without material resources, made use of a single format ill-suited to local realities (the nation-state), and was subject to intensive international intervention and rules of the game quite different from those characterizing the European experience, such as universal human rights standards. According to the author, the lack of stateness characteristic of most "postcolonial" states is the main source of their security predicament. Insecurity is the product of the lack of unconditional legitimacy of state borders and state institutions, inadequate social cohesion and lack of consensus on fundamental issues of social, economic and political organization (Ayoob 1995: 28; see too, Chapter 10). In consequence, statebuilding efforts and the struggle to build state legitimacy are viewed as key sources of violent conflict. Echoing Ayoob's analysis, Ann Hironaka (2005) argues that states in the global South, in trying to adopt the blueprints created (and universalized) by the West, exhibit perverse logics in which violent conflicts become not only likely, but more difficult to resolve, given the absence of state and governmental capacities to attend to their root causes.[9]

Resources

Greed motivation explanations are derived from the experiences of those countries in which internal war has coincided with the existence of lootable natural resources, such as oil (Nigeria, Libya, Colombia), diamonds (Angola, Democratic Republic of the Congo, Liberia, Sierra Leone), opium (Afghanistan) and cocaine (Colombia) and in which violent non-state actors seem more interested in profit than military victory or state capture. Paul Collier, both individually and in co-authorship with Anke Hoeffler, is largely responsible for the now popular idea that economic greed, not sociopolitical grievance, be it economic inequality, ethnic divisions or political repression and exclusion, is at the root of civil war (see for example, Collier 2000; Collier and Hoeffler 2004). According to these authors, the root causes of and motivations for armed rebellion are ultimately less important to understanding the onset of civil war than the capacity of armed actors to finance their activities, either via looting or contributions from diasporas residing abroad. In this sense, the likelihood of intrastate conflict is strongly linked to the economic greed of rebels, which Collier (2000) describes as quasi-criminal actors, and their utilitarian calculations concerning the availability of resources required to conduct a rebellion. Although the greed thesis does not deny the presence of collective grievances in all instances of civil war, these are viewed less as a causal variable and more as a "smokescreen" employed by rebels to justify their armed struggle and to maintain a semblance of legitimacy among the civilian population.

James Fearon and David Laitin (2003) concur that those factors associated with rebel profit opportunities have greater explanatory weight in accounting for intrastate war, and also confirm Collier and Hoeffler's argument that ethnic or religious diversity add little to the probability of civil war onset. However, they identify a causal link between state weakness and the appearance of armed insurgency. In their view, rebels weigh the viability of armed rebellion in relation to the commodities that they can extract before and during violent conflict, but the relative degree of state strength/weakness also affects the likelihood that a war will begin (or not). Taken together, the factors mentioned tend to create a "conflict trap" in which the lack of economic development and state capacity increase the likelihood of conflict, and the resilience of conflict affects the viability of economic development (Fearon and Laitin 2003; Collier and Hoeffler 2004).

The "greed" thesis has given way to more nuanced studies that attempt to identify the distinct roles played by primary goods (oil, precious stones such as diamonds, and drugs) in violent conflict. Such is the case of Michael Ross's (2004, 2015) work on the so-called "resource curse" that sustains that natural resources tend to have a negative effect on democracy, governance, economic development and the incidence of violent conflict. In testing the impact of different kinds of commodities on the onset of civil war, via looting by potential rebels, grievances of local populations or state dependence on resources that lead to state weakening, the author finds little to no causal evidence, except in the case of oil, which Ross views as a key driver of state weakening. This finding underscores the lack of consensus among those studying resources as to the causal mechanisms at play in the onset, resilience and intensity of intrastate war (Ross 2015: 250), leading to the conclusion that resources do not fate countries automatically to war or state incapacity, but that distinct trajectories are shaped by a number of factors, including state–society relations, geographical location and legal-institutional factors such as clearly defined property rights and concentration of land ownership (see Nugent and Robinson 2011; Rettberg et al. 2014).

Land

Informality and inequality in land and property rights, in particular in agrarian zones are at the root of most internal armed conflicts around the world, and are customarily exacerbated by warfare, thus constituting a key challenge to peace-building as well. And yet, they are virtually ignored by scholars who focus on greed and the resource curse. Indeed, although "research and analysis of violent conflict ... has adjusted ... to focus on categories such as ethnicity, inequalities (vertical and horizontal), poverty and unemployment, mineral resource endowment, elite bargains, economic opportunities" (Cramer and Richards 2011: 278), other equally important factors continue to be understudied. The agrarian, land-based roots of conflict are one of these, as has been observed in cases from across the globe, including Bosnia-Herzegovina, Cambodia, Burundi, Colombia, Timor-Leste, Uganda and Rwanda (see Takeuchi 2014). Indeed, it could be argued that what are typically described nowadays as wars of greed in which warlords seek out individual, selfish gain, have much deeper historical roots in principled struggles related to unequal access to land and property (Chauveau and Richards 2008; Peluso and Lund 2011).

Local inequalities in land holdings are exacerbated by global dynamics too. What the literature refers to as foreign "land grabs" are the result of processes associated with neo-liberal globalization and the rising demand for food and natural resources by Northern countries that promote large-scale commercial enterprises to satisfy these needs, to the detriment of small-scale subsistence farming (Borras et al. 2012: 403). As the crisis of the ecosystem increases, affecting food, energy and water sources, among others, understanding land ownership concentration and its links to violent conflict within a broader context of global capitalist dynamics is becoming more and more crucial.

Identity

Identity-based explanations, in turn, focus on the politics and ideology of identity, be it ethnic, religious or class as the main source of conflict. Racial, ethnic, religious and less so, class, identities are viewed as the source of privilege or inequality in different war-torn societies that fuel grievances. In interstate conflicts too, such as that existing between India and Pakistan, mutually exclusive ideas/identities of nation-state are rooted at the core of ongoing confrontation. In the greed versus grievance debate, critics have argued that although greed (of profit-seeking state elites and rebel groups) is present in most armed conflicts, and can indeed transform the nature of intrastate war, it is not the main cause of war. Similarly, while ethnic, religious and other identity-based differences may partially account for conflict in some cases (Doyle and Sambanis 2000; Sambanis 2001), material factors associated with injustices such as poverty, inequality and exclusion have to be factored into any comprehensive analysis of civil war, particularly when they are perceived as inequality and injustice between social groups and are thus capable of mobilizing collective (armed) action.

In seeking out a more satisfactory explanation that takes into account the three variables mentioned (grievances, identities and greed), Zartman and Arnson (2005) make the case for an integrated analytical framework in which need, creed and greed constitute three "acts" that lead to the onset of intrastate war. First, the deprivation of some basic need, be it security, equality or sociopolitical inclusion, combined with state corruption and clientelist practices, customarily creates a sense of injustice. Given the power vacuums created by state weakness, collective grievances provide justification for armed actors seeking to fill them. Second, in countries with low levels of sociopolitical cohesion and multiple nations, communities, ethnicities or races, identity plays a role in explaining violent conflict. Namely, the shared sense of collective discrimination (or horizontal inequality) based precisely upon such identities helps legitimate the justice of the armed struggle and popular support for it. Third, while resources are key to understanding how civil war is fueled, it is only in the more advanced stages of warfare that economic divides become a motive in themselves and violent non-state actors start behaving in predatory or criminalized fashion, dramatically altering the logic of some intrastate conflicts.[10] This framework is largely echoed by Shiping Tan (2015), who proposes a general theory about the onset of ethnic war in which emotional factors such as fear, hatred and resentment are filters through which deep drivers such as inequality, exclusion and dysfunctional political institutions necessarily pass.

Alternatives

Strictly defined categorizations of war and attention to singular causes (be they state weakness, resources, identity or grievance) tend to overlook the complex, multilevel and geoculturally situated processes through which war emerges. Equally important, the majority of the scholarly work highlighted in previous sections of this chapter, with significant exceptions such as the analysis of land rights, ignores the ways in which intrastate wars in the global South are linked to *longue-durée* dynamics associated with the political economy of colonialism and neoliberal globalization (Zeleza 2008; Barkawi 2013).

Contrary to the question of "what" causes war, post-positivist theory, of which postcolonialism, decoloniality and feminist approaches are all examples, is concerned with "how" certain questions become important, how differences become naturalized and how problems, including war, become constituted in the very act of theorizing about them. Although the analysis of war is largely absent in postcolonial accounts of IR and politics, a research agenda would entail contesting the Eurocentric nature of war studies and making the colonial assumptions central to portrayals of war in the global South visible, including what such theorizing *does* in terms of constituting the Southern other as different and inferior. By way of illustration, let us briefly remember the story that this chapter began with. As discussed in the introduction, the film *Hotel Rwanda* represents the genocide as a struggle between good, civilized and ultimately Westernized Tutsi victims (and Hutu defenders such as Paul) and their evil, uncivilized Hutu oppressors, thus creating an uncomplicated storyline that reinforces stereotypes already familiar to Western spectators and bypasses a more nuanced and historically sensitive reading of this event.

Postcolonialism

How difference is conceptualized and politicized, although a central concern of post-colonial scholars, is rarely considered in analyses of war. However, as we have seen, variances between ethnic, religious and ideological groups within countries, and the "different" nature of war-prone states in the global South, occupy a key place in most explanations. Postcolonial scholarship has long been concerned with the histor-ical processes through which difference has been coded and represented in such a way that othering occurs (see Chapter 17). Naeem Inayatullah and David Blaney (2004: 10–11) show how under colonialism and modernity, "difference becomes infer-iority, and the possibility of a common humanity requires assimilation," with which "knowledge of the other, inflicted by the equation of difference and inferiority, becomes a means for the physical destruction, enslavement, or cruel exploitation of the other."

In the case of the scholarly literature discussed above that identifies state weakness as a cause of war, the multiple adjectives used to describe deficits in stateness (quasi, failed, backward, e) reproduce representational practices in which global South states are defined in opposition to the modern nation-state model that allegedly exists in the West and North, and solely in terms of what they lack (see Chapter 8). Such "empti-ness" or "nothingness," argues Achille Mbembe (2001: 1–4), begs to be filled by colonial contents, via either insistence on statemaking (a la Tilly) or foreign interven-tion. The problem is that state "weakness," rather than proof of imperfect develop-ment and modernization in the global South, is the particular form that the state takes there, something underscored by postcolonial and dependency authors alike (Cardoso 1972; Krishna 1999). Nevertheless, in their "postcolonial anxiety" (Krishna 1999: 240–241), elites mimic processes and categories that have supposedly worked in the West/North, and employ violence against potential rivals and innocent civilians in their name, even though the modern nation-state is viewed with suspicion or even rejected as the main form of organization of political community in many parts of the non-West. Indeed, a postcolonial lens highlights the ways in which deeply entrenched colonial categories such as ethnicity, religion, culture, race or tribe become the main axes by which political, social and economic processes are organized, and how people and countries become stuck to these, to the detriment and erasure of many others (Behera 2006).

Such critiques constitute an invitation to examine more critically the theories and cat-egories used to explain war, to interrogate the assumptions of inferiorized difference that underwrite them, and to think about the power implications of such readings, including the justification of specific interventions required to "fix" them (Wai 2012). Similarly, postcolonialism suggests that a key site (typically ignored) to build more historically grounded accounts of war (both interstate and intrastate) is imperialism and colonialism (Barkawi and Laffey 2006), if not global capitalism more generally. One such account is offered by Frantz Fanon and Ashis Nandy, who explore, albeit in distinct ways, the psychology/pathology of colonialism. Both authors, psychoanalysts by training, examine the bodily effects of the physical violence underwriting colonialism and the colonization of the mind, as well as the continuation of pathologies internalized under colonial rule way beyond its formal end. Nandy (1983: 72) observes psychosocial decay in both colonizers and colonized, resulting largely from the definition of the Western and non-Western self as negation (non-Oriental) on the one hand, and inferiority (self-loathing) and mimicry on the other, even though the Oriental opposite too is a Western construct. Fanon (1952, 1963) traces a similar affectation in the case of African blacks, whose identity/culture is erased by colonization and replaced by internalization and reproduction of Western whiteness and racist attitudes. In consequence, colonialism entails "a systematic negation" of all attributes of humanity of the colonized, who are constantly asking, "who am I?" (Fanon 1963: 250). Given that for Fanon, colonial rule employs violence (that also makes the colonizer mentally ill) to convert the colonized into a dehumanized and animalized "native," violence alone provides a collective remedy through which the colonial subject releases her aggression, overcomes self-loathing, regains her humanity and takes control of her political life (an argument rejected by Nandy).

Both authors underscore the danger of national elites recycling colonial logics after independence, with which violence and war continue to be an issue. In particular, psychological affectations are transferred to and materialized in categories such as nation-state, modernization and development, and derive from the impulse of postcolonial elites to suppress traditional ones and to adjust to them, even though they are vestiges of colonialism.

Feminism

Feminism too offers a distinct reading of war and violence of particular relevance for thinking differently about this problem from/in the global South and the North. In addition to highlighting the role that gender plays in structuring knowledge about and practices of global and local politics in ways that reinforce hegemonic views of masculinity and that devalue femininity, along with the distinct social actors to which these traits are customarily ascribed, feminist theory sheds light on the links that exist between masculinity and militarism, and on the deep interdependence of distinct forms of violence practiced at all levels of human activity.

Laura Sjoberg (2013: 5) defines gender as "the socially constructed expectation that persons perceived to be members of a biological sex category will have certain characteristics." The resulting ideas of manhood and womanhood are interrelated (meaning that one cannot exist without the other) and have a profound effect on distinct realms of social practice that often go unnoticed, given their alleged correspondence to "natural" differences between men and women. Among these, "[b]inary logocentrism engenders a structuring of paired opposites that at once differentiates one term from the other, prefers one to the other, and arranges them hierarchically, displacing the subordinate term beyond the boundary of what is significant and desirable" (Peterson and True 1999: 19).

This dichotomous structure not only assigns superior value to allegedly masculine traits, among them, rationality, strength, assertiveness and independence, and inferior worth to feminine ones (irrationality, sensitivity, weakness, emotion, passivity), but also naturalizes the divide between the public sphere, where politics and war allegedly take place, and the private sphere, in which home and family prevail. The feminist slogan, "the personal is political," seeks to underscore the interrelatedness of public/private activity and the markedly political nature of personal (private) life. In the study of International Relations, nearly exclusive focus on states and on the public sphere, in which (white) males are dominant, simply reinforces women's invisibility. In her classic 1989 study, *Bananas, Beaches and Bases*, Cynthia Enloe (2014) explores distinct "private" spaces in which women's roles in activities such as diplomacy and war are critical.

Violence is one of the main global problems for which feminists have sought to undo the public/private divide. Johan Galtung (1969) is widely recognized in peace studies for expanding our understanding of violence to include its structural manifestations, defined as violence built into social and political structures that results in the unequal distribution of power and resources such as wealth, health and education. However, as Catia Confortini (2006) shows, by ignoring the gendered nature of all types of violence, the author's theorization of direct physical violence, indirect structural violence and cultural violence falls short of explaining how the three types of violence, and violences occurring at distinct scales, are strongly interrelated.

Feminist theorists also show that gender can be used as a causal variable to explain war and violence where masculinity and militarism come together. Indeed, "gendered militarism" is a common feature of social and political life across the globe, and warmaking, notwithstanding its historical transformation, continues to be rooted in gendered constructions of the military (Sjoberg and Via 2010: 3). At the most basic level, the military establishment is a key site of hypermasculinity in which success on the battlefield has long been associated with a series of masculine traits that military training seeks to cultivate. This is one reason why the presence of women, homosexuals and transgender in the military continues to be viewed as a threat (and in the latter two cases, is still illegal in some countries). However, in describing militarism as a widely accepted ideology about how humans and the world work, including the proneness to conflict, the naturalness of having enemies, and the need to prove manliness in times of crisis, Cynthia Enloe (2004: 219) underscores the strong link that exists between it, masculinity and widespread militarization.

According to the author, in addition to patriarchy, militarism is also closely intertwined with nationalism (Enloe 2004). Although war is typically portrayed as an affair in which brave and selfless masculine heroes defend feminized, innocent and helpless victims, namely women and children (the so-called "myth of protection"), as bearers of "honor" and reproducers of "nation," women's bodies are also battlegrounds for reinforcing hegemonic masculinity and humiliating and emasculating the enemy by attacking its females (Confortini 2006: 346; Sjoberg and Via 2010: 5). In consequence, wartime rape and sexual violence are widely practiced by all armed actors, including state militaries.

Finally, feminists argue that gender binarism and the privileging of (hegemonic) masculinity over non-dominant masculinities and femininity is the root cause of naturalized power relations that underwrite diverse types of asymmetry, domination and violence. Intersectionality constitutes the main way in which they propose understanding that factors such as gender, ethnicity, race, class and sexuality do not act independently of each other, but are highly interdependent and mutually reinforcing. Patricia Hill Collins and Sirma Bilge (2016: 2) argue that social inequality and the practices that are derived from it, including discrimination and violence, are "shaped not by a single axis of social division ... but by many axes that work together and influence each other." For example, the internally displaced population in Colombia, which numbers over seven million, affects poor rural (class), Afrodescendant and indigenous (race and ethnicity), women and children (gender) disproportionately in comparison to other social groups.

In the specific case of war and militarization, masculinized, racialized, classed and sexualized logics often go unnoticed. However, both postcolonialism and feminism expose how difference is otherized and inferiorized. In the specific case of feminist theory, the ways in which distinct social actors are devalued and dehumanized via feminization is of particular interest. As both Spike Peterson (2010: 20) and Cynthia Enloe (2004: 355) argue, uncivilized, incompetent, irrational and even threatening "others" in the global South tend also to be represented as "feminine" or "childlike," justifying tutelage, protection and punishment by superior actors that are civilized and masculinized. In this sense, what intersectionality *does* more than what it *is*, is of key interest (Collins and Bilge 2016: 5) (see Box 7.4).

BOX 7.4 WHEN FEMINIZATION AND OTHERIZATION MEET

Full Metal Jacket (Stanley Kubrick 1987) is a film about the Vietnam War that explores the racial, ethnic and sexist discourses employed in the social construction of U.S. soldiers and the representation of the Vietnamese enemy. In order to expose these dynamics, the director examines the everyday practices entailed in military training, and the war as experienced and represented by its American combatants. The first half of the film documents the loss of individuality and the transformation of young men into marines, a process that requires both demanding physical and tactical training, and dehumanization via verbal and physical aggression. The most visible "other" among the trainees, who threatens their collective masculinity in his slowness, incompetence, corpulence and femininity, is targeted by the drill instructor and ultimately the entire group, with humiliation and extreme violence, leading him to mental derangement. In the second half, the recently socialized and masculinized marines find themselves in Vietnam, a country that is introduced to the spectator in the figure of a prostitute, in other words, a deviant and corrupt female "gook" who is thought to also carry infectious disease (tuberculosis). Throughout this part of the film, Kubrick narrates war scenes and collective experiences in which gendered and racialized discourses about "us" and "them" are a recurring theme among the U.S. soldiers and their superiors. However, what is most striking about the constitution of the Vietnamese other is the invisibility of the Vietcong enemy throughout the film, with which the director seems to be saying that the social construction of otherness is as much a result of collective U.S. and Western imaginaries as of "realities" on the ground.

Given that the causes and the logics of violence (including war) are difficult, if not impossible to understand if envisioned through singular, exclusionary lenses (gender, class, race) or levels (public versus private), intersectionality works to show that "power relations are to be analyzed both *via their intersections*, for example, of racism and sexism, as well as *across domains of power*, namely, structural, disciplinary and interpersonal" (Collins and Bilge 2016: 55). Therefore, how violence occurring in one realm (for example, sexual and domestic violence rooted in sexism) is related to violence at other levels (excessive police violence against young men of color rooted in racism or warfare against radical Islamism) is of key analytical concern.

Conclusion

As mentioned in the introduction to this chapter, the ways in which the causes of war and violent conflict are analyzed have a strong impact on the solutions devised by the "international community" and individual states for overcoming them. For example, by describing intrastate war as a problem that is prevalent in contexts of weak or failing states, and poverty-stricken populations preyed upon by rapacious armed actors likened to organized criminals (or terrorists), many theories of civil war unwittingly represent the global South as a "corrupt," "backward" and sometimes "threatening" other in which Western/Northern tutelage and ultimately, intervention, become justifiable if not necessary.

Chimamanda Ngozi Adichie's cautionary tale about the dangers of single stories was mentioned in Chapter 1. Although few would dispute the claim that violent conflicts in the global South are the result of some combination of institutional state weakness, poor governance, political instability, poverty and inequality, and identity-based ethnic and racial infighting, it is no less true that for the most part, they are also linked to complex and intertwined logics rooted in colonialism, postcolonalism, neoliberal globalization and patriarchy. As we saw in the final section on alternatives, by adhering to singular causes and ignoring the constitutive effects of knowledge (what it *does*) many dominant explanations of war and conflict not only run the risk of reductionism, but ultimately of reproducing existing stereotypes and power relations that are operative across the globe.

Questions for discussion

1. What are the analytical advantages and disadvantages of concise definitions of war, both qualitative and quantitative?
2. Explain the argument that what war *does* as a political discourse is important for understanding war and provide an example different from those offered in the chapter to illustrate.
3. If war between states is largely a thing of the past, why should the field of International Relations continue to study this phenomenon?
4. In your opinion, which of the factors identified throughout the chapter weighs most in explaining the proneness of the global South to internal war?
5. What is the relationship between colonialism and violent conflict in the global South?
6. What does "postcolonial anxiety" consist of and how might it explain war and violent conflict?
7. How do masculinity and militarism explain war, according to feminists?
8. Identify the similarities that exist between feminist and postcolonial interpretations of war and violence.

Notes

1 I am grateful for the research assistance provided by Mateo Morales Callejas in the preparation of this chapter.
2 The Armed Conflict Dataset of the International Peace Research Institute Oslo, PRIO and the Department of Peace and Conflict Research of Uppsala University, also distinguishes between four types of war: interstate, intrastate, internationalized and related to decolonization.

3 An adequate discussion of terrorism and the war on terror is beyond the scope of this chapter. Since 9/11, the U.S. alone has waged this war in Afghanistan, Iraq, Pakistan, Syria, Libya, Yemen and Somalia through direct military intervention, proxy wars and drone strikes, inflicting alarming material and human costs in those countries, and arguably worsening the situation in each. For a comprehensive approach to terrorism as a distinct form of political violence distinguishable from war, see Chenoweth et al. (2019).

4 In an 1988 article, feminist scholar J. Ann Tickner delivered a systematic critique of Morgenthau's six principles rooted in that author's masculinized assumptions about human nature as "naturally" rooted in domination, power and conflict. See Tickner (2014).

5 The study of the role of personality in political decision-making processes that predispose leaders to warlike behavior has been most prevalent in the subfield of foreign policy analysis. See Hermann et al. (2001).

6 A similar argument was formulated in 1932 by political theorist and Nazi supporter, Carl Schmidt (2007), who deemed "the political" to be rooted in the distinction between friend and enemy. According to the author, political difference and enmity are not necessarily rooted in objective causes, but rather are socially determined. However, contrary to constructivists, Schmidt considers the very existence of the state to be rooted in the differentiation of a given political community from an "enemy" and the willingness to go to war with that "other."

7 It is important to note that civil or intrastate war is not a singular phenomenon, but rather, exhibits a number of types with varied causes, objectives and dynamics, including rebellions against the state, secessionist wars, and inter-communal wars (that may coincide with genocide). See Zeleza (2008: 6–8) for a more elaborate typology.

8 For the most recent versions of the UCDP/PRIO dataset, see the Uppsala Conflict Data Program webpages: https://ucdp.uu.se/#/(consulted July 5, 2019).

9 In contrast to these authors, Partha Chaterjee (2011: 20–21) maintains that political society rarely conforms to the Weberian state's ideal monopoly over violence, and that local politics is usually characterized by the exercise of some mutually defined "normal" level of violence. This is the case of so-called "strong men," whose governance capacities are largely a function of such violence.

10 Nazih Richani (2013) too traces the origins of war to social, economic and political exclusion, land concentration and inequality, but argues that its resilience is due to "war systems" resulting from institutional failure to mediate between antagonistic group interests. Consequently, war is perceived by distinct actors, including the state, military, guerrillas, business elites, paramilitaries and organized crime, to create a positive political economy.

Further reading

Aolaín, Fionnuala Ní, Naomi Cahn, Dina Fracesca Haynes and Nahla Valji (eds) (2018) *The Oxford Handbook of Gender and Conflict*, Oxford: Oxford University Press. A comprehensive study of the role of gender and women in violent conflicts across the globe.

Arjona, Ana, Nelson Kasfir and Zachariah Mampilly (2015) *Rebel Governance in Civil War*, Cambridge: Cambridge University Press. A comparative analysis of how rebel groups exercise governance functions in distinct civil wars in the global South and North.

Hinton, Alexander Laban, Giorgio Shani and Jeremiah Alberg (eds) (2019) *Rethinking Peace*, Lanham: Rowman & Littlefield. A critical, comprehensive and geoculturally sensitive analysis of peace studies.

Nhema, Alfred and Paul Tiyambe Zeleza (eds) (2008) *The Roots of African Conflicts: The Causes and Costs and the Resolutions of African Conflicts*, Athens: Ohio University Press. A multidimensional study of the causes and pathways to resolving conflicts in Africa authored by scholars in/from the continent.

Wai, Zubairu (2012) *Epistemologies of African Conflicts*, New York: Palgrave Macmillan. A critical study of the ways in which dominant knowledge about conflicts in Africa has constituted the continent as an inferior other subject to international tutelage.

References

Abraham, Itty (ed) (2009) *South Asian Cultures of the Bomb*, Bloomington: Indiana University Press.

Autesserre, Séverine (2012) "Dangerous Tales: Dominant Narratives on the Congo and Their Unintended Consequences," *African Affairs*, 111(443): 202–222. DOI: 10.1093/afraf/adr080

Ayoob, Mohammed (1995) *The Third World Security Predicament*, Boulder: Lynne Rienner Publishers.

Barkawi, Tarak (2013) "War, Armed Forces and Society in Postcolonial Perspective," in Sanjay Seth (ed) *Postcolonial Theory and International Relations*, London: Routledge, pp. 87–103.

Barkawi, Tarak and Mark Laffey (2006) "The Postcolonial Moment in Security Studies," *Review of International Studies*, 32(2): 329–352. DOI: 10.1017/S0260210506007054

Behera, Navnita Chadha (2006) *Demystifying Kashmir*, Washington, DC: Brookings Institution Press.

Borras, Saturino M., Cristobal Kay, Sergio Gómez and John Wilkinson (2012) "Land Grabbing and Global Capitalist Accumulation: Key Features in Latin America," *Canadian Journal of Development Studies*, 33(4): 402–416. DOI: 10.1080/02255189.2012.745394

Cardoso, Fernando Henrique (1972) *Estado y sociedad en América Latina*, Buenos Aires: Ediciones Nueva Visión.

Cashman, Greg (2014) *What Causes War? An Introduction to Theories of International Conflict*, Lanham: Rowman & Littlefield.

Chaterjee, Partha (2004) *The Politics of the Governed*, New York: Columbia University Press.

Chaterjee, Partha (2011) *Lineages of Political Society*, New York: Columbia University Press.

Chauveau, Jean-Pierre and Paul Richards (2008) "West African Insurgencies in Agrarian Perspective: Cote d'Ivoire and Sierra Leonc Compared," *Journal of Agrarian Change*, 8(4): 518–552. DOI: 10.1111/j.1471-0366.2008.00179.x

Chenoweth, Erica, Richard English, Andreas Gofas and Stathis N. Kalyvas (eds) (2019) *The Oxford Handbook of Terrorism*, Oxford: Oxford University Press.

Clausewitz, Carl von (1989) *On War* (translated by Michael Howard and Peter Paret), Princeton: Princeton University Press.

Collier, Paul (2000) "Rebellion as a Quasi-Criminal Activity," *Journal of Conflict Resolution*, 44(6): 839–853.

Collier, Paul and Anke Hoeffler (2004) "Greed and Grievance in Civil War," *Oxford Economic Papers*, 56(2004): 563–595.

Collins, Patricia Hill and Sirma Bilge (2016) *Intersectionality*, Malden: Polity Press.

Confortini, Catia C. (2006) "Galtung, Violence, and Gender: The Case for a Peace Studies/Feminism Alliance," *Peace & Change*, 31(3): 333–367. DOI: 10.1111/j.1468-0130.2006.00378.x

Cramer, Christopher and Paul Richards (2011) "Violence and War in Agrarian Perspective," *Journal of Agrarian Change*, 11(3): 277–297. DOI: 10.1111/j.1471-0366.2011.00312.x

Dawkins, Richard (1990) *The Selfish Gene* (2nd edition), Oxford: Oxford University Press.

Doyle, Michael and Nicholas Sambanis (2000) "International Peacebuilding: A Theoretical and Quantitative Analysis," *The American Political Science Review*, 94(4): 779–801. DOI: 10.2307/2586208

Doyle, Michael W. (1996) "Kant, Liberal Legacies and Foreign Affairs," in Michael G. Brown, Sean M. Lynn-Jones and Steven G. Miller (eds) *Debating the Democratic Peace*, Cambridge: The MIT Press, pp. 3–57.

Enloe, Cynthia (2004) *The Curious Feminist*, Berkeley: University of California Press.

Enloe, Cynthia (2014) *Bananas, Beaches and Bases: Making Feminist Sense of International Politics*, Berkeley: University of California Press.

Fanon, Frantz (1952) *Black Skin, White Masks*, London: Pluto Press.

Fanon, Frantz (1963) *The Wretched of the Earth*, New York: Grove Press.

Fearon, James and David Laitin (2003) "Ethnicity, Insurgency, and Civil War," *American Political Science Review* 97(1): 75–90. DOI: 10.1017/S0003055403000534

Galtung, Johan (1969) "Violence, Peace, and Peace Research," *Journal of Peace Research*, 6(3): 167–191.

Harrow, Kenneth W. (2005) "'Un train peut en cacher un autre': Narrating the Rwandan Genocide and Hotel Rwanda," *Research in African Literatures*, 36(4): 223–232. DOI: 10.1353/ral.2005.0165

Hermann, Margaret G., Thomas Preston, Baghat Korany and Timothy M. Shaw (2001) "Who Leads Matters: The Effects of Powerful Individuals," *International Studies Review*, 3(2): 83–131. DOI: 10.1111/1521-9488.00235

Hershberg, Eric and Kevin W. Moore (2002) *The Critical Views of September 11. Analyses from Around the World*, New York: The New Press.

Hironaka, Ann (2005) *Neverending Wars. The International Community, Weak States, and the Perpetuation of Civil War*, Cambridge: Harvard University Press.

Holsti, Kalevi (1996). *State, War, and the State of War*, London: Cambridge University Press.

Huntington, Samuel P. (1998) *The Clash of Civilizations and the Remaking of World Order*, New York: Simon & Schuster.

Huth, Paul K. and Todd L. Alee (2004) *The Democratic Peace and Territorial Conflict in the Twentieth Century*, New York: Columbia University Press.

Inayatullah, Naeem and David L. Blaney (2004) *International Relations and the Problem of Difference*, London: Routledge.

Ish-Shalom, Piki (2013) *Democratic Peace*, Detroit: University of Michigan.

Kaldor, Mary (1999) *New and Old Wars: Organised Violence in a Global Era*, Cambridge: Polity Press.

Kaldor, Mary (2013) "In Defense of New Wars," *Stability: International Journal of Security and Development*, 2(1): 1–16. DOI: 10.5334/sta.at

Kalyvas, Stathis (2001) "New and Old Civil Wars: A Valid Distinction?" *World Politics* 54(1): 99–118.

Krishna, Sankaran (1999) *Postcolonial Insecurities*, Minneapolis: University of Minnesota Press.

Lai, Brian and Dan Reiter (2005) "Rally 'Round the Union Jack? Public Opinion and the Use of Force in the United Kingdom 1948–2001," *International Studies Quarterly*, 49(2): 255–272, 10.1111/j.0020-8833.2005.00344.x

Lenin, V.I. (1917/1975) *El imperialismo, fase superior del capitalismo*, Beijing: Ediciones en Lenguas Extranjeras.

Levy, Jack S. and William R. Thompson (2010) *Causes of War*, Malden: Wiley-Blackwell.

Lorenz, Konrad (1966) *On Aggression*, New York: Harcourt, Brace and World.

Mamdani, Mahmood (2002) *When Victims Become Killers: Colonialism, Nativism and the Genocide in Rwanda*, Princeton: Princeton University Press.

Marez, Curtis (2004) *Drug Wars*, Minneapolis: University of Minnesota Press.

Marten, Kimberly (2012) *Warlords: Strong-Arm Brokers in Weak States*, London & Ithaca: Cornell University Press.

Mbembe, Achille (2001) *On the Postcolony*, Berkeley: University of California Press.

Mearsheimer, John J. (1994/95) "The False Promise of International Institutions," *International Security*, 19(3): 5–49.

Moravcsik, Andrew (1997) "Taking Preferences Seriously: A Liberal Theory of International Politics," *International Studies Quarterly*, 51(4): 513–553.

Morgenthau, Hans J. (2005) *Politics among Nations* (7th edition), New York: McGraw-Hill.

Nandy, Ashis (1983) *The Intimate Enemy*, Delhi: Oxford University Press.

Nugent, Jeffrey B. and James A. Robinson (2011) "Are Factor Endowments Fate?" *Journal of Iberian and Latin American Economic History*, 28(1): 45–62.

Peluso, Nancy Lee and Christian Lund (2011) "New Frontiers of Land Control: Introduction," *Journal of Peasant Studies*, 38(4): 667–681. DOI: 10.1080/03066150.2011.607692

Peterson, V. Spike (2010) "Gendered Identities, Ideologies, and Practices in the Context of War and Militarism," in Laura Sjoberg and Sandra Via (eds) *Gender, War and Militarism: Feminist Perspectives*, Santa Barbara: Praeger, pp. 17–29.

Peterson, V. Spike and Jacqui True (1999) "'New Times' and New Conversations," in Marysia Zalewski and Jane Parpart (eds) *The "Man Question" in International Relations*, Boulder: Westview Press, pp. 14–27.

Pinker, Steven (2002) *The Blank Slate: The Modern Denial of Human Nature*, New York: Viking.

Reno, William (1998) *Warlord Politics and African States*, Boulder: Lynne Rienner.

Rettberg, Angelika, Ralf Leiteritz and Carlo Nasi (2014) "Different Resources, Different Conflicts? A Framework for Understanding the Political Economy of Armed Conflict and Criminality in Colombian Regions," September 22, available at SSRN https://ssrn.com/abstract=2499580 or 10.2139/ssrn.2499580

Richani, Nazih (2013) *Systems of Violence: The Political Economy of War in Colombia*, Albany: SUNY Press.

Ross, Michael (2004) "What Do We Know about Natural Resources and Civil War?" *Journal of Peace Research*, 41(3): 337–356. DOI: 10.1177/0022343304043773

Ross, Michael (2015) "What Have We Learned about the Resource Curse?" *Annual Review of Political Science*, 18: 239–259. DOI: 10.1146/annurev-polisci-052213-040359

Rotberg, Robert I. (ed) (2004). *When States Fail: Causes and Consequences*, Princeton: Princeton University Press.

Russett, Bruce (1993) *Grasping the Democratic Peace*, Princeton: Princeton University Press.

Rwafa, Urther (2010) "Film Representations of the Rwandan Genocide," *African Identities*, 8(4): 389–408. DOI: 10.1080/14725843.2010.513254

Sambanis, Nicholas (2001) "Do Ethnic and Nonethnic Civil Wars Have the Same Causes?: A Theoretical and Empirical Inquiry," *Journal of Conflict Resolution*, 45(3): 259–282. DOI: 10.1177/0022002701045003001

Schmidt Carl (2007) *The Concept of the Political*. Expanded Edition, Chicago: University of Chicago Press.

Shaw, Martin (2009) "Conceptual and Theoretical Frameworks for Organized Violence," *International Journal of Conflict and Violence*, 3(1): 97–106. DOI: 10.4119/UNIBI/ijcv.50

Sjoberg, Laura (2013) *Gendering Global Conflict: Towards a Feminist Theory of War*, New York: Columbia University Press.

Sjoberg, Laura and Sandra Via (2010) "Introduction," in Laura Sjoberg and Sandra Via (eds) *Gender, War and Militarism: Feminist Perspectives*, Santa Barbara: Praeger, pp. 1–16.

Takeuchi, Shinichi (ed) (2014) *Confronting Land and Property Problems for Peace*, London: Routledge.

Tan, Shiping (2015) "The Onset of Ethnic War: A General Theory," *Sociological Theory*, 33(3): 250–279. DOI: 10.1177/0735275115599558

Tickner, J. Ann (2014) *A Feminist Voyage Through International Relations*, Oxford: Oxford University Press.

Tilly, Charles (1992) *Coercion, Capital and European States, AD 990–1992*, Cambridge: Basil Blackwell.

Wai, Zubairu (2012) *Epistemologies of African Conflicts*, New York: Palgrave Macmillan.

Wallerstein, Immanuel (2004) *World-Systems Analysis*, Durham: Duke University Press.

Waltz, Kenneth N. (1959/2001) *Man, the State and War: A Theoretical Analysis*, New York: Columbia University Press.

Waltz, Kenneth N. (1979) *Theory of International Politics*, New York: Random House.

Wendt, Alexander (1992) "Anarchy Is What States Make of It," *International Organization*, 46(2): 391–425.

Wilmer, Franke (2002) *The Social Construction of Man, the State, and War*, New York: Routledge.

Wrangham, Richard and Dale Peterson (1996) *Demonic Males: Apes and the Origins of Human Violence*, New York: Houghton Mifflin.

Zartman, I. William (ed) (1995) *Collapsed States: The Disintegration and Restoration of Legitimate Authority*, Boulder: Lynne Rienner.

Zartman, William and Cynthia Arnson (2005) "Need, Creed, and Greed in Intrastate Conflict," in Cynthia Arnson and William Zartman (eds), *Rethinking the Economics of War: The Intersection of Need, Creed, and Greed*, Baltimore: Johns Hopkins University, pp. 256–284.

Zeleza, Paul Tiyambe (2008) "Introduction: The Causes and Costs of War in Africa," in Alfred Nhema and Paul Tiyambe Zeleza (eds) *The Roots of African Conflicts: The Causes and Costs and the Resolutions of African Conflicts*, Athens: Ohio University Press, pp. 1–35.

Zimbardo, Philip G. (2006) *The Lucifer Effect: Understanding How Good People Turn Evil*, New York: Random House.

8 State and sovereignty

Navnita Chadha Behera

Introduction

Sylvia Mirabal was eight years old when the Taos Pueblo community celebrated the return of the Blue Lake and its surrounding 48,000 acres of land from the U.S. Congress. She had learned about the legend of the Blue Lake – the place of their origin and source of all life force. From the 16th century, Spanish and Mexicans had recognized their land rights, reaffirming their sovereignty under the Treaty of Guadalupe Hidalgo in 1848 with the U.S. government. In 1906, U.S. President Roosevelt took over their lands, incorporating these into the Carson National Forest. After 64 years of long struggle, the Taos Pueblo people got back the "trust title" for these lands and became a "sovereign nation" within the U.S. (Deverell 1987). At the 40th anniversary of this milestone event in September 2010, Mirabal was happy to celebrate her grandfathers' role in this struggle which earned them continued "free access" to the Blue Lake.[1] The apparent contradiction of being part of a "sovereign nation," which in turn was part of the territorially sovereign state of the U.S.A., made little difference.

Julie Roberts Szczepankiewicz, a young Polish girl, had often heard her mother saying "grandmother was Polish *but* they lived somewhere close to the Russian border." Much later, she understood that was because Poland did not exist as an independent nation between 1795 and 1918. Her ancestral village, Kowalewo-Opactwo in present-day Słupca County of Wielkopolskie province, was originally part of the Polish-Lithuanian Commonwealth, which was partitioned thrice among Russia, Prussia and Austrian empires during this period. However, when she inquired if these border changes implied that her ancestors were not Poles, but were really German or Russian, she soon learned that ethnicity and nationality were not necessarily the same thing, best explained by her Polish grandma who told her, "if a cat has kittens in a china cabinet, you don't call them teacups."[2]

Sovereign states are the fundamental building blocks of the international system, and are at the core of most theories of International Relations (IR). The dominant narratives casting them as permanent, primordial and somewhat unproblematic entities are, however, at deep variance with the ways in which statehood has evolved and political authority and statecraft are understood and practiced in different parts of the world. These stories illustrate that statehood and sovereignty are experienced by their respective inhabitants differently across historical spans and geographical loci, and yet IR's disciplinary debates fail to account for such diverse realities across the globe.

This chapter therefore argues that the sovereign state needs to be viewed as a historically evolving and living entity that is constantly-in-making, whose internal and external structures, constituent social forces, political choices and cultural renderings continually shape its political character. Reworking its conceptualization entails *not* using Westphalia as a ubiquitous point of reference and according due recognition to different imaginaries of political authority, statecraft and statehood. We will debate the meaning and import of the concepts of state and sovereignty from three vantage points: their theoretical notions; the underlying methodological assumptions; and the empirical realities. The rest of the chapter is broadly divided into three parts. The first part captures the key components of the existing literature, especially from a theoretical and methodological standpoint. The second part explains why such characterizations tend to give a misleading and erroneous account of these concepts owing not only to their Eurocentrism, rendering them to be ahistorical, but also because these are "unscientific" and their claims of "universality" and "objectivity" do not stand up to scrutiny. The third part discusses what needs to be done in order to arrive at a more holistic understanding of these concepts.

What's (out) there? Singular underpinnings

The state system is a distinctive form of political community, which in the contemporary international system is the primary unit that has the legitimacy, authority and recognition for organizing international life.

The classic Weberian notion of the state refers to a territorial entity with fixed and legitimate borders and a largely homogeneous populace. In addition, its institutional apparatus enjoys a monopoly over legitimate instruments of using force and commands the unquestioned loyalty of its citizens. Weber underlined four features: community, legitimacy, violence and territory as the constitutive elements of the modern state (1994: 310–311).

A modern state is sovereign because it is able to exercise absolute and legitimate authority within its territorial boundaries without being challenged by any other political community within or outside its jurisdiction. The classic notion of sovereignty denotes the power to command and rule, which is rendered legitimate through a claim to authority. Its internal dimension implies consolidation of the territory under a single authority and the recognition of that authority as legitimate by the population, and its external dimension denoted such recognition by other states.

State and sovereignty are thus understood as mutually constitutive concepts. States define the meaning of sovereignty through their engagement in practices of mutual recognition, while mutual recognition of claims of sovereignty is, in turn, an important element in the definition of the state itself (Biersteker 2002: 157). Similarly, Hinsley notes "the origin and history of the concept of sovereignty are closely linked with the nature, the origin and the history of the state" (Hinsley 1986: 2). Territoriality lies at the heart of both concepts as a state cannot exist without territory and sovereignty can be exercised only within the fixed territorial borders of a state. The Westphalian ideal of sovereignty in particular stresses "the principle of the inviolability of these borders" (Hinsley 1986: 2).

The existing debates on the concepts of state and sovereignty may be divided into two broad approaches – positivist and post-positivist – wherein each shares philosophical bases, theoretical principles and methodological orientations. Positivist philosophy stipulates that all authoritative knowledge can only be derived through scientific methods based on empirical evidence (Smith et al. 1996). So, all social phenomena that exist are knowable by human reason/rationality and can be verified through observation, experimentation and mathematical/logical proof. It rejects value judgments and its belief in objective reality leads scholars to make epistemological claims that yield *definitive* and *singular* answers to "what" counts as knowledge of any social phenomenon and "how" to determine the validity and legitimacy of such knowledge. In International Relations, realists and liberals of all persuasions abide by a positivist characterization of the sovereign state, which is viewed as a natural and permanent phenomenon and hence, an unproblematic entity. An epistemological formulation of state and sovereignty bestows them with the qualities of being "timeless" and universal phenomena.

Deploying positivist tools, realists insist that fundamental features of state and sovereignty are "given" and self-perpetuating, effectively ruling out any possibility of transformation in terms of their defining features and inner workings. They view the state as a unitary and primary actor in the international system and argue that domestic and international politics follow different logics. Hence, scholars need to firmly focus on the state's behavior in the external domain while the workings of its inner domain do not matter or simply do not fall within the purview of IR's subject matter. All states, it is argued, are functionally alike in their inner domain, perform broadly similar functions and have a benign presence in so far as they usually provide basic social values such as security, freedom, order, justice and welfare (Jackson and Sorenson 2007: 5). That is because every human being derives his/her security by virtue of being a citizen of a state, and while a citizen's life inside a state is free, secure and orderly, statelessness is a source of fear and insecurity. In the external realm, classical realist Hans Morgenthau believed that states always pursue their interests defined in terms of power, while Kenneth Waltz, a neorealist argued that there are constraints on a state's behavior imposed by the structure of the international system. Since all sovereign states are equal, the international system becomes anarchical in the absence of any overarching authority and hence IR is mainly concerned with power struggles among states. The liberal argument is different only to the extent that anarchy in the international system can be mitigated with the help of international institutions and regimes and that a state's power and authority tend to be circumscribed on account of the market forces at work, both inside and outside its borders.

Neither realists nor liberals account for different historical trajectories of state-making because their conceptual parameters are almost exclusively drawn on the basis of a particular slice of Western Europe's history, that is the Peace of Westphalia treaties signed in 1648. In fact, the modern state in the IR literature is often referred to as the "Westphalian state," though, significantly, how this model became "global" is the most neglected and perhaps least understood part of the story.

Post-positivism, by contrast, is an approach drawn on by a range of theoretical schools of thought in IR including critical theory, constructivism, Marxism, feminism, post-structuralism, post-colonialism and historical sociology. This approach rejects the foundational proposition of positivism that reality exists independently "out there" and argues that it is mediated by historicity as much as the values norms and social practices of the actors involved. It accords primacy to the ontological questions of "what is there" in terms of the nature of reality, which varies and is subject to change being a socially constructed phenomenon. Knowledge, it is argued, is created, not discovered; and knowledge is power, that is, it is produced in the form of opinions and theories by those in power whose interests it serves. Accordingly, the post-positivist approach believes in historicizing and offers a sociological understanding of the sovereign state.

Its engagement with the ontological question of what constitutes reality paves the way for recognizing that the state is neither a natural nor a permanent phenomenon but rather a historically and socially constructed phenomenon. In fact, for the better part of human history, humans have organized themselves politically in a diversity of ways, ranging from city-states, kingdoms, feudatories and colonies to empires. Accordingly, there are scholars who do not accept the state as a given, and focus on explaining how the state was made, how its boundaries were formed and maintained and how it came to appear as natural and "given." In doing so, however, scholars have pursued different lines of inquiry and reached differing conclusions.

Charles Tilly's work on the formation of European states, for instance, focuses on how they acquired the monopoly over coercive instruments of power, characterizing the state-making process as a "quintessential protection racket with the advantage of legitimacy," and terming these as the "largest examples of organized crime" in history (1985: 170). Benno Teschke deploys Marxist and historical sociological approaches to show that the modern sovereign state was born only after capitalism took root in 17th-century England, thereby drawing a clear distinction between the "absolutist sovereignty" of France (which, unlike England was present at the Peace of Westphalia in 1648) and the "capitalist sovereignty" of England (2004: 59–60). Teschke argues that this became possible only because the capitalist social formations had paved the way for the formal separation of politics and the economy, thus rendering sovereignty to become a purely political affair. Feminist scholars trace the birth of the public–private dichotomy to the early experiences of state-making of the Athenian *polis* in Greece, wherein "the propertied men acquired status, authority and resources as patriarchal heads-of-households and the new participants in the public sphere," driving women into the now-subordinated private sphere, and viewing them exclusively as biological and social reproducers (Peterson 1996: 263).

These theoretical approaches also reject the cartographic view of the state as a legal-territorial entity and question the inside–outside binary by arguing that the sovereign state must be contextualized in the social domain within which it is located. Recognizing that a society may not be homogeneous, comprising as it does different social classes and interest groups, the state–society relationship is viewed as a variable phenomenon. Society, from this standpoint, is not simply an arena where the state acts but a constitutive realm which shapes the very character of the state and informs its interests as well as its political choices.

Within the parameters of the sociological framework, however, scholars offer different perspectives. Feminists argue that the state is the chief organizer of patriarchy and manipulates gender identities to serve its narrow ends of maintaining internal unity and safeguarding its external legitimacy. They debunk the inside–outside binary which obscures the prior gendered public–private division within the states as explained above. Neo-Marxists focus on the social property relations, which they argue is the key to understanding both the character of the individual states as well as the dynamics of the inter-state system because the modern state and the capitalist mode of production have developed together (Halliday 1994; Rosenberg 1994; Teschke 2004). Modern capitalist states, for instance, are still involved in the regulation of the production process but they do not directly extract the surpluses. Earlier states were directly involved in the production process but with the separation of sovereign territorial governance and production, capitalist enterprises are now able to function internationally with much greater autonomy from state control. Linklater (1996: 127) explains how "the political architecture of global capitalism helps maintain material inequalities through a combination of coercion and efforts to win consent."

They also pay much closer attention to the political rather than territorial aspects of sovereignty. While the critical theorists and feminists highlight the exclusionary dimensions of sovereignty in so far as they privilege citizens over human beings and the masculine over the feminine respectively, constructivists focus on the ideational structures and shared understandings that underpin the concept of sovereignty.

Finally, critical theorists offer an ethical critique of state and sovereignty and challenge the somewhat benign image of the state. The feminists lay bare its implicit hierarchical power structures that render the state as a site of oppression against women. Karl Marx and Friedrich Engels had argued that the state cannot play an autonomous role, independent of the interests of the ruling bourgeoisie, and it was a mere instrument in their hands to exploit the proletariat. Among the later generation of neo-Marxists, however, Nicos Poulantzas (1975) and Peter Evans (1979) argued that the state could theoretically work against the ruling class, if it served against the broader purpose of preserving capitalism as a system. The post-modernist and critical theorists have also explained how the sovereign state can become a source of insecurity, injustice and violent conflicts and problematize its monopolizing claims of loyalties and allegiances of its citizens while exploring ways for transforming the state and rethinking the idea of a political community by instituting alternate cosmopolitan arrangements that would promote freedom, justice and equality among all.

The competing characterizations of a sovereign state as propounded by such different theoretical approaches are encapsulated in Table 8.1.

The "e" problem: Eurocentrism, epistemological frame and empiricism

Existing conceptions of state and sovereignty are neither scientific, capturing the objective truth, nor truly historical as they share a common "e" problem of Eurocentrism, that is, keeping Europe as their foundational basis for all theorizing (Alatas 2006; Amin 2009; Blaut 1992; Hobson 2012); privileging epistemological formulations at the cost of marginalizing or negating the ontologically divergent . ground realities; and making empiricist claims that do not stand historical scrutiny.

History shows that the modern sovereign state has never "universally" acquired the "timeless" attributes that supposedly form its core constitutive elements. Scholars tracing the birth of the modern state system to the Peace of Westphalia in 1648 also concede that it took several centuries for the modern state to evolve and acquire its contemporary character. Three historical junctures marking critical milestones in its evolution may be highlighted. First was the Peace of Westphalia treaties in 1648, which established the idea of the "free exercise of territorial right" (Treaty of Munster Article 64, Treaty of Osnabrück, Article VIII, 1) or the "territorial right and superiority" (Osnabrück, Article V, 30) that the princes have, thus linking political rule, or sovereignty, to land, to territory (Elden 2009: 201). Second, the birth of the United Nations in 1945 whose Charter enshrined the principle of sovereignty as a qualifying criterion for recognizing new states and the principle of sovereign equality (non-intervention in each other's internal affairs) as the cornerstone of the post-World War II international system. The third milestone refers to the period from the mid-1950s through the 1970s when decolonization resulted in a sharp increase in the total number of sovereign states from 76 to 144 within a span of about 20 years (see Table 8.2).

None of the core constituent features of a sovereign state can consistently be identified throughout this long history of state-making in Africa or Asia as much as in Europe or

Table 8.1 Conceptualizations of state and sovereignty in IR

Theoretical lens	Philosophical bases/ methodologies	Basic conception of state	Basic conception of sovereignty	Key features of state and sovereignty
Realism	Positivist and empiricist epistemology; ontology is irrelevant as Europe provides the historical basis for all theorizing	A unitary and primary actor in the international system	Territorial; sovereignty is absolute, indivisible and inalienable	a) Both are natural and permanent phenomena across time and space; b) The anarchical external domain causes the perennial security dilemma of states; c) The inner domain is secure, peaceful and orderly and fundamentally alike; states perform similar functions
Liberalism	Positivist and empiricist epistemology	A rational and central actor, embedded in international markets	Territorial, albeit powers of a sovereign state are malleable on account of transnational market forces	a) The state is a central player but non-state actors and international institutions also matter; b) The external domain is anarchical though it can be managed through international institutions; c) Markets and international institutions affect state policies and the welfare of its citizens
Critical Theory	Post-positivist; interpretative understanding upholds universal ethical norms; ontology, in principle, a must for theorizing	A distinct form of political community with particular functions, roles and responsibilities that are socially and historically determined	Political; focuses on practices of inclusion and exclusion of sovereign states that privilege its citizens over human beings	a) The state is neither natural, nor permanent; it examines how its boundaries are formed, maintained and transformed; b) An exclusionary form of political body whose "moral deficits" generate estrangement, injustice, insecurity and violent conflicts by imposing rigid boundaries between citizens of one state and other states; c) It seeks reconfiguration of political community by decentering the state with a cosmopolitan set of arrangements that will promote freedom, justice and equality across the globe
Post-modernism	Post-positivist; genealogical approach that rules out the possibility of any universal frame for theorizing; allows only for competing perspectives	The state is performatively constituted – an ontological product of continued iteration of a set of norms, not a singular act, beyond which it has no identity	Political; seeks to problematize and defy the territorial imperative of sovereignty and questions the spatial logic through which such boundaries have been constituted	a) The sovereign state is not a given; it is a subject in process that is always in the process of being constituted; b) The key is to understand how the sovereign state is made possible, naturalized and made to appear as if it had an essence (historical constitution and reconstitution of state as the primary/normal mode of subjectivity in international politics); c) It offers an ethical critique of state sovereignty and challenges its monopolizing claims over identifications, allegiances and loyalties of its members; d) It seeks to rethink the concept of the political without invoking assumptions of sovereignty and territoriality

(Continued)

Table 8.1 (Cont.)

Theoretical lens	Philosophical bases/ methodologies	Basic conception of state	Basic conception of sovereignty	Key features of state and sovereignty
Constructivism	Seeks to combine positivist epistemology with interpretative methods, historical analysis, and, intersubjective, social ontology	A socially constructed, distinct identity which is constituted by the institutionalized norms, values and ideas of the social environment in which it is embedded; it is not static but ever evolving because it interacts with its environment	A social and constitutive category since the prior condition of recognizing the sovereignty of individual states attests to a shared understanding and acceptance of the concept	a) Ideational and normative structures are as important as material structures for understanding state and sovereignty; b) The identity of a state informs its interests, and in turn, its actions; c) Agents and structures are mutually constitutive; the state and the international system both impact each other; d) Society is a constitutive realm, and the site that generates actors as knowledgeable social and political agents is the realm that makes them who they are
Feminism	Post-positivist; accords primacy to the social and historical context but primarily focuses on the gendered character of state and sovereignty irrespective of their Western or non-Western loci	Patriarchal and regarded as the centralized, main organizer of gendered power that works through the manipulation of public–private spheres; empirically, the state is (mostly) run by men, defended by men and advances the interests of men	Embodies the masculine dominance institutionalized through the parallel trajectories of sovereign contract and sexual contract, embedded in the public–private spheres	a) The state as a paramount expression of collective and historically constituted male power should not be taken as a given but explained in dynamic gender terms; b) It manipulates gender identities for its own internal unity and external legitimacy; c) The discursive separation of domestic and international politics obscures the prior gendered public–private division within states, and anarchy outside typically supports gender hierarchy at home and vice-versa; d) It disregards division between the individual, state and international system by showing how each level is preconditioned by the image of a rational man that excludes women and femininity
Neo-Marxism	Non-positivist; ontology matters as it takes social and historical context into account in challenging the thesis of the Westphalian origins of the modern state system but Europe remains the theoretical base	The socio-economic system (the mode of production) underpins the basic political character of the state	Reflects the nature of the state in capitalism where it has become purely political	a) The prevailing form of capitalism determines the basic character of state and sovereignty though they are both a historical product; b) The impersonal model of sovereignty is premised on the separation between the economic and the political domains – only possible in capitalism; b) Production shapes the nature of state power and strategic interactions between them and, in turn, it is shaped by them; d) Geo-political systems are structurally tied to different modes of production; e) The relationship between the state system and global capitalism (internationalization of relations of production) is needed to understand the structure of global hegemony and how it perpetuates inequalities of power and wealth

Table 8.2 Growth in the number of states in the international system

Number of member states of the United Nations

1945	51
1950	60
1955	76
1960	99
1965	117
1970	127
1975	144
1980	154
1985	159
1990	159
1995	185
2000	189
2005	192
2015	193

Source: www.un.org/en/members/growth.shtml

the Americas. Let us explain this by testing the claims to objectivity with reference to three such core constitutive features.

The *first* defining principle of the sovereign state – territoriality – stipulates that each state has fixed and legitimate borders within which it exercises its sovereignty. A material record of history at these critical milestones alongside the current global map clearly illustrates the constantly changing territorial configurations in every part of the world.[3] Perhaps there is not a single state in the globe whose territorial borders have remained unchanged through this period.

Even the boundaries of European states – the bedrock for theorizing the sovereign state – have been substantially redrawn over centuries since 1648. Indeed, this transpired at the end of World War I in 1919; during World War II from 1939 until 1945 and in its immediate aftermath; and then at the end of the Cold War in 1990.[4] The single most important transformation in the world's territorial map, however, took place when decolonization resulted in the creation of 68 states from the 1950s to the 1970s. This was also why the "territorial contiguity" principle characterizing a modern state's borders was not a universal practice until the mid-20th century as the imperial European powers, including the British, French, Italians, Spanish and Portuguese, had colonized large parts of the world, thereby exercising sovereignty over territories that were thousands of miles apart from the boundaries of their respective "parent" states. The number of sovereign states has continued to grow, almost quadrupling over the past 70 years. While there were 51 founding members of the United Nations in 1945, the organization's current membership stands at 193 member states.[5] The growing number of sovereign states and changing territorial boundaries clearly show that the first constitutive feature of each state having fixed territorial boundaries even in the post-1945 period is but a myth.

The *second* principle refers to two linked features of a sovereign state: exercising monopoly over legitimate instruments of violence within its territory and being a provider of security to its citizens. The realist and liberal writings, however, offer no understanding about how such a monopoly was acquired by the European states

Table 8.3 Numbers of wars between 1820 and 2007

Decade	International wars	Civil wars	Non-state wars	Total wars
1820–1829	13	08	10	31
1860–1869	19	23	06	48
1890–1899	25	16	01	42
1900–1909	21	09	00	30
1930–1939	13	08	00	21
1960–1969	09	24	01	34
1990–1999	09	40	01	51
2000–2007	05	20	00	25

Source: www.correlatesofwar.org/COW2%20Data/WarData_NEW/WarList_NEW.html as cited in Sarkees and Wayman (2010)

over the millennia, which had entailed "imposition of the state's religion on its population," extensive monitoring of people's lives for regular taxation and "disarming of all competing players including privateers and merchant shipping companies to pirates and mercenaries who were stripped of their powers to bear arms against or in competition with the state" (Devetak et al. 2012: 143). It was thus an end product of a long and bloody struggle by state builders to extract coercive capabilities from other individuals, groups and organizations within their territories (Tilly 1975: 71). While European states took four to seven centuries to emerge as fully fledged nation-states, the newly sovereign states in the wake of the decolonization period were expected to master and exercise such monopoly almost immediately after the transfer of power from the erstwhile colonial powers to the local ruling elites. This proved especially challenging as the colonial powers had destroyed their original, pre-colonial political structures and practices of statecraft. Not surprisingly, this never materialized in many states. A complete monopoly over coercive instruments of power has thus remained more of an assumption than an objective reality for the majority of the states comprising the international system, which is evident from a comparative analysis of intra-state wars and inter-state wars between 1940 and 2007, as suggested in Table 8.3 (see also Chapter 7).[6]

This also brings into sharp relief the assumption that a state commands the unquestioned allegiance of its citizens and is the provider of security to all its citizens. Scholars have shown how states have proven to be a source of insecurity and even oppression to their own populace, especially minorities, on the grounds of religion, race, language, gender, ethnicity, culture and so on and that this holds true of not only the global South but also the global North.[7] In order to meet empiricist claims on their own turf, it is worth citing R.J. Rummel's data that more than 262 million people have been killed by their own governments, which dwarfs the figure of 38.5 million people killed in international and civil wars in the 20th century alone.[8] This "democide," he noted, murdered six times more people than died in combat in all the foreign and internal wars of the century. Finally, it is not only the states located in the global South that still face secessionist demands but the political record of Eastern and Central Europe in the last two decades, and separatist demands made by Ireland and Scotland in the U.K., Quebec in Canada and Catalonia in Spain show that even the "oldest" players in the system are not immune to internal threats of disintegration.

Table 8.4 Interventions by major powers, non-major powers and international organizations, 1946–2005

	Cold War (N=690)			Post-Cold War (N= 425)		
	Number	*Percent*	*Per year*	*Number*	*Percent*	*Per year*
Major powers	193	27.9	4.3	90	21.2	5.63
U.S.A.	74	10.7	1.68	35	8.2	2.18
United Kingdom	38	5.5	0.86	13	3.1	0.81
France	35	5.1	0.79	31	7.3	1.93
Soviet Union/Russia	25	3.6	0.56	10	2.4	0.63
China	21	3	0.47	1	0.2	0.06
Non-major powers	440	63.8	10	248	58.3	15.5
International organizations	57	8.3	1.2	87	20.5	5.4

Source: Pickering and Kisangani (2009: 597)

The *third* core constituent element pertains to the principle of sovereign equality and non-interference in one another's internal affairs. Empirically, the historical record shows the violation of this principle in the post-1945 period to be the norm rather than the exception, prompting Stephen Krasner to characterize sovereignty as "organized hypocrisy" (1999: 42). This underlines the contradictory practices of asserting the inviolability of territorial boundaries on the one hand and the practices of constant interference in the affairs of other states, ostensibly on humanitarian grounds, on the other. In other words, the Westphalian ideal of sovereignty as non-interference has always been just that – an ideal. It certainly does not match the empirical realities on the ground: 690 interventions occurred in the Cold War era between 1946 to 1989, as against 425 from 1990 to 2005. Overall, intervention rates, as shown in Table 8.4, seem to have increased.

In the post-Cold War era, roughly 16 foreign military interventions were launched per year during the 44 years of the Cold War, while 26 interventions per year were initiated during the 16 years of the post-Cold War period (Pickering and Kisangani 2009: 596–597). In fact, the debate on humanitarian intervention and the doctrine of "responsibility to protect" has since then sought to bestow the sanctity of international law for devising exceptions to the principle of sovereignty and identify grounds on which states can indeed militarily intervene in other states' internal affairs on humanitarian grounds (Mamdani 2010; Thakur 2012; Chapter 7).

Indeed, how the empiricist conceptualization of the sovereign state has survived and thrived in the face of such cumulative and empirically contradictory evidence that rebuts almost all its key postulates, is a question that remains to be answered.

Though the positivist and the post-positivist theoretical approaches differ in their foundational assumptions and methods of inquiry, as explained earlier, they actually remain tethered together at a much deeper level as they share the fundamental premise of Eurocentrism. While the former is ahistorical, the latter makes only half-hearted attempts at historicizing the state because they also fail to largely see beyond Europe.

The realist scholars sought to create a parsimonious and general theory of international relations, whose explanatory power was universal; but in order to derive the abstract categories from empirical realities, these had to be located at some historical juncture. This was found in the Peace of Westphalia of 1648, which has since then been presented as "the European big bang theory of world politics" and modern state creation (Hobson 2013: 32). Eurocentrism thus remains deeply embedded in the DNA of the very idea of the modern state. This has proven to be a deeply flawed and questionable proposition on three counts.

First, it tends to assume that "the Europeans single-handedly created the sovereign state in the absence of any Eastern input," and it was a phenomenon made in Europe and then exported to the rest of the world (Hobson 2013: 32). A critical gaze into the earlier history of Western and Eastern parts of the world ranging from India, China and West Asia to Africa and the Americas offers an altogether different picture. Hobson explains that the dialogue among these civilizations involved

> diffusion of Eastern resource portfolios (ideas, institutions and technologies) in the wide ranging domain of war and military revolution to global trading patterns and their role in tracing epistemic origins of sovereignty through renaissance and the scientific revolution; that traversed across the Oriental global economy to be assimilated by the Europeans in the process of state formation especially its materialist aspects.
>
> (Hobson 2013: 32)

Second, it failed to consider the pre-1648 history even of Europe, especially the imperial encounter between the Spanish and "indigenous Americans." The year 1492 was an important milestone because "it not only preceded the rise of sovereignty but constituted an ideational crucible within which the concept of sovereignty was forged" (Hobson 2013: 46). Hobson explains how Western scholars of political theory and international law such as Francisco de Vitoria, Hugo Grotius, Albert Gentili and Emerich de Vattel along with Thomas Hobbes and John Locke generated

> a Eurocentric "standard of civilization" discourse – a conceptual device whereby the Americas were constituted as an example of the original state of nature inhabited by savages and barbarians who lacked rational institutions which were then juxtaposed with Europe's civilized institutions which meant that the European states were worthy of being awarded sovereignty.
>
> (Hobson 2013: 44)

More importantly, it became axiomatic that the lack of sovereignty of the non-European world and the later emergence of European sovereignty enshrined imperialism as a natural and legitimate policy vis-à-vis uncivilized societies. Even the United States, which declared its independence from Great Britain in 1776, had over the next century, until 1887, seized over 1.5 billon acres of land from America's indigenous people by treaties and executive orders (Saunt 2014).

Third, the problem with such Eurocentric historicism, to quote Dipesh Chakrabarty, is that it "assumes the existence of a singular, universalizing narrative of modernity and cannot countenance the existence of alternative modes of temporality each with its own concept of the political" (2000: 22–23). Such a denial renders post-colonial peoples as "people without history" (Wolf 1982) and helps legitimize the "civilizing mission" of colonialism by translating historical time into cultural distance, that is, time taken by non-Western societies to become civilized and modernized like Western societies.

The history of state formation processes outside Europe is thus not studied and a particular slice of European history is considered to suffice as the singular basis for fashioning a general theory for *all*. This has resulted in a crucial disjuncture between the singular, epistemological formulation and conceptual parameters of the sovereign state with the ontologically diverse empirical grounded realities of most states. The fundamental idea of political community and authority are reduced to the modern sovereign state, whereas there are multiple political practices going on around the world and in different times of history that offer alternative imaginaries of political community and statecraft (Walker and Mendlovitz 1990). More importantly, the non-West, as a site of knowledge creation of international politics, was thus structurally and intrinsically removed from the very genesis of its foundational parameters as their diverse "pasts" stood delegitimized, as indeed any alternative conceptions of state and sovereignty envisaged in other temporal or spatial contexts.

Significantly, this is true not only of the realist tradition but also the Marxist approach, which had coined the powerful conceptual tool of "historical materialism" to escape telling a state-centric story of international politics. Marx and Engels's attitude towards non-Western societies was also rather condescending, if not altogether contemptuous. They were convinced that Western imperialism and the spread of capitalism were necessary to liberate the "history-less people" from religious myths and the tyranny of tradition (Linklater and Burchill 2005: 133). The theoretical base of IR, thus, remained confined to Europe (and later, North America). Almost all other theoretical approaches including feminism, critical theory and post-modernism also remained somewhat complicit. So, whether Teschke traces sovereignty to the birth of capitalism in 17th-century England rather than to Westphalia, or the feminists locate the adoption of patriarchal practices in ancient Greek city-states, all throughout there is an implicit or explicit assumption of *a particular kind of state*. In other words, while the scholars have emphasized the need to study the history of state-making, an abstract notion of the sovereign state (*a la* the Westphalian model) remains deeply embedded in their consciousness and provides the ubiquitous reference point for all such scholarly debates. Histories of non-Western states continue to be mostly studied either in terms of the "*lack*" (the missing elements) or the "*distance*" (from their goalpost), that is, the time they needed to reach their "given destination," a point discussed in detail in the following section. In methodological terms, their emphasis on ontology along with epistemology turns out to be a qualified one at best. Ontology, in this context, seems to have been used more from a utilitarian point of view; it is useful to understand and help in one's search for an epistemological answer which remains "fixed" and "Eurocentric." Ontology has to be unleashed to explore the full potential for knowledge building, as discussed below.

What can be done?

The key is to ask different questions and search for answers in different places. It is important to shift the focus from looking for a *universal* idea of sovereign state to recognizing the possibility of different imaginaries of political authority, different degrees of stateness and multiple formulations shaped as they are by their diverse histories of state formation as indeed various political, social, economic, military and cultural forces continually exercising their influence from within and without. Accordingly, a state needs to be viewed as a *living* body – constantly in-the-making over the long term – whose internal and external structures, constituent social forces, political choices and cultural renderings are constantly evolving in a fundamental manner. This is potentially transformative and allows all states to create new norms, institutions and practices that are best suited to their own grounded realities.

This does not necessarily require abandoning the hitherto universal markers of having territory, sovereignty, centralized authority and so on but in providing "thick" descriptions of their diverse internal and external contexts and how these drive the state-making processes. So, a question of "what kind of a state?" merits a response *without* using Westphalia as a ubiquitous point of reference and calls for studying different organizing principles of power and authority within each state by asking: what social forces are exercising state power within and beyond (read external partners)? For whose benefit? And at whose cost?

Connecting with *histories* as distinct from *a history* (read European history) both in a spatial and temporal sense is imperative to understand how modernity and its variants of colonial modernity altered/fixed the trajectories of state-making with lasting consequences for the kind of states we have today. This might throw light on possible alternate structuring principles of political authority and the relationship with its constituent social groups and norms of public morality. Let me explain this with historical examples drawn from the Indian experiences of suzerainty, the Quranic concept of *hakkimaya* and cultural notion of sovereignty of the Americas' indigenous peoples.

Drawing upon three key theoretical texts and epics of the Hindu tradition namely the *Manusmriti*, the *Arthashstra* written by Kautilya[9] and the *Mahabharata*, Sudipto Kaviraj, for instance, points to a theory of the state that, "while recognising the requirement of unrestricted royal authority, sought to impose restrictions upon it by positing an order that was morally transcendent – an order to which it was both subject and in complex ways eventually responsible" (Kaviraj 2010: 44, 47). By distinguishing

> between "the law" (*danda*) and a fallible human agent (the king), Manu is able to construct a theoretical structure in which the king does not enjoy unconditionally absolute power over the lives of his subjects because there is a moral framework of *dharma* to which he is, in turn, subordinate.
>
> (Kaviraj 2010: 45)

In the medieval period, the Mughals followed "a theory of rule" drawn from a very different tradition of Persianate Islam that also "implicitly accepted limitations on political authority in relation to the *social* constitution, and which was parallel to those of Hindu rulers," meaning that "the Islamic state also saw itself as limited and socially distant as the Hindu state" (Kaviraj 2010: 45). Kaviraj underlines the need to

> understand the difference between actual weakness of a state and its marginality in principle. The relative autonomy of the social constitution from the state did not

arise because the state was weak [but] ... because it followed from a moral principle, which guided the relation between rulers and subjects.

(2010: 45)

Unlike the European statecraft that deeply penetrated into people's lives by imposing the
state religion and disarming, even eliminating all competitive players, as explained earlier, political authority and control in the traditional Indian order tended to be dispersed
and distributed between various levels of authority: vassal states, regional kingdoms and
empires, as distinct from a centralized political unity of the modern sovereign state.
Another critical distinction was that vassals usually became so not by "contract" but
"lawful conquest" or *dharamvijya*, which significantly did not involve the absorption of
the conquered kingdom (Bhasham 1954: 95). Mostly, the suzerain's hand weighed very
lightly, especially on the more powerful and remote vassal states, creating a fluid and
malleable political system with constantly changing political status and loyalties of kingdoms. Also, the state or its upper layers had little direct interaction or control over the
collective identities at the grassroots level. The basic unit of most kingdoms comprised
of the autonomous village communities, which were economically self-sufficient and
self-governing, which centuries later, still thrive in the form of *panchayati raj* (village-
level governing institutions) in the present-day Indian democracy. So, the following question merits further exploration: are India's democratic political practices of power sharing
an entirely "modern" political product? Or, are these *derived* in some ways by its centur-
ies-old practices of statecraft?

In the Middle Eastern context, the concept of *hakimiyyah*, derived from the
Quranic word *hokum* (to govern and to rule), is defined by Qutb as "the highest
governmental and legal authority" (cited in Khatab 2011: 98). While this might
denote "sovereignty," it is often misconstrued to mean "God's rule" – a theocratic
proposition, which Qutb totally rejected. Based on several Quranic verses (i.e.,
2:229; 4:59), he argued, "government in Islam is limited to regulations laid down
in the Qur'an and *sunnah* the primary sources of shari'ah law" (ibid.: 99), but that
symbolize a deeply democratic commitment. Unlike an elected government which
derives its legitimacy from the majority vote, this upholds the rule of law for the
entire populace. Political theorists argue that limitations of governmental power in
running the state and regulating the peoples' affairs lie at the heart of the idea of
constitutional rule. This is indeed central to Qutb's idea of *hakimiyyah*, understood
as being essential to the organs of the state, its identity and its domestic and international relations, while emphasizing the underlying unity of humanity in terms of
race, nature and origins (Qutb 1992: 501). "If the sovereignty (*hakimiyyah*) *of* the
law is accepted," Khatab points out, "the government should observe justice, freedom, power sharing, human rights, and consultation between the ruler and the
ruled" (2011: 103–104).

Shifting the gaze to another part of the world throws up a deeply cultural premise of
sovereignty by the indigenous peoples of North America, Canada and Australia. They
believe that since tribes existed long before these states came into existence, their sovereignty is inherent and ancient. Their ability to *exercise* sovereignty is, however, severely
circumscribed because "the recognition and respect necessary" for doing so has been
consistently eroded by the states' continuing colonial practices, rendering it to be
a "negotiable phenomenon" (Cobb 2005: 119). Lyons explains how the United States has
limited and eroded the Native Americans' tribal sovereignty through a process of

"rhetorical imperialism" that entails defining and redefining the parties by describing them in different ways from "sovereign" to "ward," from "nation" to "tribe" and from "treaty" to "agreement" (2000: 453; see too, Chapter 3). As the first story at the outset of this chapter illustrates, this has real, tangible consequences in the everyday experiences of Native Americans because their concepts of government and culture are inseparable. Wilkins explains that tribal sovereignty "can be said to consist more of continued cultural integrity than of political power and to the degree that a nation loses its sense of cultural identity, to that degree, it suffers a loss of sovereignty" (Wilkins 1997: 21). Sovereignty is in fact "cultural continuance," but this is no longer a natural part of an inherent sovereign, but instead becomes "a criterion, a quality, that Native nations must [continually] prove for their sovereign status to be recognized," and if they fail to do so, the Congress can simply terminate its government-to-government relationships with tribes and deny their sovereignty, as happened during the termination era of the 1950s (Cobb 2005: 121) and much earlier, as in the case of the appropriation of the Blue Lake.

In terms of inter-state relations, the Chinese philosophy of Confucianism stipulated a different principle of organizing power and authority. It held that there was a preordained natural order in which heaven is the source of all authority (Wang 2009: 111–112). "All-under-heaven," according to Chinese philosopher, Zhao Tingyang had a "triple meaning – as the land of the world; as all peoples in the world; and as a world of institution – combined in the single term, indicating a theoretical project of the necessary and inseparable connections among these three elements" (2005). Unlike the horizontal Westphalian system organized on the basis of sovereign equality, the concept of "all-under-heaven" is organized in a hierarchy – a pattern of order based on a world measure. That is to say, the issues and affairs of the world should be analyzed and measured by a world standard rather than by a nation standard, and in the world context rather than from a local perspective. The Pax Sinica or Chinese world order was based on longevity and the flexibility of its core institution – the tributary system. During the Han period, it was primarily a special trading arrangement, but later it played an important political role in keeping peace and winning allies. The tributary system envisaged an institutional complex to ensure coexistence among different entities of the Chinese empire: barbarians, tribes, kingdoms, peripheral political communities and eventually the Europeans too (Zhang 2001: 53).

An important word of caution is that any such historical exemplars must not be viewed as offering an alternate *panacea*. The Indian political system, for instance, upheld its *varna* (caste) system's discriminatory practices while the predominantly Muslim Ottoman Empire persecuted Jews and Christians as "inferior subjects." So, while one must understand the Westphalian state system in its specific European context, it is equally important to problematize the past histories of other civilizations and states. At the same time, it is imperative not to read, filter and judge such historical conceptual constructs by modern sensibilities and yardsticks – linguistic, material or normative. Divorcing them from their specific historical contexts tends to result in misconstruing, if not distorting, their meanings. For instance, non-territorial and/or cultural notions of nationalism and other modes of belonging must be understood on their own terms.

Any disjuncture between these concepts and modern-day realities should also not *automatically* result in their dismissal. The purpose of introducing students to indigenous concepts in any part of the world is not to accept these uncritically but help them learn to deploy these to ask more questions and explore when and why they emerged. How did they shape their respective state-making experiences? The idea is to expose them to multiple configurations and practices of statecraft, which are not necessarily boxed in the *a-priori* container of sovereign statehood.

Finally, it is important to drive home the point that there is a choice to be exercised in selecting any particular "lens" or a particular set of variables for studying a problem which, in turn has academic, normative and political consequences. A classroom exercise can explain how multiple understandings of the same phenomenon are derived. Let me explain this with reference to different "readings" of the sovereign state in the African context, which is predominantly cited for instances of dysfunctional, weak or failed states (see Chapter 7).

The sovereign state in Africa

Robert Jackson explains African sovereignty as part of a framework that juxtaposes "real states and positive sovereignty" in the global North with "quasi-state and negative sovereignty" in the global South (1986, 1993). Having an "unquestioned presence," real states, it is argued, possess sovereignty by merit and have an integrated political community resting on a common culture with an effective government organization (Jackson 1993, cited in Doty 1996: 151–152). The quasi-states in Africa, by contrast, are characterized by a *lack* – an "absence" of political community, "lack" of national capability, backwardness and a "soft" state, characterized by corruption and disorder, and devoid of moral values.

It is important to understand the assumptions underlying Jackson's analysis and the questions he asks or more importantly, *does not*. First, the very idea of "real statehood" is predicated on a primordial "universal," formulation, which also serves as the gold standard for every state to match. Two, the local and diverse pre-colonial pasts of African states simply do not count. Three, Africa's colonial pasts are understood purely from the standpoint of the West's "civilizing mission" in being characterized as "the moral, legal, material aid structure that maintained Africa," and generally as "a basically bloodless episode in the unfolding and development of the state system" (Doty 1996: 154). Four, it precludes any structural linkages between internal and external dynamics of state-making.

So, the African states' failure is squarely attributed to their own "lack" of indigenous capacity for self-government, their incompetence and corruption, while the "benevolent" international society is mildly chastised for unintentionally facilitating them as a result of reinforcing the principle of primordial statehood. African states alongside other third world countries are constructed as "freeloaders in the international system," who pursue collective ideologies, thereby creating "a normative dilemma" by getting sovereign independence and yet demanding development support from others (Doty 1996: 156).

However, using a different set of variables yields a very different picture of the African state. Amy Niang (2018), for instance, delves deep into the pre-colonial pasts of West Africa in order to understand the social structures that had sustained African political life. The Mossi state that had become the role model in the Voltaic region in Africa during its formative years through the 15th and 16th centuries, she explains, was constructed around the twin ideas of the *Naam* and the *Tenga*. The *Naam* – an original conception of political authority – established the political order and shaped the contours of social experience as a whole, though it had to contend with the capacity for resistance of pre-existing social structures, especially the earth priests and other first-settler figures that operated under the moral authority of *Tenga* (Niang 2018: 26–27). Together, these constituted

> analogized articulations of imaginaries of authority (an ethics of legitimation), of cultural ethos (beliefs, values, artistic expression) and positionalities (social statuses and relations, entitlements) which in reality were brought together by a juridical compact whose terms were to be regularly revisited through ritualised procedures.
>
> (Niang 2018: 26–27)

The underlying legal ideas and norms like rituals, she adds, were "deeply onto-logical," and were woven into mutually binding relationships, the legibility of which was both internal and experiential. While the pre-colonial forms of political, social and cultural order overlapped, the peculiar modalities of colonial modernity sought to carve these up into distinct spheres disrupting, instrumentalizing and discrediting their indigenous mediating mechanisms (Niang 2018: 196). Many local chiefs were co-opted into the colonial apparatus; no longer answerable to the people they governed, which effectively disempowered them. Elsewhere, they were attacked by the national-ist leadership like Kwame Nkrumah in Ghana and Thomas Sankara in Burkina Faso, who were committed to forging a modern, post-colonial state. Their state-making enterprise made it imperative for the Africans to overcome their primordial attach-ments and spiritual beliefs but in doing so, they created a post-colonial state that was "culturally void," denuded of its public morality (Niang 2018: 197). Since the omis-sion of Africa's experiential pasts and moral orders had little bearing on the state formation processes, the post-colonial state not only cemented the original divide between the state and society fostered by the imperial rulers but also invested the state power solely in the hands of the sovereign. With the state becoming a solely political instrument, it became susceptible to its continued exploitative use for the benefit of its erstwhile colonial masters, at the expense of the majority of Africans. Niang explains that when this led to

> contestations of various forms including an outright rejection of the state as a parasitic thing that had been displaced and subordinated to external exigencies and interests … people escaped from the state in resistance, informality, avoid-ance, *faire-semblant*, subversion and other means that could free them from the state tutelage.
>
> (Niang 2018: 195)

Instead of reworking the state structures to make them more accountable to people, this, paradoxically, has been construed as a sign of state weakness, if not failure.

Alternatively, Amin (1973), Rodney (1982), Mamdani (1996), Ferguson (2006) and Grovogui (2012) analyze the impact of colonial rule and often continuing neo-colonial interference in African states on their state-making processes. Doty (1996) argues that works like that of Jackson preclude the possibility that the colonial powers and/or the international system could be partially responsible for producing this condition of states whose stateness is truncated.[10] Grovogui explains that right from the period of imperial regimes, which led to the genesis and institutionalization of the slave trade, the African protectorates and colonies were sites that allowed

"European usurpation of economic sovereign power, forced labor and taxation without representation," and decolonization did not end the interference of imperial powers like France, the U.S. and the U.K. (Grovogui 2012: 132). With Africa getting embroiled in the Cold War, such neo-colonial interference often resulted in the overthrow of democratically elected but "disagreeable" African leaders. Nkrumah (who was overthrown in 1966) was a victim of both interference and removal. He was preceded by Congo's Patrice Lumumba (1961) and Togo's Sylvanius Olympia (1963). All three were replaced by military dictators. These coups were executed "by multinational alliances that included locals and yet their mechanisms of implementation and structures of legitimation were all commodities of global politics long before African independence" (Grovogui 2012: 121–122). Grovogui (132) further explains that alongside the absence of African historiography in the political sciences, its disciplinary practices marked by the particular choice of liberalism and capitalism as the ideological lens which entered the field of African studies through theories of development, modernity and good governance, have distorted the terms of inquiry. In selecting these as the key to post-colonial salvation, Africanists selectively pointed to the failures of policies of Africanization and economic nationalization pursued by Afro-Marxist regimes in the late 1970s. These states, it was argued "lacked the rule of law, preyed in citizenries, expropriated land without compensation, instituted single party regimes, and thus deprived citizens of civil liberties" (132). Thus, Ghana (under Nkrumah), Guinea (under Sekou Toure) and Tanzania (under Julius Nyerere) among others emerged as symbols of an earlier era of failure, whereas Senegal, Liberia, Cote d'Ivoire, Kenya, Tunisia and similar examples of economic liberalism were branded as successful models of development (Young 1983, 1988). Up until the mid-1990s, these countries were reliable Western allies as long as each provided much needed natural and strategic resources to them while granting a free hand to the market economy at home. This, however, also meant that the "constitutional order in these countries all but negated local conventions," and resulted in "the dispossession of the majority of Africans of land, power and rights" (Grovogui 2012: 132).

The preceding discussion makes it clear that our understanding of state and sovereignty, indeed like any other social phenomenon, depends on what kind of questions we ask, the variables we select for studying it and which terrains are explored for seeking the answers. It makes it imperative therefore to understand and accord due recognition to the specificities of the political character of each state rather than work on false assumptions to make each conform to a given set of parameters.

Conclusion

The sovereign state will remain a significant pillar of the international system in the foreseeable future and hence it is important to seek to transform its conception from its hitherto exclusivist and ahistorical underpinnings towards understanding it as a nuanced, inclusive and historical phenomenon. This requires abandoning its explicit and implicit commitment to Eurocentrism as much as the drive to coin a singular and overarching epistemological formulation because the existing conceptualizations of the sovereign state have proven to be woefully inadequate for not only capturing the diverse and complex ground realities of large parts of the global South but some parts of the global North as well. There is a need to delve deeper into the histories of those parts of the world which have thus far remained on the margins of the theory building enterprise in IR, and closely examine the structural linkages between the internal and external domains that determine the political character of a state, and which continue to evolve.

Questions for discussion

1. What are the differences and similarities between the positivist and the post-positivist notions of a sovereign state?
2. Do we need to historicize the phenomenon of the sovereign state? If so, why?
3. What do you understand by the state being a "living entity" and how does this transpire?
4. How does the choice of any particular set of variables impact our understanding of the state? Explain with relevant examples.
5. What do you understand by the political character of the state?
6. Explain the structural linkages between the internal and external domains of the state-making process.

Notes

1 https://sacredland.org/taos-blue-lake-united-states/
2 https://fromshepherdsandshoemakers.com/2017/01/15/those-infamous-border-changes-a-crash-course-in-polish-history/
3 For the map of the world in 1648 AD, see www.timemaps.com/history/world-1648ad/; for the world map in 1945 as per the United Nations, see www.un.org/en/decolonization/pdf/world1945.pdf; and for the current world map, see www.un.org/en/decolonization/pdf/world today.pdf
4 See the video that shows how the European map has changed since 400 BC: www.visualcapitalist.com/2400-years-of-european-history/
5 Also see the map of countries joining the UN by their date of admission: www.targetmap.com/viewer.aspx?reportId=2937
6 Data provided by Berman et al. (2018) that charts the incidents and effects of conflicts world-wide between 1975 and 2015 further corroborates such trends. It juxtaposes the figures plotting battle deaths in thousands for intra-state and inter-state conflicts in each year with the number of conflicts with at least 25 battle-related deaths occurring in the given year. This period too has seen far more civil wars than wars between nations.
7 The U.S. locks up more people per capita than any other nation, with deep-rooted racial and gender disparities. See Wendy Sawyer and Peter Wagner, "Mass Incarceration: The Whole Pie 2019," March 19, 2019. www.prisonpolicy.org/reports/pie2019.html
8 See Prof. R.J. Rummel's website: www.hawaii.edu/powerkills/20TH.HTM
9 He was the shrewd counselor to the first Mauryan emperor, Chandragupta, who defeated Alexander's successor, Seleucus, and established a Hindu empire.
10 In Latin America, *dependentistas* spoke of a structural trap that had been historically set up by the most powerful capitalist states to deny the possibility of these states effectively practicing their sovereignty and overcoming dependent development (Lopez-Alves, 2000, 2012). See Chapter 13.

Further reading

Chakrabarty, Dipesh (2000) *Provincializing Europe: Postcolonial Thought and Historical Difference*, Princeton: Princeton University Press. Chakrabarty explains why Europe is not the only source of all legitimate knowledge and makes room for other ways of knowing in the world.

Krasner, Stephen (1999) *Sovereignty: Organized Hypocrisy*, Princeton: Princeton University Press. Krasner offers historical accounts of actual practices of sovereign statehood to show how the Westphalian sovereignty is a durable myth because it persists despite frequent violations of its basic principles.

Niang, Amy (2018) *The Post-Colonial State in Transition: Stateness and Modes of Sovereignty*, New York: Rowman and Littlefield. Niang traces the pre-colonial pasts of African political life to highlight the diversity of human trajectories on conceptions of statecraft, legitimacy, public morality and different imaginaries of stateness and sovereignty.

Walker, R.B.J. and Saul Mendlovitz (1990) *Contending Sovereignties: Redefining Political Community*, Boulder: Lynne Rienner. Walker and Mendlovitz situate state sovereignty in a broader historical and conceptual framework to explore the middle ground between the mutually exclusive positions of the permanent and primordial presence or the immanent absence of state sovereignty.

Walter, Rodney (1982a) *How Europe Underdeveloped Africa*, Washington DC: Howard University Press. Walter offers a historical account of primitive exploitation and oppression of Africa to benefit Europe and how the latter's development and Africa's underdevelopment are dialectically linked and a product of the same historical processes.

References

Alatas, Syed Farid (2006) *Alternative Discourses in Asian Social Science: Responses to Eurocentrism*, New Delhi: Sage.

Amin, Samir (1973) *Neo Colonialism in West Africa*, Harmondsworth: Penguin Books.

Amin, Samir (2009) *Eurocentrism: Modernity, Religion and Democracy: A Critique of Eurocentrism and Culturalism*, New York: Monthly Press Review.

Berman, Eli, Joseph H. Felter, Jacob N. Shapiro and Vestal McIntyre (2018) *Small Wars, Big Data: The Information Revolution in Modern Conflict*, Princeton: Princeton University Press.

Bhasham, A.L. (1954) *The Wonder that Was India*, London: Picador.

Biersteker, Thomas J. (2002) "State, Sovereignty and Territory," in Walter Carlsnaes, Thomas Risse and Beth A. Simmons (eds) *Handbook of International Relations*, London: Sage, pp. 157–176.

Blaut, James M. (1992) *1492: The Debate on Colonialism, Eurocentrism and History*, Trenton: Africa World Press.

Chakrabarty, Dipesh (2000b) *Provincializing Europe: Postcolonial Thought and Historical Difference*, Princeton: Princeton University Press.

Cobb, Amanda J. (2005) "Understanding Tribal Sovereignty: Definitions, Conceptualizations and Interpretations," *American Studies*, 44 (3–4), Fall–Winter: pp. 115–132.

Deverell, William F. (1987) "The Return of Blue Lake to the Taos Pueblo Author(s)," *The Princeton University Library Chronicle*, 49 (1), Autumn: pp. 57–73.

Devetak, Richard, Anthony Burke and Jim George (eds) (2012) *An Introduction to International Relations*, Cambridge: Cambridge University Press.

Doty, Roxanne (1996) *Imperial Encounters: The Politics of North-South Relations*, Minneapolis: University of Minnesota Press.

Elden, Stuart (2009) "Why Is the World Divided Territorially?" in Jenny Edkins and Maja Zehfuss (eds) *Global Politics: A New Introduction*, London: Routledge, pp. 220–244.

Evans, Peter (1979) *Dependent Development: The Alliance of Multinational, State, and Local Capital in Brazil*, Princeton: Princeton University Press.

Ferguson, James (2006) *Global Shadows: Africa in the Neo Liberal World Order*, Durham: Duke University Press.

Grovogui, Siba (2012) "The State of the African State," in Arlene B. Tickner and David L. Blaney (eds) *Thinking International Relations Differently*, London: Routledge, pp. 117–138.

Halliday, Fred (1994) *Rethinking International Relations*, Basingstoke: Palgrave.

Hinsley, F.H. (1986) *Sovereignty*, Cambridge: Cambridge University Press, 2nd edition.

Hobson, John A. (2013) "The Other Side of the Westphalian Frontier," in Sanjay Seth (ed) *Postcolonial Theory and International Relations*, London: Routledge, pp. 32–48.

Hobson, John A. (2012) *The Eurocentric Concepts of World Politics: Western Political Theory 1760–2010*, Cambridge: Cambridge University Press.

Jackson, Robert H. (1993) *Quasi-States, Sovereignty, International Relations and the Third World*, Cambridge: Cambridge University Press.

Jackson, Robert H. (1986) "Negative Sovereignty in Sub-Saharan Africa," *Review of International Studies*, 12(4): 247–264. DOI: 10.1017/S0260210500113828

Jackson, Robert and Georg Sorenson (2007) *Introduction to International Relations: Theories and Approaches*, 3rd ed. New York: Oxford University Press.

Kaviraj, Sudipta (2010) *The Trajectories of the Indian State: Politics and Ideas*, New Delhi: Permanent Black.

Khatab, Sayed (2011) "International Relations of Modernity in Sayyid Qutb's thoughts on Sovereignty: The Notion of Democratic Participation in the Islamic Canon," in Robbie Shilliam (ed) *International Relations and Non-Western Thought: Imperialism, Colonialism and Investigations of Global Modernity*, London: Routledge, pp. 87–107.

Krasner, Stephen (1999) *Sovereignty: Organized Hypocrisy*, Princeton: Princeton University Press.

Linklater, Andrew (1996) "Citizenship and Sovereignty in the Post-Westphalian State," *European Journal of International Relations*, 2(1): 77–103. DOI: 10.1177/1354066196002001003

Linklater, Andrew and Scott Burchill (eds) (2005) *Theories of International Relations*, London: Palgrave Macmillan.

Lopez-Alves, F. (2000) *State Formation and Democracy in Latin America, 1810–1890*, Durham: Duke University Press.

Lopez-Alves, Fernando (2012) "The Latin American Nation-state and the International," in Arlene B. Tickner and David L. Blaney (eds) *Thinking International Relations Differently*, London: Routledge, pp. 161–180.

Lyons, Scott (2000) "Rhetorical Sovereignty: What Do American Indians Want from Writing," *College Composition and Communication*, 51 (3), February: 447–468. DOI: 10.1080/07350198.2011.530108

Mamdani, Mahmood (1996) *Citizens and Subjects; Contemporary Africa and the Legacy of Late Colonialism*, Princeton, NJ: Princeton University Press.

Mamdani, Mahmood (2010) "Responsibility to Protect or Right to Punish?," *Journal of Intervention and State Building*, 4 (1): 53–67. DOI: 10.1080/17502970903541721

Niang, Amy (2018) *The Post-Colonial State in Transition: Stateness and Modes of Sovereignty*, New York: Rowman and Littlefield.

Peterson, V.S. (1996) "The Gender of Rhetoric, Reason, and Realism," in F.A. Beer and R. Hariman (eds) *Post-Realism: The Rhetorical Turn in International Relations*, East Lansing: Michigan State University Press, pp. 257–276.

Pickering, Jeffrey and Kisangani Emizet (2009) "The International Military Intervention Dataset: An Updated Resource for Conflict Scholars," *Journal of Peace Research*, 46(4): 589–599. DOI: https://doi.org/10.1177/0022343309334634

Poulantzas, Nicos (1975) *Classes in Contemporary Capitalism*, London: New Left Books.

Qutb, S. (1992) *Fi Zilal a-Qur'an*, Cairo: al-Shuruq.

Rosenberg, Justin (1994) *The Empire of Civil Society: A Critique of the Realist Theory of International Relations*, London: Verso.

Sarkees, Meredith Reid and Frank Wayman (2010) *Resort to War: 1816–2007*, Washington DC: CQ Press.

Saunt, Claudio (2014) *West of the Revolution: An Uncommon History of 1776*, New York: W.W. Norton & Co.

Smith, Steve, Ken Booth and Marysia Zalewski (1996) (eds) *International Theory: Positivism and Beyond*, Cambridge: Cambridge University Press.

Teschke, Benno (2004), "The Origins and Evolution of the European States-System," in William Brown, Simon Bromley and Suma Athreye (eds) *Ordering the International: History, Change and Transformation*, London: Pluto Press, pp. 21–63.

Thakur, Ramesh Chandra (2012) *The Responsibility to Protect: Norms, Laws, and the Use of Force in International Politics*, Cambridge: Cambridge University Press.

Tilly, Charles (1975) "Reflections on the History of European State Making," in Charles Tilly (ed) *The Formation of National States in Western Europe*, Princeton: Princeton University Press, pp. 3–83.

Tilly, Charles (1985) "War Making and State Making as Organized Crime," in Peter Evans, Dietrich Rueschemeyer and Theda Skocpol (eds) *Bringing the State Back in*, Cambridge: Cambridge University Press, pp. 169–188.

Walker, R.B.J. and Saul Mendlovitz (1990) *Contending Sovereignties: Redefining Political Community*, Boulder: Lynne Rienner.

Walter, Rodney (1982) *How Europe Underdeveloped Africa*, Washington DC: Howard University Press.

Wang, Yiwei (2009) "China: Between Copying and Constructing," in Arlene B. Tickner and Ole Wæver (eds) *International Relations Scholarship around the World*, New York: Routledge, pp. 103–119.

Weber, Max (1994) "The Profession and Vocation of Politics (1919)," in Peter Lassman and Ronald Speirs (eds) *Weber: Political Writings*, Cambridge: Cambridge University Press, pp. 309–369.

Wilkins, David (1997) *American Indian Sovereignty and the US Supreme Court: The Masking of Justice*, Austin: University of Texas Press.

Wolf, Eric (1982) *Europe and the People without History*, Berkeley: University of California Press.

Young, Crawford (1983) *Ideology and Development in Africa*, New Haven: Yale University Press.

Young, Crawford (1988) "The Colonial State and Post-Colonial Crisis," in Prosser Gifford and Wm. Roger Louis (eds) *Decolonialization and African Independence: The Transfers of Power 1960–80*, New Haven: Yale University Press, pp. 1–32.

Zhang, Yongjin (2001) "System, Empire and State in Chinese International Relations," *Review of International Studies*, 27(5), December: pp. 43–63. DOI: 10.1017/S0260210501008026

Zhao, Tingyang (2005) *Tianxia System (All-under-heaven): Introduction to the Philosophy of World Institutions*, Nanjing: Jiangsu Higher Education Publishing House.

9 Religion, secularism and nationalism

Aparna Devare

Short stories

In 1914, Captain A.D. Chater, a soldier in the British army during World War I, wrote a letter to his mother from the trenches. He described what he called an extraordinary Christmas morning. A German soldier approached from the enemy's trenches, waving and unarmed. Suddenly, both sides emerged from the trenches and began wishing each other a merry Christmas. They then buried their dead jointly, exchanged cigarettes and began to play football. They took photos together and expressed a common desire to go home. When the military authorities later found out about the temporary truce, they threatened the soldiers with court martial and execution if they did not resume killing each other. They soon did so with great vengeance. The war went on for four more years, and by the time it ended, 37 million people had died, including civilians and military personnel (Dearden 2014).

Around 300 years ago, in a village called Chamliyal (in what is today Jammu, north India), there lived a Hindu man named Dalip Singh Manhas. Local villagers believed he had saintly powers of healing and he was known for his compassion and ideas of universal brotherhood. However, he was beheaded by some villagers who felt threatened by his growing popularity. According to local legend, his head landed in a village called Saidawali and his body in Chamliyal. Hindu, Muslim and Sikh villagers all built *dargahs*, or shrines, where his body parts fell and worshipped at them for the next several centuries. Legend has it that Baba Chamliyal (as he came to be known) visited a man afflicted with skin disease in his dreams and told him to apply *shakar* (soil) and *sharbat* (water), after which he was cured. Henceforth, Baba's shrines came to be known for curing skin conditions in particular. Much like Baba's severed body, which fell in two distinct places, India was partitioned into two nations in 1947; the shrine with Baba's head went to the Pakistani side, while the shrine with his body remained in India. Every year in June, a festival was held at both shrines on the anniversary of Baba's death. The Pakistani villagers continued to visit Chamliyal until they were barred from entering India after the two countries went to war in 1971. But the beliefs on both sides persist; the Pakistani (Muslim) villagers send a green *chadar* (considered a holy color in Islam) to cover the shrine, while the Indian (Hindu and Sikh) villagers send *shakar* and *sharbat* to their Pakistani counterparts. They cannot do this directly since the borders are tightly sealed and no exchange is allowed without the long, complicated process of obtaining visas, so an official ceremony is held every year at the border by Pakistani military personnel or Pakistani rangers and

Indian military personnel or the Indian Border Security Force (BSF) (Mohammed 2012). Because the India–Pakistan border is one of the most militarized in the world, the security forces on both sides are otherwise engaged in tense hostilities, with occasional firing at each other leading to both military and civilian casualties. However, even in the midst of ongoing tensions, these ceremonial exchanges continue to take place today.[1]

Both of these stories take place in high "conflict zones" in two distinct parts of the world and different historical periods. Yet they each indicate that everyday practices of religiosity can challenge the singular narrative of the nation-state that is so closely tied to ideas of national security. Even the border officials in the India–Pakistan story have had to capitulate to local villagers' beliefs once a year. In earlier days, the collective ideas that people normally had to conform to were religion or loyalty to the king. However, the nation, at base a *secular* concept, emerged as the most powerful idea during modern times. Over the course of centuries, nationalism gradually replaced religion as the basis of conflict under conditions of modernity.[2] Even so, religion and religiosity continue to be viewed by the modern world as the source of all evil, intolerance and hatred. Not surprisingly, dominant perspectives within International Relations (IR) carry the same residue of bias towards religion.

Introduction: "secular" International Relations and its silence towards religion

Mainstream IR perspectives tell us that the world is comprised of individual nation-states that for various reasons either cooperate, engage in conflict, or something in between (see Chapter 8). For realists, the world is anarchical, lacking any central enforcement authority and therefore constitutes a self-help global structure in which each state has to look out for its own self-interest. Two assumptions undergird these perspectives: first, that the nation-state is secular and relatedly, that it is a rational actor. Where does religion fit into all this? Only as a presence that evokes "passions," is "irrational" and "backward" and thus finds little place in a modern secular nation-state framework. IR theories were linked to modernization theories, which believed that the world would become less religious and all societies would become "proper," "rational" nation-states as modernization took place. As Fabio Petito and Pavlos Hatzopoulos (2000), editors of a special *Millennium* issue on "Religion and International Relations" ask, why has IR remained silent on religion? What is unspoken, as Shampa Biswas (2002: 185) points out, is the "secularity of the nation-state form" which is "taken for granted in accounts of international relations." Hence, mainstream IR has an "epistemological inability" to deal with religion now that there has been a resurgence in religiosity since the post-Cold War period (Biswas 2002). It can only react within the binary of "secular nation-states" versus "irrational" religious communities, states and societies fomenting conflict, largely prompted by global Islamic fundamentalism. This is not very different from Samuel Huntington's "clash of civilizations" thesis, which merely replaces civilizations with nation-states, while still treating them as internally homogeneous, self-contained units.

There are two things that need to be unpacked here, which this chapter attempts to do from a "critical global South perspective." First, secularism and the secular nation-state have been implicated in large-scale violence in the modern world and cannot claim superiority over religion in this regard; second, religion itself has become highly secularized and politicized in its engagement with secularism, making the two quite indistinguishable from each other. While this chapter is not a plea to replace secularism or a defense of religion in any simplistic manner, it does question the "hubris of secularism" and shows the ways in which secularism and religion intersect so that it becomes difficult to see them in binary ways.

IR and the Eurocentric view of religion

Mainstream IR perspectives draw from "Eurocentric" views on the role of religion. What this means is that they privilege a Western understanding situated in the histories and theories of Europe. In this view, religion is singled out as inherently conflictual, while less importance is assigned to other factors that may play a more important role, such as history, political economy, identity politics and nationalism. This is especially the case with respect to non-Western societies. While the non-West is religious, the West is not characterized in the same manner. In other words, non-Western societies are Muslim, Hindu, Buddhist, etc., but Western societies are not identified with religious identities, even if their values may be predominantly Judeo-Christian. The idea that religion should play a very limited role in society is crucial to how the "modern" is defined, specifically rooted in the European historical experience.

The idea of secularism rests, as Charles Taylor (2011: 49) argues, on not just the separation of religion from public life, but also the belief in God as *voluntary* and for some not part of their worlds at all. This would have been unthinkable, he says, in Western civilization 500 years ago. Modern secularism is thus, to paraphrase historian Dipesh Chakrabarty (2000), a "provincial" rather than a universal view towards religion, but one that has come to be universalized with European, and later Western, dominance globally. Modern religion also then emerges along with secularism; like conjoined twins, the "secular" and "religious" enter the world together, the definition, meaning and identity of each irrevocably linked to the other.

In order to understand the Eurocentric view of religion on which IR rests, it is important to understand its historical origins. Its specific location in European history indicates that people around the world do not share the same history or experience. However, an important caveat must be added here. While modern secularism did originate in Europe, this is not to say that secularizing tendencies did not exist in other religions and societies around the world. Across the centuries, in fact, every major religion in the world has been marked by debates about fundamental questions such as the role of religious authorities, who should decide what religious truths are, the role of reason in interpreting religion, individual and human agency, the influence of religion and so on. These ideas were neither unique to European Christianity nor raised for the first time there.

In the case of Islam for instance, Fatima Mernissi (cited in Soguk 2011: 38) argues the religion has been marked throughout its history by the "trends between *Aql* and *ta'a*, that is, between reason and obedience, or between questioning and forgetting." The Mutazila movement for example, which first emerged in 690 CE, comprised thinkers who used rationalism to question the fusion of theology and state power. Some scholars contend this movement's focus on reason (*Aql*) and independent opinion (*Ra'y*) in the interpretation of religious texts made it one of the world's most significant intellectual movements (Soguk 2011). As political scientist Nevzat Soguk (2011: 38) states, "The Mutazila went so far as to theorize that the Qur'an was God's revelation, but it was created (recorded) and organized by humans in time and thus open to interpretation through reason and personal deliberation." They were labelled as free thinkers and heretics because they stressed humans' free agency (*hurriyah* or freedom) versus their lacking choice (*majbur*) (Engineer 2005: 68). This movement paved the way for the principle of *ijtihad*, or independent critical thinking and reasoning, that was to remain an important resource within the critical Islamic tradition. By 813, Greek, Indian and other philosophies had made their way into the Islamic world and led to a spurt in creative thinking in the arts and sciences; by the 9th and 10th centuries, scientific thinking led to the invention of algebra, advances in astronomy and trigonometry, the field of optics and so on. This period of churning gave rise to intellectuals such as Al-Farabi who, strongly influenced by Greek philosophy, saw Islam as compatible in advocating reason to understand revelation (Ansari 2001).

In the case of Hinduism, Buddha (born a Hindu prince named Siddhartha in the 6th century BCE) launched a critique of Hindu Brahmanical practices using rationalist arguments, paving the way for several centuries of vigorous debates both between Hinduism and Buddhism and within Hinduism itself. Buddhist thought can be considered radical in that it questioned many existing ideas and practices at the time including ritualistic action, the authority of the ancient, sacred Hindu scriptures known as the Vedas, the divine basis of monarchy and the notion that the world does not have an intelligent creator (Gupta 2001: 115). Instead, the Buddha stressed individual morality and ethical conduct. Buddhism also questioned the existing caste system and allowed access to people from all social groups[3] into its collectives, known as *sanghas*, because Buddha saw society as based on a social rather than divine order (Raju 2013).

Some have pointed out he was not interested in such metaphysical questions as whether or not God exists but focused on self-reliance over dependency on an external God. Thus, as Gustavo Benavides (1997: 323) argues, Buddhist philosophy provided a radically rationalist view of the world long before modern Western rationalism.

What distinguishes trends within European Christianity is the extent to which the role of religion in social and public life was questioned along with challenges to the Catholic Church. This is in part because, unlike many other pre-modern states and empires, the Catholic Church dominated the political landscape of Europe for centuries. For instance, the state in medieval India was largely secular. Irrespective of whether the rulers were Hindu or Muslim, the state was never formally led by religious authorities but maintained a separation between temple/mosque and state.[4] The dissenting movements that took place in India generally challenged the social order rather than the state, which was not as centralized as its modern counterpart. The privatization of religion that gradually occurred from the 17th century onwards in Europe was at least in part the result of the excessive influence that religion qua the Catholic Church had acquired in European matters over the preceding centuries.

It is important to discuss these historical transformations in Europe in order to better understand the rise of new secularisms and what made them different than earlier attitudes towards religion. These transformations did not take place with a single event or thinker in Europe but were shaped over a long period of time starting in the 16th century.[5] While it is not possible here to discuss the centuries-long process of secularization in Europe, I briefly highlight some important historical events and developments that point to the rise of secular thinking and go along with new understandings of religion and its role in public life in the modern world.

On October 31, 1517, Martin Luther posted his 95 theses in Latin on the door of the Wittenberg church in Germany. Interestingly, while Luther is credited with initiating the Protestant Reformation, there is very little in his 95 theses that deal with questions of faith. Rather, he questioned corrupt practices in the Catholic Church, particularly amongst the clergy and not the Catholic faith per se. In his view, the Church authorities and clergy had become too money-minded. He demanded that the pastors in churches not be involved in public duties, just as monarchs did not perform sacraments (Philpott 2000: 206–245). As sociologist J.P.S. Uberoi (1978) suggests, it was Zwingli, a Swiss reformer, who radically questioned Catholic beliefs and practices such as the use of sacraments. Faith, according to Zwingli, was inward looking, related to individual belief and had nothing to do with drama, ritual or symbol (Uberoi 1978) (see Box 9.1).

BOX 9.1 ORIGINS OF THE WORD "SECULAR"

The origins of the word "secular" are derived from the Latin word *saeculum*, which refers to those who engaged in secular activities such as the clergy associated with this-worldly activities, including administration versus those who dealt with other-worldly concerns or were part of the monastic world (Calhoun et al. 2011: 8). But to suggest to the medieval people in Europe that *saeculum* could mean the removal of religion from public life altogether would have been a very odd idea indeed. In other words, there was a distinction made between secular and religious activities in medieval times but the formal authority of the Church was not questioned (Asad 1993: 39).

With the growing Protestant challenge posed by Zwingli, and later followed by John Calvin and others, there was a shift from emphasis on collective ritual and practices that saw divinity in the sacraments to an inner faith lodged in the *individual*. Each person could access the word of God directly through the Bible through its translations into languages other than Latin, and the work of God was increasingly carried out through missionary activity.[6] The "word" and "work" of God replaced the collective participation in various re-enactments of God's presence, such as receiving the Eucharist during mass. Faith was increasingly seen as a private individual matter and individuals were encouraged to be disciplined, take control of their own lives and be responsible for themselves (Taylor 1989: 229).[7] This allowed faith to become increasingly "privatized," or brought into the private sphere, and was related to the dismantling of the Catholic Church's institutional power. With the Catholic Church under attack, Catholicism also became much more defensive (Hendrix 2000: 572).[8] Even the new reformist movements that emerged, including Lutheranism and Calvinism, were less open to being questioned and instituted new kinds of uniformities and hierarchies. As historian Daniel Philpott (2000: 236) puts it, "the politics of toleration" was not intrinsic to either side's ideas (see Box 9.2).

BOX 9.2 TALAL ASAD OUTLINING NEW IDEAS ABOUT RELIGION

Talal Asad (1993: 207) puts it,

> in this movement we have the construction of religion as a new historical object: anchored in personal experience, expressible as belief-statements, dependent on private institutions, and practiced in one's spare time. This construction of religion ensures that it is part of what is *inessential* to our common politics, economy, science, and morality.

By initiating these changes, the Reformation both reordered the attitude and practices of religion and allowed for the rise of secular states by questioning their monarchic foundations. Protestant reformers were backed by princes in different parts of Europe, especially Germany, who in turn were breaking away from the political and economic dominance of the Catholic Church and its benefactors, such as the Hapsburg dynasty.[9] The Church and the Holy Roman Emperor Charles V sought to suppress the revolt known as the Counter-Reformation, leading to one of the bloodiest periods of modern European history (Philpott 2000). The conflict found some reprieve with the Treaty of Augsburg in 1555, which accepted Lutheranism as an official religion in the Holy Roman Empire but did not recognize Calvinism. The continuing conflict between Catholics, Lutherans and Calvinists was one of the factors leading to the outbreak of the Thirty Years War in 1618, which ended with the Treaty of Westphalia in 1648 (see Box 9.3). Historians note that over eight million people died as a result of this devastating war at a time when the European continent had only 100 million inhabitants, making it the most destructive conflict in the region prior to the world wars of the 20th century (Wilson 2008: 554–586).

BOX 9.3 THE TREATY OF WESTPHALIA AND ITS ROLE IN CREATING NEW "SECULAR" FORMS OF STATE POWER

The Treaty of Westphalia, considered momentous in establishing the principle of sovereignty in international relations and establishing secular states, is in reality more historically complex than is generally understood. Rather than making states secular, it established the principle of *cuius region eius religion* (who rules, his religion) which meant people had to follow the religion of their rulers (Catholicism, Lutheranism or Calvinism) or migrate to safer places (Calhoun et al. 2011: 15). However, the Treaty also curbed the power of the Holy Roman Emperor by giving greater autonomy to the small kingdoms and princes particularly in Germany (Watson 1992: 186). It brought an end to religious conflicts in Europe and triggered a process of secularization in Europe that was to go on until the 19th century and also impacted the Americas since large-scale migration took place there during these times. As Scott Thomas (2000: 823) points out, for the modern state "to be born, religion had to become marginalized" and this is what the princes could achieve as the Treaty curbed the Church's powers.

The European attitude of distrust towards religion was rooted in the distinctive vio-lence of the 16th and 17th centuries. Political scientist Elizabeth Shakman-Hurd (2008) refers to the belief that religion should be private as *laicism*, which is now being increas-ingly contested by the growth of minority populations living in Europe who are unen-cumbered by the traumatic histories of the Reformation and Thirty Years War. Thus, they view the relationship between religion and politics quite differently.[10]

Beginning in the 1600s, large numbers of Europeans fleeing religious persecution and seeking new opportunities went to the Americas, which was increasingly seen as a promised land imbued with religious undertones. Expansion into the wilderness of the West and defeating the "pagan" Native Americans was also undergirded with reli-gious meanings, such as fulfilling a divine mission or scriptural prophecy and taming the wilderness as a biblical necessity (Nash 1967). Protestant values of hard work and frugality were seen as foundational to these new societies (Weber 1930). There was also a proliferation of Protestant sects, or denominations, each with its own dis-tinctive character and identity, including Quakers, Amish, Mennonites, Lutherans, Presbyterians, Baptists and so on. In North America, religion was much more a part of public life than in Europe, although in the case of the United States, the Constitu-tion remained secular.[11] Shakman-Hurd (2008) points out that while political life in Europe was premised on *laicism*, or a fairly sharp separation of religion and politics, North American political life was always strongly influenced by Judeo-Christian values (see Box 9.4).

BOX 9.4 RELIGION IN AMERICAN PUBLIC LIFE

In the United States, political speeches and campaigns of politicians from both the Republican and Democratic parties often have references to God and the presiden-tial oath is generally taken by placing one hand on the Bible. Robert N. Bellah (1967: 1–21) has used the term "civil religion" to talk about the strong religious undertones of American public life unlike that of Europe. As Jose Casanova (2011: 64) puts it, "the American pattern is one of secularization combined with religious growth and recurrent religious revivals." Rather than experiencing a decline in religion, the United States has witnessed its spread and growth in recent years particularly with respect to Christian fundamentalism and extremist movements. While liberal churches have experienced a decline in membership, conservative Protestant churches have grown considerably (Bruce 1996).

Perspectives from the global South on secularism and religion

Secularism and colonialism

Europe's specific attitude towards religion, rooted in the history as discussed above, was imposed on the rest of the world via Western colonialism. By the 18th and 19th centuries, secular attitudes towards religion in Europe had become a defining feature of being "rational," "enlightened" and hence "modern." This growing secular worldview went alongside the colonization of non-European lands stretching from the Americas to Africa and Asia. The trans-Atlantic slave trade began as early as the 1500s and Columbus's "discovery" of the Americas in 1492 marked the beginning of intense and violent colonization of the non-Western world by European powers that continued for the next 500 years. What accounts for this paradox of the emergence of liberal values, including secularism in Europe, that went alongside the total dehumanization of non-Western peoples via colonial expansions across the globe? Was it a case of modern values not being appropriately applied or something intrinsic to secular modernity itself? (See Chapters 3 and 4.)

Literary scholar Walter Mignolo (2009) argues that European modernity, of which secularism is an integral part, allowed the colonization and wide-scale dehumanization of people because it placed humans on a temporal scale based on ideas of progress. Those societies that were endowed with reason, writing and science were seen to be further along in the process of development, fully civilized and temporally in the present, while those who lacked these attributes were placed further back in time, living in the past. Religion, superstition and myth came to be equated with backwardness, a defining characteristic of the colonized world. In "modern" European societies, God could be personal, inhabiting the individual's private world but could not influence science, nature or history. In the modern world, humans were now seen to be agents of change and makers of their own destinies. In this view, nature could be understood scientifically and controlled for human purposes (Merchant 1980). This was the underlying basis of the Scientific Revolution, which granted humans unprecedented belief in their own rationality and powers. "Unscientific" cultures and societies were seen as incapable of using their own lands productively or governing themselves, hence it was legitimate to dispense with them in the search for new territories and replace their rulers with "enlightened," "civilized" people. Therefore, "helping" colonial societies become "civilized" became one of the key ideological imperatives of European colonialism. Whereas early colonialism focused on converting the indigenous peoples of South America into "good Christians," apart from economic motives, the "civilizing mission," as some scholars have put it, became a distinctive feature of late liberal colonialism (Nandy 2009).

What struck European liberals, intellectuals and officials as primitive was the "natives'" inability to distinguish religion from others spheres of life. Moreover, the colonizers also could not comprehend the fluidity and porousness of religious boundaries between the various mixed religious practices and animism pervasive in the colonial world. In Africa, for instance, millions of people followed Christianity, Islam and animism at the same time (Haynes 2007: 302). This was also the case in societies like China, India, Japan and South-East Asia, where strict boundaries between religious practices and beliefs were not maintained. For instance, Chinese indigenous "religions"[12] such as Daoism and Confucianism easily accepted a later entrant, Buddhism, which introduced a monastic tradition in the 2nd and 3rd centuries. All three were practiced by ordinary Chinese people for centuries and it was difficult to draw sharp lines between them because they all comingled along with animism and folk religions. Similarly, in Japan, most Japanese followed Shintoism, a polytheistic religion that co-existed alongside Buddhism and Confucian ethics (Ellwood 2008).

The first thing the colonizers did in the colonies was classify the native populations through a census (Cohn 1987). In a colonial census, one could not belong to three religious groups at the same time – *one had to choose* – leading to increasing homogenization and fixity. This colonial legacy persists in the manner in which the modern world views religion; one has to choose a religion increasingly aligned with national boundaries that demand singularity in language, dress, culture and religion. To be modern was to separate religion from politics, which has led to religion and politics being viewed in binary terms separate from each other, although this is not the lived reality of many people across the globe. As Mohammed Arkoun (2003: 18–39) argues with respect to the Islamic world, Muslims are less concerned with secularized culture and cannot identify with this principle because it was born in a particular, changing European social context that holds little relevance to how Muslims live their lives. This is one of the biggest fault lines in the world today: that modern categories rooted in provincial histories of Europe have been globalized even though they do not speak to the lived realities of most of the world's population.

Secularism in the modern world: a view from the global South

A focus on religion has made a comeback in IR scholarship in part because the post-Cold War period has seen a rise in religious conflicts, such as those between fundamentalist groups and states and religious resurgences in the ex-communist world. Some scholars have argued that despite the efforts of communist leaders, religion never quite went away and instead appeared under guises such as nationalism or communism, ideologies whose followers often exhibited similar passions.[13] In the case of China, following Mao and his brand of communism acquired a cult status, with his followers reading his books like sacred texts and enacting rituals similar to spiritual ones even while religion was formally condemned (Poceski 2009: 252). Similarly, as Mark Juergensmeyer (2011: 197) points out, in the case of nation-worship, "secular nationalism" also required a great deal of faith, producing nations that Anthony Smith (2000: 791–814) refers to as "sacral communities."

While the passions of religion may have transferred onto nationalism and other ideologies, the nation does remain at base a secular category. Not coincidentally, then, passions associated with secular ideologies have been responsible for some of the most horrific violence of the 20th century, many of which, as Nandy (2013) argues, had nothing to do with religion at all. One could include on this list both the World Wars, the Holocaust, Hiroshima, the Vietnam War, the Cold War, the Cambodian genocide, Stalin's purges and the Cultural Revolution in China, to name only a few. He argues that more people have died in the 20th century thanks to secular ideologies of capitalism and development, socialism/Marxism, nationalism and so on than in the name of religion (Nandy 2013; see too, Chapters 7 and 8).[14]

And yet it is religion that continuously needs to be on the defensive and apologetic about interrupting modern norms, especially in the realm of public life. The recent controversies in France about women wearing the veil in public, Sikhs wearing turbans, Switzerland not allowing minarets on mosques, the banning of the veil in Turkey under Kemal Ataturk and preventing fasting during Ramadan amongst Uighur Muslims in the Xinjiang region of China are some examples. This is not to deny the role of religion in fomenting large-scale conflict; indeed, much of pre-modern history proves this to be the case. However, recent history does not exonerate secularism either, which is often portrayed as the antidote to religious conflict. Criticisms about the "intrusion" of religious norms and values into the modern, "rational" public sphere is especially targeted toward Muslim populations globally, who are seen as less capable of keeping distinctions between religion and politics intact. Hence, they are often seen as less modern and seen as posing an "uncomfortable," sometimes "threatening" presence in societies such as Europe where they now live in large numbers as immigrants. Even non-Western societies with minority Muslim populations are taking similar positions, as seen in the rise of anti-Muslim violence and rhetoric in countries like India, Burma, China and so on. This in turn has led to a backlash in many Muslim-majority countries, where a "purist" notion of Islam has growing appeal, especially amongst youth. Drawing on schools such as Wahhabism,[15] radical elements of these societies downplay local traditions and practices seen as "un-Islamic," such as in South-East Asia where the presence of Hindu, Buddhist and animist traditions have blended with Islam, in Africa where Christianity, Islam and folk religions are simultaneously practiced, or in Serbia where Muslim Serbs were hardly considered Muslims at all.

Countries that adopted communist ideologies after World War II also adopted aggressively anti-religious policies to govern their populations. They shared a modernist suspicion toward religion as irrational (Lynch 2000: 741–759) and wanted to significantly reduce, if not completely remove, the influence of religion on people's lives and the presence of religious authorities. Mao, for instance, saw popular Chinese religion, such as the belief in ancestors and spirits amongst the peasantry, as part of a patriarchal, irrational/unscientific and inegalitarian feudal past that had to be radically ruptured (Poceski 2009). The Chinese state under Mao, especially during the Cultural Revolution, destroyed most monasteries, many ancient texts and relics as well as persecuted religious figures in an attempt to stamp out all religious practices from people's lives. The most tragic example may be Cambodia, where the communist-inspired Khmer Rouge tried to eradicate Theravada Buddhism and folk religions, as they represented "tradition." Led by Pol Pot, who studied Marxism in France in the 1970s, the government killed one out of every five Cambodians, or 1.5 million people, by starvation, execution and forced labor (Haynes 2007).

Secularism and the transformation of religion

The aggressive secular critique has transformed the very nature of religion itself. As a result, religion has emerged in fundamentally new ways with the rise of secularism. In order to counter strong secular critiques, religions have adopted the self-defense strategy of increasingly aligning themselves with modernist elements drawn from secularism. Within each religion since the 18th century, there have been deep internal questionings and criticisms by intellectuals and social reformers in order to deal with secular claims that religion represents an atavistic, irrational and unscientific worldview. This process began in an aggressive manner with Christianity, where major elements of the Christian faith – "the miracles, the Virgin Birth, the bodily resurrection of Christ, the expectation of Christ's return, the reality of eternal damnation – have been quietly dropped from the teachings of the major Christian churches" (Bruce 1996: 36).

Religion, with its multiple temporalities and diversities of tradition and practice, does not fit well with modern secularism's unitary demands, especially in the case of nation-building. The scathing attacks on religion that started with Catholicism, and today are channeled increasingly against Islam, have also allowed the more authoritarian elements within these religions to take over as "authentic defenders," while moderate voices get suppressed. Conservatives are increasingly purifying religions in order to expunge them of elements that seem foreign or threatening, which often include local, folk and popular practices. In order to counter these claims and gain "self-respect" in the modern world, each religion has undergone fundamental transformations and gradually aligned with modern categories, most notably those of the nation and the individual self.

Oftentimes the demands of those who speak in the name of religion are secular rather than purely religious in nature. They often have very little to do with spiritual concerns but instead reflect hard, core material interests. The rise of religious extremism worldwide today is inextricably linked to secularism; in many ways, it is a response to secularism and has incorporated many of its key beliefs. Religious extremists focus on political economy, geopolitics, territory and the nation-state, factors similar to those that drive secular nation-states. Thus, the "clash of civilizations" that Huntington claims exists between the West and non-West may not be such a clash after all, as the interests that drive these conflicting parties are not all that different if one examines the demands coming from both sides.

In the case of political Islam, for instance, scholar Olivier Roy (2005: 148–149) argues that the focus on the individual, or individuation, that took place in Christianity had a parallel movement in Islam. He points out that Islam has become increasingly privatized, tied to an individuated form of belief much like in the West. This is especially true amongst the large numbers of Muslim migrants living in non-Muslim societies, who are more likely to search for a "purist" and de-territorialized notion of Islam, or a global *ummah*. He writes, "The definition of what it means to be a Muslim and the reconstruction of a Muslim community rests on the individual," and points out that religion is no longer embedded in social and cultural relationships (Roy 2005: 151), which has led to a "deculturation." It is this deculturation, he argues, that has spawned religious fundamentalism (Roy 2005: 155) marked by a search for "authenticity" and a return to "roots." Roy writes, "By fighting to purify religion, fundamentalists tend to objectify religion, to define it as a closed and explicit set of norms and values, separated from a surrounding culture systematically seen as corrupting" (Roy 2005: 334). Roy (2002: 5) also points out that Islamists see Islam not merely as a religion but as a political ideology that permeates all spheres of life. They acknowledge modern education, technology, politics and so on, distinguishing them from the traditional *ulama* (learned scholars). This is what accounts for the large number of modernizing, middle-class Muslims being attracted to Islamist ideologies. They are increasingly drawn from urban professionals, such as engineers (Malik 1996: 6).[16] In its encounter with the West, Islam has been politicized and secularized, including in self-proclaimed "Islamic" countries such as Iran where Roy argues, "religion does not define the place of politics but the converse" (Roy 2007: 63) (see Box 9.5).

BOX 9.5 HOW "RADICAL" WAS THE "ISLAMIC" REVOLUTION IN IRAN?

The Iranian Revolution in 1970 appears to the outside world to have ushered in a radical Islamic state and society after overthrowing the secular Westernized leader Shah Reza Pahlavi who was a close ally of the United States government at that time. However, Roy argues that there is very little that is religiously radical about the regime in Iran. In fact, he argues the new regime suppressed traditional clerics and did not bring a clerical structure into power. Leaders are chosen, he points out, from the Council of Guardians based on political and not religious criteria. Even those clerics who are included are not done so for their religious contributions but because they are part of the political class. Rather, he states, "the overemphasis on state power by Islamists has resulted in the devaluation of religion" (Roy 2007: 90) and a "decline in religious observance" (Roy 2007: 63). And many state laws are not in accordance with *sharia* or Islamic laws. Thus for him, "the question is thus not that of the persistence of an Islamic culture but of the sudden appearance of new ways of religion becoming ideological and of new forms of religiosity in the framework of the modern nation-state" (Roy 2007: 64). In Iran, however, the constitution does call for a *Faqih* or cleric (known as the principle of *Welayat al Faqih*) to be the supreme leader of government while presidents and prime ministers serve as heads of government (Messari 2015).

Therefore, what one increasingly sees is the secularization of religion or its political resurgence. It is important to distinguish between religion as practice and its more political elements, although the two do often overlap. International Relations theorist Mustapha Pasha (2004: 135–132) offers a useful definition of both. He argues that religion

> connotes no discernible political project to reshape the state or civil society but a fairly heterodox set of quotidian cultural and religious beliefs and practices. Religious resurgence is intrinsically a modern political phenomenon ... aims primarily to restructure national space, to redefine nationalisms and to redirect modernization.

A great deal of fundamentalist violence today has to do with religious resurgence as understood above because many of its demands and concerns are at base secular. This is not to say all religious practices are peaceful and cannot co-exist with their more politicized dimensions, but it is also erroneous to look at "religion" as some realm removed from political and secular concerns rather than driven by them, especially in trying to understand religious-based conflicts in recent years (see Box 9.6).

BOX 9.6 THE CRISIS IN AFGHANISTAN (1979–PRESENT DAY)

In the case of Afghanistan, the present-day problems have their origins in the
Cold War; the Soviet Union invaded the country in December 1979 precipitat-
ing a war to resist them that left a million Afghans dead, created millions of
refugees and devastated the countryside. The Soviets in turn lost 15,000 troops
and spent US$5 billion annually to maintain their presence (Barfield 2010:
341–346). The anti-Soviet fighters known as the *mujahideen* were funded by
the governments of the United States (via the CIA, see Khory 2009: 74), Pakistan (via the Pakistani intelligence known as the ISI) and Saudi intelligence
agencies (Roy 2002: 5). Once the Soviets were defeated and left Afghanistan in
1989 the power vacuum was filled by some of these heavily armed and radical-
ized Afghan Pashtun groups known as the Taliban, led by a minor religious
cleric named Mullah Omar. The Taliban received active support from Pakistan's
military establishment (Khory 2009) and attracted extremists from all over the
world especially the Middle East forming the basis of Al-Qaeda (headed by
Osama Bin Laden who spent many years in Afghanistan), whose members were
responsible for hijacking airplanes and flying them into the World Trade
Center, New York on September 11, 2001. Thus, it is apparent that these conflicts which are termed "religious" are not purely so; rather they are deeply
intertwined with "secular" concerns such as power politics, geo-politics and
political economy.

Modernity has given rise to Buddhist,[17] Jewish, Christian, Hindu and Islamic national-
isms and fundamentalisms. While each deals with its own distinctive religion, they also
share remarkable similarities in their quest for "purities" and alignment with the idea of
a nation-state based on a homogenous religious identity. Modern political economic processes in the last three decades (often termed "globalization") have also played
a significant role in generating support for right-wing movements worldwide. In the
United States, for instance, the massive transfer of manufacturing jobs, anxieties created
by rising inequality and increased feelings of powerlessness with respect to employment
security among lower- and middle-class whites, especially in rural areas, have fed into
support for Christian evangelical movements. This New Right has seen a growing
number of converts and has become more politically active since the 1970s, working
closely with the Republican Party (Gallaher 2004: 31–56). The New Right has also
played a significant role in missionary activities in Latin America, Africa and Asia, promoting evangelical sects of Christianity, such as Pentecostalism, which has seen a rapid
spread in these regions, especially in countries such as Brazil which used to be predominantly Catholic.[18] These movements are very modern in that they draw on forms of
communication such as television and mass media, encourage wealth acquisition (or
"religious entrepreneurship") (Van Dijk 2011: 386–416) and stress individualism and personal healing. They are also "global" in that they are fairly uniform in terms of their
liturgy, organization and ideology (Lehmann 2011: 75–92), although how they are
received varies depending upon the local context, as will be discussed below.

Religion as lived experience and a way of life

So far we have discussed religion in its modern avatar, as an increasingly politicized process becoming closer to secular ideologies. This secularization of religion is a worldwidex process taking place in both the West and non-West and is tied to a search for purities and uniformities that can often be a source of conflict. Yet, in much of the global South and in parts of the North too, religion continues to exist to meet people's spiritual needs and is intrinsically woven into the daily fabrics of their lives. It does not form a separate sphere that can be easily detached. This is religion as "lived experience." Modernity has not led to the decline of religious practices, a fact that is now obvious to any observer of global trends. Instead, the world over, one sees the practice of religion thriving; in China, despite the Chinese government aggressively promoting atheism, 85% of the population are said to participate in some religious practice (Marsden 2005: 251). In Taiwan, with the onset of rapid economic growth in the 1970s, there was an increase in popular forms of worship, which normally consists of worshipping gods, ancestors and ghosts (Geschiere 2011: 358–385). Ghost worship remains very popular, especially of those ghosts who are troubled because they died in the wrong way. In the seventh lunar month, all ghosts are released from the underworld to enjoy a month of feasting offered by the living, a practice known as ghost feeding rituals (Weller 1987). Most people in Japan say they are not overtly religious (only 12% identify as such), and yet their lives are woven around popular religion, or what Japanese call folk customs. For instance, people celebrate Shinto festivals as community affairs and marriages take place in Shinto shrines. Funerals are likely to be conducted in the Buddhist way. In recent years, Christmas has been celebrated in Japan, especially the gift-giving part, and weddings are held in a Christian style, even if the participants are not Christians themselves (Ellwood 2008: 18). In West Africa, belief in witchcraft and occult practices are on the rise, which can be seen to redress problems of inequality (Geschiere 2011). Similarly, one sees the emergence of new saints and cult worship in Latin America, such as the popular folk saint Santa Muerte (saint of Holy Death) in Mexico and among Mexicans in the United States. This practice represents the assertion of marginalized groups who are finding new bases of shared spiritualities, though the Catholic Church strongly denounced these forms of worship (Blumberg 2014).[19] Similarly in South Asia, despite growing polarization between religious communities, folk religion is still widely practiced, as embodied in the physical spaces known as *dargahs* or Sufi shrines that dot the landscape all over the region. People from different castes, classes and religious backgrounds visit these shrines to resolve their personal issues such as asking for a child to be born to them or be cured of a disease and so on. Even Pentecostal movements, although tied to American funding, have become increasingly popular in countries such as Korea, Brazil and Nigeria. Converts continue to draw heavily on local traditions even as they critique these practices in light of their new religious affiliation. In Korea, for instance, people borrow from the shamanistic folk religion (Mullins cited in Beckford 2011: 44) by enacting exorcisms and healing services. In Brazil and West Africa, they draw on possession cults.

Conclusion

It is apparent that lived religions continue to play an important role in people's lives the world over. Rapid modernization processes have thrown up immense changes such as rising inequality, rapid urbanization, displacement, environmental degradation, breakdown of community networks and so on. It is apparent that religion fulfills a need other ideologies cannot in dealing with some of these accelerated changes. As South-East Asian studies scholar Benedict Anderson (1983) points out, existential and spiritual needs revolving around eternal human questions like life and death cannot be answered by modern systems of thought, including secularism, ideologies of the market, nationalism or Marxism, however powerful they may be. While science has brought many aspects of human life under greater control and predictability, life still remains quite uncertain, even more so for those who live on the margins. As a result, religion as a lived experience and part of people's everyday lives continues and will persist.

Therefore, religion need not always be viewed as a threatening presence in people's public and private lives. Religion can also act as an antidote to those who speak extremist languages in its name, and it can be reclaimed by those who want to bring ethical values and norms into politics. Many figures from different parts of the world have successfully achieved this and continue to do so: Martin Luther King, Mahatma Gandhi, Desmond Tutu, the Dalai Lama, liberation theologists in South America who have brought Marxism and Christianity together to raise issues of social justice and many other unknown names and movements. Religious worldviews can act as moral frameworks that guide people in dealing with social problems. In light of the massive ecological devastation and rising inequality currently taking place in the world under an aggressive neoliberal model of development, religious ethics and frameworks critical of these models do offer hope and possibility for many. This is not to argue that religion exists in some kind of "ideal space" unsullied by politics, power and conflict. History has shown otherwise. Religion has also played its role over the centuries in fomenting social hatred and intolerance, and religion in its modern manifestation continues to do so. However, mainstream IR has singularly concentrated on the latter and thus been unable to account for religion as a lived experience that can play a positive role. Using a more critical, self-reflexive gaze could allow mainstream IR to unpack its secularist biases. This would allow IR to begin to meaningfully engage with religion as people experience it socially and not just as a threatening Other. As political theorist William Connolly (cited in Biswas 2002: 202) insightfully puts it, what we need is not to dislodge secularism but to "convert it into one perspective amongst several in a pluralistic culture." Secularist IR needs to recognize its own provincial location in a world of multiple perspectives, including religious ones.

Questions for discussion

1. How does one define secularism?
2. What are the origins of secularism?
3. How did secularism spread to the rest of the world?
4. How is religion influenced by secularism? Are the two separate?
5. Can religion play a positive role in international politics?
6. Can religion and secularism co-exist?
7. Is secularism purely a Western phenomenon?
8. How can we better understand the relationship between religion and nationalism?

Notes

1 I thank Tania Patel for her help with these stories. Tania has done field work on the Chamliyal shrine on the Indian side of the border for her ongoing PhD research and will be publishing the work soon.
2 In a 1998 ISSP poll, more than two-thirds of the population in Europe said they believed religion was intolerant and that it creates conflict (Casanova 2011: 69).

3 At first, the Buddha did not allow women in *sanghas*, but he was convinced by his disciple Ananda that women could participate (Krishna 1996: 44).

4 See Adam Bowles (2010: 61–74) for a discussion on the secular nature of the Maratha state led by the Hindu ruler Shivaji. Richard Eaton (2000: 164), who studied Islamic states in South India in the medieval period, points out that both Hindu and Muslim rulers used the Islamic title "Sultan" because early Indo-Muslim culture sharply demarcated "church" from "state." Political theorist Rajeev Bhargava (2011: 105) calls this the notion of "principled distance."

5 Some argue the beginnings of secularism are there in the work of Christian theologians like Thomas Acquinas and intellectuals like Pierre Dubois and Marsiglio of Padua as early as the 1300s in their questioning of the theological nature of the state and use reason to critique religion (Knutsen 1997).

6 The development of print media also helped spread these ideas. Between 1517 and 1520, Luther's followers printed 300 copies of his writings, which spread across Europe (Philpott 2000).

7 The most enthusiastic recipients of Protestant ideas were merchants and artisans (Philpott 2000).

8 However, Hendrix (2000) argues that the Reformation did not lead to a reduction in religiosity but rather an appeal to a return to a "pure" and "authentic" Christianity not steeped in idolatry, worship of saints, relics and so on.

9 The Hapsburg dynasty ruled significant parts of Europe (which comprised the Holy Roman Empire) from the 1400s to the 1700s with its capital in Vienna, Austria. In the 1800s, it ruled over what came to be known as the Austro-Hungarian Empire, which brought Austria and Hungary together.

10 Minorities include North African Muslims in France, South Asian Hindus and Muslims in Britain, Muslim Turks in Germany and so on.

11 Casanova (2011: 71) points out that European states are not as secular as they project themselves to be. For instance, branches of Christianity are privileged in most European countries such as the Anglican Church in England, the Presbyterian Church in Scotland, the Orthodox Church in Greece and so on. In France, many private Catholic schools are state funded.

12 Daoism and Confucianism were not religions in the Western sense of the term but were increasingly defined as such by Christian missionaries and Westerners who came to China and used their own classifications to "define" these worldviews. Something similar happened with Hinduism in the case of India.

13 Calhoun et al. (2011: 188) suggests that historically this was always the case. The French Revolution, for instance, exhibited religious-like passions in its fervor, as did the American Revolution. Secular nationalism and the manner in which it spread globally had a missionary zeal and became a new religion in its own right.

14 A point also made by Casanova (2011: 70).

15 Wahhabism is a radical Islamic philosophy that began during the 18th century to "purify" Islam. Founded by Muhammad ibn Abd-al-Wahhab (1703–1792) in a small oasis town in the Najd region (in what is now central Saudi Arabia), it focused on absolute monotheism and preached a strict adherence to Islamic codes.

16 Amitav Ghosh (2002) also makes this point.

17 Buddhist fundamentalism and nationalism is on the rise in Sri Lanka and Burma amongst other places; Jewish extremism in the case of Israel and Christian fundamentalism in the United States also persist.

18 Bruce (1996) argues this is linked to rapid urbanization; over 75% of Brazilians live in urban areas and are searching for modes of community living. Moreover, in some cases the Catholic Church failed in reaching out to the poor and often allied itself with upper-class interests.

19 See also Lois Ann Lorentzen's piece titled "*Santa Muerte*: Saint of the Dispossessed, Enemy of the Church and State." Available at: www.emisphericinstitute.org/en/emisferica-13-1-states-of-devotion/13-1-essays/santa-muerte-saint-of-the-dispossessed-enemy-of-church-and-state.html (accessed on February 16, 2020).

Further reading

Asad, Talal (2003) *Formations of the Secular: Christianity, Islam, Modernity*, Stanford: Stanford University Press. Asad discusses the emergence of the "secular" in the histories of Europe and its implications for societies with different historical trajectories.

Calhoun, Craig et al. (eds) (2011) *Rethinking Secularism*, New York: Oxford University Press. Various authors in this book explore the relationships between secularism and liberalism, democracy, citizenship, religion and violence in Western and non-Western contexts.

Haynes, Jeffery (2007) *An Introduction to International Relations and Religion*, Harlow: Pearsons. Haynes analyzes how various IR theories assess the impact of religion on global politics and the rise of religious actors and processes.

Shakman Hurd, Elizabeth (2008) *The Politics of Secularism in International Relations*, Princeton and Oxford: Princeton University Press. Shakman Hurd examines variants of modern secularism that she argues underpin international relations and the implications these have for the manner in which IR deals with questions of religion in global politics.

Soguk, Nevzat (2011) *Globalization and Islamism: Beyond Fundamentalism*, Lanham: Rowman and Littlefield Publishers. Soguk challenges dominant representations of Islam (especially in the West) and uncovers ancient, flexible and diverse traditions of Islamic cosmopolitanism in various parts of the world.

References

Anderson, Benedict (1983) *Imagined Communities*, London: Verso.

Ansari, M.T. (ed) (2001) *Secularism, Islam and Modernity: Selected Essays of Alam Khundmiri*, New Delhi: Sage. DOI: 10.1177/006996670203600313

Arkoun, Mohammed (2003) "Rethinking Islam Today," *Annals of the American Academy of Political and Social Science*, July, 588: 18–39. DOI: 10.1177/0002716203588001003

Asad, Talal (1993) *Genealogies of Religion: Discipline and Reasons of Power in Christianity and Islam*, Baltimore and London: The Johns Hopkins University Press. DOI: 10.1017/S0020743800061195

Barfield, Thomas (2010) *Afghanistan: A Cultural and Political History*, Princeton: Princeton University Press.

Beckford, James A. (2011) "Globalisation and Religion," in Veronique Altglas (ed), *Religion and Globalization: Critical Concepts in Social Studies (Religious Responses to Globalization)*, London and New York: Routledge, II, pp. 3–54.

Bellah, Robert N. (1967) "Civil Religion in America," *Daedalus: Journal of the American Academy of Arts and Sciences*, Winter, 96(1): 1–21. DOI: 10.1162/001152605774431464

Benavides, Gustavo (1997) "Magic, Religion, Materiality," *Historical Reflections/Reflexions Historiques*, 23(3): 301–330.

Bhargava, Rajeev (2000) "Rehabilitating Secularism," in Calhoun, Craig, Mark Juergensmeyer and Jonathan VanAntwerpen (eds), *Rethinking Secularism*, Oxford and New York: Oxford University Press, p. 105.

Biswas, Shampa (2002) "The 'New Cold War' Secularism, Orientalism, and Postcoloniality," in Geeta Chowdhry and Sheila Nair (eds), *Power, Postcolonialism and International Relations: Reading Race, Gender and Class*, London and New York: Routledge, pp. 184–208.

Blumberg, Antonia (2014) "Meet Santa Muerte: The Tequila-Loving Saint Comforting Both Criminals and the Marginalized," *The Huffington Post*, 11 October (accessed September 1, 2015). Available: www.huffingtonpost.com/2014/11/07/santa-muerte-saintdeath_n_6108198.html?ir=India&adsSiteOverride=in

Bowles, Adam (2010) "Governance and Religious Conflict in the Eighteenth Century: Religion and the Civil Discourse of Separateness in the Maratha Polity," *South Asia: Journal of South Asia Studies*, XXXIII(1): 61–74.

Bruce, Steve (1996) *Religion in the Modern World: From Cathedrals to Cults*, Oxford and New York: Oxford University Press.

Calhoun, Craig, Mark Juergensmeyer and Jonathan VanAntwerpen (eds) (2011) *Rethinking Secularism*, Oxford and New York: Oxford University Press.

Casanova, Jose (2011) "The Secular, Secularizations, Secularisms," in Craig Calhoun, Mark Juergensmeyer and Jonathan Van Antwerpen (eds), *Rethinking Secularism*, Oxford and New York: Oxford University Press, pp. 54–74.

Chakrabarty, Dipesh (2000) *Provincializing Europe: Postcolonial Thought and Historical Difference*, Princeton: Princeton University Press. www.tandfonline.com/doi/abs/10.1080/09502389200490221

Cohn, Bernard (1987) "The Census, Social Structure and Objectification in South Asia," in *An Anthropologist among the Historians and Other Essays*, Delhi: Oxford University Press.

Dearden, Lizzie (2014) "Christmas Day Truce 1914: Letter from Trenches Shows Football Match though Soldier's Eyes," *The Independent*, 24 December (accessed on August 26, 2015). Available: www.independent.co.uk/news/uk/home-news/christmas-truce-of-1914-letter-from-trenches-shows-football-match-through-soldiers-eyes-9942929.html

Eaton, Richard (2000) *Essays on Islam and Indian History*, New Delhi: Oxford University Press.

Ellwood, Robert (2008) *Introducing Japanese Religion*, New York and London: Routledge.

Engineer, Asghar Ali (2005) "Liberation Theology in Islam," in Rattan Lal Hangloo (ed), *Approaching Islam*, New Delhi: Black and White, pp. 66–94.

Gallaher, Carole (2004) "The Religious Right Reacts to Globalization," in Mary Ann Tetreault and Robert A. Denemark (eds), *Gods, Guns and Globalization: Religious Radicalism and International Political Economy*, Boulder and London: Lynne Rienner, pp. 31–56.

Geschiere, Peter (2011) "Globalization and the Power of Indeterminate Meaning: Witchcraft and Spirit Cults in Africa and East Asia," in Veronique Altglas (ed), *Religion and Globalization: Critical Concepts in Social Studies (Religious Responses to Globalization)*, London and New York: Routledge, II: pp. 358–385.

Ghosh, Amitav (2002) "The Fundamentalist Challenge," in *The Imam and the Indian*, Delhi: Ravi Dayal Publisher and Permanent Black.

Gupta, Bina (ed) (2001) *Explorations in Philosophy, Indian Philosophy: Essays by J.N. Mohanty*, New Delhi: Oxford University Press.

Haynes, Jeffrey (2007) *An Introduction to International Relations and Religion*, Harlow: Pearsons. DOI: 10.4324/9781315833026

Hendrix, Scott (2000) "Rerooting the Faith: The Reformation as Re-Christianization," *Church History*, 69(3): 558–577. DOI: 978131583302610.1093/jaa

Juergensmeyer, Mark (2011) "Rethinking the Secular and Religious Aspects of Violence," in Craig Calhoun, Mark Juergensmeyer and Jonathan Vanantwerpen (eds) *Rethinking Secularism*, Oxford and New York: Oxford University Press, p. 188.

Khory, Kavita (2009) "Have the Chickens Come Home to Roost?" in StigJarle Hansen, Atle Messy and Tuncay Kardas (eds), *The Borders of Islam: Exploring Huntington's Faultlines from Al-Andalus to the Virtual Ummah*, New Delhi: Foundation Books, pp. 65–82.

Knutsen, Torbjom L. (1997) *A History of International Relations Theory*, Second Edition, Manchester and New York: Manchester University Press.

Krishna, Daya (1996) *The Problematic and Conceptual Structure of Classical Indian Thought about Man, Society and Polity*, Delhi: Oxford University Press.

Lehmann, David (2011) "Religion and Globalization," in Veronique Altglas (ed), *Religion and Globalization: Critical Concepts in Social Studies (Religious Responses to Globalization)*, London and New York: Routledge, II, pp. 75–92.

Lynch, Cecelia (2000) "Dogma, Praxis and Religious Perspectives on Multiculturalism," *Millennium: Journal of International Studies*, 29(3): 741–759. DOI: 10.1177/0305829000290031701

Malik, Jamal (1996) "Muslim Identities: Suspended between Tradition and Modernity," *Comparative Studies of South Asia, Africa and the Middle East*, 16(2): 1–9. DOI: 10.1215/1089201X-16-2-1

Marsden, Magnus (2005) *Living Islam: Muslim Religious Experience in Pakistan's North-West Frontier*, Cambridge: Cambridge University Press. DOI: 10.1017/CBO9780511489549

Merchant, Carolyn (1980) *The Death of Nature: Women, Ecology and the Scientific Revolution*, San Francisco: Harper and Row Publishers.

Messari, Nizar (2015) *Personal communication*, May 31.

Mignolo, Walter (2009) "Enduring Enchantment: Secularism and the Epistemic Privileges of Modernity," in Purushottoma Bilimoria and Andrew B. Irvine (eds), *Post-colonial Philosophy of Religion*, Springer, pp. 273–292. DOI: 10.1007/978-90-481.2538-8

Mohammed, Jigar (2012) "The Shrine of Peace," in Rekha Chowdhary (ed), *Border and People: An Interface, Centre for Dialogue and Reconciliation*, Jammu: Centre for Dialogue and Reconciliation, pp. 48–55.

Nandy, Ashis (2009) *The Intimate Enemy: Loss and Recovery of Self under Colonialism*, New Delhi: Oxford University Press.

Nandy, Ashis (2013) *Regimes of Narcissism, Regimes of Despair*, New Delhi: Oxford University Press. DOI: 10.1111/1478-9302.12100_110

Nash, Roderick (1967) *Wilderness and the American Mind*, New Haven and London: Yale University Press.

Pasha, Mustapha Kamal (2004) "Modernity, Civil Society and Religious Resurgence in South Asia," in Mary Ann Tetreault and Robert A. Denemark (eds), *Gods, Guns and Globalization (IPE Yearbook)*, Boulder: Lynne Rienner, 13, pp. 135–152.

Petito, Fabio and Pavlos Hatzopoulos (2000) "Silete Theologi in Munere Alieno: An Introduction," *Millennium: Journal of International Studies (Special issue on Religion and International Relations)*, 29(3): iii–iv. DOI: 10.1177/03058298000290030301

Philpott, Daniel (2000) "The Religious Roots of Modern International Relations," *World Politics*, 52(2): 206–245. DOI: 10.1017S0043887100002604

Poceski, Mario (2009) *Introducing Chinese Religions*, London and New York: Routledge.

Raju, Raghuram (2013) "Indian Political Theory," in Gerald Gause and Fred D'Agostino (eds), *The Routledge Companion to Social and Political Philosophy*, New York: Routledge, pp. 192–204.

Roy, Oliver (2002) "Islamic Radicalism in Afghanistan and Pakistan," *UNHCR*, 6: 3–24. Available: www.refworld.org/pdfid/3c6a3f7d2.pdf

Roy, Oliver (2005) *Globalised Islam: The Search for a New Ummah*, New Delhi: Rupa.

Roy, Oliver (2007) *Secularism Confronts Islam*, New York: Columbia University Press.

Shakman-Hurd, Elizabeth (2008) *The Politics of Secularism in International Relations*, Princeton and Oxford: Princeton University Press. DOI: 10.2139/ssrn.2719206

Smith, Anthony (2000) "The Sacred Dimension of Nationalism," *Millennium Journal of International Studies (Special issue on Religion and International Relations)*, 29(3): 791–814. DOI: 10.1177/03058298000290030301

Soguk, Nevzat (2011) *Globalization and Islamism: Beyond Fundamentalism*, Lanham and Boulder: Rowman and Littlefield Publishers.

Taylor, Charles (1989) *Sources of the Self: The Making of the Modern Identity*, Cambridge: Harvard University Press.

Taylor, Charles (2011) "Western Secularity," in Craig Calhoun, Mark Juergensmeyer, and Jonathan VanAntwerpen (eds), *Rethinking Secularism*, Oxford and New York: Oxford University Press, pp. 31–53.

Thomas, Scott (2000) "Taking Religious and Cultural Pluralism Seriously: The Global Resurgence of Religion and the Transformation of International Society," *Millennium: Journal of International Studies* (Special issue on Religion and International Relations), December, 29(3): 815–841.

Uberoi, J.P.S. (1978) *Science as Culture*, New Delhi: Oxford University Press.

Van Dijk, Rjik (2011) "The Moral Life of the Gift in Ghanaian Pentecostal Churches in the Diaspora," in Veronique Altglas (ed), *Religion and Globalization: Critical Concepts in Social Studies (Religious Responses to Globalization)*, London and New York: Routledge, II, pp. 386–416.

Watson, Adam (1992) *The Evolution of International Society*, London and New York: Routledge.

Weber, Max (1930) *Protestant Ethic and the Spirit of Capitalism*, Talcott Parsons and Anthony Giddens (trans.), London and Boston: Unwin Hyman.

Weller, Robert P. (1987) *Unities and Diversities in Chinese Religion*, London: The Macmillan Press.

Wilson, Peter (2008) "The Causes of the Thirty Years War 1618–48," *English Historical Review*, CXXXIII (502): 554–586. DOI: 10.1093/ehr/cen160

10 Security

Pinar Bilgin

Introduction: an Ottoman sultan in Paris

In 1867 the Ottoman sultan, Abdülaziz, arrived in Paris to attend the World Fair as Emperor Napoleon III's guest of honor. The Sultan's visit was a significant occasion not only for his hosts but also for the Ottomans. For it was the first time an Ottoman sultan was traveling to lands outside the empire for reasons other than battle and conquest. Indeed, some at home objected to an Ottoman sultan stepping outside of what they viewed as *dar-al-sulh* (abode of peace) for reasons other than war-making. Such objections were warranted by Ottomans' hierarchical conception of the international which was legitimized by a particular cosmology that placed them at the top vis-à-vis all other peoples. More specifically, *dar-al-sulh* referred to a space where Muslims and other protected peoples enjoyed security. European powers, in turn, were viewed as located on a lower pedestal in relation to the Ottoman self. While this particular cosmology did not mandate war with non-Muslims, it nevertheless underscored the potential for their territories to be conquered sometime in the future.

Needless to say, this hierarchical view of the world hinged on the continuation of Ottoman military superiority vis-à-vis their European counterparts. From the 17th century onwards, as the empire experienced one battlefield loss after another, the Ottomans found it increasingly difficult to hold on to their own view of the international. By the time the Paris World Fair took place in 1867, the empire had succumbed to the European society of states' view of the international. The latter was another hierarchy that ranked world peoples in terms of so-called "standard of civilization" (Gong 1984) (see Box 10.1). The Ottoman leadership struggled to improve the empire's position in this hierarchy by reorganizing its bureaucracy and particularly the military. The Ottomans also started attending world fairs to improve their image and claim their place among the "civilized" (Deringil 2003). The sultan's visit to the 1867 Paris World Fair was conceived as part of this strategy.

BOX 10.1 STANDARD OF CIVILIZATION

The "standard of civilization" refers to "the assumptions, tacit and explicit, used to distinguish those that belong to a particular society (by definition the 'civilized')" (Gong 1984: 172). Initially formulated to overcome the obstacles European actors encountered in their dealings with non-Europeans, the standard of civilization also proved instrumental for the former in their colonial dealings. While those who were altogether outside the society of states (i.e. "less-then-civilized") were considered to be not deserving of self-governance (as with parts of Asia and Africa), others in the process of meeting the standards with a view to joining endured intervention of one form or another (such as China, Japan and the Ottoman Empire; see Suzuki et al. 2014).

Yet, not all in the empire were ready to let go of the Ottoman conception of the international. Some offered an ingenuous solution that would have allowed the Ottomans to hold on to their own conception of the international while at the same time enabling the sultan to leave *dar-al-sulh* and visit Paris. The solution they offered was that special shoes would be prepared for the sultan, putting in a sole layered with Ottoman soil inside the shoes. Their thinking being if he wore these special shoes, Sultan Abdülaziz would technically not be stepping outside *dar-al-sulh* (Zaptçıoğlu 2012). We do not know whether the shoes got made or the sultan chose to wear them. Nevertheless, the sultan traipsed through multiple worlds: Europe/non-Europe; civilized/less-than-civilized; *dar-al-harb/dar-al-sulh*.

Sultan Abdülaziz's visit turned out to be a momentous occasion in an unexpected way: it laid bare the fragility of the European conception of the international through challenging the civilizational hierarchy on which it hinged. Indeed, the sultan's appearance caused awe and wonder in Paris not because he was "different," but because he came across as "similar." The European hosts of the sultan expressed disappointment with his outward appearance and demeanor, passing the verdict that he was not "authentic" (Zaptçıoğlu 2012). The Ottoman sultan's apparent similarity seemed to have challenged his Parisian hosts' sense of "self" and their conception of the international which was warranted by assumptions of (civilizational) difference.

To begin with his outward appearance, Sultan Abdülaziz was dressed in military attire very similar to European military uniforms of the time. The only significant difference was his headgear: *fez*. Yet, this one item of the sultan's outfit that came across as "authentic" was a recent adoption from North Africa. It was introduced by Sultan Mahmut II in the 1820s as part of the modernization of the military; a decade later it became integral to attempts to reinforce an Ottoman identity by removing a significant marker of difference (among Muslim and non-Muslim men). It was a testimony to the rapid changes the Ottoman Empire was going through that by 1867 the *fez* appeared to be the only "different" (i.e. seemingly "authentic") item of the Ottoman civil and military officials' outfit when compared to their "European" counterparts.

It was not only the Ottoman sultan's outward appearance but also demeanor that came across as not-so-different. The way the sultan handled himself in Parisian circles, taking tea with his hosts, offering his arm to the empress when escorting her from room to room in the royal palace, were entirely in keeping with the European courts' behavioral code of the time. The point being, the Sultan Abdülaziz's Paris visit turned out to be a momentous occasion for both the sultan and his European hosts; an occasion that laid bare multiple insecurities on both sides. By putting forth an appearance and exhibiting a demeanor that was not as different as presumed by those who invented the "standard of civilization," Sultan Abdülaziz challenged his hosts' conception of the international – a conception that hinged on a hierarchical divide between civilized/less-than-civilized, Europe/non-Europe.

As will be seen below, one characteristic shared by students of world politics is scarce attention paid to others' conceptions of the international (Bilgin 2016). Indeed, when studying "others" as sources of insecurity, "we" have been orientated to look at their material capacities based on "our" assumptions regarding "their" intentions. Yet, focusing on others as sources of insecurity is not the same as being attentive to *their* insecurities. Such scarcity of attention to others' conceptions of the international and their insecurities has rendered "Eurocentrism" a persistent limitation for the study of world politics. Here, Eurocentrism is understood as the limitations engendered by theorizing from a particular narrative on "European" experiences to study the rest of the world. Over the years, insecurities experienced by "Europe" have shaped the study of world politics and have turned into theories and methods utilized in the analysis of "non-Europe."

The next section highlights the implications of Eurocentrism in the study of security around the world. Next, the chapter introduces two key concepts, the security dilemma and the insecurity dilemma. The security dilemma is widely viewed as a concept applicable in the study of inter-state security dynamics anywhere around the world. Its limitations in understanding security dynamics in the "third world" has led some scholars to offer the insecurity dilemma as an alternative. While the first/third world (or global North/South) divide of the contemporary era does not match the European/non-European divide of earlier periods, it nevertheless reflects insecurities tied up with hierarchies of world politics. In the final section, the chapter revisits the case of the Ottoman sultan's visit to the Paris World Fair to offer an alternative approach that goes beyond both concepts in addressing the limitations of Eurocentrism in the study of security. This is done by offering an alternative approach to security: inquiring into the conceptions of the international and security of all those who also constitute the international, but have, so far, been paid scarce attention in the study of world politics.

Security

Security can be defined in a deceptively simple manner: the condition of "being safe" and "feeling safe" (Booth 2007). However, as Ken Booth has highlighted, what is deceptive about this definition is that it masks the politics of "being" and "feeling" safe for different peoples in different parts of the world. Consider the following:

- Many who live in the global South are concerned about accessing scarce resources (as with food or health services). They may "be" and "feel" safe under conditions different from those who have access to plentiful resources but may have concerns such as the environmental impact of such access (as with their "carbon footprint").
- People who live in "national security states" experience their freedoms being curtailed on a daily basis for "security" reasons. They may "be" and "feel" safe under conditions different from those others who live in states with established systems of checks against state interference in citizens' lives.
- People who live under conditions of violent conflict might expect to "be" and "feel" safe when a peace agreement is signed. Yet others who have experienced "the morning after" (Enloe 1993) violent conflicts know that such efforts address mostly the public (but not always the private) aspect of "direct violence" experienced by women. There is

also "structural violence" (Galtung 1969) that is experienced disproportionately by the most vulnerable in the society, including women.

That is to say, while security may be a "universal" need, people experience and pursue it in different ways. This is not only due to differences in insecurities experienced in the global South and the global North, but also because people experience phenomena differently, attaching different meanings (and sometimes choosing *not* to address them in "security" terms; see Box 10.4 on securitization theory).

Consider the example of nuclear weapons. They were treated as the central security concern in International Relations (IR) textbooks of the Cold War period. Following their deployment against Japan by the United States during World War II, they came to be viewed as the "absolute weapon" that would change the face of war (Brodie et al. 1946). Nuclear weapons were never deployed again. This has led some to jump to the conclusion that what prevented the Cold War from turning "hot" was the strategy of nuclear deterrence "at work." It was further presumed that nuclear weapons became "objects of desire" for states other than the five (U.S., USSR/Russia, China, France, Britain) because these weapons "worked" via deterrence. Subsequently, such a Eurocentric approach to security and strategy limited our understanding of the role played by nuclear weapons in world politics (see below).

Eurocentrism is understood here as the limitations engendered by theorizing from a particular narrative on "European" experiences to study the rest of the world (compare with how Eurocentrism is understood in Chapter 12). As will be seen below, over the years, insecurities experienced in Western Europe and North America have shaped the study of world politics, being turned into theories and methods utilized in the analysis of the rest of the world (Bilgin 2016; 2017). I will identify six specific ways in which Eurocentrism has limited our understanding of security and strategy.

To begin with, the Cold War period was characterized by the absence of "hot" war only in Europe; the two superpowers continued to confront (and sometimes clash with) each other via proxies elsewhere in the world (Prashad 2008). Indeed, some thought that what kept the Cold War "cold" in Europe was "hot" wars fought elsewhere in the world – some of which brought the world to the brink of a nuclear exchange (as with the Middle East in 1967 and 1973). What is more, the Cold War period witnessed the rise of what K. J. Holsti (Holsti 1996) called "wars of the third kind" as shaped by the "insecurity dilemmas" (Job 1992) of "third world" states (see below the section on the insecurity dilemma).

Second, while it is widely assumed that Cold War was kept "cold" in Europe thanks to the strategy of nuclear deterrence as employed by the United States, scholars who have studied Cold War crises have shown that it was not nuclear brinkmanship in individual crises but the very existence of nuclear weapons that "worked" (Lebow and Stein 1994, 1998) – in other words, "existential deterrence," that is fear of nuclear annihilation. That we continue to presume that it was nuclear deterrence that kept the Cold War "cold" has to do with persistent ethnocentrism in nuclear strategic thinking in that the Soviet Union is assumed to have "played" the same deterrence "game" as the U.S. (Booth 1979). However, analysts specializing in Soviet strategy maintained that the Soviet Union developed different approaches to nuclear weapons, and that they were not practicing deterrence as assumed by their U.S. counterparts. The point being that nuclear weapons do not "work" the same way everywhere.

Three, peace maintained through the fear of nuclear annihilation has proven to be less-than-stable, as Kenneth Boulding (1978) has argued. "Stable peace," in turn, could only be created through mutual satisfaction with the existing condition. Some argued that what allowed for the creation of a "zone of peace" in Western Europe in the aftermath of World War II was not only the fear of nuclear annihilation, but also the set-up of the European Community/Union as a "security community" that sought "stable peace" (Adler and Barnett 1998; Deutsch et al. 1957). Others have highlighted the relationship between the "zone of peace" and "zone of war," maintaining that explaining the emergence of a "zone of peace" in "Europe" without considering its constitutive relationship to the "zone of war" betrays a Eurocentric approach to security (Barkawi and Laffey 1999).

Fourth, that others in some other parts of the world also seek to acquire nuclear weapons has been understood with reference to aforementioned assumptions regarding the workings of nuclear weapons in bringing about so-called "zone of peace" in Western Europe. Accordingly, the eventuality that the new nuclear powers may have "different" approaches to nuclear weapons is seldom considered. However, Itty Abraham's (1998) research on India's nuclear (weapons) program has shown that the "securityness" of nuclear weapons for India's founding leaders was not isolated to deterring adversaries. Nor was it (only) about a search for prestige by proving to the world that India was capable of building its own nuclear weapons. Scott Sagan's (1996) research suggested that similar prestige-related concerns proved integral to the French nuclear weapons program as well. There was yet another dimension to India's case in that nuclear weapons also marked its "arrival" at the world stage. By way of building its own nuclear (weapons) program, India's leaders sought to prove their country to be a "modern" state that deserved to be treated as an "equal" by the society of states (Abraham 1998), thereby revealing their conception of the international as hierarchical (see below for further discussion).

Relatedly, insofar as students of world politics have remained less-than-curious about rising powers' approach to nuclear weapons (presumably "universal" but intrinsically Eurocentric), aforementioned presumptions behind the strategy of nuclear deterrence persisted. Consequently, we have remained oblivious to India's leaders' rationale in ceasing tests on – what they called – the "peaceful bomb" for more than two decades following the first test in 1974. During that period India's leaders did not practice "atomic diplomacy" (Alperovitz 1965) in the way that other nuclear powers did, cultivating instead a "nuclear ambivalence" (Abraham 2006). The second test came as late as 1998, which reflected a change in strategy on the part of its leaders vis-à-vis their position in the hierarchy in the society of states. As a rising power of the 1990s, India's policy-makers no longer wished their country to be viewed as "postcolonial" but cast themselves as "normal" (Biswas 2014). At both moments, in 1974 and 1998, India's leaders highlighted another "use" for nuclear weapons in addressing insecurities that are rarely (if at all) considered by nuclear deterrence theorists.

Finally, the presumption that nuclear weapons "work" the same way everywhere has impoverished our understanding of the causes of nuclear proliferation and hampered the search for a nuclear-weapons-free world. This has to do with the way in which the nuclear non-proliferation treaty (NPT) regime is set up: it reinforces the hierarchy between those who acquired nuclear weapons first (the five), those whose nuclear weapons status were eventually recognized (such as Israel, India and Pakistan) and those whose acquisition of nuclear weapons is considered altogether unacceptable (as with Iran and North Korea) (Biswas 2014). As early as 1980, Ali Mazrui had characterized this situation as "nuclear apartheid," issuing the warning that as the NPT regime constitutes nuclear weapons as a status symbol, it would render nuclear weapons to be "objects of desire" in a way that is not considered by nuclear deterrence theorists. Time has proven Mazrui right (also see Biswas 2014). Our Eurocentric approach to security and strategy has limited our understanding of the role of nuclear weapons in the past and present of world politics.

The security dilemma

This section focuses on the concept of the "security dilemma," which comes across as universally applicable and apparently immune to above-discussed Eurocentric limitations of thinking about security and strategy. The concept's originator was John Herz (1950), who maintained that conflict and war were not unavoidable between states whose policy-makers remained aware of security dilemma dynamics. In their 2007 book, Ken Booth and Nicholas Wheeler further elaborated on the concept to highlight (material and non-material) dynamics that produce dilemmas of security and what can be done to prevent conflict and war (Booth and Wheeler 2007; Wheeler and Booth 1995). Over the years, the security dilemma has proven to be a key concept utilized both by policy-makers and IR scholars who recognize only a "fatalist" logic to the security dilemma *and* critical theorists who point to the ways in which it could be managed. Let us look at each in turn.

In everyday debates, policy-makers invoke the security dilemma to suggest that conflict (if not war) between states is inevitable. This is because, they argue, policy-makers of State A do not know about the intentions of State B. Even the defensive actions that the policy-makers of State B take may be interpreted as unclear (if not offensive) by their counterparts in State A. Indeed, even those policy-makers who know of each other's peaceful intentions and fully trust each other may not be able to escape the dilemma, the theory goes, because while governments may change, capabilities remain; the new government in State B may have different intentions and use their already existing capabilities for offensive purposes.

Herz offered the concept of the security dilemma to counter such everyday presumptions. He underscored that conflicts and war occurred because policy-makers were not aware of security dilemma dynamics. Wars occur, Herz argued, because policy-makers who were unsure about the intentions of the others, prepared for the worst. In doing so, they rendered their counterparts less sure and less secure, thereby creating a "vicious circle of security and power accumulation" (Herz 1950: 157). It was up to the policy-makers to forego "the 'easy' solution … of force" and choose a "policy of restraint" Herz (1950: 180) concluded.

Pointing to "war" as the "easy solution" may come across as counter-intuitive to some and distasteful to others. Yet, we know that security policy-making involves political choices – including the decision to go to war. Gone are the days when people were conditioned to think of war as a "disease" (like the common cold that one could try to avoid but still have to endure every now and then) or as "a sign of health" of the society (where the weak will perish and the strong will flourish, resulting in a renewal of the society). We know that there is a political economy to war preparation (the so-called "military-industrial-complex" and the global trade in arms) and that war-fighting may become a way of life for some in conflict zones (a style of life that may be difficult to let go of due to a lack of alternatives or the attractiveness of a "heroic" way of life for the child-soldier, the guerrilla, the black-marketeer, etc.) (Kaldor and Luckham 2001; see too, Chapter 7). Given the above-listed dynamics, choosing a policy of restraint may indeed be a "difficult" solution for policy-makers.

The innovativeness of Herz's discussion on the security dilemma was in the way in which he pointed to war as a "choice" and not as an inevitability. For portraying war as an inevitability masks the political choices involved. In contrast, once war is recognized as a choice, the reasons why that particular choice (and not some other) was made has to be explained and justified to the citizens. Hence, the politics of security is revealed.

Notwithstanding the significance of Herz's contribution, security dilemma thinking remained hostage to Cold War deterrence theorizing. Booth and Wheeler revived security dilemma theorizing in the post-Cold War era, putting emphasis on the "dilemma" dimension (Booth and Wheeler 2007; Wheeler and Booth 1995) (see below for further discussion of the security dimension). Reminding us that a dilemma involves making a difficult choice, Booth and Wheeler highlighted the ways in which IR has failed to consider security dilemma dynamics in inter-state relations. Whereas security dilemmas are about deciding whether the opponent is aggressive or not, Cold War thinking about security focused on managing opponents whose aggressive intentions were presumed but seldom inquired into.

Booth and Wheeler elaborated on the factors that rendered policy-makers less sure about each other's intentions. To begin with, absence of trust between policy-makers has meant that one's adversaries cannot be taken at their word and that their moves are "defensive." Furthermore, noted Booth and Wheeler, there is also the "other minds problem"; policy-makers find it difficult to trust each other not because of human nature, but because they cannot enter the minds of their counterparts and find out what they "think" (see Box 10.2).

BOX 10.2 THE OTHER MINDS PROBLEM

What philosophers term the "problem of other minds" was discussed by Martin Hollis and Steve Smith in *Explaining and Understanding International Relations* to highlight the difficulties involved in understanding policy-makers' decisions. "When a car makes a nasty noise and refuses to start," wrote Hollis and Smith (1990: 172–3), "the expert can infer what is wrong with it by analogy with similar cases and can check the inference by taking the engine apart." No similar procedure is available for figuring out what the policy-makers of other states think. The extra level of complexity involved, though not explicitly discussed by Hollis and Smith, is the politics of security. There is a political dimension to decision-making in states; bureaucracies and civil societal actors are also involved in the making of decisions. In the arena of world politics, there is also the need to inquire into conceptions of the international and insecurities of others (for further discussion, see the final section).

Given the "other minds problem," Booth and Wheeler (2007) concluded that dilemmas of security cannot be avoided. Yet, following Herz, they maintained that policy-makers can be educated to be more sensitive to their counterparts' fears. Such education would be geared towards developing "security dilemma sensibility," they suggested. In the authors' words,

> [s]ecurity dilemma sensibility is an actor's intention and capacity to perceive the motives behind, and to show responsiveness towards, the potential complexity of the military intentions of others. In particular, it refers to the ability to understand the role that fear might play in their attitudes and behaviour, including, crucially, the role that one's own actions may play in provoking that fear.
>
> (Booth and Wheeler 2007: 7)

Developing security dilemma sensibility, Booth and Wheeler underscored, is key to avoiding wars between states. But then, how do "we" generate "security dilemma sensibility" if we continue to remain less than curious about others' insecurities – especially if they do not fit our assumptions? The question being, is it possible to address the "other minds problem" without inquiring into others' conceptions of the international and insecurities? While security dilemma thinking urged students of world politics to be sensitive to the "complexity" of others' intentions, relatively less attention was paid to their insecurities. By pointing to internal challenges faced by "third world" states, the concept of the insecurity dilemma provided one answer to this question.

The insecurity dilemma

According to the critics, what rendered security dilemma thinking Eurocentric was that it theorized from the experiences of states in the developed world. In the "third world," they noted, the assumption that "inside" the state is characterized by "security" and that "insecurity" originates from "outside" is turned on its head. This is because external boundaries of "third world" states may be maintained through norms and principles of the United Nations system while the biggest challenges may have domestic sources. Hence the concept they offered: the insecurity dilemma (see too, Chapters 7 and 8).

Students of security in the "third world" have, for long, underscored that state development and state–society relations outside Western Europe and North America have followed a different trajectory. Edward Azar and Chung-in Moon (1988) pointed to (what they called) the "software" aspect in state–society relations in the "third world," arguing that focusing merely on the "hardware" capacity of states did not allow understanding state–society relations and regimes' vulnerability vis-à-vis the society in the "third world." Diverging from other students of security in the "third world," Baghat Korany (1986) underscored the need to pay attention to insecurities of societies vis-à-vis states, noting that security needs and interests of states and societies do not always overlap (see Box 10.3).

BOX 10.3 SOCIETAL SECURITY AND THE SOCIETAL SECURITY DILEMMA

The concept of "societal security" was offered in debates about security in Europe in the post-Cold War era in response to developments unleashed by the end of the Cold War, the dissolution of the Soviet Union and the wars of the Yugoslav break-up. Ole Wæver (1993) noted that "national security" was becoming an increasingly irrelevant framework with which to study post-Cold War developments. In its stead, he proposed the term "societal security" and a focus on the insecurities of societies vis-à-vis states. Later, the concept of the "societal security dilemma" was offered when discussing how dilemmas of security could be generated inside states between members of different ethnic/religious groups (Roe 1999). Such a concept allows studying how people, who have lived side by side for years, could turn against each other and define their neighbors as the source of their societal insecurities, as in Bosnia-Herzegovina during the 1990s. Correspondingly, such societies could rebuild trust through developing "security dilemma sensibility" (Booth and Wheeler 2007).

Building on the "third world" security scholarship outlined above, Brian Job (1992) maintained that the concept of the security dilemma hindered more than it revealed. For, the inside/outside distinction makes little sense in those contexts where the international boundaries are safeguarded by the constitutive norms of the society of states (namely, sovereignty, the non-violability of borders and non-intervention), whereas domestic threats dominate governmental security agendas. As Robert Jackson (1992: 93) argued, "instead of states or alliances defending their populations against external threats, international society is underwriting the national security of states, whether or not they convert it into domestic security for their citizens." In such cases, Job (1992) argued, the concept of the "insecurity dilemma" offered a better handle on insecurities experienced by those who are "preoccupied with internal rather than external security," as with armed uprisings against the central government, ethnic/religious strife and violence between different groups, and/or resource scarcity and limited state capacity.

What the critics of security dilemma theorizing did not point to was that it was *not only* in the "third world" that threats to the security of individuals and social groups may originate from inside the state, if not generated by the state itself. Indeed, the terms global North/South was offered to replace North/South conceived in geographical terms for exactly this reason; for "the line dividing the North from the South presently runs right through the north, the south, and across both" (Dirlik 2016). The point that citizens may experience insecurities at the hands of their own state was developed principally by feminist scholars, who pointed to the ways in which women suffered disproportionately during wartime or in the aftermath of peace agreements (Enloe 1993; Sharoni 1998). Furthermore, those who dared to voice their insecurities were made to feel guilty by their regimes – guilty for voicing their concerns when "national security" was portrayed as under threat (Mernissi 1992).

With feminist scholars' criticisms, then, discussions of the politics of security came full circle. For, viewed through gendered lenses, those governments who sell the weaponry, those regional governments who give high priority to regime security and invest in the military, and those individuals and social groups who dare not challenge the status quo out of fear of the kinds of instability and change that democracy and human rights may introduce into their daily lives could all be considered partners in crimes committed against women's security (Mernissi 1996). There is a politics to deciding whose security could be addressed at the expense of whom. Such politics do not take place purely "inside" or "outside" the state, be it in the "first" or the "third world."

Furthermore, while cognizant of the non-material dimensions of in/security, insecurity dilemma theorizing did not focus on the politics of security, in particular the ways in which policy-makers may approach security as a technique of government in the "third world" and also beyond. Understanding security as a technique of government is not isolated to the "third world," but focuses on how "security is imagined on the basis of a bounded and vulnerable identity in perpetual opposition to an outside – an *Other* – whose character and claims threaten its integrity and safety" (Burke 2001: xxii –xxiv). A case at hand is Australia, as discussed by Anthony Burke (2001) where some policy-makers have, for years, invoked an "invasion anxiety" to design specific policies toward immigrants and asylum seekers (outside), while keeping the opposition in check (inside). Another example is the United States, as discussed by David Campbell (1992), where "writing security" has been used by Cold War policy-makers to manage relations with the Soviet Union (outside) and nonconformists (inside). It is in this sense, suggested Campbell, that foreign policy can be studied as a process of representing some (inside or outside) as "foreign," thereby rendering appropriate certain security practices while sidelining some others, prioritizing the security of some while imperiling others.

The point being, while seeking to address the Eurocentric limitations of security dilemma theorizing, scholars of the insecurity dilemma did not go very far. What the Australian and U.S. examples point to is that security has been utilized by policy-makers as a technique of government not only in the "third world," where pointing to a dangerous outside has been utilized to deflect attention from troubles at home, *but also* in the "first world." Politics of security could be papered over for political purposes here, there and everywhere. It is in this sense that securitization of issues could be counterproductive vis-à-vis human needs, including democracy (Booth 2007; Wæver 1995) – especially if "security" is utilized by policy-makers to render invisible the politics of making decisions that adversely impact citizens' lives (Aradau 2004) (see Box 10.4).

BOX 10.4 "SECURITY AS TECHNOLOGY" AND "DESECURITIZATION"

Using the language of "security" mobilizes feelings and forces that have favored states since the end of World War II, when the term "national security" began to replace the narrower notion of "national defense" (Abraham 2009). Following Ole Wæver's (1995) analyses of post-World War II dynamics in Western Europe, and the securitization theory he developed together with his colleagues from the Copenhagen Peace Research Institute, it has become commonplace to understand "security" as a "conservative mechanism" employed as a policy tool by practitioners. Thus, "desecuritization" is viewed as a preferable alternative strategy (cf. Booth 2007; Aradau 2004). One way of explaining this preference is to argue that it is "absurd" to try to maximize security, for it cannot be achieved (Wæver 1995). Wæver offered another explanation: "if one has ... complete security, one does not label it 'security'" (Wæver 1995: 56). In such a situation, he noted, security may not be a relevant concern, as is the case with 20th-century inter-state dynamics of Scandinavian states or post-World War II dynamics in Western Europe (Wæver 1998).

Conclusion: the international in security

One characteristic shared by security dilemma theorists and their critics is limited attention paid to others' conceptions of the international and insecurities. Security dilemma theorizing as advanced by Booth and Wheeler sought to move beyond such limitations when they offered the notion of "security dilemma sensibility." Yet, being "responsive to others' fears" and being "ready to assure others through words and needs" also requires becoming aware of their insecurities as shaped by their conceptions of the international. Such criticism is also relevant for insecurity dilemma theorists who, while seemingly interested in different insecurities experienced in the "third world," did not consider how the international is viewed by their policy-makers. To return to a previously discussed example, if insecurities shaping India's search for nuclear weapons status are not only "external" (as presumed by security dilemma theorizing) or merely "internal" (the presumption of the insecurity dilemma) but also to do with their search for status in the international society, then there is a need to inquire into India's conception of the international as hierarchical (Bilgin 2008).

This is what is meant by inquiring into "the international in security" – that is, inquiring into the ways in which others' conceptions of the international shape (and are shaped by) their insecurities (Bilgin 2017). To elaborate on this alternative approach to the study of security, let us return to the story about the Ottoman sultan and his hosts at the 1867 Paris World Fair, and consider the insights to be gained by inquiring into the international in security.

During the 19th century, world fairs served as occasions for states and empires to showcase their technological and cultural accomplishments and locate themselves in the world (Mitchell 1992). The earliest world fairs were held in Paris (1844), London (1851 and 1862) and New York (1853). What was different about the 1867 fair was its universalist pretenses. While previous fairs focused mostly on Europe and North America, the organizers of the 1867 World Fair had made a special effort for the rest of the world also to be represented. Sultan Abdülaziz seemed to take the spirit of this invitation to heart; for he was accompanied by a large entourage including *shehzades* (princes) and officials.

Forty-one delegations in total were present at the 1867 Paris World Fair. The hosts' use of space gave away their view of the world, their own and others' place in it. At the very center was the main building where Europe's industrial and cultural achievements were displayed. In small pavilions surrounding the main building, everyday lives of those coming from outside "Europe" were put on display in their custom-built villages, coffeehouses and temples/mosques (Corbey 1995). The 19th century was a time when Europe's history was being re-written by putting it at the center of narratives on world history, drawing a straight line from Ancient Greece to Renaissance Europe, to the neglect of Europe's debts to others in terms of give-and-take, learning, self/other dynamics and other relations of mutual constitution (Mignolo 2002). The Paris Fair served to re-inscribe this new narrative, attributing most industrial achievements to Europe, leaving "others" to exhibit their "cultural" differences (Mitchell 1992).

That said, it was not only the hosts but also the invitees who brought their own agendas to world fairs (one exception being those peoples who were enslaved and forcefully brought in for showcasing purposes). As with some other delegations invited from outside Europe and North America, the Ottoman participants were there to display their own "civilization," seeking to counter their portrayal as "savages." Yet, in doing so, the Ottomans remained cognizant of their "difference" being put on display by their hosts (Deringil 2003). For world fairs crystallized power/knowledge dynamics of their time, laying bare the insecurities experienced by those who did not have the power to produce and disseminate knowledge about themselves. Indeed, as Edward W. Said (1978) argued, Orientalist representations did not only authorize colonizing practices but also helped to constitute "the Orient," shaping self-understandings and practices of peoples as "Orientals." Let us focus on the insecurities of the Ottoman visitors to the 1867 World Fair and those of their Parisian hosts.

By 1867, the Ottoman view of its own position in the world had already come under challenge (as discussed in the Introduction). Ottoman insecurities were not isolated to military losses but also rooted in the challenge to the Ottoman conception of the international. Whereas they previously considered the empire on top of a hierarchy driven from their own cosmology, the Ottomans had increasingly found themselves located on a different hierarchy as conceived by the European society of states. In this new hierarchy, the Ottomans had not only lost their top position but were not even considered an equal to the "civilized" members of the European society of states. Such placement, in turn, warranted a particular treatment. Those who were considered as "civilized" had their relations governed by international law as evolved in European diplomatic practices (Grovogui 1996). Those who were considered "less-than-civilized," in turn, were not allowed those rights and protections that were accorded by international law. Ottoman insecurities were rooted as much in such portrayals of the empire as in battlefield losses. The 1867 Paris World Fair was considered an important opportunity by the Ottoman leaders to showcase the empire's own "civilized" status and make a claim for equal treatment as a member of the European society of states (Deringil 1998).

The European hosts' insecurities were a response to the Ottoman sultan's outward appearance and demeanor: he did not come across as "different." By being less "different" than expected, the sultan challenged his hosts' conception of the international – a conception that hinged on a hierarchical divide between civilized/less-than-civilized, Europe/non-Europe. That very conception of the international shaped (and was shaped by) the practices of the European society of states (including the "civilizing mission") vis-à-vis non-members and not-yet-members. Where the non-members were subjected to colonization, not-yet-members were measured against the "standard of civilization." Falling short of the "standard" allowed members of the European society of states to interfere in the affairs of non-members (see Box 10.1). The point being, such challenge to their conception of the international came across as a threat to their efforts to render European colonialism legitimate in the eyes of domestic publics and the colonized peoples.

Furthermore, Orientalist representations that "temporalize difference" and "spatialize time" (see Box 10.5) have warranted the colonization of peoples in other parts of the world not only during the age of colonialism but also beyond. Insecurities tied up with Orientalism (as reflected in the world fairs of the 18th and 19th centuries) are often understood as isolated to the age of colonialism and/or one region of the world (the Middle East or Asia) (but see Hall 1996). However, insofar as such representations (of some as waiting to be brought into the fold of the "civilized") have shaped the self-understandings and practices of all those caught up in the dynamics of colonialism: the colonizers, the colonized and those who narrowly escaped being colonized (Bilgin 2012).

BOX 10.5 TEMPORALIZING DIFFERENCE, SPATIALIZING TIME

Through temporalizing difference, one's own contemporaries are relegated to a past where security dynamics are presumed to work differently. Through spatializing time, one's contemporaries living in some other parts of the world are relegated to a past world (Helliwell and Hindness 2005; Hindness 2007). These twin processes have implications for in/securing peoples in different parts of the world. Temporalizing difference and spatializing time have allowed portraying insecurities of some people in some other parts of the world as a passing phase in search for security, and overlook the need for investigating alternative presents and futures. Insecurities experienced in the "third world" are rendered explicable as trials and travails of shaking off ideas and institutions of that past world. Interventions of various kinds are, in turn, warranted as the only available remedy in addressing such challenges (Jabri 2013; Bilgin 2016).

To reiterate, what is meant by Eurocentrism is not the origins of IR being in Western Europe and the United States, or the centrality of the roles played by European great powers and the United States in shaping post-World War I world politics. Eurocentrism limits the study of world politics because security as viewed through the lenses of the European great powers (and later the United States) has shaped the study of world politics, being turned into theories and methods utilized in the analysis of the rest of the world; whereas insecurities as experienced by non-Europeans do not always find their way into "our" textbooks (Bilgin 2010, 2016, 2017).

Questions for discussion

1. What is Eurocentrism (see too, Chapter 12)?
2. How does Eurocentrism matter in the study of security?
3. Identify different conceptions of the international discussed in the chapter. How do they matter in the study of security?
4. What are the contributions of security dilemma theorizing to the study of world politics? Discuss with reference to examples.
5. What are the Eurocentric limitations of security dilemma theorizing? Does the concept of the "insecurity dilemma" address these limitations? Discuss with reference to examples.
6. What does it mean to study "security as technology?" Discuss with reference to examples from world politics.
7. What does it mean to study "security in the international?" Discuss its relevance with reference to examples from world politics.

Suggested readings

Bilgin, Pinar (2012) "Security in the Arab World and Turkey: Differently Different," in Tickner, Arlene B. and Blaney, D. (eds.) *Thinking International Relations Differently*, London: Routledge, pp. 27–47.

Bilgin, Pinar (2016) *The International in Security, Security in the International*, London: Routledge. This book introduces the study of "the international in security."

Bilgin, Pinar (2019) *Regional Security in the Middle East: A Critical Perspective*, London: Routledge. This is an analysis of regional security in the Middle East from a critical perspective.

Booth, Ken and Nicholas J. Wheeler (2007) *The Security Dilemma: Fear, Cooperation, and Trust in World Politics*, Basingstoke: Palgrave Macmillan. This book introduces security dilemma theorizing.

Jabri, Vivienne (2013) *The Postcolonial Subject: Claiming Politics/Governing Others in Late Modernity*, London: Routledge. Jabri analyzes the Arab uprisings as an instance of postcolonial resistance to hegemony.

Job, Brian L. (1992) "The Insecurity Dilemma: National, Regime and State Securities in the Third World," in Job, Brian L. (ed.) *The Insecurity Dilemma*, Boulder, CO: Lynne Rienner. Here Job introduces the concept of the "insecurity dilemma."

Tickner, Arlene B. and Monica Herz (2012) "No Place for Theory? Security Studies in Latin America," in Tickner, Arlene B. and Blaney, D. (eds.) *Thinking International Relations Differently*, London: Routledge, pp. 92–114. This reading and Bilgin (2012) explore conceptions of security in Latin America and the Middle East, respectively.

Bibliography

Abraham, Itty (1998) *The Making of the Indian Atomic Bomb: Science, Secrecy and the Postcolonial State*, New York: Zed Books.

Abraham, Itty (2006) "The Ambivalence of Nuclear Histories," *Osiris*, 6(21): 49–65. doi:10.1086/507135

Abraham, Itty (2009) "Seguranca/Security in Brazil and the United States," in Gluck, Carol and Tsing, Anna Lowenhaupt (eds.) *Words in Motion: Toward a Global Lexicon*, Durham and London: Duke University Press, pp. 21–39.

Adler, Emanuel and Michael N. Barnett (1998) *Security Communities*, Cambridge and New York: Cambridge University Press.

Alperovitz, Gar (1965) *Atomic Diplomacy: Hiroshima and Potsdam: The Use of the Atomic Bomb and the American Confrontation with Soviet Power*, New York: Simon and Schuster.

Aradau, Claudia. (2004) "Security and the Democratic Scene: Desecuritization and Emancipation," *Journal of International Relations and Development*, 7(4): 388–413. doi:10.1057/palgrave.jird.1800030

Azar, Edward E. and Chung-in Moon (eds.) (1988) *National Security in the Third World: The Management of Internal and External Threats*, Aldershot: Edward Elgar.

Barkawi, Tarak and Mark Laffey (1999) "The Imperial Peace: Democracy, Force and Globalization," *European Journal of International Relations*, 5(4): 403–434. doi:10.1177/1354066199005004001

Bilgin, Pinar (2008) "Thinking Past 'Western' IR?" *Third World Quarterly*, 29(1): 5–23. doi:10.1080/01436590701726392

Bilgin, Pinar (2010) "The 'Western-Centrism' of Security Studies: 'Blind Spot' or Constitutive Practice?" *Security Dialogue*, 41(6): 615. doi:10.1177/0967010610388208

Bilgin, Pinar (2012) "Globalization and In/Security," in Stetter, Stephan (ed.) *The Middle East and Globalization: Encounters and Horizons*, New York: Palgrave Macmillan, pp. 59–75. doi:10.1057/9781137031761

Bilgin, Pinar (2016) *The International in Security, Security in the International*, London: Routledge. doi:10.4324/9781315683812

Bilgin, Pinar (2017) "Inquiring into Others' Conceptions of the International and Security," *PS: Political Science & Politics*, 50(3): 652–655. doi:10.1017/S1049096517000324

Biswas, Shampa (2014) *Nuclear Desire: Power and the Postcolonial Nuclear Order*, Minneapolis, MN: University of Minnesota Press.

Booth, Ken (1979) *Strategy and Ethnocentrism*, New York: Holmes & Meier.

Booth, Ken (2007) *Theory of World Security*, Cambridge: Cambridge University Press. doi:10.1017/CBO9780511840210

Booth, Ken and Nicholas J. Wheeler (2008) *The Security Dilemma: Fear, Cooperation, and Trust in World Politics*, Basingstoke: Palgrave Macmillan.

Boulding, Kenneth E. (1978) *Stable Peace*, Austin, TX: University of Texas Press.

Brodie, Bernard, Frederick Sherwood Dunn, Arnold Wolfers, Percy Ellwood Corbett, William Fox, and Thornton Rickert (1946) *The Absolute Weapon: Atomic Power and World Order*, New York: Harcourt.

Burke, Anthony (2001) *Fear of Security: Australia's Invasion Anxiety*, Annandal: Pluto Press.

Campbell, David (1992) *Writing Security: United States Foreign Policy and the Politics of Identity*, Manchester: Manchester University Press.

Corbey, Raymond (1995) "Ethnographic Showcases, 1870–1930," in Pieterse, Jan N. and Parekh, Bhikhu C. (eds.) *The Decolonization of Imagination: Culture, Knowledge and Power*, London: Zed Books, pp. 43–56.

Deringil, Selim (1998) *The Well-Protected Domains: Ideology and the Legitimation of Power in the Ottoman Empire, 1876–1909*, London: I.B. Tauris.

Deringil, Selim (2003) "'They Live in a State of Nomadism and Savagery': The Late Ottoman Empire and the Post-Colonial Debate," *Comparative Studies in Society and History*, 45(2): 311–342. doi:10.1017/S001041750300015X

Deutsch, Karl, Sidney A. Burrell, Robert A. Kann, Lee Jr., Lichterman Maurice, Lindgren Martin, E. Raymond, Francis L. Loewenheim, and Richard W. Van Wagenen (1957) *Political Community and the North Atlantic Area: International Organization in the Light of Historical Experience*, Princeton, NJ: Princeton University Press.

Dirlik, Arif (2016) "Global South," *Voices from Around the World* [Online]. Available: https://web. archive.org/web/20161026083455/http://gssc.unikoeln.de/print/467

Enloe, Cynthia (1993) *The Morning After: Sexual Politics at the End of the Cold War*, Berkeley, CA: University of California Press.

Galtung, Johan (1969) "Violence, Peace, and Peace Research," *Journal of Peace Research*, 6(3): 167–191.

Gong, Gerrit W. (1984) *The Standard of "Civilization" in International Society*, Oxford: Clarendon Press.

Grovogui, Siba N. (1996) *Sovereigns, Quasi-Sovereigns and Africans: Race and Self-determination in International Law*, Minneapolis, MN: University of Minnesota Press.

Hall, Stuart (1996) "When Was 'The Post-colonial'? Thinking at the Limit," in Chambers, Ian and Curti, Lidia (eds.) *The Post-Colonial Question: Common Skies, Divided Horizons*, London: Routledge, pp. 242–260.

Helliwell, Christine and Barry Hindness (2005) "The Temporalizing of Difference," *Ethnicities*, 5: 414–418.

Herz, John H. (1950) "Idealist Internationalism and the Security Dilemma," *World Politics*, 2(2): 157–180.

Hindness, Barry (2007) "The Past Is Another Culture," *International Political Sociology*, 1: 325–338.

Hollis, Martin and Steve Smith (1990) *Explaining and Understanding International Relations*, New York: Oxford University Press.

Holsti, Kalevi J. (1996) *The State, War, and the State of War*, Cambridge: Cambridge University Press. doi:10.1017/CBO9780511628306

Jackson, Robert H. (1992) "The Security Dilemma in Africa," in Job, Brian L. (ed.) *The Insecurity Dilemma: National Security of Third World States*, Boulder, CO: Lynne Rienner, pp. 81–93.

Job, Brian L. (1992) "The Insecurity Dilemma: National, Regime and State Securities in the Third World," in Job, Brian L. (ed.) *The Insecurity Dilemma*, Boulder and London: Lynne Rienner, pp. 11–35.

Kaldor, Mary and Robin Luckham (2001) "Global Transformations and New Conflicts," *IDS Bulletin-Institute of Development Studies*, 32(2): 48–69. doi:10.1111/j.1759-5436.2001. mp32002005.x

Korany, Bahgat (1986) "Strategic Studies and the Third World: A Critical Evaluation," *International Social Science Journal*, 38(4): 547–562.

Lebow, Richard Ned and Janice Gross Stein (1994) *We All Lost the Cold War*, Princeton, NJ: Princeton University Press.

Lebow, Richard Ned and Janice Gross Stein (1998) "Nuclear Lessons of the Cold War," in Booth, Ken (ed.) *Statecraft and Security: The Cold War and Beyond*, Cambridge: Cambridge University Press, pp. 71–86.

Mernissi, Fatema (1992) *Islam and Democracy: Fear of the Modern World*, Reading, MA: Addison-Wesley Publishing Company.

Mernissi, Fatema (1996) "Palace Fundamentalism and Liberal Democracy: Oil, Arms and Irrationality," *Development and Change*, 27(2): 251–265. doi:10.1111/j.1467-7660.1996.tb00588.x

Mignolo, Walter (2002) "The Geopolitics of Knowledge and the Colonial Difference," *The South Atlantic Quarterly*, 101(1): 57–96. doi:10.1215/00382876-101-1-57

Mitchell, Timothy (1992) "Orientalism and the Exhibitionary Order," in Dirks, Nicholas B. (ed.) *Colonialism and Culture*, Ann Arbor, MI: The University of Michigan Press, pp. 289–318.

Prashad, Vijay (2008) *The Darker Nations: A People's History of the Third World*, New York: New Press.

Roe, Paul (1999) "The Intrastate Security Dilemma: Ethnic Conflict as a 'Tragedy'?" *Journal of Peace Research*, 36: 183–202.

Sagan, Scott D. (1996) "Why Do States Build Nuclear Weapons? Three Models in Search of a Bomb," *International Security*, 21(3): 54–86.

Said, Edward W. (1978) *Orientalism*, London: Penguin.

Sharoni, Simona (1998) "Gendering Conflict and Peace in Israel/Palestine and the North of Ireland," *Millenium: Journal of International Studies*, 27(4): 1061–1089. doi:10.1177/03058298980270040701

Suzuki, Shogo, Yongj Zhang and Joel Quirk (eds.) (2014) *International Orders in the Early Modern World: Before the Rise of the West*, London: Routledge.

Wæver, Ole (1993) "Societal Security: The Concept," in Wæver, Ole, Buzan, Barry, Kelstrup Morten and Lemaitre, Pierre (eds.) *Identity, Migration, and the New Security Agenda in Europe*, London: Pinter, pp. 17–40.

Wæver, Ole (1995) "Securitization and Desecuritization," in Lipschutz, Ronnie D. (ed.) *On Security*, New York: Columbia University Press, pp. 46–86.

Wæver, Ole (1998) "Insecurity, Security, and Security in the West European Non-war Community," in Adler, Emanuel E. and Barnett, Michael N. (eds.) *Security Communities*, Cambridge: Cambridge University Press, pp. 69–118.

Wheeler, Nicholas J. and Ken Booth (1995) "The Security Dilemma," in Baylis, John and Rengger, N. J. (eds.) *Dilemmas of World Politics*, Oxford: Oxford University Press, pp. 29–60.

Zaptçıoğlu, Dilek (2012) *"Yeterince Otantik Değilsiniz Padişahım": Modernlik, Dindarlık Ve Özgürlük ["His Excellency, You Are Not Authentic Enough": Modernity, Religiosity and Freedom]*, İstanbul: İletişim.

11 Foreign policy

Asli Calkivik

Introduction

Nelson Mandela's death on December 5, 2013 made global headlines. The whole world mourned the passing of an iconic figure of struggle against the racist, oppressive regime of settler colonialism. Although the global media's coverage of the tribute paid to "Madiba" was extensive, there was a glaring omission from most of the narratives accounting the life and deeds of the freedom fighter. In the words of an observer, what was "conspicuously absent" in the Mandela coverage was the role that Cuba had played in the struggle against apartheid, despite the fact that, in his visit to Cuba in 1991 after his release from prison, Mandela had extensively acknowledged the immense contributions of this supposedly insignificant country in the Caribbean to the downfall of the apartheid regime (Nimtz 2013). In his speech at a huge rally in Havana, Mandela had highlighted Cuba's unwavering stance against imperialism and its unceasing aid to liberation movements as a foreign policy goal, noting the defeat of the racist army at Cuito Cuanavale as the most significant turn that had opened the way to victory against the apartheid regime. "What other country," he had asked "can point to a record of greater selflessness than Cuba has displayed in its relations with Africa?" (Nimtz 2013).

This was not the first time that the Cuban state's political agency was written out of dominant narratives of world politics. The crisis that ensued between the U.S. and the USSR in 1962 after the installation of missiles on the island by the latter marked a crucial point in the history of the Cold War and became a paradigmatic case for students of foreign policy through influential accounts such as Graham Allison's (1971) decision-making models. Although recognized in name through its worldwide baptizing as the "Cuban missile crisis,"[1] there was little of Cuba in mainstream accounts except as the locale where the incident played out, thus marginalizing Cuban sovereignty. As Laffey and Weldes (2008: 555) ironically note, "Cuba didn't matter in the Cuban missile crisis." Relegated to the position of a geographic site where the two superpowers clashed over the deployment and removal of the missile arsenal, the country was rendered virtually invisible as a pawn whose concerns, stemming from a long history of imperial aggression, could simply be ignored.

In 2014, Cuba made a limited appearance in global news sources through its effort to fight the ebola crisis looming in West Africa. The country embarked upon "health diplomacy" by sending 165 health workers to Sierra Leone where 2,400 people had died from the virus and close to 5,000 were infected by it (BBC 2014). Dr. Margaret Chan, director of the World Health Organization, voiced the gratitude of the international community for "the generosity of the Cuban government and [the] health professionals in helping fellow countries on the route to progress" (BBC 2014). Cuba's efforts to help alleviate the ebola crisis are just one chapter of an uncommon form of diplomacy that also included sending hundreds of medical workers to Haiti during the 2010 earthquake.

Reading these episodes together suggests that dominant ways of thinking about foreign policy can be misleading as to what, when and why those relegated to the periphery practice what they do, and, more importantly, blind us to what is happening in the realm of foreign policy making and world politics writ large. Rooted in imperial and colonial formations and discourses that legitimate the conquest and perpetual patronage of the non-West, dominant narratives within International Relations are largely circumscribed by their assumptions about who and what counts and in what ways, in foreign policy practice and analysis. Such assumptions forestall coming to terms with the role of the non-Western Other in the making and remaking of world politics. They block recognition of the general logics (motivations, objectives, ethical concerns) that often structure the foreign policies of the global South and that cannot be exhausted within Western-centric frameworks. As Cuba's role in the struggle against apartheid or its health diplomacy demonstrate, foreign policy conduct may exceed narrow calculations of power and aggrandizement of national interest, and can be premised on political and ethical concerns about freedom and equality stemming from a shared historical experience of domination. However, such foreign policy actions remain invisible and unaccounted for if we remain within conventional parameters.

Probing into this conundrum demands a counter-hegemonic understanding of what foreign policy is and how it should be studied, and bringing these insights to bear on the foreign policies of the global South.[2] A subaltern perspective on foreign policy, this chapter argues, is informed by three main dimensions: (1) the necessity to attend to historical legacies of colonialism and persisting global hierarchies in foreign policy making and analysis; (2) the need to challenge state-centrism and problematize reifying concepts like the national interest, national security and national power; and (3) the importance of conceptualizing the foreign policy of the global South – a subaltern foreign policy – not only in terms of specific actions and decisions taken by state actors, but more broadly as a political-ethical project that is enacted by state and non-state actors.

A subaltern perspective demands that we heed the voices of the periphery by making international hierarchy – its historical constitution in colonial and imperial forms as well as in its neocolonial and neoimperial articulations – our point of departure. Premising analyses on the idea that the North and the South are mutually constituted, such a perspective will aid us in being cognizant of the erasures present in hegemonic accounts as it brings to the fore the counter-hegemonic practices and discourses of foreign policy. Rendering audible what is silenced, visible what is erased and attending more closely to the periphery, where the international system reveals its logic, has important repercussions for understanding the foreign policies of the global South – as well as those of the West.[3] It requires that we move beyond state-centric and empiricist accounts,[4] and attend to hierarchical relations of power undergirded by capitalism, imperial and colonial histories, racialized and gendered aspects of foreign policy making and behavior.

Finally, as will be argued in this chapter, a subaltern perspective calls for reconceptualizing the foreign policies of the global South as an "ethico-political positionality" (Grovogui 2003; Slater 2004: 20) that points to something beyond particular policy actions and outcomes. Adopting such a stance towards foreign policy analysis amounts to more than attending to the "weak," the "small," the peripheral. Rather, it entails coming to grips with an alternative foreign policy perspective enacted by those who are governed; a political imaginary that is intent on turning the colonizing, imperial gaze back on itself.

Exploring this ethos, however, requires that we dispense with an essentialized understanding of the global South just as we set aside a positivist, state-centric understanding of what foreign policy is. The global South is not "one," a uniform entity, given the historical, economic, political, institutional and cultural differences of the states and peoples populating the periphery. Yet, the global South is also not "one" in a different sense: being located in the global South geopolitically (being at the receiving end of relations of power and domination) does not automatically translate into an ethical stance since, as is discussed subsequently in the chapter, foreign policy processes in the global South can and do reproduce their own Other – dominated, ruled and oppressed. Consequently, when speaking of the foreign policy ethos, we are invoking the global South, not merely as a geopolitical label, but as an alternative political positionality and ethical subjectivity (see Chapter 1).

Building on these premises, the chapter starts by exploring how foreign policy has usually been understood, in what ways conventional readings in the sub-field are Western-centric, and how these narratives are contested by analyses that take peripheral perspectives as their point of departure. The main argument of this preliminary discussion is that a subaltern perspective on foreign policy takes as its main point of departure not the state, but social relations at the domestic and international level, thus making the legacy and enduring forms of colonialism and imperialism, capitalist relations of power and exploitation, central to foreign policy analysis. The following section pursues the theme of the foreign policies of the global South as an "ethos" and probes into the historical legacy of the Bandung Movement as the enactment of an alternative foreign policy subjectivity deriving from the experiences of the post-colonial states in their struggle for recognition and dignity. It also explores other instances where this ethos translates into alternative forms of foreign policy agency in relating to the international, such as the Panchsheel policy or practices of solidarity among the oppressed. The final section elaborates on recent global developments, charting the challenges for subaltern perspectives within the context of capitalist globalization and neoliberal hegemony. It attends to the increasing role played by non-state actors, not in terms of their participation in foreign policy making, but as novel agents of the foreign policy ethos of the global South and potential bearers of alternative imaginaries.

Conventional approaches to foreign policy analysis

The academic institutionalization of foreign policy analysis (FPA) dates back to the 1950s and early 1960s when three works regarded as paradigmatic for the development of this field of study were published: Snyder, Bruck and Sapin's (1954) work on the decision-making process, which focused on the policy making processes to explain the determinants of certain courses of state action; James N. Rosenau's (1966) study that contributed to the development of actor-specific theories that explain the foreign policy behavior of specific actors; and, finally, Harold and Margaret Sprout's (1956) analysis, which investigated psychological, social and political contexts of the individuals who are involved in the foreign policy making process (Hudson 2005: 12–17).

While regarded as a subfield of International Relations (IR) and incorporated within its intellectual and disciplinary domain, FPA had "an uneasy state of affairs" within the discipline (Carlsnaes 2006: 340). This is because of the predominant distinction upheld in IR between theories pertaining to international politics proper (system-level theories) and explanations that attend to the behavior of individual states (unit-level theories). Establishing the indispensability of FPA to IR and highlighting its situatedness at the cross-section of the main problematics debated within the discipline – issues such as the structure and agency problem, and developing universally applicable theories while taking note of specificities of particular cases – has been one of the points of contention within FPA debates. What complicates these debates further are the disputes over the definition of the object of study – what is to be analyzed and explained (explanandum, also called the dependent variable, foreign policy) – and the relevant factors and appropriate methodologies to explain it (explanans) (Hudson 2005; Carlsnaes 2006).

Some studies, known as policy approaches, seek to explain specific policies taken by actors such as states, bureaucracies, politicians. They focus on "a single decision or indecision [as well as] a constellation and/or sequence of decisions taken with reference to a particular situation" (Hudson 2005: 2). Alternatively, other inquiries prioritize the foreign policy decision making process itself rather than the outcomes. They investigate questions such as how a problem is perceived and framed, what kind of foreign policy goals are prioritized and how different options for action are assessed (Hudson 2005; Carlsnaes 2008).

How do group dynamics – factors that play into groupthink, such as pressures to maintain group consensus, the personal inclinations towards being accepted by one's group – influence the decision-making process? In what ways do principles, values and organizational rules in larger and more structured groups such as bureaucracies shape the development of foreign policy? These are the kinds of questions that inform a line of research developed by, among others, prominent figures of FPA such as Morton Halperin (1974) and Graham Allison (1971) (Hudson 2005).

Still focusing on the foreign policy making process, another dominant line of research investigates the role of psychological and societal factors in the making of foreign policy. They introduce cognitive factors influencing individual decisions, the political psychology of individuals in the decision making process – their perceptions, understanding, representation – shape foreign policy decision making. Rather than attending to the psychology of individuals, other studies in this line of research introduce societal and national factors, grappling with questions such as: how does the political elites' conception of the role of their state in world politics shape foreign policy? In what ways can the "two-level games" (Putnam 1988) – a game played out between the decision makers and societal actors in domestic politics, on one level, and in the course of the interaction of state representatives with the state's outside on another – play into the formulation of foreign policy course and action?

A major contention among scholars of foreign policy analysis concerns the role structures and actors play in the explanation of foreign policy actions (Carlsnaes 2008). Scholars focusing on foreign policy processes generally invoke both actors and structures understood in terms of analytically distinct levels of explanation – that of the individual, the state and the international level (Hudson 2005; Carlsnaes 2008). In a classic articulation of the level of analysis framework, Singer (1961: 90) concluded that sub-systemic explanations (in other words, those that are actor-oriented and focus on the state as actor) are a "more thorough investigation of the processes by which foreign policies are made" than the ones couched at the level of the international system. However, he refrains from privileging one over the other, concluding that the choice to focus on the micro (actor) or the macro (system) should be driven by the research question at hand.

One of the prominent representatives of structuralist accounts (in other words, accounts that prioritize systemic factors over agency – preferences, choices, actions explanations) is realism.[5] Positing the anarchic nature of the international system (the lack of an overarching, supra-national authority that can protect the survival and security of the state) as its premise, realists conceptualize foreign policy as the means through which national self-interest, defined as power, is realized (Morgenthau 1948; Wohlforth 2012). Any distraction from defending the national interest, in this view, can lead to self-destructive foreign policy behavior. Although realist thought possesses a systemic orientation in understanding world politics, there are nevertheless important disagreements among realists about explaining world politics at large and foreign policy in particular. For instance, for a neorealist scholar such as Kenneth Waltz (1979), explaining foreign policy behavior with reference to the state or the individual would ultimately be a "reductionist" form of explanation (in other words, accounting for the behavior of states solely through a focus on unit-level factors without taking into consideration the effects their environment have on those units). In contrast, while agreeing with the former on the crucial role of a state's position in the international system as determinant of their foreign policy, neoclassical realists emphasize the need to take into account domestic factors as intervening factors that shape the impact of systemic factors.

While they share with realists the idea that states inhabit an anarchic system, liberals disagree on the conclusions that one draws from this observation. They shift the emphasis away from systemic factors towards actors, moving away from treating the state as a unitary actor vying for survival and power in an anarchic international system. In other words, rather than a top-down perspective, they provide a bottom-up view of foreign policy, which gives primacy to societal actors (individuals, social groups and so forth) over political institutions (for example, the state, bureaucracies and so forth) – and thereby open the black box of state action. For instance, an important proponent of this school of thought, Andrew Moravcsik (1997), investigates the role of domestic politics and interest groups as important determinants of the foreign policy of a state. Liberals argue that political institutions such as liberal democracy, private property and capitalist markets play a central role in the shaping of foreign policy preferences, decisions and outcomes (Doyle 2012: 54–55).

Social constructivism is a relative newcomer to an area of study that is to a large extent shaped by liberal and realist traditions. Constructivism diverges from the latter two with its emphasis on the role of ideational factors such as social rules, norms and values in the making of foreign policy (Kubálková 2001). In this framework, world politics is viewed as an intersubjective realm where actors' (individuals or states) conception of themselves and the world shape the way in which they define their interests, and by extension their foreign policy. Constructivist scholars, following realist analysis, register the centrality of national interest to foreign policy, but challenge its conceptualization (Weldes 1996). Rather than taking national interest as given, treating it as *a priori*, they explore the process of interpretation and representation through which state officials make sense of their international context and thereby produce specific understanding of what "the national interest" is. They reformulate foreign policy as a process of "defining rather than defending national interest" (Finnemore 1996: ix). While sharing some aspects of cognitive approaches to foreign policy analysis, constructivists diverge from them with their focus on the societal instead of the individual level. In these accounts, the question of "why?" (why a certain course of foreign policy is taken) is compounded by the question of "how-possible?" They seek to explain "not why a particular outcome obtained, but rather how the subjects, objects, and interpretive dispositions were socially constructed such that certain practices were made possible" (Doty 1993: 298).

Foreign policy of the global South

The major obstacle conventional approaches face in accounting for and understanding foreign policies of the global South stems from the parochialism of their conceptual frameworks. Central categories and assumptions of realist, liberal, as well as constructivist theories on world politics at large and by extension foreign policy analyses in particular have their roots in and bear the imprint of a particular experience, that of the West – as evidenced in the Eurocentric nature of realist categories of thought (Walker 1993) or the imperial impetus animating liberalism (Jahn 2005). Whether it be in the form of a vision of a world where might makes right and the weak do what they have to do, or in its contesting conceptualizations that allow for the civilizing potentials of international law and norms, liberal democratic institutions and market-oriented arrangements, both realist and liberal accounts bear the residues of the modern historical trajectory and the colonial and imperial historical geographies it underwrites (Barkawi and Laffey 2001).

The taken-for-granted historical geographies – the imperial, colonial legacies and their neocolonial and neoimperial forms – that inform conventional analyses systematically understate and misrepresent the role of the global South, as the Cuban missile crisis discussed in the opening section amply demonstrates. Privileging international anarchy as the systemic condition of foreign policy and relying on juridical notions of sovereignty serves to erase the hierarchical relations of power and domination that peripheral countries find themselves in, as well as the structural constraints that they face in foreign policy making (see too, Chapters 5, 6 and 8). The division between foreign policy and domestic politics, even when those two realms are drawn together through two-level games (Putnam 1988), renders invisible the manifold ways in which the global South has always experienced the "outside" as part of the "inside": that "[f]or the societies of Latin America, Africa and Asia, the principles governing the constitution of their mode of political being are deeply structured by external penetration, by the invasiveness of foreign powers" (Slater 2004: 24). A common effect of these forms of knowledge production on foreign policy is the reproduction of international hierarchy by effacing socio-historical constraints on foreign policy action, marginalizing the periphery and rendering it inconsequential for the constitution of world politics. They close down alternative conceptualizations of the basic parameters and objectives of foreign policy practice beyond realist power struggles or the problematic of the diffusion of (and compliance with) liberal values and institutions.

It would be highly presumptuous to suggest that conventional analyses have gone uncontested. On the contrary, there are numerous formulations that attend to the particular circumstances and dynamics that make the foreign policies of peripheral countries different from those in the North. In an early articulation, for instance, Baghat Korany (1984: 8) laments the state of foreign policy theory, questioning its "applicability to the Third World." Pointing to the individualist bias of existing frameworks and arguing against an "[o]verwhelming focus on the leader's personality dispositions and other psychological factors in reaching foreign policy decisions," he highlights the importance of attending to the "operational environment" (1984: 14) – "the objective factors as distinct from subjective ones" (1984: 17) – and the ways in which "underdevelopment" has influenced third world decision making. When exploring the foreign policy actions of peripheral states, it is argued, it is important to "explore the impact of disintegrative factors, of informal networks and of patron-client relationships" (Korany 1984: 18) that affect state structure and set the foreign policy course of the global South on a different path than the North.

The importance of attending to the particular circumstances of post-colonial states and taking account of "the broader, long-term concern[s]" of third world foreign policy making have been noted by a variety of scholars (Mohamedou 2003: 65) (see Box 11.1). For instance, taking a state-centric and security-based perspective, albeit through an alternative "subaltern realist" reading, Mohammed Ayoob (2002) foregrounds the global historical context that created states in the global South, and considers how this in turn shapes their foreign policy priorities and behaviors. He argues that, because some states in the Middle East and Asia are still in the making, this leads them to prioritize security as a concern not only in foreign policy but also in domestic politics. This entails defending themselves against all actors, both internal and external, that question the state's legitimacy and monopoly over the use of force (see Chapter 10).

BOX 11.1 FROM THIRD WORLD TO THE GLOBAL SOUTH?

The term "third world" dates back to the 19th century, appearing in literature and journalism, where it referred to the three worlds (Europe, Asia and a "third world" – Russia) of the Eurasian continent (Solarz 2012). Although the origins of its distinctive semantic and political meaning in the 20th century are contested, the term's widely accepted usage is attributed to a 1952 article entitled "Three worlds, one planet," by the French scholar Alfred Sauvy (Wolf-Phillips 1987; Solarz 2012). In a global political conjuncture defined by growing waves of decolonization, ambitions of newly independent states to overturn their political, economic, cultural marginality in the world system, together with the intensification of rivalry between the liberal, capitalist bloc led by the United States and the socialist bloc led by the Soviet Union, the third world held multiple meanings. One was its socio-economic dimension, identifying it with the low-income, underdeveloped countries. Another was its political-international meaning, associating it with the Cold War. In this sense, the third world signified both a field on which the superpower rivalry played out, and a third pole of influence in the international arena. The latter materialized with the emergence of the Non-Aligned Movement in the 1960s. As a political movement, third worldism combined "romanticised interpretations of pre-colonial traditions and cultures with the utopianism embodied by Marxism and socialism" (Berger 2004: 11). With the Cold War's end and the dismantling of the Soviet bloc, coupled with the changing nature of international economic order with the globalization of capitalism and the rise of finance, the idea of the third world became the center of intellectual debate. While some assert its continuing analytical and political import, others suggest that it has become irrelevant and prefer the notion of the "global South." This new terminology not only seeks "to name patterns of wealth, privilege, and development," but also "references an entire history of colonialism, neo-imperialism" (Dados and Connell 2012: 13; see too, Chapter 1).

Carlos Escudé (2009) also develops a distinctive approach to the realist para-digm – peripheral realism – that pivots on the conception of the international system as a proto-hierarchy rather than an anarchy, comprised of three types of states: the powerful rule-makers; those that abide by the rules; and rebellious ("rogue") states that are normally punished. He suggests that peripheral state for-eign policy is determined not only by systemic restraints, but also by the specific social structures and political cultures prevalent in the states of the global South, which shape their foreign policy preferences in ways oftentimes not conducive to the general interest. Instead, the author claims that the main function of foreign policy should be to serve the citizenry and not just elite groups, a goal that can be achieved primarily through the promotion of socio-economic development (Escudé 2009: 6). Since the latter constitutes the citizen-centric (versus national, elite-based) interest, peripheral states should avoid unnecessary political confrontation with greater powers such as the United States, so as to avoid sacrificing their material interests, which are fundamental.

In keeping with Ayoob's and Escudé's concern with the specific vulnerabilities of post-colonial states and their margins of international maneuver, other analysts problematize the conventionally presumed relation between state capacities and the exercise of agency and autonomy, the constitution of foreign policy objectives and the strategies pursued to fulfill them. Focusing on the small states of the Caribbean as "foreign policy actors in a highly complex world," Jacqueline Braveboy-Wagner (2008: 13), for instance, develops a via-media approach by combining realist, lib-eral, and constructivist perspectives in her account of the differences that character-ize the countries of the non-West in their definition of the national interest and their choice of strategies to pursue it. She suggests that the latter are shaped by systemic factors such as international and regional dynamics and constraints as well as the level of development and the role of political leaders. In this analysis, "Caribbean interests" are depicted as "continually changing," prioritizing more real-ist concerns, equating national interest with military-political security issues and development prospects when those goals are perceived to be under threat, while inclining towards more liberal concerns such as "socioeconomic (human) security" issues at other times (Braveboy-Wagner 2008: 13).

Attuned to both the vulnerabilities and the resilience of small states in their diplo-macies at the turn of the 21st century, Cooper and Shaw (2009: 2) too suggest that these states make up for their lack of leverage at the systemic level through their "creative energy" by deploying "strategies to exploit globalization." Among these strategies, the authors identify the establishment of export processing zones and off-shore financial centers and less conventional ones such as "selling sovereignty, mili-tary bases, fishing rights, shipping registeries" (2009: 6). Despite the common-sense notion that small states cannot exercise foreign policy agency because of their lack of real independence, it is suggested that they can possess the potential to act out like Henry Kissinger – demonstrating the power of the powerlessness by becoming prag-matic players in a game that was not of their making (Baldacchino 2009). Yet other studies contest the general view of the foreign policy of weak states "as the manifest-ation of those states' inferior position within the international system" (Hey 1993: 201), thus complicating accounts about the relation between state weakness and pro-core foreign policy choices and behaviors. They highlight the need to distinguish between the conditions of dependence and dependency – the former understood in positivist terms via indicators such as dependence on level of trade, foreign aid and direct foreign investment, the latter implying "a contextual situation defined by both domestic and international variables that frequently defy attempts to quantify them" (Hey 1993: 204) – and assert the need to subscribe to the dependence viewpoint rather than the dependency position. From this perspective, regardless of their dependent status, weak states are seen as possessing "very rich foreign policy repertoires" that they can deploy (Hey 1993).

Analyses such as these, which constitute only a representative sample of a considerable literature produced in or on the global South on diverse issues of foreign policy, are to be commended for taking as their departure point the experiences of the non-West. The majority converge in their conceptualization of the global context of foreign policy not as anarchy but as consisting of various forms of hierarchy (an unequal and uneven system of power relations), while also attending to the political, social, economic, socio-cultural variations that set the foreign policies of the "weak," "small" countries of the global South on a different path than those of the North. They also make significant contributions to the study of foreign policy analysis by accounting for the variations that are observable within the global South itself. They explore the ways in which taken-for-granted concepts such as state, security and national interest, take on different meanings when they travel to the periphery.

While problematizing the universal applicability of Western perspectives and exposing their parochialism, however, such analyses end up affirming what they negate by relying on similar conceptual frameworks and the same basic assumptions and categories, which are simply amended to suit the concerns of peripheral states. By assuming foreign policy as the relation of self-contained communities to the international, they inadvertently subscribe to conventional thinking by implicitly relying on the West as the norm – hence, registering the particularities of the South as a deviation from the norm – and reproducing state-centric, empiricist understandings of foreign policy at the theoretical and practical level. For instance, emphasizing the different forms that insecurity takes as it travels to the periphery leaves intact the assumption that security is/has to be as a central objective of foreign policy, thereby shielding dominant understandings of the national interest from scrutiny.

Another major shortcoming pertains to the optics of power at work in much of the global South literature. Privileging compulsory and institutional forms of power comes at the expense of attending to forms of power enacted in and through social structures (such as capital–labor relations) that "allocate differential capacities" to actors occupying distinct social positions in the structure, and constitute their subjectivities and interests (Barnett and Duvall 2005: 18).

This limited conception reproduces a reductionist understanding of what it means to be in the periphery, to be "small" or "vulnerable," as well as speaking of "dependent economies" rather than of countries locked into a relationship of dependency. As the critical sociological and post-colonial perspectives that will be discussed below demonstrate, such a limited understanding of power only scratches at the surface of those (neo)colonial and (neo)imperial relations that shape global South foreign policies. Finally, these analyses reproduce the conventional assumption that agency can be exercised only if one achieves a certain level of institutional strength, possesses a certain level of material capacity, or develops strategic ways to make up for what is lacking. The effect of such assumptions is that they render invisible forms of foreign policy action that are animated, not merely by pragmatic calculations, but by ethical principles. For example, limiting foreign policy options for the vulnerable to being "good Kissingers" leaves little to no room for attending to foreign policy actions that stem from other interests, such as solidarity among the oppressed.

Simply amending dominant conceptions and hegemonic frameworks of foreign policy thinking and practice to make them "fit" the global South, although an interesting exercise *per se*, falls short of decolonizing foreign policy analysis, which calls for a more radical project of uprooting. To this end, it is important to "retrieve the imperial" in the "international" *and* to conceptualize the latter as a thick social space of "mutual constitution through which states, societies, and other international phenomenon are produced" (Barkawi and Laffey 2002: 112). Accomplishing this goal requires replacing state-centric analyses with historically grounded, sociological accounts to uncover the changing nature of the relation between states, social relations and world orders (Cox 1981). Such a reframing of foreign policy allows us to move beyond the "problem-solving" nature of positivist approaches towards a critical analysis of foreign policy that is attuned to the concerns and struggles of the governed, exploited and oppressed.

This is precisely one of the insights that the dependency school provides by laying out the determining factors of peripheral foreign policies, thus underscoring alternative objectives and strategies as compared to those of the West: namely, a perspective on international hierarchy understood as structurally ingrained, unequal and exploitative relations rooted in global capitalism and the capitalist division of labor that create a global socio-historical context that restricts the possibilities for the self-determination and self-realization of the people situated in the periphery (Cardoso and Faletto 1979, also see Chapter 13). Pushing beyond binary categories that pit the developed against the underdeveloped, the modern against the traditional and the urban against the rural, dependency frameworks expose the manifold ways in which each of those terms in the binary are implicated in each other: that wealth accumulation in the North and underdevelopment in the South proceed simultaneously; that the split between the modern and the traditional falls short of capturing the linkages between different stages of development and social structures depicted as such; that the urban (developed areas of underdeveloped countries) draw out the elements from their own hinterland (the rural) to make up for their own development (Cardoso and Faletto 1979; Stavenhagen 1968). Taking stock of "[W]estern invasiveness, penetration and intervention" (Slater 2004: 26), the role played by class relations transcending territorial borders, transnational corporations, international economic and financial institutions, renders obsolete the strict demarcations between the inside and the outside, and foreign policy and domestic politics in the periphery (Tickner 2003). Further, as post-colonial scholars alert us, not only global material inequalities produced through the combined and uneven development of capitalism, and overt and covert imperial interventions, but also the enduring colonial legacies and their contemporary articulations need to be taken into account when analyzing the construction of state identity and foreign policy interests in the global South (Grovogui 2003). The Indian nuclear tests of 1998 provide an illuminating example of the importance of attending to the foreign policy of peripheral states as an attempt at post-colonial identity construction, and the role played by the global political economy and social forces such as race and gender during this process (see Box 11.2).

BOX 11.2 INDIAN FOREIGN POLICY AND NUCLEAR PROLIFERATION

In May 1998, the Indian government conducted five nuclear tests (BBC 1998). Two weeks later Pakistan retaliated, triggering a dangerous trend of nuclear brinkmanship. In spite of undertaking a series of tests in 1974, the Indian state had been a vocal supporter of nuclear disarmament programs, expressing its commitment to work towards a nuclear-free world. Strategic analyses fall short of making sense of India's counter-intuitive and contradictory foreign policy behavior. It requires an understanding of these nuclear tests as part of an attempt to perform India's post-colonial identity and attend to its particular history and its relation to domestic political struggles. India's desire to acquire nuclear technology can also be understood as an expression of the pivotal role played by science and technology in Indian nationalist discourse (Chacko 2011a). Nuclear technology can be interpreted as expression of the desire to become modern, to "catch up with the West" and prove one's status as equals.

The creation of a nuclear establishment was also expressive of another crucial factor constitutive of the Indian state's post-colonial identity: its specific relation to the global political economy (Varadarajan 2004). Political economy had been one of the important sites differentiating the Indian nation from the British Empire during the post-independence era (Muppidi 2004). The Indian post-colonial state, unlike its colonial predecessor, set out not only to end exploitative economic relations, but also to harness the productive forces of the nation towards the promotion of the welfare of its people (Muppidi 2004). The shift in India's nuclear policy and the ensuing tests coincided with the introduction of neoliberal policies in the early 1990s (Varadarajan 2004), which essentially served to dismantle the safeguards provided by the state. At a time when such changes to the economy by the ruling elites were seen by some as undermining the sovereignty of the nation, the nuclear tests were interpreted as an "expression of sovereignty," assuaging fears that national interests were being subverted (Varadarajan 2004: 330).

Foreign policy as ethos

In this section, the question of what we can learn by making peripheral perspectives the central analytical vantage point for understanding foreign policy will be discussed. As suggested in the previous section's exploration of global South perspectives, some that claim to be alternative are still framed within dominant readings of the international (see Chapter 6). The potentially transformative lessons derived from the periphery remain inaudible, muted and mutated: in particular, they prevent registering foreign policies of the global South as the articulation of an alternative political ethos (Grovogui 2003; Pasha 2013). As Eduardo Galeano (1997: 2) reminds us, when viewed from the global South, the world reveals itself as a place where an "endless chain of dependency [is being] endlessly extended." In such a world, what might we encounter as different when we leave behind our sedimented reference points? What would an ethos of foreign policy that is animated by a different logic, a different set of values from the dominant, imperial, colonizing subject of foreign policy entail?

To explore this foreign policy ethos – a different form of relating to the international – our first stop will be a city in the global South – Bandung, Indonesia. It was in this city that 29 delegations representing newly independent states freed from colonial rule convened at the Asian-African Conference in 1955. As one observer notes, this was a conference where "[t]he despised, the insulted, the hurt, the dispossessed – in short, the underdogs of the human race were meeting" (Wright 1995 [1956]: 12). Despite their differences, what united these post-colonial states was their shared opposition to colonialism and its neocolonial articulations – the latter understood as domination by means other than territorial conquest. Bandung marked the beginning of initiatives and movements associated with the project of third worldism, which attempted to displace the confrontation between the East and West and to foreground North and South conflict (Berger 2004). From the perspective of these third world "Others," the Cold-War mystified the realities of ongoing struggles in the global South, and the political, social and economic priorities of peoples in the periphery. Their primary demands were substantive equality on the world stage and a "more dignified rate of return for labor power of their people, shared acknowledgement of the heritage of science, technology, culture" (Prashad 2007: xvii).

The Bandung Conference was the precursor to the Non-Aligned Movement (NAM), launched in Belgrade in 1961. Not merely a declaration of neutrality, non-alignment signified an attempt to open up an independent political space beyond the geopolitical pressures of the confrontation between the two superpowers. The movement convened six major meetings between 1961 and 1979. The Fourth Summit in Algiers testified to two important developments: emphasis on economic inequalities and the need for transnational economic justice, and solidarity with ongoing anti-colonial and anti-apartheid struggles (Berger 2004). At the NAM's Sixth Summit in 1973, the parties inaugurated and adopted the New International Economic Order (NIEO), which aimed at reducing the North–South divide, incorporating South–South cooperation as an important component of enabling Southern economies to break from the colonial bonds that remained intact after political independence (see Box 11.3; also see Chapter 5 on how these developments relate to the construction and contestation of global order).

BOX 11.3 G77, UNCTAD AND THE NEW INTERNATIONAL ECONOMIC ORDER

In 1962, 36 countries from Africa, Asia and Latin America signed the Cairo Declaration at the conference held specifically to tackle the socio-economic problems faced by developing countries. The declaration called for a United Nations conference that would address "all vital questions relating to international trade, primary commodity trade and economic relations between developing and developed countries" (Toye 2014: 1760). It was the outgrowth of the dissatisfaction of many developing countries on issues concerning world trade as negotiated under the UN General Agreement on Tariffs and Trade (GATT). Following this call, the first United Nations Conference on Trade and Development (UNCTAD) was convened in Geneva in 1964, where the developing countries established the Group of 77 (G77). Three years later, G77 constituted the UNCTAD as a permanent organization. In the 1970s, UNCTAD put forward a set of proposals, known as the New International Economic Order. They sought to improve their terms of trade through measures such as tariff reductions, increase their share of development assistance as well as replacing the Bretton Woods System with an international economic system that would be more favorable to third world countries.

A pivotal moment in militant third world politics was the 1966 Tricontinental Conference convened in Havana. It was the first time that three continents of the South – Latin America, Africa and Asia – were brought together in their common struggle against ongoing imperialism. The journal established at the Conference – *Tricontinental* – became the first platform for the writings of post-colonial theorists and activists (Young 2003). Rather than producing a single, overarching political position, the conference and the journal aimed to promote the general goal of popular liberation and the well-being of all peoples. As Che Guevara noted in his message to the Tricontinental:

> What is the role that we, the exploited people of the world, must play? The contribution that falls to us, the exploited and backward of the world, is to eliminate the foundations sustaining imperialism: our oppressed nations, from which capital, raw materials and cheap labor (both workers and technicians) are extracted, and to which new capital (tools of domination), arms and all kinds of goods are exported, sinking us into absolute dependence. The fundamental element of that strategic objective, then, will be the real liberation of the peoples.
>
> (quoted in Young 2003: 18)

Much more than geographic labels, the "third world" and the "tricontinental" meant an alternative political perspective and an alternative form of knowledge about the state of the world (Dodds 2005). The concern for "the real liberation of the peoples" foregrounded autonomy as the primary objective of foreign policy (Tickner 2003) (see Box 11.4). Pushing the idea of sovereignty beyond its *de jure* conception as formal equality, autonomy embodied the goal of achieving non-dependent forms of development and self-determination in a world envisioned as an "interconnected social space" (Blaney 1996: 472). Understood in relational terms, it forced "a recognition of the mutual dependence of political and economic communities and a concern for and an obligation to those political communities disadvantaged within these common social relations" (472).

BOX 11.4 DEPENDENCE, DEPENDENCY, AUTONOMY

The principle of autonomy – that is, freedom from external control and/or influence, possessing the capacity of each political community to rule itself – is one of the important principles extended by dependency theory. Dependency, defined as "a situation of objective economic subordination to outside nations and enterprises" is depicted as the main obstacle to realizing this principle (Cardoso and Faletto 1979: 21). Challenging the global hierarchy produced by the capitalist division of labor, dependency thinking embraces sovereignty and autonomous development as the path for third world states to achieve self-determination and self-realization (Cardoso and Faletto 1979). Registering the important legacy of dependency thinking while challenging its embrace of the logic of sovereignty and modernist visions of development, recent scholarship offers alternative conceptions of autonomy that closely resonate with contemporary social movements (Blaney 1996).

As an alternative form of relating to the international, other historical cases in which a relational understanding of autonomy acted as the ground for alternative foreign policy practices are worth mentioning. One example is the doctrine of peaceful coexistence, the policy of Panchsheel, elaborated by Jawaharlal Nehru. Formally codified for the first time in an agreement signed with China in 1954, the principles of Panchsheel included mutual respect for territorial integrity and sovereignty, mutual non-aggression, mutual non-interference in each other's domestic affairs, equality and peaceful coexistence (Chacko 2011b). Envisioned as an alternative to military alliances and collective pacts, as Chacko explains, Panchsheel, like the policy of non-alignment, was intended as a "means of keeping alive a notion of security that did not depend on generating insecurity in others" (191). As such, it was a counter-hegemonic understanding to the dominant security ethos of Western political thought and practice (see also Chapter 10).

Further traces of this ethos can be found in numerous acts of solidarity among the countries of the global South – such as Cuba's health diplomacy touched upon in the opening story of this chapter. The provision of an extraordinary amount of aid from the government of Guyana and the Guyanese people to Haiti following the 2010 earthquake is also exemplary in this regard (Shilliam 2013). Such a gesture cannot be adequately captured by the logic of strategic, materialist calculations when one takes into the consideration that, as a percentage of its gross domestic product, Guyana gave 80 times as much as the United States. It becomes intelligible only if one takes into account ideational elements, foremost among them sentiments of solidarity arising from a shared history of colonialism and an indebtedness to the Haitians who had been the first to revolt against their enslavement and the institution of slavery itself (Shilliam 2013). The same concern with solidarity is apparent in the political thought and practice of figures such as Michael Manley and Julius Nyerere, who were at the forefront of struggles to establish the New International Economic Order (Bogues 2011). Informed by anti-colonial, anti-imperial internationalism, such an ethos overturns dominant forms of relating self and the other as it encourages the "embrace and touch, recognizing immediately the human in the form of another" without collapsing difference into sameness or rendering the process of relating into hierarchical dominations of power (Bogues 2011: 200).

Contemporary developments, challenges and prospects

The past few decades have witnessed a break from foreign policy as a means to challenge colonial, neocolonial relations of power at the systemic level and to vocalize popular demands for equality, freedom and justice – the defining features of the subaltern perspective hinted at in the previous section. Foreign policies pursued by states in the global South dramatically shifted from a position of challenging prevailing international regimes, resisting global capital and its ideology, towards one of adherence to and internalization of the norms of global liberal governance, and adapting to the conditions of neoliberal globalization.

From the 1980s onward, the fervor and the vitality of the efforts to push for an alternative foreign policy agenda would be eclipsed by economic bottlenecks faced by countries in the global South under the twin pressures of a new global political economic order structured along neoliberal lines and the material, institutional and ideological dominance of the West following the demise of the Soviet bloc. Debt crises faced by many of these countries became an opportunity to reign them in through structural adjustment programs, which made it almost impossible for them to pursue independent economic policies (Krishna 2009). The demise of the Eastern Bloc and dismantling of the Soviet Union aggravated the situation with many developing countries losing a crucial pillar for political leverage (Braveboy-Wagner 2003). Furthermore, the economic success achieved by the newly industrializing countries of Northeast and Southeast Asia created a model of capitalist development that many third world countries tried to emulate, displacing alternative visions for addressing international inequality. Abandoning the demands for a New International Economic Order, foreign policies now became directed at making countries in the global South safe for capital, and foreign ministries increasingly became "global sales representatives for their countries" (Persaud 2003: 57).

As neoliberal globalization progressed throughout the 1990s, the differential capacities of countries to adopt to the new global political and economic landscape and to reap the economic benefits from the changing structure of global production (through technological innovation, the rise in the service industry, the outsourcing of production, among others) diluted the cohesion of the third world as an economic bloc and undermined the solidarity it had displayed in its bargaining position vis-à-vis the North (Braveboy-Wagner 2003: 4). Although creating and utilizing alternative platforms to extend their foreign policy agendas, new power centers – such as Russia, China, Brazil, India, South Africa and Turkey – have been seen as merely seeking to alter the global balance of power without changing the rules of the game (Hurrell 2006; Cooper and Flemes 2013). For instance, since the 1990s Brazilian foreign policy objectives have been reformulated in tandem with neoliberal measures adopted at the domestic level (Vigevani and Cepaluni 2007). Gearing away from a stance of distancing the country from prevailing international regimes towards a vision of "international insertion" – active adherence to and participation in "international regimes, especially more liberal ones" (Vigevani and Cepaluni 2007: 1313) – Brazil has been pursuing a strategy of diversifying its relations through agreements with "non-traditional" partners (China, the Asia-Pacific, Africa, Eastern Europe, the Middle East) so as to reduce asymmetries in external relations with powerful countries. Likewise, in the context of South Africa, foreign policy initiatives have at times reflected the embrace of neoliberalism, not only as an economic, but also as a political strategy. For example, former South African President Thabo Mbeki's "African Renaissance" initiative foresaw a post-colonial Africa that "blend[s] African tradition and symbolism with the rhetoric of free markets and global governance" (Becker 2010: 133). Under the Justice and Development Party rule, Turkish foreign policy has been following a similar path, despite the much vocalized Islamic roots and conservative tendencies of the ruling party. Not only aggressively applying neoliberal policies at the domestic level, it has been actively pushing the neoliberal agenda at the international level through free trade partnerships and development projects carried out in Asia and Africa (Demirtaş 2012).[6]

Nevertheless, as post-colonial states' foreign policies get captured by capital and neoliberal ideology, the enactment of the "Bandung Impulse" (Pasha 2013) in novel sites above and beyond the state has become more visible. In this regard, the increasing role played by non-state actors, not as participants in foreign policy making, but as novel agents of the subaltern ethos and potential bearers of alternative imaginaries, is an important piece of the global South foreign policy puzzle. Alter-globalization struggles – from #Occupy movements to the World Social Forums, from the Zapatista rebellion to the international peasant farmers' movement Via Campesina – are reinventing the project of third worldism anew, practicing an internationalism and a solidarity reminiscent of the legacy of Bandung, albeit articulating it in line with a changed historical context through their novel conceptualization of autonomy, sovereignty, justice and equality (see Chapter 15).

Repeating a geopolitical imaginary reminiscent of the one captured by authors such as Galeano (1997) yet attuned to contemporary historical conditions, the Mexican Zapatistas treat the national level as intermeshed with the global, supra-national, regional and the local (Slater 2004: 205–206):

> Chiapas is bled through thousands of veins: through oil ducts and gas ducts, over electric wires, by railroad cars, through bank accounts, by trucks and vans, by ships and planes, over clandestine paths, third-rate roads and mountain passes ... Oil, electric energy, cattle, money, coffee, bananas, honey, corn, cocoa, tobacco, sugar, soy, melons, sorghum, mamey, mangos, tamarind, avocados and Chiapan blood flow out through a 1,001 fangs sunk into the neck of southeastern Mexico ... Billions of tons of natural resources go through Mexican ports, railway stations, airports and road systems to various destinations: the United States, Canada, Holland, Germany, Italy, Japan – but all with the same destiny: to feed the empire.
>
> (Subcomandante Marcos, quoted in Slater 2004: 206)

As discussed previously, the foreign policy objectives and strategies pursued by states in the global South since the 1990s subscribe to an acquiescent understanding of autonomy – one that is equated with the active and successful integration to global capitalism and institutions of liberal governance. In contrast, rather than accepting the predominant vision of *homo economicus* – a rational, calculating and maximizing economic agent propagated by neoliberal orthodoxy – alter-globalization movements such as the Zapatista resistance endorse a different rationality informed by a different understanding of political autonomy (Evans 2008). As Evans elaborates, by returning to communal systems of organization, the Zapatistas disrupt the liberal notion of autonomy understood as juridical equality and individual freedoms. Further, by defining autonomy – in the words of Comandante Tacho – "as a community arguing, discussing, planning, deciding how we want to live, how we want to share the wealth," the Zapatistas embrace and enact it not as an ideal state to be reached or a geographical entrenchment, but as an experience whose "success depends upon whether it is a lived practice" (Evans 2008: 514).

Also exemplary in this regard is the struggle against the international food order carried out by La Via Campesina, which makes autonomy and sovereignty central to this group's aims (Patel and McMichael 2004). Organized around an alternative conception of sovereignty – food sovereignty – Via Campesina aims to protect local farming as it unites local and regional chapters of landless peasants, small farmers and indigenous communities across continents through democratic-collective mechanisms. In this view, an appropriate understanding of biodiversity is premised on human diversity, and as such, it comprises "not only flora, fauna, earth, water and ecosystems," but also "cultures, systems of production, human and economic relations, forms of government"

(Via Campesina 2000). Consequently, food sovereignty is defined not in individual, but collective terms as "the right of peoples, communities to define their own agricultural, labor, fishing, food and land policies which are ... appropriate to their unique circumstances" (Via Campesina 2002). Such a formulation performs a unique conception of rights: rights without a specific content ("the right is the right to self-determination"); rights for the state to guarantee, but ones that it cannot authorize (since it is the community itself that redefines the substance of food relationships appropriate to its geography) (Patel and McMichael 2004: 249).

Finally, solidarity, an important component of the ethos of the foreign policy of the global South, is also being re-invented through transnational activist networks such as the one created around the Zapatista rebellion. Taking more democratic and global forms, these relationships are characterized by mutuality rather a one-way flow and a clear separation between providers and beneficiaries of solidarity (Olesen 2004). Despite the limits posed by the "fault lines within the solidarity network" arising from cultural, linguistic barriers, tactical differences and different life worlds, as Olesen notes, such global solidarity activities nevertheless are indicative of increasing imbrication of local, national and global spaces without erasing difference and enacting new social and political forms (265).

The notion of *buen vivir* that emerged in the countries of the Andean region provides a potent example of how the political-ethical ethos enacted by these social movements can inform the foreign policy course adopted by the states in the global South (Walsh 2010; Gudynas 2011). It describes alternatives to development focused on the good life in a broad sense. A strong critique of classical Western development theory, it emerges from indigenous traditions and provides a powerful counter-narrative to dominant practices in the global political economy, exploring possibilities beyond the modern Eurocentric tradition. Actively used by social movements, this notion is integrated into the constitutions of Ecuador and Bolivia (see Chapter 17).

Conclusion

This chapter has probed into the foreign policies of the global South with an eye to problematizing and unraveling dominant ways of thinking about this realm of human practice by taking the perspective of those who are exploited, marginalized, rendered as Other, marginal, peripheral or even less than human in world politics. While seeking to expose the limits of dominant conceptualizations, which pre-empt other ways of thinking and practicing foreign policy in the North and the South, it explored the notion of subaltern foreign policy as a political ethos that is premised on the legacies of colonialism and neocolonial forms of rule in the contemporary era, deriving from the experiences of the global South.

Dominant forms of thinking about foreign policy, as the chapter explored, are not only limited, but also misleading in terms of grappling with the realm of foreign policy making and world politics writ large. Western-centric, modernist narratives of foreign policy obstruct the non-West in the making and re-making of world politics and in coming to terms with the political motivations, aims and ethical concerns that inform subaltern perspectives. Understanding foreign policy from the perspective of the global South does not only entail shifting our geographical focus from that of the North to that of the South. It also requires that we question and overturn ingrained assumptions about what foreign policy is, where it is formulated, by whom it is enacted and what its principle coordinates are.

Questions for discussion

1   What is foreign policy conventionally taken to be? What are the limits of such conceptions, both analytically and politically?
2   How does re-positioning our analytical lenses away from Eurocentric approaches to foreign policy towards the non-West refine our understanding?
3   What does such a shift in perspective entail in terms of the appropriate methods to study foreign policy?
4   In addition to the ones discussed in this chapter, such as the Panchsheel policy and *buen vivir*, what examples can you think of as instances of subaltern articulations of foreign policy subjectivity?

Notes

1   The hegemony of West-centric accounts of this incident is underlined by the almost complete erasure of alternative names given to the event. What the discipline recalls as the "Cuban missile crisis" appears as the "Caribbean crisis" in Soviet accounts and as the "October crisis" in Cuban accounts (Weldes 1999).
2   For an alternative conception of "counter-hegemonic" approaches to foreign policy, see Persaud (2001).
3   For one such study, which investigates the ways in which dominant foreign policy discourses in the West (particularly the United States of America) reproduce relations of power and hierarchies, see Campbell (1998).
4   Foreign policy analysis is empirical since it entails examining actual case studies and evidence. Empiricism "implies that the analysis is in some way 'neutral' and that the evidence is not tainted by the theoretical and normative lenses through which these 'facts' are seen as the ones to use rather than others." Consequently, foreign policy analysis should be empirical but its empirical grounding needs to be framed within "an explicit theoretical and normative commitment" (Smith et al. 2008: 5).
5   It should be noted that not all systemic explanations of foreign policy are formulated as outcomes of factors external to the state (i.e., the international system), however. Focusing on organizational behavior, other forms of systemic explanations make central the idea that organizations (such as bureaucracies) can dictate the action of individual decision makers (Carlsnaes 2006).
6   In the case of Brazil, South Africa and Turkey, foreign policy approaches have shifted under different administrations and so these observations have been true to a greater or lesser extent during distinct periods.

Further reading

Campbell, David (1998) *Writing Security: United States Foreign Policy and the Politics of Identity*, Minneapolis, MN: University of Minnesota Press. One of the earliest examples of critical approaches to foreign policy analysis, *Writing Security* explains the way in which state identity is constituted through foreign policy discourses and practices.

Garrison, J.A., J. Kaarbo, D. Foyle, M. Schafer, and Eric K. Stern (2003) "Foreign Policy Analysis in 20/20: A Symposium," *International Studies Review* 5(2): 155–202. Covering a broad range of theories and methodologies, this collection of essays evaluates the new paths of inquiry into foreign policy analysis that opened up since the end of the Cold War.

Hudson, V.M. (2007) *Foreign Policy Analysis: Classic and Contemporary Theory*, New York: Rowman and Littlefield. An introductory textbook for advanced undergraduate students that provides an overview of mainstream approaches to foreign policy analysis.

Persaud, Randolph B. (2001) *Counter-Hegemony and Foreign Policy: The Dialectics of Marginalized and Global Forces in Jamaica*, Albany: SUNY Press. An early example of foreign policy analysis from the perspective of the global South, this book demonstrates the ways in which marginalized states and people could enact their own agenda and challenge the hegemonic practices of dominant states in the system.

Weldes, Jutta (1999) *Constructing National Interests: The United States and the Cuban Missile Crisis*, Minneapolis, MN: University of Minnesota Press. Focusing on the Cuban missile crisis that took place during the height of the Cold War, the book adopts a critical constructivist approach and is a first attempt to decolonize the predominant approaches that had so far prevailed in the study of this event.

References

Allison, Graham (1971) *Essence of Decision: Explaining the Cuban Missile Crisis*, New York: Longman.

Ayoob, Mohammed (2002) "Inequality and Theorizing in International Relations: The Case for Subaltern Realism," *International Studies Review* 4(3): 27–48. doi:10.1111/1521-9488.00263

Baldacchino, Godfrey (2009) "Thucydides or Kissinger? A Critical Review of Smaller State Diplomacy," in Andrew F. Cooper and Timothy M. Shaw (eds.) *The Diplomacies of Small States: Between Vulnerability and Resilience*, New York: Palgrave Macmillan, pp. 21–40.

Barkawi, Tarak and Mark Laffey (eds.) (2001) *Democracy, Liberalism and War: Rethinking the Democratic Peace Debate*, Boulder, CO: Lynne Rienner.

Barkawi, Tarak and Mark Laffey (2002) "Retrieving the Imperial: Empire and International Relations," *Millennium: Journal of International Studies* 31(1): 109–127. doi:10.1177/03058298020310010601

Barnett, Michael and Raymond Duvall (2005) "Power in Global Governance," in M. Barnett and R. Duvall (eds.) *Power in Global Governance*, Cambridge: Cambridge University Press, pp. 1–32. doi:10.1017/CBO9780511491207

BBC (1998) "World Fury at Pakistan's Nuclear Tests." Available at http://news.bbc.co.uk/onthisday/hi/dates/stories/may/28/newsid_2495000/2495045.stm (accessed: 4 July 2019).

BBC (2014) "Cuba to Send Doctors to Ebola Areas." Available at www.bbc.com/news/health-29174923 (accessed: 4 July 2019).

Becker, Derick (2010) "The New Legitimacy and International Legitimation: Civilization and South African Foreign Policy," *Foreign Policy Analysis* 6: 133–146.

Berenskoetter, Felix and M.J. Williams (eds.) (2007) *Power in World Politics*, London and New York: Routledge.

Berger, Mark T. (2004) "After the Third World? History, Destiny and the Fate of Third Worldism," *Third World Quarterly* 25(1): 9–39.

Biswas, Shampa (2001) "'Nuclear Apartheid' as Political Position: Race as a Postcolonial Resource?" *Alternatives: Global, Local, Political* 26(4): 485–522. doi: 10.1177/030437540102600406

Blaney, David (1996) "Reconceptualizing Autonomy: The Difference Dependency Theory Makes," *Review of International Political Economy* 3(3): 459–497. doi:10.1080/09692299608434365

Bogues, Anthony (2011) "Radical Anti-colonial Thought, Anti-colonial Internationalism and the Politics of Human Solidarities," in Robbie Shilliam (ed.) *International Relations and Non-Western Thought: Imperialism, Colonialism and Investigations of Global Modernity*, New York and London: Routledge, pp. 197–213.

Braveboy-Wagner, Jacqueline A. (2003) "The Foreign Policies of the Global South: An Introduction," in Jacqueline A. Braveboy-Wagner (ed.) *The Foreign Policies of the Global South: Rethinking Conceptual Frameworks*, Boulder, CO: Lynne Rienner, pp. 1–12.

Braveboy-Wagner, Jacqueline A. (2008) *Small States in Global Affairs: The Foreign Policies of the Caribbean Community (Caricom)*, New York: Palgrave Macmillan.

Campbell, David (1998) *Writing Security: United States Foreign Policy and the Politics of Identity*, Minneapolis, MN: University of Minnesota Press.

Cardoso, Fernando H. and Enzo Faletto (1979) *Dependency and Development in Latin America, Berkeley*, Los Angeles, CA and London: University of California Press.

Carlsnaes, Walter (2006) "Foreign Policy," in B. Guy Peters and Jon Pierre (eds.) *Handbook of Public Policy*, London: Sage, pp. 339–364. doi:10.4135/9781848608054

Carlsnaes, Walter (2008) "Actors, Structures and Foreign Policy Analysis," in Steve Smith, Amelia Hadfield, and Tim Dunne (eds.) *Foreign Policy: Theories, Actors, Cases*, Oxford: Oxford University Press, pp. 113–129.

Chacko, Priya (2011a) "The Search for a Scientific Temper: Nuclear Technology and the Ambivalence of India's Postcolonial Modernity," *Review of International Studies* 37: 185–208. doi:10.1017/S026021051000046X

Chacko, Priya (2011b) "The Internationalist Nationalist: Pursuing an Ethical Modernity with Jawaharlal Nehru," in Robbie Shilliam (ed.) *International Relations and Non-Western Thought: Imperialism, Colonialism and Investigations of Global Modernity*, London and New York: Routledge, pp. 178–196.

Cooper, Andrew F. and Daniel Flemes (2013) "Foreign Policy Strategies of Emerging Powers in a Multipolar World: An Introductory Review," *Third World Quarterly* 34(6): 943–962. doi:10.1080/01436597.2013.802501

Cooper, Andrew F. and Timothy M. Shaw (eds.) (2009) *The Diplomacies of Small States: Between Vulnerability and Resilience*, New York: Palgrave Macmillan.

Cox, Robert W. (1981) "Social Forces, States and World Orders: Beyond International Relations Theory," *Millennium – Journal of International Studies* June (10): 126–155. doi:10.1177/03058298810100020501

Dados, Nour and Raewyn Connell (2012) "The Global South," *Contexts* 11(1): 12–13. doi:10.1177/1536504212436479

Singer, David J. (1961) "The Level-of-Analysis Problem in International Relations," *World Politics* 14(1): 77–92. doi:10.2307/2009557

Demirtaş, Birgül (2012) "Turkish Foreign Policy under the AKP Governments: An Interplay of Imperial Legacy, Neoliberal Interests and Pragmatism," in S. Coşar and G. Yücesan-Özdemir (eds.) *Silent Violence: Neoliberalism, Islamist Politics and the AKP Years in Turkey*, Ottawa: Red Quill Books, pp. 213–250.

Dodds, Klaus (2005) *Global Geopolitics: A Critical Introduction*, London: Pearson/Prentice Hall.

Doty, Roxanne Lynn (1993) "Foreign Policy as Social Construction: A Post-positivist Analysis of U.S. Counterinsurgency Policy in the Philippines," *International Studies Quarterly* 37(3): 297–320.

Doyle, Michael W. (2012) "Liberalism and Foreign Policy," in S. Smith, A. Hadfield, and Tim Dunne (eds.) *Foreign Policy: Theories, Actors, Cases*, Oxford: Oxford University Press, pp. 54–77.

Escudé, Carlos (2009) "Peripheral Realism: An Argentine Theory-Building Experience, 1986-1997," in José Flávio Sombra Saraiva (ed.) *Concepts, Histories and Theories of International Relations for the 21st Century: Regional and National Approaches*, Brasília: IBRI. Available at www.argentina-rree.com/Peripheral%20Realism%20-%20Theory%20builiding%20experience.pdf

Evans, Brad (2008) "The Zapatista Insurgency: Bringing the Political Back into Conflict Analysis," *New Political Science* 30(4): 497–520. doi:10.1080/07393140802486245

Finnemore, Martha (1996) *National Interest in International Society*, Ithaca, NY: Cornell University Press.

Galeano, Eduardo (1997) *Open Veins of Latin America: Five Centuries of the Pillage of a Continent*, New York: Monthly Review Press.

Grovogui, Siba N. (2003) "Postcoloniality in Global South Foreign Policy: A Perspective," in Jacqueline A. Braveboy-Wagner (ed.) *The Foreign Policies of the Global South*, Boulder, CO and London: Lynne Rienner, pp. 31–48.

Gudynas, Eduardo (2011) "Buen Vivir: Today's Tomorrow," *Development* 54(4): 441–447.

Halperin, Morton H. (1974) *Bureaucratic Politics and Foreign Policy*, Washington, DC: Brookings Institution.

Hey, Jeanne A.K. (1993) "Foreign Policy in Dependent States," in L. Neack, J.A.K. Hey, and P.J. Haney (eds.) *Foreign Policy Analysis: Continuity and Change in Its Second Generation*, Englewood Cliffs, NJ: Prentice Hall, pp. 201–213.

Hudson, Valerie M. (2005) "Foreign Policy Analysis: Actor-specific Theory and the Ground of International Relations," *Foreign Policy Analysis* 1: 1–30. doi:10.1111/j.1743-8594.2005.00001.x

Hurrell, Andrew (2006) "Hegemony, Liberalism and Global Order: What Space for Would-Be Great Powers?" *International Affairs* 82(1): 1–19. doi:10.1111/j.1468-2346.2006.00512.x

Jahn, Beate (2005) "Kant, Mill, and Illiberal Legacies in International Affairs," *International Organization* 59: 177–207. doi:10.1017/S0020818305050046

Korany, Bahgat (1984) "Foreign Policy in the Third World: An Introduction," *International Political Science Review* 5(1): 7–20. doi:10.1177/019251218400500102

Krishna, Sankaran (2009) *Globalization and Postcolonialism Hegemony and Resistance in the Twenty-first Century*, Boulder, New York and London: Rowman & Littlefield Publishers.

Kubálková, Vendulka (2001) (ed.) *Foreign Policy in a Constructed World*, New York: Taylor and Francis. doi:10.4324/9781315291376

Laffey, Mark and Jutta Weldes (2008) "Decolonizing the Cuban Missile Crisis," *International Studies Quarterly* 52: 555–577.

Mohamedou, Mohammad M.O. (2003) "Foreign Policy in the Arab World: The Promise of a State-Centered Approach," in Jacqueline A. Braveboy-Wagner (ed.) *The Foreign Policies of the Global South*, Boulder, CO and London: Lynne Rienner, pp. 65–78.

Moravcsik, Andrew (1997) "Taking Preferences Seriously," *International Organization* 51(4): 513–533. doi:10.1162/002081897550447

Morgenthau, Hans (1948) *Politics Among Nations: The Struggle for Power and Peace*, New York: Alfred A. Knopf.

Morgenthau, Hans (1952) "Another 'Great Debate': The National Interest of the United States," *American Political Science Review* 46(4): 961–988.

Muppidi, Himadeep (2004) *The Politics of the Global*, Minneapolis, MN and London: University of Minnesota Press.

Nimtz, August (2013) "Cuba Was Conspicuously Absent in Mandela Coverage," *Star Tribune*. Available at www.startribune.com/opinion/commentaries/235146711.html (accessed: 4 July 2019).

Olesen, Thomas (2004) "Globalising the Zapatistas: From Third World Solidarity to Global Solidarity?" *Third World Quarterly*, 25(1): 255–267. doi:10.1080/0143659042000185435

Pasha, Mustapha K. (2013) ""The Bandung Impulse and International Relations," in Sanjay Seth (ed.) *Postcolonialism and International Relations*, London and New York: Routledge, pp. 144–165.

Patel, Rajeev and Philip McMichael (2004) "Third Worldism and the Lineages of Global Fascism: The Regrouping of the Global South in the Neoliberal Era," *Third World Quarterly* 25(1): 231–254. doi:10.1080/0143659042000185426

Persaud, Randolph B. (2001) *Counter-Hegemony and Foreign Policy: The Dialectics of Marginalized and Global Forces in Jamaica*, Albany, NY: SUNY Press.

Persaud, Randolph B. (2003) "Reconceptualizing the Global South's Perspective: The End of the Bandung Spirit," in Jacqueline A. Braveboy-Wagner (ed.) *The Foreign Policies of the Global South: Rethinking Conceptual Frameworks*, Boulder, CO: Lynne Rienner, pp. 49–64.

Prashad, Vijay (2007) *The Darker Nations: A People's History of the Third World*, New York and London: The New Press.

Putnam, Robert D. (1988) "Diplomacy and Domestic Politics: The Logic of Two-level Games," *International Organization* 42(3): 427–460. doi:10.1017/S0020818300027697

Rosenau, James N. (1966) "Pre-Theories of Foreign Policy," in James N. Rosenau, *The Study of World Politics: Volume 1: Theoretical and Methodological Challenges*, London and New York: Routledge, pp. 171–199. doi:10.4324/9780203014721

Shilliam, Robbie (2013) "The Spirit of Exchange," in Sanjay Seth (ed.) *Postcolonial Theory and International Relations: A Critical Introduction*, New York: Routledge, pp. 166–182.

Slater, David (2004) *Geopolitics and the Post-Colonial Rethinking North–South Relations*, Malden, MA: Blackwell Publishing. doi:10.1002/9780470756218

Smith, Steve, Amelia Hadfield, and Tim Dunne (eds.) (2008) *Foreign Policy: Theories, Actors, Cases*, Oxford: Oxford University Press.

Snyder, Richard, H.W. Bruck, and Burton Sapin (1954) *Foreign Policy Decision Making: An Approach to the Study of International Politics*, Princeton, NJ: Princeton University Press.

Solarz, Marcin W. (2012) "'Third World': The 60th Anniversary of a Concept that Changed History," *Third World Quarterly* 33(9): 1561–1573. doi:10.1080/01436597.2012.720828

Sprout, Harold and Margaret Sprout (1956) *Man-Milieu Relationship Hypotheses in the Context of International Politics*, Princeton, NJ: Princeton University Press.

Stavenhagen, Rodolfo (1968) "Seven Fallacies about Latin America," in James Petras and Maurice Zeitlin (eds.) *Latin America: Reform or Revolution?* New York: Fawcett, pp. 13–31.

Tickner, Arlene (2003) "Hearing Latin American Voices in International Relations Studies," *International Studies Perspectives* 4: 325–350. doi:10.1111/1528-3577.404001

Toye, John (2014) "Assessing the G77: 50 Years after UNCTAD and 40 Years after the NIEO," *Third World Quarterly* 35(10): 1759–1774. doi:10.1080/01436597.2014.971589

Varadarajan, Latha (2004) "Constructivism, Identity and Neoliberal (In)Security," *Review of International Studies* 30: 319–341. doi:10.1017/S0260210504006096

Via Campesina (2000) "Biodiversity and Genetic Resources." Available at http://viacampesina.org/en/index.php/main-issues-mainmenu-27/biodiversity-and-genetic-resources-mainmenu-37/389-bio diversity-and-genetic-resources12

Via Campesina (2002) "Declaration NGO Forum FAO Summit Rome+5." Available at http://viacam pesina.org/en/index.php/main-issues-mainmenu-27/food-sovereignty-and-trade-mainmenu-38/398-declaration-ngo-forum-fao-summit-rome5

Vigevani, Tullo and Gabriel Cepaluni (2007) "Lula's Foreign Policy and the Quest for Autonomy through Diversification," *Third World Quarterly* 28(7): 1309–1326. doi:10.1080/01436590701547095

Walker, R.B.J. (1993) *Inside/Outside: International Relations as Political Theory*, Cambridge: Cambridge University Press. doi:10.1017/CBO9780511559150

Walsh, Catherine (2010) "Development as Buen Vivir: Institutional Arrangements and (De)colonial Entanglements," *Development* 53(1): 15–21.

Waltz, Kenneth (1979) *Theory of International Politics*, Reading, MA: Addison-Wesley Publishing Company.

Weldes, Jutta (1996) "Constructing National Interests," *European Journal of International Relations* 2(3): 275–318. doi:10.1177/1354066196002003001

Weldes, Jutta (1999) *Constructing National Interests: The United States and the Cuban Missile Crisis*, Minneapolis, MN: University of Minnesota Press.

Wohlforth, William C. (2012) "Realism and Foreign Policy," in S. Smith, A. Hadfield, and Tim Dunne (eds.) *Foreign Policy: Theories, Actors, Cases*, Oxford: Oxford University Press, pp. 35–53.

Wolf-Phillips, Leslie (1987) "Why 'Third World'? Origin, Definition and Usage," *Third World Quarterly* 9(4): 1311–1327. doi:10.1080/01436598708420027

Wright, Richard (1995 [1956]) *The Color Curtain: A Report on the Bandung Conference*, Jackson, MS: Banner Books/University Press of Mississippi.

Young, Robert J.C. (2003) *Postcolonialism: A Very Short Introduction*, Oxford: Oxford University Press.

Part 3

Issues

12 Globalization

John M. Hobson

Today the earth has grown small and men are everywhere in close touch. If white civilization goes down, the white race is irretrievably ruined. It will be swamped by the triumphant [barbarian] colored races, who will obliterate the [superior] white man by elimination or absorption … Unless we set our house in order, the doom [of the white race] will sooner or later overtake us all.

Lothrop Stoddard (1920: 303)

In place of the old local and national seclusion and self-sufficiency, we have intercourse in every direction, universal interdependence of nations … The bourgeoisie, by the rapid improvement of all instruments of production, by the immensely facilitated means of communication, draws all, even the most barbarian, nations into civilization … It compels all nations, on pain of extinction, to adopt the bourgeois mode of production; it compels them to introduce what it calls civilization into their midst, i.e., to become bourgeois themselves. In one word, it creates a world after its own image.

Karl Marx and Friedrich Engels (1848/1973: 70–71)

Introduction

The fact that "globalization" became a buzzword within the academy and in the popular imagination during the 1990s at first sight appears to lend credence to the notion that it is only a very recent phenomenon. Indeed it is clear that for many scholars globalization's existence is located to the post-1945 world, with some pointing to the era of the Pax Americana beginning in 1945, others to 1973 when the fixed exchange rate system came to an end, and yet others to the post-1989 era following the end of the Cold War. But whichever date we run with, the received imaginary is one in which globalization is conflated with Westernization/Americanization on the one hand and that it emerged in the second half of the twentieth century on the other. This leads on to one of this chapter's central claims: that the vast majority of International Relations (IR) theory advances various Eurocentric conceptions of globalization that are *ahistorical*. However, it is not the case that all Eurocentric theories equate globalization with the universalization of the West, for there are some that view it as issuing a rising and rampaging "barbaric threat" to Western civilization (for example, Kaplan 1994; Huntington 1996). But these remain Eurocentric because their prime concern is to defend the purity of Western civilization against the "barbarian Eastern menace." And more generally, it turns out that nearly all of our modern theories of globalization simply rehearse or replay an earlier set of

Eurocentric and scientific-racist diagnoses which were advanced between about 1760 and 1945 (see Chapters 3 and 4).

It is instructive to note that many of the classical thinkers from the mid-eighteenth century on were grappling with the idea of growing global interdependence (Hobson 2012; Armitage 2013). And they too perceived it through various Western-centric lenses, specifically "Eurocentric institutionalist" (wherein difference is ascribed to culture and institutions), or "scientific racist" (wherein difference is attributed to genes/biology, climate and environment). Moreover, the "idea" of globalization was used in different normative ways depending on which Western-centric lens was deployed. The anti-imperialist liberal-Eurocentric thinker, Immanuel Kant, writing in the second half of the eighteenth century, argued that under conditions of global interdependence, cultural heterogeneity in the world was no longer possible and that all savage and barbaric societies would need to undergo the civilizing process (according to the Western-centric model) before a federation of republican states could be established (Kant 1970a: 107–8; 1970b). Others, such as the anti-imperialist Eugenicist-racists, Lothrop Stoddard (1920) and Charles Henry Pearson (1894), viewed rising global interdependence through the predatory trope of "globalization-as-barbaric threat," in which the so-called rising yellow (Chinese) and brown (Islamic) perils had now arrived on the doorstep of the West only to threaten the existence of (Western) civilization and hence of world order – a discourse that finds its contemporary voice in Samuel Huntington's (1996) "clash of civilizations" thesis. Then again, imperialist-Eurocentric thinkers such as Karl Marx and Friedrich Engels (1848/1967) viewed globalization and imperialism as a *necessary* (albeit brutal) process of global primitive accumulation insofar as it would "uplift" the backward "barbaric" Eastern societies and retrack them onto a capitalist developmental trajectory that would culminate with the future communist terminus. Others such as the racist imperialists, Alfred Mahan (1897) and Halford Mackinder (1904), viewed globalization – or what they called "the closing of the world" – in terms of the arrival of the yellow peril on the doorstep of the West in general and the United States in particular, thereby echoing Stoddard and Pearson, but rather than retreating from empire they advocated Anglo-Saxon racial imperialism as the means to counter the "barbaric threat." And yet other racist-imperialists, often liberals, viewed globalization as enabling the natural conquest of savagery and barbarism by (white) civilization through its "progressive" universalization across the world (Dilke 1868; Fiske 1885; Roosevelt 1905) (see Box 12.1).

BOX 12.1 WHEN AND WHY DID EUROCENTRISM EMERGE?

The standard view that is bequeathed by Edward Said (1978/2003) is that Eurocentrism or Orientalism was constructed in mid-eighteenth century Europe. This seems a reasonable claim though it is noteworthy that a *nascent* form of Eurocentrism was constructed during the Spanish colonization of the Americas. Important here was Francisco de Vitoria's (1539/1991) text "On the American Indians" where a "civilization/barbarism" discourse was invented in order to "understand" the natives but which turned out to be a justification for their colonization. Moreover, the imperialist idea of "social efficiency" emerged in the early sixteenth century. This asserts that if a non-Western people fails to productively develop its land, the Europeans have a right to take over their land and do it for them "on their behalf." And some have argued that the discourse of barbarism and civilization predates 1500 (Mathieu 2020). All of which means that 1750 marks the advent of the *mature* form of Eurocentrism, given that it had emerged in cruder form after 1500. But there is also the tricky issue concerning the role of religion that tends to get sidelined within postcolonial analysis. For example, while it is all-too-often assumed that the Atlantic slave trade was an inherently racist exercise, this elides the point that Christianity played a very important role in defining Africans as inferior and as "ripe" for slavery (being the people that was bequeathed to Noah's son, Ham, and who were viewed as but hewers of wood and stone). This is reinforced by the point that scientific racism only emerged in the eighteenth century – too late for the slave trade. As to why Eurocentrism emerged, this refers to the whole process of the construction of European identity. For even as late as the seventeenth century, Europe did not exist given that it was known as Christendom. But with the identity crisis of (Catholic) Christendom that was brought on by a combination of the Renaissance (c.1450), the Reformation (1517), the rise of the sovereign state system in the seventeenth through nineteenth centuries and its challenge to the political role of the papacy, so a new identity had to be forged in order to try and maintain a sense of order. It was especially during the European Enlightenment (c.1700–c.1800) that this new European identity was forged through the invention of mature Eurocentrism.

This chapter subverts the standard Eurocentric narratives and advances an alternative *non-Eurocentric* vision of globalization. Its key claim is that globalization has long historical origins that took the principal form of Orientalization, along with the transmission of non-Western "resource portfolios" (ideas, technologies and institutions) across the non-Western-led global economy between about 1492 and 1830/1850, all of which was made possible by the prior development of non-Western-led Afro-Eurasian regionalization between c.600 and 1492.[1] The chapter proceeds in four stages. The first section provides a brief overview of the conventional Eurocentric literature on globalization, focusing largely on post-1945 Western international theory while also considering classical approaches in order to reveal the essential properties of Eurocentrism. The second section then provides an alternative "non-Eurocentric" interpretation that "brings the non-West back in" by restoring the role of non-Western agency in the making of global politics and of the global political economy between c.600 and 1830/1850. The third section then focuses on the "dialogues of civilizations" wherein early globalization took the form of Orientalization and the diffusion of Eastern resource portfolios which, in turn, enabled the rise of the West. Finally, the fourth section considers the different ways in which various parts of the East have viewed globalization in the last 150 years and paints a very different picture to that which is imagined by Eurocentric approaches; one which brings the "dialectics of civilizations" to the fore and restores the role of non-Western agency in the making of modern globalization by focusing on how non-Western actors have resisted Western imperialism and neo-imperialism.[2]

Eurocentric narratives of globalization and development, past and present

BOX 12.2 THE CONTESTED DEFINITIONS OF EUROCENTRISM

This is contested because there are two clear definitions which are radically juxtaposed. The first definition of what can be called "Eurocentrism I," defines Eurocentrism as a discourse or metanarrative that reifies Western agency in the global economy while simultaneously silencing the dark side of Western imperialism on the one hand and on the other demoting the non-West to a passive entity that is only ever acted upon and never acts as an agent (see, for example, Ling 2002; Ling 2014; Go 2016; Acharya 2018; Hobson 2020). The second, which is embraced, albeit largely implicitly, by many IR and International Political Economy (IPE) scholars – what I call "Eurocentrism II," defines Eurocentrism as a discourse or metanarrative that serves to deny, elide or normatively justify the central role that Western imperialism plays in the global economy and international system. This finds its clearest and most explicit formulation in two important pieces: Wallerstein (1997) and Sajed and Inayatullah (2016). However, while both approaches seek to bring into focus the repressive-imperial side of the West they differ radically on the issue of non-Western agency. Thus, while Eurocentrism II views Eurocentrism as denying or whitewashing the role of Western hyper-agency, Eurocentrism I views Eurocentrism as denying or whitewashing the role of non-Western agency in globalization. Naturally, this gives rise to two competing antidotes to Eurocentrism (as I explain in Box 12.3).

As with the pre-1945 historical literature, we encounter a variety of Eurocentric narratives that are contained within modern theories of globalization (see Box 12.2). One can contrast the neoliberal approach, typified by Thomas Friedman (1999) and Martin Wolf (2005), which views the spread of Western liberal capitalism through the vehicle of globalization as a global political good with the neo-Marxist approach, typified by the likes of Robert Cox (1996) and Immanuel Wallerstein (1974), which laments the spread and diffusion of capitalism from the West on the grounds that it serves merely to exacerbate global inequality between the North and South. But though there are important differences nevertheless both generic approaches, when reviewed through a non-Eurocentric lens, reappear as but minor variations on a consistent Eurocentric theme. For both view globalization as representing the ineluctable triumph of the West as it forces all non-Western societies to become assimilated to the Western standard of civilization. Then again there is the anti-imperialist Eurocentric approach advanced by Samuel Huntington in his famous text, *The Clash of Civilizations and the Remaking of World Order* (1996), which harks back to the vision constructed by Stoddard and Pearson. For he views globalization-as-barbaric threat since it brings the rampaging and atavistic Muslims and Chinese onto the doorstep of the West and threatens the culture of Western civilization and hence world order; to which he advocates the West's need to batten down the hatches and to renew Western civilizational identity.

Although globalization is thought in general to have been only a recent phenomenon, most approaches adhere to an *implicit* history in which post-1945 "thick" globalization turns out to be the very tip of a huge Eurocentric iceberg, the contours of which crystallized from the sixteenth century onwards; the time when Europe had supposedly risen to the top to become the world's first modern civilization. Such approaches rest on the Eurocentric "big bang theory/trope" of globalization, which comprises an ahistorical two-step narrative wherein the first step sees modernity exploding spontaneously into existence within Europe as a result of its own exceptional institutional genius before "civilization" expands and diffuses outwards thereafter to create a Westernized world in the second step.

The first step presumes that the story of Europe's breakthrough into modernity can be recounted through the foundational Eurocentric idiom of the "logic of immanence," wherein Europe *self-generates* through an endogenous, evolutionary process without any help or influence from the non-Western world as a result of its own *exceptional* "rational" institutions and cultural genius. In this imaginary it is assumed that from the very outset, Europe's successful breakthrough into modernity was but an historical *fait accompli*, foretold or pre-ordained. This is reflected in the standard stadial developmental models that were advanced by the likes of Adam Smith (1776/1937) and Immanuel Kant (1970b) through to Walt Rostow (1960) and Francis Fukuyama (1992) on the liberal side, and by Karl Marx and Friedrich Engels (Marx and Engels 1848/1967) through to Robert Brenner (1982) on the radical side of the intellectual ledger. A useful metaphor here is that of the "Oriental(ist) Express" (Blaut 1993; Frank 1998), wherein the European developmental train departs from Ancient Greece and then proceeds through a whole series of strictly European way-stations. Having passed through Ancient Rome, the Express steams through European feudalism and then tracks back southwards to Italy, passing through the Italian commercial and financial revolutions as well as the Renaissance before it begins its long sweeping journey north-westwards. This sees the train wending its way through the era of Dutch capitalist hegemony and then further north-westwards onto the British industrial revolution via the French Revolution before the baton of modernity ships across the Atlantic to arrive in the liberal imagination at what Rostow (1960) famously called the (American) "age of high mass consumption," in which industrial production dominates and consumers have the ability to purchase high-value products. And, of course, for Marxism the developmental trajectory culminates at the universal communist terminus.

Simultaneously, Eurocentrism presumes that development is largely (though not always) stillborn outside of the West. That is, the East is constructed as Europe's inferior Other, weighed down by only regressive, irrational institutions that block the possibility of Eastern development. Critically, East and West are entirely separated out and are thought to comprise self-constituting billiard ball-like entities. By separating out the East and the West in this way, any influences that the East had upon the West magically disappear from view. Exposing this Eurocentric sleight of hand is, *inter alia*, the task of the third section of this chapter where I discuss some of the ways in which the East enabled the rise of European modernity. But for the moment it is important to recognize that for many Eurocentric institutionalists the West is *exceptional* because only it enjoys the necessary "rational" institutions (e.g., democracy, individualism, inventiveness and science) that can deliver Europe into modernity. Conversely the "irrational" institutions of the East (e.g., Oriental despotic states or the state of nature, collectivism, imitative, superstition and mystical religions) ensure that stagnation, repression and misery are the lot of its peoples.

Having completed the first step, the second follows on immediately in its wake through which the modern West expands outwards in its mission to remake the world. Or, to complete the metaphor: in this imaginary the miraculous "big bang of modernity" exploded autonomously into existence within Europe via the exceptional Eurocentric logic of immanence, before the Western civilizational frontier expands outwards through a kind of "Genesis effect" to create an entirely new and fully Western earthly universe initially through trading post empires, later through formal and informal imperialism (i.e., proto-globalization) and subsequently through (thick) globalization after 1945. In turn, as we saw with the Eurocentric developmental narrative, so globalization is understood through the analogy of the Western relay race, wherein the baton of global power was passed from one Western imperialist runner to the next. Thus, the Iberians ran the first leg after 1492/1497, spreading Western institutions and normative practices outwards to the Americas in the far West (via Christopher Columbus) and to Asia in the East (via Vasco da Gama). The baton was then passed to the Dutch in the seventeenth century before it was handed over to the French and the British in the eighteenth and nineteenth centuries only to culminate with the American anchor man who ran the final leg in record time after 1945 to pass the line into thick globalization.

All in all, two points emerge here. First, the Eurocentric narrative invokes an ahistor-ical conception of world politics and of economic/political development, summarized by the trope of "first the West and then elsewhere" (Chakrabarty 2000: 4–11); or, if I may be permitted some interpretative license here, "first the West, then the rest." Second, Eurocentrism reifies the agency of the West, in both development and global politics, while simultaneously demoting or denying the creative agency of non-Western actors. To counter these two key assumptions, the following sections argue that the "rest" actually came first, and that only by restoring the place of non-Western agency in the making of modernity and of globalization can we begin to escape the current impasse of Eurocen-tric globalization theory (see Box 12.3).

BOX 12.3 THE CONTESTED DEFINITIONS OF ANTI-EUROCENTRISM

Because there are two contested definitions of Eurocentrism so there are two alterna-tive non-Eurocentric antidotes. Immanuel Wallerstein's seminal 1997 *New Left Review* article took aim at what he called the "avatars of Eurocentrism." By this he was refer-ring to those non-Eurocentric scholars who seek to bring the role of non-Western agency in to explaining the rise of capitalism in Europe. He views this as inherently Eurocentric for a range of reasons. Ultimately though, he views such an approach as inherently Eurocentric because it dilutes the centrality of the hyper-imperial and brutal West in the making of the modern world. As Wallerstein (1997: 102) put it, "[i]f we insist too much on non-European agency as a theme, we end up whitewashing all of Europe's sins, or at least most of them" (see also Sajed and Inayatullah 2016). Accord-ingly, in "anti-Eurocentrism II," the objective is to downplay if not ignore non-Western agency so that the brutal West can be placed center-stage of the analysis and thereby prosecuted for its crimes against global humanity in the Western academic court of social justice. In this vision the West is viewed as entirely separate and self-constituting such that it is segregated off from any non-Western influences. By contrast, "anti-Eurocentrism I" adopts a very different position. For in addition to revealing the dark side of Western imperialism in the world, most of the emphasis lies in "de-segregating" the global economy. This focuses not just on the many mutual or co-constitutive interactions and interconnectivities between West and non-West, but also brings back into focus the multiple roles and instantiations of non-Western agency both in the making of the West and of the global economy more generally (see, for example, Bhambra 2014; Go 2016; Hobson 2020). Such a position operation-alizes what the historian, Sanjay Subrahmanyam, refers to as "connected histories" and what the postcolonial historical sociologist, Gurminder Bhambra, calls "connected sociologies" (Subrahmanyam 1997; Bhambra 2014).

Inverting the Eurocentric big bang theory (I): Oriental proto-globalization and Oriental-led globalization, c.600–1850

This section begins the task of inverting the big bang trope by advancing the proposition that non-Western-led globalization *preceded* Western-led globalization (see Hobson 2004: chapters 2–4). One of the key sets of objections to the existence of globalization before 1945 is presented in the influential book, *Global Transformations* (Held et al. 1999), which asserts that proper, or what the authors call "thick" globalization, emerged only after 1945, given the existence of high degrees of *extensity, intensity, velocity* and *impact propensity* of global or trans-regional exchanges, all of which are deemed to have been at insufficient levels before 1945 and certainly before the nineteenth century. Thus with respect to extensity, the authors claim that the trade that did exist prior to the nineteenth century was in luxury goods that were consumed only by elites, or the top 10% of the world's population; that transport technologies were far too primitive to allow for significant trans-regional trade levels; that there was a lack of institutions to support trans-regional trade and that most non-Western states were "Oriental despotisms" that sought merely to stifle trade and nascent capitalism. Regarding intensity, they argue that any interactions that occurred between societies were far too sporadic to qualify as globalization and that in any case their velocity of circulation was far too slow. And finally, whatever global interactions existed, they failed to have any significant *impact* in that they were unable to promote significant changes in societies across the world.

In what follows, I argue that between c.600 and 1492 there was a non-Western-led proto-globalization/Afro-Eurasian regionalization in existence before it jumped in scale into early non-Western-led globalization between 1492 and c.1850 and which, in both cases, witnessed significant levels of extensity, intensity and impact even if velocity remained relatively low. The working definition of globalization that this discussion lends itself to is one in which *significant flows of goods, resources, currencies, capital, institutions, ideas, technologies, diseases and peoples flowed across regions to such an extent that they impacted upon and led to the transformation of societies across the globe.* All in all, Robert Holton (1998: 28, emphasis added) puts it well when he notes that:

> A global history need not take the form of a single uniting process (or metanarrative) such as the triumph of reason or Western civilization. Nor should it be taken to imply an inexorable process of homogenization to a single pattern … [T]he *minimum* that is required for us to be able to speak of a single global connecting thread is that *tangible interconnections exist between distinct regions, leading to interchange and interdependency.*

Clearly, a great deal hinges on the definition of globalization that is deployed. As a general rule of thumb, non-Eurocentric writers who date its existence before the nineteenth century deploy a relatively loose definition while Eurocentric writers utilize a very tight, modern-specific one.

Phase 1: Afro-Eurasian regionalization/proto-globalization, c.600–1450/1492

Beginning first with "extensity" I argue that after c.600 CE the Persians, Arabs, Africans, Javanese, Jews, Indians, Armenians and Chinese created and maintained a proto-global economy down to 1492, wherein all the Afro-Eurasian civilizations of the world became consistently interlinked. Second, the various regions were governed by rulers who sought not to stifle proto-capitalism but instead provided a pacified environment and kept transit taxes low in order to facilitate trans-regional trade. Moreover, a whole series of sufficiently rational capitalist institutions were created and put in place after 600 to support trans-regional trade. As Janet Abu-Lughod (1989: 8) notes:

> Distances as measured by time, were calculated in weeks and months at best, but it took years to traverse the entire [global] circuit. And yet goods were transferred, prices set, exchange rates agreed upon, contracts entered into, credit – on funds or on goods located elsewhere – extended, partnerships formed, and, obviously, records kept and agreements honoured.

While transport technologies were obviously nowhere near as advanced as they are today, nevertheless they proved to be sufficient for the regular conduct of trans-regional trade. Moreover, the assumption that trade affected only about 10% of the world's population (i.e., the elites rather than the masses) and was therefore inconsequential is contradicted by the fact that the majority of trade was conducted in mass-based consumer products such as everyday clothes and foods (Frank 1998). While it is undoubtedly true that the velocity of global transmissions was often very slow, the various flows had a major re-organizational effect (i.e., *impact*) on societies across the world (with the exception of the Americas before 1492). How then did Oriental-led proto-globalization play out when we turn to re-imagining world history?

I take 600 CE as the approximate starting date of Oriental-led proto-globalization/Afro-Eurasian regionalization. Key here was the emergence of a series of interlinked world "empires" and regions that enabled a significantly pacified trans-regional environment within which overland, as well as seaborne, trade could flourish (Bentley 1993: chapters 1 and 3). These comprised Tang China (618–907), the Islamic Ummayad/Abbasid empire in West Asia/North Africa (661–1258), as well as the Fatimids in North Africa (909–1171). The key role was played by the West Asian/Levantine Muslims after 650, as they succeeded in weaving together the Afro-Eurasian region. One of the most significant aspects of Islam was its penchant for trade and rational capitalist activity; a point that immediately stands at odds with the Eurocentric assumption, as argued especially by the famous German sociologist Max Weber, that Islam was a regressive and irrational religion that blocked the possibility of capitalist, let alone *rational* capitalist, activity (Weber 2001). This is hard to square with the fact that the Prophet Mohammed himself had been a *commenda* (or *qirād*) trader and had married a rich *Qurayshi* woman (the *Quraysh* had grown rich from the caravan trade as well as banking). Not surprisingly there are many cues for capitalist activity within the Qu'rān, such as:

> If thou profit by doing what is permitted, thy deed is a djihad ... And if thou invest it for thy family and kindred, this will be a Sadaqa [that is, a pious work of charity]; and truly, a dhiram [drachma, silver coin] lawfully gained from trade is worth more than ten dhirams gained in any other way.

Noteworthy too is that the *Sharīa* (Islamic law) set out clear provisions for contract law.

The center of Islam, Mecca, was also one of the centers of the proto-global trading network. Indeed,

The density of commercial relations within the Muslim world constituted a sort of world market ... of unprecedented dimensions. The development of exchange had made possible regional specialisation in industry and agriculture ... Not only did the Muslim world know a capitalistic sector, but this sector was apparently the most extensive and highly developed in history before the [modern period].

(Rodinson 1974: 56)

Islam's economic reach was extraordinary for the time, such that by the ninth century there was one long, continuous line of trans-continental trade pioneered by Islamic merchants, reaching from China to the Mediterranean (Hourani 1963: 62; Abu-Lughod 1989: 199) (see Figure 12.1).

Thanks to the work of Janet Abu-Lughod (1989) we now have a clear picture of the architecture of the Afro-Eurasian economy (even though she claims that it was a global economy). She argues that it comprised three prime trade routes, though the two most important ones were the Middle and Southern. The Middle route had a land component, which linked the Eastern Mediterranean with China and India, and a sea route that passed through the Persian Gulf. The Southern route linked the Alexandria-Cairo-Red Sea complex with the Arabian Sea and then, as with the Middle sea route, the Indian Ocean and beyond to Southeast Asia, China and Japan. These routes ensured that Europe was fundamentally connected to the Afro-Asian economy after about the ninth century. And *contra* Eurocentric world history, this situation continued throughout the period between 1000 and 1800, when various leading European powers were at their height.

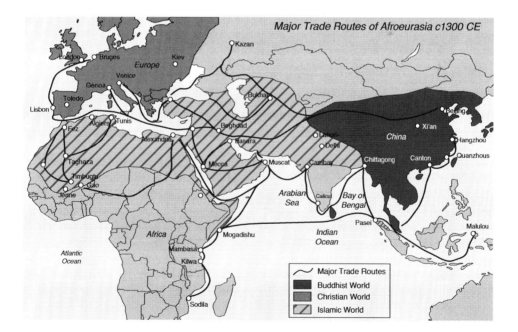

Figure 12.1 World trade routes, c.1300 CE

Source: World History for Us All, https://whfua.history.ucla.edu/eras/era5.php

With the "Fall of Acre" in 1291, which marked the end of the Crusades, the Venetians, who were the key intermediary that fed eastern trade across to Europe, came to rely on the dominant Southern route which was presided over by the Egyptians. As Abu-Lughod (1989: 149) claims, "[w]hoever controlled the sea-route to Asia could set the terms of trade for a Europe now in retreat. From the thirteenth century and up to the sixteenth that power was Egypt." Down to 1517 Venice survived because Egypt played such an important role within the global economy and after 1517 Venice continued its trading connection through the Ottomans. However, the baton of global power was passed not to the Iberians but to the Chinese during the mid-fifteenth century (even if the Muslims remained key economic players in the early global economy), who thereby opened up the phase of early globalization.

Phase 2: early globalization 1450/1492–1850: Orientalization dominant, Occidentalization emergent

Eurocentric theory assumes that 1492/1497 provided a radical break with the past in a number of key respects (Roberts 1985; Landes 1998). First, it witnessed the retreat of China from international trade following the official Ming ban in 1434. Second, it saw the Europeans "discover the world" during the so-called "European Age of Discovery" as the Portuguese and Spanish filled the vacuum that the exit of China had supposedly left in its wake. And third, it saw the Iberians initiate the primitive accumulation of globalization through the breaking down of the non-Western "barbaric" walls. In this way Eurocentric world history assumes that the world was fragmented into isolated countries and regions prior to 1492. But 1492 witnessed not the exit but the *arrival* of China at the center of early globalization (Flynn and Giráldez 1994; Frank 1998; Hobson 2004: chapter 3). Moreover, the era of early globalization did not miraculously appear after 1492/1497 as some kind of virgin birth, but was only made possible by the developments that had been achieved during the era of Oriental-led proto-globalization that had comprised Afro-Eurasian regionalization since about 600 CE. Accordingly, the so-called voyages of discovery to the East might better be labelled the European voyages of *rediscovery*.

There were three key processes associated with China's central role in the emergent global economy. First, the conversion of the Chinese economy onto a silver standard in the mid-fifteenth century was a seminal moment (which is why I delineate 1450/1492 as the birthdate of early globalization) that, when coupled with the point that China was the world's leading economy after the thirteenth century (having underwent something of an industrial miracle during the Song period, 960–1276), meant that there was a huge Chinese demand for silver that flooded in as a result of Europe's arrival in and exploitation of the Americas (Frank 1998; Hobson 2004: chapter 3). Second, China's strong economy had the effect of sucking in significant parts of the world's supply of silver in part because much of the rest of the world in general and Europe in particular, endured consistent trade deficits with China. And third, because the price of silver relative to gold in China was twice as high as the equivalent in Europe so there developed a kind of global arbitrage system (Flynn and Giráldez 1994), wherein silver flowed into China, was then converted into gold before it was shipped to Europe and converted into twice as much silver before this returned to China whence the process began anew. This occurred between the sixteenth and mid-eighteenth centuries, drawing Europe and China ever closer as profits were derived at both ends of this inter-regional connection.

While Eurocentric world history assumes that the Europeans discovered the Americas from which they extracted gold and silver, and the British set up the "triangular trading system" that linked Britain with Africa and the Americas in what is called the "Atlantic system," this obscures the point that a good deal of the silver that was plundered from the Americas found its way across to China (and India). This suggests that China and the Pacific and Indian Ocean systems helped *suck* the Europeans into playing a *direct* role in the global economy for the first time. And this is reinforced by two further noteworthy points. First, right down to 1800 the various European actors that entered the Indian Ocean system did not dominate the Asian powers but at all times were dependent upon local Asian knowledge, Asian capital (much of which was provided by rich Indian *banias*) and the goodwill of Asian rulers. Second, despite all the Eurocentric reports of Europeans monopolizing the spice trade, the fact is that the majority of European profits – around 75% – were derived from their place in this global arbitrage system (or what I call the *global silver recycling process*) and the rest of their profits were derived not from monopolizing Asian trade but by acting as intermediaries within the intra-Asian trading networks (known as the "inter-country trade").

All in all, the upshot here is that non-Western agency has been a key factor in the development of early globalization (1492–1850) as much as it was in fostering Afro-Eurasian regionalization (c.600–1492). And while the Europeans played an increasingly important role in linking up the global economy after 1492, nevertheless much of the impetus to this was provided by the Asians.

Inverting the Eurocentric big bang theory (II): Orientalization in the rise of the West

The Eurocentric big bang theory presumes that in the first step Europe single-handedly broke through into modernity before in the second step it expanded outwards initially through proto-globalization between 1492 and c.1945 and subsequently through thick globalization after 1945. In this section I invert this trope by arguing that early non-Western-led globalization came first and that it helped Europe make the breakthrough into modernity. It is particularly ironic that significant dialogues between Islam and the West were taking place at the very same time as the Crusades were raging, though these dialogues continued on after the Crusades had finished (i.e., after 1291). First, the famous European commercial/financial revolution of the post-1000 period was enabled by Italy's trading relations with Islamic West Asia/North Africa. Eurocentrism's celebration of Italy's financial and cultural genius obscures the point that many of the ideas, technologies and institutions upon which they were based were pioneered in Islamic West Asia and then diffused across in various ways. For example, while we are generally told that Italy's capitalist genius was responsible for the invention of the *collegantzia* (or *commenda*) trading partnership institution in the twelfth century, nevertheless this institution was an exact replica of the *qirād* trading partnership that was developed by the Muslims many centuries earlier. Moreover, all the remaining financial institutions, including banks, bills of exchange (*suftaja*), checks (*hawāla*) and insurance schemes originated in Sumer and Sassanid Persia before they were developed much further by the Muslims (see Hobson 2004: chapter 6).

Perhaps Italy's "unique" contribution to European modernity, Eurocentrism holds, is the Renaissance, which supposedly harked back to the pioneering rational ideas of ancient Greece. And to the extent that the Muslims played a role it was as mere librarians insofar as they held many of the Greek texts in their libraries and then dutifully returned them back to Europe whence they came. In this way, the hugely significant Islamic contributions are air-brushed out of history. It is certainly the case that at the House of Wisdom (*Bayt al-Hikmah*), which was founded in the early ninth century by the seventh Abbasid caliph, al-Ma'mūn, ancient Greek texts were translated into Arabic from which the Muslims learned a great deal. Nevertheless, Arab scholars also drew heavily on Persian, Indian, African and Chinese thinking to craft a corpus of knowledge that extended, and at times transcended, the earlier Greek texts. Moreover, the Muslims were often critical of Greek knowledge and sought to take it in new directions. How then did Islamic thinkers help shape the Renaissance and the subsequent scientific revolution?

Islamic breakthroughs in mathematics including algebra and trigonometry were vital, with the former term taken from the title of one of al-Khwārizmī's mathematical texts (as a result of the translation made by the Englishman, Robert of Ketton, in 1145). Developments in public health, hygiene and medicine were also important. Al-Rāzī's medical works were translated and reprinted in Europe some forty times between 1498 and 1866. And Ibn Sīnā's (or Avicenna's) *Canon of Medicine* became the founding text for European medical schools between the twelfth and fifteenth centuries. The Muslims developed numerous medicines and anaesthetics and pioneered the study of anatomy. Notable here is that the Egyptian physician, Ibn al-Nafis (d. 1288), whose work on the human body, which contradicted the traditional position of the Greek physician, Galen, fully pre-empted the much heralded work of William Harvey by 350 years. The Muslims were also keen cartographers and astronomers, and their ideas were avidly borrowed by the Europeans. Notably, Ibn al-Shātir's mathematical models bore an uncanny resemblance to those used by Copernicus 150 years later. And last but by no means least, the Baconian idea that science should be based on the experimental method had already been pioneered by the Muslims (not the Greeks) (Goody 2004: 56–83; Hobson 2004: 173–83; Bala 2006). The profound irony of this is that while the Renaissance thinkers were in part anxious to forge a new European identity that was independent of, and indeed differentiated from, the Islamic world, it was nevertheless from Islam that the Renaissance scholars drew so many of their new ideas.

Europe's dialogues with Islamic West Asia and China were also vital in enabling the European voyages of rediscovery. The Muslims passed on the lateen sail which, unlike the square sail, enabled European ships to sail into the strong headwinds that blew up South of Cape Bojador on the West coast of Africa. They also passed on the use of geometry and trigonometry, solar and lunar calendars, more accurate navigational charts, latitude and longitude tables, as well as the astrolabe and quadrant (Hobson 2004: 140–4; Seed 1995: 107–28), all of which were vital pre-requisites for oceanic sailing. Moreover, the Chinese passed on the all-important inventions of the square hull and stern-post rudder as well as the triple mast system and the compass. In short, in the absence of these Islamic-European and Sino-European dialogues, the Iberians would most probably have remained confined to the Islamic Mediterranean, with the rest *not* being history.

Another key turning point in the rise of the West is the British agricultural and industrial revolutions (Hobson 2004: chapter 9). The British agricultural revolution was spurred on by a series of inventions, including the iron mouldboard plough, Jethro Tull's seed drill and horse-drawn hoe, the horse-powered threshing machine and the rotary winnowing machine. But in each case, these inventions had been pioneered in China and were all in place as early as the sixth century. In the case of the plough and rotary winnowing machine, Chinese models were brought across (either by the Jesuits, European scientists or Dutch sailors). And the remainder were most likely copied from Chinese manuals that flooded into Europe after 1650.

Much the same story applies to the British industrial revolution. While Eurocentrism celebrates James Watt for his pioneering skills in inventing the steam engine, nevertheless his was developed from John Wilkinson's machine, the essentials of which go back to Wang Chên's *Treatise on Agriculture* (1313), which in turn go back to the Chinese invention of the water-powered bellows (31 CE). Moreover, the Chinese box-bellows was a double-acting force and suction pump, which at each stroke expelled the air from one side of the piston while drawing in an equal amount of air on the other side. Not only did it share a "close formal resemblance" to Watt's engine but, by the late seventeenth century, the Chinese had developed a steam turbine (Needham and Ling 1965). Moreover, its use was vital in enabling the production of Chinese iron and steel.

Given China's and especially India's substantial lead in iron and steel production, it was not surprising that British producers (including the famous Benjamin Huntsman of Sheffield) undertook detailed studies of Chinese and Indian production methods as late as the eighteenth century in order to develop their own iron and steel manufacturing techniques. The other great pillar of the British industrial revolution was cotton manufacturing. But while Eurocentrism celebrates pioneering British inventors such as John Lombe, this misses the point that some of their inventions had been pioneered in China many centuries earlier. John Lombe's silk machines became the model for the Derby cotton machines. But while Lombe's "invention" was a copy of the Italian machines, they in turn were a direct copy of the earlier Chinese inventions. More generally, it is important to note that the idea of "laissez-faire" originated in China before the Common Era and is termed "wu-wei" (Hobson 2004: chapter 9). And, when coupled with the point that many Enlightenment thinkers explicitly embraced the Confucian idea of rationality, it becomes clear that some of the key ideas of the European Enlightenment can be said to have originated in China (Clarke 1997).

All in all, then, we should not be seduced by the idea of a fundamental and inevitable clash of Europe and Islam or Europe and China, precisely because this obscures the dialogues that were conducted between them. Moreover, these dialogues were vital in enabling not just the rise of the West but in shaping Europe's cultural identity (especially through the Renaissance). Accordingly, this analysis disrupts the Eurocentric monological approach by recognizing that East and West are not separate self-constituting entities but are fundamentally *hybrid amalgams* that are constituted through iterated dialogical relations via resource portfolio transmissions (Ling 2002; see too, Chapter 17).

However, after the mid-nineteenth century this particular form of dialogical interaction receded as the transmission of non-Western resource portfolios more or less dried up at the same time as the West came to occupy the leading position in the world economy. Not only had Europe caught up with the non-West, having assimilated many of its resource portfolios, but it now subjected much of the non-Western world within a hierarchical relationship that was based on formal and informal imperialism. Not surprisingly, this has led many to believe that modern globalization can readily be conflated with Westernization or Americanization. But the simple problem that I want to emphasize is that to reify the role of the West as the sole source of globalization after 1850, as do many critical and mainstream IR theories, is to fall back into the trap of Eurocentrism. To counter this predominant tendency to reify the role of the West as the proactive subject of globalization while demoting the East to the role of an inert and largely passive "victim" (as in neo-Marxism) or "beneficiary" (as in neoliberalism) of Western-led globalization, the following section will restore the role of non-Western agency in the making of modern globalization. It does this by bringing to the fore the concept of the "dialectics of civilizations" in which the non-West has *resisted* and *contested* Western impositions of power and in so doing has shaped both the West and globalization/global politics, while also highlighting numerous "views from the South" that provide a very different picture to the one that is bequeathed by Eurocentrism.

Modern globalization and the manifold views from the South

From about 1830 onwards globalization took an imperial form and was Western-led, morphing into a neo-imperial shape after 1945. It is a common trope of modern Eurocentric IR theory that European imperial globalization constituted, in effect, a "civilizing mission" that "uplifted" the non-Western states/societies onto the rational Western standard of civilization and was a process which was mostly received by the target states in a consensual way given that they sought voluntarily to become members of (European) international society (Bull 1984a, 1984b; see too, Chapters 3, 4 and 6). For Hedley Bull, only in one arena have non-Western states resisted Western global socialization, specifically the issue of cultural independence; a "problem" that Bull views as an irrational impediment to the successful reproduction of global international society today (Bull 1984b). But what such an analysis misses is the "dialectics of civilizations" wherein the non-West sought to resist the global-imperial and neo-imperial Western incursions and, in the process, often forged its own independent path on the one hand while retracking the inner core and outward trajectory of the West as well as shaping globalization on the other. For when viewed from the global South, a number of different pictures emerge. Those countries that experienced *informal* colonial over-lordship – that is, where they were not held under direct imperial control – held various views (Suzuki 2009; Kayaoglu 2010; Zarakol 2011). William Callahan's important discussion of the Chinese "century of humiliation" (c.1839–1949) poses an apposite example. For this informal imperialist engagement with China "did not lead to order but to massive social dislocation, and ultimately violent revolution" (Callahan 2004: 313). Indeed, the various Chinese revolutions were in part stimulated by a deeply hostile reaction to this encounter with the West, with Mao's communism being the final outcome. In this way, Bull's disapproval of third world socialism and its rejection of capitalist Western values is oblivious to the role that European coercion played in stimulating its formation, at least in China (and no doubt elsewhere). Accordingly, Bull effectively naturalizes the informal global-imperial expansion of European international society. In addition, while Japan was much freer of European formal and informal imperialism, it is nevertheless often argued that Japan voluntarily industrialized after 1868 as it sought to join international society. Even so, it was precisely the threat of European and American military coercion by the West that prompted the Japanese into making this move. Put differently, it was not so much the desire to voluntarily join European society in order to become "civilized" but a desire to protect themselves from a marauding imperialist West that prompted such moves.

However, in a deeply paradoxical move, while Bull recognizes the existence of the revolt against the West, his conception has the effect of eliding the very processes of non-Western agency that brought formal imperialism to an end. Undoubtedly, many of the factors that enabled decolonization after 1945 can be traced back to the pre-World War I period, most notably the Japanese defeat of Russia in 1905; an event that had an epistemic-transforming impact both within the West and in the East, serving to raise Western anxiety levels while simultaneously boosting non-Western self-confidence. This inspired the rising nationalist revolt against the West, which developed strongly during the inter-war period and climaxed in the aftermath of World War II (see Chapter 5).

While there were many localized uprisings, the most important strategy comprised the *rhetorical* or *mimetic* challenge to empire wherein the nationalist movements appropriated Western civilizational rhetoric as a means to delegitimize it. They used, for example, the key third point of the Atlantic Charter which asserted that the signatories, Roosevelt and Churchill, "respect the right of all peoples to choose the form of government under which they will live; and they wish to see sovereign rights and self-government restored to those who have been forcibly deprived of them." Opinion leaders in the colonies used this and many other so-called Western ideas such as democracy and human rights to push for emancipation. Their rhetorical attack on racism was also extremely important. In the end, the non-Western nationalist movements successfully prosecuted the West in what in effect amounted to a global "social/epistemic court of justice" and won the case for decolonization (see Crawford 2002: chapter 7). Thus, while liberal theories tend to view decolonization as the "victory of Western ideals" and many Marxists view it as the moment when the global baton of power was passed from the European colonial powers to the neo-colonial power of the United States, thereby narrating decolonization as yet another chapter in the ongoing saga of the "triumph of the West," the argument made here restores the process of non-Western agency to the center of the story of decolonization. For in undermining the legitimacy of empire, the whole edifice was finally brought down and world politics moved into a new postcolonial era.

The upshot of this discussion is three-fold: first, that Western imperial globalization was consistently challenged by non-Western states thereby revealing the contested rather than consensual nature of Western-led imperial globalization; second, that decolonization and non-Western resistance agency impacted the West in fundamentally transformative ways, retracking the imperial powers onto new post-imperial paths; and third, that it impacted the development and architecture of the global political economy in the post-1945 era. Thus, one major outcome of decolonization was a *deepening* of globalization, since before 1960 the world had been divided up into semi-autonomous national imperial segments that retained free trade on the inside but were protectionist towards others on the outside. Following decolonization, however, the whole world was opened up in a way that enabled a deeper process of globalization to emerge on the one hand, and for free trade to be spread more widely on the other. Accordingly, this means that we need to factor in the role of non-Western agency rather than reifying the Pax Americana when trying to understand how postcolonial globalization effected a deeper process of integration to that of its Western-led imperial global predecessor.

The dialectics of globalization refers to the way in which West and non-West become entwined in a struggle. But unlike Samuel Huntington's (1996) conception of the "clash" of billiard ball-like civilizations, the dialectics is important insofar as it leads to a transformation of the inner cores of Western and non-Western societies on the one hand, and to a retracking of their outward trajectories on the other. This is significant because it transcends the Eurocentric conception of civilization and barbarism which presupposes that the West and the non-West are self-constituting billiard ball-like entities. What this reading misses is the performance of non-Western agency wherein the West and the global economy are reshaped and retracked in manifold ways, all of which is obscured by Eurocentrism's reification of Western agency in globalization. Many examples of these dialectical processes are evident. In addition to the effecting of a deeper mode of globalization that decolonization effected, a further example lies with the Organization of the Petroleum Exporting Countries (OPEC) oil crises of 1973/4 and 1979/80.

These oil crises were a means by which the Middle Eastern Muslims sought to punish the West for its support of Israel (1973/4 crisis) and for U.S. support of the Shah in Iran (1979/80). This was achieved by drastically raising oil prices which, in the process, spurred on a major recession in the West that in turn saw the response in the form of the turn to neoliberalism and later the establishment of the Washington Consensus. Moreover, this also spurred on third world debt that exploded into existence in 1982 and that was responded to in part by bringing the International Monetary Fund (IMF) back in (given that its role in managing the fixed exchange rate system had formally ended in 1973). All in all, then, the dialectics of civilizations not only led to changes in the global economy but they also initiated major transformations within the West as well as retracking the directions that the West undertook in the global economy (thereby countering the Eurocentric assumption that the West is not merely self-made but also self-directed).

Conclusion: "globalizing" globalization

There are nine key upshots of the arguments of this chapter:

1. It dispenses with the first step of the Eurocentric big bang theory of globalization, which presumes that the West was *self-made* as a result of its own exceptional qualities. Rather, the West was to an important, though by no means complete, extent "Other-made," thereby yielding the idiom that *without the rest there might be no West* – and certainly not the one that we witness today.
2. It reveals that the rise of the West occurred in significant part during the early global age in which Orientalization was the dominant process and Occidentalization the subordinate.
3. The assimilation of diffused non-Western resource portfolios provides a significant litmus test for the presence of non-Western-led globalization in the period between 1492 and 1830/1850, since it led to the fundamental reorganization of societies across the world, especially Europe.
4. Point 3 also reveals how the "dialogues of civilizations" needs to be brought to the fore.
5. As a result of these four points, this alternative vision in effect inverts the two-step Eurocentric big bang theory, in which early non-Western-led globalization came first and the rise of the West came second (in large part as a derivation of the former process).
6. Early non-Western-led globalization that existed between 1492 and 1830/1850 was only made possible by the prior existence of Afro-Eurasian regionalization/Eastern-led proto-globalization between the sixth century and 1492.
7. Modern globalization in turn was only made possible by the prior existence of non-Western-led early globalization, which formed a launch pad for Western-led globalization after 1830/1850.
8. Although the West has been the dominant regional power between 1850 and 2000, we also need to factor in the role of the "dialectics of civilizations" and recognize the role of non-Western resistance agency in shaping the global economy in general and Western civilization in particular, partly so as to counter Eurocentric accounts

that reify the West's role in globalization and partly as a means by which we can provide an intellectually democratic and truly "global" account of globalization.

9. The final upshot is that non-Western agency has constituted an enormously important factor in the making of the modern global world in general and of Western civilization in particular.

Questions for discussion

1. What is Eurocentrism, how does it understand Western development and how does it elide Eastern agency?
2. How are the major theories of globalization, including Marxism, Eurocentric? And what is meant by the Eurocentric "big bang theory" of globalization?
3. How is globalization's existence before 1945, if not the nineteenth century, discounted by Eurocentric theories?
4. Is the claim that globalization began after 1492 and that it was made possible by Eastern-led proto-globalization/Afro-Eurasian regionalization plausible?
5. How does non-Eurocentrism invert the Eurocentric "big bang theory" of globalization? And how does it disrupt Eurocentrism's linear narrative of world history?
6. What are the historical "dialogues" and "dialectics" of "civilizations" and how do these concepts differ to Huntington's "clash of civilizations"?
7. How does recognizing the different "views from the South" recalibrate our conventional understandings of globalization?
8. Is the claim that Eastern agency needs to be factored into our analysis of globalization convincing?

Notes

1 The term "Orientalization" should, of course, not be confused with "Orientalism," where the latter refers in essence to Eurocentrism.
2 For more on the "dialectics of civilizations," see Pieterse (1989).

Further reading

Barkawi, Tarak (2005) *Globalization and War*, Lanham, MD: Rowman & Littlefield. This book explores the mutually reinforcing and historical relation between globalization and war.

Frank, Andre Gunder (1998) *ReOrient*, Berkeley, CA: University of California Press. A key non-Eurocentric book on the global economy in the Asian age (1400–1800).

Hobson, John M. (2012) *The Eurocentric Conception of World Politics*, Cambridge: Cambridge University Press. Hobson provides a detailed critique of international and globalization theory between 1760 and 2010 by revealing the various forms of Eurocentrism and scientific racism that underpin these theories.

Hobson, John M. (2020) *Multicultural Origins of the Global Economy*, Cambridge: Cambridge University Press. This book provides a detailed non-Eurocentric account of the origins of the modern global economy that stems back to 1500.

Ling, L.H.M. (2002) *Postcolonial International Relations*, Houndmills: Palgrave Macmillan. A seminal non-Eurocentric take on IR, focusing on the hybrid relations between East and West.

Pieterse, Jan Neederveen (1989) *Empire and Emancipation*, London: Pluto. This book focuses in part on the dialectics of civilizations.

References

Abu-Lughod, J.L. (1989) *Before European Hegemony*, Oxford: Oxford University Press.

Acharya, Amitav (2018) *Constructing Global Order*, Cambridge: Cambridge University Press.

Armitage, David (2013) *Foundations of Modern International Thought*, Cambridge: Cambridge University Press.

Bala, Arun (2006) *The Dialogue of Civilizations in the Birth of Modern Science*, Houndmills: Palgrave Macmillan.

Bentley, Jerry H. (1993) *Old World Encounters*, New York: Oxford University Press.

Bhambra, Gurminder K. (2014) *Connected Sociologies*, London: Bloomsbury.

Blaut, James M. (1993) *The Colonizer's Model of the World*, London: Guilford Press.

Brenner, Robert (1982) "The Agrarian Roots of European Capitalism," *Past & Present*, 97: 16–113.

Bull, Hedley (1984a) "The Emergence of Universal International Society," in Hedley Bull and Adam Watson (eds), *The Expansion of International Society*, Oxford: Oxford University Press, pp. 119–26.

Bull, Hedley (1984b) "The Revolt Against the West," in Hedley Bull and Adam Watson (eds), *The Expansion of International Society*, Oxford: Oxford University Press, pp. 217–28.

Callahan, William A. (2004) "Nationalising International Theory: Race, Class, and the English School," *Global Society*, 18(4): 305–23. doi:10.1080/1360082042000272436

Chakrabarty, Dipesh (2000) *Provincializing Europe*, Princeton, NJ: Princeton University Press.

Clarke, J.J. (1997) *Oriental Enlightenment*, London: Routledge.

Cox, Robert W. (1996) *Approaches to World Order*, Cambridge: Cambridge University Press.

Crawford, Neta (2002) *Argument and Change in World Politics*, Cambridge: Cambridge University Press.

Dilke, Charles Sir (1868) *Greater Britain*, 2 vols, London: Macmillan.

Fiske, John (1885) *American Political Ideals*, New York: Harper's & Brothers.

Flynn, Dennis O. and Arturo Giráldez (1994) "China and the Manila Galleons," in Heita Kawakatsu and John Latham (eds), *Japanese Industrialization and the Asian Economy*, London: Routledge, pp. 71–90.

Frank, Andre Gunder (1998) *ReOrient*, Berkeley, CA: University of California Press.

Friedman, Thomas L. (1999) *The Lexus and the Olive Tree*, London: HarperCollins.

Fukuyama, Francis (1992) *The End of History and the Last Man*, London: Penguin.

Go, Julian (2016) *Postcolonial Thought and Social Theory*, Oxford: Oxford University Press.

Goody, Jack (2004) *Islam in Europe*, Cambridge: Polity.

Held, David, Anthony McGrew, David Goldblatt, and Jonathan Perraton (1999) *Global Transformations*, Cambridge: Polity.

Hobson, John M. (2004) *The Eastern Origins of Western Civilisation*, Cambridge: Cambridge University Press.

Hobson, John M. (2012) *The Eurocentric Conception of World Politics*, Cambridge: Cambridge University Press.

Hobson, John M. (2020) *Multicultural Origins of the Global Economy*, Cambridge: Cambridge University Press.

Holton, Robert J. (1998) *Globalization and the Nation-State*, London: Macmillan.

Hourani, George F. (1963) *Arab Seafaring in the Indian Ocean in Ancient and Early Medieval Times*, Beirut, LB: Khayats.

Huntington, Samuel P. (1996) *The Clash of Civilizations and the Remaking of World Order*, London: Touchstone.

Kant, Immanuel (1970a) "Perpetual Peace: A Philosophical Sketch," in Hans Reiss (ed), *Kant's Political Writings*, Cambridge: Cambridge University Press, pp. 93–130.

Kant, Immanuel (1970b) "Idea for a Universal History with a Cosmopolitan Purpose," in Hans Reiss (ed), *Kant's Political Writings*, Cambridge: Cambridge University Press, pp. 41–53.

Kaplan, Robert D. (1994) "The Coming Anarchy," *Atlantic Monthly* (February): www.TheAtlantic. com/atlantic/election/connection/foreign/anarcf.htm

Kayaoglu, Turan (2010) *Legal Imperialism*, Cambridge: Cambridge University Press.

Landes, David S. (1998) *The Wealth and Poverty of Nations*, Boston, MA: Little Brown.

Ling, L.H.M. (2002) *Postcolonial International Relations*, Houndmills: Palgrave Macmillan.

Ling, L.H.M. (2014) *The Dao of World Politics*, London: Routledge.

Mackinder, Halford J. (1904) "The Geographical Pivot of History," *The Geographical Journal*, 23(4): 421–37.

Mahan, Alfred T. (1897) *The Influence of Seapower upon History*, London: Sampson, Law, Marston.

Marx, Karl and Friedrich Engels (1848/1967) *The Communist Manifesto*, Harmondsworth: Penguin.

Mathieu, Xavier (2020) *Sovereignty and the Denial of International Equality*, London: Routledge.

Needham, Joseph and Wang Ling (1965) *Science and Civilisation in China*, IV(2), Cambridge: Cambridge University Press.

Pearson, Charles H. (1894) *National Life and Character*, London: Macmillan.

Pieterse, Jan Neederveen (1989b) *Empire and Emancipation*, London: Pluto.

Roberts, John M. (1985) *The Triumph of the West*, London: BBC Books.

Rodinson, Maxime (1974) *Islam and Capitalism*, London: Allen Lane.

Roosevelt, Theodore (1905) *The Strenuous Life*, New York: The Century Co.

Rostow, Walter W. (1960) *The Stages of Economic Growth*, Cambridge: Cambridge University Press.

Said, Edward W. (1978/2003) *Orientalism*, London: Penguin.

Sajed, Alina and Naeem Inayatullah (2016) "On the Perils of Lifting the Weight of Structures: An Engagement of Hobson's Critique of the Discipline of IR," *Postcolonial Studies*, 19(2): 201–09. doi:10.1080/13688790.2016.1254017

Seed, Patricia (1995) *Ceremonies of Possession in Europe's Conquest of the New World*, Cambridge: Cambridge University Press.

Smith, Adam (1776/1937) *The Wealth of Nations*, New York: The Modern Library.

Stoddard, Theodore Lothrop (1920) *The Rising Tide of Color against White World Supremacy*, New York: Charles Scribner's Sons.

Subrahmanyam, Sanjay (1997) "Connected Histories: Notes Towards a Reconfiguration of Early Modern Eurasia," *Modern Asian Studies*, 31(3): 735–62.

Suzuki, Shogo (2009) *Empire and Civilization*, London: Routledge.

Vitoria, Francisco de (1539/1991) "On the American Indians," in Anthony Pagden and Jeremy Lawrance (eds), *Vitoria: Political Writings*, Cambridge: Cambridge University Press, pp. 231–92.

Wallerstein, Immanuel (1974) *The Modern World-System*, I, London: Academic Press.

Wallerstein, Immanuel (1997) "Eurocentrism and Its Avatars: The Dilemmas of Social Science," *New Left Review*, I(226): 93–108.

Weber, Max (2001) *The Protestant Ethic and the Spirit of Capitalism*, London: Routledge.

Wolf, Martin (2005) *Why Globalization Works*, London: Yale Nota Bene.

Zarakol, Ayse (2011) *After Defeat*, Cambridge: Cambridge University Press.

13 Inequality

Joao Pontes Nogueira

Introduction

Globally, the total wealth of the world's 2,158 billionaires increased to US$8.9 trillion in 2017, the highest level in recorded history. At the same time, the number of people living in extreme poverty (defined as having an income of less than $1.90 a day) stood at 736 million in 2015 (World Bank 2018). Inequality is not only evident between individuals; there is also a regional dimension to global inequality. For example, of the world's 28 poorest countries, 27 are in Sub-Saharan Africa, and it is estimated that by 2030, based on historical growth rates, the portion of the poor living in this sub-region could be as large as 87%. In addition, poverty exhibits a strong gender component, with women suffering disproportionally from lack of access to resources. Of course, lack of income is only one indicator of poverty, and poverty is only one form of inequality.

Inequality has become one of the most discussed problems in international affairs in the past two decades. It has come a long way since the massive protests by social movements in Seattle (1999) and Genova (2001) against structural adjustment policies imposed by the International Monetary Fund (IMF) and the World Bank on developing countries. Those protests inspired the creation of the World Social Forum (WSF) in 2001, in which an agenda critical of neoliberal globalization promoted alternative solutions to reduce poverty and inequality worldwide (see Chapter 15). Today inequality is practically a mandatory item in reports and meetings of multilateral organizations and even business-oriented settings like the World Economic Forum (WEF). In 2015 the United Nations (UN) General Assembly approved the Sustainable Development Goals (SDGs) among which goal number ten aims at reducing inequality within and among countries. As noted above, despite their gains in visibility and relevance, inequality of income and wealth continues to grow during the era of globalization. When measured by income, inequality has risen in most countries in the world, both in the mature economies of Europe and the United States as well as in fast-growing emerging countries such as China and India (World Inequality Report 2018). By contrast, international inequality (or inequality between countries) has been declining since the early 2000s, mostly due to the growth of emerging economies, particularly China. Even so, the top 1% of the adult population has captured an increasing share of the result of economic growth (27% in 2016) since 1980. The disparity between the decline in international inequality and the concentration of income and wealth among a very small part of the world population is perhaps the most striking contradiction of the era of globalization. It means, basically, that even when developing economies manage to grow at higher rates and reduce the gap between them and the richest countries, inequality increases and the well-being of the world's population (measured, for instance, in access to health and education) does not improve.

How does International Relations (IR) as a discipline approach such a crucial problem? In this chapter I will discuss the limitations of its traditional views to offer an account of the nature and consequences of inequality for world politics and try to suggest alternative perspectives that consider inequality as a formative feature of the international system. My argument starts from a simple observation of the paucity of titles in IR literature dedicated to the problem of inequality. Despite its overwhelming concern with differentials of power to explain conflict and cooperation, international theories rarely address political and economic inequalities as problems in themselves. The discussion will try to foreground, however, that despite its marginality as an object of inquiry, inequality is an indispensable principle of the modern international imagination. Traditional approaches take it as an assumption that does not require elaboration; as a natural and inevitable feature of a Hobbesian world. However, as I will try to show in the following sections, this view has always been contested, both in theory and practice, by scholars and actors in the global South. Much of the remainder of the chapter will be dedicated to discussing alternative and innovative perspectives that conceptualize inequality as constitutive of world politics. I start with an analysis of inequality in the context of the debate on dependency and autonomy in the global South and then introduce more recent contributions of critical theories about the role of neoliberal disciplinary reason in the reproduction of inequalities. Finally, I explore how decolonial contributions to contemporary IR scholarship in the global South offer a productive alternative to meaningfully articulate the international and global dimensions of inequality through the introduction of coloniality as a central conceptual device.

The problem of inequality in traditional IR

Inequality as constitutive of international order

"Internationally, inequality is more nearly the whole of the political story" (Waltz 1979: 143). This quote, by neorealist Kenneth Waltz, seems to suggest that traditional IR theories consider inequality a crucial problem for understanding world politics. For any student of IR living in the global South, inequality appears as a dominant feature of everyday life as well as an important object of discussion and analysis. Greater disparities in wealth, income, access to services, living conditions, health and education have become a common trait of the processes of restructuring of state/market relations required to achieve competitiveness in the global economy. And yet, the field of International Relations has had very little to contribute to the study of inequality in world politics for much of its existence. Instead, the discipline's main concern has been the problem of how international order is created and maintained in the absence of a central authority (see Chapter 5). In this sense, the most common approaches to international relations might seem, to those who are not part of the academic universe of the developed societies of the West, of limited interest and use for the understanding of the worlds they live in. It is the argument of this chapter, however, that the systematic exclusion of inequality from IR has been changing in the past few years, for reasons that comprise social and political dynamics in global politics as well as new approaches to the problems of security, development and statehood. As a result, the theme of inequality has gained relevance in academic and policy circles in rather diverse forms. The changing intellectual environment in IR has also contributed to this trend. Perspectives from the global South have been more influential in bringing inequality into the academic debates from which they were consistently marginalized. This argument will be further developed in the third section of the chapter. For now, my goal is to discuss how inequality plays a central role in the constitution of international order; how it is silenced by the dominant theories of International Relations; and how the rule of sovereign equality creates the conditions of possibility for the reproduction of inequality (see Chapters 5 and 8).

We live in a world in which states are equal once they are recognized as sovereign entities. Despite the clear asymmetries of power and wealth between states, formal equality functions as the normative foundation for world order. Traditional IR theories separate the realm of politics, where relations of power define the dominant traits of the system, from the economic sphere, where problems such as poverty and development are a function of the domestic resources (such as technology, raw materials) of each particular state. This separation makes the discussion about the effects of inequality in world politics rather problematic, especially from the point of view of the global South.

International law similarly reflects such a separation between politics and economics. It affirms that sovereignty accords states the right to exercise authority over territories and population, and to act as agents in international society. The universalization of sovereign statehood took place in the second half of the 20th century after the demise of colonialism and the struggle for national liberation in the third world. One of its consequences was to highlight the gap between the formal equality of the new states under the rules of the UN Charter, and their actual capacities to participate in decision-making processes in world forums as well as the workings of the international economy. As we will see in the following sections, the tension between these two conceptions of equality (legal and actual) was at the center of political and economic controversies between North and South during the Cold War and after (Simpson 2004; Anghie 2005) (see Box 13.1).

BOX 13.1 SOVEREIGN INEQUALITY

The rule of sovereign equality endured in the modern era despite the contradictions between the rights it ascribed to states in general and their ability to exercise such rights. Classical theories of international relations associate sovereignty to the principle of self-help, which is mostly defined by the capacity (or power) of a state to exercise its political autonomy. In this perspective, equal sovereign rights are dependent on power (and wealth). Critics of international inequality have focused on ways to redress the asymmetries that constrained the ability of third world countries to influence world affairs and condemned them to underdevelopment. The tension between formal equality and the substance of the rights inherent to sovereignty is fundamentally problematic. It expresses a view of world politics that naturalizes inequality and restricts the rights of the majority of states to participate in the governance of the international system. The end of the Cold War ignited a process of limited reform of global governance institutions with the aim of giving more weight to emerging economies in areas such as trade and monetary policies. New arrangements such as the G20 and the BRICS (Brazil, Russia, India, China and South Africa) were created as alternatives to a U.S.-centered power structure. These efforts were balanced by competing processes that moved sovereignty away from its universal definition to a more relative understanding of its application to different kinds of states – rogue, failed, fragile states. As a result, sovereignty has often become conditional upon the adoption of liberal democratic principles and the adoption of technologies of good governance. This "anti-pluralist" movement promotes a "tolerable inequality" that legitimizes interventions in the areas of development, security and humanitarianism.

For conventional IR theories, sovereign equality is of relatively little interest as a theoretical problem. Politically, it represents the defeat of colonial and imperial experiences between the 15th and 20th centuries and the assertion of self-help as the dominant behavior adopted by states in an anarchic system. In other words, the autonomy achieved by post-imperial and postcolonial nation-states in the last century placed the responsibility of providing security and welfare to their citizens in the hands of these states themselves with whatever resources they had available. For realists, for instance, equality is, more than a normative principle, a political and material expression of self-help and as such, contingent on power (Krasner 1985; Waltz 2000) For liberals, the independence afforded by sovereignty can be preserved if institutions of collective security fulfill their objectives, an outcome largely dependent on states' self-interest and capacities – especially on the commitment of great powers to the functioning of such institutions. Because states have different resources of power and wealth, sovereign equality does not go very far in its promise of independence and autonomy. It proved to be a good solution to the unstable order of the 19th century, plagued by the territorial revisionism of imperial and hegemonic ambitions. The international order of the second half of the 20th century was regulated by the combination of great power competition and the relatively strong consensus that territorial integrity and self-help contribute to a more stable international system. The UN Charter is the most eloquent expression of how sovereign equality and territorial integrity became the pillars of the post-war international system. Paradoxically, taking the legal and functional equality of states as a starting point supports an arrangement in which a more equal distribution of resources to exercise sovereignty became marginal at best. The conventional wisdom in IR therefore begins with inequality as a natural given of political organizations in general, and of the system of states in particular. Sovereign rights are progressively extended to all states in order to redress inequalities that could no longer be legitimated (such as imperialism and colonialism). Because the exercise of equality is dependent on resources that continue to be unequally distributed, structural inequality persists. However, once legal sovereignty was accepted as the main source of legitimacy, asymmetries of power and wealth became a feature of traditional perspectives on how order is produced.

What is the problem with the traditional view?

As outlined above, traditional IR theory does not completely erase inequality from international politics but instead views it as an underlying property of how the international system is structured. In conventional accounts, inequality is framed by the dynamics of stabilization or change as states engage in cooperation and conflict. Processes of change can occur when the distribution of capabilities (mostly military but also economic) is dispersed among a greater number of states. Less concentration of power disturbs the balance of power and may lead to war. War is considered, mostly by realists, the principal mechanism of change and redistribution of power in the international system. Consequently, change is risky, even if driven by justified claims to more equality in international politics. Because inequality concentrates power among few actors, it allows for a more stable and efficient management of the balance of power. Inequality, then, according to the classical view, is only a problem when there is not enough of it.

As a theoretical problem inequality has a marginal place in the discipline's research agendas. IR theory, however, has been instrumental in depicting inequality as a given of global political life as well as a problem that has to be constantly deferred. Three points illustrate this argument. First, IR theories do not normally integrate the dynamics of capitalism in their analysis of international politics. As a mode of production based on exploitation and domination of subaltern classes, it is only reasonable to expect that capitalism should be a crucial dimension of any reflection on inequality. Efforts to integrate critiques of capitalism to explain international inequality have either fared poorly or been marginalized (Kubálková and Cruickshank 1981). For example, Waltz argues that there is no specificity to capitalist expansionism relative to other forms of imperialism.

For realist and liberal International Political Economy, often regarded as a subfield of IR, the production of wealth and its expansion globally result from either state interests or those of economic elites. Capitalism is either treated as a property of the internal organization of states or as an economic system with no direct influence on international politics. Either way, its absence in these theories enables: (a) conventional narratives about the constitution of the international system as an unintended consequence of interstate competition driven by power politics or (b) liberal views about the expansion of the global economy as the expression of the interests of states to integrate markets to produce more wealth. As a result, a good deal of the Marxist contribution to the analysis of international relations – such as theories of imperialism – is set aside from the principal debates in the field.

Conventional thinking in IR considers the particular quality of world politics as a consequence of the dangerous environment wherein it unfolds. The international system is considered a separate and distinct political space. Boundaries separate an inner sphere in which the authority of the state is based on relations of hierarchy and legitimacy from its opposite, an outside realm where the preservation of autonomy requires self-help as a guiding principle in international relations. My second observation about the reproduction of inequality addresses the "sovereign narrative" (Walker 1993). The establishment of the limits of states' jurisdiction is taken to be the legitimate product of their sovereign authority. However, sovereign practices are made possible by spatial demarcations in the first place. In the context of our discussion, the narrative of sovereignty offers a sharp insight into the ontological assumptions of the claims for equality in international relations. For the latter are based precisely on the affirmation of the rights of territorially contained political communities and their absence outside the boundaries of the state. As we have seen, however, this move instantiates a world in which the primacy of self-help legitimates inequality as an ordering principle. In other words, the separation of domestic and international realms creates the conditions to think about inequality as a natural state of affairs in world politics.

A third and final point illustrates how claims to equality in IR theory often rest on forgetting the constitutive inequality at the origins of the modern "international" itself (see Chapter 6). The colonial experience is probably the most eloquent marker of the contradictions in dominant narratives of sovereign inclusion. In the conventional story of the post-war era, the decolonization process represented the end of rules and practices of subjugation of peoples for the purpose of imperial expansion justified on standards of civilization, racism, religion and other ideological constructs. The end of colonialism also signified the expansion of the system of states as the universal model of political organization available for those whose right of self-determination was recognized. As such, decolonization was a powerful mechanism in the consolidation of the modern international system once it made the inclusion, as equal and free members, of every autonomous community that managed to acquire a state, possible. The evolution of the international system could now be interpreted as a process of modernization at the reach of all. While humanity finally seemed to share a same historical time, not everyone, however, lived in the same stage of social, political and economic development.

The post-war order was predicated on the principle of sovereign equality inscribed in the United Nations Charter. Moreover, it set the conditions for the elimination of the colonial system. Liberation and independence brought most of humanity to the sphere of rights conferred by the international community. Nations and its citizens were entitled to be free of the scourge of poverty and to dignified living conditions. Modernization and development would become the center pieces of policies designed to achieve those basic rights. However, while decolonization created a world in which all peoples were equal by right, it also gave birth to a system characterized by rising international inequality. Modernization theories claimed such inequalities were a transitory moment in the path to development. They also legitimized the Western model of political and economic organization of societies as the universal standard every developing state should aim for. For many critics, the old civilizational trope crept into notions of development and divisions between North and South, advanced and backward economies, and developed and underdeveloped countries. While these differentiations exposed hierarchies and inequalities in the post-war system, the promise of progressive inclusion into the modern world was always deferred but at the same time present in the temporal frame of international theories. Given time, adequate institutions to govern trade and finance, international cooperation and aid, development would eliminate poverty and generate shared prosperity. As we will see next, however, this dominant view was contested by third world intellectuals and policy makers who interpreted the "structural inequality" of world politics as a legacy of centuries of colonial exploitation.

Contesting inequality

Observers in the third world were not indifferent to the predicament of peripheral states in a profoundly unequal system. In fact, newly independent countries as well as less developed nations of the South were quite successful in bringing the problem of international inequality to the center of the agenda in multilateral institutions as well as in the intellectual and academic milieus of central and peripheral societies. The contrast between formal equality and the concentration of wealth in a few central states led to the contestation, during most of the Cold War, of the North–South polarization.

Without going into this historic debate in great detail, it is important to highlight several positions that, schematically, summarize a range of critical contributions from the South, especially during the decades of the 1960s and 1970s up to the early 1980s, which could be translated into a set of three strategies: neutrality, autonomy and reform, and delinking (on the foreign policy implications of these strategies, see Chapter 11). There were overlaps among these strategies according to different political contexts. The discussion will be limited to a brief outline of the theoretical underpinnings of each one in order to put the argument about contemporary contestations of inequality into perspective. The three strategies were influenced, in different ways, by a range of interpretations about the unequal nature of international relations. I will discuss the most relevant: adaptations of power-based approaches to the realities of the periphery, structural theories and variation of theories of imperialism (Kubálková and Cruickshank 1981).

As the configuration of world politics crystallized in a competition between two superpowers and their respective spheres of influence, *neutrality* appeared as the earliest manifestation of an attempt to seek alternatives to alignment and explore the contradictions of that antagonism for the benefit of the third world. This position consisted of the articulation of the principles of decolonization, development and disarmament as the basis for a potential mediating role and the flexibilization of the dynamics and arrangements of a system then seen as "frozen" by the confrontation between the two camps. These principles would sustain several important political initiatives that included the formation of the Non-Aligned Movement (NAM) in 1961, the Group of 77 and the United Nations Conference on Trade and Development (UNCTAD) in 1964. The neutrality approach, however, lost much of its appeal when the notion of "peaceful coexistence" gradually took hold of East–West relations after the Cuban missile crisis, giving relative stability to the power structure of the Cold War. In that context, Brazilian diplomat Araujo Castro observed an accentuation of the rigidity of relations of power internationally, and a considerable restriction of the possibilities of collective action by the third world (Amado 1982).

The analysis of the problem of inequality in the world economy received a fundamental contribution in the work of Raúl Prébisch, founder of the Economic Commission for Latin America (ECLA) school of economic thought, for whom the causes of underdevelopment in the periphery could be traced to the structure of the international division of labor – which attributed to the periphery the production of primary goods – and to the deteriorating terms of trade of such goods in a world market dominated by the most advanced, central economies. These structural constraints were the main obstacle to the development of the third world and required changes in the political and economic architecture of the international system, as well as substantive reforms in domestic economic policies. In the vision of ECLA the path to development should be based on the recovery of terms of trade by means of political coordination in multilateral arenas, and on state-led industrialization policies in underdeveloped countries. These two strategies illustrate well what would be the dominant approach to broader North–South relations and the more specific issue of inequality: the struggle for national *autonomy* and reform of the structures of the international system.

The third main set of arguments contesting international inequality was based on the contributions of dependency theories (for more on dependency and its implications for war and conflict, sovereignty and foreign policy, see Chapters 7, 8 and

11). I briefly discuss the works of Marxist authors who were instrumental in the formulation of strategies of *delinking*. The general argument of dependency is that underdevelopment is the product of the development of global productive forces controlled by the center of the capitalist system. It is the condition of dependency of peripheral countries that perpetuates their underdevelopment. Unequal exchange, the role of multinationals in controlling investment and innovation and the hegemony of central powers established a mechanism of extraction of surplus from the periphery and its domination and exploitation (economic and political) by the center (Santos 2000). The important distinction of dependency vis-à-vis autonomy-oriented structuralism is to situate the mechanism of domination within the dynamics of the international system itself, instead of in the dysfunctions of the international division of labor. In this sense, the strategy of autonomy and reform through modernization and changes in the rules that govern the multilateral system was, for these authors, incapable of breaking the cycle of dependency. Instead, peripheral societies should privilege national liberation and pursue anti-imperialist strategies based on alliances with revolutionary movements throughout the third world. In consequence, the periphery would acquire the power resources needed to articulate a genuinely autonomous economic model and break the ties of dependency that prevent the development of the full potential of its productive forces. Undoing the links with the world capitalist economy was, for these authors, a necessary condition for the success of this strategy (Amin 1990). Even though their impact in the policies of less developed countries was limited,[1] dependency theories have had a long-lasting influence upon intellectual debates about international inequality. They are also the best known examples of a theoretical formulation of the problem by authors from the global South.[2]

Dependency theories provided a more radical approach to the intellectual mix that composed third world visions of the time. As such, they attracted a great deal of intellectual attention and support at a time when anti-capitalist and anti-imperialist sentiments were widespread in the North and South, fueling important social movements and exerting great pressure on Western democratic governments. In Latin America, Asia and Africa, where many regimes took an authoritarian turn, dependency was used, when convenient, to denounce the unjust and unfair positions of advanced economies. In fact, dependency became influential in part because it combined an explanation of class struggle in the language of international relations with anti-imperialist theses that advocated the struggle for autonomy of national states (Kubálková and Cruickshank 1981). In this context, the political and economic make-up of third world regimes became secondary once their main function was to resist the economic policies of hegemonic states. Delinking, however, came to be perceived as a high-cost and high-risk strategy that relied on the success of revolutionary processes in peripheral states. This option was seldom pursued by elites in power in developing countries who more often adopted strategies that avoided isolation, secured access to international sources of finance and investment and provided political support against outside intervention as well as domestic opposition. In the end, the more internationalist contestation advocated by dependency was subsumed by the narrative of sovereignty, under the form of economic nationalism and frequently, authoritarian statism in much of the third world.

The critique of the liberal economic order of the post-war era coincided with the economic and political crises of the 1970s in the core of the system. Emboldened by successful experiences of development in semi-peripheral countries, the South seemed, to a point, capable of putting the dominant powers on the defensive in the debate over reforms of the multilateral system of trade and finance. As Krasner observed, "the South's ability to present an effective analysis of the global economy enhanced the unity of developing countries, weakened the capacity of the North to defend the liberal order, and facilitated the formulation of specific policy proposals" (Krasner 1985: 81) (see Box 13.2).

BOX 13.2 INTERNATIONAL INEQUALITY

International inequality refers to asymmetries of power and wealth between states. It is commonly measured in terms of differences in capabilities (usually military) or mean national income. In classical theories, inequality is an intrinsic quality of the international system. In other words, it is taken as a necessary condition of the modern age in which politics and society are organized in discrete, autonomous, sovereign states. Realist and liberal traditions coincide in privileging order and stability over alternative ways of organizing world politics aimed at redressing inequality. The classical view became untenable with the delegitimation of colonialism – a system previously insulated from claims to equality and considered part of the "natural" evolution of international society. National liberation movements and decolonization foregrounded the inequity and exploitation that structured the international order. The expansion of the system of states only made international inequality more evident in the tension between the equal rights of sovereignty and the unequal material and political conditions for their enactment. For instance, third world countries became more vocal and organized actors in multilateral institutions during the 1960s and 1970s and were able to influence agendas of international trade and development. At the same time, income inequality between countries rose steadily until the 1980s, when it started to decline, mostly as a consequence of the rapid growth of the Chinese economy. Alternatively, the inflexion in international inequality has been matched by a sharp increase in inequality within countries (national inequality). Compare with "global inequality" (see Box 13.3).

Alternative approaches to international inequality

Inequality remains a central theme of critical traditions in international thinking today – or, for some, an issue that distinguishes "left" from "right" in the global political spectrum (Noël and Thérien 2008). In this section I discuss contributions to the debate by authors who have analyzed the logic of contemporary world politics as constitutively linked to the reproduction of inequality. In line with the proposal of this chapter, I will suggest that inequality's place in international thought has recovered its centrality in a critique of world politics from the global South. This effort will include the neo-Marxist analysis of neoliberal globalization and postcolonial perspectives on how the modern international reinscribes domination in its attempts to overcome its own limits. Finally, I will suggest that inequality continues to be a contested concept and an object of intense controversy among experts and policy makers of diverse ideological convictions.

Neo-Marxist critiques of global inequality

Perhaps the most relevant distinction of contemporary debates on inequality resides in their transversal nature. Structuralist accounts, dominant from the 1960s until the 1980s, worked with discrete lines between global, international and national levels of analysis. Contemporary approaches cut across the boundaries of modern social spaces, destabilizing the coherence of once territorially contained political practices. The displacement of conventional boundaries forces us to look, for instance, into the transnational strategies of so-called global elites articulated in global networks. While many authors of a cosmopolitan orientation have considered globalization as a new political space where normative theories of justice, associated to the expansion of new forms of global governance, could address social problems more adequately than national settings,[3] neo-Marxists inspired by the work of Antonio Gramsci, such as Stephen Gill, argue that the current phase of capital accumulation has "intensified global inequalities" (Gill 1995). This shift in the scale of the analysis of the problem has foregrounded the concept of global inequality (see Box 13.3) in contrast with the more traditional concept of international inequality (see Box 13.2) (Bourguignon and Scott-Railton 2015; Milanović 2016). Two main processes constitute globalization as an unprecedented expansion of the power of capitalist social forces: disciplinary neoliberalism and new constitutionalism (Dallmayr 2002). The first captures the deepening of market values and disciplines in social life, enabling the logic of accumulation to penetrate wider spheres of social reproduction and everyday life. Disciplinary neoliberalism is the product of the internationalization of social forces and the consequent restructuration circuits of production and finance under post-Fordist capitalism (see Chapter 15).

BOX 13.3 GLOBAL INEQUALITY

The paradox of the simultaneous decline in international inequality and the rise in inequality within countries has been the main source of the debate about the effects of globalization on the contemporary disparities of wealth and well-being among individuals and countries across the world. As a result, students of inequality have increasingly focused on the phenomenon of global inequality. The concept, according to Milanovic, refers to "income inequality among citizens of the world" and can be determined by combining national inequalities and gaps in income between countries (Global Inequality 2016). What does this approach offer to better understand the problem? Basically, it takes stock with more precision of the impacts of global economic trends in stratification among groups of people (and individuals) beyond the limits of national boundaries. In other words, it widens the scope from which we can analyze and evaluate income inequalities worldwide. For instance, if we consider the reduction of international inequality (inequality between states) since 1980 we will notice that, given the accelerated growth of emerging economies (especially China and India), it has dropped consistently, either in market dollar values or in terms of purchase parity power (PPP, which weighs variations in income according to their purchase power in each national economy). If, however, we take global inequality as a measure we will see that mean income levels between countries are increasing and still very significant. In other words, it establishes a correlation between globalization and rising inequalities. Compare with "international inequality" (see Box 13.2).

These processes led to a profound reconfiguration of post-war welfare states in advanced Western economies as well as structural reforms in developing countries. As a result, different combinations of market-oriented strategies were implemented across the international system, with roughly three important outcomes: a historical shift in the balance of state and markets in the appropriation of surplus capital; the reduction of the relative power of organized labor through more flexible work legislation and the reduction of social protection programs; and the gradual displacement of policy and decision making to institutions and forums of global governance. These combined outcomes greatly increased the ability of corporations to restructure, reduce labor costs, introduce new technologies and move production plants to different regions of the planet faster. These processes, in short, were at the basis of a very dynamic phase of capital accumulation initiated in the 1970s with financial globalization.

Neoliberalism concentrated more power in the hands of global corporations that now operate with much fewer constraints than in the previous welfarist phase. In the current context, states act to regulate the global circulation of capital and integrate in the new circuits of value creation, now beyond the reach of national economic projects (Crouch 2011). The downside of deregulation is more volatility and less predictability of markets globally. Crises are harder to manage because policy instruments are more decentralized. Domestically, political support for adjustment imposes increasing costs to governments, both conservative and leftists. The rationale for the "new constitutionalism" is based precisely on the higher political risks associated with disciplinary neoliberalism. Given the breakdown of the old social pacts of welfare states in developed economies, and of populist or authoritarian regimes in developing countries, structural reforms of the institutions of the state were implemented to "contain challenges" to the neoliberal project "through cooptation, domestication and depoliticization of opposition" (Gill 1995: 48). In fact, reforms of the state were at the heart of the economic and political transformations in "new democracies" of·former socialist blocs as well as in Latin America. In general, they redefined the role of the state in the economy (through privatization, deregulation, fiscal and monetary reforms) and in social policies through welfare reform, labor legislation reform, privatization of social programs, administrative streamlining of state bureaucracies, changes in electoral systems and so forth.

While many of these initiatives faced political opposition, they were legitimized by the dominant modernization discourse associated with the assumed inevitable process of globalization. It would be an overstatement to argue that neoliberal reforms were uniformly imposed and successfully implemented across the globe. However, the analysis of new constitutionalism as an indispensable strategy to produce the necessary political and institutional environment for the success of the neoliberal program provides us with more elements for a better understanding of the contradictions and variations of neoliberalism.

For the purposes of the discussion proposed in this chapter, the neo-Gramscian approach sheds new light on the problem of inequality (see too, Chapter 15). Through it we can see how the process of internationalization of capital was led by social forces organized as global elites in institutional and corporate networks informed by a renovated ideology of modernization, crystallized around the notion of globalization (Pieterse 2004, 2009). This process created the conditions for a concentration of power and wealth by these global social forces which, as a result, intensified inequalities both at the international and the global levels. It would be difficult, however, to frame the analysis solely on the basis of these economic factors, for hegemony is, in Gramsci's words, a "war of position": it involves continuing political and ideological struggles to construct dominant historical blocs. This is where Gill's concept of "new constitutionalism" brings added analytical value. It accounts for the different mechanisms for neutralizing opposition and building consensus around a market-oriented and individualistic form of citizenship that can live side by side with inequalities of wealth, income, gender and race. These narrower, more restrictive, forms of citizenship, institutionalized by legal and institutional reforms, "lock in" modes of unequal representation within democratic constitutions, marginalizing resistance to the new global regime of governance of the political economy of capitalism. In other words, the move to the "global" which explains the rise in inequality in contemporary world politics is only made possible by the hollowing out of political commitments to social equality within states (Chandler 2009).

However, the mobility and speed of the new circuits of accumulation have, as mentioned above, produced more volatility and instability, generating institutional insecurity that affects the daily operation of markets. In the context of increasing social polarization, democracies come under pressure to adopt more extensive and complex mechanisms of control and surveillance of populations, often through legal instruments that restrict freedoms in the name of security (Bigo 2007). We can see how legal reformism is crucial for a new articulation between economics and politics, creating juridical-political frameworks that legitimize the higher social stratification resulting from the freer operation of markets and the reduction of social protections (Gill 1995; Dezalay and Garth 2011). The re-articulation of politics and economics offers a more complete perspective, lacking in many prominent liberal accounts, of how inequality is reproduced globally by capitalist dynamics that operate transnationally. It is, as most neo-Gramscian theories in IR, framed by the structural power of capital, which often appears as the ontological foundation for the constitution of disciplinary neoliberalism. The analysis consequently privileges the agency of social forces in advanced capitalist regions in its account of globalization, despite the somewhat relevant role of peripheral forces in counterhegemonic (global) movements that take place "both within and across complexes of civilizations" (Gill 1995: 51).

Inequality acquires a truly global dimension in the neoliberal regime. Moreover, inequalities rise within states as well as across a more stratified global political economy. Inequality still is a relevant measure of asymmetries of power and wealth in the international system, however, transformations in the world political economy have led to new conceptualizations to account for global processes of domination and exploitation unfolding across the old North–South divide. As the numerous studies on the subject attest, rising inequality has become an affliction of advanced industrialized societies as well as of poorer ones (Wilkinson and Pickett 2010; Stiglitz 2012; Piketty and Goldhammer 2014).

Views from the global South

Does international inequality remain, under contemporary circumstances, an issue that identifies the struggle of the peoples of the South for a more just world order? Some authors argue that dependency theory can still contribute to a "project of counter-representation" of the periphery, essential to displace the epistemic and political centrality of the West in most critical approaches to inequality in world politics.[4] Theotonio dos Santos reasserts the contention made in his landmark works that dependency still enables the extraction and transference of surplus from the periphery to the center, despite significant changes in post-Cold War forms of domination (or empire) (Santos 2000). Indeed, other scholars have also argued that the widening asymmetries of power and wealth, and the transformation of modes of domination in the shape of global governance can be interpreted as hegemony through imperial rule (Hardt and Negri 2000; Harvey 2005). While the emergence of new technologies of power in the governance of global issues is in line with most critiques of globalization, the claim that inequality results from some form of neo-imperialism is less compelling. It is true that the critique of global inequality has inspired a return to geopolitical readings of international relations and, consequently, a reassertion of sovereignty as indispensable in a strategy aimed at "independent development and autonomy" (Slater 2004). However, as the previous analysis suggests, contemporary world politics presents complexities that resist definition by general categories such as capitalism, imperialism or nation-state. These global phenomena seem, on the contrary, fragmented by transformations in spatio-temporal processes and representations that would be difficult to understand under the modern political imagination of international relations (Bhambra 2014).

Alternatively, many scholars have turned to the contribution of postcolonial theories to articulate a richer approach to the problem of inequality and formulate fresh critical views of the historical experience of domination.[5] Postcolonial thought frames the problem of inequality squarely within the constitutive relation between modernity and coloniality. For authors of the Latin American school of decolonial studies such as Anibal Quijano, Enrique Dussel, Walter Mignolo and Santiago Castro-Gomez, among others, there is a clear line of continuity between their work and the intellectual tradition of dependency (Lander and Castro-Gómez 2000). The latter made a compelling case about the historical determinants of colonialism in the processes of modernization in peripheral societies. Dependent development not only deferred modernization to an indefinite future but also reproduced and amplified dependence and inequality. Quijano articulates the concept of coloniality as an ontological condition of modernity. The modern world consists of the hierarchical separation between the West and "the rest" produced by the colonial encounter. In other words, modernity consists in the colonial organization of the world, both in time and space.

The historical process analyzed by postcolonial thought consists of two essential movements. The first is an epistemological one, which asserts the centrality of Europe in the historical cosmology of the modern world and includes an expression of universality which encompasses yet negates the particularity of the Other (the Americas). Walter Mignolo defines the "colonial difference" as the denial of "epistemic contemporaneity," in other words, a temporal and developmental gap between the civilized space of Europe and the distant, backward places beyond (Mignolo 2010). Inayatullah and Blaney (2004) use a similar image to analyze the "Westphalian deferral" as an expression of the antinomies of modernity – the affirmation of equality in a world of sovereignty which can only be ordered through the production of difference or of inferior others. Interestingly, these authors read inequality through "forms of social hierarchy" based on the "intensification of difference" as a source of threat. Such insights allow us to read inequalities as the product of differences always present in the colonial encounters since early modern cosmologies where inscribed in historical time (Inayatullah and Blaney 2004). The second distinctive movement of postcolonial thought can be found in Quijano's work when he identifies the "principle and strategy of control and domination" as the "coloniality of power" (Quijano 2010). This very modern power is based on race, geohistorical identity and civilizational hierarchy (Quijano 2010). It sustains political and economic colonial domination as the expression of its ontological foundations. It is, however and above all, a regime of power founded on a hierarchy of knowledge, an epistemology of difference geopolitically enacted (Lander and Castro-Gómez 2000).

As we can see, this approach formulates a critique of modernity that situates the emergence of the international system of states within a globality that not only precedes conventional Westphalian narratives characteristic of International Relations theories, but also argues that there can be no modernity without coloniality (see Chapter 6). To be sure, modern reason affirms the universality of modernity through the epistemological violence that excludes other knowledges than those produced in the West. Modern sciences play a central role in the management of non-Western populations, their exclusion and exploitation and the conquest of their territories. (Castro-Gómez and Grosfoguel 2007; Mignolo 2008). Furthermore, the colonial encounter establishes the production of a world system based on hierarchies of difference (ethnicity, race, civilization) that inscribe inequality in the very experience of modernity.

Decolonial theories breach the dualities through which inequalities in international relations are conventionally interpreted – development/underdevelopment, center/periphery and so forth – exposing the antinomies of a global modernity constituted by the continuous exclusion of its other, or said differently, of what is external, marginal or peripheral to it. Dussel criticizes this "total" conception of modernity because it assumes Europe's centrality in its historical project, ignoring the coloniality of its origins. His alternative is to conceive a "transmodernity" inclusive of different and marginalized cultures, whose "immense capacity of invention" and "intercultural dialogue" can affirm multiple possibilities of a transformed globality that does not renounce a universal project of emancipation (Dussel 1995, 2008: 345). The place of difference in postcolonial critiques of inequality opens important analytical avenues to problematize the gendered, racialized and culturally exclusionary dimensions of the modern international system. They offer interesting modes of analysis of global inequality that are not limited by traditional categories of power and wealth, but rather reflect on domination in world politics from conceptions of inequality based on ethnicity, race and gender (Bhambra 2007; Anievas et al. 2014; Boatcă 2015).

The postcolonial analysis of the power configuration of modernity adds an important dimension to the neo-Marxist dissection of the contemporary hegemonic order. It introduces a theorization of modern coloniality as a dynamic social formation based on a form of power that combines race and labor and separates peoples spatially and temporally in heterogeneous processes of domination. This particular social formation claims universality (and today, globality) from the standpoint of knowledges that affirm the equality of humans at the same time as it is founded on the reproduction of colonial difference. This view of the formation of the modernities of today's world enhances our understanding of the many shapes of inequality, for it sheds light on what is obscured and naturalized by the discourses and practices of globalization, governance and development: the continuation of Western superiority as the indispensable principle upon which the future of modernity is conceivable (Escobar 1995; Kapoor 2008; Mignolo 2012).

Disciplinary neoliberalism expanded the reach of capital across diverse areas of social life. In this process it reproduces and intensifies inequalities of income, race, gender and culture in a range of social spaces transformed by globalization. These changes upset the categories through which we interpret inequalities and asymmetries that shape international relations. Third world, center and periphery, North and South, dependency and imperialism were gradually set aside to make way for theoretical constructs that could account for the displacement of spatial-temporal references of an international system no longer centered on sovereign states. For many, the effacement of those categories meant that the contradictions they expressed were overcome by history. For others of a more critical orientation, new categories were needed to understand current forms of hegemony and domination. The postcolonial approach provides a critique that accounts for the multiplicities of trajectories cohabiting the world today, many of which formed in other spaces and places, "exteriorities" of the totalizing frame of the modern international system (Escobar 2004). It is from these places, these "peripheries" or "borders" of the international, that a critique of inequality as an expression of the globalization of the coloniality of power can emerge.

Conclusion

The problem of inequality has re-emerged in different intellectual and institutional sites in the past decade. As a normative condemnation of the effects of globalization on the increasing disparities in the living conditions of the great majority of human beings, the critique of inequality remains an important reminder of its centrality in the dynamics of global politics today. Its influence in policy debates, however, is limited. As we have seen, the recognition of sovereign equality as a general rule of the international system is also constitutive of a world of unequal entities. It also defined the autonomy of those states to address issues of distributive justice domestically as they please. When those issues were taken to the international arena by states claiming for fairer international rules affecting their development, egalitarianism was regarded by the great powers as a threat to the hegemony of the liberal West. Third world countries realized that to play the sovereign game the field would have to be minimally leveled by rules and institutions that would allow for development at the periphery of the system. In the long run the result was promotion of development in the form of poverty alleviation and the imposition of standards to discipline economic policy making. Inequality often becomes an issue in the agenda of global governance when western states and multilateral institutions decide the sovereign game should be changed to create the conditions for the globalization of the liberal order.

The sustained growth of big emerging economies during the last decade has affected the inequality debate in many ways, two of which are of significance here. First, the five countries comprising the BRICS group have been responsible for half of the world economy's output since 2009 and account for close to a quarter of world gross domestic product (GDP). As a result, international inequality has decreased for the first time in four decades. Alternatively, with the exception of Brazil and Russia, domestic inequality has increased in all emerging economies, especially in China. Global inequality has also increased during the two decades of steady growth of the world economy. Conscious of their new role and status, these countries have claimed, once again, changes in the distribution of political power in international institutions, given the material shifts in economic power recognized by everyone. The modest processes of reform of the IMF voting quotas have yet to produce any results and talk of reform of the multilateral system is lukewarm. Emerging powers have benefited from globalization and their agenda is to adapt policies and institutions to their development strategies. Their main concern is with disparities of representation in the institutional architecture of the international order.

The challenge lies in how to problematize inequality from an alternative, critical perspective. This is not, as has hopefully become clear in this chapter, a simple task. We have raised suspicions that the move to the "global" poses serious theoretical and political problems, potentially allowing for reductionist formulas typical of the "good governance" discourse. A more promising path lies perhaps away from the abstraction of globalism, or rather in a critique of its universal ambition, by putting into evidence the enduring violence of coloniality and in the reproduction and diffusion of multiple forms of inequality, exclusion and domination.

Questions for discussion

1. How does globalization affect inequality?
2. What is the relationship between inequality and order in traditional and critical theories of IR?
3. What are the limits of the classical approach to sovereign equality? What contributions from third world agendas can we mobilize for a critique of the classical view?
4. Inequality in world politics can be measured basically in terms of power and wealth. Discuss.
5. What is the value added of the concept of global inequality to the debate on inequality in world politics? What are its limitations?
6. Much of the debate on global inequality takes measures such as income and wealth to address the many dimensions of the problem. How can alternative perspectives from the South contribute to politicize this debate?

Notes

1 The works of Prebisch and Furtado, however, had a significant impact in domestic and international policies of third world countries.
2 For a recent and updated version of this argument see Mignolo (2007).
3 See, for instance, Linklater (2007).
4 See, for instance, Slater (2004) who argues for dependency theories as crucial interpretative keys to analyze the contemporary world order.
5 An indispensable reference for a postcolonial approach to IR is Inayatullah and Blaney (2004).

Further reading

Aalberts, Tanja E. (2014) "Rethinking the Principle of (Sovereign) Equality as a Standard of Civilization," *Millennium: Journal of International Studies* 42(3): 767–789. In this article Tanja Aalberts argues that the universalization of the rule of sovereign equality constitutes an international order based on practices of exclusion and inclusion that reproduce a colonial logic embedded in the notion of a standard of civilization.

Amin, Samir (2006) *Beyond US Hegemony? Assessing the Prospects for a Multipolar World*, London and New York: Zed Books. In this book one of the main authors of the dependency school analyzes different scenarios for an emergent multipolar world order in the context of unequal globalization.

Escobar, Arturo (1995a) *Encountering Development: The Making and Unmaking of the Third World*, Princeton: Princeton University Press. In this classical work on critical development studies, Arturo Escobar lays out the argument that the production of underdevelopment and the third world by policies and knowledges that constitute the field of development was crucial to the government of inequality in world politics.

Krishna, Sankaran (2009) *Globalization and Postcolonialism Hegemony and Resistance in the Twenty-first Century*, Lanham: Rowman & Littlefield. In this book Krishna brings together different lineages of postcolonial theory to reflect on globalization as a long historical process based on conquest, control and unequal exchange.

Milanović, Branko (2016) *Global Inequality: A New Approach for the Age of Globalization*, Cambridge: The Belknap Press of Harvard University Press. In this book Milanovic, a key reference in economic studies about inequality, articulates conceptual and methodological approaches to think inequality as a global problem.

Morana, Mabel, Enrique Dussel and Carlos A. Jauregui (Hispanic and Luso Brazilian Councils) (2008) *Coloniality at Large: Latin America and the Postcolonial Debate*, Durham: Duke University Press. A key reference and introduction to Latin American approaches and debates on coloniality and postcolonialism.

Nkrumah, Kwame (1968) *Neo-Colonialism: The Last Stage of Imperialism*, London: Heinemann Educational. A classical text on colonial inequality by the leader of the independence movement in Ghana and key intellectual of Pan-Africanism.

Rosanvallon, Pierre (2013) *The Society of Equals*, Cambridge: Harvard University Press. A reflection on the transformation of politics and democracy in times of growing inequality.

Therborn, Göran (2013) *The Killing Fields of Inequality*, Cambridge: Polity Press. A multidimensional and interdisciplinary analysis of the contemporary trends and transformations in inequality.

References

Amado, Rodrigo (1982) *Araujo Castro*, Brasiliai: Universidade de Brasilia.

Amin, Samir (1990) *Delinking: Towards a Polycentric World*, London: Zed Books.

Anghie, Anthony (2005) *Imperialism, Sovereignty and the Making of International Law*, Cambridge: Cambridge University Press. doi:10.1017/CBO9780511614262.

Anievas, Alexander, Nivi Manchanda and Robbie Shilliam (2014) *Race and Racism in International Relations: Confronting the Global Colour Line*, Abingdon: Routledge.

Bhambra, Gurminder K. (2007) *Rethinking Modernity: Postcolonialism and the Sociological Imagination*, Basingstoke and New York: Palgrave Macmillan.

Bhambra, Gurminder K. (2014) *Connected Sociologies*, London: Bloomsbury Academic.

Bigo, Didier (2007) "Detention of Foreigners, States of Exception, and the Social Practices of Control of the Banopticon," in Prem Kumar Rajaram and Carl Grundy-Warr (eds), *Borderscapes: Hidden Geographies and Politics at Territory's Edge*, Minneapolis: University of Minnesota Press, pp. 3–33.

Boatcă, Manuela (2015) *Global Inequalities Beyond Occidentalism*, London and New York: Routledge. doi:10.4324/9781315584867

Bourguignon, François and Thomas Scott-Railton (2015) *The Globalization of Inequality*, Princeton: Princeton University Press.

Castro-Gómez, Santiago and Ramón Grosfoguel (eds) (2007) *Reflexiones para una diversidad epistémica más allá del capitalismo global*, Bogotá: Siglo del Hombre Editores.

Chandler, David (2009) *Hollow Hegemony: Rethinking Global Politics, Power and Resistance*, London and New York: Pluto Press.

Crouch, Colin (2011) *The Strange Non-Death of Neo-Liberalism*, Cambridge, Malden: Polity.

Dallmayr, Fred (2002) "Globalization and Inequality: A Plea for Global Justice," in Mustapha Kamal Pasha and Craig Murphy (eds), *International Relations and the New Inequality*, Oxford: Blackwell, pp. 137–156.

Dezalay, Yves and Bryant Garth (2011) "Hegemonic Battles, Professional Rivalries, and the International Division of Labor in the Market for the Import and Export of State-Governing Expertise," *International Political Sociology* 5(3): 276–293. doi:10.1111/j.1749-5687.2011.00134.x

Dussel, Enrique (1995) "Eurocentrism and Modernity," in John Beverley, Michael Aronna and José Oviedo (eds), *The Postmodernism Debate in Latin America*, Durham: Duke University Press, pp. 65–76.

Dussel, Enrique (2008) "Philosophy of Liberation, the Postmodern Debate, and Latin American Studies," in Mabel Moraña, Enrique Dussel and Carlos A. Jáuregui (eds), *Coloniality at Large: Latin America and the Postcolonial Debate*, Durham: Duke University Press, pp. 324–349.

Escobar, Arturo (1995) *Encountering Development: The Making and Unmaking of the Third World*, Princeton: Princeton University Press.

Escobar, Arturo (2004) "Beyond the Third World: Imperial Globality, Global Coloniality and Anti-Globalisation Social Movements," *Third World Quarterly* 25(1): 207–230. doi:10.1080/0143659042000185417

Gill, Stephen. (1995) "The Global Panopticon? The Neoliberal State, Economic Life and Democratic Surveillance," *Alternatives* 20: 1–49.

Hardt, Michael and Antonio Negri (2000) *Empire*, Cambridge: Harvard University Press.

Harvey, David (2005) *The New Imperialism*, Oxford: Oxford University Press.

Inayatullah, Naeem and David Blaney (2004) *International Relations and the Problem of Difference*, New York: Routledge.

Kapoor, Ilan (2008) *The Postcolonial Politics of Development*, London and New York: Routledge.

Krasner, Stephen (1985) *Structural Conflict: The Third World Against Global Liberalism*, Berkeley: University of California Press.

Lander, Edgardo and Santiago Castro-Gómez (2000) *La Colonialidad Del Saber: Eurocentrismo Y Ciencias Sociales: Perspectivas Latinoamericanas*, Buenos Aires: Consejo Latinoamericano de Ciencias Sociales.

Kubálková, Vendulka and Albert Cruickshank (1981) *International Inequality*, New York: St: Martin's Press.

Linklater, Andrew (2007) *Critical Theory and World Politics: Citizenship, Sovereignty and Humanity*, London and New York: Routledge.

Mignolo, Walter (2007) "Delinking," *Cultural Studies* 21(2–3): 449–514. doi:10.1080/09502380601162647

Mignolo, Walter (2008) "The Geopolitics of Knowledge and the Colonial Difference," in Mabel Moraña, Enrique Dussel and Carlos A. Jáuregui (eds), *Coloniality at Large: Latin America and the Postcolonial Debate*, Durham: Duke University Press, pp. 225–258.

Mignolo, Walter (2010) "Delinking: The Rhetoric of Modernity, The Logic of Coloniality and the Grammar of De-Coloniality," in Arturo Escobar and Walter Mignolo (eds), *Globalization and the Decolonial Option*, Abingdon: Routledge, pp. 303–368.

Mignolo, Walter (2012) *Local Histories/Global Designs: Coloniality, Subaltern Knowledges, and Border Thinking*, Princeton: Princeton University Press.

Noël, Alain and Jean-Philippe Thérien (2008) *Left and Right in Global Politics*, Cambridge and New York: Cambridge University Press.

Pieterse, Jan Nederveen (2004) *Globalization or Empire?* New York: Routledge.

Pieterse, Jan Nederveen (2009) *Globalization and Emerging Societies: Development and Inequality*, Basingstoke: Palgrave Macmillan.

Piketty, Thomas and Arthur Goldhammer (2014) *Capital in the Twenty-First Century.* Cambridge: Harvard University Press.

Quijano, Anibal (2010) "Coloniality and Modernity/Rationality," in Arturo Escober and Walter Mignolo (eds), *Globalization and the Decolonial Option*, London: Routledge, pp. 22–33.

Santos, Theotonio dos (2000) *A Teoria da Dependência: Balanço e Perspectivas*, Rio de Janeiro: Civilização Brasileira.

Simpson, Gerry (2004) *Great Powers and Outlaw States: Unequal Sovereigns in the International Legal Order*, Cambridge: Cambridge University Press.

Slater, David (2004) *Geopolitics and the Post-Colonial: Rethinking North–South Relations*, Malden: Blackwell Publishing.

Stiglitz, Joseph (2012) *The Price of Inequality: How Today's Divided Society Endangers Our Future*, New York: Norton & Co.

Walker, R. B. J. (1993) *Inside/Outside: International Relations as Political Theory*, Cambridge: Cambridge University Press.

Waltz, Kenneth N. (1979) *Theory of International Politics*, New York: Random House.

Waltz, Kenneth N. (2000) "Structural Realism after the Cold War," *International Security* 25(1): 5–41.

Wilkinson, Richard and Kate Pickett (2010) *The Spirit Level: Why Greater Equality Makes Societies Stronger*, New York: Bloomsbury Press.

World Bank (2018) *Poverty and Shared Prosperity: Piecing Together the Poverty Puzzle*, www.worldbank.org/en/publication/poverty-and-shared-prosperity

World Inequality Lab (2018) *World Inequality Report*, https://wir2018.wid.world/

14 Migration

Nizar Messari

Introduction

Episode 1: the French team that won the FIFA World Cup in July 1998 was a very appealing one, and not only from a sport performance point of view. Many of its star players were the sons of immigrants, and its captain, Zineddine Zidane, nicknamed Zizou, was a Kabyle of Algerian descent. The team managed to unify France behind it, with no regard for race, religion or ethnicity. Those who were playing and those who were supporting the team in the stadiums and the streets underplayed their differences for a moment. Admittedly, this rosy picture was disturbed by a few nasty comments by extreme right-wing leaders who felt that the team did not represent them and were unhappy with the victory of *that* French team. But by and large, this was a small and insignificant minority.

Episode 2: fast-forward to October 2005, when the streets of the Parisian suburbs were the theater of a rebellion of the not so well integrated sons and daughters of immigrants. The celebration of difference of 1998 was forgotten, as the marginalized youth of the suburbs burned cars and destroyed stores and other private and public properties while they were violently repressed by the police. The French model of integration was violently questioned, both physically and rhetorically, as both sides of France (the one originating recently from migration and the one that had been French for generations) were in disbelief regarding the reaction of the other side. Although such reactions did not mean there were no success stories among families of migrants, the rebellion revealed deep fractures within French society between different ethnic, religious and cultural groups.

Episode 3: on July 21, 2019 the streets of Paris were overrun by the celebration of … the Algerian national football team's victory in the African Cup! Young people of Maghrebi descent – and not only those of Algerian descent – motivated the following headline from the very serious French newspaper *Le Monde*: "We celebrate Algeria's victory just like we celebrated France's victory last year" (referring to France's FIFA World Cup victory in July 2018, the second of its kind).[1]

Does this mean that the current generation of young French with migrant origins are better integrated and less discriminated against? That would be a hasty conclusion, although again, there are several success stories in those communities: individuals from those communities have held important ministry portfolios, been elected in local, national and European elections, held important positions in the business world and even won prestigious literary prizes. But at the same time, individuals from those same migrant communities were behind all the terrorist attacks that had struck France over the past few years, and many migrants from those same communities went to Syria and became fighters for the so-called Islamic State, commonly referred to through its acronym, ISIS.

These three episodes portray some of the key dilemmas of migration in the contemporary world, comprising integration attempts, marginalization and violence. But the migration debate goes beyond these issues: in the West, it portrays migration as a burden and a threat. Although those who support it defend migration as an opportunity to be taken or even a necessity, they often are on the defensive and usually end up arguing about how to control migration humanely. The dominant argument is that states need to act in order to protect their borders from illegal crossings and must build the capacity to do that. The establishment of agencies such as Frontex in the European Union (EU) and the Department of Homeland Security in the United States is the embodiment of this orientation.

Migration is an issue in which movements and actions of people are hindered and harmed by the actions and policies of nearly all states. Namely, the state imposes its rules and priorities in a way that impacts people's lives to degrees that did not exist before the establishment of such political entities. Indeed, migration of individuals and groups from one geographic location to the other is not a new phenomenon in the history of humanity. In fact, people have been moving around for centuries looking for better living conditions, fleeing oppression and/or epidemics, or simply looking for better lands and opportunities. The relative novelty regarding this phenomenon is the context within which it takes place: states and the borders that separate them. In geographical areas such as the American continent, the impact of the state is even more paradoxical: with the exception of Native Americans, the entire population descends from people who were migrants at a certain point in time. However, those who came earlier acquired the right to establish rules that have acted to exclude those who came later. States of all kinds reaffirm these exclusionary practices in order to establish an inside and an outside (see Chapter 8).

Today, 255 million individuals are estimated to be migrants, which is a large number per se, but a small one in terms of the total world population (between 3 and 4%). Among them, there are economic and political refugees, refugees who are victims of climate change, students and expats, as well as retired individuals and couples from wealthier states who migrate to warmer and cheaper geographical locations. This is to say that migration is neither recent nor restricted to poor people looking to improve their living conditions in wealthier economies.

This chapter begins with a brief historical perspective that aims at showing that individuals and communities have been migrating from one place to the other for a long time, and for different reasons. The second part of the chapter presents one of the most important, although relatively recent impacts of the state on migration, i.e., the securitization of migration, which translates into considering migration as a threat, and sometimes, migrants as quasi-criminals, or at least, law-violating individuals. The third and last part of the chapter presents the migrant's perspective, which is not state-centered – for starters – but that also emphasizes the human and humanitarian factors and perspectives at play in this issue.

Migration in history

Migration is not a new phenomenon in world history. In modern times, a landmark mass migration movement took place when Europeans of all social classes migrated to the Americas, looking for new opportunities and fleeing poverty and rigid political, economic and social systems. Some also had religious motivations: while some fled religious repressions and wars of religion, others wanted to convert the populations of the New World to Christianity. A subsequent migration wave took place in the second half of the nineteenth century, when new groups of Europeans migrated to the Americas, North and South. In South America in particular, the impact of positivism created an impetus for local elites, comprised essentially of European descendants, to further encourage European migration hoping that it would have a positive impact on the attitudes and values of the population, and help the region in its development efforts. Italians, Prussians and Spaniards were especially encouraged to immigrate to the New World in order to enjoy better lives. The fact that most of those migrants were poor and illiterate, and some with criminal records, was not noted by those who encouraged them to migrate to South America. During this period, droves of Europeans went to the colonies, either as soldiers, colonial administrators or small entrepreneurs. While many were from modest backgrounds in their home countries, when they landed in the colonies they enjoyed privileges granted to the colonizers, and took advantage of the locals whom they often considered to be inferior and in need of civilizing by the Europeans. A couple of decades later, Japanese, Syrians and Lebanese constituted the new group of migrants arriving to the American continent. The irony in Latin America is that since the first Syrian and Lebanese migration took place when the Levant was part of the Ottoman Empire, they are referred to as Turks, although they are actually Arabs. In the Brazilian part of the Amazon forest, the economic prosperity that resulted from the intensive and extended exploitation of rubber caused a massive migration to that region, and in particular from North African Jews, whose synagogues and descendants are still in Belem, the capital of the state of Pará, for instance.

In the first half of the twentieth century, the two world wars caused the displacement of millions of individuals. As borders were drawn and re-drawn, empires melted and new powers emerged, and as death and destruction forced many to move to other lands, groups of people changed their citizenship, sometimes against their will, as new states were formed and others lost or gained lands. After World War II, decolonization and the emergence of independent states became an opportunity for millions of individuals to move around, either seeking safety and protection (in the case of Jews who massively sought refuge in the newly created state of Israel, or Muslims who felt unsafe in India and sought to become citizens of Pakistan, to cite only two examples). Simultaneously, in the Soviet Union under Stalin, mass deportations took place with the impetus of creating a novel social and ethnic reality. The consequences of those movements are still felt in the twenty-first century, be it in Crimea or in the Caucasus. The wars in the Middle East between Israel and its Arab neighbors caused two types of population movement. The first is the most common in areas of conflict: refugees fleeing the war-torn zone and seeking what they hoped were temporary residences. These were mostly Palestinians who sought refuge in neighboring Lebanon and Jordan. The second type was more unusual in the sense that instead of fleeing war, Sephardic Jews who used to be established in North Africa in general, and in Morocco in particular, felt increasingly unsecure and fled those countries, some heading to Western destinations, mostly France, whereas many others went to Israel.

In parallel, the economic growth and prosperity that ensued after World War II in Western Europe transformed the continent for the first time from a population sending region to a host region, as it represented a pull factor for migrants not only from Southern Europe (most notably Greeks, Italians, Spanish and Portuguese), but also from North Africa as well as Sub-Saharan Africa and other former colonies (such as Indians and

Pakistanis in the U.K.) and less prosperous economies (like Turks in Germany). These were called guest workers as they were actively recruited by Western European companies to fill mostly low-skilled jobs and sustain the economic growth of those economies. But the end of the long cycle of economic growth in Western Europe, which was accelerated by the two oil crises of the 1970s and the resulting inflation hike, transformed those guest workers into undesired migrants, and eventually into an economic, social and cultural threat. At this juncture, it is important to note that all Western European states did not experience this shift at the same time. The three episodes presented at the beginning of this chapter illustrate the challenges of integrating and assimilating those migrants in Europe in general, and France in particular. While France was starting to experience this shift, Spain and Italy were just beginning to welcome migrants as they were experiencing a shortage in labor, and in the case of Spain, a significant economic boom. But by the early 1990s, migration had been securitized, as well illustrated by Wæver et al. (1993) (see too, Chapter 10). The securitization of migrants in Western Europe, which will be discussed subsequently, is only one of the consequences of this population movement. The other is a substantial population and cultural diversity that exists today in Europe, with key political and business leaders, influential cultural figures and star football players originating from the migrant populations.

As for North America, after receiving populations originating essentially from Europe, and mainly although far from exclusively from Western Europe, the second half of the twentieth century witnessed the growth of migration from South America, initially Mexico and Central America, to the United States. This migration has had long-term political, economic, cultural and ethnic impacts on the U.S., as the share of the population of Hispanic origin in the country has increased, and with it, the place of the Spanish language and Latino culture. Migration, which many consider as an asset for the U.S. economy (Hampshire 2013: 38), has come to be considered a threat by others (Hampshire 2013: 20), becoming the object of intense political controversy. Recent public debates in the United States regarding migration, detention centers and building walls illustrate the centrality of this issue in that country, as well as the radically distinct positions that surround it (see Box 14.1).[2]

BOX 14.1 REFUGEES AS A SPECIFIC TYPE OF MIGRANTS

Conceptually, refugees are hard to define. They are migrants, but they migrate involuntarily, i.e., not out of choice but out of obligation. There is also an international aspect to their migration. Otherwise, they would be referred to as "internally displaced people." And international treaties and conventions accept more easily political refugees than economic refugees, although the UNHCR (United Nations High Commissioner for Refugees) keeps trying to include economic refugees in the definition of those it seeks to protect. In sum, refugees are individuals who challenge sovereignty in a world made of sovereigns. However, the challenge they present is a soft, as opposed to a hard, one. Namely, sovereign states find themselves, due to humanitarian reasons and legal commitments, obligated to extend protection and privileges to people from other countries who have fled their country of origin because of their race, religion, nationality or membership in particular groups or organizations, to protect their lives (Haddad 2008).

Another type of migrant appeared in the second half of the twentieth century. As opposed to the more common Northbound population movement, this is a Southbound migration, consisting mostly of retiring individuals and couples from wealthy Northern European and North American economies who seek sunnier and warmer weathers for their old age. Besides a more welcoming weather, another attraction for these populations are the lower income levels in the countries of destination, which usually allow them higher standards of living in their regions of choice than in their countries of origin. While these population movements were started by the British, Germans and Scandinavians who opted for southern Spain, Portugal, Italy or even Malta for their retirement, such movements have increased over time with retirees from the United States and Canada heading to Mexico, and other Europeans relocating in North Africa. New small communities are created in the regions of destination, where consumer habits are transplanted from home and a whole system of support is put in place in order to serve that population. Tensions might arise between these migrants and the local population, but in general their higher purchasing power and older age contribute to their acceptance by the locals.

A further relatively welcome type of migration in host economies from the North is what is customarily referred to in the global South as the brain drain. These can be students from the South (and from China) who remain in the countries where they studied at the undergraduate and postgraduate levels after graduating, mainly in Western Europe and North America. Many of these individuals are from STEM (science, technology, engineering and mathematics) fields, i.e., sectors with the most innovative and transformative potential for their home economies. In fact, the prevalent practice of West European firms between the 1960s and early 1970s, consisting of offering guest visas to low-skilled workers from former European colonies, has been replaced by the targeting of highly skilled workers.

A recent new destination for North–South and South–South migrants has been the Persian Gulf, and its states rich in oil and gas. Although those economies have been destinations for North African and Middle Eastern migrants as well as Western migrants for years, the last two decades witnessed a deepening and expanding of this trend as Dubai in the United Arab Emirates and Doha in Qatar (besides Saudi Arabia) became attractive poles for all types of migrants from around the world. The need to prepare for an imminent post-oil and gas moment has resulted in fast-growing economies with substantial needs in terms of human capital in many sectors, all attracted by high and competitive salaries and benefit packages. Western, Middle Eastern and North African as well as South Asian high-skilled workers have been attracted by those packages, whereas low-skilled labor in construction and other similar sectors has also been drawn to those economies. Contrary to other migration destinations, in most of the Gulf state destinations, migrants are far more numerous than the locals. Another important characteristic of this migration is that it is precarious: the relative generosity of the work packages compensates rather shaky labor protection laws and a high level of randomness, and the lower the skills, the harsher the working conditions. The Kafala system, which gives the employer total control over the living conditions of the foreign employee (who cannot switch jobs, quit a job or leave the country without the formal approval of his/her employer) provides the best illustration of the precariousness of work in these states.

Migration driven by economic factors constitutes a less welcome form of population movement. As previously mentioned, initial population movements from poorer economies to wealthier ones in Western Europe were based on the concept of guest workers. However, after the two oil crises of the 1970s, Western European as well as North American economies became increasingly closed to migration and started imposing restrictions on incoming migrants. Nevertheless, the "migration genie" was already out: on the side of pull factors, citizens from former colonies as well as from South America who were established in Western Europe and North America had discovered the advantages of migrating and started projecting a mostly rosy picture of migration. By doing so, they encouraged individuals from their villages, neighborhoods and towns to join them, even if illegally. Those individuals also either married partners from their countries of origin and decided to bring them to Europe or felt increasingly comfortable in their countries of residence and applied for authorizations for family reunions. In either case, despite restrictions imposed on new migrants, their numbers did not stop growing over the years. On the side of push factors, significant differences in terms of job opportunity, given widespread poverty and poor economies back home, were important incentives for individuals to leave home and attempt to improve their life prospects abroad. Such migrants came to represent an important asset to their national economies, not only by alleviating the number of local job seekers but also and mainly through substantial money transfers to their families. In poor economies across the global South, remittances constitute the first or second source of foreign currency, ahead of productive sectors such as tourism or manufactures (for the Moroccan case, see Seeberg 2013).

Economically motivated movement continues to be the main stimulus for individuals to migrate. The European Union, and to a lesser extent, the United States, now understand that in order to reduce the number of migrants arriving from poorer economies, supporting development initiatives to create better living conditions in the sending countries is key. As we will discuss later on in this chapter, the European Union sought to improve living conditions in southern Mediterranean shores, establishing not only economic, but also cultural, political and environmental conditions in order to encourage young people from the region to remain at home. The results of such policies, we will soon argue, are far from conclusive, and individuals who seek better living conditions continue to migrate massively.

In sum, migration is neither a recent phenomenon, nor has it taken place in one direction only. Throughout modern history, migrants have moved in many different directions. In the second half of the twentieth century, movement from Europe to the rest of the world, and from the North to the South, was replaced by the reverse tendency, with Europe becoming a net receiver of migrants. However, Northbound population flows are not the only direction of migration, as the examples of migration to the Persian Gulf countries and the migration of retired individuals and families to warmer climates show. Additionally, migrants are not necessarily unwelcome: in the 1960s and 1970s, Western Europe sought out low-skilled labor, and in contemporary Western Europe and North America, high-skilled labor from the global South, referred to as the brain drain, is in high demand.

The securitization of migration

One facet of the public debate about migration that has been gaining traction in recent decades, mostly in the West, is related to the representation of migrants as a threat to national identity and interests, against which both states and peoples need to protect themselves by closing their borders. Throughout the 1980s, rising unemployment in Western Europe, in addition to the growth of non-European and non-Judeo-Christian migrant communities, turned migration into a hotly debated topic and a security issue. The perception of migrants as a source of threat – or to use the language of "securitization" an existential threat (see Chapter 10) – created a framework in which a security apparatus was needed to handle the alleged threat. An illustration of this perception of migrants in the European Union in particular is a map on the web page of Frontex, the EU's main agency for border management, control and protection. The map portrays a continent seemingly under siege by migrants, in which threatening multi-colored arrows show the routes migrants take to reach Europe as if they were military troops poised to invade (see http://frontex. europa.eu/trends-and-routes/migratory-routes-map/).

Admittedly, International Relations (IR) has not addressed migration until quite recently. However, the rise of critical strands of linking in the 1980s and the turn towards "identity" as a central concept in the field, led to its increasing visibility (see for example, Betts and Loescher 2011; Huysmans 2006; Bigo 2002). In 1998, Barry Buzan, Jaap de Wilde and Ole Wæver published *Security: A New Framework for Analysis*, in which they explored how distinct issues and sectors could become security problems at a given time and place. One of their main challenges was to explain how immigration had become, in the late 1980s and early 1990s, a security issue. The authors argued that in the same way that some topics are politicized, i.e., they become part of public life, others are securitized, i.e., they are "upgraded" to become part of a very closed and select group of problems that represent an existential threat against which all possible resources must be mobilized (see Chapter 10 for a more detailed discussion of securitization and desecuritization).

The securitization of migration in Europe resulted in a whole set of policies put in place to stop migrants from entering the continent, "externalization" being one of the main ones. Two kinds of "externalization" are visible in EU policies (Qadim 2015: 8). On the one hand, the European Union exports classical tools of migration control such as border control, policies combatting illegal migration and building capacities in order to be able to handle asylum requests and manage migration (Boswell 2003: 622). On the other hand, the second set of externalization instruments put together by EU authorities and member states refers to the transit role that some states started playing during the 1990s, including measures to allow

> the return of asylum seekers and illegal migrants to third countries. The main instrument here was readmission agreements with third countries committing them to readmit irregular immigrants who had passed through their territory into EU countries or were their nationals.
>
> (Boswell 2003: 622)

The objective of these procedures was to impose new and remote selection locations, and to avoid having to send back undesired migrants to their homes (or departure points) once they had already arrived in Europe. The active engagement of non-state and non-EU members in this process – along with EU states – is one of the main characteristics of this set of policies. Such procedures took African migrants who were either refused an entry visa to Europe or who did not even attempt to obtain one to look for alternative ways to reach the continent without a formal authorization. Individuals seeking to enter European territory through Morocco, Algeria, Tunisia or Libya without legal authorization, come from countries as diverse as Cameroon, Côte d'Ivoire, Congo, the Democratic Republic of the Congo, Gambia, Ghana, Guinea, Guinea-Bissau, Liberia, Mali, Mauritania, Nigeria, Senegal and Sierra Leone (Carling 2007: 12) (see Box 14.2).

BOX 14.2 FAILED ATTEMPTS AT THE EXTERNALIZATION OF EU MIGRATION POLICIES

An important aspect of cooperation between some EU member states and countries like Morocco in migration control was the establishment of Morocco-Spanish naval patrols as well as EU territorial controls within Morocco, both activities sponsored by the EU (Collyer 2007: 672). For instance, in December 2004 an EU-Morocco program of "border control management" provided institutional support to the Moroccan Ministry of the Interior, with training programs, equipment (such as radars, infrared cameras, electromagnetic sensors and so on) amounting to €40 million. In August 2006, and as a follow up step, the EU added €67.5 million in assistance for Morocco to step up its fight against what it called "clandestine immigration." Morocco has also established controls along its Mediterranean and Atlantic coasts in order to crack down on departures towards Europe from Moroccan shores (Collyer 2007: 684). The adoption in 2004 by Spain of SIVE or Sistema Integrado de Vigilancia Exterior, a technology-based sophisticated system of space control – including maritime space – allowed that country to increasingly monitor and act in the "protection" of its borders. According to Collyer (2007: 672), "[t]he number of migrants apprehended in the Straits of Gibraltar has fallen steadily since 2004." Despite all these new technological tools of unauthorized migration control, and according to Arango and Martin (2005: 266), in 2005 Spanish police estimated catching only one out of four boats attempting to cross the Strait of Gibraltar towards Spain, which emphasized the importance of having Morocco acting pre-emptively and stopping these boats before they leave its territory.

In sum, outsourcing the control of migration movements was one of the key mechanisms put together by EU authorities. It was accompanied by both pressure and European funding to encourage southern Mediterranean partners to control their maritime and land borders with Europe. Two such initiatives, MEDA I (1996–2001) and MEDA II (2001–2006) contributed significantly to funding the fight against "illegal immigration." Tellingly, at the Euro-Mediterranean Conference held in Barcelona in 1995, the need to increase development in the countries of the southern coast of the Mediterranean was linked to migration and the reduction of migratory pressure for the first time (Lacomba and Boni 2008: 130–131). The objective of these policies was to provide populations from southern Mediterranean countries with conditions that would enable them to stay at home rather than to migrate to Europe. It was hence a double strategy of increasing the risks of unauthorized migration while creating incentives for people to stay at home (Martin 2014: 236). However, according to Lacomba and Boni (2008: 141), the benefits of emigration far surpass those of international cooperation, given that "emigrants' remittances have a direct effect on their families' economies ... while development projects contribute to the collective welfare in the middle and long term" (2008: 141). Therefore, the main result of European policies was to leave migrants with illegal, and very often dangerous routes and strategies to migrate to Europe.

The Southern perspective

Until here, we have seen that migration is an ancient phenomenon. Individuals and communities have migrated throughout history either looking for a better life or fleeing wars, famine or harsh weather conditions (UNDP 2009). In the case of the African continent, current population movements are not only considered by many historians a continuation of pre-colonial trans-Saharan trade and religious routes (Berriane 2014), but also, most African migrants remain on the African continent and do not aim to travel to Europe, Asia or the United States. In 2017, according to the International Organization on Migration (2018), approximately 19 million Africans were living in another African country, as compared to 17 million who were living outside of Africa. Among these, most were in Europe (9.3 million), then Asia (4.4 million) and finally North America (2.6 million). This means that Europe hosts less than half of African migrants, most of whom prefer to remain on the continent. Clearly, this places the alleged "threat" of African migration to Europe under a new light, given that the empirical evidence shows that African migrants prefer to remain closer to home.

Notwithstanding its permanence across much of human history, two relatively developments characterize migration today: states have established population controls and limitations on human movement; and even states that were, until the mid-twentieth century, relatively open to migrants, have increasingly closed their borders (Shamir 2005). As mentioned above, multiple types of migrations took place previous to this period, given the laxer controls that were in place. In the eighteenth, nineteenth and twentieth centuries, this was the case in the Americas, of the migration and contributions of African (who were very often slaves), Asian and European migrants. This was also true of twentieth-century Europe, first with intra-European migration, which was followed by migration from Africa, Asia and South America. However, beginning in the 1980s, and more clearly in the 1990s, the securitization of migration intensified. Besides the security threat that migrants are said to pose, illegal migrants are also frequently criminalized, both in discourse and in practice through laws, since they are, by definition, illegally residing in a state. In contrast to their portrayal in the West as a source of threat, from the point of view of migrants themselves, potential host societies can become a key source of threat to them: the number of migrants who lose their lives while attempting to cross to North America or Western Europe, and the harsh treatments suffered by many of those who survive, both at the hands of security forces and in host societies and by employers, make them fear for their lives and their safety. From their point of view and that of many organizations that provide them with support and protection, they are victims of discriminations and abuses, not the perpetrators of violence and insecurity.

Let's check some recent data. The establishment of the Schengen space by members of the European Union – and the adherence of other states to that space – as well as the emphasis on illegal migration in the United States, have not stopped many individuals from attempting to reach these places through illegal means and at very high risk. Some African migrants cross substantial parts of the continent, aided by the existence of visa exemption agreements among several African states, and enter Algeria, Libya or Morocco, many times sneaking in illegally, to attempt their final and most important border crossing towards Europe. In this process, African migrants, who get impoverished along their journey, survive through small jobs they perform along the way, as well as through money transfers from their families back home to their temporary locations. According to research conducted by Collyer (2007: 684) for instance, African migrants heading to Europe spent an average of 15.4 months in Morocco before they managed to commit financially to cross to Europe, mostly using the services of smugglers. Indeed, Frontex admits that 503,811 individuals attempted to enter Europe illegally in 2016, and approximately 5,098 lost their lives trying to do so (Global Migration Data Analysis Centre 2017). This means that 1.01% of those who attempt to reach the European Union lose their lives during these attempts. In the United States, the Department of Homeland Security reveals similar although smaller numbers and trends: 415,816 individuals tried to enter in 2016 and were arrested by U.S. border patrols,

400 of whom lost their lives as they were attempting to do so (Global Migration Data Analysis Centre 2017). However, the Department of Homeland Security acknowledges that it seizes only approximately half of those who try to enter the United States illegally. Meanwhile, 450,954 migrants were deported from the U.S. back to their home countries in 2016. While alarming, these numbers indicate the relatively low risk of losing one's life while attempting to cross borders illegally. For those who have made many sacrifices in order to reach what they know very well is not an Eldorado, the risk is thus worth taking. This only underscores the fact that migrants do not represent a security threat to the North; rather, it is the North and its policies that have represented a life threat to migrants (see Box 14.3).

BOX 14.3 THE MANY LEVELS OF IMPORTANCE OF MIGRANTS TO SENDING STATES

The official discourse of the sending states on their national migrants is in general positive and consists mainly of appraisals of migrants and their contributions back home. Migrants are highly valued and appreciated in their states of origin due to two different types of factors. Their money remissions to support their families back home represent an important source of hard currency for those states and a means of alleviating poverty in their home country (Guevara 2010; and in the case of Morocco, see Seeberg 2013). Moreover, diasporas have been relevant to their countries of origin in myriad ways: some have supported their countries of origin to lobby their countries of residence on different issues, while others have supported their countries of origin directly, either by transferring knowledge or playing the role of bridges between their countries of origin and their countries of residence (Knott and McLoughlin 2010).

Giving voice to migrants

As for migrants themselves, in addition to not considering themselves a threat to others, they also do not feel protected by the state, neither the one they formally belong to, nor the ones they cross through or aim to reach. From their point of view, at best, their home state does not have the means to provide them with acceptable living conditions (education, jobs, housing, etc.) nor sometimes to protect even their physical security. The latter is largely the case in civil-war-ridden countries, or in areas where violent non-state actors, be they insurgent groups, organized criminals or terrorist organizations, are active. The examples of Boko Haram in Nigeria and of the communitarian conflicts in the Central African Republic, Mali and South Sudan are relevant here. To many of these migrants and refugees, "home" refers to their families and their communities, not their states.

An important question one might ask is why people insist on migrating, despite the high risk and the difficulties encountered by many migrants? There are many reasons that push individuals to migrate, among which the attractiveness of the European, Asian and North American job markets, the existence of unauthorized but very well known – despite their informality – routes for individuals to cross from Mexico to the United States, as well as from North Africa to Europe, and very hard conditions back home. Some of these conditions are related to economic hardship, whereas others are related to political instability and lack of security in the countries of origin. A few individual migrants bring both types of stories as explanation and justification for their choice to migrate.

As for economic reasons, many different factors push individuals to leave home. On the one hand, there is poverty and economic hardship and the resulting lack of job opportunities. On the other hand, droughts that are the result not only of natural environmental cycles, as shown by a United Nations Development Programme (UNDP 2009) report, but also of man-made developments – including climate change – impact poor rural communities by changing their survival economies. Migrants are selected by their families in order to go to Europe and try to support those back home. This means that many sacrifices are made by everyone to support such journeys: families mobilize all their savings in order to make the trip happen, and some-times, these families seek loans in order to support the member who is leaving for Europe. This support is not limited to the initial moment of departure, as it is extended throughout the journey. Cell phones allow contact through text messages and banking allows relatively easy and fast money transfers from one country to the other. In other words, poor families become even poorer in the hope of allowing one of their members to reach a place where they might be able to find a job and start supporting – and paying back – their families (see Box 14.4).

BOX 14.4 MIGRATION AND CLIMATE CHANGE

A recent United Nations climate change report (UNDP and UNFCC 2019) emphasized the case of climate refugees, i.e., individuals and communities who are forced to leave their homelands, some because of desertification, others due to rising sea waters, while others because their livelihoods are threatened by other climate changes. These popula-tions have no choice but to leave their geographical areas of origin and find themselves stranded as refugees. According to the World Bank report, "Groundswell: Preparing for Internal Climate Migration" (2018), climate change will turn more than 143 million people into climate refugees. Most of this demographic change will take place in Sub-Saharan Africa, South Asia and Latin America. But, the same report states that the 143 million climate refugees represent only 2.8% of the population in Sub-Saharan Africa, South Asia and Latin America. Moreover, much future migration will shift people from rural areas to urban areas over the next 30 years. Not surprisingly, the poor-est people in those areas will be the most affected and may not be able to move easily. Having said that, two caveats are needed: although drought is a natural phenomenon, individuals and communities who are forced to leave their homes because of it do so because policies have not been put in place to protect them from such phenomena. In other words, climate refugees are as much the outcome of natural disasters as they are the outcome of public policies or their absence, and natural disasters can be made worse by human action or its lack. This is not to argue that climate change will not worsen environmental degradation. The second caveat concerns climate refugees per se, as data show that most of them leave their homes and move for very short distances, with the hope that they would be able to quickly return home and rebuild their lives.

It is important to note here that hardship is not limited to the living conditions of migrating individuals back home. During their journey, most endure myriad kinds of physical violence inflicted by both police forces and other migrants, as well as verbal and moral abuses. No less important, they lose any reference to a place they can call home and live in makeshift shelters vulnerable to weather conditions, without proper food or care. Migrants also feel threatened by policies that reinforce and increase their vulnerabilities. Due to barriers and borders that reject them and prevent them from entering Europe or the United States, they become victims of different kinds of violence perpetrated by distinct actors, including: fellow migrants, without being able to resort to police protection due to their illegal status; official security forces,[3] be they U.S., European or those of transit states, as many of them either find themselves in detention centers or are very often badly injured physically when they attempt to cross to the United States or Europe; and sexual violence and rape, particularly in the case of women. These vulnerabilities start at home and continue throughout the journey to their new destinations.

During transit, migrants are vulnerable to the actions and deeds of other states and their security apparatuses. Scholars such as Didier Bigo (2002) and Jef Huysmans (2006) have explored the insecurities that result from the politics of security in general and in the EU in particular. According to Bigo (2002), instead of producing security, security apparatuses produce insecurity in order to justify their own existence. This sheds new light on the challenges that migrants encounter, as it suggests that security actors constantly re-define what and who is a threat and how to put in place security measures to provide protection against those threats. In *The Politics of Insecurity* (2006), Huysmans also analyzes the security implications of varying and flexible communities resulting from migrants and asylum seekers in the European Union. According to him, in the EU, migrants and asylum seekers are simultaneously distant Others who come spatially close but who at the same time actively contribute to the countries they live in, abiding by their rules and norms. Because Huysmans' assumption is that "insecurity is a politically and socially constructed phenomenon" (Huysmans 2006: 2), the securitization of migrants and asylum seekers is neither accidental nor unwanted. Instead, it actively contributes to normative debates about European political identity. Therefore, it is more a question of choice and political will that explain why immigration, rather than other issues, is forwarded and prioritized as a security threat. This indeed is the big paradox: while migrants are instrumentalized and defined as the source of threat by the EU security apparatus, they see themselves as victims of that same EU security apparatus. Huysmans (2006) argues that insecurity is not only related to the definition of threat, but also to the policy and institutional framing of the issue, within what he refers to as the "domains of insecurity." "Insecurity thus emerges from discursively and institutionally modulating practices in terms of security rationality" (Huysmans 2006: 4). It is in this way that security can be considered a governing technique (see Box 14.5).

BOX 14.5 MIGRANT TESTIMONIES

Many organizations, national, international and non-governmental alike, have made a point of meeting with migrants and listening to their voices, with an eye to gaining greater understanding of this issue and to devising more effective (and inclusive) strategies to confront it. Ideally, an alternative approach to migration would take into account more fully than the space of this chapter has allowed the lived experiences of migrants. For further information and testimonies, see: www.undp.org/content/undp/en/home/2030-agenda-for-sustainable-development/prosperity/recovery-solutions-and-human-mobility/migration-and-displacement.html; and the International Organization for Migration website, "I am a migrant," https://iamamigrant.org/

While migration has been a latecomer to the study of International Relations, the links between migration and gender have garnered even less interest within this field. For a long time, the migration literature mentioned migrants and their families generically, and ignored the specificities endured by women as migrants. It was only in the 1980s and more significantly in the 1990s that women and gender became topics of analysis and debate within the academic community that studied migration. Despite this shift, available data on women migrants is still scarce, and scholars as well as activists continue to call for the need to collect and analyze migration data according to sex and gender. One of the reasons for this necessity is that migrant women exhibit several specificities (Martin 2014: 243). For instance, high numbers of migrant women in North Africa have babies, some of whom were born during the journey from home to their destination, very often as a result of unwanted sexual relations. These women find themselves in vulnerable positions in which sexual relations are forced upon them, both by fellow migrants and by locals, including those vested with legal authority who are allegedly supposed to be protecting them. In some cases, these women seek protection from mafias or ring leaders in exchange for sexual relations. When and if these women realize they are pregnant and decide to keep the child, they find themselves in precarious conditions of pregnancy and eventually of motherhood. Because a pregnant woman is easily visible, human rights organizations very often manage to provide them with some support, but once the babies are born, these women are largely left to fend for themselves, although their newborn babies become one more motivation to continue the journey. In a sense, the gender vulnerability of migrants adds to gender vulnerability in general. As J. Ann Tickner, a leading feminist scholar, reminds us when she challenges the IR mainstream and tells its scholars that "they just don't understand" what security really is (1997), by placing gender at the center of our analyses when debating migration, it becomes clear that instead of migration as a threat, our topic of study should be the gendered dichotomy security/insecurity and its myriad consequences for individuals in general, and women in particular.

Conclusion

Migration is certainly not a recent phenomenon in human history, but the current political debate around it is new. It mixes fear of difference, of the Other, with increasingly exclusionary practices of the state that result in an excessive securitization of the issue (migration) and of individuals and communities, which, in some cases, includes the criminalization of illegal migrants. Policies aimed at integrating and better assimilating migrants have been put in place in different countries with varying levels of success, as illustrated by the three episodes mentioned at the beginning of this chapter. Despite the undeniable successes experienced by many individuals, the poorest and the least qualified migrants still suffer from a high degree of discrimination and substantial violence.

The contrast between how migrants are perceived and dealt with and how they see themselves is also considerable: while migrants, especially those of non-Western descent, are largely considered a threat, their aim is to secure a better life and to help others from their families and original surroundings benefit from their movement too. Although this is not to romanticize migration and the migrants, given that they are indeed a diverse group comprised of all different kinds of individuals, reducing their lot to "rapists" and "terrorists" that invade and contaminate the countries they arrive at – as epitomized by right-wing political leaders such as Donald Trump in the

United States – is equally, if not more, problematic. Among other things, such stereo-types act to minimize and invisibilize the ways in which migrants are victims of dis-crimination and of all kinds of violence, including rape and fear for their lives. As discussed in this chapter, instead of a threat, migrants see themselves as victims of their own societies, of transit societies and of host societies. In this sense, migration materializes the paradoxes of the relationship between the North and the global South.

Questions for discussion

1. What is new about contemporary migration that makes it such a polarizing topic in the national politics of many states?
2. Besides South–North migration, what are the other kinds of migration that are cur-rently taking place in the world?
3. Why has migration been securitized during the past decades and what are the main effects of this securitization?
4. What would putting the migrant at the center of analyses of migration consist of? What do migrants say about migration when they are heard?
5. In what ways are women affected differently by migration than men?
6. What types of relations exist between migrants and their countries of origin?
7. Do you think that migrants from the global South are treated better by other states and societies from the South than they are treated in North America or Western Europe? Why?

Notes

1   "Nous célébrons la victoire de l'Algérie comme celle de la France l'an dernier," accessed at: www.lemonde.fr/afrique/article/2019/07/20/can-2019-nous-celebrons-la-victoire-de-l-algerie-comme-celle-de-la-france-l-an-dernier_5491472_3212.html?xtor=EPR-32280629-[a-la-une]-20190720-[zone_edito_1_titre_1.
2   It is worth noting here that both Democratic and Republican administrations have fought illegal migration and treated migrants harshly, including the idea of building a separation wall, which was not solely a Trump government project.
3   In some cases, unofficial security forces are the source of violence against migrants, like in the case of the militia–mafia collaboration that was behind the slave trade in Libya until 2017, as revealed by the International Organization for Migration.

Further reading

Betts, Alexander and Gil Loescher (eds) (2011) *Refugees in International Relations*, Oxford: Oxford University Press. This volume draws on the different IR theories, from mainstream to critical, in order to deal with the challenge to the state system that refugees represent.
Haddad, Emma (2008) *The Refugee in International Society: Between Sovereigns*, Cambridge: Cambridge University Press. This book discusses the concept of refugees in world politics and explores its evolution throughout the twentieth century.
Hampshire, James (2013) *The Politics of Immigration*, Cambridge: Polity Press. This book explores different positions on migration governance, both at the national and international levels, and uncovers the politics behind it.
Huysmans, Jef (2006) *The Politics of Insecurity: Fear, Migration and Asylum in the EU*, London: Routledge. Huysmans presents a critical perspective on the study of migration in the field of IR,

arguing that the discourse on migration infuses fear and insecurity in order to justify the securitization of the migration and migrants as well as the establishment of a security apparatus to deal with them.

Martin, Susan F. (2014) *International Migration: Evolving Trends from the Early Twentieth Century to the Present*, Cambridge: Cambridge University Press. This is an excellent reference for a broad and serious discussion of international migration in contemporary world politics.

References

Arango, Joaquin and Philip Martin (2005) "Best Practices to Manage Migration: Morocco-Spain," *International Migration Review*, 39(1): 258–269. doi:10.1111/j.1747-7379.2005.tb00262.x

Berriane, Johara (2014) "Intégration symbolique à fés et ancrages sur l'ailleurs: Les Africains Subsahariens et leur rapport à la Zaouïa d'Ahmad al Tijânî," *L'Année Du Maghreb*, 11: 139–153. doi:10.4000/anneemaghreb.2277

Bigo, Didier (2002) "Security and Immigration: Toward a Critique of the Governmentality of Unease," *Alternatives*, 27: 63–92. doi:10.1177/03043754020270S105

Boswell, Christina (2003) "The 'External Dimension' of EU Immigration and Asylum Policy," *International Affairs*, 79(3): 619–638.

Buzan, Barry, Ole Wæver and Jaap de Wilde (1998) *Security: A New Framework for Analysis*, Boulder: Lynne Rienner Publishers.

Carling, Jorgen (2007) "Unauthorized Migration from Africa to Spain," *International Migration*, 45(4): 3–37. doi:10.1111/j.1468-2435.2007.00418.x

Collyer, Michael (2007) "In-Between Places: Trans-Saharan Transit Migrants in Morocco and the Fragmented Journey to Europe," *Antipode*, 39(4): 668–690. doi:10.1111/j.1467-8330.2007.00546.x

Global Migration Data Analysis Centre (2017) "Migrant Deaths and Disappearances Worldwide: 2016 Analysis," *Data Briefing Series No. 8*, https://gmdac.iom.int/gmdac-data-briefing-8 (consulted June 15, 2019).

Guevara, Anna (2010) *Marketing Dreams, Manufacturing Heroes: The Transnational Labor Brokering of Filipino Workers*, New Brunswick: Rutgers University Press.

Haddad, Emma (2008) *The Refugee in International Society: Between Sovereigns*, Cambridge: Cambridge University Press.

Hampshire, James (2013) *The Politics of Immigration*, Cambridge: Polity Press.

Huysmans, Jef (2006) *The Politics of Insecurity: Fear, Migration and Asylum in the EU*, London: Routledge.

International Organization for Migration (2018) *World Migration Report 2018*, www.iom.int/wmr/world-migration-report-2018 (consulted June 15, 2019).

Knott, Kim and Seán McLoughlin (eds) (2010) *Diasporas: Concepts, Intersections, Identities*, London: Zed Books.

Lacomba, Joan and Alejandra Boni (2008) "The Role of Emigration in Foreign Aid Policies: The Case of Spain and Morocco," *International Migration*, 46(1): 123–50. doi:10.1111/j.1468-2435.2008.00439.x

Martin, Susan F. (2014) *International Migration: Evolving Trends from the Early Twentieth Century to the Present*, Cambridge: Cambridge University Press.

Qadim, El and Nora (2015) *Le gouvernement asymétrique des migrations*, Paris: Dalloz.

Seeberg, Peter (2013) "Morocco and the EU. New Tendencies in Transnational Migration and the EU's Migration Policies," *Center for Mellmostudier*, December.

Shamir, Ronen (2005) "Without Borders? Notes on Globalization as a Mobility Regime," *Sociological Theory*, 23(2): 197–217. doi:10.1111/j.0735-2751.2005.00250.x

Tickner, J. Ann (1997) "You Just Don't Understand: Troubled Engagements between Feminists and IR Theorists," *International Studies Quarterly*, 41(4): 611–32.

UNDP (2009) *Human Development Report 2009, Overcoming Barriers: Human Mobility and Development*, New York: UNDP.

UNDP and UNFCC (2019) *The Heat Is On: Taking Stock of Global Climate Ambition*, New York: UNDP and UNFCC.

Wæver, Ole, Barry Buzan, Morten Kelstrup and Pierre Lemaitre (1993) *Identity, Migration and the New Security Agenda in Europe*, New York: St. Martin's Press.

World Bank (2018) *Groundswell: Preparing for Internal Climate Migration*, Washington, DC: World Bank, https://openknowledge.worldbank.org/handle/10986/29461 (consulted June 15, 2019).

15 Resistances

Carolina Cepeda-Másmela

Introduction

Although global South encounters with the "international" have been mediated historically by subordinate forms of insertion into the world system, the so-called periphery has also been highly proactive in seeking to transform the world. Resistance to neoliberalism has been one such activity (see too, Chapter 11). Let's take the story of Hugo, a man whose life story illustrates how neoliberalism is experienced on an everyday level across the globe and how it pushes many to seek out alternatives that challenge the existing hegemonic order. Hugo is a 60-year-old militant of the Frente Popular Darío Santillán (Popular Front Darío Santillán), an Argentine multi-sectorial movement. In a conversation I had with him as we walked around the streets of Berisso – a small working-class town close to La Plata and the capital city Buenos Aires – he talked at length about the impact of neoliberalism on his own life and that of his community.

Although the conversation took place in November 2012 we traveled through decades of contemporary Argentine history. Hugo's neighborhood is called la Nueva York, given that during the first half of the 20th century, it was where the main meat processing plants, Armor and Swift, were located. Many European immigrants who arrived in Argentina worked in these plants, and the neighborhood was a vibrant community center filled with cinemas, theaters and shops. At some point, the Armor plant shut down and only Swift remained. Hugo remembers seeing the Swift plant when he was little, but when the military came to the power in 1976, it deteriorated substantially and was finally closed in 1982.

As we moved through the neighborhood, Hugo pointed to all the shuttered-up buildings that were once shoe stores, pharmacies, hairdressers, cinemas, theaters and so on. He said that it used to be an entire world where people moved around 24 hours a day, including boarding houses and "hot beds" that were rotated between workers as they changed shifts. After 1976, the military shut the neighborhood down completely, resulting in disaster. Not only were the meat processing plants closed, but the workers left, and the privatization of state-owned companies resulted in Hugo losing his job with the national railways system. As we talked and walked, I noticed that he still wore his national railways overalls and remembered the schedules of all the provincial trains. According to him, the largest challenges both he and the community face are public health and public education, although there are many others. And yet, in la Nueva York he resists with the Darío Santillán, as he calls the movement. Its members conduct different kinds of activities. They recently recovered a little square that the port authority had taken from them. He played there when he was a small boy and now that the movement recovered it, other children play. They organize end-of-year activities with the children, rebuild the streets, fight to recover pensions and create jobs. Notwithstanding the hardships endured by their community, they have hope and they struggle every day in order to live with dignity.

Hugo's is not the only story about resistance. There are many other Hugos whose lived experiences underscore how neoliberalism affects people's lives in numerous ways across the global South and the North, as we will soon see. His story also helps to illustrate some important points about resistance. First, an adequate understanding of the expansion of neoliberalism as a political rationality (Brown 2003) and resistances to it must consider the local and the global levels as interrelated spheres of political activity. Second, social change – defined here as the sum of diverse proposals and alternatives to capitalism developed through concrete practices (Dinerstein 2013a: 161) – is a key goal of resistance that is realized everyday by people like Hugo. Third, if we want to know how to resist and how to challenge the neoliberal hegemonic order, we need to recover local forms of resistance against neoliberalism and to analyze how they contribute to envisioning alternatives.

Resistance has not been a central issue within "conventional" International Relations (IR). Admittedly, some works rooted in the liberal-constructivist perspective have considered civil society organizations and their role in the construction and circulation of international norms around human rights, free trade or environmental issues (Keck and Sikkink 2000; Khagram, Riker and Sikkink 2001; Sikkink 2005). However, such approaches fall short of considering these organizations as real challengers of political order. Other approaches such as postcolonialism and the neo-Gramscian school have considered resistance in a more comprehensive way (Chin and James 2000; Cox 2005; Eschle and Maiguashca 2005; Gills 2000, 2008; Morton 2007; Reitan 2007; Worth 2013), illustrating how different social actors challenge the current hegemonic order in political, economic and cultural ways. But, they too largely ignore how local experiences produce specific values, imaginaries, targets, strategies, allies, solidarities and symbols that are then appropriated by other actors located at distinct scales, thus helping create more globalized forms of resistance. In this way, it is crucial to understand that social organizations and movements, both local and global, enact practices of resistance that are reconceptualizing the very way in which we are accustomed to understanding this term.

In this sense, it is important to revisit the concrete practices of social movements and organizations that contribute to developing concepts and analysis of the varied ways in which the neoliberal order has been challenged around the world. This chapter links the experiences of the global South and the global North by showing that the everyday effects of neoliberal globalization and resistances to it share commonalities across the world, independently of where one lives. In doing so, it also argues that a comprehensive understanding of international relations demands an analytical framework that transcends conventional divisions between North and South, West and East, or local and global. Indeed, looking at concrete experiences of resistance exercised by social organizations and social movements in their daily lives, but that entail complex movement across such binaries, can help us visualize alternative knowledges and practices of politics.

The first section of the chapter discusses the alter-globalization process, in order to link global resistances to neoliberalism with concrete local experiences of collective resistance. We will learn that understanding these two logics together is fundamental for thinking about political alternatives derived from the practices of social movements and organizations. The second section reviews neo-Gramscian, Marxist and postcolonial approaches to hegemony and resistance. The third and fourth sections offer an alternative proposal, derived from experiences of social mobilization in concrete local settings in Argentina and Bolivia that invite us to think about the encounters between local and global practices and dynamics in the exercise of resistance against neoliberal globalization, as well as some final insights that might be drawn from this approach.

Realizing resistance

Before trying to understand the relationship between hegemony, resistance and alternatives in relation to neoliberalism, it is important that we ask some important questions, namely: who resists neoliberalism? Why and how do they resist? And where do they resist? Perhaps the best way to respond is to begin with a brief discussion of neoliberalism itself.

Since the 1970s, neoliberalism has evolved as a dominant reading of social order and politics, associated with individualism and self-care, and policies such as free trade, privatization of state-owned companies and the commodification of services such as health, social housing and education. David Harvey (2007) defines that process as the successful restoration of dominant class power, which is reflected in the fact that neoliberal policies have been implemented throughout the North and the South and are largely responsible for the unequal concentration of wealth both between and within countries, and the marginalization of broad segments of society (see Chapter 13). Given its myriad manifestations, neoliberalism is best defined as a form of political rationality (Brown 2003 2006), a logic that transforms politics, the economy, society and individuals. In this sense, it affects different spheres of social life as well as generating conditions of possibility for the organization of diverse forms of resistance against it (Cepeda-Másmela 2019). Resistances go far beyond the economic sphere, as witnessed for example, in social mobilizations against the exploitation of natural resources in indigenous lands. Rather, they are framed within discourses and practices that include diverse areas of social life in which neoliberalism has had some type of impact (see Box 15.1).

BOX 15.1 WHAT IS NEOLIBERALISM?

"Neoliberalism" is a term that has been widely discussed in academia during the last three decades. We are accustomed to "seeing" it under the guise of privatization of public enterprises or social services, and free trade agreements, but several definitions have also been coined, ranging from a set of economic policies to a form of governmentality (see Brown 2003; Harvey 2007; Restrepo 2003; Steger and Roy 2010). Wendy Brown's definition (2003) is particularly useful for describing both the effects of neoliberalism and the resistances organized against it. According to her, neoliberalism is best understood as a form of political rationality that spreads the market logic of cost–benefit to all spheres of social life, including economics, political institutions, cultural industries, law, security and the everyday In consequence, people behave as rational individuals that make calculations according to a market rationality, which has deep implications that range from inequality, accumulation by dispossession, lack of solidarity among social groups, growing power of transnational corporations and commodification of different aspects of social life. However, this same political rationality plants the seeds for resistances against neoliberalism at different levels too.

Additionally, neoliberalism has affected different social processes such as globalization. Even though this is a multidimensional phenomenon, it is possible to highlight its neoliberal side linked to free trade, delocalization and relocalization of production, deindustrialization of industrialized cities, growing economic and political power of transnational corporations and transformation of the state as a market state (Brown 2003; Gill 2008; Sassen 2007). The negative effects of this version of globalization and of the spread of neoliberalism as a political rationality are best summarized as structural violence that prevents people from enjoying their social, cultural and political rights.

Interestingly, some negative effects of neoliberalism are transformed by political actors into opportunities for social mobilization, while some of the transformations implicit in globalization create spaces for recovering and strengthening distinct forms of social solidarity (Cepeda-Másmela 2019). Many different groups of people have contested and resisted the negative effects of neoliberalism long before the onset of the 21st century, seeking alternatives at the political, social and economic levels. Indeed, technological innovation, the media, social networks and migratory flows offer increasing possibilities for the organization of social movements and other types of collectives, while greater availability of information about problems and events taking place in different parts of the world facilitates both shared knowledge at the local, national, regional and global levels, and the construction of bonds of solidarity (Florini 2002; Laïdi 1997).

As a result of the strategic use of these opportunities in the exercise of resistance, many groups have converged in the so-called alter-globalization process. Alter-globalization, rather than a single and unified actor, is better understood as a process in which different social movements, organizations and activists opposed to neoliberal globalization have converged to develop distinct alternatives to the current hegemonic order and to contribute to developing social change. Naturally, this process has been underpinned by diversity. Local political and social experiences, and the specific ways in which neoliberal policies have been implemented across the world, have led to diverse understandings of resistance and to varied proposals to counter neoliberalism. Therefore, the actors that converge in the alter-globalization process articulate their values, claims, demands and practices of resistance in ways that allow them to frame their struggles similarly, but also develop and implement concrete alternatives in their own local or national contexts.

So, how did the alter-globalization process emerge and evolve? The first time the global media paid attention to it was in 1999, during the so-called "Battle of Seattle," a massive demonstration against the Third Ministerial Summit of the World Trade Organization (WTO). In Seattle's aftermath, similar demonstrations were organized around other international summits taking placing in Washington, Prague, Melbourne and Genoa, between 2000 and 2001. From that point onward, the mass media began to talk about the "anti-globalization movement," but the same activists quickly redefined themselves as alter-globalization since their target was not globalization itself, but its neoliberal version. The process also had deep roots in mobilizations and the organization of social movements that occurred during the 1990s, as is illustrated in the following timeline (see Figure 15.1).

The global demonstrations of this initial period were primarily aimed at the implementation of neoliberal policies and specifically targeted world summits on economic and financial issues. Global activism offered an important opportunity for face-to-face meetings between different social actors who had only met previously on the internet, but also a space in which to identify shared targets of social protest, including the WTO, the International Monetary Fund (IMF), the World Bank and transnational corporations, all deemed key agents of neoliberal capitalism with tremendous power to (negatively) affect everyday people's lives (Negri 2007). Such engagements also created opportunities to exchange distinct repertoires, strategies and discourses of social action.

As a result of these first massive protests, social movements and organizations developed a number of smaller networks and coalitions, including "50 Years Is Enough!" and "Reclaim the Streets" (see Box 15.1). These were largely prepared within the framework of earlier struggles against neoliberalism conducted by organizations located in the global North. However, in the South too, similar coalitions and network formations began to appear. In Latin America, for example, the negotiation of the Free Trade Area of the Americas (FTAA) in the mid-1990s produced a strong reaction among different peasant movements, workers' unions, student movements, indigenous organizations, women's groups and environmental associations, that began to establish links with like-minded actors across the hemisphere to coordinate actions parallel to those of regional governments (Smith and Korzeniewicz 2006). This opened up the possibility

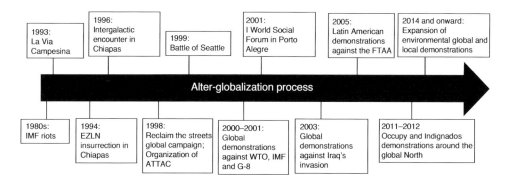

Figure 15.1 Alter-globalization process timeline
Source: Elaborated by author

for social movements from the Americas to organize regional networks and coalitions to work together on issues beyond free trade. For example, the ALBA de los Movimientos Sociales (ALBA of Social Movements), a coalition rooted in anti-neoliberal, anti-imperialist and anti-patriarchal ideas, brought together grassroots movements from across the continent with an eye to consolidating a critical project of continental integration. Such examples reflect the diversity and dynamism of the alter-globalization process, in which common concerns about the environment, trade, land and social rights, among others, converged with shared protest strategies, including demonstrations, campaigns and lobbying.

The World Social Forum (WSF), a third expression of the alter-globalization process, was formed in 2001 in order to strengthen the activities described above and to overcome some of their limitations in terms of generating effective collective action and resistance. During its first three editions, the WSF was spearheaded by globally known movements such as the Association for the Taxation of Financial Transactions and Citizens' Action (ATTAC) and the Brazilian Movimiento dos Trabalhadores Rurais sem Terra (MST) and held in Porto Alegre, Brazil, a city governed by the left-wing Partido dos Trabalhadores (PT) (Teivainen 2012). In 2004, it moved to Mumbai, India, and since then has been organized in different countries around the world. Such geographical expansion has been useful not only to increase the number of participants, but also to extend the Forum's agenda in order to include problems as diverse as war, inequality, imperialism, patriarchy, the environment and the ownership of common goods (Pleyers 2010).

As one of the main expressions of the alter-globalization process, the WSF constitutes a regular and ongoing space for the development of alternatives to neoliberal globalization rooted in the idea of justice globalism (Steger et al. 2013), and in which activist groups participate from diverse stripes of society (including empowered communities) located throughout the world (Worth 2013). These actors are all committed to the idea that another world is possible, and in many cases, they have implemented such worlds through different forms of political and socioeconomic organization and production, located outside traditional schemes of representative democracy and market economy. Take for instance, the numerous kinds of barter arrangements and networks that have appeared across the globe as an alternative to capitalist forms of exchange.

In the case of social movements located in both the global South and the North, the WSF has thus been a key space for sharing distinct experiences of struggle; for developing the discursive bases for the articulation of these struggles within the alter-globalization process; and for (re)constructing specific local struggles as a result of the exchanges, learning processes and broader articulation with this global movement. Although world events, most importantly the financial crisis of 2008, led many movements to refocus their efforts on immediate local concerns related to unemployment, impoverishment and austerity policies that have affected access to housing, education and health, global resistance against neoliberalism did not end. On the contrary, it transformed and has expanded, as illustrated by cases such as the Occupy movement and the Spanish Indignados (see Box 15.2), both of which have revitalized debates about neoliberalism and capitalism (Worth 2013).

BOX 15.2 TRANSNATIONAL COALITIONS AND DEMONSTRATIONS

One of the main manifestations of the alter-globalization process is the formation of transnational coalitions and demonstrations. While some of these are located in a single country and spread through the inclusion of new local members, many others expand to distinct national sites. Some examples of the latter include:

50 Years Is Enough! is a coalition organized since 1994 in the United States. It includes around 200 organizations, including 185 across 65 countries. Its main goal is to transform the practices and policies of the Bretton Woods institutions.

Reclaim the Streets began in London in 1995 as an initiative to vindicate the streets as a common good through street parties. This initiative spread around the world and in 1998 there was a global street party during a G-8 meeting in Birmingham; there were coordinated actions in cities such as London, Melbourne, Buenos Aires, Bogota, Kyoto and Seattle, among others.

Occupy Wall Street! is the name used to designate the different mobilizations that have taken place around the world since 2011, when the financial crisis erupted. The first of these mobilizations was in the United States with the initiative of Occupy Wall Street in New York City; it quickly expanded into other cities in the country, and since then it has been replicated in different parts of the world. The mobilizations aim to denounce and confront the political and economic actors responsible for the crisis, and to look for alternatives to current hegemonic order. It implies many actions of the activist are focused on building strong bonds of solidarity and exchanging of opinions and experiences and dissemination of information.

Indignados is the name used by the press to designate the protesters who took part in different concentrations and mass mobilizations in Spain between 2011 and 2012. These demonstrations express widespread discontent over high levels of unemployment, rising mortgage costs and laws restricting freedoms. The first big demonstration took place on May 15, was organized from the initiative of early riser groups such as Democracia Real Ya! (Real Democracy Now!), V de Vivienda (V for Housing) and Hipotecados (Mortgaged) and managed to gather a wide variety of activists and ordinary citizens who were outraged by the precarious social situation.

As we have briefly seen in this section, alter-globalization entails a dynamic process that has combined numerous strategies of opposition to neoliberalism, ranging from mega-protests, global fora and world networks, to national and localized practices rooted in concrete lived experiences. Therefore, in order to take stock of the plurality of resistances through which people are challenging the current order and constructing alternative means of organization and production, we must look beyond the broader global movement, inquire into concrete local expressions and take account of the relation and the articulation between the two.

Hegemony and resistance: a neo-Gramscian perspective

Both Hugo's story and the alter-globalization process underscore how resistance is linked to hegemony. Namely, the hegemony of neoliberalism has led to the growth of distinct forms of resistance that seek to provide alternatives for social change, based upon shared world imaginaries, discourses and practices (Bieler and Morton 2004). In order to understand more fully the interplay between these two processes, we need an analytical framework that sheds light on the encounters that take place between local and global dynamics, and from which resistance can be said to emerge. As we will now discuss, a neo-Gramscian lens is particularly well suited for the task, given its focus on the asymmetrical relations that exist between different social actors that contribute to the configuration of hegemonic orders.

Global systems and forces

Leslie Sklair (2003) proposes an approach to world politics that focuses on the concept of global system instead of international system (see Chapter 5). The global system is based on global forces and institutions that are conducive to a series of transnational practices whose main actors are not exclusively states, as shown in Table 15.1. Within this system, select groups control the most important economic, political and cultural goods that circulate within the capitalist market. Such control translates into deep asymmetries between these (dominant) groups and others, which then evolves into a form of hegemony that can be exercised by a state or by groups of states, or a specific social class with the goal of imposing their interests in the struggle for global resources (Sklair 2003).

In the same spheres it is possible to observe processes of construction and contestation of dominant ideas and practices, or in other words, resistance exercised against hegemony. Robert Cox (1986, 1996, 2002), whose work is widely inspired by the thinking of Antonio Gramsci, defines hegemony at the international level as a social, political and economic structure that contains two key features. First, it is expressed through norms, institutions and universal mechanisms that dictate the general rules of behavior sustaining the dominant mode of production for states and civil society forces that act across national boundaries (Cox 1996: 137). And second, it is produced within what Cox (1986) describes as a historical structure, a particular configuration of forces in which material capabilities, ideas and institutions interact.

Table 15.1 Synthesis of transnational practices

	Sphere	*Institution*	*Central agent*	*Central activity*	*Resources*
Transnational Practices	Economic	Transnational corporations	Transnational corporations	Production of commodities and services useful for that production	Global capital and resources
	Political	Transnational capitalist class	Transnational capitalist class	Creation of a useful political environment to commercialize products in different countries	Political power
	Ideological-cultural	Cultural ideology of consumerism	Ideological-cultural institutions	Promotion of the values that create and sustain the necessity of those products	Sphere of ideas

Source: Elaborated by author with information extracted from Sklair (2003)

Material capabilities refer to both the productive and destructive potential of social actors, including a wide array of forms such as technology, industry, natural resources, human capital, weapons and infrastructures, among others. Ideas entail inter-subjective meanings, shared notions of the nature of social relations and collective images of social order arising from different interpretations of the nature and the legitimacy of prevailing power relations. Finally, institutions are the combinations of ideas and material capabilities (Cox 1986: 219).

In practice, this structure operates across three spheres of activity: social forces, forms of state and world orders. Each sphere of activity exhibits a specific configuration of ideas, material capabilities and institutions that make hegemony something tangible, more than an ideology or a world vision, at any given historical moment (Cox 1986: 220). For example, neoliberal hegemony is expressed through ideas such as the market logic of cost–benefit that governs the behavior of institutions, such as central banks, that depend on material capabilities such as foreign investment or exports to a given country.

In the sphere of social forces, there are those engaged in the process of production as well as the organization of the process itself; social classes in a Marxist sense, for example. The sphere of the state is understood in its broadest sense, including civil society as a field in which hegemony is constructed and challenged (Gramsci 1973), called the state–civil society complex. Finally, there is the sphere of world orders, in which issues of peace and war are defined according to specific configurations of forces. Moreover, these three spheres are interrelated: changes in the organization of production can affect the state structure and these can modify issues of world order. In the same way, transnational social forces can generate transformations at the national and local levels (Cox 1986).

Both Sklair's and Cox's analyses lend themselves to the claim that hegemony is not a static condition, but rather, is constantly changing and challenged (Bieler and Morton 2004). Given that challenges to hegemony occur at the global, regional, national and local scales, tracing the potential links that exist between distinct scales is fundamental. Resistances against neoliberalism can be understood as a crucial part of a project that questions the current hegemonic order. However, as we have hinted above, not all resistances are the same: while most share common opposition to neoliberalism and to some of its key agents, their strategies and alternative projects can vary dramatically depending upon the lived experiences of those who resist. In this sense, it is important to clarify what we mean by resistance and to identify its local particularities.

Resistance

In simple terms, resistance can be understood as a local response to the uneven development of neoliberalism (Morton 2007). This means that resistances across the globe share important commonalities derived from the solidarity and empathy that emerge from recognizing one's own suffering in others (Reitan 2007). But, resistances also have important differences rooted in the specific ways in which neoliberal logics evolve locally and affect diverse communities. Barry Gills (2000: 4) proposes a definition that recognizes such variation. For this author, resistance is a form of political action that should represent general or social interest with the potential to transform the political situation and produce a real alternative against neoliberal globalization. These resistances can differ in terms of goals, objectives, strategies and alternative proposals.

In the spirit of identifying distinct forms of resistance, Christine Chin and James Mittelman (2000) offer a typology that includes counter-hegemony (Gramsci 1972, 1973, 1975), which describes actors who resist and challenge a specific hegemony in the state–civil society complex; counter-movements (Polanyi 2003), forms of resistance that demand protection measures against market expansion; and infra-politics (Scott 2000), everyday forms of resistance that can be both individual and collective but that are not openly declared contestations. Owen Worth (2013) argues that resistance is better understood as the contestation of a specific hegemonic order. According to him, these resistances can propose and construct alternatives to the established neoliberal order, as well as confront and challenge the state apparatus in the pursuit of political transformation. However, such counter-hegemonic resistances are not homogeneous in terms of the worldviews or the kinds of transformation they espouse. In this sense, Worth (2013) identifies three different forms: progressive internationalism, composed of social movements and organizations whose aim is to transform contemporary capitalism by subordinating economics to social relations; national populism, consisting of those groups who see neoliberalism as a threat to their national ways of life and culture and try to restore their traditions by promoting social change from above; and religious fundamentalism, whose goal is to establish a counter-hegemony based on specific interpretations of religious beliefs (see Figure 15.2).

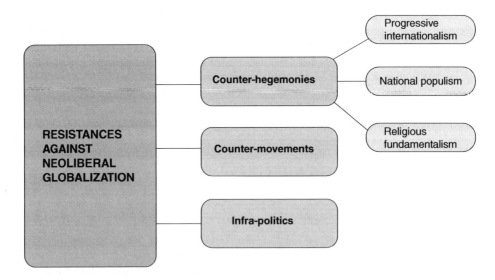

Figure 15.2 Resistances against neoliberalism

Source: Elaborated by author with information extracted from Chin and Mittelman (2000) and Worth (2013)

The kind of resistances that converge in the alter-globalization process go far beyond episodic demonstrations of discontent, individual actions in everyday life and sporadic signs of solidarity. Rather, such activities are akin to those of social movements, defined by Alberto Melucci (2002: 46) as actors that anticipate social change in the present; share recognition that they are part of the same social organization involved in conflict over valuable resources against a recognized adversary; and employ strategies that exceed the tolerance limits of the system.

Much of the literature on global social movements (Andretta et al. 2006; Della Porta 2003, 2005; Smith et al. 2008), social movement theory and transnational advocacy networks (Keck and Sikkink 2000; Khagram et al. 2001; Sikkink 2001, 2005) has tried to interrogate the links between local and global actors that exercise distinct forms of resistance, and to build bridges between political science and sociological work on social movements and IR's focus on non-state actors (Della Porta and Tarrow 2005; Sikkink 2005; Tarrow and Della Porta 2005). This work has shed important light on the features of global social movements (Andretta et al. 2006), the political structures within which these movements or networks operate (Keck and Sikkink 2000; Tarrow 2007), the actors they interact with (Khagram et al. 2001; Reitan 2007) and the opportunities they have to organize themselves (Tarrow 2007). However, scant attention is paid to the actual mechanisms through which local and global practices come into contact, the interactions that exist between them, and the implications of such efforts for change at the local and global levels. Let's turn to this now.

Encounters between "the global" and "the local"

As hinted at previously, resistances against neoliberalism cannot be properly understood by considering only one dimension, be it local or global, as there is a complex relation between the two. Similarly, concrete practices of resistance exercised by social movements and organizations located throughout the global South and the North must be factored into our analyses equally. Echoing Saskia Sassen (2007), and at the risk of stating the obvious, the study of globalization cannot be focused exclusively on global phenomena but also requires careful analysis of local practices and conditions, and their articulation globally. This is evident in cases from the global South such as the Mexican Ejército Zapatista de Liberación Nacional (EZLN) and the Argentine *piquetero* movement, both of which illustrate how neoliberalism affects societies in concrete ways, how people organize and resist it, and how they are able to link their struggles together (see Box 15.3). The same is observable in cases from the global North, including the Standing Rock movement in North and South Dakota in the United States, which congregates indigenous peoples, and Extinction Rebellion, formed by random people with trajectories of social mobilizations linked to more classical or material issues. These movements are based in the global North but fully linked to other processes occurring in the South, given that environmental issues and earth justice must be attended to simultaneously by actors around the world (see Box 15.4). Resistances such as these anchor their main goals at both the local and global scales, posing a challenge to neoliberal rationality as a whole but highlighting the local practices and alternatives (Escobar 2012).

**BOX 15.3 LOCAL SOCIAL MOVEMENTS WITHIN THE
ALTER-GLOBALIZATION PROCESS**

Notwithstanding the global character of many of the expressions of the alter-globalization process, local and national movements have been central actors in its construction. These movements discuss, produce and construct alternatives to neo-liberal political rationality in their immediate context, which is crucial to challenging the current hegemonic order. Two illustrative examples are:

Ejército Zapatista de Liberación Nacional, EZLN, a Mexican indigenous movement whose central demands are related to land possession and the recognition and participation of indigenous people in Mexican politics. Its struggle against neoliberalism is based on the fact that the Mexican state initiated an agrarian counter-reform in the 1990s to fulfill the conditions to sign the Free Trade Agreement with the United States and Canada. This process threatened indigenous communities' worldview and their collective relationship with land.
Piqueteros, a working-class movement that appeared around 1996 in Argentina, when the oil workers of the city of Cutral-Co, province of Neuquén, began mobilizations against unemployment and mass dismissals, using a strategy of roadblocks on the main streets of the city. In this event three elements came together: the term "*piqueteros*" as the central agent of the action, the roadblocks as a fundamental strategy and the logics of those actions based on the demand for jobs. Similar actions spread around the country until 2001.

BOX 15.4 RESISTANCE AND EARTH JUSTICE

Neoliberal political rationality has many effects. One of them is the commodification of natural resources and the ensuing sacrifices made by different communities in order to allow their exploitation. In consequence, environmental issues have grown within the alter-globalization process and related movements have spread since 2014, not only in the global South but also in the global North. Two examples are:

The *Standing Rock Movement* gathers people from the Sioux Nation against the construction of the Dakota Access Pipeline, given the tribe's need to honor its ancestors and protect sacred lands and water. The resistance began in 2014 with several legal actions. In 2016, the Oceti Sakowin Camp was organized in alliance with other indigenous peoples and like-minded "water protectors" (solidarity organizations). This was the largest gathering of Native Americans since the 19th century and the numbers of people who arrived and stayed at the camp at the peak of its activities reached several thousand.
Extinction Rebellion defines itself as an international movement oriented toward the achievement of a radical change that allows humanity to minimize the risk of human extinction and ecological collapse. Its main strategy is non-violent disobedience organized via small local groups connected in a global network. Since its organization, the network has conducted numerous demonstrations and public talks, and has become active in fashion revolution projects, road blockages and trainings on non-violent activism.

Two specific mechanisms enable and explain encounters between local and global resistance practices and dynamics: vernacularization and global framing. The term "vernacularization" reflects how general or abstract discourses and practices are translated in ways people can understand and appropriate them (Appadurai 1996). In the case of neoliberal globalization and resistance it entails the adaptation of each logic within national and local contexts, based upon the specific form that they adopt and the concrete ways in which they are experienced by different social actors. In other words, people understand neoliberalism in their immediate context and their daily lives according to local and national policies, and their effects on communities. So, it is possible to frame abstract struggles against neoliberal globalization and capitalism from their everyday experiences.

Vernacularization may be accompanied by subaltern strategies of localization that are designed and used by communities and social movements. These include "place-based strategies depending on their link with territory and culture, and global strategies emerging from network work that allows social movements to articulate into the production of locality establishing a politics from below" (Escobar 2012: 132). The mechanism of vernacularization/localization helps illustrate how social movements appropriate global struggles in different ways and use them to re-signify their own. For example, during the 1990s in Argentina, abstract global struggles such as the alter-globalization process materialized in local conflicts related to massive layoffs from state-owned companies. In this case, vernacularization opened opportunities to create social movements and organizations with specific and localized demands such as dignified employment, while framed within a broader struggle, that of the alter-globalization process. The opposite happened when movements from other countries and contexts, such as the Italian organization *Ya Basta!*, appropriated the Zapatista slogan, "a world in which many worlds fit," to underscore the link between different progressive resistances against neoliberalism around the world.

Communities have borrowed images, discourses and apparatuses used by state and market agents to spread neoliberal rationality, especially those cultural goods associated with mass media, such as popular music, documentaries and advertising campaigns. Activists domesticate, give another meaning and use these apparatuses to channel their struggles and their alternative projects in an exercise of appropriation of "the global" in everyday practices (Appadurai 1996). One example is the diffusion of the Zapatista struggles through the communications of the movement as well as through different kinds of music composed as a tribute by rock and punk bands around the world, including songs such as "People of the Sun" by Rage Against the Machine, "Marcos' Hall" by the Mexican band, Panteón Rococó or "Paramilitar" by the Spanish band, Ska-P.

The second mechanism, global framing, consists of the ability to see one's own demands in terms that link them with global struggles. More precisely, it can be understood as "the use of external symbols to orient national or domestic claims" (Tarrow 2007: 60). According to Tarrow, this connection is possible in two ways. One is structural equivalence, which occurs when similar reactions to the negative effects of transnational practices take place without previous coordination, as the mobilizations of students from both public and private universities against explicit commodification of education in countries such Colombia and Chile during 2011 and 2012. The other is thinking globally, framing local problems within a global frame from the beginning of social conflicts such as unemployment or privatizations of state-owned companies. In this way, globalization has the capacity to provide common targets and to bridge social movements' frames of collective action by connecting different kinds of activists (Tarrow 2007: 73).

Both subaltern strategies of localization and global framing are traversed by the process of scale shift, defined by McAdam et al. (2001: 331) as "change in the number and level of coordinated contentious actions leading to broader contention involving a wider range of actors and bridging their claims and identities." This change involves both claims (i.e. the defense of natural resources) and goals (i.e. changes in the way resistance is produced); it can be bottom-up – local actions are extended to the regional or global levels – or top-down – globalized practices are adopted at a local level. The repertories of strategies (Rossi 2017) that involve mobilization strategies as well as organizational practices can be local, national, regional or global, and they can change according to the dynamics of the same repertories, the responses of interlocutors such as the state, transnational corporations or international organizations, interactions with allies and the expansion of goals and discourses.

Ruth Reitan (2007) takes the model of scale shift developed by McAdam et al. (2001) as a starting point to analyze why and how social movements are increasingly involved in global actions and struggles. These shifts are not limited to reproducing actions and demands at different levels; they also "produce new alliances, objectives and changes in the focus of claims and maybe new identities" (Tarrow 2007: 121). Thus, there are consequences for local resistances and struggles in terms of identity, objectives and vindications, which is why Reitan (2007) proposes two additional mechanisms: structural violence and the necessity of going or being global.

The structural violence exercised by neoliberal globalization, understood as the threats and suffering produced in people's everyday lives around the world as a result of the negative effects of neoliberal policies, precedes local actions and makes activists aware of the need to be global. In other words, the fact that their problems and conflicts originate in global logics makes activists aware of the need to act beyond their local environments in their search for alternatives. In this context, brokerage and diffusion actions are crucial since they lead to a shift in claims and objectives at the transnational level, while they also imply a transformation of collective local action frames. This transformation lends itself to shared recognition of the worthiness of distinct resistances, interconnectedness and similarity, which ground the building of solidarity. Finally, transnationalization has an impact on localized actions such as the transformation or extension of objectives, the incorporation of new repertoires, changes in discourse and the establishment of new alliances.

Based upon the dynamics described, it is possible to claim there is a constant process of appropriation and re-signification of discourses, symbols, strategies, conflicts and antagonists within the alter-globalization process. Appropriation and re-signification facilitate encounters between local and global practices of resistance that are embodied in those very elements. This happens through the mechanisms of vernacularization/localization and global framing, which work in a global system characterized by the four features illustrated in Figure 15.3.

Thus, the alter-globalization process, as the sum of distinct resistances against neoliberalism, is better understood as a form of articulation of local practices and global dynamics that produces permanent horizontal encounters within the global system. This relationship is facilitated by the features of the global system mentioned throughout the chapter: the structural violence of neoliberalism; the different expressions of the alter-globalization process; communicational tools such as the internet and cheap flights; and fluxes in disjuncture relations, understood as unequal fluxes in which information and material conditions travel around the world, creating gaps between peoples' expectations and actual lived realities, but also offering channels for connecting local and global issues (Appadurai 2001: 6).

These encounters generate values, allies, strategies, symbols, targets, imaginaries and solidarity that cannot be understood exclusively through one of the two dimensions. In other words, resistances against neoliberalism are composed of all the elements in that encounter and cannot be understood as something purely local or global. Also, in such encounters, it is normally irrelevant if the actors involved are from the global South or the global North, making such a division unhelpful, at least for studying the specific issue of resistance.

Social movements, organizations and activists that are part of the alter-globalization process have different origins, backgrounds of mobilization and forms of organization. However, they share opposition to neoliberalism and they exercise that opposition in distinct ways depending on the impact of the neoliberal structural violence in their everyday lives. They also share similar targets, embodied in transnational corporations, international financial organizations and powerful states, and advocate for the importance of collective work and the necessity of struggle in different spaces of social life and at different territorial levels.

Learning from the exercise of resistance

Let's take a look at some other Hugos around the world. The Bolivian *cocalero* movement, organized in the province of Chapare during the 1980s, represents another interesting case of resistance (Cepeda-Másmela 2019). In Bolivia, the structural violence of neoliberalism was experienced in three main ways: the implementation of public policies such as privatizations; structural state abandonment; and the implementation of the so-called "war on drugs." Hence, the *cocalero* movement has exercised resistance on three fronts since its origins: claiming the right to grow and commercialize the coca leaf, to satisfy the needs of the community and to avoid the commodification of all aspects of social life. Its articulation with the alter-globalization process has occurred mainly in the realm of the imagination, understood by Arjun Appadurai (2001: 6–7) as a collective faculty facilitated by globalization that allows communities to envision dissent and to propose life alternatives, at the same time as they are disciplined and controlled by globalizing logics and their agents.

Strategies such as community radio stations and the performance of government and state functions at the local level play a central role. In the first case, the dissemination of information on local problems and social conflicts contributes to the development of a shared political awareness about them and helps to vernacularize neoliberalism in the local context. In the second, inspired by ideas frames within justice globalism, it is possible to organize community life in terms of social behavior, and in the allocation and rotation of tasks to satisfy the immediate needs of communities such as housing, employment and access to public spaces, communication routes, health and education, linking their own alternatives with the practices of other social movements.

The *cocalero* movement is a powerful form of resistance against neoliberalism that articulated its demands, practices and strategies with the alter-globalization process, although not explicitly but rather through more subtle elements. This is evident in several processes. First, the identification of some targets such as transnational corporations and international organizations such as the WTO or the United Nations; second, the appropriation of values like social solidarity, radical democracy and the political sustainability of the alternative of social change; and third, the construction of social imaginaries in which the direct exercise of popular power and political accusations are of fundamental importance for building and expanding alternatives for social change.

Another example is the multi-sectorial movements in Argentina (Cepeda-Másmela 2019), which bring Hugo, meat processing plants and Nueva York back into the picture again. In the Argentine case, neoliberalism adopted three central characteristics: the link between it and state terrorism, due to the presence of dictatorship when the model was first being implemented; the precarization of material conditions of the working class; and the impoverishment of the middle classes. The privatization of public companies was a key factor in Argentina's vernacularization of neoliberalism, given its profound economic and social impact. One of the expected effects of these policies was the depoliticization of unemployed workers who, in their new situation, should have taken refuge in their families and private support networks to mitigate unemployment. However, the opposite occurred, and unemployed workers became a fundamental political actor that demanded and claimed work, not as a final goal, but as a basic condition for the exercise of their rights (Dinerstein 2003; Sitrin 2012).

Militants of multi-sectorial organizations define themselves as "heirs of the *piqueteros.*" They emerged from several organizations of this kind, evidenced in their shared demand for decent employment and their use of picketing as a mobilization strategy. However, as the demand for employment was partially satisfied after 2003, the new movements realized there were other important issues related to employment conditions, migrant rights, education and access to public spaces. Multi-sectorial movements therefore differ from the *piqueteros* in several ways: first, the object of their struggle is what they call a "multi-sectorial subject," that is, unemployed and employed workers, students, migrants, artists, intellectuals and artists; second their organizational structure is much stronger than that of their *piquetero* predecessors; third, their demands and mobilization strategies are much broader. Thus, multi-sectorial organizations are a form of resistance against neoliberalism in its broader conception of political rationality and not only a reaction to some of its specific local dimensions.

The strategies and political practices of these organizations vary, in a clear exercise of vernacularization of neoliberalism. Some seek to obtain state resources through pickets and the occupation of public buildings, practiced also by other social movements of the alter-globalization process; others attend to the demands of local communities and promote social change in daily life through popular schools, work cooperatives and health posts; and still others are focused on the diffusion of their struggle and resistance through alternative means of communication. The use of these tools also facilitates an encounter with the alter-globalization process through the global framing of the organizations' struggles. In the opposite sense, direct democracy is vernacularized from the assembly practices that precede any action or decision taken by the organizations, from the rotation of tasks in the neighborhood to direct participation in the alter-globalization process through the construction of alliances with other organizations.

Other examples from the global North, such as Standing Rock and Extinction Rebellion, discussed briefly above (see Box 15.4) underscore that resistances against neoliberalism are increasingly linked to the environment, given that the survival of peoples, lands and traditions have been severely affected by distinct neoliberal policies. Such practices are localized in the sense that they take place within specific territorial states, but they also call on global solidarity, understood in terms of identification (Melucci 2002), translated into demonstrations, diffusion of information, organization of local camps and coordination among activists.

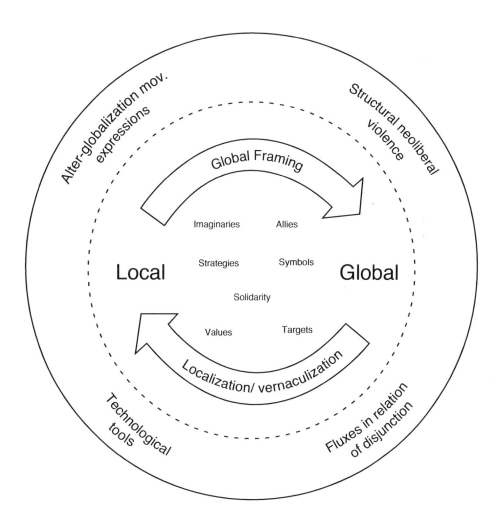

Figure 15.3 Global and local encounters of resistance
Source: Cepeda-Másmela (2018)

Conclusion

This chapter has shown that resistances to the hegemonic neoliberal order take place at multiple levels (both local and global) in both the global South and the North, adopt numerous discourses and strategies and are highly intertwined. This insight has several important implications for understanding resistance, and for envisioning and practicing alternatives to neoliberalism. First, rather than focusing our attention exclusively on specific instances of resistance and mobilization, we would be well advised to examine the connections and entanglements that exist between these, and the distinct ways in which resistances taking place locally or globally, in the South or the North, empower or magnify, constrain or hinder, and transform or confirm, those occurring elsewhere.

Second, resistance is exercised permanently and on a daily basis by people throughout the world. Although most analyses tend to focus on the most visible "peaks" of mobilization taking place via global demonstrations or at the World Social Forum, the most significant challenges to neoliberalism seem to occur locally, are less boisterous and are practiced in everyday life. Oftentimes these challenges adopt a global form through the development of solidarity networks or links with external actors, discourses, strategies and agendas. In this sense, global mobilizations are fundamental for strengthening local alternatives as they contribute to the development of solidarity bonds, and to the articulation of distinct transformative projects around common concerns and goals.

Finally, through the very exercise of resistance and the imagination of alternatives, social movements and organizations are also producers of knowledge about resistances to neoliberalism and its potential transformation. Therefore, any meaningful attempt to conceptualize resistance must take into account such voices, thus pointing to a distinctive form of scholarly practice than what is customarily recognized within conventional IR, rooted largely in intellectual activism and commitment to positive change.

Discussion questions

1. How do we conceptualize resistance in a changing world?
2. What is the relationship between resistance and change in world politics?
3. Is it useful to distinguish between the global North and global South to understand the exercise of resistance against neoliberalism?
4. How do insights from neo-Gramscian approaches help us to conceptualize resistance against neoliberalism?
5. What concepts and frames from social movements theories complement critical IR approaches to understand change in world politics?
6. What elements link local struggles and practices of resistance around the world?
7. Is it possible to identify alternatives to neoliberalism in every process of resistance against it?
8. How do we link environmental struggles with resistances against neoliberalism from the 1990s and the beginning of the 21st century?
9. What can we learn from people like Hugo, the man whose story opens this chapter, in political, epistemological and personal terms?

Further reading

Cepeda-Másmela, Carolina (2019) *Coca, desempleo y dignidad: Resistencias contra el neoliberalismo entre lo local y lo global*, Bogotá: Editorial Javeriana. A comparative analysis of *cocalero* and multi-sectorial movements within the alter-globalization movements.

Dinerstein, Ana (ed) (2013a) *Movimientos sociales y autonomía colectiva: La política de la esperanza en América Latina*, Buenos Aires: Capital Intelectual. A comprehensive study of social movements and resistances against neoliberalism in Argentina, Bolivia, Mexico and Brazil.

Mouly, Cecile and Esperanza Hernández-Delgado (eds) (2019) *Civil Resistance and Violent Conflict in Latin America*, London: Palgrave Macmillan. A comprehensive and comparative analysis of experiences of non-violent resistance in Latin America, especially within the context of violence and armed conflict.

Pleyers, Geoffrey (2010) *Alter-Globalization: Becoming Actors in the Global Age*, Cambridge: Polity Press. This book provides a comprehensive overview of the distinct strands of the alter-globalization movement.

Rossi, Federico Matias (2017) *The Poor's Struggle for Political Incorporation: The Piquetero Movement in Argentina*, Cambridge: Cambridge University Press. A historical analysis of the *piquetero* organizations in Argentina that improve theories of social movements by proposing alternative concepts such as stocks of legacies.

References

Andretta, Massimiliano, Donatella Della Porta, Lorenzo Mosca and Herbert Reiter (2006) *Globalization from Below: Transnational Activists and Protest Networks*, Minneapolis: Minnesota University Press.

Appadurai, Arjun (1996) *Modernity at Large: Cultural Dimensions of Globalization*, Minneapolis: Minnesota University Press.

Appadurai, Arjun (2001) "Grassroots Globalization and Research Imagination," in Arjun Appadurai (ed), *Globalization*, Durham: Duke University Press, pp. 1–21. doi:10.1215/08992363-12-1-1

Bieler, Andreas and Adam D. Morton (2004) "Another Europe Is Possible? Labour and Social Movements at the European Social Forum," *Globalizations*, 1(2): 305–327. doi:10.1080/1474773042000308622

Brown, Wendy (2003) "Neoliberalism and the End of Liberal Democracy," *Theory and Event*, 7(1): doi:10.1353/tae.2003.0020

Brown, Wendy (2006) "American Nightmare. Neoliberalism, Neoconservatism and De-democratization," *Political Theory*, 34(6): 690–714. doi:10.1177/0090591706293016

Cepeda-Másmela, Carolina (2018) "Resistencias contra el neoliberalismo: Una conceptualización de su ejercicio entre lo local y lo global," *Relaciones Internacionales*, (39): 59–80. doi:10.15366/relacionesinternacionales2018.39.004

Cepeda-Másmela, Carolina (2019) *Coca, desempleo y dignidad: Resistencias contra el neoliberalismo entre lo local y lo global*, Bogotá: Editorial Javeriana.

Chin, Christine and James Mittelman (2000) "Conceptualizing Resistance to Globalisation," in Barry Gills (ed), *Globalisation and the Politics of Resistance*, London: Palgrave, pp. 29–45. doi:10.1057/9780230519176_3

Cox, Robert (1986) "Social Forces, States and World Orders: Beyond International Relations Theory," in Robert Keohane (ed), *Neorealism and Its Critics*, New York: Columbia University Press, pp. 204–254.

Cox, Robert (1996) "Gramsci, Hegemony and International Relations: An Essay on Method," in Robert Cox and Timothy Sinclair (eds), *Approaches to World Order*, New York: Cambridge University Press. doi:10.1177/03058298830120020701

Cox, Robert (2002) *The Political Economy of a Plural World*, New York: Routledge. doi:10.4324/9780203116036

Cox, Robert (2005) "Civil Society at the Turn of the Millennium," in Louise Amoore (ed.) *The Global Resistance Reader*, New York: Routledge, pp. 35–47.

Della Porta, Donatella (2003) *New Global: Chi sono e cosa vogliono I critici della globalizzazione*, Bologna: Il Mulino.

Della Porta, Donatella (2005) *The Social Bases of the Global Justice Movement: Some Theoretical Reflections and Empirical Evidence from the First European Social Forum*, Suiza: Instituto de Investigación para el Desarrollo Social. Retrieved from www.unrisd.org

Della Porta, Donatella and Sidney Tarrow (2005) "Transnational Processes and Social Activism: An Introduction," in Donatella Della Porta and Sidney Tarrow (eds), *Transnational Protest and Global Activism*, Lanham: Rowman and Littlefield, pp. 1–17.

Dinerstein, Ana (2003) "Power or Counter-Power? The Dilemma of the Piquetero Movement in Argentina Post-Crisis," *Capital and Class*, 81: 1–7. doi:10.1177/030981680308100101

Dinerstein, Ana (2013b) "¿Empleo o trabajo digno? Crítica e imaginación en las organizaciones piqueteras, Argentina," in Ana Dinerstein (ed), *Movimientos sociales y autonomía colectiva: La política de la esperanza en América Latina*, Buenos Aires: Capital Intelectual, pp. 69–94.

Eschle, Catherine and Bice Maiguashca (eds) (2005) *Critical Theories, International Relations and 'The Anti-globalisation Movement': The Politics of Global Resistance*, New York: Routledge.

Escobar, Arturo (2012) "Más allá del desarrollo: Postdesarrollo y transiciones hacia el pluriverso," *Revista de Antropologia Social*, 21(1): 23–62. doi:10.5209/rev_RASO.2012.v21.40049

Florini, Ann (2002) "Who Does What? Collective Action and the Changing Nature of Authority," in Richard Higgott, Geoffrey Underhill and Aandreas Bleler (eds), *Non-State Actors and Authority in the Global System*, London: Routledge, pp. 15–31. doi:10.4324/9780203279380

Gill, Stephen (2008) *Power and Resistance in the New World Order*, New York: Palgrave Macmillan.

Gills, Barry (2000) "Introduction: Globalization and the Politics of Resistance," in Barry Gills (ed), *Globalization and the Politics of Resistance*, London: Macmillan Press, pp. 3–11. doi:10.1057/9780230519176

Gramsci, Antonio (1972) *Notas sobre Maquiavelo, sobre la política y sobre el Estado moderno*, Buenos Aires: Ediciones Nueva Visión.

Gramsci, Antonio (1973) *Selection from the Prison Notebooks*, London: Lawrence and Wishart.

Gramsci, Antonio (1975) *El materialismo histórico y la filosofía de Benedetto Croce*, México: Juan Pablos Editor.

Harvey, David (2007) *Breve historia del neoliberalismo*, Madrid: Akal.

Keck, Margaret and Kathryn Sikkink (2000) *Activistas sin fronteras*, México: Siglo XXI Editores.

Khagram, Sanjeev, James Riker and Kathryn Sikkink (2001) "From Santiago to Seattle: Transnational Advocacy Groups Restructuring World Politics," in Sanjeev Khagram, James Riker and Kathryn Sikkink (eds), *Restructuring World Politics. Transnational Social Movements, Networks and Norms*, Minneapolis: University of Minnesota Press, pp. 3–23.

Laïdi, Zaki (1997) *Un mundo sin sentido*, México: Fondo de Cultura Económica.

McAdam, Doug, Sidney Tarrow and Charles Tilly (2001) *Dynamics of Contention*, Cambridge: Cambridge University Press. doi:10.1017/CBO9780511805431

Melucci, Alberto (2002) *Acción colectiva, vida cotidiana y democracia*, México: El Colégio de México. doi:10.2307/j.ctvhn0c2h

Morton, Adam David (2007) *Unravelling Gramsci: Hegemony and Passive Revolution in the Global Political Economy*, London: Pluto Press. doi:10.1177/030981680709300116

Negri, Antonio (2007) *Goodbye Mr. Socialism: La crisis de la izquierda y los nuevos movimientos revolucionarios*, Barcelona: Paidós.

Pleyers, Geoffrey (2010b) *Alter-Globalization: Becoming Actors in the Global Age*, Cambridge: Polity Press.

Polanyi, Karl (2003) *La gran transformación: los orígenes políticos y económicos de nuestro tiempo*, Mexico: Fondo de Cultura Económica.

Restrepo, Dario (2003) "De la falacia neoliberal a la nueva política," in *La falacia neoliberal: Críticas y alternativas*, Bogotá: Universidad Nacional de Colombia, pp. 19–40.

Reitan, Ruth (2007) *Global Activism*, New York: Routledge. doi:10.4324/9780203449783

Rossi, Federico Matias (2017) *The Poor's Struggle for Political Incorporation: The Piquetero Movement in Argentina*, Cambridge: Cambridge University Press. doi:10.1177/0268580919831621

Sassen, Saskia (2007) *Una sociología de la globalización*, Madrid: Katz Editores. doi:10.4067/S0250-71612008000200008

Scott, James (2000) *Los dominados y el arte de la resistencia: Discursos ocultos*, Mexico: Ediciones Era.

Sikkink, Kathryn (2001) "Restructuring World Politics: The Limits and Asymmetries of Soft Power," in Sanjeev Khagram, James Riker and Kathryn Sikkink (eds), *Restructuring World Politics: Transnational Social Movements, Networks and Norms*, Minneapolis: University of Minnesota Press, pp. 301–318.

Sikkink, Kathryn (2005) "Patterns of Dynamic Multilevel Governance and the Insider-Outsider Coalition," in Donatella Della Porta and Sidney Tarrow (eds), *Transnational Protest and Global Activism*, Lanham: Rowman and Littlefield, pp. 151–173.

Sitrin, Marina (2012) *Everyday Revolution: Horizontalism and Autonomy in Argentina*, London: Zed Books.

Sklair, Leslie (2003) *Sociología del sistema global*, Barcelona: Gedisa.

Smith, Jackie et al. (2008) *Global Democracy and the World Social Forums*, London: Paradigm Publishers. doi:10.4324/9781315636375

Smith, William. C. and Roberto Korzeniewicz (2006) "El movimiento doble: Actores insiders y outsiders en la emergencia de una sociedad civil transnacional en las Américas," *Colombia Internacional*, (63): 40–69. doi:10.7440/colombiaint63.2006.02

Steger, Manfred, James Goodman and Erin Wilson (2013) *Justice Globalism: Ideology, Crisis, Policy*, London: Sage. doi:10.4135/9781446270080

Steger, Manfred and Ravi Roy (2010) *Neoliberalism: A Very Short Introduction*, New York: Oxford University Press. doi:10.1093/actrade/9780199560516.001.0001

Tarrow, Sidney (2007) *The New Transnational Activism*, New York: Cambridge University Press. doi:10.1017/CBO9780511791055.002

Tarrow, Sidney and Donatella Della Porta (2005) "Conclusion: 'Globalization,' Complex Internationalism and Transnational Contention," in Donatella Della Porta and Sidney Tarrow (eds), *Transnational Protest and Global Activism*, Lanham: Rowman and Littlefield, pp. 227–246.

Teivainen, Teivo (2012) "Global Democratization without Hierarchy or Leadership? The World Social Forum in the Capitalist World," in Stephen Gill (ed), *Global Crises and the Crisis of Global Leadership*, London: Cambridge University Press, pp. 181–198. doi: 10.1017/CBO9781139046596

Worth, Owen (2013) *Resistance in the Age of Austerity*, London: Zed. doi:10.1111/1478-9302.12053_98

16 Socio-environmentalism

Cristina Yumie Aoki Inoue and Matías Franchini

-

Introduction

December 22, 2018 was the 30th anniversary of the murder of Chico Mendes, recognized around the world as one of the greatest defenders of the Brazilian Amazon forest. What is less known is that Mendes was also a rural workers' leader, and one of the key figures in the creation of the National Council of Rubber Tappers (CNS) in 1985. In his efforts to satisfy both environmental and social goals – thus reflecting the conviction that rural communities were people of the forest with rights to the land and the opportunity to improve their lot – Mendes proposed the idea of extractive reserves (Resex), whereby rubber tappers could live sustainably from the Amazon.

Around the same time, in another part of the Amazon, a group of scientists, scholars, international non-governmental organizations (NGOs), bilateral cooperation agencies and the local population developed a project to protect an area of flooded forest extremely rich in biodiversity, while also improving life conditions. The result was the creation of the Mamirauá Institute (IDSM) in 1999 and the first sustainable development reserve of the same name. Both Chico Mendes and Mamirauá can be seen as instances of socio-environmentalism, a largely Brazilian enterprise that might contribute to "greening" International Relations (IR) (see Box 16.1).

BOX 16.1 THE MAMIRAUÁ RESERVE

The creation of Mamirauá Sustainable Development Reserve (RDS) in 1991 stemmed from the work of a coalition drawing together the conservation movement (conservation biology) and local communities (Movimento de Preservação de Lagos) (Inoue and Lima 2007). The project aimed at integrating research, biodiversity conservation and sustainable development. Mamirauá was the first sustainable development reserve established in Brazil. It was considered innovative at the time of its creation not only because it recognized the rights of the local population that remained within and around it, but also due to their role as actors in the elaboration and implementation of its management plan.

Mamirauá Sustainable Development Reserve and Institute's existence is in part the result of a transnational network of primatologists and other Amazonian-oriented researchers that shared similar views about biodiversity conservation and the need to include local populations in the process. The network contributed to their emergence by attracting financial support from its partner institutions and generating acceptance among conservationists worldwide. While the project underscored the difficulties of including human populations in protected areas and of balancing standard of living issues with environmental protection, it was also innovative in its attempts to overcome top-down and fenced-off approaches of biodiversity conservation.

Mamirauá illustrates the productive convergence of diverse values related to ecological sustainability, social justice and cultural diversity, and the importance of encouraging local participation in decision-making. Local ownership of conservation efforts makes sense not only on the grounds of fairness, but due to considerable knowledge that communities have of flora and fauna, and their sustainable management and use. Traditional and indigenous populations have been using natural resources in sustainable ways for centuries, and their knowledges and ways of being are said to be non-dichotomous with regards to the society/nature divide, allowing them to perceive other dimensions of reality beyond Western rationality (Narby 1999; Ramos 2013; see too, Chapter 17).

Exponential growth of human activities has caused an environmental crisis. Increasing pressures on ecosystems, soil and water, climate and the atmosphere have the potential to trigger sudden or irreparable environmental changes that can harm human and non-human lives on earth (Rockström et al. 2009; Steffen et al. 2015). As we enter the Anthropocene,[1] almost all environmental problems demand greater cooperation among societies to avoid free-riding and the tragedy of the commons (Hardin 1968). Moreover, the poor in emerging and poor countries are likely to be the most affected.

The magnitude of the socio-ecological crisis and the concrete changes needed at all levels (from the global to the local) to address it highlight the inadequacies of prevailing behaviors, policies and ultimately, IR theories. Globally, both individuals and social structures operate within short-term and egotistical considerations[2] that are largely encouraged by almost all development models and political regimes – from right to left, from democracy to autocracy – and the international system itself, whereas the construction of a safe operating space for humanity demands cooperative action (Earth System Governance 2018; Viola et al. 2013). Traditional IR responses to sustainability challenges have been problematic, as the environment has been considered a marginal area of thematic concern. Indeed, only recently has a body of green theory been developed within the field (Eckersley 2010).

Based upon the Brazilian experience in the Amazon, we argue that the concept of socio-environmentalism can nurture green IR thinking by highlighting two movements – or dialogues – that are neglected in conventional IR approaches. We call the first movement a vertical dialogue. It rearticulates different levels of analysis and scales, from the local to the global, and transcends dichotomies such as the public and the private. As we show empirically, there are cases in which developments at the global level of governance can be helpful for geographically located socio-political structures. In this sense, the global–local antithesis has to be abandoned as an a priori assumption. The Mamirauá story is a good example (see Box 16.1 and subsequent discussion). The second movement consists of horizontal dialogue. It suggests constructing dialogues and synergies between different epistemologies and worldviews. We need to move beyond cognitive and epistemological dichotomies, especially those of nature–society, global–local and even North–South, to understand socio-environmental problems and struggles that are taking place around the planet. To do so, we ultimately need to go beyond modernity.

Complexity, trans-disciplinarity and holistic knowledge paradigms seek to overcome borders that separate the sciences, philosophy, art and spiritual traditions (D'ambrosio et al. 1993; Morin 1998; Leis 1999), and to integrate reason, sensation, emotion and intuition; that is, different ways in which we perceive, know and understand reality (Adorno and Horkheimer 1997; Leis 1999; Marcuse 1975). Moreover, local populations, especially indigenous and aboriginal peoples, practice knowledge(s) of and relations with "nature" that customarily transcend the dichotomy of rationalism and the anthropocentrism of modernity (Narby 1999; Ramos 2013; Santos 2006). This chapter aims not so much to establish local knowledges as a general framework for analyzing global problems but for these to help us bridge existing gaps between different knowledge systems.

The chapter begins with a brief problematization of the way in which conventional IR theory has dealt with the environment (or not). We focus on three relevant traditions, including realism, liberal institutionalism and global governance. We argue that in terms of vertical integration, all three approaches exhibit serious deficits, mostly related to their well-known state-centrism. However, literature on governance, rooted largely in the liberal institutional tradition, has been able to integrate different levels of analysis, becoming a strong conceptual framework to assess global environmental politics that transcend simplistic dichotomies such as global/local and North/South. Regarding horizontal integration, however, neither theory offers significant progress. Both realism and liberal institutionalism are almost ontologically incapable of assimilating non-modern worldviews due to their rationalist structure of agent incentives. The governance approach, which is more constructivist with regards to social processes, is epistemologically capable of incorporating other forms of knowledge, but as far as we know, it has not yet done so. The furthest this literature has gone is a multi-disciplinary approach – earth system governance – that continues to operate under a modernist umbrella.

Following our discussion of the theoretical literature, we explore socio-environmentalism as a potential contribution to "green" IR. We not only define this concept but show how it entails dialogues among different actors, as well as between distinct worldviews. Thus, we argue that socio-environmentalism contributes to greening the field of International Relations by bridging the vertical and horizontal gaps found in mainstream IR theories. We also illustrate the concept with a brief description of the process that led to the creation of the Mamirauá Sustainable Development Reserve, located in the Brazilian state of Amazonas. We focus on the Amazon as a locus of global environmental politics as this region exemplifies some of the contradictions of modernity; namely, multiple governance experiments conducted in the Amazon since the 1980s underscore the need for epistemological changes in how we conceive of reality and how we conduct social life in such a way that we might overcome the society/nature dichotomy.

IR literature and the environment

The vertical gap

In spite of the impressive growth in international environmental treaties, activism and policies in the last decades, environmental politics is still marginal in International Relations scholarship, as environmental problems have never been a main concern in the discipline (Eckersley 2010; Green and Hale 2017; Pereira 2017). Besides this disinterest, conventional IR theories do not consider properly the diversity of actors, levels of analysis and scales in global environmental affairs, leading to a vacuum that we call the "vertical gap." Vertical dialogue is the capacity of a theoretical framework to apprehend international relations as a complex social field that integrates different actors with a wide definition of ideas, interests and incentive structures. Those agents are located on a double continuum: from local to global and from public to private. They are also involved in causal and constitutive relations among themselves, and between them and social structures. In this sense, individual citizens, nation-states, NGOs, epistemic communities and others, are capable of shaping the social outcome at the international level, depending of course, on their agency level (Biermann et al. 2009).

The absence of vertical dialogue has been especially intense in the realist tradition. Accordingly, many scholars (Haas 1992; Keck and Sikkink 1998; Keohane and Nye 2011) have highlighted the limitation of this theoretical perspective to consider actors other than the nation-state as relevant players in world politics. In this tradition, the basic dynamic of the international system is conflict between states arising from anarchy (see Chapters 5, 7 and 8). Consequently, even international regimes – which have been the main instrument of environmental international politics – are only epiphenomena of state behavior (Strange 1982).

The liberal tradition in IR has been more willing to accept environmental issues as a key part of the international agenda. Accordingly, from the 1970s onward a sub-field concerned with environmental cooperation emerged. Since then, the role of regimes within institutional liberalism has been the predominant analytical lens for studying international environmental issues. However, this tradition too contains important shortcomings in terms of vertical integration (Eckersley 2010; Okereke et al. 2009; Paterson 1996). For example, the concept of international regime has been related to interstate relations and to national responses to a set of principles, norms, rules and decision-making procedures agreed among states (Krasner 1983). Even though the definition put forward by Krasner makes it possible to consider other actors and their expectations, the way the regime concept has been used in the literature mainly concerns state decisions and actions (Porter et al. 2000). Thus, as among realist scholars, liberal institutionalists have focused primarily on state behavior to assess global environmental issues. In this tradition, the state is also a rational actor, guided by economic gains and engaging in cooperation as a more productive way to address international problems.

It is important to notice that, even though environmental concerns are marginal within mainstream IR, global environmental politics (GEP) has emerged as a sub-field, as evidenced by the growth of the Environment Studies Section in the International Studies Association (ISA) and the existence of publication venues such as *Global Environmental Politics*, *International Environment Agreements* and the recently launched *Earth System Governance*, as well as several student and professor handbooks (Betsill et al. 2014; Chasek et al. 2013; Dauvergne 2005; Elliott 2004; Stevis 2014).

The GEP research agenda covers myriad topics and perspectives, including global environmental change and governance (multilevel transnational, private); the national and the local within a global perspective (e.g., how global norms impinge/impact or diffuse to the local level (Acharya and Buzan 2009; Frank et al. 2000); global environmental change and security; and how global economic processes (production and consumption) relate to environmental change (Conca and Dabelko 2014; Park et al.

2008). There is also an emerging attempt to look at environmental politics comparatively (Franchini 2016; Steinberg and VanDeveer 2012). Moreover, awareness that we have entered a new geological epoch, the Anthropocene, has also fostered innovative reflection on the new earth politics, as suggested by a recently edited book on this subject (Nicholson and Jinnah 2016).

Many scholars have looked at global environmental politics as a sub-field of IR with an eye to tracing its trajectory (Stevis 2014), theoretical underpinnings (Eckersley 2010; Paterson 2014) and themes and research agenda (Betsill et al. 2014; Chasek et al. 2013; Dauvergne 2005; Elliott 2004). From these works, we view a field that is apparently diverse in terms of research themes, theoretical perspectives and to a certain extent the researchers' geographical locations and institutional affiliations. As a byproduct of the field, GEP has grown and acquired a life of its own, perhaps more diverse and interdisciplinary than IR itself. The sub-field covers a variety of themes linked to state/political, economics/market, societal and ecological dynamics from the global to the local. Liberalism and liberal constructivism seem to dominate theoretically in such research (Stevis 2014). Environmental security, in turn, is viewed largely through a realist lens, while critical environmental studies are rooted in eco-socialism, critical and post-structural IR, and feminism, as well as an emerging green political theory (Eckersley 2010; Paterson 1996, 2014; Stevis 2014). Notwithstanding apparent diversity, a closer look reveals that liberalism and liberal constructivism continue to prevail as theoretical frames and governance/institutions as the broad themes (Inoue and Moreira 2016; Stevis 2014).

As an analytical framework, governance seems more suitable for assessing the role of non-state actors in the international system and, hence, more convergent with the idea of vertical dialogue. However, this tradition too suffers several limits. First, the very concept of global governance is somewhat vague (Finkelstein 1995), with which the research and analysis inspired in this concept can be quite heterogeneous. Second, part of the global governance literature overlaps with liberal regime analysis in terms of their focus on the state and formal international regimes, although other strands assess global environmental politics beyond state/society, global/local and North/South dichotomies (De Búrca et al. 2014; Okereke et al. 2009; Ostrom 2009; Rosenau 1995). In particular, the notion of an earth's system of governance is a valuable tool. Biermann et al. (2009: 4) define earth system governance as:

> the interrelated and increasingly integrated system of formal and informal rules, rule-making systems, and actor-networks at all levels of human society (from local to global) that are set up to steer societies towards preventing, mitigating and adapting to global and local environmental change, and in particular, earth system transformation, within the normative context of sustainable development.

This body of literature produces a more complex and layered picture of global environmental governance (Eckersley 2010) than conventional IR theories.

The horizontal gap

By conceiving knowledge exclusively in terms of positive science – grounded in a modernist view of the world and social processes – mainstream IR theories also lack the capacity to incorporate other worldviews as well as other forms of knowledge. We call horizontal dialogue the capacity for a conceptual framework to assimilate different types of knowledge and world visions; that is, different kinds of ontologies and epistemologies. In environmental studies, the heritage of modernity reinforces a nature/society division that constitutes an epistemological obstacle to assimilating the challenges of the Anthropocene.

Leis (1999) argues that modernity is unsustainable, meaning that anthropocentrism, instrumental rationality, modern dualities, the organization of knowledge into disciplines and fields, and the consequent separation between nature and human societies are the roots that underlie the drivers of all the environmental problems we face. The domination of nature is seen to emerge from the ways in which the relation between societies and nature has been constructed. The quest for eco-development, sustainable development, green economy, low carbon economy and other blueprints has not taken us much further, and the predominant development paradigm has remained largely unchanged. Leis (1999) claims that the means to overcome the crisis would be to go beyond modernity – a universal model of rationality, science and knowledge – by incorporating pre- and post-modern ways of thinking and finding solutions, as shown in the next section. According to the author, modernity has transpired on a material plane, entailing broad scientific and technological transformations and expansion of the market. Consciousness about the ecological limits of economic growth does not depend on the free market, but on the actions of environmentalism. The author calls this project realist-utopian because it can only take place through the bridging and approximation of opposite phenomena, or the harmonization of spiritual and material experiences, and reconciliation of the transcendent and immanent plans.

In this vein, Leis (1999) argues that the society/nature, one of the main characteristics of Western culture in the modern era, has structured the ways in which societies have organized economies, political and social systems across the globe (see too Chapter 17). Socio-political life happens within nation-states with their territories organized around the idea of national and subnational boundaries that do not coincide with ecosystems or river basins. Democracies are arranged around voters and candidates that represent only present generations, whereas future generations and nature are not represented. Economics is structured in markets, profits, production and consumption, and the idea of exploitation of nature in the present, so that the pace of extracting resources and disposing of solid, liquid and gas residuals is much faster than nature's recovery capacity. Future generations do not vote or consume. There are human rights, but no rights of nature, although this has begun to change, as suggested by recent decisions in countries as diverse as Colombia, India and New Zealand that recognize the rights of rivers and other natural bodies.

In sum, the social sciences in general, and International Relations in particular, have been structured around anthropocentric cultures and epistemologies that fail to consider complex interactions and inter-relations between nature and society. Moreover, predominant Western modern views of (positivist) science tend to ignore other forms of knowledge that fail to conform to its standards. Horizontal dialogues could bring other worldviews and knowledges to the debate, with an eye to transcending anthropocentrism and the dualisms of modernity, particularly the nature/society divide. For example, in the context of India, the Tagore affords a distinct approach to human relations with nature (Behera 2009). Behera argues that modern Western belief systems premised on the separation between human beings (subject) and nature (object) are the basis for an instrumental relationship of domination. Ling (2013) too highlights other traditions that reveal ways of looking at the world beyond dichotomies. She draws on Advaita monism and Daoist dialectics to portray world politics as constantly connected and inter-related (see too, Chapter 17). Through lenses such as these, it is impossible to see North/South, environment/development or nature/society as opposite poles.

Filling the gaps

Green politics, IR and socio-environmentalism

In his critique of mainstream IR's focus on environmental regimes, Paterson (1996) argues the need to develop what he calls "green politics," a tradition that rejects the idea that the states-system and other structures of world politics can provide an adequate response to the environmental crisis. Accordingly, the author identifies two sets of literature – "green political theory" and "global ecology" – that might nurture a green position on IR and global politics. While the first body of literature rejects the anthropocentric worldview and highlights the "limits to growth" argument, the second builds on green principles and provides an analysis of the environmental crisis rooted in development as its root cause and the need to protect and reclaim the "commons."

Since the 2000s, a growing body of like-minded green IR theory has appeared. Eckersley (2010) states that a green position has emerged that draws on more radical green discourses from outside the discipline of International Relations and has helped expose what she calls the ecological blindness of IR theory. According to the author, green IR theory emerged primarily out of a critique of mainstream rationalist approaches (neorealism and neoliberalism), and has simultaneously drawn upon, and critically revised and extended, neo-Marxist-inspired International Political Economy (IPE) and normative international relations theories of cosmopolitan orientation, bringing new discourses of ecological security, sustainable development (and reflexive modernization) and environmental justice.

Eckersley (2010) subdivides green IR theory into an IPE wing and a normative or "green cosmopolitan" wing. The first offers an alternative analysis of global ecological problems to regime theory, while the second articulates new norms of environmental justice and green democracy at all levels of governance. She locates green IR theory on the critical/constructivist side of the rationalism versus constructivism debate, arguing that:

> green IR scholars seek to articulate the concerns of many voices traditionally at the margins of international relations, ranging from environmental non-government organizations, green consumers, ecological scientists, ecological economists, green political parties, indigenous peoples, and broadly, all those seeking to transform patterns of global trade, aid, and debt to promote more sustainable patterns of development in the North and South.
>
> (Eckersley 2010: 265)

In the next section, we suggest that the concept of socio-environmentalism can be considered a continuation and extension of this tradition, given the struggles that are taking place at the local level on all continents of the globe, no matter if North or South.[3] We turn to the definition and discussion of this concept within the context of the Brazilian Amazon now.

Defining socio-environmentalism

In Brazil, socio-environmentalism emerged in the Amazon in the late 1980s and early 1990s. The murder of Chico Mendes in Acre in 1988, as he struggled to keep land, the forest and the way of life of rubber tappers, is identified by Hochstetler and Keck (2007) as a key source of its emergence.[4] Mendes' death generated widespread discussion about the links between the livelihood struggles of traditional forest peoples and the protection of the Amazon.

Socio-environmentalism encompasses three main ideas (Santilli 2005). First, a new development paradigm is needed that promotes the sustainability of ecological processes, attention to species, ecosystems and all processes involved in sustaining life on earth (for example, the hydrologic, geologic and climatic cycles). Second, the social and economic needs of the present generation must be attended while not compromising the ability of future generations to meet theirs (just social-economic sustainability). Accordingly, ideas of justice and fairness, such as reduction of poverty and social inequality, are intrinsic to socio-environmentalism. Third, cultural diversity should be promoted and valued, as well as the consolidation of the democratic process, understood as broad social participation in managing the environment. Although this concept evolved in the Brazilian Amazon, it can be applied to the struggles for land, rivers, mountains, ways of living and knowing that do not separate society from nature.

Santilli (2005) considers socio-environmentalism a Brazilian "invention," even though movements that link social and environmental struggles, including access to land (justice) and protection of forests (or other natural resources) have taken place throughout the world. Indeed, Jacobs (2002: 59) asserts that grassroots organizations in many places have pursued an ecologically as well as socially just society. However, within the context of Brazil, *socioambientalismo* has acted as a political ploy to bring together social and environmental movements, organizations and local populations (traditional and indigenous peoples). According to Jacobs (2002: 64–65), the specific framing of this concept between the late 1980s and early 1990s created shared awareness of the importance of both environmental preservation and social struggles. As the socio-environmental movement grew, activists, jurists and social scientists attempted to expand its meaning to encompass not only sustainability, both ecological and social, both also justice, cultural diversity and participation. In addition to offering a broad framework within which to mobilize diverse constituencies, socio-environmentalism was also a reaction to the predominant view that environmental concerns were something foreign to Brazil. During the 1970s, for example, reactions to environmentalism were negative, as the military regime tended to dismiss environmental critiques as an international attempt to prevent Brazilian development or to threaten the country's sovereignty in the Amazon region, a reaction conceptualized as "Amazon paranoia" by Viola and Franchini (2018). This vision has experienced a comeback under the right-wing government of Jair Bolsonaro.

Mamirauá and other experiences throughout the Brazilian Amazon are expressions of socio-environmentalism. For instance, the rubber tappers in Acre, who took the lead in establishing a link between their struggle and ecological concerns, also spearheaded the creation of a coalition to protect the Amazonian rainforest named "Forest Peoples Alliance," and that brought together both rubber tappers and indigenous groups. We will return to this alliance soon. The Altamira Gathering, a five-day event in 1989 led by the Kayapo people against the projected Xingu Dam, similarly illustrates the struggle for territory combined with explicit environmental concerns (Da Cunha and Almeida 2002).

Clearly, similar developments throughout the world that link local populations to nature conservation illustrate how traditional and indigenous peoples often turn from culprits (of environmental degradations) to victims (of land dispossession and inequality), and from victims to active protagonists of environmental politics (Bodmer et al. 1997; Burch et al. 2019; Jeanrenaud 2002). In the specific case of Brazil, until the 1980s the poor were largely seen as a source of pressure over natural resources. As the impacts of development projects were increasingly more visible, Da Cunha and Almeida (2002: 81) assert that it became partially accepted that the disadvantaged were not always the culprits of environmental disaster, but rather victims of tragedies associated with ill-conceived development plans that disrupted lifestyles as well as water and forest environments. In the late 1980s, increasingly, traditional and indigenous peoples became more directly linked to environmental issues. The authors argue that such groups began to appear in public discourse on world environmental problems as legitimate stakeholders, and actors endowed with significant knowledge of the natural environment, with which they were converted into agents and authors of environmental protection measures (Da Cunha and Almeida 2002).

Filling the vertical gap

As mentioned previously, conventional IR theories are hard-pressed to address environmental issues, mainly due to the sharp separation they establish between domestic and international politics, and state and non-state actors. Socio-environmentalism offers a more complex and layered picture, linking the global and the local by crossing state jurisdictional boundaries. In this sense, it dialogues with the idea of transnational governance that is part of the earth system governance agenda. Empirically too, socio-environmentalism operates as a transnational movement that has led to non-state forms of deterritorialized governance by non-state and state actors.

The notion of earth system governance converges with socio-environmentalism in three other ways. First, it considers both natural and social factors in environmental studies. Similar to what Leis (1999) argues, the idea of earth system governance is "as much about environmental parameters as about social practices and processes" (Biermann et al. 2009: 22). Second, as a research program, earth system governance transcends IR's traditional focus on the state and regimes, since the problem is wider than "the regulation of global commons through global agreements and conventions" (23). Finally, as a research network, it integrates a variety of disciplinary knowledges: "the analysis of earth system governance thus covers the full range of social science disciplines across the scales, from anthropology to international law" (23).

Socio-environmentalism also offers a more nuanced lens through which to discuss global environmental norms (Hochstetler and Keck 2007), as it attempts to bridge the social and environmental dimensions of political struggles that gained force with Brazil's democratization in the 1990s, and is grounded in local contexts and dynamics. In this sense, socio-environmentalism does not simply reflect a norm diffusion process from the global to the local (Frank et al. 2000), as we will now see.

Socio-environmentalism: principles and norms in context

Theories of international norms diffusion account for the spread of environmental protection measures over a comparatively short period of time (Finnemore and Sikkink 1998; Hochstetler and Keck 2007). However, they ignore key dimensions of environmental politics by failing to consider the local context (Hochstetler and Keck 2007). The emergence of socio-environmentalism in Brazil reflects particular local developments, even though the global environmental movement of the 1980s and 1990s acted to reinforce this process (Hochstetler and Keck 2007; Pádua 2002; Santilli 2005). Not surprisingly, Hochstetler and Keck (2007) argue that more *nuanced* discussions of global struggle over norms are needed, given that the process of norm diffusion is much more complex than this body of literature assumes.

Even though global environmental norms have tended to diffuse from North to South, they have been significantly modified in the different contexts where they "landed." In Brazil, social justice is a strong dimension of social movement activity, including environmental activism. Hence, as already argued, socio-environmentalism displays the underlying assumption that one cannot separate ecological from social sustainability. In the Amazon, most of the struggles over land and natural resources involve protection of nature and a fight for justice and well-being of local populations. For instance, rubber tappers in Acre needed the conservation of the forest to keep their livelihoods while at the same time, they wanted access to land in opposition to farmers who were land grabbing and deforesting to establish cattle ranching or large-scale agriculture. Thus, a transnational coalition emerged between them and Northern environmentalists in which social and ecological sustainability were intrinsic to shared struggle.

Socio-environmentalism and transnational networks in the Amazon: global–local governance

In addition to redefining norms, socio-environmentalism has also established new forms of governance. Socio-environmental movements and the resulting transnational networks they have helped build, have resulted in deterritorialized governance arrangements involving governmental and non-governmental actors, and cross-scale interactions from the global to local levels, across national jurisdictions. In the Brazilian Amazon, as mentioned previously, interactions between indigenous and traditional groups[5] resulted in the creation of the Alliance of Forest Peoples in 1989 (see Box 16.2). The Alliance sought to support collaborations between indigenous people and rubber gatherers in conflict with land grabbers and timber dealers in Acre, and also to enable coordination between their organizations at a national level to claim rights and protections. The Alliance fought for the traditional populations' livelihood – both physical and cultural – which largely depended on conservation of the forest but was threatened by deforestation and depletion of natural resources (Santilli 2005). The drivers of this predatory mode of nature exploitation were the construction of big highways, forest slash-and-burn for cattle raising and farming, and the migration of thousands of settlers and farmers to the Amazon region.

BOX 16.2 PEOPLES OF THE FORESTS

In Brazil, many indigenous peoples and traditional populations (local populations that base their way of life on the extraction of natural resources such as rubber, chestnut, balata tree, vegetable oils, hunting and/or non-predatory fishing and subsistence agriculture) have become mobilized since the late 1980s. They call themselves "forest peoples" because they need forests and rivers to survive, and they claim to know how to protect and use these sustainably. According to Ailton Krenak, an indigenous leader, indigenous peoples are the original inhabitants of the forests, be it the great forest, such as the Amazon, or other forests, because their ancestral culture is based on what nature offers them. However, other Brazilian populations that have built their economy and culture on natural extractivism and the exploitation of forest resources, have learned from indigenous practices. In the specific case of rubber tappers, such learning led to an alliance in defense of the forest (Cohn 2015).

The Alliance of Forest Peoples was first established between indigenous peoples' organizations and the Rubber Tapper's National Council in the 1980s to defend the right to their lands and the protection of the forests on which they depend for their livelihoods. It was conceptualized by Chico Mendes and created under his leadership, along with Krenak and other figures. The Alliance was active during the 1990s and met again in September 2007 for the II National Meeting of the Peoples of the Forests, 21 years after the first meeting and in commemoration of the 20th anniversary of the death of Chico Mendes.

More recently, in 2019, the campaign #PovosDaFloresta was launched by the Instituto Socioambiental in partnership with indigenous peoples, extractivists, *quilombolas* (descendants of slaves) and riverine populations. The campaign seeks to support the struggle for the protection of the environment and the rights of indigenous and traditional populations. The #PovosDaFloresta is led by 25 leaders representing nine indigenous groups from the Amazon, *quilombolas* from the Vale do Ribeira in the state of São Paulo, and women from Terra do Meio in the state of Pará. The campaign upholds the diversity that characterizes the people who live and protect the forests, and also seeks to remind all Brazilians (if not the world) that the forests regulate the climate, produce rain and harbor biodiversity, which is a potential source of new medicines and cures for many diseases.

The Alliance also built coalitions with transnational networks (Keck and Sikkink 1998). The majority of ecological partnerships started in the late 1980s and early 1990s (Lima 1999), consolidating around new theoretical concepts like conservation biology. Inoue (2007) cites evidence of an epistemic community centered on conservation biology, a global biodiversity regime and local practices in Brazil. Two social movements subsequently converged, including a grassroots movement to defend natural resources essential to Amazonian livelihoods, and environmental NGOs (Lima 1999). In several cases, these socio-environmental movements have succeeded in putting political pressure on governments to legalize their proposals.

Socio-environmental organizations have promoted many programs, projects and initiatives in the Amazon, rooted in global principles such as biodiversity conversation and sustainable use, but conceived across both global and local values, including the protection of biological diversity while promoting sustainable development (WWF-Brazil and ISER 2001). In this sense, such efforts can be considered the result of international, transnational and transgovernmental collaboration among different actors, ranging from international and national NGOs, bilateral and multilateral cooperation agencies and governmental organs, to researchers and scientists, grassroots organizations and local populations. In sum, the emergence of socio-environmentalism as a discourse and practice has been intrinsically related to processes of redefining norms and concepts as well as to the emergence of new forms of governance. These bring together state and non-state actors across national jurisdictions from the global to the local.

Filling the horizontal gap

As mentioned earlier, mainstream IR environmental studies have also fallen short of incorporating other worldviews and knowledge systems, what we referred to previously as the horizontal dialogue. Socio-environmentalism brings together principles related to ecological, socio-economic sustainability, social justice and cultural diversity, and adheres to participatory approaches to decision-making. In doing so, the socio-environmental debates have brought to light issues related to worldviews, cultures and other forms of knowledge, thus moving beyond cognitive and epistemological dichotomies in IR, especially those of nature/society, global/local and even North/South. In this sense, socio-environmentalism can be considered a more robust lens to view struggles around the globe, in which the defense of land, rivers, living and non-living beings and ways of life, and social and environmental demands, are largely intertwined and inseparable.

Socio-environmentalism and socio-biodiversity: beyond modernity?

Historically, socio-environmentalism is part of a broader context of environmental thinking (Pádua 2002). Its critique of social exclusion and environmental degradation is neither European nor colonial and has largely developed out of questions regarding modernity. As a concept, socio-environmentalism can bridge the society/nature dichotomy and bring other forms of knowledge into the debate, given the participation of indigenous and traditional peoples. Its origins in the convergence between social movements in the Amazon and international environmental NGOs also bridges the divide between North and South.

During Brazil's democratic transition, social movements began to demand more participation in development projects, while global conservationists also started to change their methods. The shift in global conservationism was based on an instrumental approach to human populations, which were still seen as resources to achieve globally identified conservation objectives (Jeanrenaud, cited in Inoue and Lima 2007). In consequence, alternative perspectives started to emerge in the 1990s. While not ignoring Western science, these alternatives proposed that science should not try to produce a single, definitive set of objective laws about the environment, nor how to define environmental problems and solutions. Two key results of this dialogue have been the deconstruction (or deglobalization) of existing ideas about nature, environmental problems and their solutions, and the expansion of the number of participants in decision-making, thereby making room for a wider range of values and interests, including the promotion of human rights. The strengthening of participatory approaches has led to the development of local definitions for environmental problems and solutions, and the promotion of traditional knowledges and resource management for local needs (Inoue and Lima 2007). One example of such a local definition is socio-biodiversity, which expresses the idea that biodiversity emerges from the interaction between society and nature.[6] In this sense, socio-environmentalism has linked social-cultural diversity to biodiversity.

The United Nations Convention on Biological Diversity speaks of indigenous populations and local communities but treats each monolithically, ignoring the enormous social diversity encompassed by each category. In contrast, the term "local communities" in Brazil refers to rubber tappers, extractivists, riverine peoples, seaside peoples, *andiro-beiras* (andiroba collectors), fishers, coconut collectors (Babaçu coconut) and so on (Kaingang 2006). Indigenous populations in Brazil comprise a universe of 230 peoples with their own cultures, languages, social organizations and legal systems, as recognized by the Brazilian Federal Constitution. This represents an infinite socio-diversity that, in Kaingang's (2006) perspective, should not be conflated into a single concept. Socio-diversity accounts for mega-biodiversity (Kaingang 2006), which is well captured by the aforementioned concept of socio-biodiversity.

When addressing indigenous and traditional knowledge systems, socio-environmentalism also seeks to value them on their own terms. As a movement, it has asserted the importance of diverse knowledges and ways of being, and the participation of indigenous and traditional peoples in decision-making to shape environmental policies. Kaingang (2006) underscores the potential obstacles to such dialogues, given that indigenous knowledge is rooted primarily in oral traditions, is changing and dynamic, and cannot be divided or "categorized." However, for Santos (2006), a common understanding between "traditional" and "modern" knowledge is possible because both kinds of knowledge maintain some type of conversation with nature, however distinct, in search for solutions to shared problems. So, the question is why only one kind of knowledge, rooted in Western modern rationality, has value? The problem lies in the incapacity to recognize the worth of other ways of knowing that may not be recognized as "scientific," but that nevertheless offer interesting insights into discussion of science and technology. Thus, bringing local traditional populations and indigenous peoples into the debate means recognizing that "science" may well be rooted in a variety of different knowledge systems and worldviews.

Socio-environmentalism and modernity: a step beyond

Recognizing the legitimacy of diverse worldviews and knowledge systems may also offer a means to overcome the growing distance between the magnitude of the environmental crisis in the Anthropocene and the concrete changes needed across the global to local levels. For instance, as suggested above, shamans and scientists both dialogue with nature, albeit in different ways (Santos 2006). However, in order to make effective use of distinct kinds of knowledge, we must first recognize and transcend the power imbalances that exist in the relation between modern Western science and other knowledge systems. Doing so entails moving beyond modernity and its dichotomies (see Chapter 17).

Given the centrality of cultural diversity and the participation of indigenous and traditional peoples in environmental politics in Brazil, socio-environmentalism can also contribute to bridging the society/nature dichotomy and to bringing other forms of knowledge into the debate. We identify two dimensions in which socio-environmentalism encompasses other knowledge systems and other worldviews. One is more pragmatic and recognizes that local/traditional populations and indigenous peoples hold practical knowledge and construct local institutions that are ecologically more sustainable. The other dimension values traditional and indigenous knowledge and other worldviews per se. These are non-modern views about nature, social life, the future and so on that are simply different and should be valued as such.

In sum, socio-environmentalism represents a critique of the limits of modernity through its attempt to go beyond dichotomies (nature/society, North/South, global/local), to change the way in which development is viewed and to promote diversity in worldviews and knowledge systems. In this sense, it can contribute to the view that local peoples' struggles around the planet are more than demands for rights over land or natural "resources" but are also struggles for ways of knowing and living, in which nature and society are not separate but deeply intertwined. In IR, it may well be that socio-environmentalism could more precisely be seen as a plea to "move outside of the standpoints allowed by academic practice and institutions as a prerequisite for building knowledge more meaningful and more relevant to make the world a better place" (Tickner and Blaney 2013: 15).

Conclusion

The idea of the Anthropocene alludes to a planet in which there is no "nature" in the sense of a pristine faraway place untouched by humans. As mentioned by Rudy and White (2013: 129), humans are now a geological force on the planet which has been transformed to such an extent that there is no nature that is in any way straightforwardly "natural." Accordingly, humanity has become the main driver for the equilibrium of the earth system, with which modernity's dichotomy between nature and society no longer makes any sense. Following Leis (1999), we argue that in order to truly incorporate the environmental challenge of the Anthropocene, the social sciences, including IR, need to change their modern premises and acknowledge that: the biosphere is the basis of social life and the human species is only one of many species that live interdependently there; social action frequently produces unexpected results on the environment; and as nature and its resources are finite, there are physical and biological limits for economic growth and human society expansion (Leis 1999: 92–93).

Socio-environmentalism is a lens that can help us to go beyond modernity by providing a framework for new transnational or deterritorialized governance arrangements that gather state and non-state actors from the global and local levels; and for local struggles for lands, rivers, living and non-living beings, ways of knowing and living, or the existence of many worlds (Escobar 2016; Inoue and Moreira 2016). In brief, it can contribute to greening IR by challenging Western modernity's assumption that human beings and societies can be considered apart from nature. As Leis (1999: 141) asserts, "the relation of society to nature cannot be transformed into something passive to be controlled by science; forgetting its wild, unpredictable, and non-rational side, and, as such, uncontrollable." Today, the notions of planetary boundaries and the demands of sustainability underscore the fact that seeking to "conquer" nature is obsolete. Instead, relations between society and nature should be reconstructed and re-organized in the way we produce, consume and relate to each other as groups and individuals. Epistemologically and theoretically, this means looking for other ways of conceiving or broadening our notion of knowledge.

As Tickner and Blaney (2012: 12) have argued, we should look for how concepts get rearticulated in different parts of the world as "everything gets inflected locally." In a world that is in environmental distress, there is a growing need for efficient and equitable responses. This is the great challenge for 21st-century social science: the governance of the Anthropocene. We have claimed throughout this chapter that Amazonian socio-environmentalism has evolved as a potential bridge between global and local governance, as well as different worldviews. In the Amazon, socio-biodiversity has enabled participatory approaches that seek local definitions for environmental problems and solutions, and promotion of the role of traditional knowledge and resource management for local needs (Jeanrenaud 2002). At the local level, the programs, projects and initiatives led by a myriad of actors have evidenced this socio-environmental character and have the potential to contribute with innovative ways to re-construct relations between society and nature.

In relation to earth system governance, such experiences can also be viewed as transnational and multi-actor ways to (re)construct governance from local to global that go beyond the North–South divide that dominates the multilateral negotiation arenas and that has hampered advances among nation-states. As the global–local initiatives in the field have shown, there is room for learning and re-conceptualizing. Perhaps, also, there is room to bridge the gaps between traditional and contemporary knowledge systems.

In sum, the vertical dialogue in socio-environmentalism is evidenced by an active and status quo defiant social movement that has resulted in new global–local governance arrangements with different actors from global to local around norms that have been reframed locally. The horizontal dialogue in socio-environmentalism has brought to the floor the idea of constructing bridges and synergies between different epistemologies and worldviews. Moreover, socio-environmentalism has been conceptualized as a frame that brings together principles related to ecological, social-economic sustainability, social justice and cultural diversity, implying participatory approaches to decision-making. Thus, socio-environmentalism is a concept intrinsically about nature and about society. As such, it can contribute to our search to move outside of the conventional standpoints to find alternatives for meeting the challenges of the Anthropocene.

Questions for discussion

1. Why is the Anthropocene a major challenge for global cooperation and the field of International Relations?
2. What are the vertical and horizontal dialogues that are neglected in contemporary IR regarding the environment? Which are the major shortcomings of traditional IR theories in this regard?
3. How do the dichotomies of modernity, particularly the dualism of the nature–society divide, underlie many of the global environmental problems that humanity face?
4. What are the three major ideas encompassed by the concept and practice of socio-environmentalism?
5. Why is the Amazon region a key locus to assess the relevance of socio-environmentalism as a concept and practice?
6. How can the concept of socio-environmentalism help in the construction of a green IR?
7. How does socio-environmentalism as a concept and a practice contribute to fill the vertical and horizontal gaps in IR regarding the environment?

Notes

1 According to Rockström et al. (2009: 2), "the Earth has entered a new epoch, the Anthropocene, where humans constitute the dominant driver of change to the Earth System" and could "trigger abrupt or irreversible environmental changes that would be deleterious or even catastrophic for human well-being."

2 Egoistical considerations refer to the inclination of most actors in the political, economic and social realm to guide their behavior towards the maximization of individual interest, with little to no regard for other members of their society, both present and future.

3 For example, see the fight to protect the Peace Valley by the West Moberly and Prophet River First Nations. See www.amnesty.ca/get-involved/take-action-now/site-c-bc-government-must-do-right-thing.

4 Besides Chico Mendes' murder, Hochstetler and Keck (2007) offer two other explanations for the emergence of socio-environmentalism in Brazil: the democratic transition and the end of military dictatorship; and the preparatory process for the United Nations Conference on Environment and Development in 1992, that brought together environmental organizations, women's organizations, urban and rural trade unions, and other social movements.

5 Traditional communities and peoples are, according Brazilian legislation, groups that are culturally differentiated and that self-identify as such. Such groups practice their own ways of social organization and occupy and use territory and natural resources as a condition for their cultural, social, religious, economic and ancestral reproduction. They also use knowledge, innovations and practices that are generated and transmitted by tradition (Art 3rd of Decree 6040 of February 7, 2007). Indigenous people, by contrast, are original or native populations from the Americas, named as such because the colonizers believed they had landed in India.

6 More recent debates around the world have focused on the idea of "biocultural diversity." Ethnobiologists introduced this concept to inextricably link the variations within ecological systems to cultural and linguistic differences (Martin et al. 2012).

Further reading

Dauvergne, Peter (2018) *Environmentalism of the Rich*, Cambridge: MIT Press. A reflection on the consequences of environmentalism when based primarily on the concerns of the most affluent sectors of society.

Dryzek, John S. and Jonathan Pickering (2019) *The Politics of the Anthropocene*, First edition, Oxford: Oxford University Press. The book analyzes how humanity's institutions and political practices must change to meet the challenges of the new epoch of the Anthropocene.

Inoue, Cristina Yumie Aoki (2018) "Worlding the Study of Global Environmental Politics: Indigenous Voices from the Amazon," *Global Environmental Politics* 18(4): 25–42. doi:https://doi.org/10.1162/glep_a_00479. This article calls for recognition of indigenous ways of knowing and being in studies of global environmental politics through creative listening and speaking.

Jinnah, Sikina and Simon Nicholson (eds) (2016) *New Earth Politics Essays from the Anthropocene*, Cambridge: The MIT Press. The book offers a reflection on the limitations of governance structures to manage the impact of human activity on the earth system.

Viola, Eduardo and Matías Franchini (2018) *Brazil and Climate Change: Beyond the Amazon*, New York: Routledge. doi:https://doi.org/10.4324/9781315101651. This book offers an assessment of Brazil's role in the global political economy of climate change and provides an accessible introduction to all those studying the challenges of the international system in the Anthropocene.

Wapner, Paul Kevin and Hilal Elver (eds) (2017) *Reimagining Climate Change*, New York: Routledge. This book problematizes the most accepted responses to the climate crisis and offers alternatives.

References

Acharya, Amitav and Barry Buzan (eds) (2009) *Non-Western International Relations Theory: Perspectives on and beyond Asia*, London: Routledge. doi:https://doi.org/10.4324/9780203861431

Adorno, Theodore and Max Horkheimer (1997) *Dialetica do esclarecimento: Fragmentos filosóficos*, Rio de Janeiro: Jorge Zahar Editor.

Behera, Navnita (2009) "Re-imagining IR in India," in Amitav Acharya and Barry Buzan (eds), *Non-Western International Relations Theory: Perspectives on and beyond Asia*, London: Routledge, pp. 92–116. doi:https://doi.org/10.4324/9780203861431

Betsill, Michelle, Kathryn Hochstetler, and Dimitris Stevis (eds) (2014) *Advances in International Environmental Politics*, New York: Palgrave Macmillan. doi:https://doi.org/10.1057/9781137338976

Biermann, Frank, et al. (2009) *Earth System Governance: People, Places and the Planet*, Bonn: IHPD.

Bodmer, Richard, et al. (1997) "Linking Conservation and Local People through Sustainable Use of Natural Resources, Community-Based Management in the Peruvian Amazon," in Curtis H. Freese (ed) *Harvesting Wild Species. Implications for Biodiversity Conservation*, Baltimore: The John Hopkins University Press, pp. 315–358.

Burch, Sarah, et al. (2019) "New Directions in Earth System Governance Research," *Earth System Governance* 1: 100006.

Chasek, Pamela S., David L. Downie, and Janet Welsh Brown (2013) *Global Environmental Politics*, Boulder: Westview Press.

Cohn, Sergio (org.) (2015) *Aliton Krenak*, Coleção Encontros, 1 ed. Rio de Janeiro: Azougue.

Conca, Ken and Geoffrey D. Dabelko (2014) *Green Planet Blues: Critical Perspectives on Global Environmental Politics*, Boulder: Westview Press. doi:https://doi.org/10.4324/9780429493744

Da Cunha, Manuela and Mauro Almeida (2002) *Enciclopedia da floresta*, Rio de Janeiro: Companhia das Letras. www.estantevirtual.com.br/livros/manuela-carneiro-da-cunha/enciclopedia-da-floresta/597884057 (consulted on December 30, 2018).

D'ambrosio, Ubiratan, Roberto Crema, and Pierre Weil (1993) *Rumo à nova transdisciplinaridade: Sistemas abertos de conhecimento*, São Paulo: Summus. www.gruposummus.com.br/gruposummus/livro//Rumo+%C3%A0+Nova+Transdisciplinaridade (consulted on December 23, 2018).

Dauvergne, Peter (ed) (2005) *Handbook of Global Environmental Politics*, Cheltenham: Edward Elgar Publishers. doi:https://doi.org/10.4337/9781849809412

De Búrca, Gráinne, Robert O. Keohane, and Charles Sabel (2014) "Global Experimentalist Governance," *British Journal of Political Science* 44(03): 477–86.

Earth System Governance (2018) *Earth System Governance Science and Implementation Plan*, doi: https://doi.org/10.1016/j.esg.2019.100006 (consulted on December 23, 2018).

Eckersley, Robyn (2010) "Green Theory," in Tim Dunne, Milja Kurki, and Steve Smith (eds) *International Relations Theories: Discipline and Diversity*, Oxford: Oxford University Press, pp. 266–86.

Elliott, Lorraine (2004) *The Global Politics of the Environment*, Second edition, New York: NYU Press. doi:https://doi.org/10.1007/978-1-349-26033-1

Escobar, Arturo (2016) "Thinking-Feeling with the Earth: Territorial Struggles and the Ontological Dimension of the Epistemologies of the South," *AIBR, Revista de Antropología Iberoamericana* 11(1): 11–32.

Finkelstein, Lawrence S. (1995) "What Is Global Governance?" *Global Governance* 1(3): 367–72.

Finnemore, Martha and Kathryn Sikkink (1998) "International Norm Dynamics and Political Change," *International Organization* 52(4): 887–917.

Franchini, Matías (2016) "Trajetória e condicionantes do compromisso climático nas potências Latino-Americanas: Argentina, Brasil, Colômbia, México e Venezuela, 2007–2015," PhD dissertation, University of Brasília.

Frank, David John, Ann Hironaka, and Evan Schofer (2000) "The Nation-State and the Natural Environment over the Twentieth Century," *American Sociological Review* 65(1): 96–116.

Green, Jessica F. and Thomas N. Hale (2017) "Reversing the Marginalization of Global Environmental Politics in International Relations: An Opportunity for the Discipline," *PS: Political Science & Politics* 50(2): 473–79.

Haas, Peter M. (1992) "Introduction: Epistemic Communities and International Policy Coordination," *International Organization* 46(1): 1–35.

Hardin, Garrett (1968) "The Tragedy of the Commons," *Science* 162(3859): 1243–48.

Hochstetler, Kathryn and Margaret E. Keck (2007) *Greening Brazil*, Durham: Duke University Press.

Inoue, Cristina Yumie Aoki (2007) *Regime global de biodiversidade: O caso Mamirauá*, Brasília: Editora UnB.

Inoue, Cristina Yumie Aoki and Guilherme do Prado Lima (eds) (2007) *Reservas sustentáveis: Reflexões sobre a experiência brasileira*, Brasília: Conservação Internacional.

Inoue, Cristina Yumie Aoki and Paula Franco Moreira (2016) "Many Worlds, Many Nature(s), One Planet: Indigenous Knowledge in the Anthropocene," *Revista Brasileira de Política Internacional* 59(2): e009. doi:http://dx.doi.org/10.1590/0034-7329201600209

Jacobs, Jamie Elizabeth (2002) "Community Participation, the Environment, and Democracy: Brazil in Comparative Perspective," *Latin American Politics and Society* 44(04): 59–88.

Jeanrenaud, Sally (2002) *People-Oriented Approaches in Global Conservation: Is the Leopard Changing Its Spots?* International Institute for Environment and Development. http://pubs.iied.org/9134IIED/ (consulted on December 30, 2018).

Kaingang, Fernanda (2006) "Debates in Panel 1," in Fernando Mathias and Henry Novion (eds) *The Crossroad of Modernities: Debates on Biodiversity, Technoscience and Culture*, São Paulo: Instituto Socioambiental, pp. 39–48.

Keck, Margaret E. and Kathryn Sikkink (1998) *Activists beyond Borders: Advocacy Networks in International Politics*, Ithaca: Cornell University Press.

Keohane, Robert O. and Joseph Nye (2011) *Power and Interdependence*, Boston: Pearson.

Krasner, Stephen D. (1983) *International Regimes*, Ithaca: Cornell University Press.

Leis, Hector (1999) *A modernidade insustentavel*, Florianopolis: Vozes UFSC.

Lima, Deborah (1999) "Equity, Sustainable Development, and Biodiversity Preservation: Some Questions about Ecological Partnership in the Brazilian Amazon," in Christine Padoch (ed), *Varzea: Diversity, Development, and Conservation of Amazonia's Whitewater Floodplains*, New York: New York Botanical Garden, pp. 247–63.

Ling, L. H. M. (2013) *The Dao of World Politics: Towards a Post-Westphalian, Worldist International Relations*, London: Routledge. doi:https://doi.org/10.4324/9781315887777

Marcuse, Herbert (1975) *Eros e civilizacao*, Rio de Janeiro: Zahar Editores.

Martin, Gary, Diana Mincyte, and Ursula Münster (2012) "Why Do We Value Diversity? Biocultural Diversity in a Global Context," *RCC Perspectives* no 9. www.environmentandsociety.org/perspectives/2012/9/why-do-we-value-diversity-biocultural-diversity-global-context

Morin, Edgar (1998) *O metodo 4: As ideias*, Porto Alegre: Editora Sulina.

Narby, Jeremy (1999) *The Cosmic Serpent: DNA and the Origins of Knowledge*, New York: Tarcher.

Nicholson, Simon and Sikina Jinnah (eds) (2016) "New Earth Politics: Essays from the Anthropocene," *Global Environmental Politics* 17(1): 129–31.

Okereke, Chukwumerije, Harriet Bulkeley, and Heike Schroeder (2009) "Conceptualizing Climate Governance beyond the International Regime," *Global Environmental Politics* 9(1): 58–78.

Ostrom, Elinor (2009) *A Polycentric Approach for Coping with Climate Change*, https://openknowledge.worldbank.org/bitstream/handle/10986/4287/WPS5095.pdf

Pádua, José Augusto (2002) *Um sopro de destruição: Pensamento político e crítica ambiental no brasil escravista (1786–1888)*, Rio de Janeiro: Jorge Zahar Editor.

Park, Jacob, Ken Conca, and Matthias Finger (eds) (2008) *The Crisis of Global Environmental Governance: Towards a New Political Economy of Sustainability*, London: Routledge. https://doi.org/10.4324/9780203929100

Paterson, Matthew (1996) *Global Warming and Global Politics*, London and New York: Routledge.

Paterson, Matthew (2014) "Theoretical Perspectives on International Environmental Politics," in Michelle Betsill, Kathryn Hochstetler, and Dimitris Stevis (ed), *Advances in International Environmental Politics*, New York: Palgrave Macmillan, pp. 54–81. doi:https://doi.org/10.1057/9781137338976

Pereira, Joana Castro (2017) "The Limitations of IR Theory Regarding the Environment: Lessons from the Anthropocene," *Revista Brasileira de Política Internacional* 60(1): e018. doi:http://dx.doi.org/10.1590/0034-73292017001019

Porter, Gareth, Janet Welsh Brown, and Pamela S. Chasek (2000) *Global Environmental Politics*, Boulder: Westview Press.

Ramos, Alcida (2013) "Mentes indígenas e ecúmeno antropológico," *Série Antropologia* 439, Brasília: DAN/UnB.

Rockström, Johan et al. (2009) "Planetary Boundaries: Exploring the Safe Operating Space for Humanity," *Ecology and Society* 14(2): 32.

Rosenau, James N. (1995) "Governance, Order, and Change in World Politics," in James N. Rosenau and Ernst O. Czempiel (eds), *Governance without Government: Order and Change in World Politics*, Cambridge: Cambridge University Press, pp. 1–29.

Rudy, Alan and Carl White (2013) "Hybridity," in Carl Death (ed), *Critical Environmental Politics*, London: Routledge, pp. 121–32.

Santilli, Juliana (2005) *Socioambientalismo e novos direitos*, Brasilia – São Paulo: Editora Fundação Peirópolis.

Santos, Laymert (2006) "Replies from the Panel: The Crossroads of Modernities," in Fernando Mathias and Henry Novion (eds), *The Crossroad of Modernities: Debates on Biodiversity, Technoscience and Culture*, São Paulo: Instituto Socioambiental, pp. 197–202.

Steffen, Will et al. (2015) "Planetary Boundaries: Guiding Human Development on a Changing Planet," *Science* 347(6223), http://science.sciencemag.org/content/347/6223/1259855 (consulted on August 28, 2017).

Steinberg, Paul F. and Stacy D. VanDeveer (2012) *Comparative Environmental Politics: Theory, Practice, and Prospects*, Cambridge: The MIT Press.

Stevis, Dimitris (2014) "The Trajectory of International Environmental Politics," in Michelle Betsill, Kathryn Hochstetler, and Dimitris Stevis (eds) *Advances in International Environmental Politics*, New York: Palgrave Macmillan, pp. 13–44. doi:https://doi.org/10.1057/9781137338976

Strange, Susan (1982) "Cave! Hic Dragones: A Critique of Regime Analysis," *International Organization* 36(2): 479–96.

Tickner, Arlene B. and David L. Blaney (2012) "Introduction: Thinking Difference," in Arlene B. Tickner and David L. Blaney (eds) *Thinking International Relations Differently*, London and New York: Routledge.

Tickner, Arlene B. and David L. Blaney (2013) *Claiming the International*, Worlding Beyond the West series, London and New York: Routledge.

Viola, Eduardo and Matías A. Franchini (2018) *Brazil and Climate Change: Beyond the Amazon*, New York: Routledge. doi:https://doi.org/10.4324/9781315101651

Viola, Eduardo, Matías Franchini, and Thaís Ribeiro (2013) *Sistema internacional de hegemonia conservadora*: *Governança global e democracia na era da crise climática*, São Paulo: Annablume.

WWF-Brazil and ISER (2001) *Desenvolvimento e conservação do meio ambiente: Pesquisa de opinião com lideranças e a população a Amazônia*. Brasília: WWF-Brazil and ISER.

Part 4

Futures

17 South–South talk

L.H.M. Ling and Carolina M. Pinheiro

Introduction

> First we were populations; then [we became] issues; eventually we were recognized as peoples.
>
> Oren Lyons, Chief of the Haudenosaunee (Iroquois) Confederation[1]

In the quote above, Lyons is referring to a vote taken at the United Nations (UN) in 2007. The UN Permanent Forum on Indigenous Issues (UNPFII) finally approved the Declaration on Indigenous Rights of Indigenous Peoples after 20 years of negotiation. But to Sharon Venne, a Cree indigenous leader, this seeming success bears an original failure: another "colonizing process," the UNPFII forces indigenous peoples to fit their structures and claims into Western/Westphalian institutions, mainstream their languages to national and international discourses and acquire foreign legal concepts to attain "approval" (Venne quoted in Watson 2007: 116). Earlier, Norbet Rouland (2004: 526) had derided such tactics as a "Trojan horse." Where there is no choice but to use foreign institutions and languages, he stressed, there can be no emancipation. Colonization simply takes on another guise.

Indeed, real communication rarely takes place in world politics. Paraphrasing Thucydides on power, "the strong [speak of] what they can, the weak [listen to] what they must." Liberal internationalism may enshrine "tolerance" and "free speech" as standards of communication but, as pointed out by the case above and critics in this volume as well as elsewhere (Hutchings 2011; Jahn 2013), participants must conform to Western "modernity," "rationality" and "rule of law," among others, before any talking, let alone listening, can take place. Set by the West for the West, these prerequisites ensure who speaks and who must listen (Keene 2002). As Rajiv Malholtra (2011: 16) notes, tolerance is a "patronizing posture." It suggests a resigned acceptance that difference exists but does not necessarily deserve legitimacy or respect. Liberal internationalism, in other words, allows the West to tolerate but not always respect the Rest, thereby reinforcing the hegemony of the West.

And the results are predictable. Nineteenth-century Japan, for example, opted to emulate the West by applying "reverse Orientalism" (Nakano 2011) to its neighbors. For several decades, Japan seemed the only Asian nation "successful" enough to join the Western club of imperialist powers; it colonized Taiwan in 1895, annexed Korea in 1910 and occupied various parts of Southeast Asia during World War II. But imperial Japan ended with atomic devastation on its own people in 1945. Today, groups like al Qaeda and ISIS, the Taliban and Boko Haram ("Western education is prohibited") have embarked on a similar cycle: they take on Westphalian violence to avenge Westphalian violence. As history demonstrates, such violence against Others only begets more violence and ultimately against the Self. This is a tragedy too-oft played.

We redirect the conversation. Instead of focusing on discourse between the "West" and the "Rest," we show how the global South can speak with and listen to each other – a "chat" among friends, so to speak – and, in the process, improve communication between North and South. We extend this South–South chat to knowledge production, not just discourse. That is, we demonstrate an alignment of *epistemes* of the global South, by the global South, for the global South. We do so, in this case, by matching worldism in International Relations (IR) with another intellectual movement initiated in Latin America and southern Europe now spreading to other parts of the globe.[2] Sociologist Boaventura de Sousa Santos (2014) coins it "epistemologies of the South." This movement aims to staunch the "epistemicide" perpetrated by Northern colonialism and imperialism onto itself as well as Others for the past five centuries. Santos declares three founding principles to "epistemologies of the South":

> First, the understanding of the world by far exceeds the Western understanding of the world. Second, there is no global social justice without global cognitive justice. Third, the emancipatory transformation in the world may follow grammars and scripts other than those developed by Western-centric critical theory, and such diversity should be valorized.
>
> (Santos 2014: viii)

This chapter begins by introducing worldism and its model of dialogics or what we prefer to call "chatting."[3] We show how worldist chatting, guided by Daoist *yin/yang* dialectics, enables engagement across and within subaltern worlds on three counts: by revealing opportunities for *discursive agency* (relationality), by recognizing *political solidarity* from disparate voices at disparate sites (resonance) and by developing *ethics with compassion* as a guide to action (interbeing). Specifically, worldist chatting leads to creative listening and speaking (CLS) as a method.[4] To demonstrate, we apply CLS to two traditions never introduced: Daoism from East Asia and the Andean cosmovision from South America.[5] We call their resultant, integrated entity, *yin/yang pacha* (Figure 17.1). It offers guidelines on how to reconsider IR and world politics.

Subsequently, we do the same with worldism and "epistemologies of the South." Significant commonalities surface, producing what we call South–South talk: relationality highlights multiple understandings of the world, not just one; resonance shows where discursive and political solidarity may arise; and interbeing demonstrates emancipatory transformation as a kind of trans-subjective co-creativity. We gain additional insights and strategies as well: why some always speak, forcing Others to listen and even when the latter speak, few in the mainstream pay attention; how resonances among disparate sources enact global cognitive justice; where emancipatory transformation, with its alternative "grammars and scripts," can take us; and a recognition of epistemic "incompleteness": that is, no *episteme* can – or should – do it all. With *yin/yang pacha* as an example, South–South talk begins to build a platform for transformation on a global scale: it provides a stronger basis for North–South talk, and it articulates a conscientious Other in world politics. The conscientious Other's ancient traditions and practices serve as a check to any contemporary claims made by Westphalia-internalized, self-aggrandizing rogue Others.

Let us now review worldism: what it is, where it comes from and why it is relevant for IR.

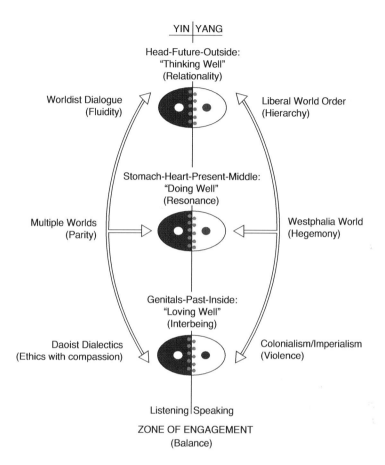

Yin/Yang Pacha

Figure 17.1 Yin/yang pacha
Source: L.H.M. Ling (2014)

Worldism

Visually, worldism resembles this painting (Figure 17.2), "Universe," by the Buddhist monk Sengai Gibon (1750–1837).

In one brush stroke, Sengai brings forth a circle, square and triangle. But each also relates to the others intimately; none could exist on its own. All three *co-create* the whole at different junctures and through different types of contact (circle and square intersect at one point, for example, compared to a whole segment linking the bottom of the circle through the middle of the square to the tip of the triangle). These nodes of interaction could induce a "clash of civilizations," as suggested by Samuel P. Huntington (1993, 1996), or "gnosis" (integration) among them, as observed by Walter Mignolo (2000). In either case, the overall picture subsumes both clashes and integrations into a larger picture of co-creativity. Yet the last brush stroke remains incomplete. It hints at the possibility of an unexpected transformation, even under a seemingly stable and overarching rubric.

Figure 17.2 "Universe"

Source: Painting by Sengai Gibon (1750–1838) titled "Universe"; see www.raisethehammer.org/
static/images/sengai.jpg

Worldism views world politics similarly, reflecting what the late Paul Feyerabend (1999) called a "richness of being." It posits that social diversity and conceptual abundance have as much significance in scientific inquiry as analytical rigor and methodological parsimony. In world politics, in particular, worldism asserts that *multiple worlds* course through and across civilizations, making them what they are. These multiple worlds register distinctions among civilizations (e.g., Daoist, Muslim, Christian) but also their cultural connections over the millennia through trade and commerce (e.g., the silk roads, European mercantilism), wars and conquests (e.g., Central African, Chinese, Mongol, Ottoman, Persian and Roman empires), not to mention pilgrimages and devotions (e.g., Buddhist treks, Muslim *hajj*, Christian crusades), culminating into various strands of trans-cultural, trans-subjectivity. For worldism, such trans-subjectivity constitutes the "stuff" of daily life, especially in globalized times.

Daoist dialectics

Daoist dialectics underpin worldism. As an epistemology, Daoism suits worldism's emphasis on interconnectivities and trans-subjectivities, change and transformation, despite conflicts and contradictions. Symbolized by *yin* (the black sphere of the female principle) and *yang* (the white sphere of the male principle), Daoist dialectics frame multiple worlds as integrating opposites. Their interweaving complicities produce an organic whole comprised of new permutations of *yin* and *yang*, blackness and whiteness, despite their confrontations as polar opposites. Unlike Hegelian/Marxian dialectics, which treat each polarity as a singular category (Cheng 2006; Brincat and Ling 2014), Daoist dialectics implicate each polarity within the other: that is, *yin*-within-*yang* (black-within-white) and *yang*-within-*yin* (white-within-black). Consequently, one polarity could not harm the other without also harming itself – and from the inside. The reverse applies as well: one polarity benefits itself by benefiting the other. These complementarities bind *despite* the conflicts and contradictions that pull the polarities apart. Indeed, change and transformation define the *dao*. "[It] is conceived as a generative unity of polarities which exist in opposition as well as in complementation," writes Chung-ying Cheng (2006: 28), "in terms of this unity, change is not only explained but the variety of things is also explained."

More than positing a model of knowledge, Daoism *senses* it. That is, Daoism values contextualizing knowledge in time, place and – significantly – feeling. "There is no view from nowhere, no external perspective, no decontextualized vantage point. We are all in the soup" (Ames and Hall 2003: 18).[6] A famous excerpt from the *Zhuangzi* illustrates this point (Ames 1998). It tells of a conversation between Master Zhuang and his dear friend and intellectual sidekick, Hui Shi. Strolling on a bridge over the River Hao one fine day, Master Zhuang remarks that the fishes must be enjoying themselves. "How do you know," challenges Hui Shi, "since you're not a fish?" In effect, Master Zhuang replies:

> How do you know I don't know? And the fact that you asked me how I know must mean that you suspect I know. I know because I'm standing here over this bridge relishing the day, the conversation, and the fishes.

In other words, explains Roger Ames, "[i]t is the situation rather than some discrete agent that is properly described (and prescribed) as happy" (Ames 1998: 221). Master Zhuang enters into subjectivity with the general condition of the day so he extrapolates that the fishes, too, must be happy. Otherwise, how could everything *feel* so right?

Creativity, suggests the *dao*, proliferates upon itself but not in isolation. Just as one wave of the sea rolls into another, so creativity rises through individual *and* collective talent. Opportunities for both "*self*-creativity and *co*-creativity [are] contextual, transactional, and multidimensional," Cheng underscores (2006: 17). Each stimulates the other. "To be fully integrative," writes Roger Ames (1998: 4) on the *Zhuangzi*, a partner text to the *Daodejing* (Classic of the Way), "individuals must overcome the sense of discreteness and discontinuity with their environment, and they must contribute personally and creatively to the emerging pattern and regularity of existence called *dao*" (Ames 1998: 4). Like drops of water, the world's "myriad things" (*wanwu*), could seem small and inconsequential on their own but, once combined, they can shape and change the universe. Ontological parity, the *dao* reminds us, inheres in all.

Worldism thus recasts IR/world politics into a complex of entwined and entwining social relations. Interactive, iterative logics operate at multiple levels and in multiple ways, constituting a *world-of-worlds*. Whereas others (Arisaka 1996; Goto-Jones 2005; Katzenstein 2009) have presented a similar notion, placing global politics under one framework like "Western modernity," worldism sees globality emanating from below. It is the exchange among multiple worlds that makes the world-of-worlds. In this way, worldism opens inter-state politics to constant interaction, change and eventually transformation, reflecting various types of trans-cultural and trans-systemic mixing, both across worlds and within them, over the millennia and ongoing today.

Worldist dialogics ("chatting")

A model of worldist dialogics emerges. We prefer to call it "chatting." Three main queries begin the chat:

- Relationality: "Who says what to whom and why?" Worldist relationality stems from the Daoist premise of ontological parity. In granting equal significance to every thing and every one, no matter how small, ontological parity posits that social power takes place *despite* structural inequities. Accordingly, relationality surveys the power relations that underpin a discourse (Enloe 2001; Tickner 2011). At the same time, another insight surfaces: "Where are the silences and how can the silenced talk back, not just speak up?"
- Resonance: "Where is change coming from and what does it mean?" Creative transformation combined with respect for local knowledge urge us to pay attention to change: what is it, where is it arising and why is it significant for local as well as global communities? The concept of resonance, as we use it here, reflects the ancient Daoist-Confucian observation that when the string of a musical instrument is plucked, it vibrates a corresponding string in another instrument nearby (Li 2004). Resonance connects the vibes, so to speak, so we may hear the common song arising from disparate voices in disparate places. Resonance implements the Daoist principle of identifying an "underlying unity and its particularities" that signal an "ethical and socio-political order *and* the divergence from order" (Li 1994: 400, original emphasis).
- Interbeing: "How can I act with ethics *and* compassion?" Worldism takes knowledge production to mean more than individual agency; it involves action in and for a larger context that demands both ethics and compassion. Ethics without compassion tends to punish; and compassion without ethics tends to dissipate into goodwill only. In worldist chatting, ethics-with-compassion guide communication across borders, identities, paradigms or any kind of subjective divide. Worldist chatting aims for what the Buddhist monk and teacher Thich Nhat Hanh (1998) calls "interbeing,"[7] an update of the ancient Sanskrit notion of "co-dependent arising" (*pratītyasamutpāda*). Interbeing treats the Self as a reverberative subjectivity: it derives meaning from "flows" through Others ("I *am* because of you, you *are* because of me").[8] Sometimes, interbeing suggests, action could take the form of stillness, presence or simply being.

In sum, relationality helps us recognize *discursive agency* of, by and for subalterns. Resonance identifies the possibility of *political solidarity* that comes with such voicing. And interbeing accounts for the purpose of both: *ethics-with-compassion* to guide action. All three contribute to a worldist method of cross-paradigmatic, trans-subjective communication: creative listening and speaking.

Creative listening and speaking

CLS explores a "third space" or what we call a "global oasis" across multiple worlds (Ling unpublished).[9] It momentarily brackets social conventions like "powerful" vs. "powerless" or "rich" vs. "poor" to enable another venue for engagement. Given its buffeted nature, a global oasis allows mutuality to develop *despite* structural asymmetries; consequently, another way of thinking and doing, being and relating emerges. This development invariably spills over into other parts of Self and Other, transforming the old and the conventional, from the individual to the world. In this way, mutual antagonisms begin to dissolve and mutually adapt, accommodate, reformulate and integrate; otherwise, the world would have blown apart long ago.

CLS thus approximates chatting. Where Self and Other may have begun as strangers, they easily attain intimacy as they listen to and speak with each other *creatively*: that is, allowing one's ontological horizons not just to meet but also engage with those of another. From this knowledge of the Other, integrated with knowledge of the Self, a new language emerges. It enables a more fluid, porous and intimate understanding of social and global relations. And yet, like the last brush stroke in Sengai's painting, CLS does not expect "completion" in any encounter, epistemic or otherwise. Simply movement towards mutual understanding would suffice, thereby perforating the binary of hegemony *or* emancipation.

By analogy, we draw on the poetic imagery of Hermann Hesse's *Siddhartha* (1957). An elegant synthesis of Buddhist philosophy with German sensibility, Hesse's novel, like the *dao*, philosophizes about life through reference to water but in the form of a river. Mystical, inspirational and generative, the river would "flo[w] and flo[w] and yet it was always there, it was always the same and yet every moment was new" (Hesse 1957: 104). Hesse suggested listening as carefully as a river, and speaking as truthfully as its flow. "Above all," Hesse wrote about his protagonist, Siddhartha, a wandering, questioning soul like the Buddha, "he learned from [the river] how to listen, to listen with a still heart, with a waiting, open soul, without passion, without desire, without judgment, without opinions" (Hesse 1957: 109). Precisely so, Siddhartha learns how to speak eloquently about the meaning and meaninglessness of life. As an old man, Siddhartha looks at the river and savors the moment: "The bird, the clear spring and voice within him was still alive, that was why he rejoiced, that was why he laughed, that was why his face was radiant under his grey hair" (Hesse 1957: 100).

CLS aims for a similar ebb and flow. It suggests tactics like reversals and intersections, mutual sharing and learning, and visions of co-presence/authority (more below). At the same time, to keep the joy of – and opening for – enlightenment alive, CLS draws on Daoism's subsidiary *wu* ("non") forms to stay vigilant against hegemony. Ames and Hall (2003: 48) explain what these are and how they work:

> [Daoism's *wu*-forms] all advocate a personal disposition that seeks to optimize relationships through collaborative actions that, in the absence of coercion, enable one to make the most of any situation. It is the uniqueness of each situation that requires any generalization about this optimal disposition to be stated in negative terms.

Augmented by Daoist *wu*-forms, CLS proceeds accordingly:

- Reversals and intersections: these alter conventional power relations. One way to do so is by (re)naming. "Nam[ing] the world," Paolo Freire ([1970] 2000: 167) observed, can "transform it." The creative, verbal act of naming triggers an engagement between listening and speaking; it releases what obstructs the free flow of communication. Two *wu*-

forms pertain especially here: *wuming* ("naming without a fixed reference")[10] and *wuzhi* ("unprincipled knowing").[11] Both emphasize knowledge-making as an undetermined process ("a feeling and a doing"). Hence, *wuming* and *wuzhi* prompt CLS to ask: "How many different names does one thing have (or could have)? Conversely, how many different things have the same name (or could have)? Why? What do these variations say about the social relations behind naming?" In this way, CLS keeps the dialogue open, fluid, creative and accepting of difference.

- Mutual learning and sharing: mutual learning indicates sources of change and where reinforcements may occur. Such resonance across disparate sites or subjects dismantles that which sustains binaries: mute listening and deaf speaking. Mute listening refers to listening without the courage to speak; and deaf speaking, a monologue without the humility to listen. *Wuzheng* ("striving without contentiousness")[12] and *wushi* ("non-interference")[13] temper this process. Both caution against power's usual tricks, such as manipulation, coercion or interference. Instead, CLS shifts the dialogical relationship from one of potential offensiveness vs. defensiveness to that approaching reconciliation. *Wuzheng* and *wushi* urge CLS to ask: "What kind of changes does mutual learning produce, and what does it signify?"
- Visions of co-presence/authority: these become possible. CLS moves dialogue beyond a presence of difference to recognition of mutuality. Here, *wuxin* ("unmediated thinking and feeling")[14] and *wuyu* ("objectless desire")[15] are especially salient. *Wuxin*, conventionally translated as "no-mind," does not mean the lack of thought; rather, it refers to refraining from imposing a predetermined intentionality to anything or anyone. Similarly, *wuyu* does not seek to abstain from or deny desire but, rather, to "celebrate and to enjoy" what *deserves* to be desired: that is, a desire based on respect (Ames and Hall 2003: 42). With these Daoist concepts, CLS addresses not only the specifics of discourse (who, what, where, how, when) but also how these produce a context of power. *Wuxin* and *wuyu* encourage CLS to ask: "Where are the silences (*yin*), undertaken by whom (*yin* or *yang*) and for what purpose (*yang*-within-*yin*)? Similarly, where are the noises (*yang*), undertaken by whom (*yin* or *yang*) and for what purpose (*yin*-within-*yang*)? And, most profoundly, what kinds of desire are in effect and how can they be reframed?"

The next two sections show CLS in action. *Yin/yang pacha* from Daoism and Andcanism demonstrates CLS in substance; South–South talk from worldism and "epistemologies of the South," as a mode of inquiry. Both cases underscore how epistemic reversals and intersections can shift power relations in discourse (relationality), and mutual learning and sharing (resonance) addresses the demand for global cognitive justice. In so doing, CLS shifts the "grammars and scripts" of emancipatory transformation (interbeing) beyond the usual parameters of Western knowledge. Hegemony crumbles in due course, not just for the mind and the body, but also the heart and the soul. Equally important, visions of co-presence/authority *sustain* emancipatory transformation.[16]

Yin/yang pacha

Yin/yang pacha urges us to "live well" in, through and across "multiple worlds." Integrating Daoism's ontological parity for all things with Andeanism's principle of "living well," *yin/yang pacha* revolves around three key concepts: pairing, balancing and harmonizing. To understand how such worldist trans-subjectivity can take place, we must first explain the Andean notion of "living well."

Andean "living well"

"Living well" comes from the indigenous peoples of the Andes: the Quechuas, Aymaras and other communities in the region. They regard life's objective as "seeking for and creating the spiritual and material conditions to build and sustain the *good life* or the *harmonious life*" (Gualinga 2002: 1). The Quechua refer to this state of mind – also considered the greatest level of development – as *alli káusai* or *súmac káusai*, translating into the general concept of "living well." Living well means harmonizing with Mother Earth or *pachamama* in whose being everything lives and which constantly evolves: mountains, rivers, insects, trees, stones, our ancestors and so on. All creatures are integral to a permanent transformative process that never happens in isolation. Everything is interconnected, interrelated and interdependent. Living well requires, therefore, respecting the cycles of life while staying aware that "the deterioration of one species is the deterioration of the whole" (Huanacuni 2010).

Two interrelated concepts guide the Andean goal of harmony: complementarity and reciprocity. The squared cross (*chakana*) and crossed hands (*manos cruzadas*) symbolize these principles, respectively.

Pairing in complementarity: squared cross

Like Daoist *yin* and *yang*, Andeanism recognizes a "proportional confrontation" (*yanan-tinkuy*) or complementarity in opposition (Lajo 2006). Everything and everyone has a pair: cold/hot, darkness/light, male/female, West/rest and so on. No pairing can cause destruction. On the contrary, all complementarity between things, thoughts or peoples indicates a path to harmony or interconnected growth. If something seems singular, without a pair, that is only temporary or an illusion.

The squared cross (*chakana*) symbolizes complementarity (Ureña 2004) for its symmetry (see Figure 17.3). It ritually expresses the dimension of time and space by a cyclic movement in which constant confrontation occurs between complementary dualities (e.g., up/down, left/right) resulting in a continuous process of transition, fusion and transformation. Human beings locate at the center, representing our continuous attempts to balance all dual forces.

In organizing the world into pairs, the Andean cosmovision not only considers the circumstances for balance, but also those for imbalance. From time to time, when complementarity is disrupted, the world requires a *re*-balancing (*pachakuti*)[17] that comes through either catastrophe or renovation (Rivera 1991). This can be applied to a vast range of crises, whether environmental, economic and/or political. For instance, Andean populations have prophesied a *pachakuti* that will redress current ecological imbalances including climate change. Global terrorism and recent attacks on U.S. missions overseas also signify a kind of re-balancing through destruction.

Balancing from reciprocity: to receive, one must first give

Along with complementarity, Andeanism values reciprocity (*ayni*). It comes not only with observations about the cycles of nature but also in the community's responsibilities *to* nature, as expressed in this statement:

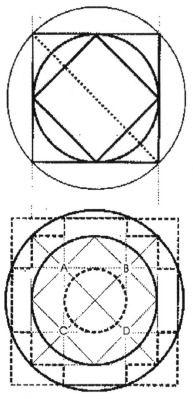

Figure 17.3 The Andean cross or *chakana*
Source: Javier Lajo (2006). Use for publication authorized by Javier Lajo

> The Sun is Wak'a in Capac Raymi, Summer Solstice in December. When it is strong, it gives us heat. But during winter, it is only a weak member of the Andean community. In fulfilling the mandate of Ayni, we must reciprocate for its past assistance. Thus, the Community symbolically warms the sun by lighting bonfires and sending it a comforting ceremonial bowl with meat.[18]

This passage tells of our moral obligation to reciprocate or engage in permanent exchange for every action and thought in nature and amongst human beings, including the sun. If the sun warms us during summer, we should warm the sun during the winter.

The icon of "crossed hands" represents *ayni* or the Andean law of reciprocity. Milla Villena (2003, 2011) has studied almost 20 artifacts of this icon. The oldest piece dates from almost 5,000 years ago and the most recent 20 years ago. In some of these icons, "the act of giving is expressed by placing the palm of the right hand over the heart and the action of receiving the palm of the left hand placed on the stomach" (Milla Villena 2003: 127). In other cases, the hands are represented as a mirror: the right hand is turned

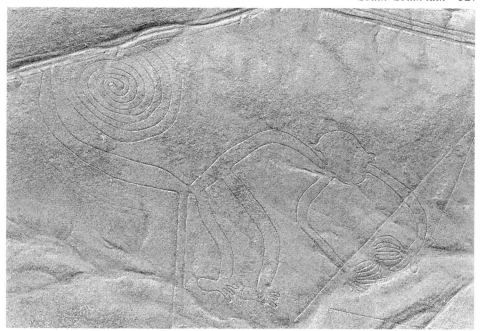

Figure 17.4 Nazca monkey

Source: Wikicommons

Note: See https://commons.wikimedia.org/wiki/File:Nazca_monkey.jpg#file *Pacha* (time-space-body) stems from complementarity and reciprocity

up while the left hand faces downward, to indicate giving and receiving.[19] A drawing of a monkey has five fingers on the left hand and four on the right (see Figure 17.4). The difference is due to the drawing perspective of the left hand receiving and the right hand giving. Its uncrossed arms show the cyclical nature of this principle: if you receive, you must give back and if you give, you receive.

Harmonizing through *pacha*: Andean time-space-body

Pacha crystallizes the Andean principles of complementarity and reciprocity. In one sense, *pacha* can be translated as "nature" or "reality" (Rodriguez 1999). For instance, *pachamama* is usually understood as Mother Earth and *pachakamaz*, the world creator. Reality for the Andean peoples comprises everything that exists, both material and spiritual, animate and inanimate (Huanacuni 2010). This implies that human interaction with reality encompasses communication with all things and beings, including the unseen and the unfelt. Spiritual communication becomes logical when the time dimension of *pacha* reveals not a linear understanding of past, present and future but a spherical one. In linear understanding, the past is behind us; whereas, in a spherical notion, the past is not dead but very much alive. This understanding implies that the world *always has the potential to change* since the past can turn into the future. Everything is alive and inter-connected, even when it belongs to the past or has not been born yet. In so doing, the Andean cosmovision renders "the past ... capable of redeeming the future" (Mamami quoted in Rivera Cusicanqui 1991: 21). Thus while on earth time passes and humans age, in the Andean cosmos, humans are alive even when dead, and the universe develops eternally (Milla Villena 2011).

Three concentric spheres graph *pacha* (see Figure 17.5). These convey *pacha* as time that flows from the inside-past (our origin) to the outside-future (our goal), and back again, returning and recycling constantly.

The external sphere, *hanan pacha*, expresses the future or potential world. It is the world that is becoming: an "outside" world that remains yet unknown. The future exists but in potential form only. *Uku pacha* signifies the "inside," the past, a world that one does not always remember, as it might belong to a different life. And *kay pacha* indicates the "here and now." It reflects what humans can capture from the complementarity between the outside-potential (*hanan pacha*) and the inside-past (*uku pacha*). The here-and-now results from either equilibrium or imbalance between the fundamental pairing of past and potential (Lajo 2006).

Complementarity (*yanan-tinkuy*) manifests most explicitly in the here-and-now. Examples echo *yin-yang* dialectics: cold/hot, female/male, darkness/light and so on. The here-and-now itself, though, is also a product of complementarity. The dimension of here-and-now (*kay pacha*) bridges the other spheres (*hanan pacha* and *uku pacha*). It is at this juncture that humans develop their abilities and knowledge to create and recreate harmony. Harmony thus is a dynamic state.

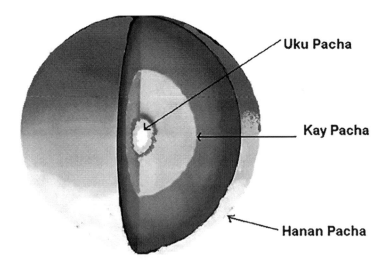

Figure 17.5 Andean time-space

Source: Javier Lajo (2006). Use for publication authorized by Javier Lajo

While imbalance produces abnormalities, too much equilibrium also harms because it can immobilize the world (Lajo 2006). This is why living well requires an art of equilibrium between complementary pairs. But how is harmony achieved? Three principles apply: we must "think well" (*allin yachay*) for the outside-future; we must "do well" (*allin ruay*) in the here-and-now; and we must "love well" (*allin munay*) in the inside-past. Moreover, each activity relates to a part of the human body: head, heart/stomach and genitals, respectively (see Figure 17.6).

All is equal in value and significance. "To think well" (*allin yachay*) represents the principle of knowledge or wisdom through which one can decipher "reasons and words, but not more than that" (Lajo 2006: 152). Given the potentiality (abstractness) of ideas and thoughts, "to think well" is linked with the outside-future and associated with the head, through which human intelligence manifests as much as communication with spiritual entities guides. "To love well" (*allin munay*) conveys the principle of loving or

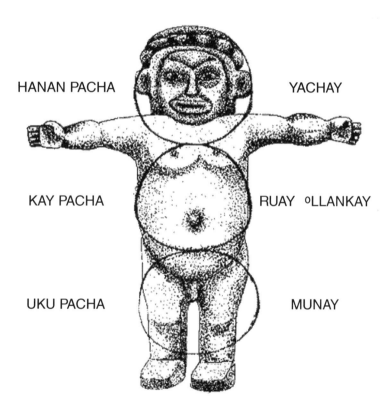

Figure 17.6 Andean time-space-body

Source: Javier Lajo (2006). Use for publication authorized by Javier Lajo

wanting. It also signifies a conscious will that projects the ability to feel and guarantees physical and cultural reproduction. "To love well" reflects a history of living and loving; consequently, it is associated with the inside-past and symbolized by the genitals. But "to love well" encompasses much more: it emphasizes the need to know *how* to feel and love not just oneself or one's beloved but also one's community, the environment, Mother Earth and the cosmos. "To do well" (*allin ruay*) stems from guidance from the other two principles as one works or seeks to "do" in the world. Associated with the heart and stomach, "to do well" pairs with the notion of the here-and-now so it could expand to be closer to or retract from the inside-past or the outside-future. For Andeans, disconnecting the present (our hearts and stomachs) from the future (our heads) or the past (our genitals) always causes imbalance and becomes a source of illness (Lajo 2006). To do well in the here-and-now, then, reflects thinking well about the outside-future and loving well in the inside-past. Maintaining harmony requires a constant movement between time-space-body towards harmony.

In sum, the Andean cosmovision invites us to view human beings and their civilizations as a kind of diversity in unity.[20] Andeanism's laws of complementarity and reciprocity demand constant interaction and connections through life. Moreover, this philosophy provides us with concrete and practical guidance towards balance and harmony as individuals and collectives, whether it is psychologically, materially, temporally and/or spiritually. To live well requires harmonizing across all three levels of being: knowing well from the head about the outside-future in conjunction with loving well from the inside-past as remembered by the genitals to enable doing well in the here-present as felt by the heart and digested by the stomach. In this way, the process remains always open and subject to change.

Yin/yang pacha gives us another take on world politics (see Figure 17.1). First and foremost, hegemony in world politics (*yang*) accounts for only half the picture; the other half (*yin*) consists of multiplicity, dialogue and ethics-with-compassion. Because little global norths exist within the global South (*yang*-within-*yin*), much as little global souths exist within the global North (*yin*-within-*yang*), their dialectical interaction compels change and transformation. Accordingly, global relations *necessarily* operate in an open system, making engagement in world politics both a goal and a fact of daily life. Given the time-space-body dynamic of *pacha*, we see, also, that future designs for global relations (e.g., a liberal world order) based on but not accounting for past atrocities (e.g., colonialism and imperialism) renders hegemony as the only course possible for the present. Only by suppressing the past could the same heinous acts enter the future as glory. For this reason, mainstream IR emphasizes the *yang* side of world politics only, whether in affirmation ("this is the way things are and always will be") or rejection ("Revolution!"). *Yin/yang pacha* reveals: we need to reconcile the future with the past to achieve any kind of justice for the present. *Yin* and *yang*, as in the *pacha*, must balance. South–South talk paves the way.

South–South talk

"Epistemologies of the South" and worldism share a common epistemic and political agenda. It centers on the following: relationality foregrounds multiple *epistemes* at work by examining the power relations in discourse; resonance advances global justice by identifying and connecting various voices of subaltern cognition at various sites; and interbeing reinterprets emancipatory transformation as a kind of trans-subjective co-creativity. This convergence stimulates additional queries: why do some always speak, putting others in the position of listening more than they are listened to? How does discursive solidarity turn into political solidarity? Where do alternative "grammars and scripts" of emancipatory transformation take us? And what's the significance of recognizing "incompleteness": that is, no *episteme* can or should do it all? These queries help to shift world politics from hegemony to engagement. Let us now review "epistemologies of the South."

Epistemologies of the South

Boaventura de Sousa Santos identifies two main pillars to "epistemologies of the South": ecologies of knowledges and intercultural translation. He defines the former accordingly: "[T]he ecology of knowledges confronts the logic of the monoculture of scientific knowledge and rigor by identifying other knowledges and criteria of rigor and validity that operate credibly in social practices pronounced nonexistent by metonymic reason" (Santos 2014: 188).[21] Pursuit of such epistemic ecologies involves the following:

- Cumulative learning: "[L]earning new and less familiar knowledges without necessarily having to forget the old ones and one's own" (Santos 2014: 188).
- Dialogue across paradigms: "[F]inding credibility for non-scientific knowledges does not entail discrediting scientific knowledge. It implies, rather, using it in a broader context of dialogue with other knowledges" (Santos 2014: 189). In particular, Santos emphasizes the notion of "incompleteness": that is, no *episteme* can account for everything.
- New epistemic relations: "The ecology of knowledges aims to create a new kind of relation, a pragmatic relation, between scientific knowledge and other kinds of knowledge" (Santos 2014: 190).
- Radical co-presence: "The ecology of knowledges lies in the idea of radical copresence [sic] … [It] means equating simultaneity with contemporaneity, which can only be accomplished if the linear conception of time is abandoned" (Santos 2014: 191).

Translation *across* epistemic ecologies follows logically. Santos defines intercultural translation broadly:

> [I]ntercultural translation consists of searching for isomorphic concerns and underlying assumptions among cultures, identifying differences and similarities, and developing, whenever appropriate, new hybrid forms of cultural understanding and intercommunication that may be useful in favoring interactions and strengthening alliances among social movements fighting, in different cultural contexts, against capitalism, colonialism, and patriarchy and for social justice, human dignity, or human decency.
>
> (Santos 2014: 212)

As with epistemic ecologies, intercultural translation poses a *political*, not just technical, challenge to hegemony. Intercultural translation involves:

- An intermovement of counter-hegemonic politics. Santos makes plain intercultural translation's political purpose: "[I]ntercultural translation is also interpolitical translation, a procedure that promotes the intermovement of politics at the source of counterhegemonic globalization" (Santos 2014: 213).

- Dismantling dichotomies. For this reason, intercultural translation begins by dismantling "reified dichotomies" that confine one set of knowledges (e.g., indigenous knowledge) to a "valid claim of identity" while asserting another (e.g., scientific knowledge) as a "valid claim of truth" (Santos 2014: 212–213).
- Shared authority. Echoing co-presence in epistemic ecologies, intercultural translation aims for parity and the partnerships it entails. "Ideally, only equal power relations, that is, relations of shared authority, fit the purposes of intercultural translation, since only then can reciprocity among social groups or movements be obtained" (Santos 2014: 214).
- Emancipatory commitment. Still, Santos cautions the need for self-consciousness in intercultural translation. It must remain true to social and political emancipation. He asks: "How to make sure that intercultural translation does not become the newest version of … imperialism and colonialism?" (Santos 2014: 213).

Language figures prominently in any translation. Here, Santos (2014: 216) focuses on two main concerns: the technicalities of translation and the context in which it happens. How do we handle differences between languages, he asks, and what effect does this have on the translation itself as well as its process? Also important are the "non-linguistic" and "paralinguistic" ways of communication: e.g., "body language, gestures, laughter, facial expressions, silences, the organizational and architecture of space, the management of time and rhythm and so on" (Santos 2014: 216). Santos raises issues of "appropriation," "asymmetry," "identity" and "motivation." He identifies the location of translation as a "third space" or "contact zone" where "hybrid cultural constellations" can "resist, reject, assimilate, imitate, translate, and subvert each other," thereby reinforcing or reducing "the inequality of exchanges" (Santos 2014: 218). Ultimately, Santos concludes, intercultural translation mobilizes "transformative practices" into "alliances for collective action" (Santos 2014: 214–215). Herein lies the true purpose of intercultural translation: it is "a bottom-up political aggregation, the alternative to a top-down aggregation imposed by a general theory or a privileged social actor" (Santos 2104: 235).

Convergences

Worldism and "epistemologies of the South" converge along the following lines:

- Relationality ⇔ Multiple *Epistemes*. Worldist relationality surveys the discursive context to cumulative learning, as urged by "epistemologies of the South," and highlights the power relations that underpin it. In so doing, worldist relationality reveals the multiple *epistemes* at play: that is, which ones dominate/silence others and why. With this recognition comes a moral imperative: cumulative learning must integrate new and old knowledges. Only by intersecting it with infusions of creativity/co-creativity can we begin to reverse the usual power plays of coercion and hegemony (Ling 2016a). In this sense, worldism and "epistemologies of the South" may serve as different names for the same thing or, dialectically, introduce different things under the same name. Resonance across paradigms begins this process of mutual understanding and its extension, global justice.
- Resonance ⇔ Global Justice. "Epistemologies of the South" urge dialogue across paradigms to know Others. CLS aims precisely to do so by, first, dismantling

dichotomies. In connecting disparate voices at disparate sites, worldist resonance makes possible a "third space" or "global oasis" to enable mutual learning and sharing. From this basis, new epistemic horizons and their socio-political relations can arise to mitigate the global injustice of subaltern "epistemicide." An inter-movement of counter-hegemonic politics thus becomes possible. Not restricted to politics only, this movement may also entail a kind of emancipation not confined to Western "grammars and scripts" of transformation: i.e., interbeing.

- Interbeing ⇔ Emancipatory Transformation. "Epistemologies of the South" seek to develop "a new kind of relation" between conventional and marginalized/erased knowledges. Worldism does so by finding commonalities between previously alien-ated traditions like Daoism and Andeanism. Their resonance with concepts like pairing, balancing and harmonizing brings about a spiritual awakening through interbeing. *Yin/yang pacha* demonstrates that one, celestial body (*pacha*) can link multiple worlds despite their dialectically induced contradictions and complicities (*yin* and *yang*). Accordingly, singular linearity – whether applied as hegemony or its heir, revolution – *can no longer define IR*. New epistemic relations enable a "radical co-presence," if not co-authority, in global relations. Silenced voices intertwine and dominant voices can no longer dominate. To heal from the past, dominant voices surface in every relation as a reminder of learning towards trans-formation. In other words, "epistemologies of the South" do not "get rid" of dom-inant voices, but embrace them as an everyday revolution, transforming them into learning steps and experiences that – despite their roots in hegemony – become linked to emancipatory, multiple worlds.
- "Incompleteness." Radical co-presence/authority in "epistemologies of the South" or interbeing in worldism perforates dichotomies in time (now vs. then), space (here vs. there) and subjectivity (Self vs. Other). But this process remains crucially and neces-sarily incomplete. Just as the last brush stroke in Sengai's painting suggests an open-ing so, too, do "epistemologies of the South." Both recognize that no single *episteme* can – or should – do it all. Mutuality is needed for humanity to survive and thrive. Here, Daoism's *wu* or "non" forms help. They inject much-needed cautionary mech-anisms to stay vigilant from hegemony.

Table 17.1 summarizes these entwinements and correspondences between worldism and "epistemologies of the South."

Implications for IR/world politics

South–South talk reconstructs IR accordingly:

- Epistemic change *and* political change. World politics can transform over time due to changes in *episteme*, even in parts, like *yin/yang pacha*. Epistemic parts may con-flict but still effect change, not necessarily due to any single attribute within each, but to their collective dynamic in time (past/present/future), space (here/there, inside/outside) and subjectivity (Self/Other, West/rest). These provide opportunities for rec-ognizing and connecting counter-hegemonic politics across disparate locations, thereby introducing structural change. Such is the very epitome of South–South talk.
- Epistemic compassion. Acknowledging simultaneity and contemporaneity in world politics – e.g., hegemony *and* openness, hierarchy *and* harmony, singularity *and*

Table 17.1 Entwinements and correspondences: worldism and "epistemologies of the South"

	Worldism	*Epistemologies of the South*
Ecologies of knowledges	Multiple worlds/world-of-worlds	Cumulative learning
	CLS	Dialogue across paradigms
	Yin/yang pacha	New epistemic relations
	Interbeing	Radical co-presence
Intercultural translation	Reversals and intersections	Intermovement of counter-hegemonic politics
	Mutual learning and sharing	Dismantling dichotomies
	Visions of co-presence/authority	Shared presence
	Daoist wu forms	Emancipatory commitment

multiplicity – ensures an emancipatory check for each on the other while at the same time leaving the system open to change. From this basis, another realization emerges: epistemic compassion. It pushes South–South talk to not just dismantle dichotomies but also *reconcile* them, and at ontological/epistemological levels (Ling unpublished). Only with epistemic compassion could we heal the global South's "epistemicide." From this basis, both North and South may finally emerge from the twin shadows of imperialism and colonialism.

- Co-presence/co-authority. A new vision becomes possible. It involves a radical co-presence or co-authority between center and periphery, hegemon and subaltern, North and South. Co-authority here does not mean "international cooperation" in its conventional sense: that is, all march behind the banner of one, hegemonic "standard of civilization" led by certain state elites. Rather, co-presence/co-authority stems from strategies of epistemic compassion from inside-and-below as well as across-and-beyond. The usual boundaries, in short, dissolve and a new kind of world politics (interbeing) becomes possible.

Another set of global relations emerges. As *pacha* notes, Rogue Others may seek to re-balance world politics through the destructive power of global terrorism. But Daoist dialectics also identify a *yin* to balance this *yang*: that is, the Conscientious Other. Its ancient archive of knowledges and practices *remains alive*. "We are still here," indigenous activist, Humberto Cholango, wrote to Pope Benedict XVI from the Andes in 2007 (Cholango quoted in Cadena 2010: 335): "[We] have always been here, and will continue to be here." No nativist trick or what colonizers had dismissed as "naïveté," such subaltern resilience stems from a philosophical worldliness. "Our religions NEVER DIED," Cholango stressed, because "we learned how to merge our beliefs and symbols with the ones of the invaders and oppressors" (Cholango quoted in Cadena 2010: 334, original emphasis). Put differently, the subaltern endures through an ability to absorb and adapt, reframe and reformulate even that which seems "foreign" or "alien." And such resilience now extends to a collective conscientious Other through South–South talk.

Conclusion

In sum, we are not alone. Thucydides notwithstanding, we can transform world politics from power relations (hegemony) to imminent change (worldism) to new kinds of global action through transcultural learning (epistemologies of the South). Under these circumstances, hegemony becomes irrelevant. It dissolves as the global South celebrates the notion of "incompleteness": that is, because no single *episteme* can or should account for everything, interconnectedness ensures survival. And the *dao* completes the link with the south within the North and the north within the South, thereby enhancing North–South communication as well.

Emancipation thus remains possible even when there seems "no choice but to use foreign institutions and languages." No matter how hegemonic they may seem, institutions can and should be transformed, not destroyed; otherwise, we would be wasting precious human experience and knowledge. "Chatting" and other forms of intercultural translation respect an ecology of knowledges: it represents a way to attain *wuyu* or desire based on respect.

From South–South talk come new languages and the social relations they express (e.g., *yin/yang pacha*). Different narratives can *coexist* with *equal* validity, leading eventually to a *co-created* social reality. No one person, thing, system or *episteme* can or should undertake the struggle alone. Worldism adds the water-like nature of the *dao* to characterize our world-of-worlds and how we can know it. So-called pristine opposites – e.g., a "superior," "enlightened" colonizing-Self versus an "inferior," "backward" colonized-Other – no longer hold. Attention to Andeanism's natural cycles between balance and imbalance reconciles what seems opposite, irreconcilable or barely tolerable.

Lastly, South–South talk articulates a conscientious Other. Rooted in millennial-old experience, it teaches us how to speak with and listen to others *creatively*. Rogue Others would do well to take note. We are not alone, after all.

Questions for discussion

1. In world politics, *worldism asserts that multiple worlds course through and across civilizations, making them what they are.* Choose a research subject or a study topic and explore the three main queries of "chatting," the worldist model of dialogics, by asking:

    a. Who says what to whom and why (relationality)?

    b. Where is change coming from and what does it mean (resonance)? What is it, where is it arising and why is it significant for local as well as global communities?

    c. How can I act with ethics *and* compassion (interbeing)?

2. *Creative listening/speaking (CLS) as a wordlist method, "momentarily brackets social conventions like 'powerful' vs. 'powerless' or 'rich' vs. 'poor' to enable another venue for engagement"*. Choose a research subject or a study topic, identify one or more power relations and analyze the "powerful" vs. "powerless" initial opposition through an ontological parity lens by applying one to three CLS tactics (*reversals and intersections*; *mutual learning or visions of co-presence*) and summarize any new language, reconciliatory scenarios and possibilities that emerged from the exercise.

Table 17.2 South–South talk: creating a platform for transformation on a global scale

	Worldism	Epistemologies of the South
Ecologies of knowledges	Multiple worlds/ world-of-worlds	Cumulative learning
	CLS	Dialogue across paradigms
	Yin/yang pacha	New epistemic relations
	Interbeing	Radical co-presence
Intercultural translation	Reversals and intersections	Intermovement of counter-hegemonic politics
	Mutual learning and sharing	Dismantling dichotomies
	Visions of co-presence/ authority	Shared presence
	Daoist wu forms	Emancipatory commitment

3. How can the Andean spherical understanding of time-space (*outside-future*; *here-now*; *inside-past*) and connected principles (respectively *think well*; *do well* and *love well*) change world politics?

4. Fill out the last column of Table 17.2 by using other Southern worldviews approaches to IR included in the present publication and to indicate other convergences in the global South? Note any difference that you consider worthwhile noting and explain why so.

Notes

1 "Chief Oren Lyons Discusses Sovereignty," *Taos News* (www.youtube.com/watch?v=SOw6 S_immM4) (downloaded: 20 April 2010).

2 The first "International Colloquium: Epistemologies of the South" was held in Coimbra, Portugal from 10–12 July 2014. Participants came primarily from Latin America, Africa and South Asia. See (http://alice.ces.uc.pt/coloquio_alice/) (downloaded: 15 September 2015).

3 We frame this form of discourse as a "chat" to indicate its intimate, friendly and seemingly meandering (agenda-less) nature. Nonetheless, a chat often bears great potential for transformation for both the chat and its participants given its sheer delight and, consequently, the kind of information that flows from it.

4 Pinheiro (2012) first coined the concept of "creative listening."

5 These selections are not random. See Ling (2014) for the prevalence of *yin/yang* theory in daily life in East and Southeast Asia despite a general lack of awareness of Daoism's formal philosophy. As for the Andean cosmovision, the Constitutions of Bolivia (2007) and Ecuador (2008) have incorporated this worldview as a core element of their commitment to multicultural engagement.

6 We rely on Ames and Hall for translations of the *Daodejing* and other texts like the *Zhuangzi*, given their sensitivity to the philosophical, not just linguistic, journeys between English and Chinese. Santos raises precisely these concerns about intercultural translation (see below).

7 The term is pronounced *tiep hien* in Vietnamese. It is based on the Chinese characters, *xiang ji*. Both mean "facing each other *now*." Ling's translation.

8 Traditions from across the globe support this notion of interbeing. Like Buddhists, Sufis teach that "I am in you, and you are in me." See, for example, the twelfth-century Persian epic, *Manṭiq-uṭ-Ṭayr* ("Conference of the Birds"). Non-religious philosophies also embrace interbeing: *poiesis* ("reverberations") from the ancient Greeks (Agathangelou and Ling 2005); *ren* ("humaneness") from Confucians (Agathangelou and Ling 2005); and *ubuntu* ("human-ness") from the Bantus of southern Africa (see Chapter 5, this volume).

9 Soja (1996) first coins the term "thirdspace," applying it to hybrid developments in urban spaces. It resembles what Ling (2002) calls "interstitial learning" in postcolonial states. In both

cases, "thirdspace" and "interstitial learning" delineate how new ideas, practices and institutions can emerge when contending forces mix, whether these are imposed from above (e.g., colonialism) or locally generated (e.g., living in the same city). "Global oasis" extends this inquiry by asking: what happens *after* hybrid learning takes place? Global oasis recognizes transformative possibilities not just in the Self or the Other due to interstitial mixing but also how this interaction transforms relations *between* Self and Other.

10 "Daoist naming personalizes a relationship and, abjuring any temptation to fix what is referenced, instead understands the name as a shared ground of growing intimacy. Such naming is presentational rather than just representational, normative rather than just descriptive, perlocutionary rather than just locutionary, a doing and a knowing rather than just saying ... Naming is more importantly the responsiveness that attends familiarity. Hence such knowing is a feeling and a doing: it is value-added. It is naming without the kind of fixed reference that allows one to 'master' something, a naming that does not arrest or control. It is a discriminating naming that in fact appreciates rather than depreciates a situation" (Ames and Hall 2003: 45–46).

11 "[T]he absence of a certain kind of knowledge – the kind of knowledge that is dependent upon ontological presence: that is, the assumption that there is some unchanging reality behind appearance ... Knowledge, as unprincipled knowing, is the acceptance of the world on its own terms without recourse to rules of discrimination that separate one sort of thing from another" (Ames and Hall 2003: 40).

12 *Wuzheng* considers "the conduct of the sages: 'Is it not because they strive without contentiousness that no one in the world is able to contend with them?'" (Ames and Hall 2003: 48).

13 *Wushi* "has a specifically political application that explains itself:

The more prohibitions and taboos there are in the world,
The poorer the people will be ...
[Hence] We do things noncoercively
And the common people develop along their own lines...".
(Ames and Hall 2003: 47–48)

14 "The sages do not compose the score for social and political order. The music is the natural expression of the common people. The role of the sages is to listen carefully to the songs of the common people and to orchestrate their thoughts and feelings into consummate harmony" (Ames and Hall 2003: 46). Gramsci had a similar notion in the "organic intellectual" (Femia 1987).

15 "[R]ather than involving the cessation and absence of desire, [*wuyu*] represents the achievement of *deferential desire* ... [It aims] simply to celebrate and to enjoy. It is deference. Desire is directed at those things desirable because they *stand to be desired*. But those things which stand to be desired must themselves be deferential, which means that they cannot *demand* to be desired. For to demand to be desired is to exercise a kind of mesmerizing control over the desirer. In a world of events and processes in which discriminations are recognized as conventional and transient, desire is predicated upon one's ability at any given moment to 'let go'. It is in this sense that *wuyu* is a nonconstruing, objectless, desire" (Ames and Hall 2003: 42, original emphases).

16 Revolutionary movements need more than a political goal. History tells us that without a moral or ethical vision to check on politics, they can – and often do – turn into the despotic/authoritarian regimes that the revolution sought to overthrow in the first place. In this sense, the civil rights movement in the U.S. served as a post-*hoc* reminder for the American Revolution.

17 *Pacha* means "time-space-body" and *kuti* "turn" or "revolution."

18 The original reads: "*El Sol es Wak'a en el Capac Raymi, Solsticio de Verano en Diciembre, cuando es fuerte y nos da calor, pero en el Invierno es solo un debil miembro de la comunidad andina, a quien, cunpliendo el mandato del Ayuni debemos reciprocar por su ayuda pasada. Para esto, la ocmunidad simbolicamente lo 'calienta' con fogatas y le envía un Kero con chichi reconfortante*" (Milla Villena 2003: 29). Translation by Carolina Pinheiro.

19 This image of giving and receiving hands also features prominently in the Sufi tradition of Islam.
20 A comparable image comes from Buddhism. It depicts a compassionate humanity as "a thousand arms and eyes" operating in tandem in one, celestial body.
21 Santos (2014: 165) defines metonymic reason as "a kind of reason that claims to be the only form of rationality and therefore does not exert itself to discover other kinds of rationality or, if it does, it only does so to turn them into raw material." He uses "metonymy" as a figure of speech to connote how one part is taken for the whole.

Further reading

Ames, Roger T. and David L. Hall (2003) *Dao de jing, "Making this Life Significant": A Philosophical Translation*, New York: Ballantine Books. Ames and Hall feature the original Chinese texts of the *Dao de jing* and translate them into crisp, chiseled English that reads like poetry.
Ling, L.H.M. (2014) *The Dao of World Politics: Towards a Post-Westphalian, Worldist International Relations*, London: Routledge. This book draws on Daoist *yin/yang* dialectics to move world politics from the current stasis of hegemony, hierarchy and violence to a more balanced engagement with parity, fluidity and ethics.
Santos, Boaventura de Sousa (2014) *Epistemologies of the South: Justice Against Epistemicide*, Boulder: Paradigm Publishers. This book shows why cognitive injustice underlies all the other dimensions; global social justice is not possible without global cognitive justice.
Santos, Boaventura de Sousa (2018) *The End of the Cognitive Empire: The Coming of Age of Epistemologies of the South*, Durham: Duke University Press. In this book Santos further develops his concept of the "epistemologies of the South," in which he outlines a theoretical, methodological and pedagogical framework for challenging the dominance of Eurocentric thought.

References

Agathangelou, Anna M. and L.H.M. Ling (2005) "Power and Play through *Poiesis*: Reconstructing Self and Other in the 9/11 Commission Report," *Millennium: Journal of International Studies* 33 (3): 827–853. doi:10.1177/03058298050330030701
Ames, Roger T. (ed.) (1998) *Wandering at Ease in the Zhuangzi*, Albany, NY: State University of New York. doi:10.1017/S0041977X00008818
Ames, Roger T. and David L. Hall (2003) *Daodejing, "Making this Life Significant": A Philosophical Translation*, New York: Ballantine Books.
Arisaka, Yoko (1996) "The Nishida Enigma: The Principle of the New World Order," *Monumenta Nipponica* 51 (1) Spring: 81–99. doi:10.2307/2385317
Brincat, Shannon and L.H.M. Ling (2014) "Dialectics for IR: Hegel and the *Dao*," *Globalizations* 11 (3): 1–27. doi:10.1080/14747731.2014.940246
Cadena, Marisol de la (2010) "Indigenous Cosmopolitics in the Andes: Conceptual Reflections beyond 'Politics'," *Cultural Anthropology* 25 (2): 335. doi:10.1111/j.1548-1360.2010.01061.x
Cheng, Chung-ying (2006) "Toward Constructing a Dialectics of Harmonization: Harmony and Conflict in Chinese Philosophy," *Journal of Chinese Philosophy* 33 (1) December: 28. doi:10.1111/j.1540-6253.2006.00389.x
Enloe, Cynthia (2001) *Bananas, Beaches and Bases: Making Feminist Sense of International Politics*, Updated Edition, Berkeley, CA: University of California Press. doi:10.1525/9780520957282
Femia, Joseph V. (1987) *Gramsci's Political Thought: Hegemony, Consciousness and the Revolutionary Process*, Oxford: Clarendon Press.
Feyerabend, Paul (1999) *Conquest of Abundance: A Tale of Abstraction versus the Richness of Being*, Chicago, IL: University of Chicago Press.

Freire, Paulo ([1970] 2000) *Pedagogy of the Oppressed*, 30th Anniversary Edition, New York: The Continuum International Publishing Group, Inc.

Goto-Jones, Christopher S. (2005) *Political Philosophy in Japan: Nishida, the Kyoto School, and Co-Prosperity*, London: Routledge.

Gualinga, C.V. (2002) "Visión indígena del desarrollo en la Amazonía," *Polis, Revista de la Universidad Bolivariana* 1 (3): 1–6.

Hesse, Hermann (1957) *Siddhartha*, New York: New Directions Publishing Corporation.

Huanacuni, Fernando (2010) "Everything Is Interconnected, Interrelated and Interdependent," Indigenouspeoplesissues.com (http://indigenouspeoplesissues.com/index.php?option=com_content&view=article&id=3837:the-good-life-of-andean-indigenous-peoples-transcript-of-aymara-fernando-huanacuni-presentation&catid=23:south-america-indigenous-peoples&Itemid=56) (downloaded: 6 June 2014).

Huntington, Samuel P. (1993) "The Clash of Civilizations?" *Foreign Affairs* 72 (3): 22–49. doi:10.2307/20045621

Huntington, Samuel P. (1996) *The Clash of Civilizations and the Remaking of World-Order*, New York: Simon and Schuster.

Hutchings, Kimberley (2011) "Dialogue between Whom? The Role of the West/Non-West Distinction in Promoting Global Dialogue in IR," *Millennium: Journal of International Studies* 39 (3): 639–647. doi:10.1177/0305829811401941

Jahn, Beate (2013) *Liberal Internationalism*, London: Palgrave Macmillan.

Katzenstein, Peter J. (ed.) (2009) *Civilizations in World Politics: Plural and Pluralist Perspectives*, London: Routledge. doi:10.4324/9780203872482

Keene, Edward (2002) *Beyond the Anarchical Society: Grotius, Colonialism and Order in World Politics*, Cambridge: Cambridge University Press. doi:10.1017/CBO9780511491474

Lajo, Javier (2006) *Qhapaq Ñan: La ruta Inka de Sabiduría*, Ibarra, Ecuador: Abya-Yala.

Lederach, John Paul (2005) *Moral Imagination: The Art and Soul of Building Peace*, Cary, NC: Oxford University Press. doi:10.1093/0195174542.001.0001

Li, Chenyang (2004) "Zhongyong as Grand Harmony: An Alternative Reading to Ames and Hall's *Focusing the Familiar*," *Dao: A Journal of Comparative Philosophy* 3 (2) June: 173–188.

Li, Wai-Yee (1994) "The Idea of Authority in the *Shih Chi* (*Records of the Historian*)," *Harvard Journal of Asiatic Studies* 54 (2) December: 345–405. doi:10.2307/2719434

Ling, L.H.M. (2002) *Postcolonial International Relations: Conquest and Desire between Asia and the West*, London: Palgrave Macmillan.

Ling, L.H.M. (2014) *The Dao of World Politics: Towards a Post-Westphalian, Worldist International Relations*, London: Routledge. doi:10.4324/9781315887777

Ling, L.H.M. (2016a) "Orientalism ReFashioned: 'Eastern Moon' on 'Western Waters' Reflecting on the East China Sea," in Andreas Behnke (ed.) *The International Politics of Fashion. Being Fab in a Dangerous World: Fashion and World Politics*, London: Routledge, pp. 69–96. doi:10.4324/9781315765082

Ling, L.H.M. (unpublished) "A Worldly World Order: Epistemic Compassion for International Relations."

Malholtra, Rajiv (2011) *Being Different: An Indian Challenge to Western Universalism*, New Delhi: HarperCollins.

Mignolo, Walter D. (2000) *Local Histories/Global Designs: Coloniality, Subaltern Knowledges, and Border Thinking*, Princeton, NJ: Princeton University Press.

Milla Villena, Carlos (2003) *Ayni*, Lima: Amaru Wayra.

Milla Villena, Carlos (2011) *Genesis de la cultura Andina*, Lima: Amaru Wayra.

Nakano, Ryoko (2011) "Beyond Orientalism and 'Reverse Orientalism': Through the Looking Glass of Japanese Humanism," in Robbie Shilliam (ed.) *International Relations and Non-Western Thought: Imperialism, Colonialism and Investigations of Global Modernity*, London: Routledge, pp. 125–138. doi:10.1057/9781137290519_1

Pinheiro, Carolina M. (2012) "Creative Listening: An Emancipatory Art of Empowerment," Master's Thesis, Julien J. Studley Graduate Program in International Affairs, Milano School of International Affairs, Management, and Urban Policy, The New School.

Rivera Cusicanqui, Silvia (1991) "Aymara Past, Aymara Future," *NACLA Report on the Americas* 25 (3): 18–45. doi:10.1080/10714839.1991.11723133

Rodriguez, Germán (1999) *La sabiduría del kóndor: Un ensayo sobre la validez del saber Andino*, Quito: Abya-Yala.

Rouland, Norbet (ed.) (2004) *Direito das minorias e dos povos autóctones*, Brasília: Editora UnB.

Santos, Boaventura de Sousa (2014) *Epistemologies of the South: Justice against Epistemicide*, Boulder, CO: Paradigm Publishers.

Soja, Edward (1996) *Thirdspace: Journeys to Los Angeles and Other Real-and-Imagined Places*, Malden, MA: Blackwell Publishers.

Thich Nhat, Hanh (1988) *Interbeing: Fourteen Guidelines for Engaged Buddhism*, Berkeley, CA: Parallax Press.

Tickner, J. Ann (2011) "Dealing with Difference: Problems and Possibilities for Dialogue in International Relations," *Millennium: Journal of International Studies* 39 (3): 607–618. doi:10.1177/0305829811400655

Ureña, Guerro Marcos (2004) *Los dos máximos sistemas del mundo*, Lima: Abya-Yala.

Watson, Irene (2007) "De-Colonization and Aboriginal Peoples: Past and Future Strategies," *The Australian Feminist Law Journal* (26): 111–122. doi:10.1080/13200968.2007.10854381

Index

Page numbers in **bold** refer to tables; those in *italics* to figures; and <u>underlined</u> page numbers indicate boxes.